Law in Our Lives

An Introduction

David O. Friedrichs
University of Scranton

Roxbury Publishing Company
Los Angeles, California

Library of Congress Cataloging-in-Publication Data

Law in our lives: an introduction/David O. Friedrichs
p. cm.
Includes bibliographical references (p.) and index.
ISBN 1-891487-41-8
1. Law—United States. 2. Sociological jurisprudence. I. Title.
KF380.F75 2001
349.73–dc21 99-037461

Publisher: Claude Teweles
Managing Editor: Dawn VanDercreek
Production Editor: Carla Max-Ryan
Assistant Editor: Kate Sterner Shaffar
Copy Editor: Arlyne Lazerson
Graphics Editor: Bonnie Gillespie
Typography: Rebecca Evans & Associates/Synergistic Data Systems
Cover Design: Marnie Kenney

Printed on acid-free paper in the United States of America. This paper meets the standards for recycling of the Environmental Protection Agency.

ISBN 1-891487-41-8

Roxbury Publishing Company
P.O. Box 491044
Los Angeles, California 90049-9044
Tel.: (310) 473-3312 • Fax: (310) 473-4490
E-mail: roxbury@roxbury.net
Web site: www.roxbury.net

For Jessica and Bryan

Contents

Foreword

All too frequently law has been viewed exclusively to be what lawyers and judges do and what law students study. American society and popular culture certainly view law primarily in this way. Legal commentators are almost invariably law professors and lawyers who look upon, and speak about, law through the lens of a profession. But law is also a social and cultural institution, one that influences and is influenced by society. The legal realist movement fostered this perspective early in the twentieth century, providing a foundation for the work of sociolegal scholars, critical legal studies theorists, feminist jurisprudence scholars, and postmodernists of all kinds.

This ferment in thinking about law within a broader social context found its way into undergraduate teaching, where the liberal arts provided a natural home. Nowhere was the impact more evident than in political science. Where constitutional law (i.e., the study of doctrinal law) once comprised virtually all of the discipline's teaching about law, by the latter half of the twentieth century it comprised only one part; courses on the judiciary, trial courts, law and politics, and rights theory now are viewed by many as the core of "public law."

At the same time, other disciplines, including sociology, anthropology, psychology, history, and philosophy, also came to view "law" more expansively or anew. Thus, by the 1960s, a new *interdisciplinary* field—usually referred to as "law and society"—emerged. The Law and Society Association became the organizational embodiment of this field, offering interdisciplinary scholars in the law schools and social scientists an opportunity to meet, interact, debate, publish, and forge common intellectual ground. The American Legal Studies Association played a smaller but parallel role for legal scholars and humanities faculty.

Curricular innovations soon followed. Undergraduate programs (majors) in law and legal studies were established at Hampshire College and the University of Massachusetts at Amherst in the early 1970s. Today, more than sixty colleges and universities have organized programs that focus on law as a liberal art, drawing on most social science and humanities disciplines. Nearly all colleges offer a wide variety of law-focused courses, even in the absence of a formal program, major, or minor.

Not only has the number of programs grown, but so too has their quality. In the 1970s and 1980s, many programs offered students a loose collection of law-related courses from several disciplines. By the 1990s, faculty teaching these courses began to integrate the learning experience for students on campus, much as a department or field might. As a result, new introductory courses were developed, course requirements began to reflect intellectual rather than administrative goals, and capstone experiences (including seminars, internships, and service learning programs) were formulated. These efforts resulted in more truly interdisciplinary programs, both for participating faculty and for the students.

But where are all the textbooks for this field of "law and society"? Disciplines, fields, even areas of study are marked by texts, which define the parameters of study and introduce the subject to newcomers. But this interdisciplinary field has been resistant to texts. In surveys that I conducted as the Director of the American Bar Association's Commission on College and University Legal Studies, I found that faculty teaching in this area used a wide variety of books—narratives, case studies, biographies, anthologies, even novels. Some textbooks were used occasionally, including Lawrence Friedman's *Law and Society* and Robert Kidder's *Connecting Law and Society*. These interdisciplinary texts are now out of print.

At the same time, there are signs that the resistance to textbooks is breaking down. The interdisciplinary field of law and society is becoming larger and more diversified. As a result, a leading sociolegal scholar, Austin Sarat, advocates strengthening the field of law and society by articulating a canon—something that provides "a unifying field that helps us recognize what we share" as well as a "fruitful terrain of conflict and contestation." In a complementary way, textbooks also help to establish and situate these field discussions and place them in a comprehensible framework.

David Friedrichs' *Law in Our Lives: An Introduction* is a welcome addition to the law and society field. A sociologist by training, Friedrichs offers a new generation of undergraduate students a sophisticated yet understandable introduction to law, legal theory, legal institutions, and topical legal issues—i.e., to the full range of subjects that engage law and society scholars and teachers today.

Law in Our Lives has four special strengths. First and most important, it treats law as a complex, multidimensional subject. Friedrichs is neither consistently celebratory nor critical of law and legal institutions. Rather, he points up the strengths and limitations, the benefits and harms, both potential and actual, as well as ordinary Americans' ambivalence toward law and lawyers. Second, this book is interdisciplinary at every turn, explicating legal phenomena in historical, political, cross-national, and sociological perspectives. Friedrichs shows how law itself can be the subject of inquiry, not merely the tool through which to explicate disciplinary truths. Third, the text offers a good balance between legal theory (jurisprudence) and the "law in action," thereby suggesting both why and where law matters. Finally, the book offers a timely discussion of many topical issues for which the law does (or will) matter—e.g., physician-assisted suicide, genetic engineering, privacy, sexual orientation, and abortion—squarely grounding the text in twenty-first century issues.

David Friedrichs observes that law is everywhere, although it is not always clearly visible to us. *Law in Our Lives* will help students see more clearly the many faces of law.

John Paul Ryan, Ph.D.
The Education, Public Policy, and Marketing Group, Inc.
Director, American Bar Association Commission
on College & University Legal Studies, 1984-1997

Preface

Law is all over. Law is everywhere. And it may seem to some that law books and books about law are all over and everywhere as well. This book about law was inspired by a certain sense of frustration. I have taught a course entitled "Law and Society" for more than twenty years. This course is required for criminal justice majors, and it is recommended that they take the course in their sophomore year. It is also taken by students in many other majors who have some interest in law, and perhaps especially by those who plan to attend law school. A well-known reader edited by the faculty of the Legal Studies department at the University of Massachusetts–Amherst—John Bonsignore et al., *Before the Law,* Sixth Edition (1998)—serves as a basic text in this course, but for some years I was unable to find a textbook still in print that provides students with an interdisciplinary framework for understanding law and society.

Several books served as important sources of inspiration for this book. In the late 1960s, as a graduate student and college instructor, I read Edwin M. Schur's (1968) *Law and Society: A Sociological View,* and it made a great impression on me. It certainly inspired in me a deeper interest in the sociology of law and the whole literature on the many challenging questions that arise in this realm. The book was never revised and eventually went out of print. Schur moved on to produce a distinguished list of books on various aspects of deviance, crime (especially victimless crime), gender, and sexuality, among other topics. Then Richard Quinney's (1974) *Critique of Legal Order,* published when I was an assistant professor at City University of New York (Staten Island), was also a seminal influence, as it articulated in a stark form the critical view of law that was so widely promoted during the turbulent era of the late 1960s and early 1970s, and my consciousness of the oppressive and unequal dimensions of law has certainly stayed with me. Quinney also produced many subsequent and original books on various dimensions of crime, spirituality, peacemaking, and personal reflection. Lawrence M. Friedman's (1977) *Law and Society: An Introduction* was fortuitously published about the time I joined the faculty of the University of Scranton and assumed responsibility for the Law and Society course. I assigned that book in the course for many years because it seemed to me that it clearly and concisely identified some elements key to understanding the interrelationship between the legal and the social. This book also was not revised and eventually went out of print, and Friedman himself has produced a series of landmark books on legal history, the nature of law in American society, and other sociolegal topics.

All of the books mentioned, then, provided me with a perspective on and a mapping of an intriguing and absorbing area of scholarly inquiry. They provided signposts, or starting points, or a window and opening for further investigation. It is my hope that the present text will in some way inspire such an interest in its readers, and will at least introduce them to the vast, rich literature on law and society, in its many layers and diverse dimensions. This book is emphatically not about "black letter law"—the specific content of the different branches of our formal law—although, of course, many references are made to such law. Rather, the book is intended to provide students with a fundamental literacy about law as an immensely important and ubiquitous presence in our social existence. Some of the topics addressed in this book are as follows: the celebration of law and the critique of law; contemporary legal issues confronting society; the definition and meaning of law, the different dimensions or models of law, and the nature of legal reasoning; law in relation to justice, to morality, to religion, and to interests; traditional and contemporary schools of jurisprudence as approaches to understanding law; the law and society movement and the sociology of law as approaches to understanding law; anthropological, comparative, historical, and contextual approaches to understanding law; the legal profession in contemporary society; the basic attributes of the coexisting systems of law, or justice, within our society; some important aspects of legal culture and legal behavior; and the nature of the relationship between law and social change. The chapters of this book are arranged in an order that makes sense to the author, but each chapter is quite autonomous. Instructors who assign this book to their students should be able to reorder the sequence of the chapters on their syllabi to suit the needs of their courses.

The literature pertaining to law is vast. The issues arising in relation to law are endlessly complex and nuanced. A comprehensive guide to understanding law in all its many aspects would inevitably run to thousands of pages. Any number of sentences in this book could give rise to a long and very detailed footnote or commentary, with elaboration, qualifications, and the like. Again, the intent here is to provide a basic understanding and point of departure for important dimensions of law as a social phenomenon. As do many others, the author has found much of the "technical" literature on law dry and tedious. On the other hand, many of the questions arising out of law have been experienced as endlessly fascinating. Readers of this book will inevitably make some choices on the perspectives, insights, or concepts they find most useful in understanding law. Ideally, readers will be inspired to undertake a lifelong pilgrimage in pursuit of a richer, fuller, and deeper understanding of that remarkable and ever-present dimension of our social existence, law.

A final note to readers: The author of this book welcomes any comments from readers. Any such comments can de directed to:

David O. Friedrichs
Dept. of Sociology/Criminal Justice
University of Scranton
Scranton, PA 18510-4605
friedrichsd1@uofs.edu

About the Author

David O. Friedrichs is Professor of Sociology/Criminal Justice at the University of Scranton (Pennsylvania). He was educated at New York University and taught for nine years at City University of New York (Staten Island). He is author of *Trusted Criminals: White Collar Crime in Contemporary Society* (ITP/Wadsworth, 1996), and the Editor of *State Crime*, Volumes I and II (Ashgate/Dartmouth, 1998). He has published some 80 journal articles, book chapters, and essays on such topics as the legitimation of legal order, legal studies, radical/critical criminology, violence, narrative jurisprudence, postmodernism, white collar crime, and state crime. His articles have been published in such journals as *Criminology, Justice Quarterly, Crime & Delinquency, Criminal Justice Review, Crime, Law, & Social Change, International Journal of Comparative and Applied Criminal Justice, Caribbean Journal of Criminology and Social Psychology, Critical Criminology, Journal of Human Justice, Humanity & Society, Social Research, Social Problems, Qualitative Sociology, Journal of Legal Education, Journal of Criminal Justice Education*, and *Teaching Sociology*, as well as in numerous books. He is also the author of some 300 published book reviews. He served as Editor of the *Legal Studies Forum* between 1985 and 1989. He has also been active with numerous professional associations and has chaired or served on committees of a number of these associations, and he has served on the editorial boards of various journals. He has been a visiting professor or guest lecturer at a number of colleges and universities, including the University of South Africa and Ohio University (as Rufus Putnam Visiting Professor). He has presented some 80 papers at professional conferences; he organized and chaired panels on law in South Africa at international meetings of the Law and Society Association (held in Amsterdam 1991; in Glasgow 1996).

Acknowledgments

A text such as this is inevitably a collaborative work. My primary debt is to the numerous scholars and journalists whose work is cited throughout this book. I can only hope that I have cited their work accurately and fairly.

My service as Editor of the *Legal Studies Forum* (1985–1989), and as an editorial board member in subsequent years, was an invaluable learning experience for me in relation to developing an interdisciplinary understanding of law, and I am especially indebted to Jim Elkins, David Papke, John Bonsignore, and Ron Pipkin for what I learned from this experience. Several of these individuals also encouraged me in connection with this book.

Professional acquaintances and personal friends with whom I discussed this book project, or who provided some form of encouragement, advice, or assistance, include Fran Buntman, Lief Carter, Roy Domenico, David F. Greenberg, Dolph Grundman, Felice Levine, David Neubauer, Jeffrey Ian Ross, Martin D. Schwartz, Javier Trevino, and Susan Will. Graduate courses with the late H. Laurence Ross and with Richard Quinney provided early inspiration for my interest in the sociology of law. I am grateful to John Paul Ryan, for many years Director of the American Bar Association Commission on College and University Legal Studies, for writing a Foreword to this book. John was the primary organizer of several stimulating American Bar Association conferences (on law and undergraduate education; law and globalization; and law, morality, and religion) in which I participated.

At the University of Scranton, the Faculty Research Committee, the Faculty Development Committee, and the University Travel Committee provided absolutely crucial support in several forms: annual faculty research grants, which enabled me to visit research and law libraries, acquire essential research materials, and defray numerous production costs; a sabbatical leave in the spring of 1999; a summer research grant in 1998; a student research assistant grant (summer 1999); and travel grants that allowed me to attend and participate in professional meetings. The provost of the university, Richard Passon; the graduate dean and director of research, Robert Powell; the dean of my college, Joseph Dreisbach; and the chairman of my department, John Pryle, have all been supportive of this project, in various ways. My department secretary, Judith Lestansky, has provided efficient assistance on many aspects of this project. I am especially indebted to Ann Marie Lutz, a criminal justice major at the University of Scranton, who worked very closely with me on this project during the summer of 1999 and the fall of 1999. Ann Marie reviewed the manuscript line-for-line, made numerous suggestions and corrections, and produced the instructor's manual/test bank accompanying this text. She is primarily responsible for the listing of key terms and discussion questions at the end of each chapter and worked on the Web site for the book. Robert Grosse and Martyna Sleszynska, two other students, worked with me on this book project during the spring, 2000, semester, and made various contributions in terms of evaluations of draft chapters, the production of boxes, and preparation of the Web site. Kara Kosiorowski, another student, contributed a list of relevant Web sites. And I have learned useful things from many of the students in my Law and Society course at the University of Scranton over a period of some twenty years.

I visited many libraries in connection with doing research for this book, and am grateful to librarians at the following law schools for providing access to their collections and assistance on inquiries: Cornell, Fordham, Georgetown, New York University, Rutgers, Toronto, and Yeshiva. I also took advantage of access to libraries at John Jay College, Pennsylvania State University, and Rutgers–Newark/NCCD (with special thanks to the awesomely well-informed Phyllis Schultze of Rutgers–Newark/NCCD). Reference librarians at the University of Scranton, especially Linda Neyer, Kevin Norris, and Bonnie Strohl, have my thanks for their assistance.

Claude Teweles, the publisher, has been encouraging and helpful at all stages of the process of producing this book. The efficient work of Carla Max-Ryan, Project Editor, and Kate Sterner Shaffar, Assistant Editor, is also appreciated. Arlyne Lazerson, Copy Editor, has contributed to the accuracy and clarity of this book in countless ways, and I thank her for her painstaking attention to every line of my manuscript.

I am grateful, as well, to external peer reviewers of my original prospectus and my manuscript. These reviewers made numerous suggestions, each of which I seriously considered and many of which I adopted. I especially appreciated the exceptionally positive and encouraging comments of many of these reviewers. The reviewers of the prospectus or the manuscript are: Ronald Akers (University of Florida); Mary W. Atwell (Radford University); Steven E. Barkan (University of Maine); James A. Black (University of Tennessee–Knoxville); Sheldon Ekland-Olson (University of Texas–Austin); Gary Feinberg (St. Thomas University); Gilbert Geis (University of California–Irvine); Robert Granfield (University of Denver); Roger E. Hartley (Roanoke College); W. Richard Janikowski (University of Memphis); Robert L. Kidder (Temple University); M. Joan McDermott (Southern Illinois University–Carbondale); Austin Sarat (Amherst College); Ric S. Sheffield (Kenyon College); Matthew Silberman (Bucknell University); and Thomas Franklin Waters (Northern Arizona University–Yuma). In some cases, I have perhaps perversely rejected the advice of these reviewers, as well as that of the Copy Editor. Any shortcomings or inaccuracies that can be identified in this book are, of course, my responsibility.

A professional involvement with law extends over many generations in my family. An ancestor practiced law in the middle of the nineteenth century; a grandfather wrote about law in the earlier years of the twentieth century; a niece, Natasha Friedrichs, begins her formal study at Georgetown University School of Law at the outset of the twenty-first century, coincident with the publication of this book. A brother-in-law, Frank Salt, is a detective with the NYPD, and a nephew, Jeff Maira, contemplates a career in law. These associations are one form of inspiration for my own interest in law.

Finally, my wife Jeanne, as always, is a source of great joy in my private life, and distracts me when she can from the call of work (recently by encouraging me to take up ballroom dancing with her). My two children, Jessica and Bryan, by being so successful and well adjusted in their own lives, have helped make it possible for me to concentrate on writing a book. Accordingly, this book is dedicated to them, with great pride and much love.

Chapter One

Introduction

"The life of the law has not been logic: it has been experience."

—*Oliver Wendell Holmes Jr., 1881*

"Once understood in the context of the narratives that give it meaning, law becomes not merely a system of rules to be observed, but a world in which we live."

—*Robert M. Cover, 1983*

Law is all over. Law is everywhere. Law is an enduring presence in our lives.

Over a period of many years, I have opened my Law and Society class with the following questions for students: What was your most recent encounter with law? What was your most memorable encounter with law? I specifically instruct students not to ask me what I mean by "law." It is their understanding of the term, their image of law, that I am interested in discussing. The responses do not surprise me. The most recent encounter is typically being pulled over by the police or the breaking up of a beer blast by police. The most memorable encounter is also likely to involve the police: for example, being arrested. We Americans tend to be socialized to think most readily of the police, and more specifically the police in their enforcement or crime-fighting role, when the notion of law is raised. The terms "police" and "law" are sometimes used interchangeably. The police are one conspicuous and important representation of law in our society, but law is a far more pervasive feature of our daily lives (Post 1963, 1–2; Friedman 1998a, 13–14).

The very building in which you are attending class is governed by legal codes. If, before class, you stopped somewhere for a meal, you were in a circumstance governed by health codes. If you went to work before class, you were subject to labor law and possibly occupational and workplace safety standards. If you made a purchase prior to class, liability law or contract law may have been involved. If you stopped at the library before class to photocopy some research material, copyright law was involved. If you engaged in some form of search or communication on the Internet, you were subject to an emerging body of law governing this new medium.

You may encounter law as well if you need to consult a lawyer about such matters as divorce or a dispute with a landlord; if you are called for jury duty; if you do an internship with the probation department; or if you are sued in civil court in connection with an automobile accident. You should also recognize that you are more than likely to encounter law any time you hear the news on the radio or television or read a newspaper or newsmagazine; you are exposed to accounts of important court decisions, proposed new legislation, alleged violations of international law, polls of public opinion concerning ongoing legal controversies, high-profile trials, and the like.

Making Sense of Law

No single framework for understanding law, no one perspective on law, no core thesis about law is adopted here. Rather, law is viewed as many-hued, multi-faceted, often complex and contradictory. Law is everywhere; law is not always visible to us; law matters, and law does not matter; law is beneficial, and law is harmful. Perhaps Franz Kafka, the celebrated early twentieth-century author and native of Prague, had it right; he formulated several parables about law that suggest that it cannot be fully understood and comprehended by conventional accounts. It seemed to me to be false, then, and a distortion of a complex reality, to attempt to impose a unified framework on the study of how law and society interact. Nevertheless, it will be evident as readers progress that the author regards some perspectives as more useful and insightful than others and some themes as more central and powerful than others.

My own graduate education was in sociology, with a specialization in criminology. Over the past several decades I have always taught in multidisciplinary departments, and have specifically taught, in addition to sociology, criminal justice, philosophy, and anthropology courses. The influence of all these disciplines should be evident to readers of this book. I have also edited an interdisciplinary, law-focused journal (*Legal Studies Forum*) and have had considerable exposure to many other disciplinary perspectives on law, including jurisprudence, history, political science, psychology, economics, and literature. Accordingly, this text draws upon the scholarship of a broad range of disciplines, using whatever seems helpful in making sense of law in our lives.

Law is studied in different ways. Some of the literature on law is purely descriptive, and prescriptive. In other words this literature simply states what the law is and what practical procedures to follow to implement the law. Law professors have produced a large volume of such literature (commonly described as doctrinal analysis). Here some law or legal ruling is subjected to analysis in terms of its consistency or inconsistency with some relevant set of legal principles or objectives.

Very little of the literature drawn upon in this book falls into the categories of law-related writing just identified. Rather, most of the literature discussed here draws upon one of two traditions of social scientific analysis.

The *positivistic* tradition looks to the natural sciences for its model. Theories are formulated, and hypotheses are generated and subjected to empirical verification. This approach aspires to dispassionately discover, explain, and make valid predictions about law-related phenomena. The ultimate complexity and variability of the human and legal world, the difficulty of being objective about this world, and the practical or ethical constraints of subjecting humans to scientific tests, however, all act as barriers to the goal of achieving a true science of the sociolegal, that is, the relationship between law and society. Specific methods used within this model include experiments, surveys, observational studies, content analysis, and secondary data analysis.

The *humanistic* tradition looks to the humanities—philosophy, history, and literature—for its model. It adopts the premise that the world of the sociolegal is fundamentally different from the natural and physical world, and accordingly it rejects the positivistic approach. In the humanistic tradition, law and the sociolegal are more likely to be interpreted than explained, and stories about law are preferred to statistical analyses relating to law. Through applying relevant philosophical concepts to the sociolegal, or providing a detailed historical account, or looking to literary explorations of it, students can presumably arrive at a rich understanding of how law and society affect each other. The humanistic approach has been criticized for its possible biases, the difficulty of verifying its claims, and its failure to produce helpful generalizations.

Each approach has its limitations. Ideally, a multiplicity of different approaches complement each other, although it seems unlikely that anyone will wholly eliminate contradictions emanating from these different approaches.

One objective of this book is to introduce students to the scholarly literature on law and society, literature from all the disciplines listed earlier. This literature is vast, and to do full justice to it would require an impossibly large book. The objective here is to provide some preliminary guideposts to this literature, and to distill some of its essential themes.

No matter whether our knowledge about the law comes from direct experience or from vicarious experience, each of us is likely to evaluate our images and understanding of law through an *ideological* prism. We all come to the study of law with a certain set of beliefs. These beliefs may be rooted in such systems as a religious doctrine, a partisan political identification, or a broad philosophy of life and human existence. Individuals' reactions to law and legal phenomena are strongly influenced, then, by a complex of beliefs they hold. Also, people have a tendency to see what they want to see.

As you approach the study of law and society, you should recognize the tensions and contradictions between the ways in which people experience law (directly or vicariously), what they learn about it through scholarly study, and what their beliefs tell them about law (see Box 1.1).

Images of Law

A fundamental tension exists between the idealized image of law and what we may discover about the "realities of law." In our time, it is difficult to sustain an image of law as a source of perfect order, impartiality, and justice. In a per-

Box 1.1

Is Law Rational? The Evidence of Odd Laws and Legal Procedures

One element of the image of law in a modern, complex society is that law is, or ought to be, a *rational* enterprise. For our purposes here, "rational" means that law is logical, understandable, fair-minded, predictable, and sound. There are some, however, who view law as illogical, incomprehensible, discriminatory, arbitrary, and counterproductive. In terms of the *substance* of law and decisions at law, many examples of "odd" laws can be provided. Listings of odd laws have been collected in some books (e.g., Hyman 1977; Napier-Andrews 1976; Shook and Meyer 1995). It has been illegal in Memphis, Tennessee, to drive a car while asleep; in Bexley, Ohio, to install slot machines in outhouses; in Lexington, Kentucky, to carry an ice cream cone in one's pocket; in Oklahoma, to take a bite out of another person's hamburger; and in New Jersey, to slurp soup in a public restaurant. It has been illegal in London to congregate with Egyptians and in Boston to take a bath. Numerous other such examples could be cited. These odd, or silly, laws remind us that laws are human creations. Almost anything can be declared against the law. We have to remind ourselves that such laws come into existence in a particular historical context and often spring from a particular circumstance. A decade later, the "particular circumstance" may have disappeared, but the law remains on the books.

Again, odd laws impress on us the point that laws need not be rational, at least by conventional, contemporary standards. On a more serious note, there is ongoing debate within our society over questions of whether existing laws prohibiting the use of marijuana or consensual homosexual relations are rational and justifiable.

In terms of the *procedures* of law, legal cases have not always been resolved by rational means. "Trials by ordeal" and "animal trials" are good examples. The trial by ordeal was a basic mechanism for resolving criminal cases in a tradition rooted in ancient Anglo-Saxon law; it was still used in some form in our own system of law into the nineteenth century; and it survives among certain societies in the contemporary world (Custer 1986; Tewksbury 1967). The essence of such trials was that the criminal defendant was subjected to an ordeal to determine guilt or innocence, and for an extended period of time in the English law an ordeal was the sole means for resolving questions of guilt or innocence. Ordeals ranged from requiring suspected wrongdoers to walk over hot coals to requiring the suspect to touch the victim's corpse.

Trials of animals were held in Europe between the fourteenth and eighteenth centuries, and apparently became quite common between the fifteenth and seventeenth centuries (E. Cohen 1986). In France, in 1457, a pig and some piglets were tried for killing a five-year-old child. The pig was convicted and hung; the piglets were released to their owner on probationary status, insofar as there was no conclusive proof that they actually committed the killing. In France, in 1587, some flies were sued for destroying a vineyard, and a lawyer was appointed to handle their defense. In another French case, when rats failed to appear in court in response to a formal summons, their advocate pleaded their fear of cats as an excuse, and requested safe conduct for them. While these animal trials may appear to be bizarre by contemporary standards, we should also ask ourselves how some of our own adjudicatory procedures—trials for young juvenile offenders, for example—will look in some future time.

son's own experience with law, he or she may witness abuses and cynical tradeoffs; such occurrences may be especially likely if the person belongs to a minority group. In the recent era, wrongdoing on all levels of lawmaking and law enforcement has been relentlessly exposed. Films and television dramas have for the most part incorporated a gritty, sometimes cynical, realism about law and lawmakers. They have largely abandoned earlier tendencies to portray law enforcement officers and judges in mythic or heroic terms.

College students who undertake the formal study of law and legal institutions, as you are doing now, become exposed to the many documented gaps between official standards and actual practices. But a general loss of innocence about law need not be equated with the adoption of a cynical outlook. It is possible to sustain a strong allegiance to "the rule of law" without being naive about the law's biases, abuses, and limitations. Law is indeed all over; law is everywhere.

One other dimension of the image of law must be addressed: What is the nature of the relation between the law and society, or the legal and the social? In one view, law is *autonomous* and must be understood wholly on its own terms, independent of a social context. In an extreme version of this view, law could be seen as equivalent to mathematics. Everyone understands that the laws of mathematics and fundamental mathematical precepts are universals, the same in the People's Republic of China and in the United States. The question of whether it makes any sense to think of law in this way is explored later in this text.

In another view, law and society are *homologous,* they correspond in origin and structure and cannot be understood independently of each other. In an extreme version of this view, law is wholly a reflection of a particular social order. Law in the People's Republic of China merely implements the values and objectives of that system, and law in the United States does the same for a very different system. Again, the question of the validity of such a way of thinking about law will be considered later.

There is a third basic perspective on the relation between law and society. In this view law and society are best thought of in *interactive* terms. This view recognizes that law and society each have some unique and independent dimensions but that they also interact on many levels, with reciprocal influences. Some version of this view is the most widely held; and it informs the perspective adopted throughout this book (see Figure 1.1).

The interactive model could alternatively be illustrated as in Figure 1.2, with reciprocal influences between social structure (e.g., social class), social processes (e.g., socialization), and law.

The Celebration of Law

In the conventional view, promoted by many of our political leaders, taught in high school civics classes, and held by many ordinary citizens, law is not only something "good" in itself, it is the principal means for ensuring that people can enjoy all the good things in life (Friedman 1990; Rodes 1976). Law in this view guarantees the possibility of a civilized existence and contributes to the enhancement of such an existence. Law alone makes freedom possible, along with the choices and rights associated with living in a free society. Law in some form, and the rule of law, is universally embraced by all

Figure 1.1 Relationship of Law and Society

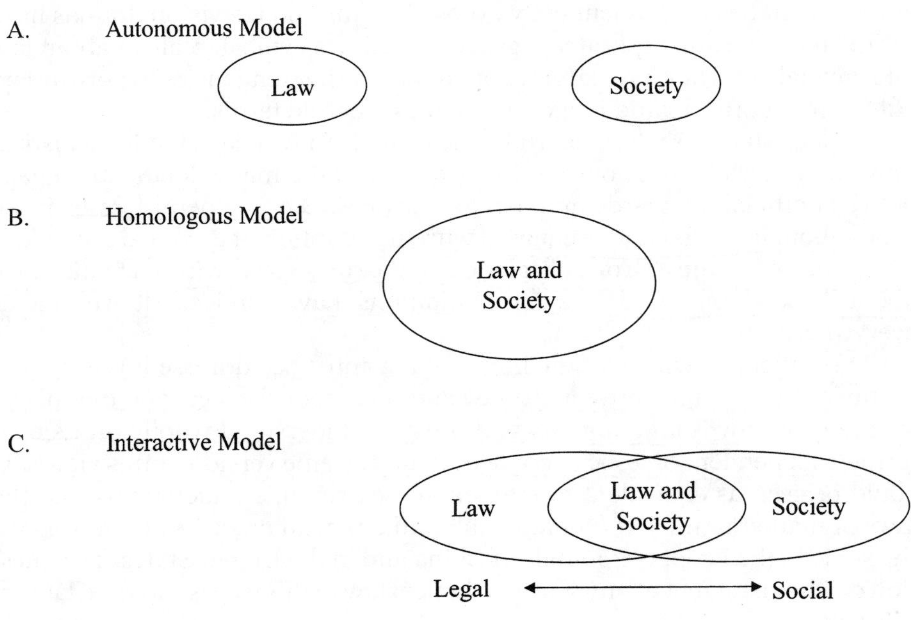

Figure 1.2 Relationship of Law, Social Structure and Social Process

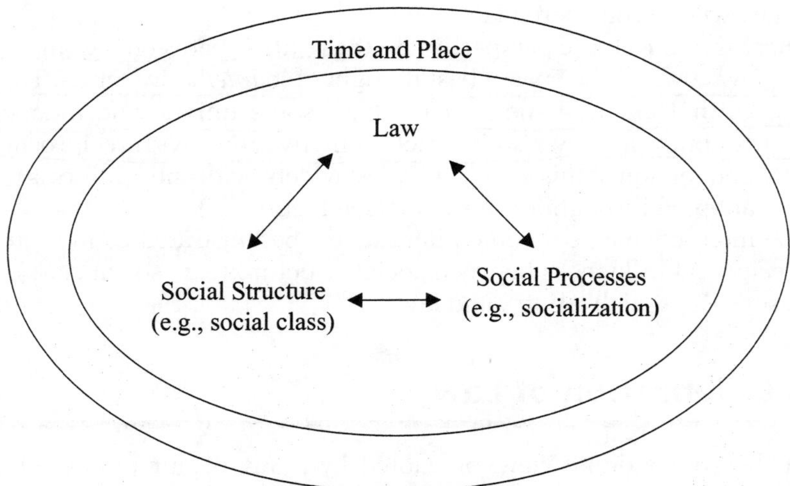

Representation of the interactive perspective on the relation of law and society. It shows that although both law and society have some unique and independent dimensions, they also have reciprocal influences.

societies aspiring to an orderly and productive existence. Ideally, and emphatically in the American tradition, law is rooted in democratic consensus. And law in this view is regarded as a profoundly rational entity with an inherent commitment to the promotion of justice and fairness. William Penn said, "Any government is free to the people under it . . . where the laws rule, and the people are a party to those laws, and more than this is tyranny, oligarchy, and confusion" (Shapiro 1993, 239).

In the conventional view, law fulfills some essential functions (Friedman 1977; Summers 1972). Law not only maintains order; it makes order possible. Law provides for the orderly, nonviolent resolution of all manner of conflicts and disputes. More specifically, law allows for social catharsis, or the release of justifiable anger and outrage directed at those seen as willfully engaging in harmful and destructive behavior, and it does so in a form minimizing the potential for further suffering and loss. Law more broadly is an instrument for the realization of justice. Law restores what has been lost, to the extent possible, to plaintiffs and victims, allocates responsibility and costs, and imposes appropriate penalties on guilty and negligent parties.

Law should serve, in the positive view, as a key element in the fostering and maintenance of a democratic political system. Law provides a fundamental constraint on the exercise of power by the political leadership and is the primary form of protection against tyranny. Law provides the framework for identifying human rights and for protecting those rights. Law allocates power and at the same time supervises the exercise of power.

Law both creates and promotes desirable social values. Law symbolically defines normative boundaries within society, clearly delineating the differences between right and wrong and between fundamentally acceptable and unacceptable behavior. Law both encourages and compels us to respect the life and personhood of others and to respect the rights as well as the privacy of others. Law tells us to pay our taxes; law tells us not to snort cocaine. Law promotes a healthier environment, better work conditions, and safer consumer products. And law may transcend the symbolic promotion of rights when it becomes the specific means of creating or providing opportunities. Antidiscrimination law and equal opportunity law can be cited as obvious illustrations of this function of law. Affirmative action law, although controversial, is a specific legal initiative to extend opportunities for employment and advancement to members of disadvantaged groups who might otherwise not have enjoyed such opportunities.

Law has some practical and mundane functions. Law provides a structure for, and facilitates, a broad range of private transactions and productive activities. Law defines what constitutes wealth and property and provides opportunities for acquiring wealth and property. Law identifies and distributes all manner of benefits to qualified citizens. Law is a mechanism through which society may formally define relationships—including the most intimate relations between family members—and the obligations attached to such relationships. Law provides a structure (and site) for depositing and maintaining many different types of records.

While many scholars and legal professionals embrace and propound the positive views of law and its functions discussed here, there is also a body of literature, by other scholars and legal professionals, that criticizes the law.

Table 1.1 Law's Functions

A. Law's Positive Functions
   1. Maintains order.
   2. Settles disputes.
   3. Allows for social catharsis.
   4. Promotes justice.
   5. Promotes desirable social values.
   6. Administers practical needs.

B. Law's Negative Functions
   1. Maintains the status quo.
   2. Divides people.
   3. Exploits people.
   4. Promotes conflict and violence.
   5. Promotes oppression and greed.
   6. Extends state power.

The Critique of Law

Law has been characterized as a profoundly negative dimension of the human environment. Thomas Cooper wrote, in 1830, that "the law, unfortunately, has always been retained on the side of power; laws have uniformly been enacted for the protection and perpetuation of power" (quoted in Shapiro 1993, 241). The critique of law comes from many sources. In the radical or anarchic version of the critique of law, it has been portrayed as an instrument of oppression and exploitation (Beirne and Quinney 1982; Kairys 1998). In this view law advances and protects elite interests and values. Law is a mechanism that the powerful use to coerce, dominate, and intimidate the powerless.

The Radical Critique

In the *radical critique*, law is inherently oriented toward the preservation of the status quo. Law plays an instrumental role, more specifically, in the preservation of private property—and a grossly disproportionate share of the wealth generally—in the hands of the few. Law is either directly a tool of the ownership class or is "relatively autonomous" but oriented toward the long-term survival of the system. Insofar as law contributes to the maintenance of "order," this purpose is fulfilled on behalf of the interests of the elite class.

In the radical critique, law contributes importantly to the legitimation of domination and the maintenance of hierarchy. In other words, law helps justify the concentration of power in the hands of the few and the privileges of some members of society in relation to everyone else. What law ordains is accepted simply because it is law. Law is violence, we are told (Cover, 1986). Law is terror put into words (d'Errico 1975). Law legitimates its own violence, then. Law promotes attitudes and actions harmful to people, and it does so through the use of language.

Law in the negative view is seen as promoting conflict rather than resolving it. And rather than eliminating differences between people and bringing them together, law contributes to categorizing people in terms of perceived differences and thereby reinforcing prejudice, discrimination, and misunderstanding (Minow 1990, 9). Law all too often, in many different ways, creates confrontations between citizens and the state.

In sum, in the radical critique, law perpetuates injustice, fosters conflict, and promotes selfish interests. Table 1.1 summarizes the positive and negative functions that have been attributed to law.

The Conservative Critique

A critique of law is also associated with the right, or conservative forces, going back at least to Edmund Burke's criticism of the legal order established in the wake of the French Revolution (O'Hagan 1984, 21). In the modern era, ultraconservative forces and the far right have been especially critical of law being used as an instrument for achieving a liberal agenda and of its ultimate infringement of individual rights. A central thesis of the right-wing critique of law, then, highlights the claim that law interferes with the natural freedom citizens are entitled to enjoy. For example, some rightist critics have attacked tax law and gun control laws as unjustifiable attempts by the state, through the mechanism of law, to confiscate the property of citizens and to deprive them of weapons they are naturally entitled to own. In somewhat less extreme conservative views, law all too often interferes with the natural law of the market and accordingly has a damaging or destructive impact on productive activity and the creation of new wealth. This right-wing critique of law, except at its extreme fringes, is less focused on law as an institution than it is on the perceived misuse and misapplication of law. Although conservative forces typically favor less application of law to the activities of businesses, they favor more vigorous application of law to conventional lower-class offenders.

Law's Unfulfilled Promises

The critique of law is not limited to those at the far ends of the ideological spectrum. The rule of law tends to be strongly supported within mainstream ideological thought, but there is much criticism of the perversion of law to fulfill the purposes of special interest groups or to improperly implement the law or to incur waste of time or money.

Virtually all of us can find some specific law, or some legal ruling, or some action undertaken by an official of law to be offensive. Law by its very nature cannot fulfill everyone's expectations and perceptions of justice. One of the paradoxes of living in a society that claims to venerate the rule of law is the production of unrealistic aspirations for what law can accomplish. Passage of the Civil Rights Acts of 1964 and 1968 swept away formal barriers to integration and equal opportunity but could not legislate racism per se out of existence; it could not obliterate deeply embedded social and psychological patterns of behavior that impeded the realization of equality. Accordingly, there has been much frustration and anger over the gap between the superficial promise of such law and the disadvantaged conditions that too many African Americans and other minority groups have continued to experience.

The Internal Critique of Law

The critique of law comes not only from those who are "outsiders," that is, who are not legal professionals, but also from those within the profession of law. Some of these critics rank at the top of their profession. Such critiques, however, are typically focused not on law as an institution but rather on the way it is used, or abused. Warren Burger (a Chief Justice of the U.S. Supreme Court) complained during his tenure in the 1970s and 1980s about the incompetence of a high percentage of lawyers who practice before the Court, the filing of frivolous lawsuits, inexcusable delaying tactics, and unseemly advertising by lawyers (Footlick 1978; Margolick 1984). Derek Bok, a former law professor, Dean of the Harvard Law School, and President of Harvard University, in a widely noted speech in 1983, was critical of the cost and inefficiency of the legal system, its emphasis on conflict, its extension of substantial advantage to the privileged, and its diversion of so many of our best and brightest minds to essentially nonproductive activity (Fiske 1983). Law professor Paul F. Campos (1998) has argued that a perverted worship of legal reasoning and the endless call for more law is symptomatic of some form of collective mental illness!

Those who have run for high political office in recent American history have often found that criticism of law—specific laws and legal rulings, judges and other lawmakers, and the legal profession—are popular themes that resonate with many voters. Following his re-election in 1936, Franklin D. Roosevelt attacked the "nine old men" of the U.S. Supreme Court, primarily on the grounds that they were trying to overturn or block New Deal legislation, and he tried, unsuccessfully, to increase the size of the Court so that he could appoint judges sympathetic to his causes (White 1976, 192). President Jimmy Carter observed, in 1978, that "ninety percent of our lawyers serve ten percent of our people. We are over-lawyered and under-represented" (Roth and Roth 1989, 152). Ronald Reagan attacked governmental regulation and government lawyers (Schechter 1990). President George Bush and his vice president Dan Quayle attacked the civil justice system for an alleged epidemic of costly lawsuits. Although this campaign was unsuccessful, it is remarkable that the antilawyer theme was pursued by a vice president who was himself a lawyer and the husband of a lawyer.

Hyperlexis: 'Too Much Law'

Other paradoxes pertaining to law often present themselves. If, on the one hand, we have come to expect law to provide solutions to an exceptionally broad range of social problems and conditions, we also tend to find law overblown and excessively intrusive. The claim that there is "too much law" (and too many lawyers) is commonplace. The term *hyperlexis* refers to the excessive growth of law (Manning 1977). By almost any measure, law has indeed been a growth industry in America (Footlick 1977; Friedman 1998a). Legislative bodies (from local to federal) add more than 150,000 new laws to the books each year. More laws mean more lawsuits, and the number of cases filed, at least in some jurisdictions, has led to a widely perceived "litigation explosion." Defining and measuring litigation is more complicated than one might think, but for now, we will say that litigation is a pursuit of some goal by using the courts. (There is more discussion of this topic later.)

The scope of litigation has broadened; some forms of litigation (e.g., medical malpractice suits) have increased exponentially, and case filings in the federal courts have risen dramatically. Class action lawsuits, where a large number of plaintiffs (sometimes many thousands) are joined in a legal action, became far more common in the 1970s than earlier; although their numbers declined in the 1980s, they were certainly a controversial element of the legal landscape in the 1990s (Martin 1988; Institute for Civil Justice 1997). Class action lawsuits were controversial because they were said to have bankrupted many companies and to have enriched lawyers rather than having adequately compensated plaintiffs. The growth of litigation was accompanied by growth in the size of the legal profession: it almost quadrupled during the second half of the twentieth century, and it grew at a substantially faster rate than did the population.

Law Versus Common Sense

Another critique of law focuses on its defiance of common sense and its imposition of burdensome, unnecessary, and counterproductive rules and requirements in an ever-widening range of circumstances. New York lawyer Philip K. Howard (1994), in his best-selling *The Death of Common Sense: How Law Is Suffocating America,* pursued this thesis. His book begins with an account of the failed attempt in 1988 of Mother Teresa's Missionaries of Charity to transform an abandoned building in the Bronx into a homeless shelter. The attempt failed as a result of the onerous (and allegedly unreasonable) requirements of the New York City municipal code. (For example, the code called for the installation of a costly elevator.)

Howard's book identifies many other cases where allegedly excessive legal red tape, or the extension of ever more rights and entitlements, frustrated the realization of socially worthwhile endeavors and where adherence to the rules and regulations seemingly became an end in itself. In a similar vein Walter Olson's (1997) *The Excuse Factory: How Employment Law Is Paralyzing the American Workplace* argues that American companies are increasingly constrained from conducting their business—particularly, in hiring and firing—in a sensible way because of the threat of lawsuits claiming discrimination, defamation, wrongful termination, sexual harassment, and the like. In this view, the present character of the law, on the pretext of protecting the rights of various classes of people, sabotages productive economic activity.

The Paradox

In the final analysis, whether people are better off or worse off if they have "more law" today is a matter of ongoing dispute. On the one hand, an argument can be put forth that people's rights are more fully protected, harmful activities are more fully addressed, and inequities and injustices are more likely to be corrected with the extension of law. On the other hand, arguments can be put forth that the law has become too intrusive, that economic inefficiencies and job losses result from excessive litigation, and that the privileged and powerful always have the advantage in the long term when there is more law. In sum, in America an enduring love/hate relationship with law persists. There are many historical contradictions and cultural sources of ambivalence. The American republic was, after all, founded on a "lawless" rebellion, or revolution; from the outset, nevertheless, the Founding Fathers professed a commitment to a nation of laws. The Constitution is one of the "sacred" objects of American history and an icon of the American rule of law. It is widely venerated and has been a source of inspiration for constitutions in many developing countries. On the other hand, in American history, there has been the frontier tradition with its resistance to formal legal controls; this stance is also widely celebrated in the present. In an America of the twentieth century an ongoing tension existed between the demand for more and more law in a rapidly growing, exceptionally heterogeneous, and increasingly complex society; at the same time a certain proportion of the citizenry has vigorously protested a perceived expansion and growing oppressiveness of the law. This paradox of wanting both more and less law is a source of tension in American society. It is not, however, the only issue that provokes contention. The following section presents a number of law-related issues around which debate currently swirls.

Current Issues Before the Law

From all sides, it often seems, we are confronted with contentious debates on law-related issues (Katsh 1998; Roleff 1996). On some matters pertaining to law there is broad agreement: That willful homicide or the sexual molestation of children should be forbidden by law is a matter of general consensus. In a large, complex society, however, one can always find some individuals or small groups who dissent from or challenge any law or social norm. An entity known as the National Association for Man/Boy Love (NAMBL), for example, advocated the position that even young children should be permitted to engage in consensual sexual relations with adults (Leo 1983). Such a group is marginalized in the extreme within our society and is subject to condemnation or prosecution. On the other end of the scale, a high level of consensus exists that parents should have the right to establish bedtimes for their minor children and require their participation in household chores and that such matters should not be addressed by governmental laws. Even here one might find extreme proponents of children's rights who would object to the imposition of any such constraints on the freedom of children, but again they would tend to be wholly marginalized within society and devoid of any measurable influence.

Between those issues on which there is a high level of consensus, whether in favor of the law or against it, there are many law-related issues on which members of society are divided. Some of the legal issues identified here have been debated over a long period of time; capital punishment is one such issue. Other issues have only surfaced recently: the use of surrogate mothers is one such issue. Many issues that were once heatedly debated—including witchcraft trials, slavery, Jim Crow laws (sanctioning segregation), voting rights for women, and the prohibition of liquor—are no longer live issues in American society. And some issues that currently divide people in other countries around the world, including genital mutilation of young girls (in some African countries), religious control over marriage (in Israel), basic rights of women (in some Muslim countries), and the right to dissent (in China, among other countries)—are also not live issues in American society.

Sanctity of Life Issues

One set of contentious legal issues can be called "sanctity of life" issues. Abortion, euthanasia, and capital punishment are three such issues; each involves the deliberate termination of life in some sense. (Questions concerning participation in warfare, hunting, and medical experimentation on animals could also be classified as sanctity of life issues.) Those who support capital punishment do not necessarily support the legalization of abortion, and vice versa. A person's position on the various sanctity of life issues seems to be related to his or her attitudes on such matters as punitiveness (Cook 1998). The issue of abortion—whether or not it should be legally available—has been exceptionally contentious in America, especially since the controversial U.S. Supreme Court decision in *Roe v. Wade* (1973) (Binion 1997; O'Connor 1996; Solinger 1998).

The status of the human fetus beyond the specific issue of abortion has also raised questions about fetal protection and crimes of mothers against developing fetuses through substance abuse (Daniels 1993).

Questions pertaining to some forms of euthanasia have become increasingly important in conjunction with medical advances allowing for the maintenance of "life" in extreme circumstances (e.g., of the profoundly injured or the terminally ill) (Dworkin, Frey, and Bok 1998). Specifically, the issue of whether physician-assisted suicide should be legally permitted has arisen.

Although polls continue to suggest that a majority of Americans support the death penalty, a significant and articulate minority campaigns actively against this extreme penalty (Bedau 1998). Insofar as positions on these sanctity of life issues are likely to reflect deeply felt and often highly personal moral intuitions, they tend to be intractable and difficult to reconcile. Some extremists, a very small number of proponents of the pro-life position on abortion, have committed murders against abortion clinic personnel, and a small number of right-to-die proponents have subjected themselves to criminal prosecution by participating in assisted suicides.

If Americans are beset with some complex legal questions relating to the termination of life, we also face challenging issues relating to the creation of life (Dolgin 1997). Advances in reproductive technology and biogenetics have generated issues about surrogate motherhood, age limitations on motherhood, the ownership of embryos, multiple pregnancies resulting from the use of fertility drugs, genetic engineering, and the possibility of cloning human beings (Brownsword, Cornish, and Llewelyn 1998; Pence 1998; Rae 1994). More specifically, these issues include the question of whether women who serve as surrogate mothers for couples unable to have a child of their own should have a right to renege on the arrangement and keep the child after birth, or should at least have some custodial rights; conversely, what happens if the contracting couple no longer wants the child after birth, especially if the child is born with significant defects?

Should surrogate motherhood itself be legally banned as a form of baby selling? If new reproductive technology makes it possible for women to sustain a pregnancy and give birth even after age sixty, should legal prohibitions be imposed on the grounds that the child (and society) is likely to experience significant adverse consequences? Should a woman retain the right to attempt to have a child from an embryo even if she is now divorced from the husband who provided the sperm and he objects? Should a woman be allowed to continue with a pregnancy involving many fetuses as a consequence of using fertility drugs, even if the multiple fetuses threaten her health, have a high probability of being born with serious defects, and are certain to impose astronomical medical costs on other parties? Should any legal restrictions be placed on an expanding technological capability of "engineering" the genetic endowment of children, or is such engineering purely beneficial for all parties? And if we develop the capability of actually cloning human beings, should this be legally permitted?

Rights Issues

One of the principal law-related themes of the latter half of the twentieth century was the dramatic increase in "rights consciousness." The Civil Rights Movement of the 1950s and early 1960s, challenging segregation and second-class citizenship of African Americans, highlighted the fact that some social groups have been systematically deprived of fundamental rights and that through collective action such a deprivation could be challenged (Kluger 1975). The success of this movement in sweeping away the legal barriers confronting African Americans inspired and influenced other disadvantaged groups. Although some of the legal victories on behalf of African Americans and minority groups generally have been widely accepted by the mainstream of society, other such victories have been the focus of heated, ongoing debate (Bell 1980; Greene 1989). For example, the abolition of official segregation

Box 1.2

Gay Marriage

At the end of 1999 the Supreme Court of Vermont instructed the legislature either to legalize gay marriage or to ensure that gay couples receive the same benefits extended to heterosexual couples (Goldberg 1999). At the outset of the twenty-first century Vermont has adopted, and several states were moving toward, the recognition of same-sex unions. On the other hand, laws against gay marriage had been adopted in some twenty-seven states, and such laws were being considered in various other states. This issue is certain to remain a contentious one in the years ahead.

has been widely accepted, whereas court-enforced busing and affirmative action have often been opposed.

The final decades of the twentieth century witnessed the emergence of a vigorous women's rights movement, as well as a gay rights movement, and somewhat lower-profile rights movements on behalf of the physically disabled, the mentally challenged and the mentally ill, illegal aliens, prisoners, and children. Each of these movements has encountered, in varying degrees, resistance, which may range from the highly organized to the subtle and personal. For example, despite the removal of most formal discrimination against women, they continue to experience disadvantages and informal discrimination (Dusky 1996).

Legal protection against housing and employment discrimination directed at gay people has been widely supported, but attempts to openly allow gays in the military encountered strong resistance. Initiatives on behalf of gay custodial or adoption rights, as well as legally sanctioned gay marriages (see Box 1.2), have provoked especially vigorous resistance (Baird and Rosenbaum 1997; Blasius 1994). Americans are far from a full consensus on the scope of accommodations that should be made for the handicapped; the right of the mentally ill to reject involuntary treatment; or the specific nature of privileges (such as conjugal visits) to which prisoners are entitled (Alpert 1980; Lotito, Soltis, and Pimentel 1992; Sales and Shah 1996). Finally, any children's rights movement, if it can be truly said to exist, is in its infancy (Freeman 1996). In one landmark case a minor child won the legal right to be emancipated from negligent parents, rendering him available for adoption by foster parents (DePalma 1992). It remains to be seen, however, whether such a case anticipates a broader extension of rights to children or is something of an aberration.

Age has always been a criterion for certain legal rights, responsibilities, and restrictions, but many issues pertaining to age-related law are unsettled. In the United States a fundamental contradiction concerning age long existed, namely, that a young man could be old enough to be drafted, and possibly fight for his country and lose his life, without being old enough to cast a vote for local municipal officers. This contradiction was resolved with the Twenty-sixth Amendment to the Constitution, which lowered the voting age to eighteen. The legal age for drinking, however, has varied among the states, although now it has been raised by most states to twenty-one; it remains a contentious issue for many young people (Wolfson 1995). On the other end of the age spectrum, the abolition of mandatory retirement continues to be a source of some debate (Levine 1988). As the twenty-first century progresses, changes in the age distribution of the population will surely have an impact on this issue.

Changing social values or patterns of behavior have generated new legal standards and new forms of "rights." Until recently in America, no right to a smoke-free environment was widely recognized, but an antismoking movement developed rapidly toward the end of the twentieth century, pushing through legislation that banned smoking in many public places, including some workplaces (Rabin and Sugarman 1993). In response, some smokers have made claims for recognition of their rights as smokers.

Even though sexual harassment has surely existed since time immemorial, the right to be free from such harassment, at least in the workplace, has also gained recent recognition (Conte 1990). On the other hand, there are those who argue that sexual harassment has been too broadly defined, so it has negative consequences for workplace relationships. While sexual harassment and smoking laws are relatively recent matters of contention, there are issues that have been the focus of contention in America since the time the Constitution was ratified. Many forms of these arguments continue through today. These are matters of free speech and privacy.

Free Speech and Privacy Issues

Freedom of speech and a free press are among the most sacred tenets of a democratic society such as the United States, and are rights guaranteed by the First Amendment to the Constitution. It is widely understood that the proclamation of heretical, blasphemous and thoroughly unpopular ideas cannot be suppressed, but many other issues arise in this context: for example, does the right to free speech encompass such diverse forms of expression as libel of public figures, obscenity, inciting illegal activity, and hate speech? The specific scope of free speech and press rights as protected by the First Amendment has led to a large body of judge-made law (Kalven 1988). In a landmark decision, *New York Times v. Sullivan* (1964), the United States Supreme Court held that critics of offical conduct could not be found guilty of libel unless they had disseminated deliberate or reckless falsehoods. This ruling did not inhibit some public officials from suing critics; for example, General William Westmoreland, Commander of U.S. forces in Vietnam, sued CBS for libel in a high-profile case (Abrams 1985). The network had claimed in a documentary that the General had suppressed information about enemy numbers. Westmoreland eventually withdrew his suit. Such lawsuits raise the question of whether the media are often inhibited from exposing or criticizing public figures because they fear undertaking the large expense of defending themselves in a lawsuit.

In another important case, a well-known fundamentalist preacher, Reverend Jerry Falwell, sued the notorious men's magazine *Hustler* after the magazine published a crude and obscene representation of him in a drunken incestuous rendezvous with his mother in an outhouse; although the jury awarded a sum of money to Falwell, the United States Supreme Court overturned the award, reinforcing the right to criticize (or make fun of) public figures (Taylor 1988). This case was featured in a popular film about the publisher of *Hustler, The People v. Larry Flynt.* Just as there is dispute about what constitutes libel, there is a long and torturous legal history of trying to discriminate between "art," which should be protected as a form of free expression, and blatantly pornographic material subject to legal controls (deGrazia 1992). The Supreme Court over a period of decades attempted to produce a standard for identifying pornography (including "of no redeeming social value" and "offensive to community standards"), but these attempts have been seen as difficult to enforce (Robel 1989). The dissemination of pornographic material and images through the Internet has been a special concern, since children have easy access to some of this material. Even so, the Supreme Court overturned a restrictive Communications Decency Act as overly broad and in violation of the First Amendment (Godwin 1998; Mendels 1999). The question of whether pornography should be legally suppressed or should be tolerated has been heatedly debated in the past few years, with at least some feminists aligned with the conservative forces calling for suppression.

In a related vein, legal cases have arisen in connection with attempts to ban certain "inappropriate" books from public libraries and with attempts by school administrations to censor student-run newspapers that publish material offensive to school personnel (Lony 1990). The issue of whether flag burning is a form of free speech has provoked especially strong reactions from self-described American patriots (Goldstein 1996). Provocation in another sense arises in connection with speech that wantonly offends or demeans some group (i.e., that is racist, sexist, homophobic, and so on). While the Courts have generally held that such speech is protected by the First Amendment, school administrators have often regarded this type of speech as a form of harassment that they should ban (Wolfson 1997). College campuses in particular have grappled with the dilemma of encouraging free speech while acting against speech that has a poisonous influence on the campus environment or that is experienced as harassment (including sexual harassment) (Shiell 1998).

When some form of speech or expression is alleged to be a direct cause of harmful behavior, the issue becomes especially complicated. Indeed, just such a connection is claimed by feminist critics of pornography, that is, that it encourages debasing and violent behavior toward women, including rape (MacKinnon 1993). In the 1970s, NBC-TV was sued after a young girl was raped by four youths apparently imitating a rape they had just seen in an NBC film, *Born Free* (*Time*, 1978). A publisher of "action books," Peder Lund (Paladin Press), was sued in the 1990s when a man who committed an especially savage triple murder was found to have purchased and specifically followed instructions in a book entitled *Hit Man: A Technical Manual for Contractors*, which Lund had published (Brooke 1996). The courts have also been reluctant to establish precedents in such cases for fear they might encourage broad censorship.

At first glance, it might seem difficult to see a connection between political campaign funding and free speech. But from 1976 on, the United States Supreme Court has consistently held that campaign donations cannot be constitutionally limited in amount or source because they represent a form of free speech (Turow 1997). Of course, a practical consequence of this position is that wealthy individuals and organizations continue to have a highly disproportionate influence in our political system and that meaningful campaign-financing reform is difficult to accomplish. Although the defense of free speech has been historically associated with those on the liberal or leftist side of the political spectrum, in the recent era this constituency has sometimes called for restrictions (e.g., on hate speech), while conservative and corporate constituencies have called for fewer restrictions, not only on campaign spending but on advertising for such products as tobacco (Lewis 1998). Also, the extraordinarily rapid expansion of the worldwide Internet has generated a variety of legal issues about what can be disseminated through this medium and what types of controls, if any, are permissible. Altogether, contentious issues in the realm of free speech and press are likely to persist for some time.

The right to privacy is another sacred tenet of American society. It is not specifically mentioned in the Constitution, but the Supreme Court has recognized that a general right to privacy is implicit in this document (McWhirter and Bible 1992). The right to privacy issue intersects with other issues, such as reproductive freedom, abortion, and physician-assisted suicide. The legitimate objective of law enforcement agencies to investigate possible criminal activity can clash with privacy rights of individuals, and the right of the press to report news can create the same type of conflict. In *The Right to Privacy* Ellen Alderman and Caroline Kennedy (1995) claim that Americans experience today a growing number of intrusions on their privacy. These intrusions include some justice system practices, such as strip searches following arrests on minor offenses; drug and school searches; prosecutions of pregnant women; interventions against the right to die; the relentless invasions by the media into the lives of both famous and ordinary citizens; and employer investigations and surveillance of employees.

Modern technology has created newer and even broader opportunities for invading privacy. One invention is the telephone listening device. In the landmark decision of *Katz v. U.S.*(1967), the United States Supreme Court affirmed the proposition that conversations carried on over a telephone wire enjoy a presumption of privacy; accordingly, listening in on such conversations requires a search warrant. The capacity to engage in observing citizens or gathering confidential information about them has been greatly extended by contemporary methods of surveillance and computerized data banks. Various controversies arise, then, on where to draw the line between protecting privacy and realizing other legitimate purposes of investigation or information gathering.

Issues of privacy are closely linked with issues of confidentiality. It is well known that confidences between priest and parishioner, lawyer and client, doctor/therapist and patient, and welfare agency and client and records pertaining to these realtionships are generally protected by law from public, involuntary disclosures. But the ultimate scope of such confidentiality is not always clear. If a confession to a priest produces crucial information about serious criminal activity; if a lawyer's client discloses engagement in ongoing fraud; if a doctor's patient is HIV-positive and at high risk to infect unknowing parties; if a therapist's patient discloses homicidal intent or sexual abuse of a minor; or if a welfare agency client has been implicated in the death of a child, do the confidentiality provisions apply? The legal system has produced various formal responses to such questions.

Family Issues

The dissolution of the family is hardly new, although the breakup of families through divorce has increased exponentially in the past few decades. In one interpretation, legal reforms such as no-fault divorce were actually introduced with the hope of discouraging divorce, but such laws obviously failed (DiFonzo 1997). Both the increase in divorce and other changes pertaining to gender roles have produced new and sometimes painful controversies (Dusky 1996). For example: Is reliance on mediation in divorce cases likely to work to the disadvantage of women? Is community property division or some other formula more or less fair? Should divorced spouses who remarry still be eligible for alimony? Should maternal custody of children be privileged over "most qualified parent"? At what age, if any, should minor children be allowed to choose their preferred custodial arrangement? And so on.

Although no-fault divorce became the norm in most states in the final decades of the twentieth century, by the century's end there was some backlash against this standard, and there has been a call for making it somewhat more difficult to obtain divorces. It remains to be seen how far this backlash movement will go.

Issues Concerning Legal Processes

Enduring legal controversies arise in connection with so-called *victimless crimes* (Meier and Geis 1997). Willful homicide, rape, burglary, armed robbery, larceny, auto theft, arson, and other forms of conventional crime are prohibited by law, and that is not a matter of controversy. By the same token, few people, if any, say that poor table manners, personal rudeness, tardiness, or bad taste in clothing should be classified as crimes, punishable by law. A category of activities does exist, however, which has been the focus of considerable public disagreement. People argue about whether these activities should be proscribed by formal law, and if so, with what penalties. These activities have included gambling, illicit drug use, prostitution, pornography, and consensual homosexual activity.

Gambling has become widely legalized in many, but not all, forms and has been actively promoted by state and local governments eager for the relevant tax income. Public sentiment is still strongly supportive of laws making distribution and sale of various so-called illicit drugs, from marijuana to cocaine to heroin, illegal, although the level of support varies according to the particular drug; calls for decriminalization or outright legalization are fairly widespread.

Prostitution and pornography represent two forms of the commercialization of sex. They have long existed and have inspired a range of law-related responses in different historical contexts. Within contemporary American society, there is less support for legalization of prostitution than for legalization of pornography, but in both cases there has been a fair amount of *de facto* legalization, or unwillingness of police and courts to enforce laws that remain on the books.

Box 1.3

Drunk Drivers and Auto Confiscation

In New York City, in 1999, Mayor Rudolph Giuliani ordered the city's permanent seizure of cars whose drivers were found to be driving drunk, including first offenders (Finder 1999). Although civil libertarians (or the drivers themselves) complained that this was a punishment which presumed guilt prior to any such finding in the court, the practice is in line with long-standing principles in Anglo-American law, which authorize property confiscation in connection with various illegal acts. Since the value of cars varies greatly, as does the wealth of those charged with drunken driving, a forfeiture might be far more punitive in one case than in another.

The United States has a long history of legal proscriptions against almost every imaginable form of intimate sexual behavior, with the exception of marital, procreative, missionary-position sexual intercourse in a private setting. These illegal forms of sexual activity have included everything from consensual homosexual relations to masturbation to fornication to adultery to oral-genital sex. If many of the relevant laws are no longer enforced, some are still on the books. In the case of consensual homosexual relations, approximately half the states define it as criminal activity.

Criminal Justice

Crime and criminal justice are major preoccupations of both the general public and politicians, so they generate ongoing debate on many enduring issues as well as newly raised issues.

Our legal system contends with an ever-expanding range of controversial defenses offered for criminal conduct, including black rage, parental abuse, premenstrual syndrome, battered wife, and even obsessed fan syndrome (Dershowitz 1994; Wilson 1997). These defenses have been collectively labeled the "abuse excuse." In one interpretation, any acceptance of such defenses reflects a reaction to the increasing toughness of our justice system's response to crime, as they provide juries or judges with a rationale for excusing an accused whom they do not think deserves the prevailing legal penalty. Such defenses in most cases are unsuccessful. But it remains to be seen whether they will, over time, be more widely embraced by both the general public and the justice system.

Many other ongoing controversies are associated with the criminal justice system. They include questions about plea bargaining, preventive detention, sentencing practices, and victim impact statements. Some of these controversies are explored in later chapters (see Box 1.3).

Business

A general increase in consciousness of the harmful consequences of some corporate activities conflicts with pro-business claims that interference with free market activities has harmful economic consequences. Accordingly, there are ongoing debates on product liability law; environmental protection and workplace safety standards; and the criteria for antitrust actions or insider trading prosecutions. Product liability refers to a company's responsibility when its products cause harm; antitrust actions refer to efforts to challenge anticompetitive or monopolistic business practices; and insider trading refers to trading on the basis of information not available to the general public, which is prohibited by law (see Box 1.4).

Tobacco companies have been successfully sued by states to compensate them for the high health costs associated with tobacco use; gun makers are also facing lawsuits claiming their responsibility for gun-related violence (Higgins 1998; Fried 1999). Whether such lawsuits will be initiated against still more types of businesses, and whether these initiatives will be supported by both the public and the justice system, remains to be seen.

Box 1.4

Copyrights and Patents

Copyrights and patents did not exist before 1790 in the United States, and artists and would-be inventors were free to copy and use the ideas of others. The basic and generally commendable objective of the copyright and patent law was to ensure that both creative individuals and corporations would get a fair return for their efforts. In 1790, the first year of the patent law, examiners (including Thomas Jefferson) issued three patents; in 1998, 147,521 patents were issued to Americans alone (Gleick 2000; Lewis 2000). Copyright protection is in effect for twenty-eight years and was made renewable for a second twenty-eight year period (greatly benefiting such corporations as Disney, who can then extend their control over the use of Disney characters).

The present era has witnessed pervasive foreign piracy of American-produced intellectual property, with annual losses in the billions to the film, music, software, and book publishing industries. In this sense, holders of copyrights have been victimized. Some critics claim, however, that granting of copyright protection has become too broad and liberal, with aspiring artists and the general public as victims of greedy copyright holders.

Health and Medicine

In the realm of physical health a new threat such as AIDS generates a whole series of complicated legal issues: for example, mandatory testing; exceptions to general standards of confidentiality; distribution of clean needles and condoms; standards for discrimination or exclusion; and liability to criminal charges against HIV-positive individuals who knowingly have unprotected sex (Dalton et al. 1987). At century's end, an increasing number of states were adopting laws intended to protect the public from HIV infection (Richardson 1998). The future direction of law on this matter was going to be guided by the balance between public fear of AIDS and sympathy for HIV-positive individuals and those afflicted with AIDS.

Conclusion

Within virtually any branch of law today—tax law, consumer law, environmental law, labor law, welfare law, and so on—we can identify public policy controversies. Also, in a world increasingly described in terms of "globalization," issues such as international bans on nuclear weapons and land mines or the desirability of establishing a permanent international criminal court arise.

The identification here of law-related controversies is by no means exhaustive. Indeed, such a listing might go on almost endlessly. The issues identified in the preceding paragraphs can be, and surely will be, endlessly debated. Many different arguments, from the highly principled to the purely pragmatic, can be and will continue to be put forth on behalf of one or the other side of these issues. These issues should be of special interest to students of law and society because they bring into sharp relief the interaction of legal and social variables; those who acknowledge and work from this point of view have a *sociolegal perspective*. This perspective allows one to understand the following: What are the primary social factors that influence or shape both the character of an issue (such as euthanasia or affirmative action) and the public perception of it or the specific response to it? Conversely, what are the identifiable social (and behavioral) consequences of existing legal policy pertaining to the issue, or a hypothetical legal policy at odds with existing policy? Scholars with the sociolegal perspective want to know how the social influences the legal and how the legal affects the social. In the final chapter of this book at least some of these issues are explored in more depth, specifically within the context of the relation between law and social change.

Law in America Today

Law is all over. Law is everywhere. In America an ongoing love/hate relationship with law persists.

On the one hand, Americans generally venerate the tradition of "a nation under law." The Constitution and the Bill of Rights are sacred documents in American history. Key concepts of these documents, including "due process" and "equal protection," are deeply ingrained in the national consciousness. Americans have come to expect "total justice," as Lawrence M. Friedman (1985), puts it, that is, a proper legal remedy for any blameworthy loss or injury. Certainly, when Americans are victims of crime or suffer a private injury of some kind, they want the law to be there for them. And if legislators are constantly enacting new laws, it is surely because at least some of their constituents are demanding such laws to address a wide range of perceived problems.

On the other hand, we have always had, as David Ray Papke (1998) puts it, *Heretics in the Temple: Americans Who Reject the Nation's Legal Faith*. Anti-abortion activists and members of right-wing militias are contemporary representatives of this tradition. But many ordinary Americans also express considerable frustration (or anger) with a nation of lawyers. Most Americans hope to avoid contact with legal authorities and lawyers and may take this into account in planning their daily lives.

The preceding two paragraphs have set forth American views of law in exceptionally broad terms. More specifically, the well-off and well-connected and those who belong to the historically dominant group in society are more likely to view law in positive terms than those who are poor and who belong to a minority group.

In their illuminating study of law in the everyday lives of ordinary Americans (*The Common Place of Law*), Patricia Ewick and Susan Silbey (1998) find that Americans tend to experience law in contradictory ways: magisterial and remote at some times and all-too-human at other times. Unsurprisingly, however, most Americans do not spend much time at all specifically thinking about law. In that sense, law would seem to be at best a marginal presence in their lives. Of course, for a minor proportion of Americans—those being processed by the felony courts; those involved in a major civil lawsuit; those engaged in a complicated divorce and child custody case—law becomes for a time an all-consuming dimension of their lives. As suggested earlier, law lies invisibly behind many of our mundane, daily activities. We can hardly avoid law entirely when it is so pervasively highlighted in our media. But these considerations aside, people in their everyday lives generally prefer to think about things other than law, and most people initiate legal action only reluctantly. According to Ewick and Silbey (1998, 196), people are often disappointed in law's inability to address the troubles that plague their everyday lives.

The reactions of Americans to the role of law in the Clinton scandals, at the end of the twentieth century, captured well some of the contradictory perceptions of law. Americans as a whole expect their President to uphold the law and comply with it, and it would be contrary to traditional American values to consider the President above the law. However, a majority of Americans were apparently distressed by the Independent Counsel's relentless legalistic pursuit of the President, and especially his intrusive exploration of Clinton's sexual conduct. Although Americans want a law-abiding President, they did not in this case display much appetite for a seemingly endless legal investigation and proceeding against the President.

Americans departed the twentieth century and entered the twenty-first, then, with profound ambivalence toward law and many contradictory perceptions of it. In the inevitably complex, dynamic, and expanding society of the future, law will be an unavoidable, and arguably growing, presence. The need to understand law as fully as possible will surely increase. But the traditional American love/hate relationship to law is also sure to endure.

Key Terms and Concepts

abuse excuse
autonomous model
copyright/patent
homologous model
humanistic tradition
hyperlexis
ideological prism
interactive model
litigation explosion
odd laws
positivistic tradition
radical critique of law
sanctity of life issues
total justice
trials by ordeal
victimless crimes

Discussion Questions

1. Explain why it might be difficult to effectively study law following the positivistic tradition. What are the advantages and disadvantages of a humanistic approach to the study of law?
2. Discuss the three views that explain the realtionship between law and society—autonomous, homologous, and interactive.
3. According to the radical critique of law, how does law discriminate?
4. Explain America's love/hate relationship with the law.
5. Which legal policy issues are especially difficult to resolve, and why?

Chapter Two

Law: Its Meaning and Logic

What is law? The word itself is familiar to all literate members of society, but defining the term is more challenging than one might expect. Much scholarship has been devoted to this question, but it has not yet produced either a perfect definition of "law" or a broad consensus on how to best define the term. Indeed, the search for a perfect definition may well be an exercise in futility; rather, those who study law should acknowledge that there are simply more useful and less useful definitions, depending on the context within which the term is invoked (Cohen 1935, 835).

In the course of Western history alone, "law" has had many meanings (Friedrich 1963). It has been equated with the will of God, as a mirror of a divine world order. Law has also been viewed as an expression of human nature; pure reason; general will; and class ideology. Law has been seen as historical fact, and as a command. Law is most broadly conceived of as a form, or type, of social control (Davis 1962). It is a universal feature of the human experience that some human beings have always, and everywhere, attempted to exercise control over other human beings. However, not all observers regard law itself as universal, and one critic declares law to be a "eurocentric enterprise" to promote Western European values and interests (Nunn 1997). Donald Black (1983) provocatively argues that what we call crime is also a form of social control, or self-help, in the sense that crimes are often committed in pursuit of the offender's idea of justice. For example, assassination is defined as a criminal act by society, but the perpetrator may regard his act as appropriate and a necessary way of addressing wrongs against him or his group.

"Control" has been identified as the central concept of sociology (Gibbs 1989). Social control is accomplished by different types of means: normative, utilitarian, and coercive (Etzioni 1968). The normative approach attempts to obtain compliance by fostering belief in the rules of the social order; the utilitarian approach offers some practical rewards or inducements for compliance; the coercive approach threatens or uses force to achieve compliance. Churches rely primarily on the normative; businesses rely primarily on the utilitarian; and prisons rely primarily on the coercive. But most social institutions—including parents attempting to control the behavior of their children—rely upon some mixture of these approaches; this is true as well for legal institutions.

The Orders of Law and Social Control

A person who uses the term "law" may be referring to a social institution, a specific legal system, or some element of a system. The term law, then, is used both very broadly, to refer to a virtually universal form of social control, and very narrowly, to refer to a specific rule or act within a particular legal system. Social control itself exists on many different levels, in many different forms. The term "law" is most typically, but not uniformly, reserved for formal governmental social control. Even with this definition, however, law takes different forms and operates on different levels. Within any society, then, we find co-existing systems of social control and law; which systems of social control are appropriately called "legal" is a matter of controversy (Tamanaha 1993). In order to examine the relationship between law and social control, it is necessary to look at the different levels, or orders, on which the law operates: universal; international; national; state; local; organizational; and community (see Table 2.1).

Table 2.1 Levels of Law

Universal Law	Divine rules (e.g., Ten Commandments)
International Law	Treaties (e.g., laws of war)
Regional Law	Treaties (e.g., Eurolaw)
Federal Law	National legislature; statutes (e.g., law against treason)
State Law	State legislature; statutes (e.g., law against larceny)
Local Law	City/town council; ordinances (e.g., zoning law)
Organizational Law	Formal organization—rules (e.g., rules against cheating)
Community Law	Social group—rules and norms (e.g., assignment of chores)

Universal Law

On a *universal* level, some laws are taken to be divine in origin, and all human beings are urged to honor them (Golding 1966). The golden rule, "Do unto others as you would have them do unto you," is a prime example; the Ten Commandments are also widely regarded as universal laws. Of course, a person's sense of commitment to any such universal law is importantly determined by his or her religious commitments; avowed atheists, for example, may or may not adopt personal codes of behavior that coincide with such universal (and divinely ordained) laws, but they do not experience the same compulsion to obey these laws that religious people experience. In an ultimate sense, obedience to or disobedience of such laws is only sanctioned or rewarded (in some religious faiths) in the next life, through eternal salvation or damnation. A church will also exercise some control here; for example the Catholic church canonizes those who adhere to divine law in an exceptionally outstanding way and excommunicates those who defy divine law. Such control can only be exercised over those who feel themselves to be believers and followers of the church. (A long history of conflict exists between universal laws identified by a particular church and some secular laws, and this issue will be further explored in Chapter 3.)

International Law and Regional Law

Although most law is something created and implemented within the boundaries of a particular state, or country, increasingly in the modern era *international* law is becoming important (von Glahn 1992). Such law comes into being through international treaties, accords, and other forms of agreement between states. International law faces the challenge that it is unlikely to achieve truly universal support among states, and it is fundamentally more difficult to enforce than is national law.

In a noteworthy invocation of international law, the surviving Nazi leadership and other Nazis directly involved in their various crimes of war, crimes against peace, and crimes against humanity, were tried after World War II in the Nuremberg trials. These surviving Nazis were charged with violations of various treaties between various nations, signed at the Hague, Versailles, Locarno, and elsewhere, from 1899 on. Jurisdiction over the Nazi defendants was based upon the newly ratified United Nations charter and an agreement between the principal allied World War II victors (the United States, the Soviet Union, Great Britain, and France) (Conot 1983). More recently, individuals involved in genocidal atrocities in Bosnia and in Rwanda have also been indicted by international tribunals (Minow 1998). Others widely viewed as major violators of international law were not or have not to date been brought before international tribunals. They include the late Pol Pot, the Khmer Rouge leader in Cambodia alleged to have masterminded the slaughter of well over a million of his fellow citizens in the late 1970s, and Saddam Hussein, the Iraqi dictator alleged to have overseen various genocidal and war-related actions. Some large questions for the twenty-first century are these: Will international law become an ever-larger presence in the world? Will a truly effective permanent international criminal court be established? Will nations collectively become more successful in controlling major crimes against peace and humanity carried out on behalf of states or by major political entities within states?

The states that compose the continent of Europe can, collectivity, be called a region. At the end of the twentieth century, the formation of a European Union and the establishment of a European Court of Justice (in Luxembourg) and a European Court of Human Rights (in Strasbourg) was giving rise to an evolving "Eurolaw" (Cohen 2000; Taylor 1999). At the onset of the twenty-first century, European law was increasingly taking precedence over national law on such matters as human rights, the environment, trade, and working conditions. Nations eager to join the European Union (e.g., Hungary, Romania, and Turkey) were influenced to conform to broader European norms on resolving conflicts and on human rights issues, and Europeans in growing numbers appeared to be embracing a European (as opposed to a solely national) identity. Although economic unity and the adoption of a single European currency was the principal objective of the Maastricht Treaty of 1993, it has followed that European countries increasingly cooperate on cross-border policing and a range of other legal issues. Accordingly, one should recognize the existence of an emerging regional law, in addition to national and international law.

Federal Law

Most people think of law as a creation of states, or countries. In many countries—Spain, for example—national law is the single most comprehensive and important body of law to which people are subject. In the United States, however, a federation of states exists, and federal (national) law has had a considerably more limited reach, since state laws and municipal laws also regulate behavior. Nevertheless, during the course of the twentieth century, the scope of federal law in the United States expanded. Federal law covers, among other matters, crimes against U.S. criminal law (including treason, attacks on federal officials, bank robbery, kidnapping, and the like); disputes between states or between citizens of different states; and regulation of a wide range of activities, from interstate commerce to environmental pollution. Federal law is generally more significant in the realm of corporate activity and white-collar crime than in the realm of conventional crime, and in disputes between corporations than in disputes between individual parties.

State Law

In countries like the United States, a confederation of states, the principal formal legal order toward which citizens must orient themselves is state law. In some cases, both state and federal law apply (for example, a business fraud violates state common law and also violates federal anti-racketeering law) (Vandevelde 1996, 17). State law in America typically covers such matters as homicide, burglary, rape, arson, auto theft, larceny, and the like, and in civil law it covers disputes between citizens of the state. Most of the lawbreakers in the news have violated state laws and are prosecuted in the name of the state. In the civil realm as well, matters such as landlord/tenant disputes, divorces, estates, automobile accident lawsuits, and the like are governed by state laws.

Although the commonalities between the U.S. states in both their criminal law and their civil law tend to outweigh the differences, some noteworthy differences do exist (Mayers 1973, 7–9). All states, for example, have laws prohibiting homicide; not all states, however, have a death penalty for those convicted of homicide. All states have laws prohibiting rape; different states may define rape in different ways. In approximately half of the American states, consensual sodomy is prohibited under the criminal law; in about half the states, no such prohibition exists. All states have laws permitting divorce; grounds for divorce are not necessarily identical between states, and different formulas for the division of marital property exist. All states allow victims of automobile accidents to sue liable parties, but different states have different provisions governing such lawsuits and obligations pertaining to automobile insurance.

Altogether, then, a general survey of all U.S. states would produce a general impression of what state law prohibits and what it allows, but it would vary on particular details of the state's law. For example, as you drive an automobile across state lines on an interstate highway, you cannot assume that the speed limit in the state you are entering is the same as the speed limit in the state you are leaving.

Why do variations between laws of states exist? To begin with, such variations reflect different histories. As one especially striking example, law in the state of Louisiana for a long time retained elements of traditional French law, as a reflection of that state's origins and heritage (Herman 1993). Then, different conditions in different states influence the law. As a rather prosaic example, Western states with their broad expanses and low density of people have traditionally permitted higher vehicle speed limits than congested Eastern states. Differences of law between states can also reflect successes and failures of lobbying groups and lawmaking coalitions, and in some cases the power of an idiosyncratic lawmaker.

Local Law

Citizens must also orient themselves to the requirements of *local* law. Such law, for the most part, addresses fairly minor matters, such as jaywalking and littering, but it also deals with some consequential matters, such as zoning (e.g., whether a business can be established in a particular neighborhood). It is on the local level that one is most likely to find odd or idiosyncratic laws, insofar as a single influential member of a local council empowered to pass such laws may be able to get a particular personal hang-up or obsession enshrined in local law. For most of us, most of the time, local law is hardly a significant preoccupation.

Organizational Law

One of the defining features of contemporary society is participation in formal organizations. All such organizations (or "private governments") have rules; whether such rules, and the procedures for administering them, add up to a system of law is a matter of some dispute (Macaulay 1986). In the case of military organizations, which are, of course, a division of the state, there is widespread recognition of the existence of military law and a military system of justice (Bishop 1974). In the cases of corporations and other types of businesses, universities, unions, professional associations, and clubs (or fraternities and sororities), formal rules and adjudicative procedures typically exist but are less likely to be characterized as law (see Box 2.1).

Organizational rules (and sanctions associated with their violation) can assume great importance for employees, faculty and students, union members, doctors and lawyers, and club or fraternity/sorority members. An employee fired for tardiness, a faculty member stripped of tenure for sexual harassment, a student dismissed for cheating, a union member ostracized for defying a strike call, a doctor stripped of a license to practice medicine or a

Box 2.1

The College Campus System of Justice

College and university campuses are significant communities. In some cases, tens of thousands of people live, study, and work in these communities. Inevitably, many instances of illegal or improper behavior occur there (Matthews 1993). In some cases, substantial violations of the larger society's laws occur: for example, theft, (date) rape, and even homicide. More mundane violations of criminal law—including use of illicit drugs and underage drinking—are extremely common. When college authorities become aware of such violations, they may call in the police, refer the offenders to the criminal justice system, or attempt to handle these cases internally (N. Bernstein 1996; Lively 1997).

A date rape case, for example, might be handled by college disciplinary procedures. The college may claim that it must act more swiftly than the criminal justice system can to protect members of the college community. However, the college disciplinary procedure is likely to be conducted in secret and without traditional due process protections and standards of proof. The alleged victim of rape may claim that the college is attempting to avoid bad publicity and to cover up the incident; the accused rapist may claim that his reputation is ruined and he is penalized without an opportunity to make a proper defense (Gose 1996).

Although no one disputes that colleges are entitled to enforce disciplinary rules against students (and staff), a question arises about whether colleges can properly penalize students for off-campus behavior (Gose 1998). In addition to taking action over violations of criminal law, colleges and universities also have their own codes of conduct to administer (for example, pertaining to cheating and plagiarism or to the violation of dormitory visitation rules). Students attending public universities are entitled to certain constitutional safeguards in disciplinary hearings, but this is not necessarily so at private universities; altogether, many students accused of disciplinary violations do not experience procedural fairness (Berger and Berger 1999).

Controversy can arise when college rules conflict with other beliefs or commitments students may have. For example, in a widely reported case, five Orthodox Jewish students sued Yale University over its rule that freshmen must live in university dormitories on the grounds that mixed-sex living in the dorms was offensive to their religious beliefs (Cloud 1997). Furthermore, colleges have long attempted to discipline faculty members for conduct in violation of the community's rules and standards. In the recent era, many colleges and universities have adopted codes to deal with sexual harassment, and cases have been pursued internally even though charges may also result in civil lawsuits. Finally, colleges and universities have long claimed allegiance to protecting academic freedom and free speech on campus, but this commitment can come into conflict with the religious mission of a college or pressures to take action against "politically incorrect" speech and action.

In the 1960s era, students rebelled against many traditional college rules, and on many campuses such rules were liberalized or abandoned (Bronner 1999). By the end of the twentieth century, however, many college campuses were reimposing controls over students' lives, at least in part in response to the expectations of parents.

lawyer disbarred for serious professional misconduct, or a club member ousted for failing to attend to mandated responsibilities may all experience significant personal trauma and shame plus loss of status, income, and possibly livelihood. Of course, aggrieved parties who believe they have been unjustly sanctioned under organizational rules may well turn to the formal civil law system to seek justice. For the most part, the state would prefer not to become involved with the internal rules of organizations, but in a society where people tend to develop a strong sense of their rights, civil courts may have to provide a final resolution of some disputes.

Community Law

Finally, we are all members of social groups and communities: for most of us that means a family, perhaps a wider circle of relatives and friends, and a neighborhood Such social groups and communities (another form of "private government") have, at a minimum, some generalized norms that members are expected to adhere to. Social control in such settings is exercised quite informally, sometimes by no more than a look of disapproval. On the other hand, a neighborhood (or other entity) may have formal proceedings to address rule violations.

What does any of this have to do with law? This is a question that does not have a single answer; the response to the question depends upon one's conception of law. Michael Reisman (1999), in *Law in Brief Encounters*, argues that the complex system of unofficial norms governing our everyday interactions with others—including staring and glaring, standing in line and cutting in, and talking to the boss—constitute social laws, which he calls microlaw.

Specific Definitions of Law

Throughout history sages and scholars have offered up some specific definitions of law, although these definitions vary considerably (see Box 2.2).

As was noted earlier, it may make the most sense for one to adopt a definition of law useful for a given purpose, or in a particular context, rather than to try to come up with a single, all-purpose definition of law. For example, a useful conception of one important form of law, criminal law, might include the following elements: it is formal (although some disagreement exists over whether law must necessarily take a written form as opposed to simply being orally proclaimed); it is imperative (that is, it most typically proscribes certain types of conduct); it has sanctions, or "teeth" (that is, external controls); it is political (it emanates from the state); it is specific (that is, it does not as a rule simply proscribe "bad behavior" but specifies what is forbidden; "disorderly conduct" can be considered one exception to this proposition); it is ongoing (that is, it is not imposed on an ad hoc, or case-by-case, basis, and it is not imposed ex post facto, or after the fact); and officials are empowered to enforce and administer it.

Box 2.2

Some Classical Definitions of Law

Definitions of law by philosophers and sages include the following:

Law is intelligence without passion. (Aristotle)

Law is the highest reason, implanted in nature, which commands what ought to be done and forbids the opposite. (Cicero)

(Law) is nothing other than a certain rule of reason for the purpose of the common good, laid down by him who is entrusted with the welfare of the community and promulgated. (Aquinas)

The law is the last result of human wisdom acting upon human experience for the benefit of the public. (Samuel Johnson)

From U.S. Supreme Court justices we have the following definitions:

The prophecies of what the courts will do in fact, and nothing more pretentious, is what I mean by law. (Oliver Wendell Holmes Jr.)

We shall unite in viewing as law that body of principle and dogma which with a reasonable measure of probability may be predicted as the basis for judgment in pending or in future controversies. (Benjamin Cardozo)

Law... the sum total of all those rules of conduct for which there is state sanction. (Harlan Fiske Stone)

From those writing in the tradition of the social sciences, just two definitional efforts are included here:

An order shall be called law when it is guaranteed by the likelihood that (physical or psychological) coercion aiming at bringing about conduct in conformity with the order, or at avenging its violations, will be exercised by a staff of people especially holding themselves ready for this purpose. (Max Weber)

(Law is) governmental social control. (Donald Black)

It is evident, then, that law has been conceived of, or defined, in different ways over time.

Sources: Aristotle, Cicero, and Stone from Shrager and Frost 1986; Aquinas, Johnson, and Holmes, from McNamara 1960; Cardozo, from Shapiro 1993; Weber 1978, 34; Black 1976, 2.

The term "law" is also incorporated into many familiar and commonplace expressions. Western, democratic nations in particular—and many other nations as well—claim to adhere to "the rule of law." This term is generally taken to mean that decisions are made and disputes are resolved in accord with what the law requires rather than by the brute exercise of power or in a state of anarchy. In one interpretation, the commitment to a government of law, not men, was most clearly affirmed in the American experience in the landmark U.S. Supreme Court decision *Marbury v. Madison* (1803) (Kahn 1997, 4). In this decision the Court held that officials of the government's executive branch are subject to correction by the Court when they violate a legal obligation and that the Court has the power to rule on the constitutionality of Congressional acts.

Box 2.3

The Rule of Law

Is "the rule of law" a truly neutral and objective standard for resolving disputes within a society, or is it actually a rhetorical devise used to justify politically motivated prosecutions (Kyle and Lauderdale 2000)? The case against President Clinton, which led to an impeachment trial, was championed on the claim that it reflected the rule of law and a government of laws, not men. Critics claimed, however, that this case was driven mainly by politically committed enemies of the President (Scheuerman 1999).

It is important to point out that the rule of law has been invoked in societies with differing legal systems, some repressive, and that the rule of law can be interpreted or applied in different ways. The rule of law has been attacked as a "myth" that masks dominance by the power structure; if this is so, a commitment to authentic liberty requires a repudiation of the "rule of law" (Hasnas 1995; Kahn 1997).

In a parallel vein, a commitment to "law and order" (in contrast to crime and disorder) is commonly expressed in Western societies, but the call for "law and order" was also one of the rallying cries of the Nazis when they were seeking political power. In at least one sense of the term, the Holocaust (the extermination of some six million people) was carried out in the name of law and order (Mueller 1991). Somewhat ironically, Richard Nixon ran for the American presidency in 1968 on a pledge to restore law and order and was then the first president forced to resign as a result of major violations of law by himself and his close associates (Blum 1991).

To what, then, does a claim of support for law and order really refer? It might refer to an institution, or a particular system, or a particular regime; more narrowly, it has been an expression of commitment to a particular (conservative) ideology, or a particular component (the police) of the justice system. For Stanley Diamond (1973, 339), "Law and order is the historical illusion; law versus order is the historical reality." It is indisputable, in any case, that some terrible crimes have been carried out in the name of law and order.

Origins of Law

How did law originate (Davis 1962; Friedman 1975)? Social control on some level has been a part of human experience since the beginning of human existence. In this section we are asking about origins of a more formal conception of law, an officially proclaimed system of rules with associated formal sanctions and officials empowered to administer this system. There are three different views on the origin of such laws: value/consensus; rational/contract; and power/coercion (see Table 2.2).

Table 2.2 Origins of Law

I. Value/Consensus
   A. Natural
   B. Customary
   C. Democratic
II. Rational/Contract
   A. State of Nature > Contract
   B. Pragmatic
   C. Negotiated
III. Power/Coercion
   A. Sovereign
   B. Class Conflict
   C. Interest Group

Value/Consensus

Law is seen as a formalization of deeply held, widely shared values. This viewpoint has several different versions. First, there is "natural law" theory: that law is, or surely ought to be, based upon divinely ordained rules, or the natural rights to which human beings are entitled (Bix 1996). Natural law, in this sense, has both a specifically religious and a secular version. In either case, however, the emphasis is on rules or rights that everyone ought to be able to recognize and honor. The Roman Catholic theologian St. Thomas Aquinas is among those identified with the divine version of this form of explanation; the English philosopher John Locke is among those identified with a secular version of "natural rights" (Friedrich 1963). The American Founding Fathers were much influenced by Locke, and the Declaration of Independence specifically invokes the notion of "natural rights" as the appropriate foundation for American law.

An alternative value/consensus view of law regards it as the "crystallization of the mores," or a formalization of customs that emerged within particular societies over a long period of time. A nineteenth-century German student of law, Friedrich von Savigny ([1831] 1986), was an early proponent of this view of law's origins. Stanley Diamond (1973), a contemporary American anthropologist, challenges the view that law (an instrument of state power) reflects a crystallization of customary norms. In his view, law is imposed from above, often at odds with custom.

A third value/consensus view of law has a distinctly modern theme and emphasizes that law is a product of democratization: that is, law reflects the values of the popular majority, as expressed through the political process. Of course, any such account is only applicable to laws created in societies that have adopted a democratic system. Jurgen Habermas (1996), a contemporary German social philosopher, is associated with a position that societies should be moving toward the creation of an "ideal speech" situation wherein citizens can in a truly meaningful and well-informed manner engage in a dialogue leading to consensus and the adoption of mutually agreed-upon rules and laws.

Rational/Contract

A second view of the origin of law shifts attention away from values to agreement based upon a contract. The English philosopher Thomas Hobbes ([1651] 1958), in his book *Leviathan*, advanced an especially celebrated version of social contract theory. Hobbes held that human beings in a "state of nature" were engaged in a "war of all against all." In such a condition, in Hobbes' further famous formulation, the life of each person would be "solitary, poor, nasty, brutish and short." Although human beings in a state of nature live like animals, they also have one important faculty, reason, that makes them different from other creatures. And through reason they arrive at the realization that it is in the long-term interest of all individuals to form a social contract with others, wherein they give up certain powers (delegated to the state, or "the Leviathan"), in return for which the state will provide them with a measure of security against their fellow human beings.

In the contemporary context, law may be viewed as a product of pragmatic necessity, or agreement based upon practical considerations. In this view, the very conditions of modern life create circumstances requiring an ever-widening net of rules and regulations. Laws that protect people from the dangers of unrestricted operation of various forms of modern technology could be said to fall in this category.

Negotiation can be identified as a specific mechanism closely associated with a contractual conception of the origins of law. In this view, law comes out of a process involving compromises and trade-offs, having a focus on achieving an instrumental objective.

Power/Coercion

A third basic view of the origins of law adopts a position fundamentally at odds with either a value/consensus or a rational/contractual view. In this view law is an expression of the will (and interests) of the sovereign or of the power elite. One classic version of this way of looking at law was advanced by the Italian philosopher Machiavelli ([1513] 1976), in *The Prince*, a famous source for the proposition that the ends justify the means, and power makes right. Machiavelli specifically advised rulers to adopt cynical, manipulative means to achieve their political ends, and the law can be a part of this enterprise.

Karl Marx regarded law as a creation of the privileged classes to maintain an inherently exploitative economic system (Cain and Hunt 1979). Marx, with his emphasis on class conflict, highlighted the fundamental conflicts of interest between the ownership class and the wage-earning class, with the law serving the interests of the former. In at least one reading, Marx regarded the very form of law as an inevitable instrument of exploitation, with the strong implication that in a truly communist society there would be no law (and no need for law).

A view of law as a product of the exercise of power and a reflection of conflicts of interest need not be specifically Marxist, or ideological. For example, Austin Turk (1969), a contemporary criminologist, has been a leading proponent of a nonpartisan, interest-group perspective on how law is formed. The perspective holds that these interest groups are not necessarily aligned with the capitalist ownership class and that one can analyze the role of power in lawmaking without choosing to say whether capitalism should be condemned or supported.

Which of these diverse views on the origin of law is "right"? This question also lacks a simple answer. First, we can all think of laws that appear to reflect a very high level of value consensus. For example, almost all citizens strongly support legal prohibitions on the sexual exploitation of children. Other laws, for example, traffic law, seem to reflect the practical realities of living in a complex, modern society (where people drive cars that are inherently dangerous vehicles unless their movement is regulated). There are also laws (vagrancy law is one classic example) that seem to reflect the powerful imposing their interests on the powerless. Nevertheless, different students of law have put more or less emphasis on one or the other of these forms of explanation for the origins of law, in accordance with their own ideological commitments. Historically, much emphasis has been put on the consensual view of law, despite considerable evidence of the central role of power and the unequal distribution of wealth in shaping law.

Models of Law

Law clearly has many different dimensions and aspects. In order to make sense of law, one needs to make a number of distinctions. The "ideal type," proposed by the great German sociologist Max Weber (1949), provides one starting point for any such distinctions. By ideal type, Weber meant an illustrative type that incorporates essential elements of something that occurs in the real world without necessarily being identical to the real-world phenomenon. For example, many legal decisions are based on "what a reasonable man would do under similar circumstances." This legalistic notion of the "reasonable man" can be considered an abstraction, or ideal type. The "reasonable man" of the law is not synonymous with any real, living person. Relatedly, dichotomies making sharp contrasts can also be useful in making sense of the law's many aspects (see Table 2.3). But reality is more complex, multifaceted, and nuanced than any such ideal types or dichotomies might suggest.

In the pages that follow, fifteen "models" of law are identified and defined, in the form of dichotomies of ideal types. The term "model" is used here to encompass a variety of patterns, conceptions, sources, contexts, forms, types, orientations, structures, foci, and contents of law. At least some of these models relate to characteristics of law. An understanding of and familiarity with these models and the key terms associated with them is a necessary undertaking for anyone who hopes to claim literacy about our system of law.

Fundamental Dimensions of Law

The Basic Conception of Law: Principles vs. Practices

One conception of law stresses the abstract in the sense of law as an ideal, law as a statement of principles. Such ideals and principles are then incorpo-

Table 2.3 Law and the Legal System: Models and Conceptions

I.	*Basic Conception*		
	Abstract	vs.	Concrete
	Law in principle (written)	vs.	Law in practice (action)
	Documents/code books/case reporters	vs.	Courts/police/corrections officers
II.	*Fundamental Source*		
	Natural (divine) (revelation/values)	vs.	Positive (human sovereign) (pragmatism/power)
III.	*Societal Context*		
	Consensus (contractual)	vs.	Conflict (domination)
IV.	*Basic Function*		
	Restitutive (order/equity)	vs.	Repressive (control/exploitation)
V.	*Theoretical Conception*		
	Epiphenomenal (social product)	vs.	Holistic (autonomous)
VI.	*Historical Origin*		
	Roman (canon/continental/civil)	vs.	Common/English (customary/communal/judge-made)
VII.	*Written Form*		
	Statutory/codes/Constitutional	vs.	Case/opinion
VIII.	*Political Source*		
	International	vs.	State-based
	Legislative	vs.	Judicial
	Executive (Administrative)	vs.	Justice system personnel (e.g., police)
IX.	*Orientation*		
	Nonrational (supernatural/intuition)	vs.	Rational (scientific/empirical)
X.	*Structure* (Judiciary)		
	A. Organization: Dual	vs.	Unitary
	B. Power: Hierarchical	vs.	Horizontal
XI.	*Form of Dispute Settlement*		
	Court model (triad)	vs.	Bargain model (dyad)
	Adjudication	vs.	Negotiation
XII.	*Type of Court Procedure*		
	Adversarial	vs.	Inquisitorial
XIII.	*Focus of Law*		
	Public/criminal (crime)	vs.	Private/civil (tort)
XIV.	*Objective* (of Criminal Law/Justice System)		
	Crime control	vs.	Due process
XV.	*Content* (of Criminal Law)		
	Substantive	vs.	Procedural

rated into written documents, from constitutions to local codes. On the constitutional level, law may take the form of a general principle; statutes and case opinions, on the other hand, tend to be specific. Statutes and case opinions are different forms of written law and are more fully defined later in this section.

In contrast, one can begin with the concrete manifestation of law in behavior, in the practices of those who implement law. Law here is a form of action: what judges do, what parole board members do, what police officers do.

Imagine for a moment being approached by an extraterrestrial who has been given the assignment to discover what this thing called "law"—which supposedly exists in your society—is. On the one hand, you might direct this alien toward the library, with the instruction to visit the "KF" section, to examine copies of the Constitution, the federal code, the volumes reporting case (judge-made) law, and the like: there law can be found. On the other hand, you might direct this alien toward the courthouse and the police station, with the instruction to observe what transpires in the courtroom and on the police officer's patrol; here, too, law could be witnessed. If these are two different approaches to getting at the essence of law, it should also be obvious that they complement each other. However, some references to law treat it as essentially a matter of principles, or written rules, and other references to law treat it as essentially a matter of practices, or specific actions.

The Fundamental Source of Law: Natural vs. Positive

Law as natural suggests that human law is (or surely ought to be) rooted in some transcendent order, that is, that it reflects divine (God-given) imperatives or natural rights that human beings can discover intuitively. Law as positive suggests that human law is simply a human creation produced in specific historical circumstances, that is, that it is made by sovereigns or other parties who are in a position to make laws. The natural conception of law tends to stress revelation, in some form, and the intimate relationship between law and moral values. The positive conception of law tends to stress power, in some form, and the practical or instrumental character of law. Of course, it is possible to view some parts of law (e.g., pertaining to homicide) as a reflection of the natural order, and other parts of law (e.g., pertaining to business contracts) as a purely practical, human creation. But the basic division between proponents of natural law and those of positive law has been influential in the history of jurisprudence; it will be discussed further in Chapter 4.

The Basic Orientation of Law: Nonrational vs. Rational

Through much of history legal decision-making was guided by what could be considered nonrational (supernatural, or intuitive) considerations. Chapter 1 described trials by ordeal, which at one time were the sole formal means of determining guilt or innocence in criminal cases. One of the defining features of law in the modern world is a movement increasingly toward rational (empirically based, or scientific) grounds for legal decision making (Weber [1954] 1967, 349–356). Judges (or juries) are expected to base decisions upon evidence that supports, or fails to support, a case. The introduction of expert witnesses and DNA evidence are elements of the ever-greater reliance upon "science." But our legal system is by no means purely rational, since biases, intuitions, and interpretations by judges and juries certainly continue to play a role in legal decision making. A wholly rational legal system would perhaps be one where decisions are rendered by infallible machines (or computers), if we can imagine such a thing.

Social Dimensions of Law

The Societal Context of Law: Consensus vs. Conflict

One of the most important, and most enduring, questions in social theory has been this: How is social order possible? All introductory sociology students are exposed to the basic dichotomy between viewing society as rooted in a broad consensus (or agreement) between members of a society and viewing society as rooted in conflict between major social groups, with the powerful imposing their will on the weak. The question of whether law is based principally upon agreement, or upon domination, is considered more fully in Chapters 4, 5, and 9.

The Basic Function of Law: Restitutive vs. Repressive

On the one hand, law either maintains or restores order and ensures, in an orderly manner, that those who have suffered injury or loss at the hands of another are appropriately compensated. On the other hand, law is a mechanism for controlling people on behalf of special interests and facilitates the exploitation of the powerless. Law's principal functions were discussed more fully in Chapter 1.

The Theoretical Conception of Law: Epiphenomenal vs. Autonomous

In the epiphenomenal view, law cannot be understood independent of the society within which it exists; in the extreme version of this view, law is nothing more than the reflection of society. In the autonomous view, law has certain universal attributes that render it at least relatively autonomous from the particular society (and political economy) within which it operates; in the extreme version of this view law is no more dependent upon social context than is mathematics. These contrasting views are entangled in jurisprudential and sociological approaches to making sense of the law, and are considered more fully in Chapters 4 and 5.

Political Dimensions of Law

The Specific Historical Origin of Law: Civil vs. Common

One encounters many different stories about law's historical development. In the history of Western civilization, however, the basic contrast has been between the civil law tradition and the common law tradition. The civil, or Roman, law tradition has been the more dominant one, in at least some form. (The term "civil" law is unfortunate here, since it inevitably leads to confusion with the criminal/civil law contrast, discussed later in this section.) In civil law countries, which include most European countries, legislative bodies draft codes of law, and judges are only supposed to apply the law. In common law countries (principally England and its former colonies), judges "find," or define, law in an evolving communal tradition of norms and precedents. The United States is typically classified as a common law country; the lawmaking activity of the U.S. Supreme Court is a prime exemplification of this tradition. It has also incorporated some attributes of the civil law countries. Of course, this dichotomy does not fully capture the world's families of law. Elaboration on these families of law is undertaken in Chapter 6.

The Political Source of Law: International vs. State

Most people are socialized to think of law as a product of the state. Within the United States and in some other countries there is a contrast between federal law and state (or individual state) law. More broadly still, there is the contrast between state (federal or individual state) law and international law. Historically, law has been most effectively legitimated and implemented within the boundaries of a sovereign state. But the world also has a long history of international treaties and accords that have produced a form of international law. As mentioned earlier, some international tribunals have been convened to implement this form of law. If we accept the proposition that "globalization" is becoming an increasingly dominant feature of our world, then it seems likely that international law will become more important during the course of the twenty-first century.

The Written Form of Law: Statutory vs. Case Law

On the one hand, our written law can be found in such documents as the Constitution and in federal or state codes. Legislative bodies (including a constitutional convention as a special type of legislative body) produce constitutional and statutory law. On the other hand, an important part of our written law can be found in appellate court case opinions. Appellate court judges, at least in the common law tradition, produce this type of written law. An ongoing tension of sorts exists between legislative bodies and judges on law: Should the will of the legislative body or the interpretation of the judge (or justices) prevail?

The Implementation of Law: Executive and Administrative

Although lawmaking is most readily associated with the legislative and judicial branches, in important respects the executive branch and administrative or justice system agencies linked with it also make law. The executive branch is empowered to issue executive orders; the president (or governor) can grant pardons, effectively negating law in particular cases. Most importantly, the executive branch oversees the enforcement of the law, and in its choices about such enforcement, as well as its allocation of enforcement resources, it has an impact on the reality of what law does and does not mean. In the same vein, justice system personnel, down to the police officer on the beat and the corrections officer on rounds, "make" law through their decisions of what laws or rules to enforce and what to disregard. For example, so-called "blue laws"—prohibitions on doing business on Sunday—remain on the books in many parts of the United States and have been upheld by the Courts but are simply not enforced; in this sense they lack substance as law. In a somewhat more formal way, administrative agencies, such as the Securities and Exchange Commission and the Environmental Protection Agency, have been empowered to make, enforce, and adjudicate many laws or rules in their realm. Accordingly, such agencies represent an important, although somewhat lower profile, source of law.

Dimensions of Legal Systems

The Structure of the Legal System: Dual vs. Unitary; Hierarchical vs. Horizontal

The American legal system is one with a dual structure, with a co-existing federal system of law and state systems of law (see Figure 2.1). In some countries the legal system is unitary, with a single system for the entire country.

In terms of judicial power, the United States—and most legal systems in developed nations—has a hierarchical structure, with higher courts empowered to overrule the decisions of lower courts. In some places, for example, in the Ottoman Empire in an earlier time, one could find an essentially horizontal structure of judicial power, with co-existing courts for different constituencies (e.g., Christian citizens; Islamic citizens; Jewish citizens) (Friedman 1977, 71). Of course, within the American system of law, different states can be considered to exercise "horizontal" judicial powers within their borders, and within states different courts (e.g., civil courts and criminal courts) exercise horizontal judicial powers within their particular jurisdictions.

Figure 2.1 The Organization of Legal Systems

A. **Dual Legal System:**
Federal – State

Unitary Legal System:
Unified National System

B. **Hierarchical Legal System:**
U.S. Supreme Court
↓
Circuit Court of Appeals
↓
District Court
↓
Magistrate's Court

Horizontal Legal System: Muslim Court - Christian Court - Jewish Court

---

The Form of Dispute Settlement: Court Model (Adjudication) vs. Bargain Model (Negotiation)

In the court model (exemplified by either the criminal court or the civil court), there are three essential parties: a defendant; a plaintiff or prosecutor; and a judge (and/or jury). The last of these three parties imposes a decision on the other parties. In the bargain model (exemplified by labor union/management dealings), there are only two essential parties, who meet on a theoretically level "playing field." The two parties, in the pure version of this model, must arrive at a mutually agreed-upon resolution of their differences. In the first model (at least on the criminal court side), a case is adjudicated; in the second model, a dispute is negotiated. Of course, in reality a large percentage of both criminal and civil cases are actually resolved by negotiation between two parties, with a judge's decision a formal declaration of this resolution. And when a labor union and management are unable to resolve their differences by bargaining and negotiating, they may agree to have the matter resolved by bringing in a third party, an arbitrator, who will impose a decision on them. In some cases, they may also turn to the courts to resolve their dispute. So the realities of dispute settlement are not infrequently at odds with the formal process.

Court Procedure: Adversarial vs. Inquisitorial

In the adversarial model, there is what amounts to a contest between two sides, with a judge presiding, or refereeing, and with either a judge or a jury making a determination about who won the contest (in accordance with whatever standard of proof is in effect). In the American criminal justice system, the adversarial model is used in major felony cases. On the plus side, adherents of the adversarial model claim that the truth in a criminal case is most likely to emerge when each side is best able to put forth its case. Furthermore, the defendant in a major criminal case, up against the intimidating resources of the state, has the best chance to put forward a case with the capacity to introduce evidence and witnesses and to challenge the state's evidence and cross-examine the state's witnesses. On the minus side, critics of the adversarial model claim that the whole thrust of such proceedings becomes a contest to win on points, with each side trying to prevent admission of the other side's version of the truth and to present its own one-sided version (Strick 1978). Some critics contend that defendants with substantial resources can win cases on the basis of legal pyrotechnics rather than on the basis of revealing truth. Such critics might well cite the O. J. Simpson criminal case as an illustrative example of this tendency.

The inquisitorial model takes the form of an inquiry, with a judge (or panel of judges) interrogating not only the defendant but victims, witnesses, lawyers, justice system personnel, and any other pertinent parties. The civil (or Roman) law courts operate essentially in terms of this approach. On the plus side, a judge (or panel of judges) who is wise and fair-minded can, with considerable efficiency, direct appropriate questions to various parties, focusing on extracting the truth of the matter at hand. On the minus side, such a system may be seen as incorporating an assumption of guilt; it puts the defendant at a considerable disadvantage with no real control over the direction of the inquiry; and when directed by a biased judge it may simply provide an opportunity for highlighting the judge's own preferred version of the truth.

France is one of the countries where an inquisitorial system is in effect (Provine 1996). An examining magistrate plays an active role in the investigation of an alleged crime. If a case goes to trial, the judge dominates the process. He or she interrogates witnesses, or must approve questions put to witnesses by others, and interrogates the accused as well, with no cross-examination. The scope of the interrogation is very broad, exploring the past record and character of the accused as well as the case at hand. If a jury is involved, the judge participates in the jury deliberations.

In the American system of justice many proceedings—for example, grand jury hearings, Senatorial inquiries, and minor criminal or juvenile delinquency trials—actually take the form of an inquisition as opposed to an adversarial proceeding. Formal inquisitorial proceedings may incorporate some adversarial elements, if lawyers or witnesses aggressively challenge the judge or judges. But the basic differences between these models remain pronounced and consequential.

Basic Focus of the Law: Civil (Torts) vs. Criminal

If we go back to the early stages of recorded history, law, for the most part, took the form of civil law (Holmes 1881). That is, one party made a complaint of having been wronged in some way by another party, and the king or whoever administered justice would make a ruling on whether anything, which might include the life of the accused, was owed to the injured party. Civil law is that part of law which addresses private grievances. Criminal law is that part of law which addresses "public" offenses. Over time, especially during the Middle Ages, a growing list of harmful acts came to be defined as crimes against the "King's peace" and were ultimately prosecuted in the name of the state (Jeffery 1962). The state administers any punishment imposed upon the wrongdoer, and the state collects any fine.

In a civil proceeding, one private party initiates a legal proceeding—say, for a divorce, for a contractual violation, or for compensation in the case of an accidental injury—against another private party. If the plaintiff's case is successful and there are monetary damages, the award goes directly to the plaintiff. A crime, then, can be thought of as a violation against a person's right as a citizen to be secure in her or his person and property; a tort (a civil wrong) can be thought of as a purely private wrong against a person as an individual. But any such broad generalizations require some qualification, and the relationship between crimes and torts is not entirely clear-cut (Fleming 1967; Gross 1979).

Crimes are not necessarily more harmful or injurious than torts; indeed, some "crimes," such as possession of small amounts of marijuana or picking pockets, cause minor harm. In contrast, some torts, such as negligence leading to another person's becoming a quadriplegic or the destruction of another person's reputation, cause immense harm.

Crimes are not necessarily intentional acts and torts unintentional; for example, corporations may be held strictly liable for environmental damage under criminal law even if there is no specific intent to do harm; the civil tort of maligning another person's reputation is typically intentional.

Crimes and torts are not necessarily mutually exclusive. In other words, the same harmful action—for example, driving an automobile while intoxicated, causing an accident and injury to another—may give rise to both a criminal prosecution and a civil lawsuit. Indeed, in any case where some party believes itself to have been harmed by another party, a civil lawsuit may be pursued, although not necessarily successfully. People rarely attempt to sue someone who has mugged them, perhaps mainly because even if the lawsuit is successful, there will be no assets to pay damages.

Wealthy offenders—corporations, professionals, or individuals such as O. J. Simpson—are often sued in conjunction with criminal prosecutions against them.

The penalties for some criminal convictions are quite minor—a small fine, probation, or some community service—while judgments in civil cases may be in the millions of dollars and can cause financial ruin. Finally, the status of an activity as a criminal matter or a civil matter may change over time. In the case of marijuana, some states have in recent years decriminalized possession of small amounts of it (relegating it to the civil law), while environmental harm (always potentially subject to civil action) has increasingly come to be defined as a matter of criminal law. In the final analysis, we should recognize that both "crime" and "tort" are social constructs.

The Basic Orientation of the Criminal Justice System: Crime Control vs. Due Process

What is law attempting to accomplish? On the one hand, achieving crime control is obviously a primary objective of the criminal justice system. On the other hand, in a democratic system (such as that of the United States), there is also concern with ensuring due process (Packer 1968). Of course, the criminal justice system may have other important objectives as well, such as avenging wrongdoing, imposing just penalties, rehabilitating and reintegrating offenders, and reconciling offenders and victims, while overseeing appropriate restitution. Nevertheless, crime control and due process are commonly regarded as primary objectives, yet they are also inherently at odds with each other. If one's only objective is crime control, one empowers the criminal justice system to move quickly and ruthlessly against any and all suspected offenders. Such an approach, however, will inevitably sweep up many innocent parties as well and will violate the privacy and rights of any number of ordinary citizens. If one insists on adhering fully to all the due process guidelines, a certain proportion of guilty offenders will escape processing or punishment, although this approach is far less likely to compromise the rights of innocent parties. The challenge has always been to achieve the right balance between these objectives. In the 1960s, a series of landmark due-process decisions by the U.S. Supreme Court (with Earl Warren as Chief Justice) had given significant momentum to the due-process objective (Graham 1970). With the rising crime rate in the 1970s, and the resurgence of political conservatism into the 1980s, the crime-control objective achieved dominance (Beckett 1997). The impact of a declining conventional crime rate at the end of the twentieth century remains to be seen.

The Content of the Criminal Law: Substantive vs. Procedural

One part of the criminal law prohibits certain behavior and identifies the penalties for engaging in such activity (Wallace and Roberson 1996). This is the substantive aspect of the criminal law. For example, murder is prohibited, and those convicted of murder are liable for severe penalties. Rape, assault, burglary, larceny, auto theft, and arson are among the other conventional offenses prohibited by the substantive law. One enduring issue for substantive criminal law is this: What is the proper scope for the law? Controversies continually arise. For example, people who call themselves "pro-life" argue that substantive criminal law in the United States fails to include an activity that it should include: abortion. In contrast, many constituencies argue that the substantive criminal law presently includes many activities that it should not include, such as possession and use of marijuana and consensual homosexual acts.

The procedural criminal law refers to that part of the law that governs procedures once an individual (or group) is suspected of a crime, apprehended, indicted, tried, or convicted (Israel, Kamisar, and LaFave 1993). Here the principal controversies center on whether those accused of crimes have too many—or too few—rights at any of these stages. In the more conservative political environment of the final decades of the twentieth century, many challenges to the accused's due-process rights arose on different levels, and these challenges were often successful.

In a simplified view, the substantive criminal law is intended to protect citizens from those who would do them harm, and the procedural criminal law is intended to protect accused criminals from persecution by the state. However, the substantive criminal law, as it relates to so-called victimless crimes for example, may be seen as an infringement on the rights of ordinary citizens. The procedural criminal law, meant to protect all of us, insofar as anyone could be mistakenly accused of a crime, has been used in totalitarian societies to empower the police to break down doors, arrest people at will, hold them indefinitely without formal charges, and so on. Accordingly, we should not confuse substantive and procedural criminal law by definition with their character in particular societies.

Conclusion

The preceding section, then, defines and distinguishes between a range of concepts essential to the understanding of law—and criminal law in particular. Surely the form of reasoning adopted within any system of law is among the most basic elements of that system of law. In the section that follows, then, the matter of legal reasoning is addressed.

Legal Reasoning

If one of the defining attributes of modern law is its commitment to rationality (as opposed to superstition), it follows that we expect legal decision

Box 2.4

Law and Emotions

The claim that law is a rational enterprise has been mentioned at various points in this text, but emotions such as disgust and shame, revenge and remorse, and love, forgiveness, and cowardice, can all influence law and legal decision making (Bandes 1999). In many complex ways, an interplay between law and emotions often occurs. Legislators, judges, and lawyers can claim that their actions in relation to law are made independent of emotions, but such claims can be challenged. Chief Justice Stuart Hughes instructed a new justice, William O. Douglas: "At the constitutional level where we work, ninety percent of any decision is emotional. The rational part of us supplies the reasons for supporting our predilections." (Douglas 1980, 8). On the lower court level, legal matters ranging from sentencing decisions in cases of mass murder to the awarding of custody in divorce cases engage the most intensely experienced emotions.

making to be based upon coherent, logical reasoning. Reasoning by analogy (finding connections between cases) and by deduction from rules (identifying conclusions that follow from valid premises) have been identified as two basic forms of legal reasoning (Burton 1985; Levi 1949; Sunstein 1996).

Legal decisions occur on many different levels, and in many settings. Not only judges, but prosecutors, probation officers, and police officers may engage in some form of legal reasoning and decision making. In the following paragraphs, however, judges are the focus of attention. In American society, there is a general expectation that an important legal decision (such as that rendered by the United States Supreme Court) will be accompanied by some form of justification for the decision. Many lower-level legal decisions are so routine or straightforward that they are not seen as requiring elaborate justifications; in many such cases a simple rule is cited or is shown to be implicit.

Legal reasoning can refer not only to justification but also to the psychology of choosing (L. Carter 1998). On one end of the spectrum, legal reasoning has been regarded as a purely intellectual exercise, akin to the application of mathematical logic to a problem. It follows from this view of legal reasoning that there is a single correct answer to a legal case, and if the appropriate legal principles are applied in an accurate way to a particular case, the appropriate decision will be produced. At the other end of the spectrum, legal reasoning has been regarded as a purely subjective phenomenon, a product of social, psychological, or ideological influences. In this view two judges who are looking at the same case may arrive at opposite conclusions, and no case has a single inevitable outcome.

In the traditional view, then, judges apply the relevant law (L) to the relevant facts (F) and arrive at a decision (D) (i.e., $L + F > D$); in the alternative, modern view (or its extreme version), the judge is biased (for social, psychological, or ideological reasons) in favor of a particular decision and then selects legal rules and facts to justify that decision (i.e., $D < L + F$) (Frank 1930). The first view has been associated with legal *formalism* and positivism, the second with legal *skepticism* or realism and critical legal studies. In Chapter 4 more detailed attention is devoted to the schools of jurisprudence associated with these different views (see Box 2.4).

Appellate court justices and trial court judges render decisions that can have a profound impact on both individual lives and on social groups, or even on society as a whole. They are compelled to make decisions, typically choosing between competing options, and these decisions can be influenced by many factors. All justices, or judges, adopt or internalize a judicial philosophy that serves as one important basis for their decisions (see Table 2.4). Some judges have a specific, fully developed judicial philosophy that they identify in the context of their judicial opinions or in books and articles they write (see Box 2.5). Other judges may choose not to articulate a judicial philosophy, and may even claim to have no such philosophy, deciding each case before them on its own merits, but this approach itself can be characterized as a perspective on how cases should be decided. Appellate court justices, in rendering their decisions, may look to what was done in the *past*, what is called for in the *present* case before them, and what impact their decision might have on society, law, and individual persons in the *future*.

Judicial Restraint

In view of the importance of appellate court decisions, especially on constitutional questions, the judicial philosophies of U.S. Supreme Court justices have received much attention (L. Carter 1998; White 1976). First, there is *judicial restraint*, which is typically regarded as a conservative judicial philosophy. Adherents of this philosophy tend to hold the view that the court is "the least democratic branch of government" and should defer to the will of the people's elected representatives in the legislative branch. Accordingly, the justices should scrupulously avoid making new law and should restrict themselves to fairly narrow questions that may arise in cases brought before them: For example, did a defendant's actions violate or fail to violate a legislatively produced statute, according to the statute's specific language or the intentions of the legislative body that produced it? Is a legislatively produced statute in conflict with a constitutional clause or amendment?

On constitutional questions specifically, adherents of judicial restraint favor the position that a judge should not interpret or apply a constitutional provision in a manner that goes beyond the "original intent" of the Framers or the specific language of the provision (Jaffa 1994). An enduring debate has focused on the issue of whether the Framers themselves meant for the Constitution to be read in this way; whether, even if they did, it is in fact possible to correctly identify a specific intent (indeed, exactly whose "intent" should count: that of the Framers or that of the ratifiers of the Constitution?); and whether, in any case, it makes sense to attempt to apply constitutional provisions formulated in an earlier and very different time to circumstances in today's world?

The conservative approach called "originalism" locates constitutional authority in the meaning of the Constitution's provisions at the time of its authorship and enactment; this view continues to be controversial. In a parallel vein, the term "strict constructionism" refers to the position that the application of a law (or constitutional provision) must not go beyond the literal meaning of the wording of the law.

Table 2.4 The basic types of judicial philosophy and their characteristics.

I. *Judicial Restraint*
   Originalism; Strict Construction

II. *Judicial Interpretation*
   Conceptualism; Historical/Referential

III. *Judicial Activism*
   Functionalism; Pragmatism

Box 2.5

Justice William O. Douglas as a Judicial Activist

William O. Douglas (1898–1980) served for over thirty-six years on the United States Supreme Court, longer than any other justice in American history. He was appointed by Franklin Roosevelt in 1939, to succeed Justice Louis Brandeis, and he resigned in 1975, some time after suffering a debilitating stroke. Douglas was also one of the most controversial justices in the history of the Court, owing to his arch-liberal and libertarian views; his outspokenness; and his unconventional personal life (Simon, J. 1980). He was an uncompromising defender of the First Amendment right to freedom of expression; he wrote for *Playboy* magazine; he was married four times (his last wife was 44 years his junior). Several attempts were made to impeach Douglas; all failed.

Douglas was a supremely American type: a rugged individualist, immensely energetic, strong-willed, stubborn, a demanding taskmaster, and a convivial companion. Although many justices have come from privileged circumstances, Douglas and his siblings were raised by their widowed mother in poor circumstances. He rode the rails from his native Washington State to New York City to enroll at Columbia University Law School, and he worked his way through the school. Douglas was a self-made man who maintained throughout his life a strong empathy for humble people at the bottom of the social order. He also believed that judges who failed to engage fully with life became "dried husks." Douglas was a dedicated mountain climber and outdoorsman; he traveled widely, wrote numerous books, and spoke out on controversial matters.

Douglas was wholly committed to individual freedom and to social justice. Although Douglas (originally a law professor at Yale and then Commissioner of the Securities and Exchange Commission—SEC) was regarded as a legal genius by some of his peers, he was utterly unpedantic. His characterization of the purpose of the Constitution—"to keep the Government off the backs of people"—is clear even to a young child.

Douglas has been described as an "anti-judge" because he was almost indifferent to precedent and judicial convention; he was result-oriented in his votes and written case opinions on the Court (White 1988). His decisions and case opinions were based upon intuitions, as well as on a romantic affinity with the natural environment and his dedication to its preservation (Ray 1999). Douglas was an important participant in the landmark due-process decisions of the Warren Court of the 1960s. He was an activist in every sense of the term, both on and off the bench.

Judicial Interpretation

A second judicial philosophy, which can be called *judicial interpretation*, adheres to the view that justices should interpret the Constitution while remaining true to, and constrained by, an evolving tradition of such interpretation. In this view, typically identified with those with a liberal or moderate outlook, justices should be respectful of the interpretations of constitutional concepts adopted by their judicial predecessors. The Constitution is viewed here less as a document than as an interpretive tradition rooted in a document. Perhaps the principal matter of controversy here is the specific principles that should guide such interpretation. One version of judicial interpretation (*historical/referential*) stresses the historical evolution of public and judicial understanding of constitutional doctrine; another version (*conceptualism*) focuses on a valid and coherent notion of constitutional concepts, such as due process.

Judicial Activism

A third judicial philosophy, known as *judicial activism*, is most commonly associated with liberals. Adherents of this judicial philosophy believe that it is wholly appropriate for justices to declare law in accordance with the perceived needs of the times. Such justices essentially believe that constitutional doctrine should provide a fundamental point of departure for creating legal doctrine that is specifically responsive to the dominant values and practical necessities of the present. The terms "functionalism" and "pragmatism" have been applied to this approach, with its stress on a currently useful interpretation. Any such judicial philosophy is bound to be controversial, and adherents of judicial activism have been bitterly attacked for arrogantly implementing their own value preferences and applying them to the rest of the citizenry.

Philosophy Versus Action

The association of a judicial philosophy with a particular political outlook has to be qualified here. Historically, conservatives have tended to interpret legal doctrine quite flexibly, or actively, when it has suited their purposes—for example, to extend more power to the executive branch, the police, and employers. Liberals have tended to read the Constitution quite strictly, or with restraint, when an amendment is in line with their beliefs—for example, the First Amendment stipulation that Congress shall make no law restricting freedom of speech.

The Constitution contains both rules and standards (Sunstein 1996). The interpretation of rules, for example, people under 35 cannot be president, has been quite straightforward and uncomplicated. It is the standards, for example, equal protection of law or unreasonable search and seizure, that have given rise to an immense body of case law.

In the final years of the twentieth century, the U.S. Supreme Court avoided broad, wide-ranging rulings; rather, it focused on deciding specific cases correctly. Cass R. Sunstein (1999), a professor at the University of Chicago Law School, defends this minimalist approach. In Sunstein's view, it is appropriate in a democratic society for the Court to alert the public to important issues of public policy, but the Court should not impose a far-reaching ruling on such issues because the Court is not the best vehicle for progressive social change. When the Supreme Court has ruled broadly on such matters as slavery (*Dred Scott*) and abortion (*Roe v. Wade*), it has done more harm than good, in Sunstein's view.

Stare Decisis and the Rule of Precedent

In the common law tradition, the doctrine of *stare decisis* (stâré di sísis)—literally, let the decision stand—has prevailed, and the rule of precedent has been adopted (L. Carter 1998; Llewellyn [1930] 1951). In their decisions in appellate court cases, then, judges look back to how other such cases were decided, and seek guidance from these earlier rulings. Two principal rationales exist for this practice. First, if the courts rule as they did in the past in the same types of case, they achieve *consistency*. Such consistency would certainly seem to be one means of achieving justice: that is, the same type of case produces the same type of outcome. Second, such consistency should also more easily allow people to orient their conduct toward the law and should enhance respect for the law and the legal system. After all, if the courts constantly handed down decisions that contradicted earlier decisions, people would likely become both confused about and disillusioned with the law. In addition, the invocation of an earlier decision fulfills the goal of *efficiency*. If the same kinds of cases arise, with the same kinds of issues, the court does not have to go back to ground zero and painstakingly work its way through all these issues. Rather, once it has been determined that the case before it fits into a particular category, the court can apply the reasoning and ruling of the earlier cases.

On the other hand, the doctrine of *stare decisis* has some definite drawbacks. First, and perhaps obviously, no two cases are truly identical. In relying upon precedent, the court may not be sufficiently attentive to unique features of the present case (or defendant) and may accordingly impose an unjust, inequitable, or unfair decision in the present case. Second, the earlier decision itself may have been a bad or erroneous decision, and invoking it in a present case simply perpetuates injustice. More generally, social circumstances, values, and interests tend to change over time, so a decision that may have seemed appropriate in an earlier time may no longer be suitable or appropriate at the present time.

A court of appeals is not bound by its own precedents, although in the interest of maintaining consistency and respect, courts have tended to be reluctant to overturn their earlier decisions. In one famous exception, in *Brown v. Board of Education* (1954), the U.S. Supreme Court ruled against segregation. In so doing it effectively overruled the precedent of *Plessy v. Ferguson* (1896), which had found no constitutional barrier to segregation.

Although the more conservative justices of the present-day U.S. Supreme Court are not favorably disposed toward the Warren Court due-process decisions of the 1960s, they have not specifically overruled them. Rather, in a series of decisions, the Court has narrowed somewhat the scope of these decisions, recognizing various circumstances in which they do not apply. U.S. Supreme Court justices throughout the history of the Court have mainly been guided by adherence to their own outlook rather than by unreflective adherence to the doctrine of *stare decisis* (Spaeth and Segal 1999). When U.S. Supreme Court justices uphold a precedent, it does not necessarily mean that they personally agree with the precedent.

Lower courts within the jurisdiction of a higher court of appeals are in fact bound to uphold the precedent established by the higher court. As a practical matter, such courts may have some leeway in determining whether the present case does, in fact, raise issues resolved in an earlier appellate court decision.

Lawyers in their briefs setting forth their argument on one side or the other of a legal dispute will also cite earlier cases in support of their argument. However, as the celebrated law professor Karl Llewellyn ([1930] 1951) demonstrated, the doctrine of *stare decisis* is "Janus-faced." If a previous decision is in line with the case a lawyer wants to make (a welcome precedent), the lawyer will claim that the principle enunciated in the earlier case is also applicable to the present case, even if some factual differences exist between the two cases. On the other hand, if a lawyer finds that the ruling in an earlier case does not support the present case (an unwelcome precedent), then the lawyer will argue that the facts in the earlier case render it fundamentally different from the present case and that the precedent is not applicable. Clearly, then, some interpretive leeway exists in the application of precedents.

Conclusion

Law is endlessly complex, because it has many different aspects, dimensions, and levels, and its origins are explained in quite different ways. A basic assumption of this chapter holds that if people are to be "literate" about law, they must recognize and understand the many manifestations of law and implications of the various accounts of law. Whenever you encounter the term "law," or related terms such as "the rule of law" and "law and order," you should attend to the context in which these terms are invoked. The "models" of law identified in this chapter should be helpful toward recognizing basic aspects of law.

Law in the Western tradition is intimately linked with a process of reasoning. An understanding of legal reasoning, then, is central to understanding law in contemporary society. Sociolegal scholarship has served as one source of challenge to the notion that judges operate as some type of "legal scientists," objectively and dispassionately applying law to cases. In an alternative reading, judges make decisions reflecting the various social and psychological influences to which they have been exposed or the beliefs and policy preferences they hold. In a more moderate view, legal reasoning combines objective and subjective dimensions, insofar as judges are strongly constrained by traditions and peer pressures from within the legal system but also are responding to other, external influences. It is important to recognize, as well, that no consensus exists on whether one gets better justice if judges are simply expected to apply the law logically and objectively or if they are expected to apply some discretionary judgment based upon their own experience and knowledge. Some of the implications of this last point are explored in Chapters 3 and 4.

Key Terms and Concepts

adjudication
adversarial model
bargain model
case law
civil/continental law tradition
common law tradition
court model
crime
crime control
crystallization of the mores
democratization
dual structure
due process
hierarchical power
horizontal power
inquisitorial model
judicial activism
judicial interpretation
judicial restraint
legal pluralism
models of law
modern view of legal reasoning
natural law
natural law theory
negotiation
orderings of law and social control
original intent
positive law
power/coercion
procedural law
rational contract
stare decisis
statutory law
strict constructionism
substantive law
tort
traditional view of legal reasoning
unitary structure
value consensus

Discussion Questions

1. What are the basic limitations of universal law, international law, and regional law.

2. Why is it that the repercussions associated with violating occupational laws can at times be worse than the penalties that might result from a conventional criminal offense?

3. When specific events occur on college campuses (e.g., date rape), is it best for the situation to be handled internally? Why or why not? Who would tend to benefit the most in a college campus date rape incident that was resolved by the college disciplinary board?

4. Compare and contrast the adversarial model of court procedure to the inquisitorial model. Is one procedure more fair than the other? Explain.

5. Explain how both judicial philosophies and the doctrine of *stare decisis* are a reflection of, or application of, partisan and instrumental purposes.

Chapter Three

Law, Justice, and the Moral Order

You live in a world where you are constantly confronted by choices. You must make choices in relation to law, and law itself reflects choices of some values over others. Law coexists with, and is interrelated with, other systems of values. It is a common assumption that law is linked with justice, but the specific character of the relationship between law and justice is not simple; it is explored in the first section of this chapter. Many people also see law as intertwined with morality. The second section of this chapter examines the relationship of morality to law. Also, at least some part of the American legal code has important points of origin with religion, so the third section of this chapter considers some of the ways in which religion has either influenced or been in conflict with law. Finally, law is also interrelated with and shaped by considerations independent of justice, morality, and religion. These considerations are here classified under the term "interests" and include everything from facilitating safe movement of automobile traffic to the promotion of efficient business practices. A brief final section of this chapter discusses such interests in relation to law.

Justice and Law

The terms "law" and "justice" are sometimes used interchangeably. We speak of the legal system and the justice system, of the rule of law and the principles of justice, of issues of law and of justice. Law, then, is sometimes treated as a synonym for justice. Alternatively, law may be considered an instrument either for achieving justice *or* for subverting justice.

But law and justice have also been seen as independent of each other. The great Associate Justice of the U.S. Supreme Court, Oliver Wendell Holmes Jr., has been quoted as responding to a plea to "Do justice" by stating: "That is not my job. It is my job to apply the law" (Bork 1990, 6). What is lawful has not always been in accord with what is just. The death sentence imposed on Socrates in ancient Athens may have been lawful, but it was not necessarily just. Socrates was indicted, tried, and condemned to death by a jury of his peers because they believed that his teaching was corrupting the city's youth. Although Socrates regarded the verdict as unjust, he refused an opportunity to escape since the verdict was lawful and one is ethically obliged to comply with law. He believed that society was harmed when people disobeyed the law (Parsons 1998, 184). We can probably all think of contemporary examples where the lawful and the just failed to coincide. Civil rights protesters in the South in the early 1960s were jailed for violating laws supporting racial segregation; the jailing may have been legal, but few today would argue that it was just. The relationship between law and justice is complex. Some of the questions posed about the relationship are as follows:

> Do we believe the law good because it is just, or is it just because we think it is good? To what degree or under what circumstances should the law be judged by a standard external to the community that creates it? To what degree is our understanding of justice determined by the laws under which we live? Is there a body of laws, a way of life regulated by law, that is simply the most just? Are there certain universal requirements that any tolerably just law or constitution must follow? (Rubin 1997, vii)

The challenge of arriving at a wholly satisfactory definition of justice is considerable. Edmond Cahn, a law professor at Columbia University for many years, adopted a creative approach to this challenge. In *The Sense of Injustice,* Cahn (1949) begins with the observation that if justice is the ultimate end of law, we should recognize that the ultimate meaning of justice is also beyond our reach. It may then be useful to think of justice as an active process of remedying or preventing what would create a sense of *in*justice. A sense of injustice has been defined as "the special kind of anger we feel when we are denied promised benefits and when we do not get what we believe is our due" (Shklar 1990, 83). Cahn thus lays out the following criteria for avoiding the creation of a sense of injustice: First, inequalities of law, where they exist, must make sense; second, law must give people what they deserve; third, law must operate in a manner consistent with maximizing human dignity; fourth, procedural proprieties must be exercised when law is implemented; fifth, governmental powers must not be exceeded; and sixth, insofar as society experiences changing needs over time, the sense of injustice must also necessarily vary over time and space.

Cahn's general criteria are certainly helpful, but they leave us with many difficult issues to resolve. Examples are questions like the following: Is the requirement that welfare mothers accept job assignments or lose their benefits just or not? Do people who commit murder deserve the death penalty? Are strip searches necessary security procedures or affronts to human dignity?

To add to the difficulty of definition, the sense of injustice is not experienced uniformly, and in the same circumstance one individual may believe the legal system has achieved justice; another, injustice (see Box 3.1).

The desire to see justice realized seems in some sense to be universal. Some scientists (naturalists) suggest that there is evidence of a biological (or evolutionary) basis for the desire for justice (Masters 1990). Social psychological study has provided us with the notion that people want to believe they live in a "just world," where all get their just desserts (Lerner and Lerner

Box 3.1

Justice Defined

"... [J]ustice is equality." Socrates, in Plato's *Gorgias*

"This ... is what the just is—the proportional; the unjust is what violates the proportion." Aristotle, *Ethics*

"There is no more ridiculous opinion than to believe that all customs and laws of nations are inherently just." Cicero, *Laws*

"Revenge is a kind of wild justice; which the more man's nature runs to, the more ought law to weed it out." Bacon, *Of Revenge*

"... when a covenant is made, then to break it is unjust; and the definition of injustice is no other than the not performance of a covenant. And whatsoever is not unjust is just." Hobbes, *Leviathan*

"Under a government which imprisons any unjustly, the true place for a just man is also prison." Thoreau, *Civil Disobedience*

"Perhaps we shall even find that when talking about justice, the quality we have to mind is charity." Cardozo, *The Growth of Law*

"To take appropriate measures in order to avert injustice even toward a member of a despised group is to enforce justice." Felix Frankfurter, *Dennis v. U.S.*, 1950

"There is no such thing as justice—in or out of court." Clarence Darrow, Interview, 1936

"One receives only imperfect justice in this world: only fools, children, left-wing Democrats, social scientists, and a few demented judges expect anything better." Walter F. Murphy, *The Vicar of Christ*

(Sources: Socrates, Aristotle, Cicero, Bacon, Hobbes, and Thoreau from Adler and Van Doren 1977. Cardozo, Darrow, Murphy, and Frankfurter from Shapiro 1993.)

1981). Cross-cultural studies undertaken by anthropologists find that people attempt to settle disputes justly (Nader and Todd 1978). Of course, the specific content of "just desserts" and justly settled disputes varies between individuals, groups, and whole cultures. Is probation or imprisonment or the amputation of a hand the just penalty for theft? Is a person who has been crippled through the negligent actions of another entitled to ten thousand dollars, a hundred thousand dollars, or a million dollars? Is a homemaker wife entitled to half the wealth of a successful entrepreneurial husband she is divorcing, or less?

The specific content of an individual's sense of justice may have various sources. In developmental psychology, as pioneered by Jean Piaget (1932) and Lawrence Kohlberg (1981), moral development (and an attendant sense of justice) is a matter of logically ordered sequences of cognitive development. In the earliest stages of life, human beings have a "premoral" orientation, where what is good is equated with pleasure and what is bad is equated with pain. As young children experience the socialization process, they are likely to acquire a conventional orientation, where moral evaluations are guided by what is approved of and disapproved of by one's most important reference group. Only a minority of individuals move on to a "principled" orientation, where moral evaluations are based upon some coherent philosophical perspective on the proper grounds for morality and justice. Developmental psychology, accordingly, provides us with one way of understanding the basis of our sense of justice, although Harvard psychologist Carol Gilligan (1982), in her book *In a Different Voice*, criticized the Kohlberg interpretation as based only upon studies of males. Gilligan made a case for the view that females tend to use a different form of moral reasoning from that favored by males.

Philosophers over a period of thousands of years have set forth conceptions of justice. Several different such conceptions can be briefly identified (see Table 3.1). First, there is an *intuitionist* conception of justice. The eighteenth-century German philosopher Immanuel Kant ([1785] 1998) advanced the view that people know justice, or the good, a priori (before experience). His *categorical imperative* is a test of the good, or just; it calls for acting on such principles as you would want to be adopted as universal law, or acting as you would have all others act.

Table 3.1 Philosophical Concepts of Justice

Intuitive	Known a priori; universal principle
Utilitarian	Practical calculus; greatest good
Contractual	By agreement; as fairness
Egalitarian	Organization of society; as equality

The late eighteenth- through early nineteenth-century British philosopher Jeremy Bentham ([1789] 1970) is associated with a *utilitarian*, or pragmatic, conception of justice. In this view, people determine what is good, or just, by a calculus: Does the action in question serve the greatest good or benefit the largest number?

A late twentieth-century American philosopher, John Rawls (1971), is especially associated with a *contractual* conception of justice. The guiding principle here is the equation of justice with fairness. Justice is achieved by implementing rules in society to maximize fairness. The question we must ask about the governing rules of society is this: If we were in the *original* position of not knowing, from behind a "veil of ignorance," whether we would end up among the advantaged or disadvantaged, what rules would we choose?

Finally, the nineteenth-century social philosopher Karl Marx ([1867] 1962) advanced an *egalitarian* conception of justice that at least implicitly equates it with equality. A contemporary American philosopher, Jeffrey Reiman (1990), has derived from the Marxist conception the following principle for evaluating justice within a society: Conditions under which humans are *not* subjugated. For Marx, in one common interpretation, the rhetoric of justice and rights is an artifact of a capitalist society, and irrelevant to a truly communist society (Buchanan 1982). In this sense, a society that has eliminated the conditions producing socioeconomic inequality is inherently just.

When the notion of justice is invoked in relation to law we must recognize that different conceptions of justice may be involved (Feinberg and Gross 1977). At different times and places, different conceptions of justice have tended to be dominant. What was regarded as just in the Middle Ages is unlikely to be regarded as just today, and the standards of justice in some other country—for example, Iraq—might be seen as very much at odds with ours. Even within one society, lawmakers and judges vary in their specific conceptions of justice.

Although discussions of justice tend to be most readily associated with theologians, philosophers, and judges, ordinary members of society also form ideas of justice and are concerned to see justice realized. Some current research has shown that people's judgments about justice influence their attitudes and behavior toward others on such matters as accepting decisions of others, helping a group of others, and their willingness to support authority figures (Tyler, et al. 1997, 6). This social justice research suggests that people's beliefs and attitudes may be more influenced by a sense of justice than by pure self-interest, and people will support just policies or processes even if they do not directly benefit from them. Furthermore, when people are in a position to render actual verdicts in cases, they may be guided more by their sense of justice than by the formal requirements of the law (Robinson and Darley 1995, 212). The concept of "jury nullification" refers specifically to a circumstance where a trial jury returns a verdict that it believes to be just, even if the verdict is arrived at through reasoning at odds with what is called for by the formal law. In at least one reading of the matter, in the Clinton impeachment case, the American people collectively had a different sense of what was called for in the interest of justice than did those attempting to prosecute (and remove) the president on the basis of a legalistic argument.

Scholars have identified principles of justice applicable to the resolution of legal cases (see Table 3.2) (A. Heller 1987; Sadurski 1984; Shklar 1990). First, *commutative* (or legalistic, corrective, and restitutive) criteria can be adopted. This formula calls for restoring "balance" following some wrongdoing or making redress in accordance with formal entitlement. Second, *distributive* (or primary, moralistic, and equitable) criteria can be adopted. This formula calls for resolution through proportional merit, or in accordance with a moral calculus. Third, *retributive* criteria can be adopted. This formula calls for resolution through the imposition of suffering on those who have done harm.

Table 3.2 Applied Conceptions of Justice

Commutative	Formal, legal entitlement
Distributive	Equal division
Retributive	In relation to blame or fault

To illustrate the differences between different conceptions of justice, we can consider examples in the form of a *criminal* case and a *civil* case. First, in a case of white-collar crime (e.g., fraud), a commutative resolution would emphasize making restitution to the victim or victims; a distributive resolution would settle the case according to who could best afford the losses; and a retributive resolution would impose punitive damages on the offender. Second, in a case of property division arising out of a divorce case, a commutative resolution would assign property in terms of formal ownership (traditionally, favoring husbands); a distributive resolution would adopt the "community property" standard and would divide marital assets equally; and a retributive resolution would compensate the wronged party with a larger share of property. Of course, in many cases the resolution may combine, in varying degrees, these different criteria for resolution. Historically, the legal profession has been biased in favor of commutative criteria for the resolution of cases, but other social forces (the public or special interest groups) have succeeded in promoting legal reforms based upon other criteria of justice.

Individual Justice and Social Justice

The distinction between individual justice and social justice is clear, at least conceptually. If society is to implement individual justice, it must ensure that individuals receive what they are entitled to, merit, or deserve. To implement social justice, society must ensure that groups receive what they are entitled to, merit, or deserve, or that the general social welfare is advanced. Historically, legal justice has been defined in terms of doing justice in specific cases and ensuring justice for the individual parties in these cases. Can *legal* justice be differentiated from *social* justice (Sadurski 1984)? Some argue that true legal justice is inseparable from social justice and not independent of it. Others hold that legal justice only pertains to the individual case at hand and must be separated from issues of social justice. In particular cases, it is sometimes difficult to reconcile individual with social justice.

The policy of affirmative action brings the conflict between individual and social justice into sharp relief (Skedsvold and Mann 1996). Affirmative action policies have as their principal rationale the advancement of social justice. By making certain concessions to increase the representation of traditionally disadvantaged groups (e.g., women; African Americans), society is addressing historical injustices and benefiting all its members by diversifying various professions and enterprises. If the policy facilitates the admission of African Americans to law school or to the police force, the society is atoning for their past exclusion, compensating them for possible disadvantages due to racism and discrimination, and providing itself with more African-American lawyers and police officers, who are likely to work for underserviced communities or provide more empathetic law enforcers.

Hiring more female professors or business executives can fulfill similar purposes. Because women have been discriminated against historically, they may face some enduring disadvantages in the socialization process; also, they are much-needed role models for female students and business employees.

Society as a whole may be said to benefit from affirmative action policies. On the other hand, it should be obvious that injustice is done to individual white males who are accordingly excluded from admissions or positions, despite their superior formal qualifications. It could be said that these white males are expected to pay the price for past practices they had no part in and for future social benefits that may exclude them. There is no formula that can ensure maximizing both individual and social justice in all cases, and the proper balance between these objectives is always going to be somewhat contentious. For much of American history, however, white males have benefited from a form of affirmative action; custom had long excluded African Americans and women from even competing for many opportunities (e.g., joining professional athletic teams or entering a university). Also in many cases special connections (such as an alumnus parent or father who is the boss)—rather than talent and aptitude—gained white men admission to programs and career opportunities. By the late 1990s, however, a significant backlash to affirmative action had developed in America. This topic is discussed more fully in Chapter 10.

In a democratic society such as the United States, an inherent conflict exists about whether the rights of individuals or the needs of the community should be given precedence (Selznick 1992; Wellman 1995). Libertarians are associated with the position that individual rights (and freedom) must be preserved above all other objectives (Nozick 1974). Socialists are identified with the view that choices must promote a humane, egalitarian community over the uncompromised rights of individuals (Harrington 1973). In the more recent era, communitarians have argued that the challenge today is to achieve a better balance between individual rights on the one hand and duties to the community, or society, on the other hand (Elshtain 1995). Accordingly, Americans are likely to engage in an ongoing debate over which specific allocation of rights and duties produces a truly just society.

Procedural Justice and Substantive Justice

Procedural justice refers to achieving fairness in the legal procedure (Sadurski 1984). Substantive justice refers to achieving a correct or appropriate outcome in a legal case. Obviously, one hopes that fair procedures will result in appropriate outcomes, but this is far from guaranteed. In our system of law, procedural fairness is especially associated with the notion that the accused, or the defendant, should enjoy the fullest measure of due process and have every opportunity to raise a reasonable doubt or challenge evidence. In the American system, the appropriate outcome should be one consistent with truth, imposing deserved sanctions on wrongdoers and providing satisfaction or resolution for authentic victims, and at the same time protecting or appropriately compensating the larger community.

Supporters (typically conservatives) of a crime control model have held that the more emphasis the system puts on ensuring procedural fairness (for the accused and defendants), the less likely it is to achieve substantive justice for authentic victims and society (Uviller 1999). In the final decades of the twentieth century, the U.S. Supreme Court and other appellate courts issued opinions that, on balance, strengthened the hand of prosecutors and sent record numbers of people to prison.

The debate over the exclusionary rule highlights this fairness dilemma (Senna and Siegel 1999, 270–275). This rule requires the exclusion of improperly (or illegally) obtained evidence from a trial; if such evidence has been used to obtain a conviction, the conviction must be overturned. An example of improperly obtained evidence could be a confession secured without providing the accused with a recital of his or her rights as a suspect (a Miranda warning), or physical evidence seized without a proper search warrant. The rationale for the exclusionary rule is that criminal justice personnel should fully adhere to the requirements of the law in making cases against criminal suspects. Inevitably, many people will experience a sense of outrage if an obviously guilty criminal obtains a reversal of conviction on the basis of the exclusionary rule and ends up avoiding punishment. This happens rarely. Nevertheless, the argument is made that the exclusionary rule, in the name of procedural justice, subverts or blocks the realization of substantive justice. On the other hand, if one wants to absolutely minimize the chances that the guilty will escape justice, one is likely to compromise standards of procedural justice.

It is difficult, then, to develop in practice a balance between attention to procedural justice and substantive justice that will satisfy all. Scholars who focus on the relation between law and society shifted their attention in the recent past, according to Garth and Sarat (1998a, 1), to procedural justice, from an earlier concern with substantive justice. For example, an earlier generation of scholars had focused more on such matters as the complicity of law in producing poverty and segregation; subsequently, more scholars studied unfair legal procedures, such as denying bail or allowing the introduction of tainted evidence. A primary focus on substantive justice may well be coming back, however. In the recent past, the inequities between the principles underlying procedural law and actual practices were especially glaring (e.g., illegal searches, lack of counsel, coerced confessions) but case law since the time of the Warren Supreme Court of the 1960s has made some progress in addressing these inequities. Perhaps relatively less progress has been made in addressing many of the substantive inequities that still separate the privileged and the underprivileged.

Justice and the Criminal Justice System

Although the realization of justice is a widely espoused objective for the legal system, and for the criminal justice system specifically, much controversy exists over how this objective could be best realized (Beckett 1997; Eskridge 1996; Kappeler, Blumberg, and Potter 1996). Do we need more laws, or fewer, to achieve justice? Do we rely more upon law as a formal means of social control, or upon alternative, informal means of social control? With regard to the police, do we need strict controls on their activities or should we extend broad discretion to them? In the courts, do we get better justice when we rely on judges or on juries? Is it better to impose sentencing guidelines on judges or to give them a broad measure of discretion? Is justice more likely to come out of plea bargaining (when defendants waive their right to trial and plead guilty to a charge in return for some form of leniency) or out of a formal trial? And when we have trials, do we get closer to just outcomes when we have an adversarial model, involving a contest between the prosecution and the defense, or an inquisitorial model, involving an inquiry by a judge or panel of judges? Finally, in the realm of the corrections system, is justice accomplished when the system is based on retribution, incapacitation, and deterrence or when it is based on rehabilitation and restitution?

The questions posed in the preceding paragraph constitute ongoing controversies about, and within, the criminal justice system. This system contends with many tensions and conflicts: justice for the victim versus justice for the perpetrator; justice for the accused versus justice for society; individualized justice versus uniform justice; and so on. It is in the operation of the criminal justice system that we can witness the inevitable dilemmas surrounding issues of justice in especially sharp relief.

Law, Violence, and Justice

The meaning of justice is inevitably influenced by the political context. To put this more directly, those in power have a disproportionate say in how justice is defined. The state declares its own violence as necessary to ensure order and justice and considers the violence of individuals and anti-state groups criminal. However, throughout history, revolutionary and anti-state violence has often been carried out in the name of achieving justice (Coblentz 1970; Graham and Gurr 1969). Such violence includes the acts of American revolutionaries, vigilantes, early labor unionists, and oppressed racial minorities.

The idea of challenging unjust institutions can be traced far back in America's political history. The English philosopher John Locke ([1690] 1965), who greatly influenced the Founding Fathers, held that in a democratic society people had the right to alter or abolish institutions found to be detrimental to justice. The twentieth-century philosopher Herbert Marcuse (1966) argued that revolutionary violence was really a form of *counter* violence, carried out against the existing violence of the state. The Algerian psychiatrist Frantz Fanon (1968), in *The Wretched of the Earth*, advocated violence in the struggle against colonial oppressors as necessary both to overthrow the oppressors and to liberate the oppressed (through a cathartic release from their experience); this thesis was endorsed by the French existentialist philosopher Jean-Paul Sartre (1968). Some of the radicals and black militants of the 1960s era called for violence against the state in the name of realizing justice (Gitlin 1987).

Political assassinations have long been justified as a form of "alternative justice" (Ben-Yehuda 1997). In the present era, terrorism is a particular concern, but terrorism too has typically been justified as a necessary response to existing injustice and as a necessary means to achieve authentic justice (Oliverio 1997). And even conventional lawbreaking, including homicide and assault, is at least sometimes driven by a moralistic impulse, aimed at avenging some injustice or pursuing some notion of justice (Black 1983).

Although in the modern code of conduct, vengeance is not regarded as legitimate in the same sense that the pursuit of justice is so regarded, the ancient desire to avenge wrongdoing is hardly extinct (Jacoby 1983). If the state is seen as failing to avenge some wrongdoing, groups or individuals may take this form of pursuing justice into their own hands. Altogether, the relationship between law, violence, and justice is more complex than it is sometimes portrayed (see Box 3.2).

Conclusion

Perfect justice, as the nineteenth-century U.S. Supreme Court Associate Justice Joseph Story once observed, is an aspiration. Certainly we should have no illusion that it is possible to achieve perfect justice through law. Our legal institutions have sometimes been more concerned with fostering the *appearance* of justice than with achieving justice per se. Any number of failures to realize either procedural justice or substantive justice are identified at various points in this book. Law has clearly been an instrument complicit in the realization of some of the worst cases of historical injustice, including

Box 3.2

Law and Transitional Justice

One complex issue that arises when considering the relationship between law and justice is this: How is it possible to realize justice when dealing with fallen regimes under which many injustices occurred? More specifically, the term "transitional justice" has been used with reference to the process undertaken by new democracies attempting to resolve past human rights abuses by former authoritarian or totalitarian regimes (Crocker 1998; Kritz 1995; McAdams 1997).

This issue arose after World War II in connection with the defeat of Nazi Germany and militarist Japan, when somewhat controversial trials were held by the victors rather than by new regimes. In the more recent era, this issue has arisen in some Latin American countries (e.g., Bolivia, Argentina, and Chile), some Eastern European countries (e.g., Hungary, Poland, and East Germany), and in South Africa. In some countries (e.g., France and Cambodia), the efforts to achieve justice with regard to the wrongdoing of officials of past regimes was addressed only decades after the fall of the earlier regime. In other countries (e.g., Bosnia and Rwanda), these issues have arisen while atrocities, conflict, and governmental instability were still ongoing. In the case of the former Yugoslavia, in particular, deep-rooted historical antagonisms led to warfare and brutal "ethnic cleansing," or genocidal actions, and to many unresolved questions at the outset of the twenty-first century.

Different approaches to the problem of transitional justice have been adopted in the various countries. The fundamental challenge is often seen as one of finding the right balance between outright vengeance and total forgiveness, between extracting the truth of what happened and responding to the suffering of surviving victims, and between achieving reconciliation and doing justice. An overly aggressive pursuit of wrongdoers from past regimes may frighten and anger many citizens who have at least some ties to those regimes, and in extreme cases it could precipitate terrorism or civil war. Furthermore, new regimes must often choose between devoting time and resources to challenges of the present and future or to resolving issues of the past. Such regimes must also address the question of how the rule of law can be applied retrospectively to what was often lawful or condoned during past regimes. Some specific cases of transitional justice are addressed elsewhere in this book.

slavery in America and the Holocaust in Nazi Germany. More broadly, some claim that law is complicit in sustaining conditions of fundamental, ongoing inequality and injustice in society.

The call for promoting justice through law certainly endures. It encounters many challenges. The preceding section has documented the existence of different conceptions of justice, or criteria for accomplishing just outcomes in legal cases, and it seems highly unlikely that members of a society can ever achieve a full consensus on matters of justice. Even where people are agreed on their perception of justice and injustice, there is what Judith Shklar (1990) calls "passive injustice," or the unwillingness of people to intervene because it is too much trouble and too disruptive. Also, there is the fact of human fallibility: Human beings, even the wisest and most intelligent of judges, make mistakes. In addition, some human beings will always be among us who are not interested in doing justice and who choose rather to do that which is unjust. And still another challenge confounding the realization of justice through law is this: In some legal cases equally valid rights, precepts, or objectives are in conflict. For example, citizens are entitled to enjoy a pollution-free environment, but some productive business enterprises cannot operate without producing a certain level of pollution. In a free society, some individuals will argue that they should have the right to smoke, but others will claim that their fresh air is contaminated by cigarette smoke. Citizens are entitled to privacy, but the state has to collect taxes and may infringe on citizens' privacy rights in order to do so. In the case of affirmative action, as mentioned earlier, rights of specific individuals cannot be satisfactorily reconciled with the realization of some desirable social goals.

Finally, there is this: As long as socioeconomic and other forms of inequality persist, a certain level of injustice will be inevitable. Those who have more resources will more often have advantages before the law than those with more modest resources. Any number of poor but innocent people have been convicted of crimes and punished, and sometimes executed, because good legal counsel was not available to them. Wealthy criminal defendants, such as O. J. Simpson, have been able to hire a "dream team" of attorneys and overcome substantial evidence of guilt. Individuals engaged in civil lawsuits with wealthier, more powerful businesses tend also to be at a substantial disadvantage. In the absence of a level playing field, the hope of realizing justice for all is necessarily an illusion. The pursuit of justice is one challenge confronting the law. Another is reconciliation of the legal and the moral.

Law and Morality

According to W. G. Sumner ([1906] 1960, 89), an early twentieth-century sociologist at Yale University, you can't legislate morality. Is this familiar proposition true, or not true? The answer to this question has to be explored in some depth.

First, what is morality; what is moral? There is no broad consensus on morality, and no uniform conception of the moral. Different general standards of morality can be identified if we make cross-cultural comparisons (between different cultures or societies); historical comparisons (between past and present within a culture or society); and intrasocietal comparisons (between different segments, or subcultures, within a particular society). Are there any moral "universals," or forms of behavior that are considered immoral in all societies, in all times, and among all segments of a particular society? Homicide, rape, and incest might easily come to mind as possible examples of such moral universals. In each case, however, one can find circumstances where homicide, rape, and incest are tolerated or even expected.

Traditional anthropological scholarship tended to emphasize cultural diversity with regard to morality (Westermarck 1906). Accordingly, anthropologists identified societies that condoned ritual killing, cannibalism, sex with children, and many other practices outlawed by developed Western societies. Some contemporary scholarship, however, has stressed uniformities of morality across many different cultures. For example, Newman (1976) examined public perceptions of deviant behavior in six countries (India,

Indonesia, Iran, Italy, Yugoslavia, and the United States) and found considerable uniformity in perceptions in these different countries.

In sociology there is the contrast between ethnocentrism and cultural relativity. Ethnocentrism is the belief that one's own culture, encompassing its system of moral beliefs, is superior to other cultures. Cultural relativity refers to the practice of evaluating a culture, including its moral beliefs, in its own terms. Ethnocentrism is obviously one form of the various types of chauvinism, including racism and sexism, that have been complicit in much human oppression and discrimination, with genocide, imperialism, slavery, and wife-battering as some of the more extreme manifestations. It thus appears that we should want to separate ourselves from an ethnocentric outlook and attempt to understand the moral order of another culture in its own terms. If we do so, does it follow that we make no moral judgments about the practices of this culture? For example, it is one thing to try to understand why the practice of genital mutilation of young girls has been adopted by some African cultures; it is another thing to say that we cannot express moral repugnance at this practice (Dugger 1996). We should recognize, of course, that some of our own cultural practices, such as imposing the death penalty on some convicted murderers, are viewed as immoral or barbaric by people in many other countries.

The whole matter of moral relativism continues to be debated on a number of different levels. The eminent sociologist Dennis Wrong (1995, 128) has suggested four basic questions emerging from this debate: First, is there a common human nature cutting across or underlying cultural diversity? Second, assuming such a nature, does it include a moral component resembling conscience, or Freud's "superego"? Third, assuming such a component, what combination of nature and nurture, biology and culture, produces it? Fourth, does such a component provide a cross-cultural standard for evaluating cultures that could overrule relativism? These are large and complex questions that cannot be covered in any depth here, but it is necessary to keep such questions in mind as you consider the relationship between law and morality.

Moral beliefs profoundly influence the law. They influence the making of laws, their enforcement, and—if it comes to that—the repeal of laws. In a democratic society a certain tension exists between the view that the law should simply reflect the morality and will of the majority and the view that law should reflect substantive moral principles that protect minorities and dissidents. For example, should broad legal rights be extended to homosexuals on the principle that minorities should enjoy the same rights as other members of society, or should they be denied certain rights (for example, to marry) because the majority of society's members regard same-sex marriages as morally repugnant or untenable? Should abortion be outlawed because it can be regarded as at odds with a sanctity of life principle, or should abortion be legally available because the majority of society's members favor that status either on practical grounds (to prevent death from illegal abortions or the birth of unwanted children) or on the moral principle that the pregnant woman's right to choose should prevail? Legislators and other elected officials charged with making and implementing laws must sometimes confront the dilemma of following either their principles or the will of their constituents (the voters); to make the principled choice may cost them their office the next time they are up for election. Historically, it seems fair to say that practi-

Box 3.3

A Case of Conflict Between Legal and Moral Duty

The moral and the legal are not synonymous. In a much publicized case in 1997, a 19-year-old man, David Cash, witnessed a good friend initiating an attack on a 7-year-old child, Sherrice Iverson, in the bathroom of a Nevada casino and did nothing to interfere, seek help for the child, or report the crime subsequently to the police (Terry 1998). The child was sexually assaulted and strangled, and her killer was convicted of the crime, but no criminal prosecution was initiated against Cash. All reasonable people would surely agree that his behavior was immoral and reprehensible; under existing law it was not illegal.

cal political considerations have more often taken precedence over moral principles when such dilemmas have arisen.

Law and morality are not necessarily synonymous. Dennis Lloyd (1970, 68–69) identifies three basic models for understanding the relationship between the legal and the moral. First, they may coincide if morality dictates the content of law or if morality is fully reflected in the law. Second, they may be seen as separate but with the moral judgment a higher form of law by which the man-made law can be evaluated. And third, they may be viewed as quite separate spheres, with each evaluated in accordance with its own criteria. Lloyd's three models provide a useful point of departure for more narrowly focused discussions of law and morality.

Judith Shklar ([1964] 1986), the late Cowles Professor of Government at Harvard University, made some concise and useful comparisons in her book *Legalism*. First, Shklar reminds us of the basic thesis that for natural law the moral and the legal intersect, whereas for positivistic law the moral and the legal are separable. More narrowly, law is concerned with external action, while morality is directed at the inner state of the mind; law demands mere conformity of behavior, while for morality action is motivated by the voice of conscience; law is social, objective, and coercive, while morality is individual, subjective, and voluntary; law calls for abstention from the forbidden, while morality calls for fulfillment of positive duties; law is subject to fairly quick change, while morality is more enduring. These generalizations seem valid, for the most part, but also may call for some qualifications. For example, one might argue that laws proscribing fornication (or voluntary sexual relations outside marriage) remained on the books long after the moral center of American society had shifted toward at least grudging tolerance of premarital sex.

Philosophers have long grappled with a range of questions pertaining to the relationship between law and morality. One set of questions focuses on whether it is an appropriate function of the law to dictate moral conduct. In the case of some forms of immoral conduct, such as willful homicide, there is no real controversy. In the case of other forms of conduct viewed by many as immoral—for example, gambling; promoting prostitution; engaging in consensual homosexual relations; selling pornography; purchasing and using marijuana; and the like—there is considerable controversy, although the degree of controversy varies by the issue. The nineteenth-century British philosopher John Stuart Mill ([1859] 1963) made a celebrated argument on behalf of the view that the state has no business criminalizing activities that are not demonstrably harmful to others. Some argue, however, that even though the harm done by so-called victimless crimes is far less obvious than the harm done by predatory crimes, they cause real and identifiable harm and should retain criminal status.

Another set of fundamental issues on the relation between law and morality addresses such matters as these: Is an immoral law still law? Does one have an absolute duty to obey law, even when law is immoral? These aspects of the relation between the moral and legal are certainly important, and are discussed at length in Chapter 9.

The relation between the legal and the moral is complex, and we should not imagine that there are any simple formulas for defining either the actual nature of this relationship or what it could be. Basil Mitchell (1970), in *Law, Morality, and Religion in a Secular Society,* has made one stab at delineating the parameters of the relationship. He puts forth the following propositions:

1. The function of the law is not only to protect individuals from harm, but to protect the essential institutions of a society.
2. The law should not punish behavior solely on the ground that it is—or is generally thought to be—immoral. But it cannot be, in all respects, morally neutral.
3. The morality which law presupposes is not beyond criticism, and ought to be open to informed discussion and debate.
4. The protection of institutions—and legitimate concern for the ethos of society—may justify the reinforcement of morality.

If lawmakers endorse the proposition that law may appropriately play a role in reinforcing morality, Mitchell (1970) suggests that they can be guided by the following principles:

1. Respect human privacy, wherever possible.
2. Recognize that it is undesirable to pass unenforceable laws.
3. Recognize that it is undesirable to pass laws which are unlikely to be respected by reasonable people.
4. Avoid passing laws that will cause suffering, or fail to prevent it.
5. Avoid passing laws that punish people for things they cannot help doing.

No one should imagine, of course, that any such set of propositions or principles can resolve the many complex issues arising out of the relation between law and morality, but they at least provide a point of departure for further discussion. And it is at the least implicit in these propositions and principles that sociological and psychological research must be undertaken if we are to successfully identify the prevailing moral values and needs of society, the nature of laws likely to be enforceable and respected, and the capacity of people to comply with particular laws.

Law and Morality in American History

Even though morality has been a major influence on the substance of American law, one still has to ask: Whose morality? After all, American society over time has become increasingly heterogeneous and has long included numerous groups and subcultures subscribing to radically different moral belief systems. The morality reflected in American law has surely been disproportionately the morality of "WASPs"—white Anglo-Saxon Protestants of middle- and upper-class social status; it has also been disproportionately a patriarchal, male-oriented morality, as well as a morality of middle-aged and older people. Throughout American history those whose belief systems have been different from or directly at odds with this dominant morality have contended with formidable pressures to conform or to face ostracism, persecution, and formal legal prosecution. On the one hand, moral dissidents have included abolitionists and civil rights workers, suffragists and feminists, free love proponents and gay activists, Mormons and Moonies; a number of these groups have been legitimized, or at least many Americans believe they should be tolerated. On the other hand, moral dissidents include Ku Klux Klan members, skinheads, satanists, and survivalists, for whom the society offers far less sympathy (Zellner 1995). An ongoing tension exists, then, between a certain level of tolerance for moral dissent and widespread intolerance for some specific forms of moral dissent.

The moral values of the politically dominant classes naturally shape the law when these laws are made, enforced, and administered by white Anglo-Saxon, Protestant, middle- or upper-class, middle-aged or older, males. But morality also becomes a force shaping law when "moral entrepreneurs" consciously lobby for laws reflecting their moral belief system, and succeed in getting them enacted (Becker 1963, 147). Moral entrepreneurs are crusaders who hope to enlist the law as one means of stamping out some condition they regard as evil. Prohibition of alcoholic beverages in the early part of the twentieth century was one of the most dramatic cases of moral entrepreneurism shaping American law (Gusfield 1963; Pegram 1998).

Prohibition of Alcohol

A "Temperance Movement" calling for the prohibition of alcohol had long existed in America and was quite successful in many states in securing laws against alcohol. But in the period immediately following World War I a series of circumstances came together allowing the Temperance Movement to achieve its long-standing dream of a national prohibition on the sale and distribution of alcohol. The circumstances included the disproportionate representation of legislators from rural and small-town jurisdictions, who were more favorably disposed toward prohibition than the underrepresented big city jurisdictions, and the nation's receptivity to such an initiative in the wake of the successful resolution of World War I. This victory for the Temperance Movement has sometimes been interpreted as the last triumph of a traditional, agriculturally based moral ethos over the rapidly encroaching forces of a modern, urban-dominated society. The Volstead Act, and the Eighteenth

Amendment, implemented in 1920, were the specific mechanisms putting Prohibition into effect. The hope of those who promoted prohibition was that in the face of legal prohibition, Americans as a whole would embrace the view that the consumption of alcohol was an inherently immoral activity, and people would voluntarily and happily comply with the law.

Much has been written about the failure of the "Noble Experiment." Millions of Americans, including President Harding and any number of other high-level government officials, simply did not comply with the law, and flagrant violation was widespread. Organized crime, including Al Capone's operation in Chicago, thrived in an environment where a high level of demand for alcohol persisted despite the absence of a legal supply; organized crime cartels, as well as independent bootleggers, enriched themselves, and "speakeasies" (or camouflaged bars) emerged all over. Ironically, the 1920s eventually came to be known as "the Roaring Twenties," characterized by a rejection of many aspects of the Victorian, pre-World War I moral order, with changing styles, tastes, and habits.

Over time, disenchantment with Prohibition grew among various segments of society. Many citizens became alarmed over the amount of crime and violence seen as one consequence of the competitive, lawless market in alcohol. Corruption of many enforcement agents and politicians on all levels was also a concern. Legitimate businesses believed that they were paying a disproportionate part of the tax burden because the hugely lucrative liquor trade, being illegal, could not be taxed. Also, political reapportionment began to give a stronger measure of political power to big city jurisdictions, which had never been especially supportive of Prohibition. If the "drys" who were still actively engaged with the Temperance Movement had been willing to consider compromise measures—for example, controlled legalization of beers and other such liquors—they might have preserved at least a partial prohibition, but the most active "drys" were somewhat fanatical and uncompromising. Accordingly, in 1933, the "Noble Experiment" ended, and Prohibition was repealed with the Twenty-first Amendment.

From one point of view, the failure of Prohibition to realize its stated goal of obliterating alcohol from American life has been tragic. The costs of alcohol in terms of its complicity in a high percentage of crimes (especially violent crimes), in accidents (including automobile accidents), in domestic abuse and discord, in school- and job-related failures, in premature death due to cirrhosis of the liver and other illnesses aggravated by alcohol, and in personal unhappiness and suicide, is literally incalculable.

If the legal prohibition on the sale and distribution of alcohol obviously did not come even close to eliminating alcohol consumption, there is some evidence that overall levels of such consumption declined during the Prohibition era; for many decades after repeal, levels of alcohol seemingly rose quite steadily (Goode 1997, 187–191). If such data are accurate, it suggests that one may, in fact, not be able to legislate morality, as Sumner proposed. Laws prohibiting the sale and distribution of alcohol, however, did deter a certain proportion of citizens who might otherwise drink from doing so and may have reduced somewhat the level of drinking of other citizens. Moral condemnation of alcohol-related excesses has persisted in the face of broad support for the legal availability of alcohol for social drinking. We continue to experience some cultural ambivalence about alcohol; drunkenness is the focus of much humor, along with bitter attacks on it. Consumption of alcohol on some level is too deeply engrained in our culture for anyone to seriously imagine that it could be prohibited in the foreseeable future. Since the 1970s, however, a more limited movement against alcohol, promoted by a new generation of moral entrepreneurs such as MADD (Mothers Against Drunk Driving), has led to tougher penalties in cases where a driver is charged with driving under the influence of alcohol; to broader liability in connection with alcohol-related accidents; and to a higher age for legal drinking (Gusfield 1996; Jacobs 1989). Whether the new laws have had a substantial impact on drinking and driving has been questioned.

Recent Controversies

The last half of the twentieth century witnessed many fierce confrontations between those who believe the law must reflect and incorporate traditional (or conservative) moral values and those who have campaigned for broad legal tolerance of deviant lifestyles and practices, and for individual choice over socially imposed morality. In the latter part of the 1960s, into the 1970s, the emergence of a "counterculture" and both a feminist movement and a gay rights movement contributed to an environment where abandonment or repeal of traditional legal proscription of some forms of sexual deviance could occur. During much the same period millions of Americans began experimenting with or using various illicit drugs—especially marijuana—and many opposed or simply disregarded the legal prohibitions pertaining to such drugs.

The immensely controversial 1973 U.S. Supreme Court decision in the case of *Roe v. Wade*, which struck down state laws prohibiting abortion, contributed to the unleashing of an ongoing, large-scale moral battle over this issue. Subsequent developments led to the intensification of debate on legalized euthanasia, such as physician-assisted suicide. On some of these issues liberal or progressive moral forces have tended to prevail: for example, on the general legal availability of pornography and of abortion. On other issues, people more aligned with conservative or traditional moral forces have been more successful: for example, the ongoing illegal status of illicit drugs and of euthanasia. On still other issues, such as the rights of homosexuals, results in the recent era have been mixed, with victories for both sides.

Clearly, many different forces can come into play in determining the legal outcome of these battles over morality. On at least some of these issues unusual coalitions are formed. For example, in the campaign to criminalize the sale and distribution of pornography, conservative fundamentalists and at least some feminists find themselves on the same side, calling for censorship of pornography, even though they object to it on different grounds. Of course, traditionalists and feminists are at odds on other issues. But good timing, the effectiveness of moral constituencies in their lobbying efforts, the particular makeup of the U.S. Supreme Court and other appellate courts, and various other factors can determine the character of law and legal reform on such issues. Some of these issues tend to be especially difficult to resolve insofar as people's most heartfelt moral beliefs are involved. Abortion is surely one such issue. Some other contentious issues are discussed in Chapter 10, in the context of an examination of law and social change.

Law and Religion

Law and religion are separate but interrelated realms (Berman 1974, 1993). Concerns with obligation, order, responsibility, and restitution are common to both law and religion; legal concepts such as crime, contract, rehabilitation and justice parallel religious concepts such as sin, covenant, redemption, and righteousness (Witte 1996, 5, 7). In past societies, law and religion were sometimes inseparable. In Western European society, for a long period of time, the Canon law of the Roman Catholic Church was a dominant force; indeed, the Canon law of the Church has been described as the first modern Western legal system (Berman 1983). Also, the Puritan society of early colonial Massachusetts largely took the form of a theocracy. Religious leaders also served as lawmakers and judges, and much of the law was taken directly from the Bible (Erikson 1966, 54–64). Over time, as the colonial society evolved and became more heterogeneous, the dominance of religion declined. But we can certainly identify societies in the modern world—for example, Iran—where religious forces are the core feature of the legal system.

The substantive content of law, including American law, has been profoundly influenced by religion. At least some of the Ten Commandments—Thou shalt not kill; Thou shalt not steal—are key elements of our criminal law. Of course, there are large bodies of law, such as commercial law, where there is little or no religious dimension. Much law in modern society is a reflection of the practical realities of such a society. But for many people, the core values of the law are seen as rooted in religious doctrine.

Conflicts

Conflicts between religious principles and law inevitably arise in some circumstances (Kephart and Zellner 1991). In the nineteenth century, for example, Mormons in America found themselves in conflict with the larger legal system because of their practice of polygamy, or multiple wives. Christian Scientists have been opposed to the application of modern medicine; this opposition has sometimes come into conflict with the expectation within our law that parents will provide proper care for their children. Jehovah's Witnesses, and the Old Order Amish, are opposed to warfare on religious grounds and have in the past come into conflict with the draft laws. In this case a resolution of the conflict has been achieved by allowing those who object to military service on the basis of religious belief to provide alternative forms of service. Traditional Catholics, as well as some of those affiliated with other religions, regard legal abortion as an abomination, fundamentally at odds with their understanding of divine law. The ongoing battle over the abortion issue is at least in part a conflict between religious and secular values.

Some Native American religious groups have claimed the right to smoke marijuana in accord with their traditional ceremonial practices, although this use of an illicit drug is at odds with the law. Within prisons, conflicts have sometimes arisen when inmate demands to be allowed freedom of worship, on Constitutional grounds, are seen as compromising prison security or other institutional objectives. And in the case of some newer religious sects, such as the Unification Church of the Reverend Sun Myung Moon, conflicts have arisen when parents of young recruits have seized their children and subjected them to "deprogramming," on the grounds that the Unification Church is less an authentic religious entity than an evil, manipulative cult. But the courts have generally upheld the right of those who are no longer minors to choose their religious affiliations, however unorthodox, and has upheld criminal prosecutions against those engaged in kidnapping such recruits.

The question of what constitutes an authentic religion is significant here as well, insofar as religious organizations are entitled to certain state-ordained benefits, such as immunity from taxation. The Church of Scientology, for example, is regarded by many people as a somewhat bizarre and sinister enterprise that is more of a cult and profit-making business than an authentic religious organization (Horwitz 1997). The Church of Scientology engaged in many years of litigation with the Internal Revenue Service before receiving some recognition, for tax purposes, as a religious entity.

The conflicts and tensions between commitment to religious principle and commitment to law are not easily resolved. Many people have gone to prison rather than compromise their religious principles. The Jesuit priest Father Daniel Berrigan and his brother (a former priest), Phillip Berrigan, endured prison sentences at various times during the final decades of the twentieth century because their understanding of their religious duty led them to engage in illegal actions such as the burning of draft board records (during the Vietnam War era) and attacks on nuclear facilities (Berrigan 1970; Dear 1997). The Reverend Martin Luther King (1963) engaged in acts of civil disobedience during the Civil Rights era, leading to his being sent to jail (Branch 1988, 1998). His famous "Letter from Birmingham City Jail," in response to criticism from some Baptist ministers who felt he was setting a bad example as a religious leader by breaking laws, reminds us that those who share the same religious faith may interpret their moral obligations in different ways.

The ongoing controversy on the abortion issue has generated a considerable dilemma for at least some of those who regard themselves as law-abiding citizens but regard the legal status of abortion as profoundly immoral and at odds with their most deeply felt religious convictions. In the most extreme cases, those opposed to legalized abortion have carried out violent attacks on abortion clinic personnel or have firebombed such facilities (Papke 1998). Many have engaged in attempts to block entrances to abortion facilities or harass those attempting to enter. Still others have undertaken less intrusive forms of protest. One view of the sensitive issue of conflicting obligations toward both the law of the state and religious law in response to abortion has been stated by the late Cardinal John J. O'Connor (1984) of New York City:

> You have to *uphold* the law, the Constitution says. It does not say that you must *agree* with the law or that you cannot work to *change* the law. It will simply not do to argue that "laws" won't work or "we can't legislate morality." Nor will it do to argue "I won't impose my morality on others." There is nothing personal or private in the morality that teaches that the taking of unborn life is wrong.

According to Cardinal O'Connor, respect for "law" should not be confused with respect for bad laws. In the view of foes of legal abortion, the seven justices in the majority in the landmark U.S. Supreme Court decision *Roe v. Wade* (1973), which struck down state laws prohibiting legal abortions, were imposing their (secular) morality on the American public and were effectively making bad law. Of course, supporters of the decision tend to believe that the Supreme Court justices recognized that decisions about abortion fall in the realm of private, not public, morality, and should be left up to individual consciences.

Doctrine Declaring Separation of Church and State

The United States has a long history, stretching over hundreds of years, of unresolved tensions and conflicts between religion and law (Fish 1997; Saunders 1997). This tension is experienced too by those who teach about law or practice law (Cochran 1997). In America the doctrine of separation of church and state was adopted by the Founding Fathers. Some of the earliest settlers were escaping from religious persecution sponsored by, or condoned by, a European state. By the late eighteenth century, at the time of the writing of the Constitution, various religious groups were coexisting in America. The Founding Fathers were concerned with preventing a circumstance where the state would engage in the persecution of religious minorities.

The exact meaning of the doctrine separating church and state, and the prohibition of state "establishment" of religion, however, has been a source of ongoing tension and conflict throughout American history. The establishment clause of the First Amendment of the Constitution reads as follows: "Congress shall make no law respecting an establishment of religion, or prohibiting the free exercise thereof." Some have interpreted this to mean that the national government should refrain from involvement with or support of religion in any form. Others say that this clause only prohibits the national government from literally establishing a state religion, but it allows for individual states to provide support for churches and religions in whatever form the state chooses. In *The Godless Constitution: The Case Against Religious Correctness*, Isaac Kramnick and Lawrence Moore (1996) (of Cornell University) argue that evidence from the Constitutional ratification debates supports the view that the Framers wanted to maintain a godly nation but believed this could be best done by defining religion as a private pursuit, not subject to governmental policy (see Box 3.4).

Contemporary Issues

In the contemporary era religion has become a basis for divisiveness and conflict, with at least some religious fundamentalists calling for the establishment of a Christian state and some ardent secularists opposing any form of state support for religious activities. The question of whether prayer in some form should be allowed in public schools is just one issue that has led to acrimonious debate and to a number of landmark cases. Yale University law professor Stephen Carter (1993), in *The Culture of Disbelief: How American Law and Politics Trivialize Religious Devotion*, has made a provocative argu-

Box 3.4

The Controversy Over Publicly Funded Vouchers and Religiously Affiliated Schools

Dissatisfaction with the public school system has been widespread in recent decades. Support for programs making publicly funded vouchers for schooling available to parents of school-age children, to be used at schools of the family's choice, has been expressed by many members of the general public, as well as by many politicians. A number of states have adopted voucher programs. But should publicly funded vouchers be made available to pay for an education at a religiously affiliated school? Teresa Stanton Collett (1999) argues that such a provision is both constitutionally permissible and is desirable as a matter of public policy. A voucher program applicable to religiously oriented schools allows parents to choose what vision of the good life their children should be exposed to; the professed neutrality of public schools all too often is alleged to promote values directly hostile to those supported by established religions, and in the recent era the Supreme Court has acknowledged this. Accordingly, a properly constructed school voucher program would not exclude religiously affiliated schools.

On the other hand, Caren Dubnoff (1999) argues that allowing public vouchers to be used for religiously affiliated schools violates the doctrine of separation of church and state of the First Amendment. Such vouchers would inevitably provide substantial public aid to particular religions. This program would promote religious divisions and would contribute to further deterioration of public education, with the most disadvantaged suffering the consequences.

ment that many major institutions, including the courts, have been complicit in denigrating religion and banishing it from public life. He observes that the separation of church and state was originally intended to protect religion from state interference and persecution, but contemporary legal rules take the form of protecting the state from religion! Carter acknowledges that it is difficult to strike the right balance between accommodating religious beliefs and implementing direct state involvement with religious expression, but he expresses the view that contemporary trends have too often tipped the balance against the former objective. In a subsequent book, *The Dissent of the Governed: A Meditation on Law, Religion, and Loyalty*, Carter (1998) claims that growing numbers of Americans find it necessary to choose between following the law and following the word of (their) God, and he controversially calls for some form of protection for those who break laws out of religious conviction.

By the mid-1990s some presidential initiatives, legislative acts, and U.S. Supreme Court decisions had recognized, in modest ways, the need to accommodate religious expression more fully. In 1999 the U.S. Senate was considering a bill, the Religious Liberty Protection Act, that is intended by its sponsors to deter or prevent government actions that disrupt religion (such actions might include zoning laws that exclude churches; school restrictions on wearing religious symbols; and coroner autopsies in violation of religious beliefs about the treatment of corpses) (Cloud 1999). Would such a bill reaffirm a historical tradition of courts generally favoring religious claims or would it have the unintended consequence of enabling religious cults to make creative claims protecting some of their bizarre or dangerous practices? During the same period, the U.S. Supreme Court was hearing cases that addressed issues such as the constitutionality of student-led prayer at public school graduations and athletic events; state tax exemptions for religious publications; and state tax credits and other tuition assistance for the costs of religious education (Greenhouse 1999b). The satisfactory resolution of such issues is difficult to accomplish if people feel that their heartfelt religious convictions are threatened by a judicial ruling. The ultimate meaning of the establishment clause would clearly continue to be a contested terrain.

Law and Interests

The preceding sections have considered how values—in terms of conceptions of justice, in terms of morality, and in terms of religious beliefs—intersect with the law. But much of law is also shaped by, or interacts with, other types of considerations that fall outside the realm of values as conventionally defined. These considerations can be called "interests." Roscoe Pound (1942), a celebrated dean of Harvard Law School, put forth a view of law as a mechanism for adjudicating (or settling) conflicts between competing interests. In all realms of law there are competing interests in the sense that different parties are attempting to realize different specific goals. In the criminal law and criminal justice system some of the competing interests include the following: avenging wrongdoing (retribution); protecting society (incapacitation); discouraging lawbreaking generally and the repetition of lawbreaking by specific offenders (deterrence); transforming lawbreakers into constructive, law-abiding citizens (rehabilitation); and returning to victims of lawbreaking what they have lost (restitution). Obviously, priorities among these competing interests or objectives may be said to reflect in some part particular conceptions of justice—some scheme of morality, religious beliefs, and purely practical concerns. So interests can hardly be separated from values, or the moral order. But the emphasis on interests, as here defined, is on outcomes as opposed to underlying principles. When different parties want to maximize their material gain and minimize their material loss, then we typically think of these objectives as practical interests. Examples might include a corporation's interest in achieving maximum economic efficiency and profit, or a husband's interest in minimizing financial responsibility for a wife he is in the process of divorcing.

If competing interests are the norm in legal issues, whose interests prevail? If it comes down to might versus right—or power on the one hand versus a more persuasive moral entitlement on the other hand—many students of law will argue that might has all too often prevailed. However, three basic models of the relationship between interests and law, or public policy, can be identified (Olsen 1970). First, there is the *power elite* model. In this model the interests of the power elite prevail; in C. Wright Mills' (1959) famous analysis, in American society the top people in the government, the military, and the business community constitute a power elite with various ties. A second model is the *pluralist* model. In this model competing interest groups vie for influence, and different groups are successful at different times. A third model is the *democratic* model. In this model law and public policy reflect principally the will of the majority of the public, as implemented by the public's representatives. Altogether, American law reflects a complex mix of interests. The last of these models has been especially celebrated in American culture, yet much evidence suggests that a mix of the first two models is more relevant to understanding whose interests are translated into law.

The relation of interests to law has been discussed only briefly here. However, these connections are explored more fully in particular contexts addressed by later chapters.

Conclusion

Law is intimately entangled with questions of justice, morality, and religious belief. This chapter has attempted to identify some of the principal parameters of this entanglement and some of the critical issues involved. The ongoing tensions and conflicts arising in this context should be evident. The final brief section of the chapter acknowledges the significance of interests reflecting practical objectives in relation to law. While the pursuit or promotion of such interests can be viewed independently of purely normative questions, in the long term we have to recognize that there are connections between the promotion of specific interests and a conception of justice.

Key Terms and Concepts

alternative justice
categorical imperative
commutative principle of justice
contractual conception of justice
cultural relativity
democratic model
distributive principle of justice
egalitarian conception of justice
ethnocentrism
intuitionist conception of justice
jury nullification
moral entrepreneurs
passive injustice
pluralist model
power elite model
practical interests
procedural justice
retributive principle of justice
substantive justice
transitional justice
utilitarian conception of justice

Discussion Questions

1. Do you think that affirmative action policies are just? Should they continue to exist? Why or why not? What stand would libertarians, socialists, and communitarians each take on affirmative action issues?

2. The exclusionary rule exists as one way of protecting the rights to due process that accused persons have. Is such a rule really fair? Is it more impor-

tant for our legal system to put an emphasis on achieving procedural or substantive justice?

3. Can violence ever be justified as a way of achieving justice? Should a mother be prosecuted for attempting to kill the man that molested and took the life of her 6-year-old, if in her mind she was "doing justice"?
4. There is no law that says an ordinary citizen has a legal duty to save the life of a drowning person. Should laws be created that criminalize the act of "doing nothing" in a situation where one has the capability of coming to another's aid? In your answer, include comments on the 1997 David Cash case, as well as the example here.
5. In *The Dissent of the Governed: A Meditation on Law, Religion, and Loyalty,* Stephen Carter calls for some form of protection for those who break laws out of religious conviction. Do you agree or disagree with his belief? What problems might occur if this became a regular practice in our system?

Chapter Four

Jurisprudence and the Study of Law

Law is rules. Law is principles. Law is practices. Those who have studied law and taught law want to be able to explain what the rules are based upon, what the principles are or should be, and what those who practice law in some sense look to when they make their decisions, or what it is that influences those decisions. Making sense of law in this way is the work of jurisprudence.

Jurisprudence

The term "jurisprudence" is derived from Latin, as is true of so much legal terminology. *Juris prudentes* can be translated as "wise in the law." In broad terms, the term jurisprudence encompasses general forms of intellectual inquiry about law (Bodenheimer 1974; Duxbury 1995; Kelly 1992; Morrison 1997). It may refer to legal philosophy or to a science of law. While no one would dispute the notion of a philosophy of law, the claim that a science of law is also possible is a matter of contention. The term jurisprudence, then, is applied to different types of inquiry and practice.

Jurisprudence may focus on legal principles, or on the actual practices of legal institutions; on what the law ought to be or on what the law as implemented actually is; on law as a system of rules with its own internal logic or on law as a social institution shaped by outside influences.

All justices who render legal decisions and issue legal opinions adopt a jurisprudential philosophy, whether or not they specifically acknowledge this. But there has been significant disagreement on how justices arrive at their decisions. The term *mechanical jurisprudence* suggests that judges are judicial scientists who, if they apply the appropriate legal principles correctly in a particular case, will arrive at the right decision (Pound 1908). The term *nihilistic jurisprudence* suggests that judges are idiosyncratic individuals who arrive at decisions according to their political biases or personal inclinations (or hunches) and that one should not pretend law itself dictates correct answers (Stick 1986). These terms present a stark contrast and do not necessarily capture the complex mix of considerations that enter into judicial decision making. But this dichotomy should be kept in mind as you read about different schools of jurisprudence, some of which are clearly aligned with one or the other of these two ways of thinking about what judges do.

Schools of Jurisprudence

Law is an inherently contentious enterprise. Accordingly, the fact that there are many competing schools of jurisprudence, each incorporating premises starkly at odds with many of the premises of the competing schools, should hardly be surprising. In this chapter seven traditional schools of jurisprudence and seven contemporary schools of jurisprudence are identified and briefly described. These schools of jurisprudence are discussed roughly in chronological order, in terms of when they were first introduced. "Traditional," in this context, refers to schools of jurisprudence originating early in history or by the mid-twentieth century; of course, many of these schools of jurisprudence, in some form, have vigorous adherents today. "Contemporary" schools of jurisprudence refer here to jurisprudential perspectives originating for the most part in recent decades, principally from the 1970s on (see Table 4.1). The number of schools identified here, and the classifications themselves, may be somewhat arbitrary, but they should at least provide a good appreciation of the diversity of jurisprudential approaches. In the context of the sociolegal focus of this book, some attention will be directed toward the relationship of the particular school of jurisprudence to social context and social variables.

Traditional Schools of Jurisprudence

Natural Law

The oldest and most enduring school of jurisprudence, with origins among classical Greek and Roman philosophers, is natural law (Bix 1996; Smith 1997; Weinreb 1987). Contemporary proponents of natural law insist that its way of understanding fundamental issues of law, morality, and justice remains superior to competing approaches (George 1999). The key attribute of this school of thought is that the human law is (or ought to be) rooted in a transcendent law of divine origin or as part of nature itself. Among the ancient philosophers, the Greek Aristotle and, to a lesser extent, Plato, and the Roman Cicero are viewed as progenitors (Morrison 1997).

The jurisprudence of the great Roman Catholic theologians, especially St. Thomas Aquinas (1266–1272; 1993), is also regarded as part of this tradition. In the natural law approach of Aquinas, the validity of law is dependent

Table 4.1 Traditional Schools of Jurisprudence

I.	*Natural Law:* B.C., Ancient Greece and Rome Law as a reflection of the moral/divine order.
II.	*Positive Law:* Early 19th century Law as the will of the sovereign; law as science.
III.	*Utilitarianism:* Early 19th century Law as the greatest good for the greatest number; pragmatism.
IV.	*Cultural/Historical:* 19th century Law as a reflection of historical circumstances; of particular cultures.
V.	*Sociological Jurisprudence:* Early 20th century Law in relation to social reality; social engineering through law.
VI.	*Legal Realism:* First half of the 20th century Social and psychological influences on legal decision making; focus on trial courts.
VII.	*Process Theory:* Mid-20th century Emphasis on procedural consistency in law; legal process.

on its relation to some higher law or principle; a specific law must be in accord with this higher law (which emanates from God) or it is not valid. In natural law thinking, there can be no separation between law and morality. The seventeenth-century English philosopher John Locke ([1690] 1965), for example, proposed that human beings possess certain fundamental rights in a state of nature, and when they are members of a civil society they are entitled to these rights. If the state infringes upon these natural rights of citizens, the authority of the state is nullified. These ideas of Locke's were, of course, immensely influential with the framers of the Constitution of the United States. The famous reference in the Declaration of Independence to "inalienable rights" reflects Locke's version of natural law theory. Although the commitment to this core concept has remained strong, over time various other schools of jurisprudence described here have been embraced.

In the contemporary era, natural law jurisprudence takes a number of different forms. Traditional Catholics continue to identify with a version of natural law theory rooted in Aquinas. A more philosophically oriented natural law jurisprudence is based on work by the German philosopher Immanuel Kant ([1785] 1998) and his categorical imperative (calling for laws based upon principles that can be applied universally) for its basic point of departure.

A sociological version of natural law jurisprudence suggests that one can empirically investigate issues of human needs and draw upon these data to formulate laws that might contribute to the filling of such needs. One prominent contemporary proponent of natural law, John Finnis (1980), argues that "human" (positive) law, while it has some important functions, must ultimately be reconciled with the criteria of natural law. In Finnis' conception, natural law integrates ethics with political philosophy and may be defined as "the set of principles of practical reasonableness in ordering human life and human community." Basic human goods such as life, knowledge, play, aesthetic experience, friendship, and religion must in this view be reconciled with "practical reasonableness." Also in the natural law tradition, Robert Clinton (1997) calls for a return to a God-centered Constitution because he sees the secularist interpretation of the Constitution as having various undesirable consequences.

On the whole, natural law jurisprudence is leery of social science, as opposed to theological or philosophical texts, as a basis for law. Natural law tends to be associated with an ideologically conservative perspective. In the famous *Lochner v. New York* (1905) case early in the twentieth century, a predominantly conservative United States Supreme Court invoked natural law in upholding the "right" of employers to be free from laws limiting the number of hours in an employee's workday. Although natural law has been cited to support free enterprise and property rights, it has probably more often been associated with fundamentalist religious belief and the position that state law is obliged to proscribe morally offensive and decadent activity while promoting biblical virtues.

Natural law also provided one foundation for the Nuremberg Trials and the prosecution of surviving Nazi leaders and perpetrators of the Holocaust. The crimes of the Nazis were interpreted as contrary in the extreme to long-recognized, widely accepted principles of natural law. During the civil rights era in the United States, in the 1950s and 1960s, Martin Luther King Jr. (1963) also referred to natural law as providing grounds for disobeying inherently immoral laws perpetuating segregation.

A fundamental problem with natural law has to be acknowledged, then. The substantive content of such law is open to interpretation. Although natural law has been invoked against genocide and segregation, it has also been invoked, historically, to vindicate slavery and the apartheid system (denying blacks basic rights) in South Africa, and to discriminate against women (Margolick 1990; Shea 1997). It is far from clear that a single natural law position on the death penalty exists. Identification with a natural law jurisprudence, then, is seen as attractive to some on the grounds that it is principled and maintains a strong connection between the moral and the legal, but the specific principles called for are open to ongoing debate (see Box 4.1).

Legal Positivism

Legal positivism is often represented as an approach to law in stark contrast to the approach taken by natural law jurisprudence (Coleman and Leiter 1996; George 1996). This jurisprudential school of thought is of much more recent vintage than natural law, with principal early contributions made in the nineteenth century. Legal positivism, in contrast to natural law jurisprudence, treats the legal and the moral—the "is" and the " ought"—as separate realms. In this approach the validity of law is determined by its source, as opposed to its content. Law is a human product of a political system, and valid law is accordingly produced by appropriate procedures. Legal rules are part of a formal, logical, closed system. The English legal philosophers Jeremy Bentham ([1776] 1960, [1789] 1970) and John Austin ([1832] 1954), writing in the late eighteenth and early nineteenth centuries, are considered

Box 4.1

Lon Fuller and Legal Naturalism

Legal naturalism is a term sometimes applied to the views of Lon Fuller (1940, 1969, 1981), a twentieth-century professor of law at Harvard University. For Fuller, law is the enterprise of subjecting human conduct to the governance of rules. Law has an *external* morality. In other words, one can ask the question of whether the substantive content of law is in accord with some defensible scheme of morality. For example, can laws permitting abortion or mandatory sterilization or physician-assisted suicide be defended on moral grounds? Of course, as we have seen elsewhere, heated debate in response to such questions is the norm.

In his book *The Morality of Law* Fuller (1969) put forth the novel argument that law also has an *internal* morality that is indifferent to the substantive content, or aims, of the law. This internal morality is one of duty and aspiration and is a precondition for valid law. To illustrate what he means by the internal morality of law, Fuller tells the story of King Rex, a fictitious monarch who attempts to establish a system of law in his country. Without here going into the details of Fuller's fable, one can simply note that King Rex encounters a series of frustrations and failures with each new tactic he adopts in this effort to create a system of law, and each of these failures generates a principle that is a critical element of a valid system of law. In brief, these principles are as follows:

1. There must be general rules, or laws.
2. These laws must be made known.
3. Laws must not be retroactive.
4. Laws must be clear and understandable.
5. Laws should not be contradictory.
6. Laws should not require the impossible or the extremely unreasonable.
7. Insofar as possible, laws should be reasonably constant through time.
8. Laws and the administration of laws should not be in conflict.

It should be immediately evident that these eight propositions tell one nothing about the substantive morality of laws or whether laws permitting abortion, enforced sterilization, or physician-assisted suicide are moral or immoral. Rather, they identify the basic attributes of a valid system of law. For Fuller, a system of law that fails on any one of these eight criteria is not really a valid system of law (Wueste 1986). On the one hand, Fuller rejects the formalist position (associated with legal positivists) that any command of the sovereign constitutes law. But Fuller also rejects the natural law position that a law whose content is at odds with natural law principles is not law. Rather, Fuller's "legal naturalism" may be viewed as a compromise perspective that emphasizes the form as opposed to the content of law. Yet Fuller clearly believed that a legal system encompassing his procedural criteria was also highly likely to adopt good and defensible substantive laws.

Following World War II, Fuller engaged in a famous debate with H. L. A. Hart, a leading proponent of legal positivism, on whether or not Nazi law was really law (Minda 1995, 50). For the legal positivists it was law, even if it was bad law. In the view of traditional adherents of natural law, who were influential in identifying grounds for trying the surviving Nazi leadership after the war, Nazi law was not law because of its inherently evil content (at odds with the moral criteria of natural law). But for Fuller, Nazi law was not really law for a different reason: it was ☞

> procedurally defective, insofar as it did not meet the criteria for a valid system of law. In other words, whatever its failures in terms of external morality, it was also internally immoral and therefore was not law. Such ideas have been controversial, but at a minimum Fuller has provided a provocative alternative to the traditional viewpoint on the relationship between the legal and the moral.

to be the founding fathers of legal positivism. For Austin, law is the command of the sovereign (or the head of the state). Commands, in this view, are orders backed by threats. The citizen's duty to obey the law is linked with the legitimacy of the source of the command rather than a moral evaluation of the command. Such moral evaluation may be important and appropriate in some contexts, but it is separate from the legal question of a command's, or law's, validity.

In the late nineteenth century Christopher Columbus Langdell became dean of the Harvard Law School. Langdell adopted a version of legal positivism that became exceptionally influential in legal education. For Langdell (1871) law was a complete, formal, and conceptually ordered system. Accordingly, law could be considered a form of science, and the student of law could take on the role of a scientist of law. Langdell believed that the appropriate way to educate law students called for the analysis of appellate case opinions. Students could arrive at the correct solution to a particular case—even if the justice or justices who actually wrote the opinion had failed to do so—by identifying the right legal principles underlying the particular case and by applying a rigorous form of legal analysis to the case. This approach to legal education was widely adopted on the premise that it would teach students to "think like a lawyer," but it also came to be subjected to increasing criticism. (Such criticism is discussed more fully in Chapter 7.)

In the twentieth century, law professor Hans Kelsen ([1934] 1967), a refugee from Nazi Germany, developed a version of legal positivism that begins with the characterization of the legal system as a hierarchy, or pyramid, of norms. Kelsen labeled the basic, or foundational, norm the "grundnorm"; other norms must be understood in their relation to this norm and in terms of how they derive authority from such fundamental norms. Accordingly, a pure science of law is regarded as possible by Kelsen, with laws understood as logical outcomes of fundamental principles.

The English legal philosopher H. L. A. Hart's (1961) *The Concept of Law* is regarded as a major statement of modern legal positivism (Mayes 1989). In Hart's view law, a self-regulating system rooted in social fact and convention, has both primary and secodary rules. The secondary rules (of recognition) are the basic sources of the validity of primary rules, or rules pertaining to individual rights and obligations (Minda 1995, 48). For example, the federal law prohibiting bank robbery is a primary rule, and Article II of the Constitution, granting the power to Congress to legislate, is a secondary rule.

The emergence of legal positivism as a school of jurisprudence can be seen as reflecting the aspiration of some students of law to emulate the obvious success of the physical and natural sciences in the realm of the law. It could also be regarded as reflecting the modern drive toward imposing rationality and order on life and social existence. In its most extreme form, it seems to suggest an image of law virtually analogous to mathematics. In this view, even if law originates with human commands and norms, it then seems to take on a life of its own, and operates almost independently of the social context.

Critics of this approach to law have found it unrealistic and morally offensive and have noted that any such approach inevitably tends to endorse or legitimate the status quo and the authority of the power elite who create, interpret, or apply law. Despite such criticism, legal positivism has persisted, and by the end of the twentieth century may even have experienced a revival. One defender of legal positivism disputes the widely held view that it is indifferent to moral principles (Sebok 1998). Two other proponents (Schauer and Wise 1997) argue that legal positivism alone is capable of differentiating clearly between law and other categories of knowledge.

Historical/Cultural Jurisprudence

During the nineteenth century another school of jurisprudence—most commonly called Historical Jurisprudence—also emerged. At odds with legal positivism, this school of jurisprudence stongly emphasized the interdependence of law and the social world. In this view, law can only be properly understood in a particular historical and cultural context. Law is regarded as a dependent variable, or a product of social forces. In the interpretation of the nineteenth-century German law professor Friedrich Karl von Savigny ([1831] 1986), a leading early proponent of historical jurisprudence, law is best understood as the slow, organic distillation of the spirit of a particular people (*Volkgeist*). The validity of law, then, is not linked with its emanating from a legitimate "sovereign" but rather is dependent on whether it accurately reflects this spirit, or national character.

Since the "spirit" of a people and its moral belief system are intimately interconnected, the positivist separation of the legal from the moral is not really applicable here. But the notion of a folk spirit has not lent itself to easy measurement and has been criticized on a number of grounds. If law reflects, or ought to reflect, a national cultural outlook, it is not easy to explain obvious variations in the law that arise between different jurisdictions within a particular nation. Also, the notion of "folk spirit" that was proclaimed by romantic nationalists in the nineteenth century was embraced and then transformed for pernicious purposes by some of the demagogues and tyrants of the twentieth century.

The nineteenth-century English legal historian Sir Henry Maine ([1861] 1970) is also associated with this school of jurisprudence. In his celebrated book *Ancient Law*, Maine explored the historical development of law and identified as a basic trend a movement from law oriented toward status to law oriented toward contract. In other words, in ancient legal systems one's status (in terms of social class, gender, and so on) determined one's standing before the law and the law's treatment. In modern, developed societies, a contract—a free agreement between two or more parties—was at the center of legal matters. Maine celebrated this perceived movement from status to contract as a sign of progress.

Maine's view of contracts, however, has been criticized as somewhat starry-eyed and naive. In many—perhaps most—contracts, one party has significant advantages over the other, and the contract itself ends up favoring that party. Although Maine was attuned to long-term social changes, he was somewhat insensitive to the immense consequences of social inequality in many legal matters in the modern world. It is perhaps ironic that the growing recognition in the modern world of the fundamental unfairness of social inequality has led to the reintroduction of status as an important element in the legal order. Now, however, social status as a disadvantaged person (e.g., as a minority group member or a woman) may translate into a legal advantage under affirmative action law. Maine was right in recognizing that law must be understood in a sociohistorical context and that the tenor of law may evolve and change significantly over time. At the same time, students and scholars have to be leery of sweeping generalizations about the changing character of law, insofar as that character is often complex and contradictory in certain respects.

Utilitarianism

All students who have taken an introductory philosophy course are likely to have been introduced to the core ideas of utilitarianism. This school of philosophy, emerging in the late eighteenth and early nineteenth centuries, became very influential, especially in the practical realm of legal reform. The British philosopher Jeremy Bentham ([1789] 1970), although he has been identified as a founder of legal positivism, is best known for espousing utilitarianism. The core principle here is that utility should govern. More specifically, that which promotes the greatest happiness, or good, for the greatest number is what society should strive for. It should be a primary objective of philosophers of law to determine which laws or policies would best promote this outcome. Bentham was a somewhat eccentric personality, and much of his work may seem dated or naive by contemporary standards. But he was immensely influential in promoting the criteria of social utility for legal reform, and his ideas challenged in a fundamental way the abstract or superstition-ridden ways of interpreting the world still common in his time. One of his best-known disciples, John Stuart Mill ([1859] 1963), produced the celebrated essay "On Liberty," with the core argument that the government should only make criminal laws proscribing identifiably harmful behavior toward others.

The eighteenth-century Italian nobleman and economist Cesare Beccaria ([1764] 1988), typically identified in criminology textbooks as the founder of a "classical" school of thought, developed ideas somewhat parallel to those of utilitarianism. Beccaria is especially associated with the notion of introducing rationality into the criminal justice system and imposing punishments that fit the crime. In Beccaria's view, rational punishments would both deter people from committing crimes in the first place and deter convicted offenders from repeating their offenses. Both Beccaria and Bentham adopted a fundamental assumption about human nature as being rational, self-interested, and naturally oriented toward maximizing pleasure and minimizing pain. Their basic stress on the capability of humans to make rational choices is incorporated in modern law and has been adopted by at least some prominent social philosophers and criminologists.

The whole tenor of the utilitarian way of thinking about law inevitably tips it toward the notion that law must not be interpreted independent of the social context within which it arises and of social consequences. This pragmatic, policy-oriented approach to law is clearly reflected in some contemporary schools of jurisprudence. It has been criticized as based upon a simplistic and distorted view of human nature, excessive emphasis on practical consequences as opposed to support of higher principles, and insufficient concern with the rights of minorities.

Sociological Jurisprudence

With the emergence of a sociological jurisprudence, principally in the early decades of the twentieth century, the connections between the legal and the social came to be even more sharply highlighted. This school of jurisprudence is most readily associated with the Austrian scholar Eugen Ehrlich ([1913] 1936) and the American Harvard law professor (and dean) Roscoe Pound (1907, 1910). During the period that Ehrlich and Pound wrote, sociology was emerging as an autonomous, clearly recognizable discipline. In the United States, in particular, early sociologists were concerned with developing sociological knowledge that could provide guidance for social reform. Ehrlich and Pound came to believe that sociological knowledge also had a specific role to play in reforming the law.

They recognized that law coexisted with other social rules and norms and that social order is dependent upon a high level of acceptance of such rules. Ehrlich emphasized that the formal law was most effective when it was in accord with the living law, or the complex of rules and norms by which members of society actually lived. Accordingly, students of law must not remain content to simply study legal treatises but must turn to the real world in which people live to understand law as a part of that world. Roscoe Pound called for the study of "law in action" to determine the extent to which a correspondence existed between the formal law and the rules that people actually tried to follow. In addition, Pound directed attention to the frequent discrepancy between claims about what legal institutions were doing and what in fact they were doing. Empirical sociological research could be applied to the investigation of such questions as these: Are the formal proclamations of the courts in conformity with the actual decisions or practices of the courts? Are the specific aims and objectives of legislative statutes realized through the process of implementing these statutes?

Roscoe Pound (1942, 1943, 1945) is also associated with a theory of interests. For Pound it is important to identify the specific social interests underlying laws and to expose some of the inevitable conflicts between these interests. Inevitably one has to recognize that individualistic (legalistic) justice is not always in accord with social (humanistic) justice: for example, even if the formal law does not require that workers injured in the workplace be compensated, social justice does require such compensation. The formal law should be adapted to the prevailing standards of social justice, in this view. A sociological (or social) jurisprudence, according to Pound, should identify the most important social interests and the crucial values of a modern society, and law reformers (as social engineers) should devise a scheme to realize these values. The influence of utilitarianism and pragmatism is evident here in the view that the law as a social institution should play a central role in enabling society to fulfill its aspirations.

Box 4.2

The Brandeis Brief

Some judges and other legal actors became more attuned to the realities of the societal environment, influenced by the sociological jurisprudential school. The so-called "Brandeis Brief" reflects this influence (Schur 1968, 42). A brief is a written argument highlighting facts, laws, legal principles, and opinions of respected authorities relevant to and in support of a lawyer's application to a court of law to take some action or render a particular decision. As a Boston lawyer Louis Brandeis prepared a brief in an early twentieth century case (*Muller v. Oregon*, 1908) about the hours of working women. His brief highlighted many forms of evidence demonstrating the pernicious effects of long workdays on the health of women. This type of brief, drawing upon social data, represented an important break with traditional legal arguments, which were framed wholly in technical legal terms. Brandeis himself became a distinguished justice of the U.S. Supreme Court, and that court and other courts came to accept the type of evidence highlighted in the Brandeis brief as relevant to their decisions. One famous example is the landmark desegregation case, *Brown v. Board of Education* (1954). The unanimous opinion of the U.S. Supreme Court in this case did not rely simply on internal legal doctrine. Rather, social science evidence of the harmful consequences of prevailing segregation practices was taken into account in the opinion, which determined that segregated schools were in violation of the Constitution.

Legal Realism

The repudiation of the abstract manner of viewing law, which was characteristic of the earliest schools of jurisprudence, reached a climax of sorts with legal realism (Aichele 1990). This repudiation has been labeled "the revolt against formalism." Although legal realism is clearly related to, and sometimes confused with, sociological jurisprudence, it has a somewhat different emphasis and focus (White 1972). Legal realism challenged a traditional view that judges simply identify what the law is by "finding" what has been recognized as the law; it insisted on recognizing that judges make new law when they render their opinions.

The celebrated Associate Justice of the U.S. Supreme Court Oliver Wendell Holmes Jr. (1881, 1897) is typically identified as a major source of inspiration for legal realism. The utilitarianism of Bentham and the historical jurisprudence of Maine were clearly important influences on Holmes. Although he also incorporated some aspects of Austin's positivistic approach—for example, on the fundamental difference between the legal and the moral—Holmes differed with the positivists on where one should look to discern the essence of law. Holmes said to look to human practices, whereas positivists relied on formal principles. Holmes was also influenced by a pragmatic orientation toward law, with special attention to results as opposed to general principles. In the most famous of his Supreme Court dissenting opinions, in *Lochner v. New York* (1905), Holmes took exception to the majority's view that New York could not pass a law limiting the working hours of bakers (on the pretext that it violated a Fourteenth Amendment due process right to freedom of contract); for Holmes, the majority view was simply a reflection of

Box 4.3

Oliver Wendell Holmes Jr. as a Legal Icon

Oliver Wendell Holmes Jr. is a towering figure in American legal history, arguably the most frequently cited of all legal writers, and perhaps second only to John Marshall among the most famous U.S. Supreme Court justices (Schnayerson 1986; Schwartz 1974; Voss 1989). Holmes was born in 1841, fought (and was wounded) in the Civil War, and lived to witness the New Deal, dying only in 1935. His father, Oliver Wendell Holmes, Sr., was a physician, celebrated wit, and well-known writer, but in time the son's fame came to overshadow that of the father. Holmes was related to a number of prominent American families; growing up, he knew his father's friend Ralph Emerson. Among his own contemporaries, he knew the psychologist William James and his brother, the writer Henry James. During the course of his long life Holmes knew and corresponded with many leading figures of his time.

Holmes was educated at Harvard and practiced law for some years. In 1881 his famous book, *The Common Law,* was published; this work emphasizes the influence of external forces on the formation of the common law and the need to see law in terms independent from morality. In 1882 Holmes was appointed Professor of Law at Harvard. In the same year, however, he was appointed an Associate Justice of the Massachusetts Supreme Court, becoming Chief Justice in 1899.

Holmes was sixty-one years old when Theodore Roosevelt appointed him to the U.S. Supreme Court in 1902; he then served as Associate Justice for almost thirty years, retiring from the bench when he was over ninety. Although he produced some 2,000 opinions, he is especially famous for his dissenting opinions, which, although few, were influential and earned him a reputation as "the great dissenter." Holmes observed that "great cases like hard cases make bad law." Accordingly, in such cases, he felt that a dissenting opinion served a useful function. Holmes was especially uncompromising in his opposition to any efforts to limit free speech and is known for his tough-minded insistence upon tolerance of dissenting viewpoints. For the most part, Holmes argued that judges should defer to the will of the people's representatives in the legislative branch, even if much of the resulting legislation was "humbug." As Holmes famously observed:

> About seventy-five years ago, I learned that I was not God. And so, when people want to do something that I can't find anything in the Constitution expressly forbidding them to do, I say, whether I like it or not, Goddamit, let 'em do it. (Schwartz 1974, 191)

the majority's economic conservatism and also was inconsistent with earlier court rulings.

In *The Common Law* (1881, 1) Holmes set forth, on the first page, his oft-quoted observation, "The life of the law has not been logic: it has been experience." Holmes was here urging students of law to turn away from a treatment of law as an exercise in abstract reasoning and to focus rather on law as it was in the real world. For Holmes, the substance of the law inevitably reflected the "felt necessities" of the times and other social and practical influences, not abstract legal logic. In his landmark *Harvard Law Review* essay of 1897 (460–461), "The Path of the Law," Holmes offered up a provocative assertion that "The prophecies of what the courts will do in fact, and nothing more pretentious, are what I mean by the law." If this is so, Holmes suggests, we have to look at the law as the "bad man" does. The bad man, in this view, is really not concerned with abstract principles and moral reasoning. The bad man is simply interested in the actual decision of the court, and ideally in being able to predict what the courts will do. It follows from this reasoning that the judicial process, and the decision making of judges, should be an important focus of jurisprudential analysis, as indeed has been the case since the time of Holmes.

The legal realist movement thrived mainly during the 1920s and 1930s. It was more of a movement than a unified school of jurisprudence. A varied group of law professors adopted the Holmesian attention to practices, as opposed to principles, as a fundamental point of departure. Karl Llewellyn ([1930] 1962), a law professor at Yale (and later, at the University of Chicago), was among the most respected of this group. Llewellyn provided one vivid demonstration of the realist perspective in his discussion of the doctrine of *stare decisis*, or precedent. The citation of precedents—or the lending of an aura of authority to the present case opinion by reference to a similar opinion in an earlier, parallel case—has always been a core feature of the common law. Llewellyn demonstrated that the doctrine of precedent is actually two-sided: If judges find that precedents are inconsistent with the favored opinion in the case under study, the precedents are read narrowly (or strictly) by emphasizing basic factual differences; if precedents are consistent with the favored opinion in the case under consideration, they are read broadly (or loosely) by emphasizing the general principle involved as applicable to a category of cases. In other words, Llewellyn sought to show that precedents are not applied in a mechanical fashion but rather are interpreted by judges who have a good deal of discretion in this regard. Altogether, for Llewellyn, law students must learn that any substantive body of law can only be understood by focusing on the procedures through which it is produced and the human actors (e.g., judges) who produce it.

Jerome Frank (1930, 1949), a lawyer and Yale law professor who eventually became a federal judge, is another leading figure in the legal realist movement. Frank called for more attention to the trial courts and the judges who sit on them; traditionally, most attention had focused on appellate courts. Although students of jurisprudence sometimes promoted skepticism about rules and the process of making rules, Frank stressed the importance of skepticism about facts, or rather attention to how facts are determined in legal cases. Frank advanced the proposition, which most people today take for granted but was heresy in the view of traditional jurisprudence, that judges are human. Accordingly, he called for attention to the social and psychological factors that influence or determine judicial decision making. Traditional jurisprudence suggested that judges apply legal rules to case facts to produce the proper legal outcome (or decision); Frank argued, provocatively, that judges often decide first and then seek to identify rules and facts that support this opinion.

Legal realism has had considerable influence. The Yale Law School, from the 1930s on, pioneered the incorporation of realist principles into the legal education curriculum (Kalman 1986). Legal realism led to more attention by at least some legal scholars to social and behavioral dimensions of law; it provided one important foundation for the Law and Society movement, or the interdisciplinary study of sociolegal phenomena, as well as for some contemporary schools of jurisprudence. As a practical matter legal realism has promoted far greater attention to what actually goes on in courts of law and to the need to adopt any available strategies to minimize the improper influence of bias within the law. Many of the tenets of legal realism have simply become part of the conventional wisdom in law, with the result that legal realism as an identifiable intellectual movement is less evident today. The primary contribution of legal realism, in the view of most commentators, has been the exposure of limitations and distortions inherent in traditional forms of jurisprudence. But if legal realism has been successful in injecting a measure of realism in the understanding of law, it has its own inherent limitation in not providing any clear foundation for discriminating between good and bad laws, and for dismissing too fully the role formal law plays in constraining the abuse of judicial discretion.

Process Theory

In the 1940s and 1950s a number of law professors at Yale (Myres McDougal, and political scientist Harold Lasswell), Harvard (Henry Hart and Albert Sacks), and Columbia (Herbert Wechsler), although strongly influenced by legal realism, were concerned with reestablishing a more objective and neutral grounding for legal decision making (Grey 1996, 502–505). The so-called "process theory" emanating from their approach also reflects the specific influences of utilitarianism and sociological jurisprudence. These legal scholars argued for the importance of attending to the specific functions and responsibilities of the different branches of the government, with special emphasis on the formal process through which decisions were reached. In this view reason is again elevated to an important status, since it should guide the legal decision-making process. Judges should not make decisions based upon their personal or ideological preferences but should dispassionately analyze the competing interests in particular cases and arrive at judgments based upon procedural consistency (establishing by sound reasoning that the present case is being decided in a manner logically consistent with that applied in earlier cases). Principled decision making and appropriate respect for legal procedures should produce socially desirable outcomes. Associate Justice Ruth Ginsburg, of the United States Supreme Court, has been identified as one of those strongly influenced by the legal process approach. On balance, this jurisprudential school has not had an especially enduring influence, other than in the realm of international law. Perhaps the faith of process school adherents in the possibility of neutral decision making in law has been largely rejected by more skeptical subsequent generations.

Contemporary Schools of Jurisprudence

The term "contemporary" is applied here to schools of jurisprudence that emerged principally in the final decades of the twentieth century. Of course, the traditional schools of jurisprudence have survived, with varying degrees of influence. Students of law continue to identify strongly with a natural law or a positivist law tradition, for example, and utilitarianism and pragmatism in some form remain influential. The contemporary schools of jurisprudence typically take the form of modifications or extensions of a traditional school of jurisprudence, as opposed to a wholly new set of premises. They have in common an especially pronounced interdisciplinary character, integrating many elements from a wide range of disciplines (Minda 1995). The social sciences—in particular, economics, sociology, and political science—have been especially important, but such disciplines as philosophy, history, and even literature have also exerted a significant influence. These contemporary schools of jurisprudence also tend to be oriented more toward intellectual challenges pertaining to meaning (i.e., not assuming that terms and concepts have a single, fixed meaning), the sources of knowledge (i.e., exploring where one's knowledge of legal phenomena comes from), and the proper grounds for morally defensible choices than with the practical problems confronting lawyers. At least some of these schools of jurisprudence differ from the traditional schools in their focus on special questions within the realm of law, such as the standing of women or people of color before the law (see Table 4.2).

Table 4.2 Contemporary Schools of Jurisprudence

I.	*Law and Economics* 1960s Economic analysis of law; economic efficiency and wealth maximization.
II.	*Interpretive Jurisprudence* 1970s Law as principle; faithfulness to evolving interpretation.
III.	*Critical Legal Studies* 1970s Law as politics, as hierarchy; indeterminancy of law.
IV.	*Critical Race Theory* 1980s Law as racist; integrating concerns and views of people of color into law.
V.	*Feminist Jurisprudence* 1970s Law as patriarchal; integrating concerns and views of women into law.
VI.	*Narrative Jurisprudence* 1970s Law as storytelling; literature and law.
VII.	*Postmodern Jurisprudence* 1990s Law in an emerging postmodern world; challenging truth claims of law.

Law and Economics

This school of jurisprudence is one contemporary extension of the utilitarian tradition. It emerged principally in the 1970s, with the University of Chicago as an important center of activity (Cooter and Ulen 1987; Polinsky 1989; Posner 1987). Several prominent economists at that university began developing innovative recastings of classical free market economic theory, and some law professors began to pay attention to these developments. Among the economists, Ronald Coase was especially influential. In a famous article, "The Problem of Social Cost," Coase (1960), who eventually won a Nobel Prize for this work, proposed a theorem challenging conventional assumptions about governmental regulation of economic activity. The essence of his theory is this: legal regulation of private economic activity, such as the government's compelling private parties to bear costs for harmful conditions they cause, can produce "transaction costs" that can be avoided, in many cases, if private parties are allowed to negotiate their own arrangements with each other. In other words, if some economic activity of mine is imposing costs on you, it is likely to be more efficient to allow us as private parties to negotiate a solution than to have the government impose a solution and costs on the first party. This theorem provided inspiration for a Law and Economics jurisprudence stressing that economic considerations should take precedence in the resolution of legal cases.

Law and Economics jurisprudence argues that traditional ideas of abstract individual rights should be abandoned in favor of the principle of achieving economic efficiency or maximizing wealth. Although it is conceded that there are circumstances requiring legal intervention, judges should defer, whenever possible, to the free market or some other consideration promoting economic efficiency. In other words, the Law and Economics school of jurisprudence adopted Adam Smith's celebrated laissez faire principle and applied it to the realm of the law. In its early arguments, such principles were applied inflexibly, but in the work of one of Law and Economics' leading lights, Richard Posner (1990, 1995a, 1998), the emphasis shifted from economic efficiency to wealth maximization (i.e., favoring legal decisions that can be affected to increase monetary wealth in society), and from purely economic considerations to more pragmatic, broader considerations of what works best in maximizing human goals and aspirations (or helps people achieve appropriate objectives that do not impinge on the rights of others). Other strands of Law and Economics jurisprudence emphasize such factors as the impact of legal rules on individual incentives; the collective consequences of individual choices; and the economic significance of how institutions (for example, administrative agencies) are organized (Scheppele 1994, 389). Yale law professor (and former Dean) Guido Calabresi, in *The Cost of Accidents* (1970) and in *Tragic Choices* (with Phillip Bobbitt, 1978) addressed such matters as shifting attention away from fault to focusing on ways to best avoid accidents and negotiate responsibility, and how to reach decisions to maximize public benefits and minimize losses.

Law and Economics was very influential during the Reagan/Bush era of the 1980s, for the obvious reason that its outlook on legal matters was in accord with the conservative economic ideology of these administrations. A disproportionate percentage of judges appointed to the Federal bench (including Richard Posner) were identified with this school of thought, as were several nominees to the United States Supreme Court.

Unsurprisingly, much criticism has been directed at the Law and Economics school. Critics allege that it embraces a questionable view of human beings as wholly rational creatures and slights many noneconomic interests and values that law is or should be concerned with. They say that it tends to favor the status quo and those who have the advantage in terms of wealth and power and that it incorporates an unrealistic view of the free market, with

Box 4.4

Richard Posner and Pragmatic Jurisprudence

Not all jurisprudential approaches can be easily classified by schools identified here. Federal judge Richard Posner (1990), for example, is a prodigiously prolific writer on jurisprudential topics who identifies *pragmatism* as the key to an alternative approach (Brint and Weaver 1991). Posner (b. 1939), a native of New York City, graduated first in his class at Harvard Law and then served as a clerk for U.S. Supreme Court Associate Justice William Brennan (Current Biography 1993). Posner has also worked as a government lawyer and has been a professor of law at the University of Chicago. He was appointed to the U.S. Court of Appeals, 7th circuit, by President Reagan in 1981. He is one of the founders of Law and Economics jurisprudence and the author of one of the leading texts (1998). Posner has published over twenty-five books and hundreds of articles, not only on law and economics but also on jurisprudence, on moral philosophy, on law and literature, on sex and reason, on aging, and on the Clinton impeachment case, among other topics (Posner 1988, 1990, 1992, 1995a, 1995b, 1999a, 1999b). Posner is highly contentious and provocative. For example, he suggested at one point that legalizing the sale of babies could be a market-driven solution to the glut of unwanted children; he has also applied a purely economic approach to the sensitive topics of abortion and rape. Richard Posner's (1995a, 1999a) pragmatic jurisprudence holds that law is an activity (as opposed to a set of rules) and that judicial decision making should be guided by attention to consequences and by the objective of achieving sound and defensible solutions, based on practical knowledge or science.

inadequate consideration of the possibilities for fraud and exploitation within such a market.

Interpretive Jurisprudence

At least one version of liberalism survives within jurisprudence in the work of the remarkably prolific law professor Ronald Dworkin (affiliated with both Oxford University in England and New York University), among others (Cohen 1984; Guest 1997). Dworkin has been described as "our leading public philosopher" and "the most original, provocative, and prominent American legal philosopher"(Kress 1987, 834; McCaffery 1997, 1043). His jurisprudential approach (sometimes referred to as Rights and Principles) has been strongly influenced by certain developments within philosophy, especially the work of Harvard University philosopher John Rawls (1971). Rawls sets forth a scheme upon which social ethics can be grounded and calls for a social contract based upon a principle of fairness, with rules determined on the basis of maximixing opportunity for the least advantaged. Interpretive Jurisprudence also parallels some developments in literary interpretation, carried over to the realm of law.

Dworkin (1977, 1985, 1986, 1993, 1996) has produced a series of works in which he both has set forth a distinctive jurisprudential philosophy and has applied this philosophy to an understanding of a range of challenging contemporary issues (including abortion, euthanasia, pornography, homosexuality, affirmative action, and free speech). Dworkin's approach rejects the positivists' claim that legal rules dictate legal outcomes, but it also rejects a nihilistic claim that law is nothing more than subjective opinion. For Dworkin, law is about policy and principle as well as about rules. Arguments of policy are goal oriented, in the spirit of Bentham's utilitarianism, and try to show that the community would be better off, on the whole, if a particular program were pursued. Arguments of principle are rights-based, in the spirit of Kant's idealism, and claim that particular programs must be carried out or abandoned because of their impact on particular people, even if the community is worse off.

When judges decide cases on principle, they are not necessarily applying rules. Dworkin illustrates this point through the oft-cited case of *Riggs v. Palmer,* 1889 (NY). In this case the central question was whether a young man who poisoned his grandfather should nevertheless inherit his grandfather's estate, as called for in the grandfather's will. A judge following the standard *rule* in probate cases would indeed allow the grandson to inherit, insofar as that rule calls for respecting the wishes of the person who made the will. However, a judge applying the widely recognized *principle* that people should not benefit from their evil acts would deny the grandson his inheritance, as was the outcome in this case. Principles, then, may take precedence over rules in legal cases.

For Dworkin, jurisprudence can play a useful role in identifying the enduring principles that have evolved within a legal tradition. One must first identify fundamental background rights (e.g., "Equal concern and respect for each other" and "Freedom of political speech") and find the appropriate balance between individual rights and the communal sense of justice or needs. Judges should neither apply rules mechanically nor base judgments on their personal preferences; rather, they should feel constrained to decide cases in ways consistent with the principles that have evolved within a legal and political community. A right to privacy is one example of such a principle. Dworkin invokes the metaphor of the "chain novel" to make this point. In a chain novel each chapter is written by a different author, but all of the authors have to remain faithful to the narrative line of the book, to provide it with coherence and consistency. Analogously, in legal cases, each judge must be faithful to the shared decisions, structures, conventions, and practices of the legal community within which she or he functions. In this sense, if these guidelines are followed, Dworkin believes that "right answers" in particular cases can be identified.

Dworkin's Interpretive Jurisprudence has been criticized on many grounds (e.g., Kerruish 1988; McCaffery 1997; Posner 1990, 1995a). If indeed there are "fundamental rights," can one really obtain a consensus on the criteria for identifying such rights? Is this approach too wedded to traditional values and interests, and accordingly is it aligned with the status quo and the rights of dominant groups? Does it have any relevance for the everyday practice of most lawyers, who in many cases apply rather than interpret straightforward legal rules? Does an interpretive approach ultimately create a philosophical hall of mirrors that leaves practitioners bereft of any firm grounding for discriminating between good and bad legal rulings?

Critical Legal Studies

Surely no school of jurisprudence has been at the center of more controversy than Critical Legal Studies (Altman 1990; Friedrichs 1986a; Kairys 1998; Kelman 1987; Schlegel 1984). The first Critical Legal Conference was held in 1977, organized by a group of younger law professors. Critical Legal Studies (CLS) became a conspicuous presence throughout the 1980s, with annual well-attended conferences, a steady stream of law review articles and provocative books, and symposium issues of reviews featuring heated exchanges between adherents and critics. It also was at the center of a number of high-profile law school battles over hiring and tenure cases, with CLS law professors claiming ideologically based discrimination against its adherents and mainstream law professors flinging back parallel charges.

CLS law professors had been influenced by the radicalizing events of the late 1960s and early 1970s and were disenchanted with the inherent conservatism of much jurisprudence and the law school curriculum. CLS also reflected the intellectual influences of legal realism, neo-Marxist theory, and some strains of continental European (predominantly French) critical theory, especially postmodernism. "Law is politics" may be identified as a basic premise of CLS (D. Kennedy 1997). One mission of CLS scholarship, then, is the *deconstruction* (or trashing, in more colloquial terms) of mainstream legal doctrine, to uncover the political agenda (and fundamental contradictions) beneath the formal, purportedly neutral, legal rhetoric. Indeed, CLS adopted an especially uncompromising repudiation of legal "formalism," and of "false necessity" (i.e., the notion that legal rules objectively dictate certain outcomes). Claims of objectivity and a neutral form of "legal logic" are challenged in case law (or judge-made law) as well as statutory law.

The proposition that the law—and law school—is oriented toward the maintenance of hierarchy, privilege, and the status quo is a central claim of CLS scholarship. Accordingly, a certain percentage of CLS scholarship has been devoted to challenging (or promoting the delegitimation) of mainstream claims about the appropriate focus of legal education and the role of legal professionals. The promotion of egalitarianism, or equality on all levels, is one of the key objectives of the CLS program. In one celebrated critique of the CLS program, Paul Carrington (1984), at that time Dean of the School of Law at Duke University, argued that CLS scholars had no business teaching in law schools because they had a "nihilistic" orientation toward law—did not believe in law, as it were—and if the principal mission of law schools is to prepare their students for careers as lawyers, CLS-oriented professors could not contribute to that mission. The CLS response to this critique, in the most concise form possible, is that the exposure of traditional myths about law is a necessary and constructive dimension of the law student's education, and ideally it will open these students to the possibilities of law careers more consistent with the realization of authentic social justice (Gordon 1985).

Through the 1990s, the original energy of the CLS movement dissipitated somewhat; some fragmentation took place in the form of alternative critical perspectives on law developing their own identity; and some conflict surfaced between the original group of CLS scholars and a younger generation of such scholars (Minda 1995, 126). Despite some of its excesses, CLS continues to provide an immensely provocative challenge to the tenets of mainstream jurisprudence and legal education.

Critical Race Theory

The leading lights of Critical Legal Studies have been, for the most part, white males, even though from the outset women and people of color were better represented among CLS scholars than in the ranks of traditional or mainstream schools of jurisprudence (an overwhelmingly white male enterprise throughout most of history). Critical Race Theory emerged, principally in the 1980s, on the premise that people of color bring a unique perspective to the legal system, and this perspective can advance people's understanding of some challenges confronting the system of law as well as society generally (Delgado 1995; Goldberg 1992; Lewis 1997; Minda 1995). The principal impetus for Critical Race Theory has been the realization that the experience and perspective of people of color has either been absent from or inaccurately represented in traditional jurisprudence, and even in Critical Legal Studies. Derrick Bell, the first tenured African-American professor of law at Harvard, is one spokesman for this theory. In his more recent work, Bell (1987, 1992) has used narrative and storytelling as a device for representing the experience of law endured by African-American women.

Other Critical Race Theory scholars in law include Richard Delgado of the University of Colorado and Mari Matsuda of Georgetown Law School. These scholars have campaigned for greater diversity on law school faculties; have called for bans on racial hate speech; have attempted to devise new approaches to enduring civil rights challenges; and have sought new ways to express the voice of people of color in legal scholarship (Goldberg 1992).

Although the First Amendment doctrine of free speech is among the most venerated principles in American law, Critical Race Theorists (Matsuda et al. 1993) argue that it has been used (in the form of hate speech) to keep minority students from participating fully on campus. This concern with the misuse of the First Amendment parallels the concern of some feminist law scholars with First Amendment protection of pornography.

Kimberle Williams Crenshaw (1989), of the University of Pennsylvania School of Law, has made the argument that the experience and circumstances of African-American women is not fully captured by either the experience of women generally or people of color generally. The term "intersectionalism" is invoked to capture some of the unique dimensions and circumstances of being both a women and a person of color. For Crenshaw and other adherents of this position, a just system of law finds ways to acknowledge this uniqueness.

The Critical Race Theorists have been criticized for too often being indifferent to truth in the name of advancing their agenda (Farber and Sherry 1997). They have been criticized as well for wholly disparaging merit, conventional standards of fairness, and tolerance for alternative points of view. These are contentious claims, of course, but at a minimum the Critical Race Theorists have challenged the dominance and complacency of white people in the world of law.

Feminist Jurisprudence

The contemporary Feminist Movement that emerged principally in the 1970s has had an immense influence in many different disciplines and fields, and law is certainly among these (Chamallas 1999; Goldstein 1992; Lewin 1988; Olsen 1995; Smart 1989). One basic premise of feminist jurisprudence is that law is predominantly a product of males and therefore has a patriarchal character. A feminist jurisprudence is dedicated to exposing the patriarchal bias of law and legal principles and to identifying and articulating the perspective, needs, and rights of women (West 1997). More specifically, feminists say, within the Anglo-American jurisprudential and legal tradition, doctrine based on liberal notions of individual rights, freedom, and reasonableness, while purporting to be value-neutral and objective, actually favors the interests of men and reinforces male domination (Anleu 1992, 423). Historically, as one dimension of such dominance, the law has restricted the entry of women into the public sphere and has done little to hinder or intervene with male dominance (and abuse) in the private sphere. Although feminist jurisprudence is not a monolithic enterprise and adherents are divided on some important issues, the general neglect by male-dominated jurisprudence of the values, fears, and harms experienced by women is one shared premise.

Feminists are divided on the significance of common experiences of women and the appropriate response of law to the difference between women and men (Baer 1999). Should feminists emphasize the commonality of the female experience, or should they stress the varieties of such experience? Does the difference between women and men require special treatment for women or simply truly equal treatment with men? And if women are different from men, why is this so and what are its significant manifestations?

Harvard University psychologist Carol Gilligan (1982) provided one influential answer to the "differentness" question. According to her research, a young boy and a young girl respond differently when presented with the hypothetical dilemma of a man considering whether to steal a drug he cannot afford in order to save his wife's life. The boy relies on the legal system to provide a just result; the girl goes beyond the confines of the narrow legal question and looks at the matter in terms of a broader network of relationships. Gilligan labels the male response a "justice approach" and the female response an "ethics of care" approach. One of the implications of these different ways of looking at such cases is that women are more amenable than men to mediation for the resolution of legal cases, although there is some controversy over whether women are really better off or worse off with mediation (for example, in domestic dispute cases).

For feminists who embrace the view that women are fundamentally different from men and have different experiences, it follows that laws should be reformed to take these differences into account and that the judicial process should be changed as well. For example, in the realm of contracts, the way in which women are socialized should be taken into account, as opposed to reliance solely on the traditional "reasonable man" standard, and damages should attend to relational losses, not simply monetary losses. For example, a woman defrauded by a man with whom she had both a personal relationship and a business contract has lost more than just money. In the realm of torts (or personal injury), feminine values of caring and concern should be more fully integrated, as opposed to reliance on traditional male standards oriented toward efficiency and profit (Bender 1990). A feminist law professor who teaches a seminar entitled "A Feminist Revisit to the First-Year Curriculum" reports that she incorporates into this course discussion of elements of

Box 4.5

Catharine MacKinnon and the Feminist War on Pornography

Catharine MacKinnon (of the University of Michigan School of Law) is arguably the best-known (and most controversial) promoter of feminist jurisprudence (Current Biography 1994; Jackson 1992). Mackinnon was born in 1946; her father was a Republican politician and federal appellate court judge. In 1974, prior to receiving her law degree from Yale, MacKinnon became involved in an early sexual harassment case and wrote a pioneering work on the subject. In the 1980s she shifted her attention to the pornography issue. Despite outstanding academic credentials and many widely discussed articles and books, MacKinnon for many years was a visiting professor at various law schools, only receiving a tenured offer from the University of Michigan in 1988. She is an intense and dynamic speaker who has given lectures in numerous forums.

MacKinnon rejects biological determinism and the notion that gender is basically a difference rather than a hierarchy. MacKinnon (1987) characterizes the modern liberal state as an entity organized on behalf of men; the law of such a state reflects the rule of men over women and male-oriented norms. Furthermore, sex and the sexual relation is at the core of a society where men dominate and women submit. MacKinnon (1993), with the feminist writer Andrea Dworkin, has been a leading feminist advocate of the legal banning of pornography, on the grounds that pornography is a key means of "actualizing" the dynamic of social inequality and sexual domination. In other words, pornography turns sex inequality into sexuality and turns male dominance into sex difference. Pornography, in this reasoning, should be banned because it contributes both to the ongoing dominance of women and to the actual practice of males inflicting physical harm, including rape, on women.

Feminists have been divided on the issue of pornography, with some arguing that it is a mistake to become aligned with conservative, fundamentalist groups on this issue, since these groups, even though opposed to pornography, are opposed to equality for women. They argue that a precedent on behalf of censorship can ultimately provide a basis for censorship of work or representations supported by feminists. Some argue that it is counterproductive to the feminist agenda to portray women principally as victims, as opposed to active agents in their own destiny. Finally, some say there are more important issues confronting women than pornography (Ellis et al. 1986; Lacombe 1994). MacKinnon has been widely criticized by law professors and others with a range of ideological commitments, including some feminists. She herself has concisely summarized this criticism: "My work is considered not law by lawyers, not scholarship by academics, too practical by intellectuals, too intellectual by practitioners, and neither politics nor science by political scientists" (Current Biography 1994, 366). Her importance in the debate on law and feminism is not in dispute, however.

a "missing curriculum," including seduction as a tort, marital rape, battered women's syndrome, prenuptial agreements, division of marital property, and exclusion of women from jury service (A. Bernstein 1996, 219).

In addition to the issue of pornography, feminists have been concerned with and have influenced legal developments on many issues. They have played a role in the reform of rape law and in the introduction of laws pertaining to sexual harassment in the workplace. They have been involved in the defense of battered wives who have killed their husbands, or abused women who have killed their partners. They have, of course, been concerned with the many forms of gender discrimination that still have impact on women, in the workplace and elsewhere. Law schools have not been immune to the charge of gender discrimination (Moss 1988). Indeed, all forms of economic discrimination against women, subtle and not-so-subtle, are matters of concern. For example, feminists have exposed some of the specific disadvantages confronting women under traditional legal standards and practices pertaining to divorce. And they have generally been advocates of all forms of expanding options and choices available to women, including the right to legal abortion. They have exposed and opposed laws that in various ways impose disadvantages and liabilities on pregnant women. (A specifically "lesbian legal theory" argues that legal scholarship has explicitly or implicitly denigrated lesbians and has paid little attention to many issues of importance to lesbians, including same-sex marriage, lesbian mothers' custody rights, and lesbianism and violence; Robson 1998.) Altogether, for many feminist students of law, conceptions of gender, the role of women, the status of motherhood, and the meaning of privacy, of autonomy, and of equality remain contested arenas and require the exposure of standards and practices unfair to women, as well as reforms effectively addressing such unfairness.

Narrative Jurisprudence

Narrative jurisprudence emerged in the 1970s and became increasingly conspicuous in the late 1980s and into the 1990s (Abrams 1991; Delgado 1989; Elkins 1990; Friedrichs 1990a; Papke 1991). On the one hand, narrative jurisprudence has been concerned with law-in-literature; on the other hand, it is also concerned with law-as-literature (Ferguson 1984; Weisberg 1984). In other words, proponents look to the treatment of law and justice in literature, and they also recognize that law is a form of literary activity that can be analyzed like any other literary activity. One proponent argues that various legal problems (e.g., capital punishment sentencing) can be usefully analyzed through reference to specific works of literature (Heald 1998). The narrative form—storytelling—is a way of conveying important truths about law.

James Boyd White ([1973] 1985, 1984) has argued that the study of literature should be part of legal education and that literary studies have something distinctive to say about law. Richard Weisberg (1992) promotes the view that the study of literature can influence lawyers to be more ethical in their professional conduct. Shakespeare's *The Merchant of Venice*, Herman Melville's *Billy Budd*, Dostoyevsky's *The Brothers Karamazov*, and Kafka's *The Trial* are just a few of the great works of Western literature that address, in some profound way, issues of law and justice.

Some critics have questioned whether literature can promote deeper ethical sensitivity in lawyers; these critics have also insisted that law and literature are different forms with different purposes, and, accordingly, the lessons they might learn from each other are limited. Even Judge Posner (1988), however, who expresses critical views of the law and literature movement, concedes that lawyers and judges can benefit from exposure to great literature if it encourages them to write legal opinions with an enhanced sense of style, clarity, and human empathy.

James R. Elkins (1985a) of West Virginia University School of Law has been a leading promoter of narrative jurisprudence, with special emphasis on its role in legal education. Elkins (1990, 1) observes:

> Lawyers are, by profession, storytellers: we relish a good tale and tell stories as a fundamental and functional part of our craft. . . . Law and legal education surround us with stories. . . . Law is a compendium of stories about how we use and abuse rules to manage our social relations and resolve both our differences and commonality. . . . It is the story of law (as it is set alongside other stories) that locates us in relation to others: to family, community, work. We use legal narratives, as we use other stories, to give meaning to social existence, to ourselves as women and men, as people of color, as persons the culture welcomes or fears.

David Ray Papke (1987, 1998) of Indiana University–Indianapolis School of Law has, in particular, applied narrative jurisprudence to recovering and understanding just those who are especially feared by mainstream, law-abiding society: conventional criminals, ideological heretics, and militant, radical groups. Papke does this by recounting the stories of such legal heretics as the abolitionist William Lloyd Garrison, the suffragist Elizabeth Cady Stanton, and the socialist Eugene Debs.

Adherents of feminist jurisprudence and of critical race theory have been especially receptive to using the narrative form as a means of bringing the different voices of historically marginalized people—women and people of color—into the dialogue about law and legal issues. Robin West (1988, 65) has argued that women in law must "flood the market" with their stories to counter the traditional dominance of stories coming from men, since there are significant differences between female and male stories. Perhaps women have been more willing than men to bring honest autobiographical accounts of their experiences into their accounts of law and legal matters. In a landmark article on rape law, Susan Estrich (1986, 1087) begins this way:

> Eleven years ago, a man held an ice pick to my throat and said: "Push over, shut up, or I'll kill you." I did what he said, but I couldn't stop crying. A hundred years later, I jumped out of my car as he drove away. (Estrich 1986, 1087)

This is not a conventional opening for an article in a major law review. The author goes on to examine essential elements in the existing legal response to rape and to offer an alternative to deficient aspects of this response. Does the introduction of her own story and experience with rape make a difference? Does it enhance or diminish the impact and validity of her analysis? Or is it utterly irrelevant? Susan Estrich, the author, states that she has made a conscious decision to invoke her own story:

> I cannot imagine anyone writing an article on prosecutorial discretion without disclosing that he or she had been a prosecutor. I cannot imagine myself writing on rape without disclosing how I learned my first lessons or why I care so much. (Estrich 1986, 1089)

Perhaps one need not have experienced rape personally to be able to write cogently on its legal dimensions. One may even write empathetically without having experienced rape. But if the experience is in fact part of one's story, telling the story would seem to be the honest thing to do, leaving it to the reader to decide whether or not it is relevant. An emphasis on the relevance of personal experience, then, is certainly one central theme of a narrative jurisprudence.

Derrick Bell (1987), a Critical Race theorist, uses the narrative form to expose the harsh realities of the struggle for justice by African Americans. Specifically, he has created an imaginary character, Geneva Crenshaw, to explore both the strategies that black people have used in this struggle as well as the means used by the dominant white forces to deny the struggle. Clearly, Bell (1992) believes that storytelling is a more powerful way of addressing these issues than through some form of dispassionate legal or historical analysis.

Narrative jurisprudence, then, challenges the traditional tendency within law to engage in dry, dispassionate, and disengaged forms of analysis, all too often with more attention to technical, formal legal questions than to raw human consequences. It has been criticized as introducing a wholly subjective dimension into discussions of law and legal issues, which interferes with rigorous analyses and open-minded argumentation (Farber and Sherry 1997). Narrative jurisprudence attempts to fully reintroduce the human dimension into the study of law, to make connections between legal issues and the larger questions of the meaning of human existence, and to facilitate the dialogue between law and the humanities.

Postmodern Jurisprudence

The last of the contemporary schools of jurisprudence to be considered here is the most recent to surface and the most difficult to clearly define (Carty 1990; Douzinas, Warrington, and McVeigh 1991; Litowitz 1997). Indeed, some of those associated with Critical Legal Studies, Critical Race Theory, and Feminist Jurisprudence incorporate themes and terms associated with postmodern thought, and, accordingly, there are no sharp boundaries between these jurisprudential perspectives and a Postmodern Jurisprudence (Minda 1995). Nevertheless, the distinctive themes associated with the postmodern merit some attention independent of any discussion of other perspectives.

Postmodern thought and jurisprudence reject claims of anyone's exclusive possession of "truth" and of the notion of a stable, fixed meaning in the world; it rejects totalizing concepts (such as the state) and totalistic visions (such as that of communism, or liberal democracy) that claim to wholly capture human experience; it celebrates difference and multiculturalism; it emphasizes the local and is profoundly skeptical of the potential of collective action to transform society; it repudiates positivism, or the scientific method, as an appropriate methodology for understanding human existence (Rosenau 1992).

In postmodern jurisprudence, then, there can be no single, solid foundation for law or for legal opinions. When judges and lawyers act as though law is objective and culturally neutral, they are deluding themselves and others. One mission for a postmodern jurisprudence is the exposure of how law as an enterprise systematically excludes many voices and experiences in a culturally diverse society. A postmodern jurisprudence seeks to open law up to a multiplicity of interpretations and to liberate law from the myth of determinancy.

Boaventura de Sousa Santos (1995), of the University of Coimbra, Portugal, provides us with one vision of a postmodern jurisprudence. Santos makes the provocative argument that in our time mainstream science no longer provides a framework for understanding our world and we must therefore look to other sources upon which we can establish a decent human life. In the context of increasing globalization, Western standards of human rights are hypocritical and insufficient, and we must learn to recognize new rights (including the right to bring historical capitalism to trial in a world tribunal!). For Santos, postmodern critical theory must displace the dominant, traditional forms of power, law, and knowledge and must provide us with a new map for making sense of our world.

Unsurprisingly, postmodern thought and postmodern jurisprudence have been strongly criticized (Handler 1992; Jamieson 1991; Litowitz 1997; Patterson 1996a). They have been attacked for being nihilistic, or denying belief in anything; for failing to provide a vision for transforming society and law in a progressive direction; and for being pretentious in their use of arcane and obscure terminology. It remains to be seen whether postmodern jurisprudence will be discredited as a passing intellectual fad or will broadly transform our way of understanding law and human existence in relation to law.

Conclusion

It may seem bewildering to the novice student of law to be confronted with such a diversity of jurisprudential perspectives. Figure 4.1 shows roughly how the perspectives discussed in this chapter are related to each other. The different schools suggest very different bases for understanding what law is, what it ought to be, and what legal decision making is based upon, as well as what it ought to be based upon. Some schools of jurisprudence clearly treat law as relatively autonomous. For other schools of jurisprudence, law can only be understood in relation to a social context or in terms of particular variables (e.g., wealth, power, gender, or race). In the more recent era, there has been a strong tendency within jurisprudence to look to disciplines outside of law—including economics, history, philosophy and literature—but the field of law is divided, and many law professors continue to adopt a jurisprudential perspective that emphasizes the internal concerns of law. The world of legal scholarship itself has been characterized as divided between those who engage in "committed argument" and those who engage in "detached observation"; those who engage in doctrinal analysis (or the technical analysis of legal principles found in judicial opinions) and those who engage in analysis driven by social science; and those who engage in lawyerly advocacy and those who engage in the scholarly pursuit of truth (Underwood 1981).

The "mainstream" of legal scholarship is criticized by many of the adherents of emerging schools of jurisprudence as reinforcing conventional legal thought, taking the world we live in as a given, and being boring. The adher-

Figure 4.1 Schools of Jurisprudence: An Approximate Genealogy

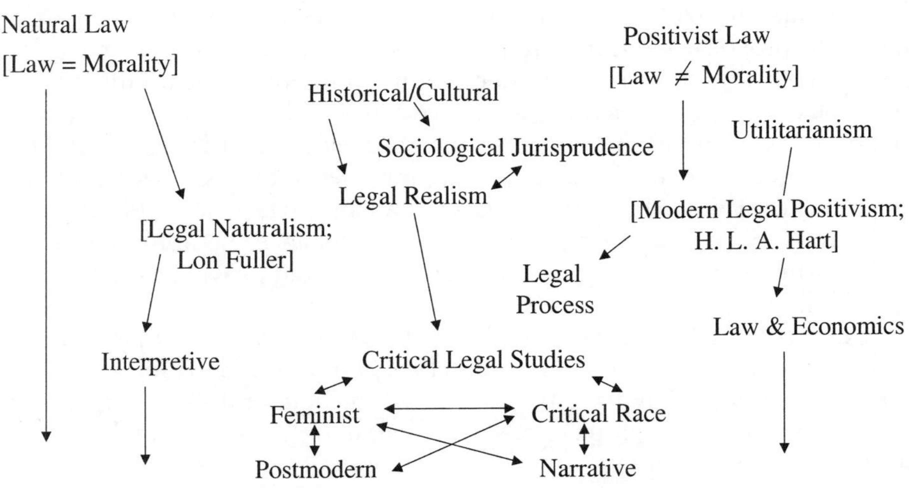

The relationship between the different schools of jurisprudence is complex, and accordingly can be diagrammed in different ways. The relationships suggested here are approximate and provisional.

ents of the new schools of jurisprudence are criticized in turn by mainstream scholars as elitists, engaged in pretentious wordplay, utterly out of touch with the real world, and promoters of a nihilistic, destructive orientation toward law (Schlag 1987). This stand-off between very different approaches to making sense of law endures. Despite the many attacks, from any number of vantage points, legal positivism survives, and by some measures it has even been reinforced. Arguments for pragmatism and practical reasoning staying close to the particulars of actual cases, as well as the traditional logic of law and legal rules, have been advanced against the efforts to bring the perspectives of various other disciplines upon matters of law (Dickstein 1999; Patterson 1996a).

In the final analysis, the different schools of jurisprudence impress on us recognition of the ultimate complexity of law and its many dimensions. Any school of jurisprudence can be challenged on some grounds, and this is true of the contemporary schools as well as the traditional schools. But Law and Economics, Interpretive Jurisprudence, Critical Legal Studies, Feminist Jurisprudence, Critical Race Theory, Narrative Jurisprudence, and Postmodern Jurisprudence all sensitize us, in provocative and fruitful ways, to dimensions and aspects of law not readily visible through the perspective of traditional schools of jurisprudence. As you encounter particular issues within law, and particular legal cases, it is surely valuable to ask yourself how these perspectives might enrich your understanding of the issue or case. A diversity of jurisprudential perspectives will certainly prevail in the future. New schools of jurisprudence are likely to emerge, and some of the existing schools are likely to become marginalized, or largely discredited. If the postmodern premise is correct, the search for "truth" about law is an open-ended process that will continue in some form indefinitely.

Key Terms and Concepts

Brandeis Brief
chain novel
Coase Theorem
contemporary schools of jurisprudence
critical legal studies
critical race theory
external morality
feminist jurisprudence
grundnorm
historical/cultural jurisprudence
internal morality
interpretive jurisprudence
intersectionalism
jurisprudence
law and economics
legal naturalism
legal positivism
legal realism
mechanical jurisprudence
narrative jurisprudence
natural law
nihilistic jurisprudence
postmodern jurisprudence
pragmatism
process theory
sociological jurisprudence
traditional schools of jurisprudence
utilitarianism

Discussion Questions

1. An understanding of law can come from any number of sources. Which of the schools of jurisprudence, in your opinion, most accurately explains, or attempts to explain, law in our society today?
2. Compare and contrast sociological jurisprudence with legal realism. Give reactions to the specific quotations and suggestions made by Oliver Wendell Holmes. Would Ehrlich and Pound tend to agree or disagree with his views?
3. Discuss some of the major contributions feminists such as Carol Gilligan and Catharine MacKinnon have made. Why is it important to have such a school of jurisprudence? Will women ever have an equal voice in the law?
4. What can narrative jurisprudence bring to the study of law? Do you think law can accurately be portrayed through literary works?
5. Discuss the major premise of postmodern jurisprudence and whether or not this school of thought has the potential of becoming a major influence for future legal studies.

Chapter Five

The Law and Society Movement

The Law and Society Movement is not a unified enterprise; it encompasses the work of historians, literary critics, anthropologists, political scientists, economists, psychologists, sociologists, and others who study some dimension of the interrelationship of the legal and the social (Abel 1995a; Lipson and Wheeler 1986). Much crossing of boundaries occurs between these disciplines, and between the traditional realms of the legal and the social (Sarat et al. 1998b). At least some law professors have become involved with the Law and Society Movement by drawing heavily upon one or more of the various disciplines in their study of law and legal issues, and by focusing on law as a social phenomenon (Friedman 1975; Macaulay, Friedman, and Stookey 1995). But the Law and Society Movement is best thought of as an endeavor to make sense of law from a vantage point outside of the professional study of law; jurisprudence—the focus of Chapter 4—is the work of law professors making sense of the law from within the context of legal education and practice.

Those engaged in sociolegal scholarship adopt diverse methods. The methods range from interpretive, critical analyses to detailed case histories to highly quantitative, empirical studies. Students of law and society do tend to share a general assumption that law must be understood as a product of sociohistorical, cultural, political, economic, and psychological forces and that law in turn has an impact in each one of these areas.

An interest in the relationship between the legal and the social goes far back in history. The emergence of a recognizable Law and Society Movement is much more recent (Garth and Sterling 1998). The founding of the Law and Society Association in 1962 signified a formal recognition of interest in interdisciplinary sociolegal scholarship. It brought together scholars from many of the disciplines referred to earlier who had developed a special interest in law and legal phenomena, as well as law professors who were drawing upon one or more of these disciplines in their own studies of law. These objectives are sometimes at odds with each other. Despite the involvement of a growing number of law professors in the Law and Society Movement, it has continued to occupy a somewhat marginal status in law schools, with most law professors focused on internal issues and questions of legal policies and practices.

In the recent era sociolegal scholarship has expanded in many countries around the world and the Law and Society Movement has become increasingly transnational, with international meetings in Amsterdam (1991), Glasgow (1996), and Budapest (2001).

Disciplines Contributing to the Law and Society Movement

Various humanistic and social science disciplines in many countries contribute to our understanding of law and legal phenomena (see Figure 5.1). The perspective of several of these disciplines is briefly reviewed in the paragraphs that follow. Two significant disciplinary perspectives—anthropology and history—are discussed more fully in Chapter 6.

Philosophy

Philosophers are concerned with the meaning of justice and law and with the relationship between them (MacCormick 1996; Murphy and Coleman 1990; Patterson 1996b). Ethics as a branch of philosophy is concerned with formulating principles for identifying goodness and morality; of course, ethical questions intersect with legal issues at many points. Philosophers grapple with the complex relation between morality and law. Metaphysics as a branch of philosophy is concerned with such matters as the nature of reality and of human beings. The enduring question of whether human beings have a free will (voluntarism) or human behavior is a product of various forces acting upon people (determinism), or some mixture of voluntarism and determinism, obviously has major implications for law. Still another dimension of philosophy is concerned with principles of logic and the role of language in making sense of the world. Again, logic is intimately involved in legal reasoning, and issues of language usage and interpretation are critically important in legal opinions.

Indeed, all those who engage in the study of and practice of law come into contact at various points with the kinds of philosophical questions just mentioned. All such study and practice involves the adoption of explicit or implicit assumptions on such matters as the nature of justice, morality, reality, and human nature itself. Many of these philosophical matters have already been mentioned in the first several chapters and will inevitably show up at other points in this text. But precisely because philosophy is in some respects so central to the study of law, and so intertwined with jurisprudence, it is not a major component of the Law and Society Movement, other than in the sense of being part of the background and context of this movement.

Political Science

Law in one interpretation is an expression of power, and the use of power is one major preoccupation of political science. The use, as well as the abuse,

Figure 5.1 The Law and Society Movement: An Approximate Genealogy

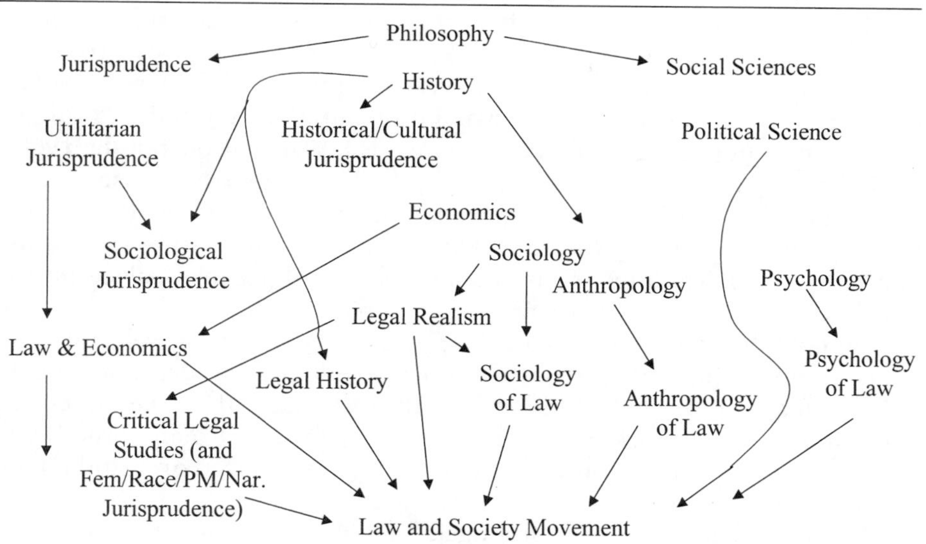

The relationship between the different disciplines and the Law and Society Movement is complex, and accordingly can be diagrammed in different ways. The relationships suggested here are approximate and provisional.

of power in connection with law is studied by political scientists (Jacob 1995; Vincent 1996; Yarnold 1992). Law both imposes constraints on the use of political power and serves as a means of exercising political power. Furthermore, political power is most effective in promoting law and persuading people to comply with it when the power holder is viewed as legitimate, or entitled to respect and obedience. The legitimation of law is studied by political scientists, among others; this topic is more fully discussed in Chapter 9.

In developed nations it is the formal political institutions (in the American system the legislative branch, the judicial branch, and the executive branch of government) that make, administer, and enforce the laws. Political scientists are interested in both the formal processes for the making, administration, and enforcement of law, and the informal political pressures and behind-the-scenes negotiations involved (Abraham 1973; Mayhew 1986). In the United States there are especially strong links between the political and the legal realms. Political officials greatly influence the legal system through the appointment of judges and prosecutors. Elected judges, in particular, can be influenced in their decision making by political considerations and public opinion. The decisions of the courts can also have impact on the political process in many ways.

Crime and crime control are major issues in American political life; accordingly, the courts can be subjected to unusually intense attention and pressure from officials and from the public, while crime-related decisions in turn help determine the response of political officials. Although the criminal justice system has received a disproportionate amount of attention, political scientists have also become interested in how the legal system resolves civil cases (Jacob 1996). Divorce law, automobile insurance cases, product liability, and many other civil matters have become important political issues.

Americans are especially likely to turn to the courts to resolve political controversies (Goldman and Jahnige 1971; Jacob 1996). These controversies range from abortion to zoning, and everything in between. The American courts play an important role in formulating public policy and accordingly can become entangled in political disputes. The Warren Court of the 1960s, for example, was widely denounced, especially by political conservatives, who claimed that it broadened the rights of criminals and handcuffed the police, and consequently fueled a rising wave of crime during this period (Graham 1970). The most conspicuous policy making takes place on the appellate court level. Political scientists have played a key role in the study of the United States Supreme Court: the process involved in the selection and confirmation of justices; the role of political ideology in the decision making of individual justices; factors influencing the response in the larger American community to landmark Supreme Court decisions; and many other such questions. Increasingly, political scientists have recognized and studied the political dynamics of the lower courts as well.

Many political scientists have judged the law—and the institutions of law, such as the courts—as inherently conservative, with a strong vested interest in the established order and the maintenance of orderliness and compliance. They have declared that historically, the poor and the powerless have been at a major disadvantage in the legal systems and they have documented some of the political ramifications of this disadvantage. Political scientists have explored the political factors leading to some increase for the disadvantaged in accessibility to the courts, as well as ongoing limitations of this accessibility. Altogether, political scientists have had to sort out the relationship between beliefs about law and such other factors as the political organization of the system in determining who litigates, and why.

Economics

The existence of a Law and Economics school of jurisprudence was discussed in Chapter 4, and the connections between economists who study law and law professors who adopt economic analysis are especially pronounced (Deakin 1996; Mercuro and Medema 1997). Economic approaches to the understanding of law often include complex quantitative analyses and mathematical formulas, and in this sense economic analysis is closest to the rigor of the physical and natural sciences (Kitch 1986). Originally, the economic analysis of law addressed such legal areas as taxation, regulation, and antitrust matters, where economic dimensions are central and obvious, but in the more recent era this analysis has been extended to other matters, including contracts, torts, property rights, and crime (Barreto, Husted, and Witte 1984). In one sense, this new interest reflects a return to the concerns of pioneering political economists in the eighteenth and nineteenth centuries, although the contemporary focus tends to be narrower and more technical.

An economic analysis of law might focus on the interrelationship between a particular type of economic system and law. Capitalism as an economic system can be shown to shape the legal system in many ways (for example, with laws favoring free markets and free enterprise); it can also be shown that a particular type of legal ideology (i.e., that of the European bourgeoisie) helped promote the growth of capitalism (Tigar and Levy 1977). The ideological orientation of contemporary economists (for example, conservative or leftist) may influence whether they attempt to identify legal rules and procedures compatible with the efficient expansion of capitalist growth or expose legal rules and procedures that contribute to economic exploitation and inequality.

From an economic perspective one seeks to identify ways in which law provides incentives (or disincentives) for productive economic activity and growth. This type of analysis has been applied to the problem of pollution, where the challenge has been to identify the legal response that minimizes pollution without producing unacceptable economic costs. It has also been applied to the problem of drug abuse, where the challenge has been to identify the legal response that raises the cost of such abuse to a level discouraging it without imposing excessive economic costs on society. Although economic efficiency and wealth maximization is a central theme in the economic analysis of law, some recent work has focused more neutrally on the character of different types of transactions and the impact of different types of institutional arrangements on these transactions.

The economic approach to understanding law is often insensitive to human values and considerations that are independent of economic efficiency (for example, realizing justice and fairness). The economic analysis of law can also be criticized on the basis that it is inherently conservative, theoretically impressive but impractical, and adopts the questionable assumption that human beings act rationally, choosing the means (on the basis of what is known) that most efficiently realize their ends. On this last point, the alternative view is that many factors other than rational calculation determine human behavior, and much human behavior is not rational in the sense identified by economists.

Psychology

The individual and the dynamics of individual behavior are the primary focus of psychology. The impact of groups on individuals, and of individuals on the group, is the province of social psychology. Since decision making is obviously one key element of legal behavior, it follows that psychological factors play an important role in law (Kapardis 1997; Lloyd-Bostock 1996; Robinson 1980; Wrightsman 1991). First, do people who violate laws do so with an understanding of the wrongness of their actions, and with the capacity to control their conduct? And by what criteria should people be deprived of their liberty and committed to mental institutions? Psychology has been intimately involved with the assessment of sanity in cases of lawbreaking, and with a broader range of legal issues arising out of the problem of mental illness.

Psychology has also studied factors influencing the behavior of bystanders and witnesses in legal cases. Various personal attributes as well as situational factors influence how people respond when they witness a crime, accident, or some other event that has legal repercussions. Psychological studies have established that past traumas, perceptual deficiencies, memory gaps, and emotional stresses can interfere with or distort memories of past events for witnesses in legal cases. Such findings are in conflict with the general expectation in courts of law that witnesses are capable of providing accurate and reliable testimony (Marshall 1966).

Psychologists have also investigated the relationship between a range of psychological factors, including personality type, and decisions made by judges, jurors, police officers, and other legal actors (Lloyd-Bostock 1988). Many studies have addressed the social psychology of jury decision making, as well as the various sources of bias in judicial decision making. Psychologists have in some cases produced profiles of individuals most likely to be jurors sympathetic to one side or the other in a legal case, although some observers are uncomfortable with this type of direct involvement in jury selection. Psychologists have also investigated the psychological impact of being subjected to the legal process, as one of the accused, a plaintiff, or a witness. The need for psychological counseling of such parties was established, in part, through such investigations.

Finally, Tom Tyler and colleagues (e.g., Lind and Tyler 1988; Tyler 1990, 1998; Tyler et al. 1997) have been especially active contributors to the sociolegal literature with studies of such psychological issues as how people perceive and respond to the procedural justice of the legal system (e.g., do they experience it as fair or unfair), and why people choose to obey or disobey the law. Some of these issues are addressed more fully in Chapter 9. Table 5.1 summarizes the disciplinary perspectives on law discussed here.

Table 5.1 A Summary of Selected Disciplinary Perspectives on Law

Philosophy	Fundamental assumptions (e.g., on human nature) and law; law and justice; law and morality.
Political Science	Law and the use of power; the role of formal institutions of law (e.g., the legislative branch); law and politics.
Economics	Law and the economic system; legal policy and economic principles; law and economic costs.
Psychology	Law and individual behavior and mental processes; psychological dimensions of legal decision making and testimony; perceptions of law and legal institutions.
Sociology	Law and society; social and group dimensions of legal behavior; the social organization of legal institutions.

The Origins of a Sociolegal Perspective

Even though the formal emergence of a Law and Society Movement and a sociology of law is quite recent, an interest in the relation between the social and the legal goes far back in history. In the sections that follow, some of the principal stages in the evolution of this interest are identified and discussed. The review here is limited to work emerging in the Western European tradition. This limitation reflects constraints of space, as well as of the author's own knowledge.

The Classical Greek Philosophers

It is always remarkable to realize how much contemporary thought has its roots in the ideas of a relatively small number of philosophers living in Greece thousands of years ago (Rubin 1997). References to law and justice can be found in the thought of the Sophists, Plato, and Aristotle. The Sophists (late 5th and early 4th century B.C.) were divided between those who regarded human laws as being at odds with the superior laws of nature and those who believed law could fulfill some worthwhile purposes for human society.

Plato's (427–347 B.C.) *The Republic* and *Laws* introduce ideas and issues with which we are still contending (Gouldner 1966). He was concerned in these works with the kinds of laws needed to govern human society and to avoid anomia, or a sense of confusion about the rules to be followed. Plato viewed law as a necessary constraint on human nature. For Plato, law educates, and law has the capacity to create a sphere of equality (which was not, however, to be extended to all). Plato called for the rule of the Philosopher/King.

Aristotle (384–322 B.C.) also regarded the rule of law as an absolutely necessary element in the survival of the state (Rubin 1997). Aristotle believed that the law should promote the common welfare of the citizenry. He recognized the role of popular will in the making of law, but especially emphasized the responsibility of well-trained legislators. Aristotle believed that a certain amount of judicial discretion was inevitable and desirable and that customary laws sometimes took precedence over formal, written laws.

The ideas of the Greek philosophers provided one starting point for subsequent efforts to understand the relation between the social and the legal.

European Social Philosophers

Observations about the relation between law and society can be extracted from the works of social philosophers throughout the ages, but attention to this relation intensified during the Enlightenment, in the seventeenth and eighteenth centuries. Although it is difficult to apply broad generalizations to the diverse social philosophers of this period, the Enlightenment is associated with an emphasis on the powers of reason, the potential of science, and the prospect of progress toward a more advanced society and way of life. The English philosopher Thomas Hobbes (1588–1679), in the early stages of the Enlightenment, is credited with having raised directly the question of social order, or how it is possible for human beings to live together in a state of relative harmony. In *Leviathan* Hobbes ([1651] 1958) answers this question by asserting that in a "state of nature" human beings live in a situation of a "war of all against all." However, human beings differ from other creatures in that they have the power of reason, and reason leads them to recognize that it is in their interest to delegate power over themselves to the state (the Leviathan) in return for security. This is the essence of Hobbes' social contract, and it has influenced one way of thinking about the basis of law in human society.

For another English philosopher, John Locke (1632–1704), writing some decades after Hobbes, humans are naturally inclined to form social bonds with each other. Locke expressed the view that human beings have certain "natural rights," and the social contract is formed to ensure that a government's primary mission is the promotion and protection of these rights. As every American schoolchild learns, these ideas greatly influenced the founding fathers of the new American republic and were incorporated into the formative document on American law, the Constitution.

The French/Swiss philosopher Jean-Jacques Rousseau (1712–1778) also made an important contribution to the idea of the social contract, although his views were at odds with those of both Hobbes and Locke. Rousseau's thought was original, and he is not easily classified; the romantic strain in his work, for example, is at odds with the Enlightenment celebration of reason. For Rousseau, human beings in the original state of nature lived freely and harmoniously; civilization has had a corrupting and oppressive impact on human existence. The social contract, then, should be based upon the "general will" of the people, expressed through the state, not the government, which only enjoys delegated power. This centralized power of the state should be absolute, once the general will has been expressed. These ideas have been interpreted as supportive of both totalitarianism and democracy. Rousseau's thought was influential during the French Revolution—reflected, some would say, in the reign of terror—but it also inspired the utopian aspect of Marx's vision of a society of liberated and equal human beings, working together cooperatively.

Baron Charles de Montesquieu (1689–1755), the French essayist, is considered an important forefather of the sociology of law specifically. Montesquieu (who had studied law as a young man) challenged the core assumption of natural law, that the source of law lies outside human experience, and argued instead for a view of law as a product of history, custom, the climate, and the environment human beings live in. He was concerned with identifying the totality of factors that account for the laws people live by (divided into civil, or family-related, criminal, and political law). For Montesquieu, laws are only understandable in a particular social context. Laws vary between different societies, in different climates, and during different periods. Each society, in this view, should have the laws most suited to its needs.

Another Frenchman, Alexis de Tocqueville (1805–1859), produced a famous account ([1835–1840] 1945) of his visit to the new American republic early in the nineteenth century. The official purpose of his visit, in 1831, was to examine and report back on the prison system being developed in the United States, but the book he produced described and analyzed many dimensions of the dynamic new country he toured. Montesquieu was living in a time of, and writing about, traditional monarchical republics, but Tocqueville was addressing an emerging modern type of society. Tocqueville, also a law student in his youth, admired and was greatly influenced by Montesquieu. His book *Democracy in America* has been an enduring classic in part because Tocqueville's observations about the essence of the new republic were remarkably astute. He recognized that the federal Constitution provided many benefits to American citizens and that law generally played a central and influential role in American life. He was especially interested in the way that the legal structure in the United States provided some balance between the will of the general population and the capacity of the political leadership to govern with some authority. Tocqueville also observed that lawyers had moved into the power vacuum created by the repudiation of an aristocracy as one consequence of the American Revolution. Altogether, he produced an inspirational model of analysis for later students of the relation between the legal and the social.

During the nineteenth century other social historians set forth interpretations of the social basis and the changing nature of law with the evolution of society. In Chapter 4, on Jurisprudence, Savigny's thesis of law as an expression of the national spirit (or "volkgeist") was discussed, as well as Maine's thesis on the shifting character of law from status to contract.

Founding Fathers of Sociology

The most influential contributions to sociological theory were made during the latter part of the nineteenth century and the early years of the twentieth. The "founding fathers" of sociology (see Table 5.2) clearly recognized the importance of law as a dimension of society, perhaps more so than many later sociologists.

Table 5.2 Founding Fathers of Sociology: Key Ideas

Karl Marx	Law as a reflection of the political economy; law as complicit in oppression and exploitation.
Herbert Spencer	The application of Darwinist principles to the understanding of law; survival of the fittest.
Emile Durkheim	Law as a social fact; changing forms of law as society evolves; law and social cohesion.
Max Weber	Law defined in social terms; law and legitimation; the growing import of rationality and law.

Karl Marx

Karl Marx (1818–1883), although best known as the principal critic of capitalism and the leading exponent of communism, has also been influential within the social sciences, including sociology. Marx studied law early in his career as a university student, although he found the study of law unrewarding. His personal encounters with law, principally in the form of experiencing censorship, were negative. Although Marx and his collaborator, Friedrich Engels, did not engage in a systematic treatise on law as an aspect of society, they made various observations on law throughout their work (Cain and Hunt 1979). Since Marx's views on some matters changed over time and some of his work was unfinished, it is possible to come up with different interpretations of law in his work.

Marx did come to regard law as epiphenomenal, or a reflection of the material conditions of society. Marx exposed the contradiction in bourgeois (or capitalist) law, which claims to protect rights and promote justice when it actually is complicit in preserving privileges and denying the majority of members a fulfilling life. In the *instrumentalist* interpretation of Marx's work, law is viewed as directly controlled by the ownership class and an important instrument in the maintenance of social inequality and the exploitation and oppression of the working classes. In the *structural* interpretation, the state and the law are principally oriented toward the long-term survival of the system, and the law is therefore relatively autonomous. This second interpretation, which is more sophisticated and persuasive, allows one to account for laws prohibiting especially outrageous capitalist activities (for example, monopolistic practices and polluting the environment) while not denying the basic role of law in maintaining an inherently unjust system. For Marx, there should be no need for law in an authentically communist society, where people would live cooperatively and the motivations for predatory conduct would have disappeared. In its broad outlines, then, Marx's conception of law has been an influence on social theories that address the negative role of law in modern societies.

Herbert Spencer

Although Spencer is little read today, he had a large influence in his own time, and some of his core ideas have been revived in contemporary society. Herbert Spencer (1820–1903) was an Englishman who, despite relatively little formal education, produced a series of works on the basic principles of ethics, biology, psychology, and sociology. Writing in the wake of the introduction of Darwin's theory of evolution, Spencer (1898) applied the Darwinian perspective on human evolution to whole societies; just as the individual organism evolves, so analogously can society be regarded as an organism that evolves over time. Law itself evolves from an orientation stressing individual interests and privileges, to inherited custom, divine orders, the will of leaders, and finally consensual, contractual equality before the law.

Spencer's ideas were adopted by Social Darwinists to support the notion that law should not interfere with the process of natural selection; the government's role should be confined to the protection of personal safety and the enforcement of contracts. On this view, the law should not specifically discriminate against the disadvantaged but it should also refrain from "social engineering" in an effort to improve their circumstances. In the late twentieth century, American conservatives, without necessarily invoking Spencer, have embraced some of the premises of Social Darwinism in their successful campaign to reduce the scope of welfare law and other law-based programs to aid the disadvantaged.

Emile Durkheim

Still another Frenchman, Emile Durkheim (1858–1917), provides us with an influential approach to understanding law and its role in society (Cotterrell 1991; Lukes and Scull 1983). Durkheim (who wrote a dissertation on Montesquieu) occupied the first professorship of sociology in France and has been considered the ultimate sociologist, insofar as he attempted to explain human activities almost wholly in sociological (as opposed to psychological) terms. For example, in his famous book *Suicide* ([1897] 1951), Durkheim sought to demonstrate that this most "individualistic" of human acts is in fact best understood in terms of sociological factors, such as the relative absence of ties to social groups or supportive others.

In his first book, *The Division of Labor in Society* ([1893] 1984), Durkheim identified law broadly defined as an important social fact worthy of study (by ethnographic means), both in terms of its origins and its functions for society.

On the origins of law, Durkheim held that in primitive societies a *repressive* form of law was the norm, but in modern society law took on a *restitutive* form. Repressive law stresses control of people while restitutive law stresses the equitable settlement of conflicts. Much criticism has been directed toward this familiar Durkheimian dichotomy. First, it is simplistic in its contrast between primitive and modern societies, with no consideration of the intermediary stages in the evolution of society. Second, much evidence suggests that Durkheim is simply mistaken both in regarding primitive societies as having a uniformly repressive law and in regarding modern societies as having a law that lacks this character and is restitutive (Spitzer 1975). Indeed, the contrary argument has been made, that law becomes more controlling and severe in modern societies and is more flexible and reconciliative in so-called primitive societies. Nevertheless, Durkheim was among the influential early promoters of a comparative approach to the understanding of law.

Throughout his career Durkheim was preoccupied with the nature of social solidarity, or the forces binding members of society together. For Durkheim, law could be regarded as an expression of the collective sentiments of society and the nature of social solidarity. Law, through the administration of punishment to those who deviate from society's norms, promotes social cohesion, in this view. Crime itself is declared to be both normal and inevitable—normal in the sense that it exists in every society, and inevitable in the sense that the needs of society and of individuals will never be wholly in accord. Crime is functional as well, insofar as the societal response to crime clarifies society's standards and reinforces social solidarity.

Here, again, Durkheim's interpretation has been justly criticized, although it has been very influential. First, Durkheim naively assumed that law expressed the will of society as a whole, when in fact there is much evidence that the powerful and privileged disproportionately determine the content of the law. Second, Durkheim neglected the many ways in which conflict occurring in connection with law and law itself can promote social conflict and divisiveness. In spite of these serious limitations of Durkheim's interpretation of law, he articulated one influential way of understanding law and its functions.

Max Weber

The German sociologist Max Weber (1864–1920) has been called the last universal genius of the social sciences. Weber, like Marx, was the son of a lawyer who himself studied law as a university student; some of his earliest published work addressed issues in legal history, and he taught law at the outset of his academic career. But, also like Marx, Weber ultimately assumed an immensely ambitious project of making sense of the modern world. It has been said that Weber engaged in a lifelong dialogue with the ghost of Karl Marx, because Weber's whole approach to understanding the modern world, and his interpretation of it, both paralleled and was at odds with Marx's on many key points (Loewith 1960). Weber viewed history and human society as more complex, contradictory, and pluralistic than did Marx.

Weber's work is immensely erudite; it is also difficult and subtle, and it does not lend itself readily to concise summaries. He is associated with the position that the social scientist must assume a "value free" approach to the study of social phenomena; in other words, the social scientist should strive for objective analysis in her or his work, as opposed to taking sides and advocating social reforms. Weber also promoted the use of the "ideal type"—abstractions through which social reality can be categorized—in his study of society and law.

In his massive unfinished work *Economy and Society,* Weber (1978) explored many aspects of law in relation to the nature of freedom, authority, secularization, bureaucracy, and the rise of capitalism. He identified the basic attributes of the bureaucracies that assumed such central importance in modern societies, and in the operation of the legal system itself. A bureaucracy has a hierarchy of authority (or chain of command), specialization (or a division of labor), reliance upon a system of rules, and impersonal, formal criteria for advancement.

Weber's definition of law can be cited again here: "An order will be called *law* if it is externally guaranteed by the probability that coercion (physical or psychological), to bring about conformity or avenge violation, will be applied by a *staff* of people holding themselves specially ready for that purpose" (Weber 1978, 34). The notion that in the course of the evolution of Western society rationality becomes an increasingly important attribute of law can be identified as a central theme in Weber's sociology of law. Although the term "rationality" was used in different ways by Weber, here it refers to a movement away from superstition and spontaneity in social control to reliance upon an orderly, logical legal system.

Weber argued that a rational orientation was becoming increasingly important in the modern world, relative to tradition or personal charisma as a ground for legitimation (people's belief that they have an obligation to comply with a system of authority). On the other hand, a legal system emphasizing formal justice and guaranteed rights, in Weber's interpretation, both facilitated the rise of a capitalist economic system and was in turn reinforced by such a system. Capitalism and formal, rational legal systems, then, have important affinities (Ewing 1987). Although for Weber these developments were inevitable in certain respects and a reflection of the general evolution of society, they could also be regarded with some ambivalence. Disenchantment with modern law occurs when people become increasingly reliant upon the technical expertise of bureaucrats of the legal order, and in Weber's famous metaphor people develop a sense of being imprisoned in an "iron cage." Law in modern society, then, contributes to a sense of alienation.

Although critics tend to acknowledge the breadth of Weber's knowledge, his specific interpretations of the evolving character of law in society have been challenged on many grounds. Indeed, the understandings of law of all the founding fathers of sociology discussed here have been criticized (e.g., see Sheleff 1997), but they have nevertheless been influential and widely cited.

Jurisprudential, Historical, and Anthropological Influences on Sociolegal Scholarship

In Chapter 4 some attention was devoted to sociological jurisprudence and legal realism as early twentieth-century schools of jurisprudence. The call for more attention to sociological factors, social and behavioral science research, and social policy had an impact on the development of jurispru-

Box 5.1

Contemporary European Social Philosophers and Law

In the final decades of the twentieth century several European social philosophers produced work that was widely discussed and quite influential. Michel Foucault and Jurgen Habermas are two of the most important of these social philosophers. Much of their work is exceptionally dense and difficult, and it is unlikely to be comprehensible to most undergraduates. In light of how often their names and ideas are invoked, however, it seems worthwhile here to summarize a few key themes of their work as they relate to the sociology of law.

Michel Foucault (1926–1984), born in Poitiers, France, was a social philosopher and cultural historian (Turkel 1990, 1996). Foucault challenged the conventional idea that the modern era represented progress toward a more rational legal order, with broader rights and more freedom for individuals. Rather, in Foucault's interpretation, the state and other social institutions in the modern era are oriented to achieve greater and more efficient control over human beings. The law plays a key role in this process by cataloging and imposing judgment on individuals. In his celebrated book *Discipline and Punish* (1977), Foucault sought to document the transformation of punishment from the traditional forms of public spectacles with direct punishment of the body to the modern form of imprisonment and therapeutic control over the mind. In the modern capitalist society, law, power, and knowledge are concentrated in the hands of a relatively small elite who achieve an ever greater capacity to watch over people, intrude on their privacy, and control them.

Jurgen Habermas, born 1929 in Dusseldorf, Germany, is an immensely erudite and prolific social philosopher, whose work has been widely discussed and debated in intellectual circles (Rosenfeld and Arato 1998; Salter 1997). In his book *Between Facts and Norms* (1996), Habermas describes modern society as fragmented and ridden with cynicism and moral relativism, which leads to political disenchantment. In these circumstances, society faces a formidable challenge to regenerate social solidarity and heartfelt belief in law and other social institutions. Liberalism puts too much emphasis on individual rights, with a commensurate cost in terms of social solidarity; collectivism puts too much emphasis on social solidarity, with a resulting denigration of individual rights. The most effective response to the circumstances of contemporary society, then, requires a movement toward a radical form of democracy, where citizens can freely and fully communicate with others (the "ideal speech" situation). Law based upon mutual understanding and a rational, democratic consensus is most likely to be supported and legitimated.

dence, but it also encouraged sociologists and other social scientists to attend to the relationship between the social and the legal.

Historical scholarship on law traditionally took the form of a narrative account of legal doctrine and decisions, with a stress on appellate court opinions and great cases, but James Willard Hurst (1950) directed attention to the impact of social and economic factors on the law, and the operation of less conspicuous legal institutions and ordinary cases. Hurst was a major inspiration for and influence on some of the leading sociolegal scholars of the recent era.

Morton Horwitz (1977) exemplifies the critical approach to sociohistorical analysis, with its thesis that in the nineteenth century American judges ruled on many issues in ways that benefitted the wealthy and powerful while having negative impact on other citizens. This historical perspective is considered more fully in Chapter 6.

An anthropological approach to the study of law and society has been influential as well. In the nineteenth century, Sir Henry Maine ([1861] 1970) claimed that the nature of law was transformed in the movement from simpler to more complex modern societies. In the twentieth century, anthropologists such as Bronislaw Malinowski (1926) and E. Adamson Hoebel ([1954] 1967) explored what law meant in the world of preliterate peoples. In the recent era, some anthropologists (e.g., Merry 1990; Yngvesson 1993) have studied the meaning of legal consciousness and legal culture in contemporary American communities. The anthropological perspective on law is also explored in more depth in Chapters 6 and 9.

The Sociology of Law and the Law and Society Movement

The sociology of law is principally a development of the post-World War II era, although earlier contributions can be identified (e.g., Eugen Ehrlich's (1922) "The Sociology of Law" and Nicholas Timasheff's ([1939] 1974) *An Introduction to the Sociology of Law*). It is best described as a subdisciplinary field within the discipline of sociology; the American Sociological Association, for example, has a Sociology of Law section. The related Law and Society Movement, which has blossomed since the founding of the Law and Society Association in 1962, is a more broadly interdisciplinary movement, including not only sociologists but psychologists, historians, economists, and political scientists, as well as law professors; all are drawn together by a common interest in the interrelation between the legal and the social, broadly defined (Friedman 1986; Garth and Sterling 1998; Munger 1998). The term sociolegal scholarship is also sometimes used to describe this interest.

The development of general theories that explain social processes in which law is involved is one mission of a sociology of law; the empirical study of and analysis of interrelations between legal and social factors and variables is another mission (Cotterrell 1986; Tomasic 1985; Sarat et al. 1998b). Scholars ask: How do social factors affect and shape the law and legal institutions, and how do the law and legal institutions influence and shape society or social behavior? (See Box 5.2)

A Positivist Approach

Sociologist Donald Black (1995) is a proponent of positivism, or the application of the perspective and method of the natural sciences to the sociology of law. His work is very much in the tradition of Durkheim. Such an approach calls for the formulation of hypotheses that can be systematically tested by empirical means. Black (1976) defines law, quite simply, as governmental social control. Law is a quantitative variable: law is arrests, cases, trials, deci-

Box 5.2

The Jurisprudential and the Sociological

Although the concerns of the sociology of law parallel (and sometimes intersect with) the concerns of jurisprudence, there are significant differences of emphasis. The sociologist Donald Black (1989, 21) has compared the two approaches concisely (if somewhat artificially):

	Jurisprudential	*Sociological*
Focus	Rules	Social Structure
Process	Logic	Behavior
Scope	Universal	Variable
Perspective	Participant	Observer
Purpose	Practical	Scientific
Goal	Decision	Explanation

sions, complaints, and accusations. Law is a dependent variable and can be measured. Law increases and decreases from one setting to another.

Some specific empirical hypotheses formulated by Black include the following:

- Law varies inversely with other forms of social control (in other words, the more law you have, the less you need other forms of social control, and vice versa).

- More stratification produces more law (in other words, the more social and economic inequality in a society, the more law).

- Downward law is greater than upward law (in other words, more law is produced by the powerful and wealthy that has impact on the powerless and poor).

- Law increases as intimacy decreases, but law declines when people are wholly unconnected to each other (in other words, there is a curvilinear relationship, and there is little law between people intimately connected with each other and between people so removed from each other's lives that they have no contact, with the most law between people who have regular contact with each other without intimacy).

Black has continued to put forth striking, if controversial, claims. Black (1989) argues that the field of law has largely neglected legal sociology. Contrary to the traditional view of legal formalism that law is a matter of rules and that cases are resolved by the logical application of these rules, law is in fact socially relative. This means that the social attributes of the parties involved in a case—not only victims and perpetrators, but judges and jurors as well—predict how a case will be handled and how it will turn out. Here, too, Black has formulated some basic propositions; for example:

Third parties socially superior to the adversaries in a legal case are more likely to invoke rules than those closer in social status.

The more equal and intimate parties in legal cases are, the less likely they are to use rules.

Rules become more prominent as society grows and becomes more complex.

Black believes that his approach here, and the propositions he has generated, have important implications for both legal education and for legal reform. Law students should learn to assess the sociological as well as the legal merits of a case; even if a case seems strong on legal grounds, it may be weak on sociological grounds. He argues that legal sociology exposes more clearly the discriminatory way in which the law operates in the real world; such exposure may promote the adoption of reforms that diminish the effects of social inequality.

Donald Black's contribution to the sociology of law has inevitably been controversial, with some commentators hailing it as a major advance in the field and others criticizing it on the grounds of an absence of logical connections between the propositions and the failure of empirical testing to support the propositions (e.g., Baumgartner 1999; Gottfredson and Hindelang 1979; Greenberg 1983). Other research has claimed to find at least limited support for Black's propositions (e.g., Lessan and Sheley 1992). Black's work is also attacked on the grounds that it misses the important and interesting questions of how and why people behave and believe as they do, and how law itself is a "linguistic practice" through which various moral choices are justified (Frankford 1995). Black, then, provides a stimulating if controversial approach to making sense of the relation between the legal and the social.

A Normative Approach

Philippe Nonet and Philip Selznick (1978) promote a *normative* sociology of law. This approach is influenced by the natural law tradition and accepts Lon Fuller's notion of an internal morality of law (see Chapter 4). For Nonet and Selznick, the task of the sociologist of law is to study the nature of legality and the conditions that encourage its development. Legality is equated with "the rule of law," or the reduction of the arbitrary element in the formation and administration of the formal law. Legal systems, then, can be evaluated in terms of how well they are in accord with such standards. The ideal is to foster a society where citizens have the "civic competence" to participate effectively in the legal order, which should lead to "rational consensus," or agreement on the restraints that states must adhere to and the degree of freedom citizens should enjoy. In such circumstances, authentic legality may be said to exist.

Philip Selznick (1992) builds on some of these ideas. His basic proposition holds that the sum of morality is that all social practice should serve human needs, discovered in the course of human experience. He promotes a form of communitarian justice that reconciles competing interests in society without eliminating all differences. Selznick identifies some specific principles consistent with this idea, such as the protection and integration of minorities, government advancement of communal well-being, and political participation rooted in social ties. The ideal social order, then, serves the needs of individuals in the context of a vibrant, supportive community. Critics ask, however, whether this approach provides answers to the many specific conflicts that arise between individual and community needs.

An Ideological Approach

A third approach to making sense of the relation between the law and society can be called *ideological*. Many sociolegal scholars, reflecting in part the influence of Marx, have attempted to expose the political basis and agenda of law (Beirne and Quinney 1982; Chambliss and Seidman 1982; Hunt 1993). An ideological perspective on law is exemplified by Richard Quinney's (1974) *Critique of Legal Order*. Quinney begins with the query, can we imagine a world not regulated by law? The "rule of law" tends to be treated as a moral absolute, but Quinney here suggests that law may not be necessary, and is not necessarily good. Law is produced by special interests, representing the goals of the ruling (or capitalist) class. Law in a capitalist society fulfills a number of functions. First, law *mystifies* through its pretence of autonomy and disinterested commitment to justice, obscuring the actual power relationships within society. Then, law *legitimates* by suggesting that legal forms of power are available to all, when in reality only the elite classes are in a position to fully use that power. Law also *oppresses*, insofar as it exercises control over the powerless and administers punishment to them far more than it protects their rights. Finally, law *exploits*, because it is used by the elite classes to maintain and extend their power, property, and privileges. If all this is so, Quinney concludes, we would be better off abolishing law, or retaining law simply for guidelines and for symbolic reasons, to represent desirable behavior. Also, in view of the functions of the existing law just identified, the obligation to obey law is problematic.

Quinney, then, provides us with one striking version of an ideological interpretation of law as a part of the social order. One part of Quinney's (1991) later work took the form of a call for a peacemaking criminology—making peace on crime—as an alternative to the mainstream "war on crime" approach. Quinney's work has inevitably been criticized as blatantly ideological, either implicitly supportive of existing communist regimes or utopian and out of touch with reality.

This section has reviewed some theoretical perspectives on law and society. Such perspectives enrich our understanding of the complex relationship between the legal and the social, as do some of the jurisprudential perspectives considered in Chapter 4. But sociology is strongly committed to generating empirical knowledge, or knowledge based on systematic, direct observation.

Empirical Research and the Sociology of Law

How should one go about studying the relationship between the legal and the social? The *positivistic* approach adopts the methods of the natural and physical sciences. Hypotheses are generated from theories and then sub-

Box 5.3

A Positivist Sociolegal Study: The Effects of Severe Penalties for Drunk Driving

In the 1980s a judge in the Ohio community of New Philadelphia decided to impose severe penalties on those convicted of drunk driving. Penalties called for jail time, excluded plea bargaining, and provided for license-plate identification of offenders. Social scientists H. Laurence Ross and Robert B. Voas (1989) undertook an empirical study of the impact of these severe penalties: Did they deter people from drinking and driving? Arriving at an accurate answer to this question is difficult. A traditional approach has measured patterns of traffic-related fatalities following the adoption of the new drunk-driving policies, but this method is unreliable because the number of such deaths is relatively small in any given community and because the role that drinking alcohol has played cannot always be clearly established. Ross and Voas chose to carry out, with the cooperation of local police, a stop-and-question survey of drivers in the New Philadelphia area and in another Ohio community, Cambridge, where the judge had not adopted this tough approach to drunk drivers. Were a higher proportion of drivers in the "control" community, Cambridge, driving after drinking; were New Philadelphia drivers aware of and deterred by the prospect of severe penalties? The researchers also compared post-conviction drunk-driving records in both communities.

Perhaps disappointingly, neither measurement supported the proposition that severe penalties could deter drinking and driving. Although Ross and Voas found some evidence of community awareness of the severe penalties in New Philadelphia, they concluded that drivers focused on the relatively low likelihood of being caught rather than on the severity of the penalties. Accordingly, deterrence of drunk driving may depend more on proactive police activities than on the policies of judges.

Ross and Voas acknowledge that their stop-and-question survey may not have been able to detect differences in deterrence between the two communities studied. Since they felt that it was necessary to announce in these communities that the survey would be undertaken on two weekends, the study itself may have affected the drinking and driving patterns on those weekends. The relatively small size of the survey sample, and the fact that it was conducted only during two brief periods of time, may also limit the conclusions that can be drawn from this study.

jected to systematic observation, testing, and analysis. A positivistic approach claims to be objective. Its purpose is to discover, explain, and predict. Quantitative data play a central role in this approach. Much sociology of law research adopts some version of this model. On the whole, however, positivistic research in the sociology of law (and on social phenomena generally) has been less successful in producing law-like propositions and patterns leading to reliable predictions than has been true in the natural and physical sciences. This difference has been explained on a number of grounds.

Ultimately, sociolegal phenomena tend to be more complex than natural phenomena, with many more variables in the social environment and variations between human beings involved. The hypothetical capacity of human beings to choose their actions by will, as opposed to in response to forces acting upon them, further complicates the explanatory challenge. Insofar as sociolegal research calls for human beings studying other human beings, and matters that may intersect with personal experiences and beliefs, it may be more difficult to maintain objectivity. And both practical and ethical constraints often make it more difficult to systematically test sociolegal hypotheses than hypotheses in the natural and physical sciences.

An alternative approach to the study of sociolegal phenomena can be described as *humanistic*. This approach looks to humanistic disciplines such as philosophy, history, and literature rather than to the natural and physical sciences for guidance and inspiration. One core assumption is that the human world is fundamentally different from the natural and physical world and accordingly cannot be studied in the same way. Objectivity is less likely to be claimed in this approach, and it may be specifically disavowed. Indeed, at least some proponents of the humanistic approach affirm the need to make commitments to the advancement of an agenda of reform or social transformation. Interpretation based upon analysis and observation and qualitative data, as opposed to systematic testing and quantitative data, is at the heart of a humanistic approach (Ewick and Silbey 1995). Work in this tradition explores how law and legal institutions differ between societies and different segments of a society; how meanings and understandings of law and legal institutions are constructed; and how our understanding of law in our lives can be enriched and deepened by attending to narratives, or stories, about law.

The humanistic approach to the study of law has been criticized as subjective and impressionistic and accordingly filled with unverifiable or unrepresentative observations about law and society (see Box 5.4).

Topics of Research

A wide range of empirical and interpretive studies have been carried out by students of law and society, especially since the mid-twentieth century. Table 5.3 lists a number of scholarly journals that report such studies.

Table 5.3 Journals Featuring Sociolegal Research

Australian Journal of Law and Society
Canadian Journal of Law & Society
Crime, Law & Social Change
International Journal of the Sociology of Law
Journal of Law & Society
Law & Contemporary Problems
Law and Human Behavior
Law & Policy
Law & Social Inquiry
Law & Society Review
Legal Studies Forum
Social and Legal Studies

Box 5.4

Sociolegal Research and the Confidentiality Principle

It is well known that certain forms of communication are "privileged" in federal law, and typically in state law. That is, some matters have the privilege of remaining private; the state cannot force them to be made public. Confidential communications between attorney and client cannot be aired without consent. Spouses cannot be required to testify against each other or about confidential marital communications. Some medical information and physician-patient communications are privileged. Also, a clergyman cannot be forced to disclose confidential confessions from a penitent. The identity of informants, mainly in criminal cases, may be concealed (although a defense lawyer can challenge this). And reporters or journalists have at least a qualified privilege in federal law not to divulge sources, but they do not have an absolute privilege to refuse to testify in grand jury investigations of crime (McLaughlin 1999).

The overriding rationale for extending these privileges is that they each contribute to the protection of a socially valued interest or relationship: legal clients, medical patients, and religious penitents must be able to communicate openly and freely with their lawyers, physicians, and clergymen and receive the full benefit of their representation, care, or comfort without fearing that sensitive and confidential personal information will be publicly disclosed. Prosecutors should be able to obtain information crucial to making criminal cases and journalists should be able to obtain information crucial to the interests of the general public without the key informers having to fear that they will be publicly identified and possibly suffer adverse personal circumstances.

Should such a privilege also be extended to academic researchers who have promised confidentiality to those who have provided information related to their research? The U.S. Supreme Court has not specifically ruled on this issue, although some federal and state courts have recognized at least a limited privilege. In 1999, Senator Daniel Patrick Moynihan (New York) introduced the Thomas Jefferson Researcher's Privilege Act (S. 1437).

Here are two cases involving young sociologists that exemplify the question of privilege in research. Rik Scarce was studying the Animal Rights Movement. After a break-in occurred at a university animal research laboratory, Scarce was called before a federal grand jury to answer questions about what he might know, and he refused to do so. Scarce spent more than five months in jail on contempt charges.

Mario Brajuha was studying the restaurant industy (from his vantage point as a waiter). When a suspicious fire broke out in one of the restaurants in his study, prosecutors subpoenaed his field notes, which he refused to turn over. A federal district court ruled in his favor (but conveyed that he might have to turn over the notes if a grand jury convened and subpoenaed the notes).

Robert McLaughlin (1999) argues that in a democratic society scholarly research makes an important contribution to the public's need to be well informed, and at least a qualified research privilege should be granted to scholars to enable them to gather and protect information from confidential sources.

Status Differences

The study of law and society has attended to law in relation to differences of power, wealth, race, gender, age, and other such variables, as well as differences of cultural traditions and values (Baumgartner 1999; Garth and Sarat 1998a). Sociologists of law who adopt a progressive, conflict, or critical perspective, in particular, have sought to demonstrate how law both reflects and reinforces the interests of the wealthy and the powerful, how it discriminates against and oppresses women and minorities, how its formal processes (such as trials) often have a political agenda, and how legal institutions in socialistic countries differ from those in capitalist countries. Within American society, access to law, then, is found to differ significantly between the various strata or layers of society. How do people, or groups of people, mobilize law or initiate legal action and legal reform? When and why do people turn to the courts and the formal institutions of law, as opposed to alternative, more informal processes, to resolve their disputes?

Acquiring Attitudes About Law

The process of being socialized about law and acquiring attitudes toward legal issues has also been studied. Sociologists have studied the "legal culture" and the values people hold that relate to law; the views people form on law-related issues; and the impact of law or law-related actions on people's attitudes. Under what circumstances do people feel obliged to comply with law, and why do people fail to comply? For example, studies have been undertaken identifying reasons why most people comply with tax law, and why laws designed to deter drunken drivers often fail (Ross 1992a; Smith and Kinsey 1987). Patterns of compliance and noncompliance with law have been linked with the nature of legal authority and with the degree to which people regard the law as legitimate. These matters are addressed in more depth in Chapter 9.

Rules of Law Versus Actual Practices

The "gap" between the formal rules of law and the realities of how law operates has been a persistent topic of interest to sociological students of law. The concept of "discretion" in decision making has also been central here, insofar as it suggests that legal decision making is not mechanical or programmed (Friedman 1975, 32–39). Sociologists of law have been especially interested in identifying social and situational factors that influence the exercise of discretionary decision making within legal institutions. Sociologists of law, then, have carried out research on what goes on behind closed doors within such institutions. Jerome Skolnick's (1966) *Justice Without Trial* is a contemporary classic exploring the actual practices of police officers in a large city police department; these practices are often at odds with the formal guidelines for policing. Harry Kalven and Hans Zeisel's (1966) *The American Jury* was a pioneering study of how juries actually arrive at their decisions (and how jury decision making varies from that of judges). Still another book, Arthur Rosett and Donald R. Cressey's (1976) *Justice by Consent*, was an influential study of plea bargaining, where informal negotiations between prosecution and defense result in a guilty plea in return for some consideration (e.g., a lesser charge) for the defendant. Contrary to many people's perspective that plea bargaining is an improper procedure that extends excessive lenience to criminals, Rosett and Cressey found it to be both an inevitable feature of contemporary court operations and a defensible device for tailoring justice to the particulars of each case.

The Legal Profession

The legal profession is obviously a central element of our legal system, and accordingly has been extensively studied by sociologists of law. These studies have looked at lawyers who service the poor and lawyers who service the rich—for example, Jerome Carlin's *Lawyers on Their Own* (1962) and Erwin Smigel's *The Wall Street Lawyer* (1969)—and lawyers within particular specialties—for example, Arthur Wood's *Criminal Lawyer* (1967) and William Felstiner and Austin Sarat's *Divorce Lawyers and Their Clients* (1995). There are studies of the process of becoming lawyers—for example, Robert Granfield's *Making Elite Lawyers* (1992)—and of lawyers who are distinctive because of some attribute, such as gender—for example, Cynthia Epstein's *Women in Law* (1993). There are also studies of the bar in a particular city—for example, Chicago, in J. P. Heinz and Edward Laumann's *Chicago Lawyers*(1982); within a country—for example, the United States, in Richard Abel's (1989) *American Lawyers*; and within many different countries—for example, Richard Abel and Philip Lewis's (1988, 1989) *Lawyers in Society* Volumes I–III. Some of the findings of these studies are drawn upon in Chapter 7.

Sociologists of law also recognize that as society changes over time, law changes as well and, conversely, changes in law can have an impact on aspects of society. Law has been studied, then, as both a dependent variable and an independent variable. The specific relation between law and social change is addressed in the final chapter of this book.

Comparative Studies

Many of the founding fathers of sociology discussed earlier in this chapter (e.g., Marx, Durkheim, and Weber) were concerned with the comparative study of different types of societies. Much of the early American sociological research on law, however, focused on law and legal institutions in the United States. In the more recent era, there has been a substantial increase of studies of law, legal institutions, and legal processes in other countries (e.g., Germany; Japan); the expansion of law and society research in many countries (e.g., France; Korea); and work that is increasingly comparative in nature (e.g, Jacob et al. 1995; Noreau and Arnaud 1998; Yang 1989). A study comparing attributions of legal responsibility in the United States and in Japan (Sanders and Hamilton 1992) exemplifies the comparative approach to law and society. A study of law and legality in Cuba (Zatz 1994) is a good example of an in-depth exploration of law in a noncapitalist society.

The growth of law and society scholarship in many countries, as well as a growing interest in comparative approaches, is signified by International Law and Society meetings attended by scholars from all over the world. Although law cutting across national boundaries has been important for a long time, especially in connection with international commercial transactions, it has increasingly expanded into other areas; the explosive growth of concern with human rights law is an example (Friedman 1996a). In a world of increasing interdependence of people in many different countries, traditional borders have become less important. The emergence of a European community and European law (discussed briefly in Chapter 2) is one obvious example of the eroding status of traditional national borders.

The specific social and law-related impact of globalization, or the spreading web of worldwide interconnections (facilitated by new forms of communication and transportation), can be interpreted in different ways. Susan Silbey (1997), in a presidential address to the Law and Society Association, provocatively characterizes globalization as a form of "postmodern colonialism," insofar as it facilitates the divide between the rich and the poor and the concentration of power in the hands of few, through the domination of increasingly larger numbers of people by those who shape and control law and communication in first-world countries. In the twenty-first century the attention of sociologists of law to transnational law and the impact of globalization will surely expand.

Key Terms

Coase theorem
empirical approach
founding fathers of sociology
humanistic approach
ideological approach
Law and Society Movement
normative approach
positivistic approach
postmodern colonialism
rational consensus
Social Darwinism

Discussion Questions

1. It seems ironic that sociolegal scholarship has expanded in many countries, yet only occupies a marginal status in law schools. Do you think that the Law and Society Movement should be given more attention, especially in law schools that are supposedly preparing men and women for careers in which they will be serving society? Explain.

2. Discuss Herbert Spencer's application of the Darwinian perspective on human evolution to whole societies. What is the main idea of his Social Darwinism? How could this have an impact on welfare laws as the author suggests?

3. Compare and contrast the theories of Karl Marx with those of Emile Durkheim. In what ways do their ideas differ the most, especially in their view of law?

4. Examine the three approaches explaining the relationship between the legal and the social (i.e., empirical, normative, and ideological). How does each approach add to a greater understanding of the Law and Society Movement?

5. Do you agree with Susan Silbey when she characterizes globalization as a form of "postmodern colonialism"? Do you feel that as we move into the twenty-first century, the expansion of transnational law and the concern of globalization will do more harm than good?

Chapter Six

Comparative and Historical Perspectives on Law and Society

Is law universal, and do all human societies have law? In particular, what has "law" meant in the world of preliterate and indigenous peoples, and specifically what role has law played in the history of American Indians? How does the form and nature of law differ between the developed nations of the world, and how should one classify the different "families" of law? In particular, how has the law of nondemocratic communist nations differed from American law? And how did law in the past, within the Western tradition of which America is a part, evolve over time? What forces and influences shaped American law, and specifically what was the significance of the African-American experience with law? Finally, what does law mean in the context of war, or a specific war such as that which occurred in Vietnam? These are some of the fundamental—and endlessly fascinating—questions explored in this chapter. Those who wish to acquire a deeper and richer understanding of the relationship between the legal and the social must address such matters. The disciplines of anthropology and history are especially useful in the search for answers to the questions raised here.

The Anthropological Perspective on Law

Social and cultural anthropology has as its focus the understanding of the whole of human cultures, but it is especially associated with the study of preliterate (primitive, in past terms) societies. With surviving preliterate cultures, anthropologists use an ethnographic approach to research, which calls for intensive, extended fieldwork among the people being studied. Analysis of the findings produces a rich descriptive account of the culture as a whole and of the interrelationship of its different parts and aspects. The principal legal issues are: Is law universal? What are the means of social control among preliterate peoples? What does law have in common with, and how does it differ from, other means of social control?

Even though social philosophers and historians, including Sir Henry Maine ([1861] 1970), had long speculated about the differences between law and social control in primitive and modern societies, cultural anthropology is principally a twentieth-century enterprise. Because the question of whether law is a universal feature of human societies is one of the important issues investigated by twentieth-century cultural anthropologists, the challenge of coming up with an acceptable definition of "law" arises; in fact, anthropologists have adopted quite different definitions. In *Crime and Custom in Savage Society*, Bronislaw Malinowski (1926) rejected the notion that law is necessarily a product of the state. Preliterate tribes in the Trobriand Islands (located in the South Pacific) did not have formal, state-based laws, but they did have rules governing proper human conduct, rights of individuals, and obligations, and they had mechanisms by which people were induced to conform to these rules and expectations. For Malinowski, this was a system of law, and such a system could be found in all human societies. Other anthropologists have criticized this conception of law as too inclusive or broad.

Another landmark study was carried out by law professor Karl Llewellyn (discussed in Chapter 4 as one of the leading figures in Realist jurisprudence) and anthropologist E. Adamson Hoebel among the Cheyenne Indians of the Great Plains of North America, in the 1930s. This work used interviews and drew upon earlier published accounts to recapture the traditional ways of these people, and led to publication of *The Cheyenne Way* in 1941. Hoebel ([1954] 1967) on his own subsequently published a more general work on legal anthropology. The approach pioneered by Llewellyn and Hoebel looked at "trouble cases" to identify the law of the Cheyenne; these cases arise when some traditional rule within the tribe has been infringed and the tribe's leaders come together to deliberate and resolve the dispute at hand. For Llewellyn and Hoebel, law is not defined in terms of rules or institutions but is rather identified with the *process* of social control. According to Llewellyn and Hoebel, this process seldom results in a winner and a loser. Rather, because members of these small tribes were so dependent on one another for survival and would have to continue to associate with each other after resolution of a dispute, a compromise permitting both parties to win a little was the resolution most conducive to ongoing harmonious relations.

In the decades following these pioneering studies of dispute resolution among preliterate peoples, cultural anthropologists traveled to many remote parts of the world to study this process among indigenous people and preliterate tribes—in Africa, the South Pacific, Latin America, and elsewhere (Nader and Todd 1978; Sack and Aleck 1992). Anthropologists have embraced diverse conceptions of law (Moore 1986; Snyder 1996). Some have followed the lead of Malinowski, viewing law in broad and inclusive terms to include "rules," customs, and any identifiable means of social control. Others have adopted a view that says a systematic application of explicit rules is the minimum criterion for an identifiable system of law. The most conservative approach to this issue limits the notion of law to a system where a political state, courts, and written legal codes exist.

The claim that law in some sense is a cultural universal, found in some form in every human culture, has been challenged. Among the Andaman

Table 6.1 From No Law to Full Law

Level of Law	No Law	Minimal Law	Medium Law	Full Law
Character of Law	Spontaneous; informal social control	Established norms; informal "courts"	Specific codes/ compensation; popular tribunals	Written codes; courts
Setting	Andaman Islanders	Zuni Indians	Yurok Indians	U.S.A.

Islanders, for example, there was apparently no agreed-upon means of settling disputes and no specific sanctions for acting contrary to norms (Radcliffe-Brown 1922); this would indeed be a culture with no law. Among many other preliterate people or indigenous tribes, law could be described as minimal (for example, where public pressure is imposed on disputants to resolve their differences) to rudimentary (for example, where a code exists that one party who has done harm to another must provide compensation) (Redfield 1967). Table 6.1 summarizes the nature of "law" known to be practiced by various cultures—from no law to full law. The Eskimo Drum Song "Court" is an especially remarkable procedure for settling disputes (Hoebel [1954] 1967). When a dispute between Eskimos developed, a drumming contest would be arranged. This contest, which could extend over years, took the form of an exchange of accusations and insults, and sometimes included head butting and wrestling. Spectators would ultimately signify which contestant had won the contest in the sense of getting the better of, or shaming, the other contestant. The loser might be exiled, or some form of reconciliation might occur. Other cases of such song contests among preliterate peoples have been reported in parts of the South Pacific and Africa. Indeed, in contemporary society the inner-city ritual called "the dozens," where disputants hurl insults at each other while being egged on by onlookers, bears a close relationship to this singular process for resolving disputes.

Whether one calls the various means of dispute resolution used by preliterate people "law" or something else depends on one's definition of law. The relationship between customs and laws has been characterized in different ways. For Paul Bohannon (1967a), law is best seen as "double institutionalized" customary rules: that is, rules that have first become adopted naturally within a culture and then are formalized with specific institutions and procedures. Anthropologist Stanley Diamond (1973), however, has argued that customs and laws are fundamentally different: customs are the natural reflection of the beliefs and values of a tribe or social group, whereas law is imposed on people by the state, at least sometimes to achieve the purposes of the state and powerful interests. However one views this issue, it is indisputable that most Westerners who moved into underdeveloped countries, even those well beyond the preliterate stage of cultural development, did not regard the indigenous means of dispute settlement as law. Accordingly, Western law was largely imposed on people in colonized third-world countries (Burman and Harrell-Bond 1979). The claim that no system of law existed among indigenous people was used to justify this imposition. Although the rationale for this imposition of law was that it would enable these traditional

Box 6.1

Cultural Pluralism and the Limits of Tolerance: The Case of Female Genital Mutilation

How does one find the right balance between tolerance for the cultural and religious values of people different from ourselves and rejection of repellent and harmful practices (Crosette 1999)? For example, Americans are unlikely to adopt a tolerant attitude toward the practice, traditional in India, of sacrificing widows on the funeral pyres of their husbands. In some cultures, murder has been deemed an appropriate response to an offense against the family's honor, but American law has never formally endorsed this cultural value.

Female circumcision—or female genital cutting and mutilation—has existed for some 2,500 years and is practiced in some forty countries (mainly in Africa). Over one hundred million females are affected and about two million are at risk each year (Sussman 1998, 197). The principal objective of this practice is to diminish the possibility of female premarital sex and sexual infidelity by removal of the clitoris and stitching together the genital lips. At least some of those who immigrate to the United States from countries where this practice is customary want to continue the practice in the United States. A small number of women have fled their native country to avoid genital mutilation and have sought political asylum in the the United States on these grounds. In 1996, the U.S. Congress passed into law the Female Genital Mutilation Act, which criminalizes circumcision of females under eighteen, requires federal health agencies to educate immigrant communities about the harm of genital cutting, and imposes economic sanctions on countries that fail to take steps to prevent such practices (Dugger 1996; Sussman 1998). The difficulties of effectively enforcing such a law, which challenges deeply held religious or cultural beliefs, are great. Most Americans are in agreement with this law and regard female genital cutting, or mutilation, as barbaric. Of course, male circumcision has been widely practiced and accepted in the United States on religious, health-related, or aesthetic grounds. Any effort to outlaw the practice of male circumcision would encounter fierce resistance, especially from a politically active American Jewish community, since circumcision is required for all Jewish males. Most Americans regard circumcision, which simply involves the removal of the foreskin from the penis, as fundamentally different from female genital cutting. But at least some Americans regard male circumcision as an unwarranted (and even barbaric) form of mutilation.

societies to advance and join the family of civilized nations, it is also obvious that Western law became a critically important means for controlling and exploiting indigenous people in many parts of the world. Furthermore, traditional means of dispute settlement typically survived in these third-world countries, co-existing with and sometimes in conflict with the formal, Western legal system. The term *legal pluralism* was formulated by cultural anthropologists in recognition of the fact that formal systems of law typically co-exist with one or more other systems of social control or dispute settlement (Griffiths 1986). Of course, legal pluralism is not restricted to underdeveloped countries (see Box 6.1).

Indigenous Peoples and the Law: The Case of American Indians

The issues surrounding American Indians and the law are related to the broader problem of law and "indigenous" or "aboriginal" peoples. This term refers to descendants of the original inhabitants of a particular geographic area. About 4 percent of the world's population, or approximately 200 million people, are considered to belong to this category, with some 3,000 indigenous nations within some 200 nation-states (Rosen 1992; Lauderdale 1997: 140). Most of these indigenous peoples, whether in Africa, Asia, Australia, the Americas, or elsewhere, have had outsiders, or colonizers, come in, conquering, exploiting, and in some cases virtually exterminating them. The colonizers then imposed on survivors the outsider's own law and legal system. This imposed legal system then typically became a mechanism for controlling and further exploiting the indigenous people. In the modern era, in response to outside pressures, demands of indigenous militants, and some acknowledgment of past injustices, questions on the rights of indigenous peoples have arisen. Here we examine questions that arise in connection with American Indians and the law.

Indian Law

First, what was the nature of the "law" of American Indians prior to their contact with Europeans? We cannot come up with a definitive answer to this question, partly because there is no written history among American Indians. Furthermore, the term "American Indian" encompasses peoples with very different histories, identities, and practices. Through oral history and observational reports, scholars have gathered accounts of traditional American Indian law, although the reported forms of American Indian law may already have been affected, in some ways, by contact with European and American government agents, soldiers, and settlers. Indeed, one scholar believes that "so-called customary law is a product of colonization" (Sierra 1995, 228).

The work of Llewellyn and Hoebel (1941), referred to earlier, on the Cheyenne of the Great Plains, is one of the most famous accounts of indigenous law. Hoebel (1960), in a brief summary, notes that among the Cheyenne the law was collectively declared by the tribal leaders. Its purpose was primarily to define relations, allocate authority, address conflicts of interest, and take appropriate action against crimes such as murder or threats to the communal hunt, upon which the Cheyenne were so dependent. When a member of the tribe violated important tribal norms, the leadership class would meet and effectively resolve the matter, sometimes imposing a temporary banishment of the offender. Typically, the ultimate objective of this juristic process was to rehabilitate the offender and reintegrate him into the group. In a parallel vein, "traditional justice among the Navajo tends to be swift, direct, personal and emphasizes the restoration of harmony and reacceptance by the community rather than punishment and ostracism" (Armstrong, Guilfoyle, and Melton 1996, 51). In a contemporary idiom, this is justice as peacemaking.

Although American Indian law for the most part seems to have emphasized justice-as-healing and to have avoided repressive punishment, it may be a mistake to romanticize the original Indian cultures as uniformly reconciliatory (Lauderdale 1997). There were great differences in the legal practices and penal attitudes of Indian groups; the Aztecs and Mayans, for example, had laws and punishments similar to those of traditional European cultures. In the modern era the law administered within Indian communities can sometimes be harsh and oppressive (Sierra 1995). Ironically, in at least some cases, members of the Indian community may look to the law of the larger society to protect them from some aspects of their own community's law.

Taking Land and the Law

A second question that must be asked with reference to American Indians has to do with the law of colonizers: By what legal (or jurisprudential) theory was the expropriation of Indian lands carried out or justified? Was the "conquest of paradise" (in other words, the European settlement of North and South America) the greatest crime in Western history? Was it genocide on a monumental scale? On the first of these questions, Western explorers and colonizers justified what they did in terms of a right of discovery, the need to save the souls of irrational heathens, and the divine right of entitlement to develop and control the under utilized land occupied by indigenous peoples (Williams 1990). Certainly from the perspective of American Indians, the conquest of their lands is considered a crime on a very grand scale. The native people of the Caribbean islands—the Caribs and Arawaks—were largely exterminated; many massacres continued against Indian populations for hundreds of years, culminating in the Wounded Knee massacre in 1890 (Brown 1971). Many other Indians died from diseases contracted from Europeans; in battle; and from the loss of traditional sources of food. In the modern era, American Indian communities have had extraordinarily high rates of unemployment and such pathologies as alcoholism, child abuse, and suicide, linked with the conditions imposed upon them (Egan 1998a, 1998b). Obviously American Indians have also had many positive achievements and experiences, but in historical terms the law and the legal system are more readily associated with negative experiences, which are accordingly emphasized here.

The continued oppression of American Indians through the present era has been characterized by Indian activists and their sympathizers as a war against the Indian nations; the dramatic overrepresentation of Indians among prison inmates is seen as one outcome of this war (Nielsen 1996; Weyler 1992). The American Indian Movement (AIM), founded in 1968, is a militant group dedicated to challenging this oppression and the historic theft of Indian lands. Inevitably, this Movement has found itself in conflict with the laws and agents of the federal government. In one especially celebrated confrontation at the Pine Ridge Reservation in South Dakota in June 1975, an exchange of gunfire between AIM members and the FBI resulted in the death of one Indian and two FBI agents (Weyler 1992). As of this writing Leonard Peltier, an AIM leader, is still in prison in connection with this incident, although many questions have been raised about both his culpability in the original incident and his treatment at the hands of the justice system and the penal system in the years since.

Every American schoolchild learns at some point that various treaties were signed by American Indians and representatives of white American society. But what was the understanding of American Indians of these treaties and other agreements with white people? Did the Indians who "sold" Manhattan to Dutch settlers (for the equivalent of twenty-four dollars worth of trinkets and implements) have the same understanding of property law that the Europeans did? It is generally recognized that they did not, and they certainly did not understand that they were giving up for all time the right to hunt, fish, and settle on Manhattan island.

Did the white Americans, who had every advantage in drawing up the treaties in the first place, comply with the terms of these treaties? On the contrary. Despite the principle embedded in Article VI of the Constitution (that treaties backed by Congress are the law of the land), provisions of treaties were systematically violated by the American state and white settlers, and reservation land promised to Indians was taken away from them and opened up to white homesteaders (Bordewich 1996; Egan 1998a). One might say that the European colonizers and white American settlers violated natural law by expropriating Indian lands in the first place, and then violated the conditions of their own positive law.

In a series of early nineteenth-century decisions (*Johnson v. McIntosh*, 1823; *Cherokee Nation v. Georgia*, 1831; *Worcester v. Georgia*, 1832), the United States Supreme Court, under the leadership of John Marshall, asserted the basic right of the United States over the Indians through discovery and conquest, although the Court also acknowledged the duties of the central government toward the Indians and the right of Indians to manage their own affairs (Egan 1998a; Rosen 1992, 367–368). For much of the subsequent history, the "duty" aspect, if it was acknowledged at all, was interpreted in a paternalistic manner, providing modest forms of support in return for submissiveness on the part of Indians. From the 1880s through the first part of the twentieth century, the dominant policy, known as "allotment," broke up many of the Indian reservations into private holdings, with the principal objective being integration of Indians into the larger society and assurance that non-Indians would not be subjected to control by Indians (Bordewich 1996).

Tribal Sovereignty

This allotment policy began to change significantly in the 1970s, when the federal government adopted a policy favoring tribal sovereignty, or more direct control of Indians over their own affairs (Wunder 1996). What is the basis of tribal sovereignty? In one interpretation, tribal sovereignty is preconstitutional and extraconstitutional (Valencia-Weber 1994). This means that the sovereignty of Indian tribes existed prior to the adoption of the American Constitution, and under principles of international law the United States was never entitled to preempt the original sovereignty of the indigenous peoples of the Americas. The new policy has generated a host of complex questions. First, what is a "tribe" and exactly who belongs to the tribe (Tsosie 1997)? The term has had a dual meaning in American law, referring sometimes to an ethnologically defined group of people who share a common heritage and community and sometimes to a legally recognized political entity (Goldberg-Ambrose 1994). Tribe and tribal membership has been defined by outsiders and by Indians themselves. Some Indian groups have defined tribal membership principally in terms of common ancestry; others have expanded the idea of tribe to include Indians sharing a residential area, having an affinity for a tribe, or performing service for a tribe (Goldberg-Ambrose 1994, 1128–1129).

If American Indian tribes have sovereignty over their own domain, which law should prevail when a conflict arises between state law and tribal law? For example, how much authority should the state have to regulate tribal gaming enterprises and environmental protection (Valencia-Weber 1994)? In an extreme case, if an Indian community sanctions the assassination of alleged witches, should the state intervene and prosecute the matter as a violation of state laws pertaining to homicide (Sierra 1995)? Indians, as American citizens—a status formally recognized by Congress in 1924—are subject to the same laws as other citizens except for minor crimes and some civil matters occurring on reservations, where tribal courts have jurisdiction (Egan 1998a, 1998b).

The doctrine of tribal sovereignty has in some cases led to Indian demands for the return of sacred lands, ancestral bones, and artifacts; local economies, non-Indian landowners, and museums have felt threatened by such demands (Bordewich 1996). The resulting litigation has sometimes had unintended consequences: it has produced conflict between American Indians concerned with maintaining traditional cultural identity and those concerned with practical gains—sometimes within the same tribe (Kempers 1989). By the late 1990s, a backlash against tribal sovereignty had developed, in response to the anger of non-Indians increasingly affected by this sovereignty (for example, through attempted imposition of taxes on them if they reside on Indian lands); jealousy over the new casino-based wealth of some Indian tribes; and increasing unease in Congress and on the Supreme Court about the creation of parallel nations within the United States (Egan 1998a, 1998b). Altogether, the relation between American law and the American Indian community has been filled with injustice, contradiction, and ambivalence.

The Comparative Perspective on Law

Whether law is a universal phenomenon in the sense that it can be found in some form among all human societies, it is indisputably an aspect of all developed nations and of all societies more complex than tribal societies. Looking around the world, one also becomes conscious that there are diverse legal traditions and systems and that law exists on many different levels. A comparative, or cross-cultural, perspective on law is important for several reasons. Such a perspective enables one to overcome ethnocentric tendencies toward glorifying one's own system of law, and it reinforces one's appreciation of the fact that law does not emerge in a social vacuum but rather both reflects and influences the society of which it is a part. Also, in a world of increasing international contacts, eroding borders, and globablization, a comparative perspective is necessary to promote greater cooperation and understanding (Fields and Moore 1996; Moore 1986; Reichel 1999; Terrill 1992).

Table 6.2 The Major Families of Law

Common Law	Legal system where judicial finding of law is central; legal precedents rather than legislative statutes; of English origin.
Civil Law	Legal system where legislative codes are central; statutes rather than judicial opinions are dominant; of Continental European origin.
Socialist Law	Legal system where socialist practices and objectives provide fundamental guidance; popular justice; Communist countries.
Sacred Law	Legal system where sacred (religious) text—e.g., the Koran—provides fundamental guidance; religious laws enforced; countries where religious fundamentalism is dominant.

There are "families" of legal traditions; then, within these traditions, there are different legal systems in particular nations; within nations, there may be differences between states; and within states, there may be differences between local (e.g., city or town) legal systems or laws. The understanding of law as a social phenomenon is necessarily comparative, then, and must begin with identifying the major families of law. As is always true with such classifications, no full consensus exists on just how many such families can be identified, and how to divide up the world's legal systems. Furthermore, any typology of legal families inevitably distorts the reality that specific legal systems are rarely pure types but incorporate in varying degrees elements of different families of law and specific legal systems. Some legal systems with distinctive attributes, such as the ancient Egyptian and Mesopotamian systems, essentially became extinct with the passing of these cultures, although elements survived in later systems of law (Reichel 1999, 80–83). In any case, despite inherent limitations, a typology of legal families is a necessary starting point for the comparative study of law. For our purposes, we identify civil law, common law, socialist law, and sacred law families (see Table 6.2).

Civil Law

The oldest, largest, and most enduring legal family within the Western tradition is called the *Civil Law* tradition, also sometimes known as Roman law or Continental law. The term "civil law" is somewhat unfortunate here because this term is also used for the U.S. system of private law, which inevitably causes some confusion. The so-called civil law family derives from various continental European sources, including elements of classical Roman law, customary law, the canon law of the church, judicial decrees, the law of merchants, and monarchical law. A centerpiece of the civil law tradition is codification, or the absolute primacy of written codes of law. (Codes, however, are not unique to civil law legal systems, nor are they central to all legal systems so classified.) As an example of such codes, there is the ancient code—

and for some the true starting point of civil law—called the "Twelve Tables" set forth in about 450 B.C. in Rome. This code was not the only source of law for Romans, however, as various legislative bodies, magistrates, and judges also promulgated laws applicable to different classes of people and different circumstances (Watson 1995).

In the sixth century A.D. the Institutes of Justinian (an emperor) attempted to address the inevitable confusion and conflicts created by multiple sources of law. Through creation of a comprehensive code, this notion became central to the civil law tradition. In the early nineteenth century, in France, the Napoleonic Code (1804) was another influential effort at comprehensive codification, as was the German Civil Code (1896) later in the century, following the unification of Germany.

Much earlier in Western European history, with the emergence of a Catholic church of growing influence, a legal system known as *Canon Law* emerged. Although its origins go back at least to the fourth century, the publication of the *Concordat of Discordant Canons*, by Gratian in about 1150, extended its influence (Caenegem 1992, 60–62). Canon law, claiming its roots in divine law as decreed by the Pope and other church authorities, and administered by ecclesiastical courts (presided over by officials of the Church), was intended to apply in cases involving Christians, especially in matters pertaining to moral issues (Berman 1983). (It is principally, although not exclusively, associated with the Roman Catholic Church.) Inevitably, over time, conflicts between the law of the state and of the Church developed, and much of the jurisdiction of the Church was coopted by emerging national states. Canon law had an important influence on secular Western laws of marriage, inheritance, property, contracts, and crimes and torts, as well as on rules of judicial procedure (Berman 1983, 225–254). It has survived into the present to govern matters purely within the province of the Church, such as the granting of marriage annulments.

Judges in the civil law tradition are generally expected to defer to the will of the legislative bodies that produce the codes and to apply (rather than broadly interpret) relevant provisions of codes in specific cases; in the recent era, however, they have also been influenced (but not bound) by earlier judicial rulings (Merryman 1969, 54–55). At the same time, this tradition is associated with an inquisitorial system, with a judge (or panel of judges) exercising fairly direct control over the inquiry into the facts of cases before them (as in France), as opposed to lawyers directing this process (as in the United States). Judges are typically civil servants who specialized in training to become judges early in their legal education, which is not an option in common law countries. The pretrial investigation by prosecutors is especially important in determining guilt or innocence in criminal cases, and the accused generally have more limited rights; indeed, they do not have a right to bail, do not necessarily enjoy a presumption of innocence once their case has reached the trial stage, and have more limited options on appeal. Juries either are not used at all or have a severely limited role. This civil law tradition is dominant in Western Europe, among the Scandinavian countries and continental European countries such as Germany, the Netherlands, France, Italy, Spain, and Portugal; it also shaped the legal systems of most of the countries colonized by these European countries, especially in Latin America, Asia, and Africa.

Common Law

The *Common Law* tradition is specifically a product of English history. Its roots go far back in the law of the Anglo-Saxon tribes, an amalgam of compilations of customs, royal proclamations, early statutes, and manuals on practices (Caenegem 1988). After the conquest of England by the Normans under William I in 1066, this law was largely preserved, and it was formalized during the reign of William's descendant, Henry II, in the twelfth century. The common law became the law of the royal courts, common to all citizens (as opposed to local law, which applied only to local citizens). Starting with prominent judges such as Glanvill during Henry II's reign, with his listing of writs available in the king's courts, and Henry de Bracton in the thirteenth century, with his articulation of fundamental common law principles in *De Legibus*, and culminating with the great commentary by Oxford law professor William Blackstone in the middle of the eighteenth century, attempts were made to identify and bring together some of the core elements of the common law.

The common law principally emerged out of case law rather than from legislatively produced codes of law. In this tradition the judge plays a much more central role, because judges "find" the law in what has come to be recognized as law in the tradition of the community; they seek the law in findings of judges in earlier cases (precedent, or the principle of *stare decisis*). Since judges have considerable interpretive leeway in this tradition, it is sometimes claimed that, for all practical purposes, judges make law and that the notion of "finding" law in past decisions is a fiction. On the other hand, the common law tradition is also associated with an adversarial system where the lawyers—prosecutors and defense counsel in criminal cases—take the lead in questioning witnesses and other parties to the case and engage in a contest over the evidence. The judge presides over this contest, especially by ruling on procedural issues. The use of a jury to determine guilt or innocence, at least in cases with serious charges and claims, is also a central feature of this system. Defendants are generally regarded as having more rights within this tradition, including a fairly extensive right of appeal.

The common law is principally associated with England and its former colonies. The United States is regarded as a common law country in the sense that the U.S. Supreme Court, with its power to produce important law through its interpretations and decisions, operates in this tradition. But from the country's earliest history, written codes of law have been a conspicuous and over time an increasingly important source of law. Furthermore, although in the nineteenth century in some frontier states it was still possible to be charged with "common law" violations, or violations of what was understood to be the law, through the twentieth century and into the present century Americans can only be charged with violations of written laws.

Socialist Law

Socialist law is the most recent of the families of law and is a product of the revolutionary establishment of communist or socialist regimes in the twentieth century. The status and character of law in such countries has been a matter of considerable dispute (Hirst 1986; Shichor and Heeren 1989). In one view no valid system of law exists in communist countries, insofar as "legal procedures" and "legal decrees" are cynically used simply to serve the purposes of the regime. In this view, as there is no recognized constitutional basis for state power, such systems are really "anti-legal." In a second view, what exists in socialist countries that have systematic legal provisions is a system of law, but it is best classified as being within the civil law tradition, with some socialistic elements incorporated. A third view does recognize a system of law that is socialist and has such distinctive features that it cannot be considered simply a version of a civil law system. Which of these views is correct? The answer depends at least in part on one's ideological outlook, and in part on the specific country and period (e.g., the Soviet Union under Stalin or during the Gorbachev years). The view adopted here is that for the most part legal systems do exist in communist and socialist countries and that their socialist features do set them apart from nonsocialist legal systems.

One dimension of law in socialist countries is *idealistic*, in the sense that the law incorporates Marxist, socialistic, or revolutionary principles (e.g., profit-making private enterprise may be declared illegal) (Berman 1966, 205). A second dimension is *traditional*, in the sense that the indigenous legal norms and traditions of the country in question have not been abolished but have been adapted by the new regime (e.g., Russian secret police became Soviet secret police). And a third dimension is *pragmatic*, since the conditions of modern industrialized nations—capitalist or communist—and international commerce impose demands for certain legal norms and procedures (e.g., traffic law in the People's Republic of China).

The status of law in communist countries has inevitably been influenced by the views of Karl Marx, although these views have by no means been uniformly adopted. Marx's basic stance was one of general hostility toward law. Marx and his lifelong collaborator Friedrich Engels did not produce a systematic treatise on law, but many observations pertaining to law are scattered through their work (Beirne and Quinney 1982; Cain and Hunt 1979; Kelsen 1955). Marx (and Engels) characterized law as "epiphenomenal," meaning that law reflects the society in which it developed. In Western European states, then, law is simply a reflection of the capitalist economy, and as an element of capitalism, law is complicit in the oppression, exploitation, and alienation of ordinary people, or workers. Law is an aspect of class domination, or the domination of the working class (proletariat) by the ownership class (the bourgeoisie). In a truly communist society there would be no need for law, and law (along with the state) would "wither away."

Since Marx's observations about law are simply scattered through work produced over many years, and since the pronouncements are not always consistent, interpretations of Marx's views on law beyond such general themes have varied. For example, in an *instrumental* interpretation, Marx is understood to hold the view that the capitalist ownership class directly controls the lawmaking and law-enforcing process. In a *structural* interpretation, the law (and the state) is seen as "relatively autonomous," which means that it is not directly controlled by the capitalist ownership class but nevertheless is oriented toward the long-term survival of the capitalist system. This second interpretation appears to be more sophisticated and credible because it allows one to understand how laws (and prosecutions) can be directed against at least some capitalist practices (and capitalists) in capitalist societies, contributing to the long-term survival of these societies by fostering the notion that the law is neutral and fair.

Given the inconsistent observations on law found in the work of Marx, it is not surprising that students and followers of Marx have adopted different interpretations of the proper role of law in socialist, or communist, societies. Karl Renner (1870–1950), a native of the Austro-Hungarian empire (and for a time President of the Austrian Republic), produced an influential interpretation ([1904] 1949). For Renner, the uniformity of legal concepts across different ecoomic systems suggests that Marx was wrong in characterizing law as "epiphenomenal." Rather, legal norms as such are neutral and are based upon human relationships. Nevertheless, in capitalist societies these norms, and legal institutions generally, are manipulated to advance the interests of capitalism. It is this process of manipulation, not law itself, that should be abolished. In a similar vein the British socialist historian E. P. Thompson (1978, 258–269) argued that law was an inevitable feature of any complex society, that on balance the "rule of law" has historically been a force for good on behalf of ordinary people, and that accordingly law has a necessary role in any authentic socialist society.

The early Soviet legal scholar E. B. Pashukanis is most closely associated with the view that law by its very nature is incompatible with a truly socialistic society (Beirne and Sharlet 1980; Milovanovic 1981). Although Pashukanis rejected the instrumentalist interpretation of law as a naked instrument of coercion controlled by the capitalist class, he replaced it with his "commodity exchange theory of law." For Pashukanis the very form of law reflects the commodity form of a capitalist society, and in law the "juridic subject" is the legal parallel to the exploited worker. In a fully developed socialistic society, then, policy and planning should replace law. Pashukanis was writing in the 1920s, when the newly established communist regime in the Soviet Union was still exploring how Russia might be transformed in a way consistent with Marx's vision. By the 1930s the Soviet dictator Stalin had discovered that law and legal institutions could be used to consolidate his power and control; Pashukanis was attacked as a "legal nihilist" and disappeared in 1937, presumably murdered by Stalinist secret police.

The role of law in socialist and communist societies—and whether it has any proper role at all—was a historically contested terrain throughout the twentieth century. The typical pattern after a communist revolution has been an attempt to abolish law and legal institutions and to replace these institutions with "popular tribunals," administering justice in accord with the goals of a true communism (Tay 1990). Over time, formal law and legal institutions have tended to reemerge. By any criteria, horrendous injustices and genocidal campaigns have been carried out in the name of abolishing all remnants of a bourgeois, capitalist society and its "rule of law." This was conspicuously the case with the Chinese "cultural revolution"(1966–1976), where the fanatical Red Guard openly attacked all institutions and individuals deemed counter-revolutionary. It occurred as well during the genocidal campaign of the Khmer Rouge in Cambodia (1975–1979), where well over a million people were summarily executed on the grounds that they were a threat to, or did not fit in with, a projected radical agrarian Communist society.

Whether these crimes can be blamed on a Marxist philosophy vaunting "collective" justice over a concern for individual human rights or should be blamed principally on specific communist systems and leaders has been debated (Comaroff 1991). Of course, parallel horrors in the twentieth century have occurred in many countries, from Hitler's Nazi Germany to Idi Amin's Uganda, which were totalitarian but hardly communist.

The Russian/Soviet Case

The Stalinist regime of the Soviet Union (from the 1920s to the 1950s) is widely regarded as one of the worst nightmares of the twentieth century and a prime case of law and legal institutions being used to achieve horrendous ends. Any consideration of the status of law in the Soviet Union, however, must begin with some attention to prerevolutionary Russian law (Berman 1963). The Russian system of law was broadly rooted in the civil (Roman) law tradition but reflected as well the primitive and harsh customary law of the Mongols and other Russian ethnic tribes. The system of law that evolved under the Russian tsars was exceedingly autocratic. This law did not even pretend to embrace a principle of equality before the law; rather, separate courts and punishments were applied to serfs and to the nobility. Nor was there any allegiance to a rule of law, due process, or rational decision making. Secret police had almost limitless powers; judges were typically uneducated, immoral, and corrupt; trials were generally secret, taking the form of written presentations of evidence with no appeal possible. Lawyers were few and far between and were rarely involved in trials. Extremes of indulgence and severity were evident, with Draconian punishments possible, including exile, imprisonment, torture, and execution. Although some efforts were made under Tsar Peter the Great and Catherine the Great to Westernize the law, and some progressive reforms (including public trials, juries, the right to legal representation, and elected judges) were introduced in 1864 under Tsar Alexander II, these reforms were not widely understood or adopted, and eventually the legal system reverted to autocratic rule by, or on behalf, of the tsar's successors. It is important to appreciate, then, that the Soviet legal system did not replace a progessive and fair-minded system of law; in fact, the Soviets adapted such traditional Russian institutions as the secret police for their own purposes.

Law in Soviet Russia after the Revolution was characterized by novelist Aleksandr Solzhenitsyn (1976, 522) as follows: "Our law is powerful, slippery, and unlike anything else on earth known as law."

The Russian Revolution in 1917 was one of the most dramatic events in twentieth-century history. Vladimir Lenin, the leader of the revolutionary Bolsheviks, basically adopted the interpretation of Marx calling for a dictatorship of the proletariat and the withering away of law (Beirne and Hunt 1988). Although revolutionary tribunals were initially established and an effort was made to dismantle the existing system of law, a need for legal standards quickly became evident. Through much of the 1920s, in the era of "the New Economic Policy," much new law was passed, and a Soviet legal system was established, on the rationale that it would contribute to paving the way for a truly communist society. The promotion of the revolutionary agenda—including a broad definition of counterrevolutionary activity and abolition of profit-making private enterprise—was one central objective of the law adopted during this period.

By the late 1920s, after the premature death of Lenin, there was a long period of growing domination by Joseph Stalin (until his own death in 1953), which began with forced collectivization of peasant farms and moved on to "show trials" of people perceived as threats to the regime; also, huge numbers of people deemed politically unreliable on some grounds or other were arrested and shipped off to the Gulag (Siberian prison camps). The jurist Andrei Vyshinsky played a key role in developing the "jurisprudence of terror" that transformed law during the Stalin era into a naked instrument operating on behalf of the regime (Sharlet and Beirne 1984). The powers of the police and courts were extended during this period. People were arrested and convicted without violating specific laws but on the basis that their actions (or words) were "analogous" to prohibited conduct.

In the Khrushchev Era (1953–1966), after Stalin's death, a rejection of the "excesses" of the Stalinist regime occurred, with some liberalization of laws. Reform took the form of attention to acts, not simply persons, and to circumstances, not simply ideological considerations. After Nikita Khrushchev was forced out of office in the mid-1960s, a second post-Stalinist era (1966–1990) took place, with a series of leaders—from Brezhnev to Gorbachev—who had survived and risen in the Byzantine world of Soviet politics. During this era renewed emphasis on law as a means for promoting social order, discipline, and morality occurred. Although efforts were made to eliminate some of the more arbitrary aspects of law and render it more orderly and predictable, it continued to face interference from and be subordinate to the needs of the communist state (which had clearly failed to wither away!). The size of the legal profession expanded considerably during this period, although it remained small relative to the American bar by a factor of at least ten. In the face of growing dissatisfaction with this legal system, especially its general indifference to individual human rights, Gorbachev, through his "glasnost" and "perestroika" program, initiated some liberalizing reforms to acknowledge such rights (Hazard 1990).

It is remarkable that the formal presumption of innocence—so central to Anglo-American criminal law—was only established in Russia in 1989, in a revision of the criminal law. But by this time any such reforms were too late to salvage the corrupt, disintegrating Soviet communist system itself, which collapsed in September 1991.

Legal developments in post-Soviet Union Russia cannot be explored here, but it is striking to note that after wholly dominating Russia for over seventy years, the Communist Party found itself on trial before a constitutional court following the new Russian president Boris Yeltsin's declaration banning it and seizing its assets (Kohan 1992). The Communist party was accused of a long list of historical crimes, including the attempted destruction of the church, starvation of peasants, resettlement of ethnic groups, purging of political opponents, financing of terrorists, personal enrichment of party leaders, and the squandering of the country's economic resources in various ways. In 1992, in a harsh retrospective assessment of Soviet law, Russian president Yeltsin noted:

> For many years, the laws in this country played a decorative role. Many of them contradicted both common sense and human nature. They were openly violated or bypassed. Legal and state nihilism are deeply rooted. (Erlanger 1992, A8)

Russia, then, can expect to spend many more years contending with this legacy and developing a legal system more consistent with its democratic aspirations.

The Case of China

In Oriental culture generally, and in the case of China specifically, law and formal legal proceedings—at least in their Western form—have been looked upon with disfavor. In part, this rejection reflects Confucianism, with its view of human nature as fundamentally good and capable of perfection. In this view the elites of society should act in accord with unwritten ethical and moral codes. To the extent that laws and courts are necessary, they should address only the activities of the common people, not the leadership class. In traditional Chinese culture the patriarchal family, rather than the isolated individual, was the primary focus of concern (Tanner 1995), so social control was viewed primarily as a responsibility for the family, and by extension the community. Furthermore, in a cultural value system emphasizing conformity to the group and self-control, conflicts, when they arise, are best handled by mediation and compromise rather than by litigation. Although a formal legal system with written codes, police, and prisons long existed in China, the country only adopted some Western-style legal codes and practices, and allowed private practice lawyers, in the first half of the twentieth century (Xu 1995). The formal system of law coexisted with the informal system of law, and this form of coexistence has continued into the present era. The informal legal system consists of the justice dispensed by relatives, friends, colleagues, and workplace or community leaders through informal proceedings; all people in China are subject to such justice.

Mao Tse-tung (or Zedong) led a successful communist revolution in China and established a new regime, the People's Republic of China (PRC), on the Chinese mainland in 1949. After the revolution, the Western-influenced legal system was largely abolished, along with the legal profession (Hipkin 1980; Xu 1995). As has been typically true in such circumstances, revolutionary tribunals administered a form of "popular justice," dedicated to advancing the aims of the revolution. To the extent that formal codes and procedures were adopted, they followed the Soviet model quite closely.

With disintegrating ties between China and the Soviet Union, and the emergence of the Cultural Revolution in 1966, much of the remaining formal legal system (including the written code of law) was swept away in the name of an anti-rightist, ongoing revolutionary struggle; an editorial in the *People's Daily* during this period was entitled "In Praise of Lawlessness" (Leng 1977, 359). The revolutionary Red Guard ruled supreme, and mass trials of perceived enemies of the revolution were widely conducted, although by wholly political as opposed to traditional legal standards. Many Chinese, including some who would resurface later among the top leadership class, suffered greatly from the arbitrary form of justice administered (Ward 1997a). Following China's reestablishment of contacts with the West (including the United States) in the 1970s, and its efforts to stimulate greater economic development, reestablishment of a formal legal system began. This movement probably reflected the recognition that a reliable system of law was necessary if business relations with other nations were to be fostered.

From the early 1980s on, private enterprise was increasingly encouraged or permitted, as a means of promoting economic development. A rising crime rate, including delinquency, gangs, drug trafficking, and conventional crime, was undoubtedly one consequence of this expansion of private enterprise, more freedom, and a growing gap between the well-off and the poor. The government responded with tough anti-crime programs and punishments (Ma 1995; Ward 1997a, 1997b; Yisheng 1997). An increase in corruption involving Chinese officials and their families was another consequence of these developments. In the face of understandable popular resentment of such corruption, the Chinese government passed laws against official profiteering and attempted to crack down on such crime (Gaylord and Levine 1997).

China not only faced formidable challenges in transforming its economy, it also contended with a long history of repression in a world increasingly concerned with human rights. In June 1989, state military forces suppressed and massacred some 5,000 unarmed students and workers participating in a pro-democracy protest demonstration in Tiananmen Square in Beijing; in the wake of this event, show trials were instituted in an attempt by the state to confront global criticism of the massacre and to affirm its commitment to resolving internal conflict by law and not simply by military might (Findlay 1989). By the mid-1990s, many legal reforms had been instituted, with the introduction of numerous new laws, including a Criminal Procedure Law (Elliott 1996; Ward 1997b). Civil liberties were extended, with the police now prohibited from detaining people indefinitely without formal charges; lawyers were made more readily accessible; and the presumption of innocence was affirmed. However, the government reserved the right to charge people with antistate activity and to jail people on this charge. To Westerners, this power is viewed as a means of cracking down on dissidents. On the civil side, with international trade expanding steadily, many new law firms were opening in Beijing. Furthermore, it became possible for citizens to sue the government civilly, and the Chinese people began to turn more readily to law to resolve their grievances (Rosenthal 1998). With judges often poorly educated about law, corrupt, and beholden to local authorities, court decisions continued to be somewhat unpredictable.

Through much of the history of the People's Republic of China, the criminal law has been administered in a way much at odds with procedures in the United States (Rojek 1985). Informal processes have dominated the control of crime, with self-criticism and answering to one's immediate group emphasized. Neighborhood associations and mediation units (known as Danwei) were empowered to administer justice for a wide range of disputes and offenses and could issue warnings or impose fines. The far more limited formal court system was largely reserved for serious crimes or for criminal recidivists. Prosecutors (or procurators) had broad powers, and the matter of guilt or innocence would be determined largely by their investigation. A trial took the form of an inquisition as opposed to an adversarial contest. No exclusionary rule (exclusion of improperly seized evidence) existed, nor did a presumption of innocence (labeled by one commentator as "a worm-eaten dogma of bourgeois doctrine"). Defendants did not enjoy a right against self-incrimination; rather, a strong emphasis on a guilty plea and confession—regarded as therapeutic—governed. Furthermore, a defendant was encouraged to view his offense in terms of an ideological failure on his part, in a manner unimaginable in an American criminal proceeding. For example, in a transcript of a trial (in 1979) of a man accused of stabbing a young woman who spurned him, we find the defendant addressing the Court as follows:

> I committed this crime because I wasn't spending much time studying political thought, and I have a very low political and socialist consciousness. During the Cultural Revolution, I came under the influence of Lin Biao and the Gang of Four. I don't know what the law is and I have bourgeois ideas. (Chi and Chi 1979, 62, 67)

The legal profession, into the 1980s, remained extraordinarily small (estimated to number between 3,000 and 15,000), and these few lawyers were state employees as opposed to private practitioners; legal education was essentially an undergraduate enterprise. Defendants in criminal cases often had to defend themselves or look to a relative or friend for assistance. When defense lawyers did become involved in criminal cases, it was only after the decision to prosecute had been made. The defense lawyer was not expected to contest the claims of the prosecutor but rather might make a plea for mercy or bring some mitigating circumstances on behalf of the defendant to the attention of the Court.

Two "People's Assessors,"—or lay judges without formal legal training—would determine the outcome of a case in conjunction with the judge, and a majority vote governed. These People's Assessors were viewed as representing the conscience of the community. Contrary to what some might imagine, sentences could be mild, emphasizing ideological rehabilitation and prevention. Of course, those who committed heinous crimes or antistate activities could expect harsh sentences, which might include lengthy confinement or summary execution.

The marginal status of law in the People's Republic of China, then, is a reflection of both traditional Chinese influences and the specific agenda of the Communist party. The dominance of informal mechanisms of social control resulted in both harsh and humane outcomes. A rapidly changing and modernizing China will probably depend increasingly on formal law (see Box 6.2).

The Case of Cuba

The revolution in Cuba is the most recent among the socialist countries considered here—occurring in 1959—but by the end of the twentieth century Cuba remained the regime most committed to the principles of communism. Cuba was originally a Spanish colony; after independence, it eventually became a dictatorship under Fulgencio Batista. The prerevolutionary legal system, derived from Spanish law, was structured to favor the privileged classes. Fidel Castro, communist leader of Cuba from 1959 on, was trained as a lawyer, and in 1953 he attempted to challenge the Batista dictatorship in court (Berman 1969; Cantor 1973, 5). His legal challenge was unsuccessful, so he turned to revolutionary means of overthrowing the Batista dictatorship. Castro became contemptuous of the formal legal system and the legal profession, regarding them as corrupt instruments of privilege and oppression (Zatz 1994, 100).

After the 1959 revolution a series of laws were passed that addressed socioeconomic injustices by redistributing land and property (Cantor 1973).

Box 6.2

Lawyers in China Today

In the final decade of the twentieth century, China overhauled its legal system, expanding the rights of those accused of crimes (e.g., giving the right to legal representation), and training thousands of new lawyers (Rosenthal 2000). However, in this new environment, criminal defense lawyers confronted many challenges. The police could deny them access to clients, the court could deny them access to trial transcripts and other essential legal documents, and their witnesses could be intimidated by the authorities. A considerable gap still existed between formally granted rights and the actual implementation of those rights. Confessions were still beaten out of prisoners, despite the ban on such methods in the formal law. In some cases, criminal defense lawyers themselves, if they were especially proactive in representing their clients, were prosecuted and jailed.

The legal profession declined in both size and prestige, and, at least initially, the crime rate apparently declined as well (Cantor 1973, 3; Michalowski 1995, 81). "Popular Tribunals" were established in place of traditional courts to administer justice (Berman 1969). The tribunal judges were laypeople, not trained lawyers. They would handle disputes and grievances with the objective of educating the parties before them about the goals of their revolutionary new society and ideally inducing conformity with these goals. The proceedings, initially witnessed by many ordinary citizens, were highly informal in nature, and inquisitorial as opposed to adversarial.

As was the experience in Russia and China, in Cuba a more formal legal system was eventually reintroduced, in part because the early mass participation in the Popular Tribunals could not be maintained (Irons 1981). Court proceedings, however, focused on getting at the truth in the case, as opposed to legal formalities. Inevitably, the Cuban legal system has evolved and adapted in response to changing conditions (Zatz 1994). Although perceived enemies of the state have been dealt with harshly throughout this period, in other respects this legal system may be well attuned to popular notions of justice and fairness.

Sacred Law

Religion has been one important source of influence on law. The canon law of the Roman Catholic church influenced civil law, and biblical principles have been incorporated into common law. The traditional legal systems of Asian countries reflect religious values as well, from Confucianism in China to Hinduism in India. For some systems of law, however, religious doctrine is the dominant, if not the exclusive, source of law, and there is no clear separation between the religious and the legal. As noted in Chapter 3, this was the case with the early American Pilgrim colony, where the law was derived directly from the Bible. In a sacred law system, some sacred text—be it the Bible, the Talmud, or the Koran—is the basic source of law. No centuries-old sacred text, however, could anticipate the vast range of legal issues surfacing in the modern world. Accordingly, judges in such systems have creatively sought to find legal solutions for new problems by claiming they are being faithful to the wording of the sacred text, even when their ruling appears to be at odds with it. The term "legal fiction" has been applied to this type of legal creativity. As an example:

> In Jewish law, travel on the Sabbath was forbidden; people might walk 2,000 cubits from their towns, but no more. If a person needed to go a bit further, however, he or she could deposit some food at a place at the limit. The Rabbis treated this cache as a "temporary home", giving the person the right to go another 2,000 cubits. (Friedman 1977, 82)

Israel, founded as a Jewish state, has a legal system substantially dominated by religious doctrine, although there is some inevitable tension between religious and secular values. In the Mideast generally the reemergence of Islamic fundamentalism has inspired closer attention to its impact on law. Some 900 million people—or approximately a fifth of the world's population, living in about 60 countries—subscribe to the Muslim faith. At least some countries with a dominantly Muslim population, including Saudi Arabia, Iran, and Libya, base their law on Islamic principles; in the case of the last two of these countries, recent fundamentalist counterrevolutions led to a synthesis of the religious and the legal. Many other countries with a dominantly Muslim population (e.g., Syria, Egypt, Iraq, Lebanon, and Kuwait) have adopted much Western law, although they retain Islamic law on certain matters (e.g., family-related issues) (Freeland 1997).

Because Islam is regarded by the faithful as a whole way of life—not something that can be compartmentalized as a religious practice—it follows that for true believers a valid system of law must be wholly consistent with Islamic doctrine. The Koran, the doctrine communicated by God through the prophet Muhammad in the seventh century A.D., is the sacred text of Islam. The Koran, then, is one source of Islamic law (or "the path to follow"). There are other sources, including collections of teachings and sayings of Muhammad; judicial rulings on issues not specifically addressed by the sacred text; and reports of new principles established by jurists through analogy with established principles of Islamic law (Moore 1996). It must be emphasized that any ruling, whatever its source, cannot be inconsistent with the basic tenets of the Koran. The judgment (fatwa) against Salman Rushdie was a legal ruling issued in 1989 by the Iranian religious and political leader, the Ayatollah Khomeini, that Rushdie's book *The Satanic Verses* was gravely offensive to those of the Muslim faith; it proclaimed that Rushdie and his publishers were deserving of death and offered a monetary reward to any Muslim who killed Rushdie (Pipes 1990).

The criminal justice system under Islamic law operates differently from Western systems. Since there is no clear separation between public and private wrongs, accusers must initiate cases and must provide credible witnesses to support their accusations (Reichel 1999, 106). Ultimately, the parties involved may be required to take an oath to support their claims, with the prospect of a day of reckoning in the afterlife for lying—a powerful force toward inducing honesty. The concerns of victims tend to be taken seriously, and even in serious cases the court will allow the matter to be settled by restitution, if victims are agreeable. Proceedings tend to be conducted informally before a judge (there is no jury); defendants are generally expected to represent themselves, although counsel may assist them; trials on "moral" matters may be closed to the public; judges are expected to apply the principles of sacred law to the evidence at hand (Moore 1996). The process of reviewing judicial decisions is somewhat informal; it may be undertaken by the trial judge himself, and only in limited circumstances does it go to a higher court (Powers 1992). Altogether, Islamic law proceedings tend to move along swiftly, although from a Western vantage point with somewhat inadequate attention to procedural safeguards.

Islamic law, at least as interpreted and applied in countries where fundamentalism is dominant, is viewed by many Westerners as reactionary, irrational, and barbaric (Collier 1994; Freeland 1997). Women's options and activities are very restricted; charging interest for loans is proscribed; ritual religious practices are required; and such penalties as flogging for drinking alcoholic beverages, cutting off a hand for theft, or stoning people to death for adultery are sometimes implemented. From within, and among at least some Western students, Islamic law is viewed as quite flexible and adaptable to modern conditions and at the same time as a means of maintaining the integrity of traditional Muslim values in the face of Western imperialism (Collier 1994; Fluehr-Lobban 1987; Rosen 1989). Susan Hirsch (1998) argues, at odds with a commonly held view, that Muslim women employ the legal process quite effectively to address problems in their domestic lives. Whether the Islamic approach to law effectively deters crime is open to question; while Saudi Arabia has a low crime rate, Iran does not, which suggests that other factors (e.g., the economy) may play a critical role (Kusha 1998). In a world of increasing contacts between Westerners and Muslims, a correct understanding of Islamic law becomes all the more important. The preceding review of "Families of Law" should not be taken to encompass the legal systems of every country (see Box 6.3).

The Historical Perspective on Law

American law is a product of our history and has also been a significant influence on our history. As the great associate justice of the United States, Oliver Wendell Holmes Jr. once put it: "This abstraction called the Law is a magic mirror, [wherein] we see reflected, not only our own lives, but the lives of all men that have been" (Hall 1989, 3).

History is an ancient discipline and an enduring one. History has been used as a means of glorifying and celebrating the past; history meant to glorify is usually selective, disregarding events that might reflect poorly on that history's subject. History has also been used as a means of trying to learn from the past, and here history is far more likely to attend to the discreditable. History also serves as a rich source of entertainment, as many stories from our past are filled with drama and pathos. In the modern era historians have been divided on the question of whether it is possible to provide a truly objective account of the past.

American law professors as a whole have not been all that interested in the history of law. Histories of law that were produced focused principally on

Box 6.3

The Case of Japan

Some legal systems do not fit neatly within one of the recognized families of law. For example, many former colonial nations in Africa and elsewhere are not easily categorized (Moore 1986). Also, some highly developed nations such as Japan are hybrids of different legal systems. The case of Japan is of particular interest to American students of the sociolegal because Japan's experience with law is so different from that of the United States. First, a traditional Oriental aversion to formal law is one important dimension of the Japanese experience. The earliest codes of law introduced into Japan, principally addressing rights of victims of crime and introducing harsh measures for offenders, were based on Chinese law of the period prior to the seventeenth century. During the so-called Tokugawa Period (1600–1868) social control was exercised largely by adherence to Confucian principles of conduct and communal family standards rather than by formal written law. The criminal law that did exist was exceptionally harsh, with torture as one element (Westermann and Burfeind 1991).

After 1868, Japan renewed contact with the West (after a long period of self-imposed isolation). During the latter part of the nineteenth century a constitution reflecting Western influences (including many elements of French and, later, German law) was introduced into the Japanese legal system. These Western elements, however, came to be somewhat overshadowed by the country's growing militarism, which culminated with World War II. After the defeat of Japan in that war and the American occupation, a postwar era witnessed the adoption of a new constitution that reflected the American influence; it decreed diminished powers for the Emperor. Despite the borrowing of many elements of other legal systems—Chinese, French, German, and American—the Japanese legal system is not synonymous with any of these.

Japan apparently has the lowest crime rate of any developed nation. How can one explain this? For violent crime, the rate is close to thirty times lower than that in the United States; furthermore, both the crime rate and the imprisonment rate dropped dramatically through most of the post-World War II era (Reichel 1999, 323–324; Sanders 1996, 329–330). On the one hand, traditional cultural values emphasizing moral obligation to the community, compliance, and habits of order constrain criminal conduct; on the other hand, the broad network of police surveillance of citizens, strong neighborhood police programs, and extensive police powers in connection with arrest, detention, and interrogation also play a role in the low crime rate (Sanders 1996; Steinhoff 1993). In Japan, a strong emphasis on confession in criminal cases leads to some 85 percent of those accused of crimes confessing (Sanders 1996, 335). Trial by jury has not been in use since World War II. The low crime rate, then, is perhaps best understood in terms of the interrelationship between cultural values and justice system practices.

Japan also has an extraordinarily low rate of civil litigation. By some measures, the rate of civil litigation in Japan is about one-twentieth of what it is in an American state (Sanders 1996, 329). Why is this so? The traditional answer has stressed Japanese cultural aversion to invoking the formal processes of law. An alternative answer points to the institutional difficulties of engaging in litigation: cumbersome procedures, high fees, limited numbers of lawyers and judges, and the like (Miyazawa 1987). Furthermore, a Civil Liberties Bureau provides extensive opportunities to mediate cases. Both the traditional and the alternative answers have a measure of truth. There can be little question that Japan has traditionally had an "informalist antilaw ideology of harmony and consensus," which ☞

☞ has been deliberately promoted or encouraged by its leadership; its outlook has been likened to that of the Amish of Pennsylvania (Kidder and Hostetler 1990, 896). A strong cultural emphasis on apology also minimizes civil litigation (Wagatsuma and Rosett 1986; Westermann and Burfeind 1991). For example, when the President of Japan Airlines personally called on and apologized to the families of crash victims following a crash in 1982 where the pilot was apparently liable, no lawsuits resulted (Wagatsuma and Rosett 1986, 488). The Japanese are also less focused on individual rights and more on a network of social relationships and on the importance of resolving differences within this network (Hamilton and Sanders 1992). Japan's lower reliance on formal law can be seen in a positive and in a negative light. There may be less crime and civil litigation in Japan, but people in Japan have fewer rights and are less likely to realize personal justice than Americans.

the development of legal doctrine, on the English common law, and on the adoption of such law by the American system. James Willard Hurst, of the University of Wisconsin law school, is generally credited with having pioneered a new approach to legal history in the mid-twentieth century. In his *The Growth of American Law* (1950) Hurst explored the social and economic factors that shaped American law over time; in this sense, Hurst applied the tenets of legal realism to legal history (Soifer 1992). Hurst shifted attention away from the great cases in appellate court decisions to the other institutions of law, such as the legislature. He saw an erosion of a sense of community in American life, which led to the development of law that basically ignored economic exploitation and conservation of the environment. His book expressed the faith that if law was to be reformed in a constructive way, such reform would have to be based upon a deep understanding of the historical facts that shaped law. With this book and subsequent work, Hurst greatly influenced future generations of legal historians to immerse themselves in the realities of economic, political, and social life and the impact these forces have upon law.

Lawrence M. Friedman of Stanford University Law School, writing in the Hurst tradition in *A History of American Law* ([1973] 1986) and elsewhere, has described American law as a mirror of society, constantly changing, adaptable, and functional, responding to real economic interests, concrete political groups, and various social forces. And Kermit Hall (1989), in *The Magic Mirror: Law in American History*, emphasizes that American law is pluralistic. In addition to law produced by courts and lawyers, legislatures, administrative agencies, and the executive branch produce law; so, too, in a sense, do such informal, nongovernmental institutions as the family, private associations, and trade groups. A history of American law must appreciate the complex of interactions between these different sources of law.

The work of Hurst and Friedman has been criticized (fairly or not) as a form of functionalism, with too much stress on consensus and on law as responding to external economic and social forces (Soifer 1988, 1992). An alternative historical interpretation of American law views it as relatively autonomous (or independent), an instrument of power, and a force that lends legitimacy to the status quo. Such a view, for example, is advanced in Morton J. Horwitz's (1977) *The Transformation of American Law, 1780–1860*. Horwitz attempts to reveal how American law in the nineteenth century was significantly shaped to advance and protect the interests of the rising business class. Law in the critical historical interpretation also has an ideological function: to help persuade the oppressed to accept the existing political and social system, and to enable the oppressors to regard this system as just and fair (Tushnet 1977). Furthermore, the traditional accounts of legal history are viewed as tending to neglect or deemphasize the situation of marginal members of society, which for most of this history includes women and people of color.

Principal Influences on American Law

What are the principal influences on American law? First, and obviously, American law reflects a Western European heritage, with the British (and Anglo-Saxon) heritage dominant. It seems reasonable to suppose, then, that those Americans who are also part of this cultural heritage have adapted more easily to American law than would be true of those from non-Western cultures. A second general influence was surely the character and mission of the early colonists. Many of them—with the Pilgrims as the exemplary case—had suffered from some form of persecution in the Old World, and they were dedicated to creating a society based upon new principles. The extent to which this was true varied among the different colonies, of course, and all of them, over time, would find themselves in conflict with the mother country on some matters.

The harsh living conditions prevailing in the early history of the colonies (and continuing in the American frontier through the later nineteenth century) required a system of law and justice that was often rough, informal, and practical. The American Revolution, which was all about legal rights (as opposed to the maldistribution of material wealth), obviously produced a whole new framework for a legal system based upon democratic principles that were influenced by Enlightenment ideas of "inalienable human rights." The American legal system was also importantly shaped by the needs of an evolving capitalist economy, with its strong emphasis on individual enterprise and a free market. Of course, cultural values other than economic, such as patriarchy (male dominance) and racism, were also reflected in the law. Also, the "nation of immigrants" became increasingly heterogeneous, and the system of law was under some pressure to recognize such diversity, for example with bilingual programs. Even in the earliest period, at least some colonists came from countries and cultures other than British and introduced into American law aspects of their own heritage.

Some important influences on American law can be identified more specifically. First, the Bible has been influential in providing a moral foundation for American law; the law of the Pilgrim colony came quite directly out of the Bible. Second, from the outset, charters, codes, and constitutions have been important in American law, based on a strong inclination to produce a framework for a new type of society. American charters and the Constitution itself were influenced by earlier charters such as the English Magna Carta and the English Bill of Rights, both of which imposed constraints on centralized governmental authority (originally, the Monarch). At the same time the colonies were formed by private company charters and were subject to British control, at least until the Revolution. Third, the English common law was an impor-

Box 6.4

Louisiana Law and the French Influence

Louisiana was for a long time the only American state to retain the direct influence of a French legal heritage and the Napoleonic Code, in particular (Wiehl 1989). Louisiana retained some elements of French contract law and laws affirming the specific privileges of husbands in relation to marital property. Over time, especially in the interest of facilitating commercial transactions with other states, Louisiana law has been revised to conform with the principles of law derived from the English common law tradition.

tant source, both in terms of its according judges the central role of interpreting law and in terms of specific legal principles and rules that came out of this tradition. Sir William Blackstone's ([1765–1769] 1979) *Commentaries on the Laws of England*, which fortuitously appeared shortly before the American Revolution, was a comprehensive summary of the core principles of the English common law, organized into four areas (rights of persons; rights of things, or property; private wrongs, or torts; public wrongs, or crimes), with rationales provided for the law. Although some Americans—notably Thomas Jefferson—criticized Blackstone for a conservative view of the legal system, his work provided a basic source for early American law and was a key text in early legal education (for example, Abraham Lincoln learned law by reading Blackstone).

The common law was originally the law of the king's courts, however, and did not address all of the minor legal issues that might arise on a daily basis. Such issues were addressed by manorial (or local) law, and this aspect of law was especially familiar to colonists who came from small farming villages.

The civil law tradition of continental Europe, while less broadly influential than the English common law, also had some influence. First, from the outset, at least a certain proportion of colonists came from civil law countries, and over time this proportion increased dramatically. In certain colonies, such as that established in Louisiana by the French, the civil law tradition was dominant; in other colonies, in varying degrees, civil law elements were introduced (see Box 6.4). Second, The American Revolution was inevitably accompanied by strong anti-British sentiment, and this inspired lawmakers to look to the traditions of other European countries. And third, the civil law stress on the importance of the legislature was appealing to a new, democractic nation, since legislators are directly elected by the people whereas federal judges are not. American law reformers in the nineteenth and twentieth centuries who attempted to bring order to the maze of legislatively produced laws by producing codes of law were also influenced by this tradition; codes have had the most impact in certain branches of law, such as commercial law or tax law. Despite the legislative bias and the efforts at codification, however, the traditional common law norm according judges considerable power over the interpretation of both Constitutional provisions and legislatively passed laws survived.

Slavery and the African-American Experience of Law

Of the numerous threads that make up the tapestry of American legal history, it would be difficult to identify one more troublesome than the law's complicity in slavery and the overall African-American experience of law (Higginbotham 1978, 1996). From the outset the American colonies contended with a shortage of labor. The use of indentured servants was one early response to this problem. The passage of these servants was paid for by a master, to whom the indentured servant owed between four and seven years of service. Although such servants were not entirely without rights, as a practical matter they were little more than the personal property of the master for the period of indenture and could be easily abused. The first black African slaves, brought to the American mainland in 1619 by John Rolfe of the Virginia colony, had a status equivalent in some respects to that of indentured servants; some who gained freedom became slave owners themselves (Berlin 1998). But from the outset, race cast blacks into a different situation from that of white servants (Morris 1996). Permanent slavery was unknown in the English common law, however, and only became formalized in the latter part of the seventeenth century. The basic law of slavery ("the peculiar institution") in America, then, was in existence for some two hundred years (between 1660 and 1860). The nature of North American slavery varied considerably between different parts of the country, and over time (Berlin 1998). In the deep South, however, the law was shaped by the increasing economic dependence on slave labor; by owners' fear of the growing number of slaves and the need to control them for the safety of whites; and by a racist ideology, which provided rationales for denying blacks full-fledged recognition as human beings.

Over time the slave codes became increasingly race-specific, with slave status inherited through the mother. In the interpretation of historian Frank Tannenbaum (1946), in *Slave and Citizen*, both the conditions of slavery itself and the intensity of racism ultimately took a more extreme form in North America than in Latin America. Tannenbaum attributed this difference to both the influence of the Catholic Church in Latin America (which accorded slaves recognition as souls, entitled to receive the sacraments) and the civil law tradition (which locked in some legal protections); in the predominantly Protestant United States, the humanity of slaves was less easily protected, and the more flexible common law tradition allowed for increasing control over slaves.

By the time of the American Revolution, then, all American colonies had legally sanctioned slavery, although beginning in 1780 with Pennsylvania, the Northern states moved toward its gradual abolition (Hall 1989). This period was also witness to one of the most profound contradictions in American legal history. Many of the same venerated founding fathers (notably Thomas Jefferson) who produced the Constitution and provided the framework for legal rights for future generations of Americans also owned other human beings. John Noonan ([1976] 1994), in addressing the paradox of the "Virginia liberators," invokes the metaphor of "masks" of the law: that is, by seeing slavery in legal terms, and imposing on slaves the "mask" of a legal concept, property, the Virginia liberators were able to avoid confronting the inherent inhumanity of the slave system. And as Noonan ([1970] 1994, 529) observes:

> Slavery's survival in Virginia after the Revolution . . . was assured by the cataloguing power, the rule-making capacity, the indifference to persons of—the law? That is to depersonalize those responsible: better say—the lawyers. Without their professional craftsmanship, without their management of metaphor, without their loyalty to the system, the enslavement by words more comprehensive than any shackles could not have been forged.

Although Jefferson, in his *Notes on the State of Virginia*([1781] 1998), objected to a proposal calling for the emancipation of slaves born after a certain date, it would be a distortion to say that he (and other white Southerners) were wholly indifferent to the humanitarian issues surrounding slavery. (Washington, for example, provided for the emancipation of his slaves following his death.) The Constitution itself did not officially recognize slavery (in fact, the words "slave" and "slavery" do not appear in this document), but several clauses pertaining to rights over those in service and means of calculating the population for purposes of representation and taxation implicitly supported the rights of slaveholders (Hall 1989). On the one hand, the framers of the Constitution can be viewed as having missed a unique opportunity to renounce slavery (and racism), and accordingly they helped set the stage for the Civil War (Bell 1987). On the other hand, some say that the broad language and perspective of the Declaration of Independence and the Constitution made the dissolution of slavery inevitable (West 1998).

In the decades leading up to the Civil War the law of slavery followed a somewhat uneven and inconsistent path, subject to conflicting influences. Slave states all adopted slave codes reaffirming almost total control over slaves by the master; their status as property shifted from real property to personal property (Morris 1996). With a growing anxiety on the part of white Southerners about the increasing size of the black population, and the threat of free black people, the right to manumission (freeing slaves) was limited. But slaves had always been treated as persons as opposed to property when it came to misbehavior on their part and were subject to exceedingly harsh discipline and punishment. Of course, in the context of slavery, such acts as running away or attempting to poison the master could be interpreted as acts of rebellion against an unjust system (Schwarz 1988). Although over time some formal protections against physical abuse and being overworked, and some limited procedural rights, were extended to slaves, as a practical matter slave owners pretty much had a free hand (Morris 1996). Black people could not testify in court against a white person. An ironic historical footnote on this is the following story: George Wythe, a prominent legal authority in colonial Virginia who played a role in drafting laws pertaining to black people, was murdered by a grandnephew; the murderer could not be convicted for the crime, however, because the primary witness against him was a black woman, who was precluded by law from testifying (Bonsignore et al. 1998, 267). The principal form of protection for slaves from ultimate forms of abuse, including being murdered by the master, was this: they were valuable property (Hall 1989). Nevertheless, horrendous abuses were obviously perpetrated on slaves (see Box 6.5).

A landmark legal case in the 1850s brought into sharp relief the status of slaves in the eyes of American law. The case of *Dred Scott v. Sandford* (1857) involved a slave (Dred Scott) who had traveled with his master to a free state territory (Minnesota) and then returned to a slave state (Missouri). Scott's

Box 6.5

The *Amistad* Case and the Law

Over the years various cases arose addressing in some form the question of the ultimate parameters of the slave's status as property. One famous case arose out of a slave mutiny on the ship *Amistad* (celebrated in a 1997 Steven Spielberg film of that name). In 1839 a group of Africans being transported to North America by Portuguese slave merchants mutinied, killed the ship's captain and cook, and ordered the slave traders (held hostage) to sail the ship back to Africa (Jones 1987). The traders deceived the Africans and their leader, Joseph Cinque, and sailed north, to Long Island. The 39 surviving Africans were taken into custody and transported to New London, Connecticut. The question arose whether these Africans had to be returned to their "owners" or were entitled to freedom. Anti-slavery activists took up their cause, and a lawyer, Roger Baldwin, was contracted to represent them. The legal case on behalf of the Africans was based upon two arguably contradictory principles. On the one hand, an argument rooted in natural law theory claimed that since kidnapping and enslaving people was inherently wrong, the Africans could not be considered legal property. On the other hand, an argument rooted in positive law theory held that the Africans had never been formally enslaved by their captors. A Federal District judge ruled that insofar as the Africans had been "born free," they were not slaves and should be released and returned to their homeland. Despite an appeal of this decision to the U.S. Supreme Court by the American president at this time, Martin van Buren, Associate Justice Joseph Story ruled in favor of the African mutineers, although his ruling did not address the question of the legality of American slavery itself. The mutineers were sent back to Africa (and, according to at least one controversial account, their leader Cinque there became involved in the slave trade). But this is one famous case where the law came down on the side of freedom as opposed to slavery.

claim was that he should be recognized as a citizen of Missouri and should be able to sue in federal court for his freedom. Chief Justice Roger Taney of the U.S. Supreme Court denied Scott's petition and held that a black person, whether free or slave, was not entitled to citizenship. This notorious decision, which might be read as the culmination of a long series of common law decisions that had reduced blacks to the status of property, is credited with having contributed to the contentious political environment that brought about the Civil War.

The Thirteenth Amendment of the Constitution, as every American schoolchild learns, declared the emancipation of slaves from their bondage. The history of the Fourteenth Amendment, however, is generally less familiar. The formal rationale for this amendment, which implements rights to "equal protection" and "due process" for all citizens, was to ensure that the Southern states would not pass laws stripping the newly emancipated former slaves of their basic rights (although behind-the-scenes concerns about the redistribution of political power were involved). Despite the Fourteenth Amendment, the Southern states in the latter part of the nineteenth century passed a series of laws, known as Jim Crow laws (or Black Codes), that effectively disenfranchised black Americans, reduced them to second-class citizenship, and imposed upon them segregation from white people in many settings (for example, in schools, hotels, clubs, and on buses and trains) (Woodward 1957). In a series of decisions the United States Supreme Court basically upheld these laws. *Plessy v. Ferguson* (1896) was the single most notorious of these decisions, setting forth a doctrine of "separate but equal." With this doctrine the Supreme Court held that there was no constitutional barrier to segregated (or separate) facilities for blacks and whites, although it also held that such facilities should be "equal." Through the middle of the twentieth century, then, black Americans in the South—and to some extent in the North—endured many forms of discrimination and disadvantage.

The landmark U.S. Supreme Court decision in *Brown v. Board of Education* (1954) repudiated the separate but equal doctrine and called for the end of formal segregation with "all deliberate speed." The decision was not simply based upon principles of legal reason; rather, social and behavioral science studies documenting the damaging effects of segregation on black schoolchildren were cited in the opinion. Many years of resistance and turmoil followed this decision, with the Civil Rights Movement leading the ongoing challenge to segregation and discrimination, sometimes by specifically violating the segregationist laws and policies that continued to be enforced. The passage of the Civil Rights Act of 1964, declaring discrimination illegal as a matter of national policy, is taken to signal the final renunciation of formal segregation. Unfortunately, no such law is able to resolve the deeply ingrained attitudes and patterns of behavior that had developed over a long period of time in the relations between black and white Americans.

At the onset of the twenty-first century, the tragic legacy of the slave laws and the laws upholding segregation in various forms endures in American society. If law has been able to abolish formal segregation, it has not been able to legislate racism out of existence. Indeed, law has been directly complicit in the construction of race and the resulting racism (Lopez 1996). Many black Americans continue to suspect, with some justification, that elements of white racism influence a wide range of decisions and actions, including those of white officers of the law (e.g., the police, prosecutors, judges, and correctional personnel) (Mann 1993). Black Americans are disproportionately represented among those who are arrested, tried, convicted, and incarcerated (and executed) for conventional lawbreaking, and this indisputable fact can be interpreted in a number of different ways: as a reflection of blacks having less respect for law because of their historically negative experience with law; as a consequence of the enduring psychic and social damage brought about through slavery, segregation, and discrimination; and as a result of the racist decision making of a white-dominated system of criminal justice.

Legal measures intended to compensate on some level for past injustices to black Americans and for their continuing underrepresentation in many privileged sectors of American life (e.g., politics; elite schools; the professions) have recently been promoted and adopted. But affirmative action law, busing law, and voting rights law (e.g., race-based districting designed to ensure the election of African-American candidates) have encountered resistance and in some cases a backlash from whites on claims of reverse discrimination. At least some African Americans have also questioned whether affirmative action policies are ultimately self-defeating if they continue to perpetuate the notion that African Americans can only succeed when special accommodations are made for them (Lawrence 1998). Altogether, the movement toward any ultimate resolution of the legacy of slavery was sure to be reflected in developments within law as well as in attitudes and behavior responding to law.

The Contextual Perspective on Law

Is law operational in every context, and what does law mean in extreme circumstances? In many aspects of our private lives, for example, we tend to think of ourselves as living independent of the law. Historically, heads of families were pretty much free to "govern" their family life as they pleased, with little prospect of outside interference. School principals and teachers in the classroom have also been accorded considerable leeway in making and administering their own rules and regulations. Private businesses, as well, have traditionally been left alone to determine procedures and practices governing the workplace. In the modern era, for better or worse, the law has become an increasingly obtrusive presence in the home, in the classroom, and in the workplace. For example, we expect the law to intervene if children or spouses are abused. Principals and teachers are more liable to legal action if their discipline of schoolchildren is deemed excessive. And laws pertaining to minimum wages, safety standards, and (more recently) sexual harassment are among the constraints on the freedom of employers. The ongoing challenge in these contexts, then, is to determine what the proper balance should be between the rights of family members, teachers and students, and employers and employees in terms of self-determination and external law. When should the law intervene, and when should it leave people alone?

A second set of questions arises in the context of a new domain or one not clearly covered by existing legal jurisdiction. Human beings sometimes find themselves in circumstances where they have no recourse to a formal system of law and must rely upon some other means for resolving disputes. Although the lawlessness and violence of the mythic American Western frontier has been overstated, according to some historians, certainly there were circumstances where men (and it was largely men) resolved disputes by whatever means were available to them, and outside the boundaries of formal law (Friedman 1993, 172–192). Increasingly in the modern world, disputes involving corporations occur in a transnational context—in "the space between the laws" (Michalowski and Kramer 1987)—where it is far from clear who has jurisdiction.

This type of issue long arose in connection with crimes and disputes occurring at sea. International maritime agreements spelled out some legal guidelines for such situations, however. And as humans increasingly find themselves engaged in space travel in the twenty-first century, these issues will also arise; indeed, we already have some international agreements on law in outer space.

A parallel set of questions arises in what can be called extreme situations and desperate circumstances. A famous nineteenth-century case in English law, *Queen v. Dudley and Stephens* (1882), addressed the situation of two seamen who killed a dying young sailor and consumed his flesh when they were all shipwrecked off the coast of Africa and found themselves floating in a small lifeboat for days on end (Simpson 1984). The survivors were eventually rescued and brought back to England to stand trial on homicide charges. Many sympathetic members of the British public felt that the ordinary law of homicide should not be applicable in such extreme circumstances, where survival was at stake. The Court disagreed, however, and found the accused guilty and liable to the death penalty (the sentence was commuted to six months in prison by the reigning queen, Victoria, who had followed the case with some interest, as did her subjects).

The circumstance of *war* provides a context that calls into question many conventional assumptions about law. War operates on principles diametrically at odds with the principles upon which legal institutions operate. War addresses disputes (or contending claims) with direct violence, whereas law addresses such disputes and claims with nonviolent (although often coercive) means. As Telford Taylor (1970, 19), a prominent student of law and warfare, has observed: "War consists largely of acts that would be criminal if performed in time of peace—killing, wounding, kidnapping, destroying, or carrying off other peoples' property." Of course, war over the ages has taken many different forms, and wars have been initiated or undertaken for very different reasons. At least some acts of war might be defended on the grounds that they are an extreme if absolutely necessary form of social control exercised in response to the actions of criminal states. Certainly the Allied involvement in World War II against Adolf Hitler and Nazi Germany was justified in this way. At the end of the twentieth century, the intervention of NATO in the Bosnia crisis was widely supported, although it inspired some criticism as well.

Although law and acts of war would seem to be directly at odds, a long history of attempts to impose some legal constraints on war-related activities exists (Falk, Kolko, and Lifton 1971; Howard, Andreopoulos, and Shulman 1994). The general guiding principle has been that the ravages of war should be mitigated as far as possible by prohibiting needless cruelties and other acts that spread death and destruction and are not reasonably related to the conduct of hostilities. In the medieval era, the laws of chivalry required the proper treatment of enemy soldiers taken into custody, as well as respectful treatment of civilians. International conferences in the nineteenth and twentieth centuries led to the adoption of rules of war (e.g., the Geneva Conventions), in response to the development of increasingly destructive weapons; to civilian populations made both more aware (e.g., through photography) of war's brutalities and more vulnerable to military action; and to the onset of the age of "total war." Obviously the rules of war have been widely violated. Furthermore:

> It is one of the many darker ironies of twentieth-century history that, just as the codification of laws respecting noncombatants achieved further refinements, a whole surge of revolutionary struggles, civil wars, and insurgencies have made discriminate warfare more difficult than ever to implement. (Kennedy and Adreopoulos 1994, 215)

Going into the twenty-first century, the single greatest threat was surely the possible use of nuclear weapons (Kauzlarich and Kramer 1998). Despite an International Court of Justice advisory opinion that the use or threat of nuclear weapons would be illegal, it was evident that the nuclear nations (including the United States) were not about to abandon these weapons.

Box 6.6

The My Lai Case

In the single highest-profile case of charging a military officer with war-related crimes, Lieutenant William Calley was tried for acts committed by himself and soldiers under his command in the village of My Lai during the Vietnam War (Taylor, T. 1970). Several hundred Vietnamese children, women, and old men were massacred by Calley and his forces, who had entered the village on the pretext that they were seeking Viet Cong (guerrillas affiliated with the North Vietnamese forces). Photos depicting this atrocity were featured in *Life* magazine. Although many Americans were shocked by this event, Americans were divided on who or what was to blame, and the majority did not support the prosecution of Lt. Calley. Richard Falk (1971, 5), an authority on international law, raised the question of whether there was a truly meaningful difference between killing civilians on the ground, as Calley and his forces did, and killing civilians through bombs and napalm dropped on villages by American B-52s. In response to public sentiment President Nixon commuted Calley's life sentence to a brief term of house arrest on a military base.

It is well understood that the effective operation of any military force requires a command structure, with subordinates obeying and carrying out the commands of superior officers. But how far should this principle be carried, especially when subordinates carry out atrocities either in response to a specific command or on the basis of their understanding of what is expected of them. The Nuremberg Trials of the surviving Nazi leadership and of those complicit in crimes of war or crimes against humanity established the principle that superiors' orders do not provide an uncontestable defense against charges of having committed acts at odds with international law and international accords on the laws of war (Harris [1954] 1995). Soldiers have faced charges for deserting the battlefield or refusing to participate in acts of war. But they have also faced charges for acts carried out in the context of military operations. In his book *A Rumor of War* Philip Caputo (1977), who served as a lieutenant in Vietnam, provides us with a vivid sense of some contradictions involved in training soldiers to kill and then charging them with the crime of killing. In Caputo's case he and his men killed two Vietnamese they took to be enemies and then found themselves facing charges by the legal office of the Army (see Box 6.6).

As is well known, large numbers of Americans challenged the legality of American involvement in the Vietnam War, calling it an immoral imperialistic adventure. Since war was never specifically declared by Congress, its legality was challenged on Constitutional grounds as well, but there were not enough votes on the United States Supreme Court in favor of hearing this case (Ely 1990). An International Tribunal held in Sweden and chaired by the eminent philosopher Bertrand Russell found the United States guilty of war crimes under international law, but this tribunal had no means of implementing its finding against a powerful nation and its leadership (Falk, Kolko, and Lifton 1971, 73). Although at least one of the primary architects of the American involvement in the Vietnam War, Robert McNamara (1995), Secretary of

Defense under Presidents Kennedy and Johnson, later conceded that decisions made by the American leadership were wrong, no member of this leadership was ever formally tried before a legal tribunal.

Since the end of the Vietnam War other military engagements have raised questions from a legalistic perspective. For example, the International Court of Law found the United States guilty of crimes against international law for its complicity in the mining of the Nicaragua capital city's harbor during the civil war in that country (Simon 1999, 196). Other American military initiatives (including invasions of Grenada and Panama), although generally supported by the American people, were also challenged in relation to international law.

The relation between law, war, and violence is complex, then, and the circumstance of war offers us a singular context for thinking about law.

Conclusion

The anthropological, comparative, historical, and contextual perspectives on law considered in this chapter raise endlessly fascinating and persistently important questions about the nature of law in relation to social existence. These perspectives, then, provide us with vantage points for studying and understanding law that differ from conventional, everyday ways of relating to law. Such perspectives should deepen and enrich our grasp of law in our lives.

Key Terms

allotment
American Indian Movement (AIM)
Amistad
Brown v. Board of Education (1954)
canon law
civil law tradition
codification
commodity exchange theory of law
common law tradition
double institutionalized
Dred Scott v. Sandford (1857)
Eskimo Drum Song "Court"
idealistic, traditional, and pragmatic views of law
instrumental interpretation
Jim Crow laws
the Koran
legal fiction
manumission
masks of the law
Plessy v. Ferguson (1896)
Queen v. Dudley and Stephens (1882)
sacred law tradition
social and cultural anthropology
socialist law tradition
structural interpretation
the dozens
tribal sovereignty

Discussion Questions

1. Does law necessarily have to be an established set of rules with sanctions? Can customs such as the Eskimo Drum Song be law?
2. If American Indians are recognized as American citizens, why should minor crimes and some civil matters occurring on reservations be dealt with in tribal courts as opposed to state courts?
3. Discuss the principal, general influences on American law. Discuss specifically the role both the civil and common law traditions played in influencing the law. As we enter the twenty-first century, what do you think will become the major influences on law?
4. Explain John Noonan's metaphor of "masks" of law. Discuss how Thomas Jefferson played a role in the slavery issue. Does Noonan's metaphor offer any possible explanation as to why slavery was able to endure for more than two hundred years?
5. Should soldiers in the military be prosecuted for the killing of enemies in war? What if the killing is unnecessary or excessively cruel? Include comments on the William Calley case in your response.

Chapter Seven

The Legal Profession

Lawyers are all over; lawyers are everywhere. At least in America, lawyers seem to be everywhere. The highest political officials in the American political system are disproportionately lawyers. When these political officials get into trouble, armies of lawyers are involved in both prosecuting and defending them. Still more lawyers are called upon to comment on and make sense of these cases for the general public. The many different legal charges made against President William Jefferson Clinton, culminating in an impeachment trial, exemplified this situation.

Since matters involving law—from sensational murder cases to major civil lawsuits—dominate the news generally, the public is also exposed to the actions of still more lawyers. Inevitably, then, newsmagazines and newspapers devote much space to law-related matters, with the role of lawyers highlighted. Judges and prosecutors are among the public officials most frequently in the news. Television has also increasingly featured real trials. Court TV is a cable channel exclusively devoted to such trials, and for a time in the mid-1990s the O. J. Simpson trial became a national obsession. Numerous books on the O. J. Simpson case were published, and nonfiction accounts of legal cases featuring lawyers have been staples of the best seller lists.

The fascination with legal matters is reflected in the entertainment side of the media as well. Shows featuring lawyers are staples of prime-time television. They have included *Perry Mason*, *The Defenders*, and *Owen Marshall* in an earlier era; *L.A. Law*, *Ally McBeal*, and *The Practice* more recently. On daytime TV such shows as *The People's Court*, *Judge Judy*, and *Divorce Court* have been popular fare, featuring judges resolving actual or dramatized cases. Countless films feature lawyers, often portrayed in heroic terms in earlier films but more negatively in recent films (Greenfield and Osborn 1995).

Reflecting traditional patterns and values, the lawyers portrayed have been principally male and white. Historically, when women lawyers appeared in films, they were often portrayed in stereotypical or negative terms; only some more recent films—e.g., *Jagged Edge* (1985) and *The Client* (1994)—have featured women lawyers as relatively independent professionals (Bailey and Hale 1998, 185–191; Caplow 1999). Many best-selling novels—for example, those of John Grisham and Scott Turow—focus on lawyers as well. As

David Ray Papke (1995, 3) has observed, "No other culture so frequently and prominently features lawyers in its plays, novels, and movies." Stewart Macaulay (1987, 197) claims that "more Americans learn about their legal system from television and film than from firsthand experience." Although such observers note that media representations of lawyers and the legal process are often distorted, they agree that such representations are very influential in how people think about lawyers. They may not only inspire some to apply for law school, they may even affect the courtroom behavior of lawyers themselves (Margolick 1990). Any serious understanding of lawyers, then, must attend to how lawyers are portrayed in the popular culture.

Many members of society may harbor the hope that they will not personally have to retain a lawyer; in the long haul, however, some contact is inevitable: a real estate closing occurs; an accident happens, followed by a lawsuit; a will must be implemented; a divorce is sought, and child custody is in question; personal bankruptcy arises; an investment loss raises questions of fraud; and so on. In all such circumstances, and not simply the obvious but generally unanticipated circumstance where one finds oneself charged with a criminal act, a lawyer is likely to be retained. Lawyers, then, are all over; lawyers are everywhere. This chapter attempts to provide a general understanding of the nature and character of the legal profession and legal education.

A Brief History of the Legal Profession

Americans today generally assume that if they find themselves charged with a significant violation of law or become parties to a major lawsuit they will be represented by a lawyer. Through most of history, however, those in trouble with the law or parties to litigation were not represented by lawyers (Friedman 1977; Vago [1994] 1996). In preliterate societies nothing that we might recognize as a legal profession has ever existed. Even if lawyers in some rudimentary form can be traced far back in the tradition of Western developed nations, it does not follow that those who found themselves in a court of law also had lawyers. Rather, through most of history people generally were expected to make their own case; this remains true in many countries today.

The origins of the legal profession in the Western tradition are traced principally back to ancient Rome, where certain individuals were allowed to argue cases on behalf of others (Friedman 1977, 21). Those who were especially knowledgeable about law, and were consulted on legal issues, were known as Juris Prudentes (Vago 1994, 256). It is certainly ironic from the modern perspective that the orators who represented people before courts or tribunals were not permitted to collect a fee for this service. Over time, as the Roman Empire expanded during the Imperial Period, a legal profession emerged in response to the increasing complexity of the law itself. With the fall of Rome and the coming of the Dark Ages, the role of lawyers shrank. Such lawyers as could be found in premodern Europe were often affiliated with the Church and addressed issues arising in canon law (Berman 1983). The reemergence of the legal profession as an important force in continental European countries is linked with the emergence of a capitalist economy, since such an economic system creates a substantial demand for legal services.

The American legal profession is primarily descended from the English tradition. Originally in England litigants represented themselves, and the role of lawyer only emerged in the late thirteenth century (Harding 1973). Early legal practitioners received their training through apprenticeship and in some cases at the Inns of Court, where judges and other parties with court-related business resided (and socialized) during the trial term (Prest 1986). In the Middle Ages English lawyers had several different functions: as agents, appearing in court on behalf of someone else; as advocates, trained in oratory to make arguments before court on behalf of clients; and as jurisconsults, or advisers on legal matters (Jeffery 1962, 314–315). Into the eighteenth century no conception of lawyer in the modern sense existed, since many different parties provided various legal services; these parties included scriveners, or writers of legal documents; pleaders, or those who filed pleas; and conveyancers, or those who prepared instruments for transfer of property. Only by the end of the eighteenth century does the legal profession emerge as a full-time occupation, with licensing for practice, a professional association, an emerging monopoly over legal services, a code of ethics, and growing emphasis on formal education in law. In England a basic division emerged between barristers, or trial lawyers, and solicitors, or office lawyers.

Lawyers in America

In America none of the first settlers in the seventeenth century was a lawyer (Hall 1989). Certainly, life in the early colonies had little to attract lawyers. Furthermore, many of the original settlers were antagonistic toward lawyers, who were associated with the upper classes and with the religious persecution many of these settlers had endured in England. Indeed, laws were passed in the seventeenth century in a number of colonies prohibiting the collection of fees for legal services, and an early visitor to Pennsylvania reported that

> they have no lawyers. Everyone is to tell his own case, or some friend for him . . . 'Tis a happy country. (Roth and Roth 1989, 49)

Only gradually did some individuals begin to practice law on a part-time basis; the law they practiced was less technical than that in England. Typically these lawyers were educated in law by apprenticeship, although some traveled to England to learn law at the Inns of Court. With the evolution of colonies into rapidly growing centers of commerce and trade throughout the eighteenth century, greater reliance upon lawyers became inevitable, and hostility toward them declined (Burrage 1988). Accordingly, by the time of the American Revolution, lawyers were conspicuously present. Some of the most famous leaders in the revolutionary cause—including John Adams, Thomas Jefferson, and John Marshall—were lawyers, and lawyers were especially well represented among the signers of the Declaration of Independence, members of the Constitutional Convention, and representatives to the first Congress (Schwartz 1974, 17). For the most part, however, members of the legal profession tended to be conservatives who sided with the King, and many left the Colonies at this time.

Box 7.1

Lawyer Presidents

American presidents who were lawyers or had a legal education, taught law, or held a legal (e.g., judicial) post include: Adams (John and John Quincy), Jefferson, Madison, Jackson, Van Buren, Tyler, Polk, Fillmore, Pierce, Buchanan, Lincoln, Hayes, Garfield, Arthur, Cleveland, Benjamin Harrison, McKinley, Taft, Wilson, Coolidge, Franklin D. Roosevelt, Truman, Nixon, Ford, and Clinton.

When the Frenchman Alexis de Tocqueville ([1835–1840] 1945) visited the relatively young republic of the United States in the 1820s, he made the astute observation that lawyers had become the "new aristocracy," having moved into the power vacuum created by a society that repudiated the notion of a ruling class of the nobility. It has continued to be the case in the subsequent history of the United States that lawyers have been vastly overrepresented in the government and political system. As of the end of the twentieth century, well over half—or 26 of 41—American presidents had been lawyers. One American president, William Howard Taft, later served as Chief Justice of the United States Supreme Court. With the last presidency of the twentieth century, both the president (Bill Clinton) and, for the first time, the first lady (Hillary Rodham Clinton), were lawyers (see Box 7.1).

At times, as much as two-thirds of the U.S. Senate and one-half of the House have been lawyers (Glendon 1994, 12). Among state governors and legislators, as well as among local elected officials, lawyers have been overrepresented (Meinhold and Hadley 1995, 366). By the end of the twentieth century the representation of the legal profession among state legislators in particular had declined quite significantly (e.g., in New York State from 61 percent in 1969 to 34 percent in 1999) (Perez-Pena 1999). Legislative duties had expanded to the point where it had become increasingly difficult to maintain a legal practice on the side; state legislative salaries were no longer competitive with private practice income; and financial disclosure requirements for legislators compelled lawyers to reveal more than they wished about their legal practice and clients.

Despite some proportional decline, lawyers remain a dominant force in American political life. Although this situation is not unique to the United States, since lawyers are overrepresented in the governments of at least some other countries, the American case is especially striking. Even when lawyers do not hold elective or appointive office here, they wield extraordinary political influence as power brokers and lobbyists.

Tocqueville ([1835–1840] 1945) recognized that lawyers as a whole tend to be conservative, since their own interests are aligned with a stable order governed by formal rules. Of course, numerous exceptions to this tendency can be identified. Jerome Auerbach has argued (1976) that elite lawyers from the nineteenth century on have been directly complicit in perpetuating many forms of injustice and inequality in America. Throughout much of the nineteenth century, however, most lawyers were unaffiliated solo practitioners who rode the circuit to appear before courts in session in their general area (Friedman [1973] 1986, 270–271). Also, at this time neither a law degree nor a college education was required to practice law, and admission to practice was open. Most lawyers acquired their legal knowledge principally through self-education and apprenticeship (Abel 1986). In the first half of the nineteenth century, in particular, there was relatively little regulation of legal practice (Burrage 1988). Great oratorical skills—famously represented by Daniel Webster—were much emphasized in an era when argument before the court was at the heart of legal practice.

By the latter part of the nineteenth century, in response to the exploding growth of industrial capitalism and expanding cities teeming with new immigrants, the legal profession also grew and changed (Hall 1989). During this period, for example, large law firms closely affiliated with major corporations and big businesses began to appear, and "office lawyering" skills involving drafting of legal documents and negotiation with adversaries became increasingly important.

Twentieth-Century Lawyers

Throughout the twentieth century, the legal profession in the United States experienced periods of little growth, followed by periods of formidable growth and diversification (Abel 1989). At the beginning of this century a tightening of requirements for entrance into the legal profession took place (Abel 1986). The apprenticeship system was almost entirely replaced as a mode of entry into the profession by college education and law school, with a three-year curriculum ultimately becoming the standard (although as late as 1917 no American state required law school attendance as a condition for engaging in legal practice; Abel 1986, 382). Law schools affiliated with elite universities had the most prestige and provided the most probable route to a successful career with a prominent law firm or eventual service in a high position within the government.

Passing the bar exam became a universal condition for admittance to legal practice (Abel 1986, 380). Bar exams became more rigorous from 1876 on (Abel 1986, 380). Passing a state bar exam was a condition for admittance to legal practice in every state by 1940 (Hall 1989, 258). The American Bar Association and state bar associations, through the course of the twentieth century, adopted various requirements and rules that would enhance their control over who would be allowed to practice law and would protect the economic interests of private lawyers. Accordingly, those without formal credentials were largely excluded from practicing law, and minimum fee schedules were adopted to deter lawyers from engaging in costly price-cutting.

Although the dominance of white Anglo-Saxon Protestant males declined somewhat in the first half of the twentieth century, with the entry into legal practice of second-generation offspring of the immigrants who had poured into the country, women and blacks were systematically (and formally) excluded for much of this period. Only in the last several decades of the twentieth century was there a significant movement of women into the legal profession. (The influx of women and their experience is discussed later in this chapter.) People of color also entered the legal profession in larger numbers during this period. Despite the rapidly changing makeup of the legal profession, it is still clearly the case, early in the twenty-first century, that white males disproportionately occupy the most prestigious judgeships and law firm partnerships, and continue to dominate the American Bar Association, as well as the legal profession itself (see Box 7.2).

Box 7.2

Law Licenses and Good Character

To win admission to the bar, it is not sufficient that prospective lawyers have acquired a law degree and passed the bar exam; they must also be found to be "of good character." The standards for good character have varied historically and between states and have been applied somewhat inconsistently (e.g., rejecting a candidate with parking offenses but approving a convicted child molester) (Allen 1999). Applicants have been turned down if they were in arrears on child support payments; had neglected to settle overdue debts; or had been convicted of substance abuse and had not sought treatment. Altogether, however, denial of admission to the bar on the character issue is rare.

Some cases have raised exceptional or provocative issues for the character test. In a New York case, a lawyer who had bludgeoned his wife and three children to death and had been found not guilty by reason of insanity sought restoration of his license to practice law after having completed many years of psychiatric treatment (Margolick 1993a). In an Arizona case a man who had shot another man to death in a failed drug deal and had served eighteen years in prison sought admission to law school (Gross 1993). One question in this case was whether a record as a model prisoner and academic excellence should offset the original crime on the character issue. In an Illinois case a man who headed a white supremacist group was denied admission to the bar (Allen 1999). Some lawyers argue that the character question should focus solely on matters that might directly harm clients (such as an embezzlement conviction) and that denial to a white supremacist raises free speech issues.

The ABA

The American Bar Association (ABA), founded in 1878, and state bar associations came to play especially important roles in the development of the legal profession in the twentieth century (Flood 1985). For most of this history the ABA has been dominated by white males, only declaring in 1943 that members would not be excluded on the basis of race, creed, or color. By the end of the century, the ABA had become the largest professional association in the world (Segal 1983). The bar association has taken an active role in promoting reform in legal education, establishing standards for admission to the bar, and drafting uniform laws for adoption by the states. It engages in many other activities, including the sponsorship of research and the publication of various journals and reports. In 1908 it adopted Canons of Professional Ethics (replaced, in 1969, with the Code of Professional Responsibility). Despite its adoption of such codes and initiatives to promote more equal access to justice, the primary objective of the ABA, in one standard interpretation, has been the protection and advancement of the professional and economic interests of lawyers.

What Contemporary Lawyers Do

Through the mid-twentieth century, the vast majority of American lawyers (some 90 percent) were in private practice, and of these the majority (some 60 percent) were solo practitioners (Abel 1989). In the second half of the twentieth century the American legal profession underwent changes. It began to grow rapidly in response to an expanding economy. Law school applications multiplied dramatically. Law schools were able to be more selective. Also, from the early 1970s on, they began to admit growing numbers of women and minorities. The law profession became increasingly competitive, especially during periods of economic stagnancy and downsizing (for example, in the early 1990s). In the 1970s the U.S. Supreme Court struck down bar association minimum-fee schedules and bans on lawyers' advertising, which allowed lawyers to compete more aggressively for clients.

In a series of decisions in the 1960s and 1970s the Court also struck down state rules prohibiting (as unlawful solicitation) labor union lawyers from voluntarily advising injured union members and dependents (Seron 1993, 400). With the expansion of rights to representation for poor people accused of crimes (with the government supplying or at least paying for the lawyers), as well as the growth of governmental regulatory agencies, the percentage of lawyers in private practice declined, while the numbers working for the government on some level increased.

In the private sector lawyers increasingly joined law firms, and some law firms became huge, with thousands of lawyers working in branches spread across the country (Galanter and Palay 1991; Nelson 1988). The partners in such law firms may well draw seven-figure annual incomes, depending upon the size of profits. Firms such as Skadden Arps and Baker & MacKenzie had, by the mid-1990s, gross incomes exceeding $500 million (Nader and Smith 1996, 370). Most of the lawyers working in such firms are salaried associates, who may hope to make partner after seven years of service; the majority in a large firm will not be invited to be partners and will have to move on. "Rainmakers," partners who are able to attract a significant number of high-paying clients to the law firm, are inevitably prized as partners; some high-profile politicians are offered partnerships in major law firms less for their skills as lawyers than for their rainmaking potential.

Corporations and businesses also hired lawyers as full-time employees (in-house lawyers) in increasing numbers. At the same time, legal clinics began to open, to provide ordinary citizens with convenient, economical legal services. Jacoby and Meyer pioneered this approach in the late 1970s and by the 1990s had some 150 branch offices nationwide. Franchise law firms provided mass production of standardized legal services, although this also meant that lawyers in these firms were less autonomous, less well compensated, and less satisfied (Van Hoy 1997a). Prepaid legal service plans also became more common. With these plans, individuals or associations pay a preset monthly fee giving them access to a lawyer's services for such matters as house closings or reviews of contracts. In the mid-twentieth century the great majority of American lawyers (perhaps 85 percent) were self-employed, but by the end of the century less than half were, and most of those coming out of law school secured their first jobs as employees (Abel 1989). The increasing percentage of lawyers who find themselves working for an organization of some kind must adjust to the needs of the organization (Spangler 1986). The traditional status of lawyers as independent and autonomous was obviously eroding.

Lawyers were being called upon to address an expanding repertoire of matters, beyond such traditional legal issues as wills, contracts, personal injury lawsuits, and the like. Corporate lawyers were becoming increasingly involved in a range of business-related issues on behalf of clients, and the lines of demarcation between legal and financial matters were eroding. Lawyers for ordinary private citizens faced increasing competition from banks, real estate agents, and other providers of services, and had to be creative in offering new services to their clients. In many areas of legal practice, lawyers have to find the right balance between aggressive pursuit of their client's case and flexibility toward negotiating a resolution of conflict; the emotional minefield of divorce law exemplifies this issue (Sarat and Felstiner 1995). They also have to persuade clients who may be determined to achieve vengeance to focus on a legally realistic settlement of their case. The work of lawyers has been described as involving the "management of uncertainty" in a constant process of interaction with clients and other lawyers, among other parties (Flood 1991; Shamir 1995). With the emergence of a variety of social movements, lawyers were called upon to represent new constituencies and new types of claims, such as women's rights, gay rights, environmental protection, and consumer protection.

Lawyers' Ideological Orientations

As noted earlier, lawyers as a whole have tended to be conservative, and they have disproportionately represented the privileged and the powerful. It is also a long-standing tradition for many law firms to do a certain amount of "pro bono" (free) legal work for clients who cannot afford to pay legal fees. The American Bar Association encourages but does not require law firms to do a certain amount of such work. One law firm, Hale and Dorr, describes its pro bono work as including

> criminal defense for the indigent, drug treatment programs, death row cases, representation of handicapped advocacy groups, public policy cases, and cases involving freedom of speech . . . real estate work for community development corporations and other organizations dedicated to providing shelter to low-income and homeless individuals, battered women, the elderly, and people with HIV/AIDS. (Quoted in Nader and Smith 1996, 341)

On the whole, however, pro bono work tends to be carried out on a modest scale, if at all, and rarely draws upon the skill, knowledge, and connections of powerful law firms to challenge fundamental inequities, as opposed to commonplace injustices (Nader and Smith 1996, 339–347). The advantages of the powerful and privileged are generally unaffected by pro bono work.

Some lawyers have been liberal in orientation. The American Civil Liberties Union, for example, has ardently championed the defense of the Bill of Rights, broadly interpreted, since its founding in 1917 (Walker 1990). The National Lawyers Guild, founded in 1936, has promoted a leftist agenda. It has been active in advocating progressive legislation on such matters as rent control, in defense of union workers, on behalf of international justice and human rights, in opposition to repressive legislation directed at political dissidents, and on behalf of women, gays, and other beleaguered or discriminated-against constituencies (Black 1971; Brown 1938). In the 1960s era in particular some lawyers came to be identified with radical causes; William Kunstler, a key lawyer in the Chicago 7 case involving leading radicals of the

Box 7.3

Paralegals

The demand for paralegals was expanding at the outset of the twenty-first century, and it was one of the fastest-growing occupations in the United States (Fried 2000; Carlson 1997). The number of paralegals was expected to increase from approximately 136,000 in 1998 to some 220,000 by 2008. The paralegal is employed by a law firm or lawyer to do legal research, draw up court papers, and double-check the accuracy of briefs prepared by lawyers. A paralegal cannot offer legal advice, set fees, or present cases in court. Since lawyers today may earn as much as several hundred dollars an hour, it is much more cost-efficient to assign certain routine legal tasks to paralegals, at a cost closer to $100 an hour.

No hard and fast qualifications for becoming a paralegal presently exist, and no states presently require licensing for paralegals. Some 800 programs preparing people for paralegal work range from certificate courses over several months to selective baccalaureate programs. While some paralegals pursue this work as a long-term career, others are prospective lawyers postponing application to law school and exploring their affinity for careers as lawyers.

time, was arguably the most famous of these (Black 1971; Margolick 1993b). More recently, the term "cause lawyering" has been adopted for lawyers whose highest priority is their ideological commitment and dedication to bringing about social change in the form of reducing social, economic, and political inequality (Sarat and Scheingold 1998). The term is principally associated with leftists promoting progressive reforms, although, of course, some lawyers are dedicated to promoting right-wing and fundamentalist causes (for example, putting prayer back in the schools and criminalizing abortion). In authoritarian third-world countries, cause lawyering has been primarily associated with defensive tactics in challenging repression of dissidents and other "enemies of the state"; in liberal, developed countries, cause lawyers have typically had more freedom to affirmatively promote basic reforms (Sarat and Scheingold 1998). Cause lawyers are centrally involved in human rights issues, such as the Israel/Palestinian situation (Hajjar 1997). In the current generally conservative political environment in the United States, cause lawyers have often been fighting a losing battle, and must settle for occasional minor victories (for example, keeping death row clients alive a little longer as opposed to bringing about the abolition of the death penalty).

By the beginning of the twenty-first century the American legal profession was extraordinarily large, heterogeneous, and divided; it was less autonomous, more specialized, and more competitive than in previous times (Abel 1989; Heinz and Laumann 1997; Kelly 1994) (see Box 7.3). The legal profession in an emerging postmodern world has been interpreted as playing a critically important role in determining the distribution of power and wealth in society, all too often on behalf of the powerful and privileged (Cain and Harrington 1994).

A Comparative Perspective on the Legal Profession

The legal profession in civil law, Islamic, and socialist countries differs significantly from the form it takes in the United States (Abel 1988; Abel and Lewis 1995). To begin with, no unified legal profession represented by a common association such as the American Bar Association exists. Judges and practicing lawyers are educated with different curriculums and do not share a common identity. Law is studied as part of an undergraduate curriculum, and both the content and the pedagogical style of legal education is different from that in common law countries. The largest percentage of those who study law go into the civil service, serve as judges or prosecutors, or work for a commercial enterprise rather than becoming private practitioners. Although many forces in the recent era have led to an expansion of the numbers going into some form of legal practice in civil law countries, as has been true in common law countries, numerous differences in terms of self-identification, mode of entry into the field, and form of practice persist between the two systems.

The case of Japan, which was substantially influenced by the civil law tradition, is especially striking. Recognition of a distinctive legal profession did not exist prior to the 1860s (Rokumoto 1988). A legal system, roughly modeled on that of Germany, was introduced only at about this time, and the special standing of judges and prosecutors was recognized. Due to the traditional Japanese aversion to formal litigation, the legal profession grew very slowly. The ratio of lawyers to the general population is only 1 to 10,000, about a sixth of what it is in European civil law countries and a fraction of the ratio in the United States (Rokumoto 1988, 163; Harnett 1984, 37). This ratio is misleading in certain respects because many "legal" functions in Japan are carried out by others, including the equivalent of paralegals (Sanders 1996, 321). Lawyers, for the most part, are part of the civil service; they are not likely to specialize; and much of their work is quite routine. Less than 2 percent of those who take the legal examination that is a necessary precondition for becoming a lawyer pass; and of those who do pass, many do not go on to the formal practice of law but may go into business or some other pursuit. Despite the poor odds of being admitted to legal practice, for those who do succeed it is not an especially prestigious or necessarily lucrative career—in contrast to a career in law in the United States.

The Stratification of the Bar and the Organization of Legal Practice

All American lawyers have some things in common. In our era they have almost certainly completed three years of law school, have passed a bar exam, and are subject to a professional code of ethics. All lawyers have acquired some familiarity with basic principles of law, the language of law, and standard legal practices. And in a very general sense all lawyers share a professional status with a mix of positive and negative connotations. But beyond this, the legal profession is highly stratified, with vast differences in the nature of lawyers' practices, incomes, lifestyles, and identities. Indeed, some scholars say that lawyers reflect class divisions within the larger society, with some lawyers part of a capitalist class and others part of a worker class (Hagan, Huxter, and Parker 1988).

Strata

On the high end, in terms of income and social prestige, we find corporate lawyers, or Wall Street lawyers. They are most likely to be white males from privileged backgrounds, graduates of elite universities and law schools (such as Harvard, Yale, and Stanford), enjoying six- and seven-figure annual incomes, and representing wealthy and powerful corporations, financial enterprises, and individuals (Smigel 1964; Nader and Smith 1996). They spend most of their time not in courtrooms but in meetings with clients (whom they advise) and other parties, and drafting letters, reviewing complex legal documents, negotiating settlements, and the like (Flood 1991).

On the other end of the scale we find struggling solo practitioners, working out of small offices in inner-city neighborhoods (Carlin 1994). They are more likely to be members of ethnic, racial, or religious minorities who have attended public colleges and night law schools. Most earn a modest income by providing moderate- or low-income individual clients with a variety of services, including representation against criminal charges, drawing up of wills, representation in landlord–tenant disputes, and the like. Of course, between these extremes, there are lawyers practicing in a great diversity of settings and circumstances. Nevertheless, according to one major study of the Chicago bar, lawyers are likely to have far more in common with their clients than with each other (Heinz and Laumann 1982).

Organization

With the beginning of the twenty-first century, legal practice was increasingly specialized, with corporate practice growing and business litigation increasing; the number of solo lawyers continued to decline (Heinz et al. 1998). Among lawyers who continue to work solo or in small firms, some adhere to a traditional style of lawyering (emphasizing independence, autonomy, client service, and community networks) and some have adopted a commercial or entrepreneurial style (emphasizing business and market concerns) (Seron 1996). In the emerging economy those with a commercial orientation may be better positioned to survive in a competitive environment. While most of these lawyers are generalists, some concentrate in one of the following areas: business-corporate, real estate, tax, personal injury, divorce, will-probate-estate, criminal, and collections (Carlin 1994). Much of the work performed in these areas is routine, and requires little in the way of professional skills.

The characteristics described in the preceding paragraphs pertain to the great majority of American lawyers (over 85 percent), who are concentrated in metropolitan areas. A study of country lawyers found that they operated differently from their big-city counterparts (Landon 1990). Country lawyers have to be especially sensitive to the perceptions and values of their community, which makes it difficult for them to take on controversial cases (e.g., defending an alleged sexual abuser, filing a civil suit against the local school board, or suing a popular local doctor for malpractice). These lawyers are especially likely to become deeply involved in the lives of their clients, who may well be relatives, neighbors, or friends. Although such lawyers are typically conservative in their outlook, they also tend to embrace a small-town sympathy for the underdog, or the beleaguered individual up against an impersonal bureaucratic institution.

Lawyer-Client Relationships

Whose interest is the lawyer truly representing? Ralph Nader and Wesley J. Smith (1996, xvi) differentiate between the role of attorney, who represents the client's interests, and lawyer, who is a professional with duties to the justice system and the public interest. Although the more familiar term lawyer is adopted in the discussion that follows, the majority surely function more as attorneys in the sense just suggested. Any lawyer typically contends with conflicting pressures and obligations. Obviously a lawyer is supposed to represent the best interests of the client. But lawyers are also sworn officers of the court, as well as members of a larger public. The lawyer is formally obligated not to be a party to a sworn falsehood in court. Also, the lawyer may be oriented toward cooperating with other court figures (the "courtroom workgroup," including the judge and opposing lawyer) with whom the lawyer must maintain an ongoing relationship. The lawyer cannot easily be indifferent to the views and well-being of the larger public, since both professional and personal relationships can be jeopardized if the lawyer takes steps seen as harmful to the public interest. Lawyers in a more direct sense naturally are concerned with their own self-interest, including maximizing their income.

The richer and more powerful the client, the more likely that the client will dominate the lawyer, and the lawyer will have to do the client's bidding. But corporate lawyers, and those representing the rich, are not necessarily simply hired guns. First, they often come from a background similar to that of corporate executives and share the same values and outlook. Second, wherever possible, they may put their own interests before those of the client. In a study of elite lawyers during the New Deal era, for example, Ronen Shamir (1995) found that these lawyers' crusade against the New Deal was driven more by its perceived threats to their own interests as lawyers than threats to the interests of their corporate clients. At the same time, corporate lawyers have been accused of zealously protecting and advancing the interests of powerful corporations in ways that compromise the rights, interests, and physical well-being of ordinary citizens, consumers, and workers. Ralph Nader and Wesley J. Smith (1996) set forth a potent and thorough indictment of the ways in which corporate lawyers lobby, negotiate, obfuscate, manipulate, and even break laws on behalf of their clients, resulting in multiple forms of harm to the rest of society. More specifically, power lawyering leads to

> the radical concealment of vital health and safety information, the chronic delay, obstructionism, corporate destruction of documents, makework,

> overbilling, the stifling of competition against investors and small business, the hamstringing of proper law enforcement, the merger deals driven by the enrichment of a few at the expense of workers and investors. (Nader and Smith 1996, 346)

When corporate lawyers find it necessary to settle with plaintiffs, they negotiate a confidential settlement, which results in monetary compensation for the plaintiffs but the absence of information and warnings to the general public. The silicon breast implant case was one example of this practice.

Lawyers whose clients are ordinary citizens are supposed to represent the best interests of their clients, and ideally in a manner that is socially constructive. Unfortunately, many empirical studies suggest that lawyers all too often put their own interests before those of the client, with overlawyering (providing unnecessary services) and overbilling especially egregious examples of such self-interest (Felstiner 1998). If corporate lawyers are at least sometimes dominated by their clients, lawyers for ordinary citizens are more likely to dominate the clients (Abel 1989, 204). Of course, this is a somewhat broad generalization, and many factors can come into play in determining whether lawyer or client assumes the upper hand or they work together on strategy in the particular case. Much evidence suggests that clients often experience their lawyers as arrogant, paternalistic, unempathetic, uncommunicative, inattentive, and the like (Felstiner 1998, 63). In part, such responses might be attributed to the professional socialization of lawyers, who learn to focus on the legal logic in a case as opposed to the emotional dimensions often experienced by clients. In divorce cases, in particular, lawyers are likely to face special challenges in keeping emotionally overwrought clients focused on legal realities (Sarat and Felstiner 1995). If lawyers fail to return calls and to move forward on cases, however, this is mainly a consequence of the fact that lawyers, typically insecure about sources of future income, take on more cases than they can comfortably handle (Felstiner 1998). Clients, then, are not infrequently frustrated (and sometimes angered) in their dealings with lawyers, and lawyers seem to be disproportionately stressed, overwhelmed, and alienated. Of course, there are numerous exceptions to such generalizations (i.e., satisfied clients and fulfilled lawyers).

Public Defenders

Historically, lawyers have disproportionately worked for the rich and the middle class. The poor, for the most part, had to represent themselves, and they were obviously at a great disadvantage in doing so. In the late nineteenth century, legal services for the poor were funded by private sources, primarily to represent the working poor who were owed money or who had suffered uncompensated injury or some other injustice (Katz 1982). In the last several decades of the twentieth century, legal services for the poor came to be primarily funded by the state, and (perhaps ironically) the legal matters often targeted discriminatory state policies against the poor. By the latter part of the twentieth century, these services had become quasi-private (while funded by states) and had shifted from focusing on reforming the law to providing direct services to the poor (Kessler 1987). Legal services and aid to the poor expanded substantially during this period. Nevertheless, "the American Bar

Box 7.4

The Declining Support for Legal Services for the Poor

From the time of the Reagan Administration in the 1980s, conservative forces have engaged in an ongoing, ultimately successful effort to cut support for legal services to the poor (Besharov 1990; Kilborn 1995). These forces were especially angry about lawyers for the poor filing class action suits on behalf of their clients against the government or private businesses. Congress then passed a law imposing restrictions on the use of federal money by the Legal Services Corporation; in April 2000, the U.S. Supreme Court was considering a challenge to these restrictions (Greenhouse 2000b).

By the end of 1999, New York City was contending with a drastic shortage in lawyers willing to represent the poor (Rohde 1999). As a consequence, many indigent defendants had to spend as long as a year in jail simply waiting for a lawyer to become available to represent them.

Association estimates that 80 percent of the legal problems faced by poor citizens go unassisted" (Nader and Smith 1996, 339). These problems include the most basic issues of adequate food, decent shelter, and protection from abuse (see Box 7.4).

Public defenders who represent indigents charged with crimes occupy a somewhat paradoxical position in the U.S. legal system (McIntyre 1987). We have a tradition, affirmed by the highest courts, that those charged with serious crimes are entitled to a defense. The landmark case of *Gideon v. Wainwright* (1963) established the constitutional right to representation for indigents facing felony charges; this right was extended, in 1972, in *Argersinger v. Hamlin*, to misdemeanor cases involving jail time. Although many states had already provided indigent defendants with attorneys, it now became necessary to provide all such defendants who could not afford lawyers with legal counsel. It must be stated that many of the criminally accused are social pariahs whom the public wants to see incarcerated. The paradox lies in the state supporting public defenders who represent people the state is vigorously attempting to prosecute. Some commentators say that the principal purpose of the public defenders office is to legitimate the system of law and its claims of due process and fairness. Whether public defenders are truly committed to their clients' interests or to the interest of the court system has been debated. Public defenders may not experience the same anxieties about generating enough clients to pay the bills as private practice lawyers do, but they often contend with severe pressures, including excessively large caseloads.

In an oft-cited study, Abraham Blumberg (1967) found that the person who most frequently suggested that a defendant in a criminal case plead guilty was the defense lawyer. In Blumberg's interpretation, these lawyers "con" their clients into waiving their constitutional rights because (1) a guilty plea is the most efficient means of settling cases, and (2) the defense lawyer's primary commitment is to cooperating with the agenda of the courtroom workgroup (including the prosecutor and the judge) rather than to the client's interest. Of course, in an alternative interpretation, it is often in the client's interest to plead guilty in return for some form of leniency, and the defense lawyer's advice may indeed serve the client's interest. Almost certainly, public defenders fall somewhere along a continuum, with those on one end zealously committed to giving clients the best possible defense and those on the other end cynically focused on disposing of cases efficiently.

Women in the Legal Profession

The legal profession, through most of its history, has been an overwhelmingly male profession. As Richard Abel (1988, 202) has noted:

> No women were admitted to practice until the 1870s, and about a dozen of the forty-five jurisdictions continued to exclude them as late as 1900. Some professional associations barred women until 1937, and some law schools continued to do so until 1972.

As late as 1963, only 3 percent of American lawyers were women. Beginning in the late 1960s, however, this began to change. In the sixteen-year period between 1967 and 1983, for example, enrollment of women in ABA-accredited law schools increased from 4.5 percent to 37.5 percent of the total (Abel 1989). By the end of the twentieth century almost half of law school graduates were women, and at the outset of the new millenium women constituted roughly 33 percent of the American legal profession (in Canada the numbers are even more striking: from a ratio of 1 woman to 38 men in 1961 to 1 to 2.4 by 1991) (Hagan and Kay 1995). By any measure, then, there has been a dramatic transformation in the gender composition of the profession (Kay 1997). What difference has it made?

Jobs and Money

Although the formal barriers against admission of women to the bar have been swept away, much discrimination has persisted. Originally, many law firms resisted taking on women lawyers because they believed that their principal clients would not accept women as lawyers; for the most part, however, this did not become a problem (Epstein 1993). At the beginning of the twenty-first century, only two of the nine justices of the U.S. Supreme Court were women, and such underrepresentation in the higher reaches of the profession was typical. When the first female Supreme Court justice, Sandra Day O'Connor, graduated from Stanford Law School in the 1950s, she received no job offers as a lawyer, only an offer to be a legal secretary. There are more women judges today, but they are still a fairly small minority.

Women lawyers have been proportionally more likely to work for the government or for legal aid than men (Abel 1988, 203). Women are also greatly underrepresented among partners of private law firms, especially in leadership positions and in smaller firms; they encounter a "glass ceiling" that blocks advancement (Dixon and Seron 1995; Epstein 1993; Kay 1997). Some evidence suggests that women who are associates must exceed the performance and productivity of their male counterparts if they are to be promoted to partner (Kay and Hagan 1998). They tend to earn significantly less money than male lawyers, although the gap in pay is decreasing (Epstein 1993; Hagan and Kay 1995). The size of the gap varies across different organizational settings (private, corporate, and governmental), but women are clustered in lower-paying specialties (Dixon and Seron 1995; Epstein 1993). For various reasons women are less likely than men to make choices that might maximize their opportunities and are less likely to be in a position to make professionally advantageous contacts. But the extent to which the disadvantaged position of women (relative to men) in the legal profession can be attributed to discrimination against them or to choices they make because they tend to have different priorities than men continues to be debated.

Cultural Values and Styles

The legal profession has been dominated by males historically, and so it has also reflected strongly male cultural values and styles (Menkel-Meadow 1985). Even after women began to be admitted to law schools (in the case of Harvard Law School, only from 1950 on), they continued to face resentment and harassment and a form of education strongly biased to favor males (A. Bernstein 1996). In a study entitled *Becoming Gentlemen: Women, Law School, and Institutional Change*, Lani Guinier, Michelle Fine, and Jane Balin (1997) found that women law students are substantially more likely to enter law school committed to public interest law and to fighting for social justice than their male counterparts, but by the time they graduate, their outlook and aspirations are much more like that of male students. In addition, female students are more likely than males to experience alienation and to feel excluded in law school. They generally do not do as well academically as males and are more likely to regard themselves as psychologically damaged by the law school experience. The authors of this study conclude that the law school environment and pedagogical approach must be transformed in ways that are more encouraging to female students.

The very nature of the adversary system is based on aggressive confrontation, conflict, and domination, values traditionally associated with males. When growing numbers of women enter the legal profession, do they adapt to this masculine, even "macho," culture, or do they transform it? Apparently there is no simple answer to this question (Bogoch 1997; Pierce 1995; Thornton 1996). At least some women adopt the aggressive, competitive, and combative male role and may even exceed most male lawyers on these attributes; many others adopt a style that puts more emphasis on a humane, caring, and mediation-oriented approach to legal matters and to client relations. One study of male and female divorce lawyers found that both sexes tended to be reluctant to get involved with the emotional issues clients typically raise, but female lawyers were at least more likely to be willing to put aside purely legal questions and address such issues (Bogoch 1997). At the same time, according to this study, female clients (as well as male clients) in divorce cases tend to be more deferential toward male lawyers than toward female lawyers.

Work and Family

Many women have clearly found great satisfaction in their careers as lawyers, but women also encounter special pressures and conditions somewhat less likely to affect men (Epstein 1993). The time pressures involved in the early stages of a legal career, to qualify for partnership or build up a clientele, sometimes call for 80-hour work weeks and coincide with a stage of life (their twenties and thirties) when many women hope to marry and have children. The traditional assumption of the male-dominated legal profession was that young (male) lawyers had wives at home to attend to all domestic and child-care responsibilies; young female lawyers typically don't have wives, and they are somewhat less likely than males to have male spouses (or partners) willing to fully share such responsibilities. Female lawyers tend to face more intense conflicts between their work and personal lives and pay a heavier toll in their personal lives if they put their careers first. Successful female lawyers are less likely than their male counterparts to be married and have children (Abramson 1988; Epstein 1993).

Even when women in major law firms receive essentially the same pay as men, they are likely to perceive themselves as disadvantaged when it comes to job assignments, promotions, and opportunities to litigate cases (Lewin 1989). They find themselves with fewer opportunities to cultivate the after-hours networking that is so crucial for advancement in legal careers. Furthermore, some 60 percent of women lawyers, in one survey, reported that they had experienced unwanted sexual attention on the job (Lewin 1989). Altogether, it is not surprising that a higher percentage of women than men become disenchanted with the legal profession, and women leave legal practice 60 percent more quickly than men (Bach 1995; Kay 1997). They become disillusioned with long hours and large workloads, inadequate pay for what they do, the perception that they will not be made partner, boring or distasteful work, and a general discomfort with the adversarial nature of their work. Although such problems are also experienced by some male lawyers, the evidence suggests that the problems are more widespread or intense for female lawyers. Although some law firms have taken steps to improve the conditions for women in order to retain their services—for example, by installing on-site child care—it seems clear that both the culture and the institutional practices of the legal profession will have to change significantly before women are fully integrated into the profession.

Legal Ethics

What is the difference between a lawyer and a vampire bat? One is a blood-sucking parasite and the other is a mouselike creature with wings. What is the difference between a hooker and a lawyer? There are some things a hooker won't do for money. What is a lawyer? Someone who makes sure he gets what's coming to you (Shook and Meyer 1995, 97). As these jokes suggest, lawyers are widely regarded as unethical or immoral—or, at the least, amoral. This low regard is hardly new; unflattering views of the ethics of lawyers are attributed to Socrates in ancient Greece, a medieval saint, the eighteenth-century philosopher Kant, and so on (Luban 1994, xi). Contemporary surveys suggest that at least a significant percentage of the general public is dubious about the ethics of lawyers and distrustful of lawyers (Reasons, Bray, and Chappell 1989).

Law School Offerings

Formal attention to professional ethics has only been widely incorporated into the law school curriculum in the recent era, essentially after the high-profile exposure of unethical conduct by lawyers in the Watergate Affair in the early 1970s. Indeed, at that time the American Bar Association began requiring an ethics course in all accredited law school programs (Mangan 1998). While some law schools have adopted reasonably creative approaches to education in ethics, many have simply taken the narrow approach of familiarizing students with Bar Association rules and informing them how to avoid being disciplined by the bar (Metzloff and Wilkins 1995). In the view of James Elkins (1985c), the problem of teaching ethics cannot be separated from contemplation of the nature of legal education itself, which tends to promote ethical insensitivity.

Law students seem to dislike being required to take a "professional responsibility" course, on the grounds that such courses tend to be preachy, patronizing, and unnecessary. Also, it is difficult to demonstrate that exposure to such a course will produce ethical behavior when law school graduates are faced with the ambiguities and formidable pressures encountered in real-life legal practices (Mangan 1998; Mello 1996). At least some law professors believe that existing professional responsibility courses are largely useless when they only teach law students how to comply with bar codes of ethics but fail to address the broader ethical dilemmas intertwined with the daily work of lawyers (Chemerinsky 1985). They would like to see education in ethical matters integrated into all courses, rather than being "ghettoized" in a single course.

Ambulance Chasing

What is unethical behavior for a lawyer? In the extreme case, lawyers become criminals, or part of criminal mobs (as in the case of the *consigliere* for a Mafia family). Lawyers who represent major criminals, such as illicit drug smugglers, may be suspected of complicity with their clients. One government response to such a concern has taken the form of seizing fees to lawyers that can be shown to come from illegal enterprises.

The establishment of the legal profession has historically regarded solicitation of legal clients as unethical. Lawyers who approached accident victims and survivors, for example, and offered their services, were historically stigmatized as "ambulance chasers." In recent times the Supreme Court has upheld state bans on approaching accident victims for business. Although the U.S. Supreme Court in 1977 struck down the ban on advertising by lawyers, some specific forms of advertising (e.g., a female lawyer in a seductive pose; a male lawyer in a boxing outfit, prepared to do battle for clients) have been viewed as undignified and arguably unethical (Glendon 1994, 54).

Adversarial Issues

Complex ethical issues come into especially sharp relief in the context of legal practice. First, in the course of their legal education, lawyers become conscious of and are expected to adopt an adversarial ethic holding that the lawyer has a primary responsibility to the welfare of her or his client and that this responsibility must take precedence over most (but not necessarily all) other obligations. Furthermore, as part of the adversarial ethic, a lawyer is expected to make the best possible case on behalf of the client, or on behalf of the state if the lawyer is a prosecutor, rather than to attempt getting at the truth by laying out all available evidence on both sides of a case in an even-handed and dispassionate way. At least on the defense side, it is not the obligation of lawyers to discriminate right from wrong and ensure just outcomes.

The lawyer-client confidentiality principle is involved here as well. This principle holds that lawyers should not disclose possibly incriminating revelations made to them by clients in the course of consultations. The rationale for this principle is that a client can only obtain full-fledged representation and an effective defense if the client does not have to be concerned that the lawyer will report incriminating or otherwise harmful disclosures made during lawyer-client conferences. However, by the standards of the American Bar Association, if a client discloses the intent to take actions that might cause death or do bodily harm to another person, the lawyer is permitted (but not required) to report this in violation of the confidentiality principle (Nader and Smith 1996, 350). Aside from such extreme circumstances, the Bar Association Code effectively prohibits lawyers from taking any direct action when they are aware of ongoing criminality by their client, although they may attempt to talk the client out of such action or they may withdraw from representing the client.

Of course, it should also be emphasized that ethical issues are not entirely restricted to the defense side. Prosecutors may engage in various forms of unethical conduct, especially when they are so eager to obtain convictions that they deliberately conceal evidence favorable to the defense (exculpatory evidence) or even knowingly present false evidence unfavorable to the defense in court. For example, in one case that was the subject of two books, a 17-year-old boy was convicted of murdering his mother in a trial where a key witness known to the prosecutor was not called, even though that witness would have raised fundamental questions about the prosecution's case (Barthel 1977; Connery 1977). The boy was acquitted in a subsequent trial. Many other such cases could be cited.

The adversarial ethic has been endorsed on the claim that the truth in any particular case is most likely to emerge at the end of the adjudicatory process if the two sides are allowed to make the strongest possible cases for their version of the facts. In criminal cases in particular, the adversarial ethic allows the defense to counter more effectively the great power of the state, minimizes the chances of harsh punishments being imposed unjustly, and helps protect constitutional rights and civil liberties (Luban 1994). Some lawyers fully internalize this ethic and claim to be entirely comfortable with it; others report that they experience discomfort or chagrin when they find themselves expected to engage in advocacy on behalf of a client who is not believable to them and who they may believe is guilty of heinous wrongdoing (Mills 1971; Wishman 1981). More generally, lawyers have been somewhat divided on whether this duty to serve clients zealously should indeed take precedence over all other duties (e.g., to religious faith or to society) and whether it is acceptable for a lawyer to knowingly present a false case (Allegretti 1996; Lieberman 1978; Luban 1994; Subin 1987). Furthermore, commitment to the adversarial ethic can clash dramatically with the value system of the lay culture. The title of a book by one defense lawyer quite concisely captures a common public attitude: *How Can You Defend Those People?* (Kunen 1983).

Representing Social Pariahs

Representing social pariahs, such as Timothy McVeigh, the Oklahoma City bomber, or Ted Kaczynski, the Unabomber, is regarded as ethically appropriate (and even commendable) within the legal culture. The general public, however, may be both perplexed and angry when lawyers vigorously defend people who are believed to have committed heinous crimes. Motivations for taking on social pariahs as clients vary and may include the belief that our system of justice works best when even those accused of the most heinous crimes receive the best possible defense. A lawyer may also be motivated to take on such cases because they represent a special opportunity to demonstrate outstanding legal skills and because such cases are likely to enhance the lawyer's fame and may lead to various opportunities to earn large fees or royalties.

The confidentiality principle has sometimes produced a harsh clash between the lay value system and the internal ethic of the legal profession. In one well-known case in 1973, in upstate New York, a man named Robert Garrow was suspected of being guilty of a string of rape/murders of several young co-eds (Alibrandt and Armani 1991). He informed his lawyer, Frank Armani, of the location of the corpses of two of these co-eds. The lawyer then visited this location, a cave in the woods, and took photographs of the corpses. But when the prosecutor in this high-profile case refused to consider negotiating for a lighter sentence in return for information on the crimes, Armani refrained from sharing with the prosecutor, or the anguished father of one of the missing girls, what he had learned from his client. When all of this came out many months later, during Garrow's trial, many people were outraged over the lawyer's actions. But when the prosecutor brought the matter before the state bar association, they supported the lawyer's claim that he had only acted in the best interest of his client as his professional role required of him. As a somewhat ironic sequel to this case, the lawyer assisted the police with information when Garrow escaped from prison some five years later, and Garrow was tracked down and killed. Since the lawyer no longer represented Garrow, he had no special reservations about cooperating in the hunt for the fugitive.

In a more recent Canadian case a lawyer for a man (Paul Bernardo) accused of kidnapping, sexually assaulting, and murdering two young girls removed hidden videotapes of the crime from his client's house and viewed them, following the client's instructions, and held onto these tapes for sixteen months before turning them over to the authorities (DePalma 1997). The lawyer, Kenneth Murray, was charged with professional violations by his bar association. The lawyers' confidentiality standard defense was rejected in this case on the grounds that lawyers cannot knowingly conceal physical evidence of a crime, and the videotapes fit into this category.

An ethical gray zone may also arise when a lawyer (or law firm) becomes aware of ongoing illegal conduct by a client. In one case, for example, a prominent New York City law firm became aware that its major client was engaged in an ongoing computer leasing fraud and did not blow the whistle on the client (Taylor 1983). Was this in line with the firm's obligation to honor confidentiality between itself and the client, as the firm later claimed, or was this an unethical effort by the law firm to continue receiving a lucrative retainer fee from its major client? The bar association has generally held that lawyers should not blow the whistle on clients in such cases. Lawyers may, however, attempt to dissuade a client from behaving illegally or unethically and may choose to withdraw from representing a client who disregards such advice.

When a lawyer or law firm offers advice to a client on how to commit illegal acts while minimizing chances of being caught, a line has been crossed, and the lawyer becomes liable to criminal charges. More than one prestigious law firm was accused of complicity in the Savings and Loan frauds of the 1980s, which resulted in billions of dollars of losses to the federal banking insurance system and the American taxpayers; the American Bar Association was more critical of the federal agency initiating the charges against the lawyers than of the lawyers involved (Simon 1998).

Lying and Perjury

Since a lawyer is a sworn officer of the court as well as an advocate for clients, the lawyer is not supposed to persuade a client to lie under oath or knowingly elicit false testimony (or knowingly introduce fraudulent documents and evidence) in sworn statements in court, and the lawyer who is found to have violated this rule can be prosecuted. In the famous Watergate case of the 1970s, for example, the Counsel to the President, John Dean, went to prison because he was found to have coached other parties in the case to lie before the grand jury. The lawyer is supposed to attempt to persuade clients not to perjure themselves, and here the bar association has held that the lawyer does have an obligation to blow the whistle on a client who cannot be persuaded to refrain from lying under oath. Alternatively, a lawyer might drop a client or stand mute while a client testifies in such circumstances.

Obviously, a significant tension exists between the rules of legal ethics prohibiting a lawyer from putting a witness on the stand whom she or he knows will lie and a lawyer's obligation to protect the confidentiality of a client's conversations. Of course, there is much reason to believe that lawyers all too often either know or strongly suspect that the client is lying under oath, but lawyers may typically protect themselves by not attempting to independently establish the veracity of the client's account. In strategic terms, the lawyer may simply choose to focus on what facts can and cannot be established by the prosecutor (or the opposing side) and what challenges can be directed at this case. A lawyer may adopt the stance of being morally neutral.

Other Ethical Issues

In addition to the ethical issues surrounding perjury and lawyer-client confidentiality, there are many other ethical issues bearing on the legal profession. With the power of attorney that may be granted lawyers (which gives them unusual control over clients' financial affairs) and with many other circumstances in which lawyers become privy to confidences, lawyers have special opportunities to take advantage of and steal from clients, and some do. Contingency fees, which provide lawyers with a percentage share (which may be 40 percent or more) of any recovery made in civil cases (with no money to the lawyers if they lose the case), have been defended as a device enabling clients who are not wealthy to sue richer and more powerful entities who have done some harm to them. But at least in some cases the size of the contingency fee seems obscenely large, and in certain class action suits the lawyers may seem to be the primary beneficiaries (Meier and Abramson 1998). In 1998, for example, lawyers representing three states (Florida, Mississippi, and Texas) in cases against tobacco companies were awarded a staggering $8.2 billion in contingency fees (Meier and Oppel 1999). One lawyer, who seems to have been only marginally involved in the litigation, was demanding over $200 million in fees. Does a contingency fee system facilitate much-needed litigation on behalf of ordinary people against powerful corporate entities engaged in harmful actions, or does it promote a form of legalized extortion principally benefitting greedy lawyers?

Lawyers have also been regarded as unethical when they initiate meritless suits (for example, against hospitals and doctors) on the chance that they will be able to persuade a jury to favor a sympathetic client. On the other hand, lawyers can face an ethical dilemma when they are committed to representing a client who for various reasons, they may no longer wish to represent, because when lawyers drop their clients they may put them in legal jeopardy. The ultimate form of unethical conduct by lawyers, as was suggested earlier, arises when lawyers themselves become party to, or even initiate and direct, illegal and harmful activity.

Disciplining Wrongdoers

Historically, the ethical codes and actions of the bar association have been driven more by the objective of advancing and protecting the economic interests of the profession than by the objective of ensuring that lawyers act ethically. The American Bar Association Code of Ethics has always been full of contradictions. For example, it has been permissible for lawyers to get what amounts to kickbacks on title insurance sold to their home-buying clients (without necessarily revealing this arrangement to clients), but it has been deemed unethical for attorneys to proffer advice to people about their rights and then accept a fee, to help vindicate those rights (Lieberman 1978). Historically, according to the ABA Code, it was unethical to charge too low a fee, but the code did not recognize a fee that was unethical because it was too high; in a 1975 decision, however, the U.S. Supreme Court declared the minimum fee rule of the code illegal. If a lawyer is sued by a client, or attempts to collect an unpaid fee, the Bar Code allows for violation of the confidentiality rule.

Traditionally the bar association assumed the primary responsibility for disciplining lawyers, although in the more recent era judicially appointed commissions have taken over this responsibility in most American states (Arnold and Kay 1995, 323). The disbarment of unethical lawyers (taking away from them their license to practice) has been applied rarely, and then mainly against lawyers whose behavior is so egregious that it threatens the reputation of the legal profession itself (Schneyer 1991). More specifically, solo practitioners with a modest practice have been far more vulnerable to being targets of ethical complaints and disciplinary action than have lawyers affiliated with large, prosperous law firms (Arnold and Kay 1995). With a strong trend toward globalization at the start of the twenty-first century and the proliferation of international tribunals, the need for an international code of ethics has been recognized (Vagts 1996). The challenge of policing legal practice across borders is formidable, however.

Legal Education

Through most of history, education to be a lawyer principally took the form of apprenticeship with a lawyer and of the reading of legal treatises, such as Blackstone's *Commentaries*. In the English tradition this process became somewhat formalized at the Inns of Court, where lawyers resided while court was in session, socialized with each other, and acquired a fuller knowledge of the law. However, law was regarded as a largely practical skill and was not deemed a suitable topic for higher education. Sir William Blackstone, in the mid-eighteenth century, occupied the first university chair in law at Oxford. In the American colonies, at this time, George Wythe in Virginia offered a short course of study (lasting weeks, not years) on law, ultimately situated at William and Mary College. It is a truly remarkable fact that for some of the giants in American legal history, including Thomas Jefferson and the great U.S. Supreme Court Chief Justice John Marshall, this course was the sum total of their formal legal education. Some Americans during the pre-Revolutionary period did travel to England for their legal education.

The first full-fledged American law school was established in Litchfield, Connecticut, in 1784, by Judge Tapping Reeve (Friedman 1973, 279). This independent school educated many leading legal figures of the nineteenth century and helped firmly establish the notion of formal legal education. In the nineteenth century major universities (such as Harvard, Yale, and Columbia) established law schools, although through much of that century most lawyers continued to get their education through apprenticeship and self-study. In the university law schools, lectures by legal practitioners on such topics as evidence, equity, contracts, and wills, were the standard pedagogical style until the last part of the century.

In 1870 Christopher Columbus Langdell was appointed dean of the Harvard Law School (Sutherland 1967). Langdell had been somewhat unsuccessful as a practitioner but was highly regarded as a legal analyst. He viewed law as a science, best learned by having students read appellate case opinions and then analyze the principles that governed, or should have governed, the outcome. Despite some initial resistance, this case method approach to law became dominant over the next century or so. Texts increasingly took the form of collections of case opinions, with commentary.

The so-called Socratic method was Langdell's other influential—although controversial—contribution to legal education (LaPiana 1995; Schlegel 1995b). The essence of this method involves a dialogue between professor and student, with the professor directing probing questions about case opinions at students; the process is intended to sharpen the student's ability to identify

Box 7.5

The Law School Curriculum

The first-year curriculum at law schools typically might include the following: Contracts (the legal interpretation of private agreements); Torts (personal injuries); Property (rights of ownership; conditions of transfer); Constitutional Law (historical interpretation of the U.S. Constitution); Procedure (rules for litigation); and Criminal Law (substantive and procedural). Other core courses typically taken in the second year of law school could include: Wills and Trusts; Taxation; Evidence; Corporations; and Administrative Law. In the third year, which at least some students regard as wasteful, there is more opportunity to pursue elective courses, which might include Jurisprudence; International Law; Legal History; Labor Law; Women and the Law; Poverty Law; and so on. As noted earlier, accredited law schools are required to offer a course on legal ethics, or professional responsibility.

core principles and refine their understanding of legal reasoning. Whether this method succeeds in teaching students to "think like a lawyer" and be fast on their feet in legal contests or is a means of terrorizing and humiliating students with reasoning skills irrelevant to much of the work they will be doing continues to be debated.

Throughout the twentieth century the completion of law school, with a course of study over three years, has been the conventional means of acquiring a legal education and becoming a lawyer. The elite law schools (such as Harvard) and the organized bar association cooperated in developing standards for admissions, curriculum, and entry into practice (Stevens 1983). The three-year curriculum became standard in law schools in the twentieth century. There is an old adage that "first year they scare you to death, second year they work you to death, and third year they bore you to death" (Kahlenberg 1992, 159) (see Box 7.5).

Most law schools publish a law review, and some law schools publish several reviews. Law reviews are journals originally established at law schools to provide students with training in legal writing; today they publish law-related scholarship varying greatly in style and focus. Altogether, some 425 law reviews are published in America (Glendon 1994, 205). Historically, law students with the best grades received prestigious appointments as law review editors, although in the more recent era writing samples and affirmative action criteria have also played a role in these appointments. That students play such a key role in determining which law professor's scholarly work gets published, and edit the work accepted for publication, is a unique (and controversial) practice among scholarly publications (Friedman 1998b; Harnsberger 1997). Since tenure is importantly dependent upon a professor's publishing in reputable law reviews, this power is hardly trivial.

Recent Changes

From the 1960s on, some significant changes occurred in legal education (McKay 1985). As the applicant pool increased dramatically, existing law schools expanded and new law schools opened; law schools became more selective in accepting applicants; women (and to a lesser degree, people of color), who had been historically excluded or admitted in small numbers, flocked to law schools; and school accreditation standards were tightened. Law school applications have periodically experienced upsurges of applications. An upsurge in the early 1990s, for example, was attributed at least in part to the influence of a popular television show, *L.A. Law,* which offered a glamorous and exciting image of legal practice (Flood 1994; Margolick 1990). By the latter half of the 1990s, however, the number of applications had declined significantly at many law schools. This decline may reflect awareness of the downsizing of law firms in a fiercely competitive environment, as well as the effects of relentless criticism of the legal profession.

Critiques of Legal Education

Legal education has been criticized on many grounds (Shaffer and Redmount 1977). Derek Bok (1983), former President of Harvard University and previously professor and dean of the Law School, complained, in a widely cited speech, that too many of the best and brightest students were going to law school to prepare themselves for careers engaging in expensive litigation on behalf of privileged clients, instead of pursuing careers in such fields as science and engineering, focusing on curing diseases and designing better products. Law professor Roger Cramton (1978) has written of the "ordinary religion of the law school classroom" as including the following dogma: "a moral relativism tending toward nihilism, a pragmatism tending toward an amoral instrumentalism, a realism tending toward cynicism, an individualism tending toward atomism, and a faith in reason and democratic processes tending toward mere credulity and idolatry." The Socratic approach, as suggested earlier, has been criticized as autocratic, demeaning, male-dominated, and irrelevant to much of legal practice. A best-selling account of the first year at Harvard Law, Scott Turow's (1977) *One L,* documents how law school education seems to transform people, displacing appropriate emotional responses and ethical concerns with logical reasoning and strategic thinking. James Elkins (1979, 143), who has written extensively on legal education and legal ethics, calls attention to "the tragedy of a legal education which successfully indoctrinates students into 'thinking like a lawyer' but stifles idealism, social consciousness and creativity." For Peter d'Errico (1975), law school fosters the pathology of legalism and teaches students to seek and use power as opposed to truth and justice. For Duncan Kennedy (1983), law school reinforces the hierarchies that divide society into unequal strata, and the elite law schools direct students to careers representing the rich and the powerful. For Patricia Williams (1991), legal education is complicit in reinforcing racist images. For Nancy Erickson and Nadine Taub (1990), the law school curriculum suffers from a gender bias.

Quite a number of studies have documented a turning away from idealism among law students (Erlanger et al. 1996; Granfield 1992; Stover 1989). Most of the students who enter law school expressing an interest in pursuing a career in public interest law (here defined as representation of the poor and powerless or the protection of consumers and citizens) have abandoned that interest by the end of their law school years. Anecdotal accounts have supported this thesis of eroding idealism as well (Kahlenberg 1992). The best stu-

Box 7.6

Law Schools and Religious Faith

A legal education is typically thought of as a thoroughly secular enterprise. Although there are some thirty-seven religiously affiliated law schools in the United States, most do not emphasize the religious association (Glaberson 1998a). Some law schools, however, specifically embrace a religious commitment. Pepperdine University School of Law in California, for example, is committed to a Christian approach to law (Glaberson 1998a). The Ave Maria School of Law, funded by Domino Pizza mogul Thomas Monaghan, opened in the year 2000, in Ann Arbor, Michigan, with a specific commitment to promote Catholic religious values (Mangan 2000). Such schools emphasize the importance of natural law over court precedent. Although students are not necessarily instructed to reject clients who are accused of activities (e.g., selling pornography) repugnant to their Christian values, they are taught to raise moral issues with such clients, and ideally to promote a commitment to a religious outlook.

dents disproportionately go to work for elite law firms that represent large corporations and wealthy individuals. Although it is not entirely clear how much of the shift away from public interest work can be attributed to the law school experience—pressure to pay off law school loans may also play a role in determining career choices—there is at a minimum little reason to believe that this experience vigorously promotes idealism and public interest concerns (see Box 7.6).

Legal education continues to contend with the basic tension between promoting an intellectual understanding of and critical thinking toward legal issues and the practical objective of preparing students to obtain jobs and function as working lawyers. Much of daily legal practice involves negotiation as opposed to analysis of legal opinions, but the former skill was little emphasized in the traditional law school curriculum. However, in the recent era, many alternatives to doctrinal analysis and the Socratic method have been introduced into the law school curriculum. Clinical (hands-on) practice, role-playing, moot court, negotiating skills, computer-aided instruction, and the like receive more emphasis. Lawrence Friedman has called for replacing the present curriculum with one that is half clinical training and half training in such disciplines as history, sociology, economics, philosophy, and comparative law (Margolick 1983, 30). In other words, law students would spend half their time learning to be lawyers and half their time being educated. The Queens Law School of the City University of New York is one of the schools that has introduced a curriculum roughly along these lines; on the down side, this school in its early years experienced a very high rate of failure on the bar exam.

The Critique of the Legal Profession

The image of the legal profession in American life is remarkably contradictory. On the one hand, some of the most venerated heroes in American history have been lawyers, including Thomas Jefferson and Abraham Lincoln among presidents, John Marshall and Oliver Wendell Holmes Jr. among Supreme Court justices, Daniel Webster and Sam Ervin Jr. among statesmen, and Clarence Darrow and Ralph Nader among lawyers for the people. The legal profession in many respects is viewed as a prestigious occupation; many parents have encouraged their children to pursue legal careers, and large numbers apply annually for admission to law school. Lawyers have not infrequently been portrayed heroically in the media, whether as crusading reformers or courageous advocates on behalf of the wrongfully accused. That lawyers are so often elected to high office cannot be reconciled with the notion of a uniformly negative image of lawyers.

On the other hand, an enduring tradition that reviles lawyers and is critical of them is also part of the American cultural heritage. Relatively high levels of hostility are directed toward lawyers in America, and confidence in their integrity has been relatively low. Lawyers are commonly accused of dishonesty, amorality, greed, and incompetence; the claim is made that there are too many of them and that they are responsible for an excess of litigation (Black and Rothman 1998; Re 1994). In the recent era a number of presidents (Carter, Reagan, and Bush, for example) have considered it politically advantageous to attack lawyers on various grounds (for promoting unequal justice; for stifling economic growth; for initiating frivolous lawsuits). A Chief Justice of the Supreme Court during this era, Warren Burger, claimed that about half of all lawyers were fundamentally incompetent (Footlick 1978, 98). A judge on the U.S. Court of Appeals, Laurence Silberman (1998), expressed concern that excessive lawyering harms both politics and the economy. A retired justice of the California Court of Appeals, Macklin Fleming (1997), claimed that contemporary legal practice was too much driven, with pernicious consequences, by an obsession with money. A dean of the Yale Law School, Anthony Kronman (1993), claimed that the profession has lost sight of an earlier ideal of a lawyer-statesman. A law professor and leading student of the legal profession, Richard Abel (1986), has argued that the American legal profession's practices are shaped by, and reflect, capitalist inequality. A distinguished lawyer (and corporate CEO), Sol Linowitz (1994), claimed that lawyers had lost their independence and were too beholden to the marketplace. And many working lawyers admit to being disillusioned with what is required of them and dissatisfied with their professional lives (Bachman 1995; Glendon 1994; E. Gross, 1998). An internal critique of the legal profession is quite pervasive, then.

With the great growth in the size of the legal profession, it has become fiercely competitive, and the suspicion of "overlawyering"—lawyers generating unnecessary work and unsupported billing—frequently arises. Legal costs in the contemporary era rose more rapidly than the rate of inflation, and tens of billions of dollars are annually expended on legal bills. Furthermore, tens of thousands of complaints against lawyers are filed annually on a national level, and legal malpractice cases have increased. Calls for reforms are commonplace. Recommended reforms would make legal representation available to the poor and more affordable to other members of society; would take various measures to discourage needless litigation; would create more alternatives to resolving disputes not dependent upon lawyers; and would impose more oversight on unethical or exploitative practices of lawyers.

The Legal Profession in the Twenty-First Century

It seems unavoidable that the legal profession will continue to play a central role in American life in the twenty-first century. However, some questions concerning the future of the profession are unsettled. Will it continue to grow and expand exponentially, as it did in the final decades of the twentieth century? Will the massive movement of women into the legal profession—and, to a lesser extent, the movement of minorities—fundamentally transform the character of the profession, or is it women and minorities who will be transformed? Will the changes in the market for legal services that occurred during the latter part of the twentieth century continue to transform the profession, with the virtual disappearance of solo practitioners and the continuing growth of law mega-firms, legal clinics, and public sector lawyers? The massive expansion of information technology, in conjunction with forces promoting rational, economically efficient use of resources, is sure to influence legal practice in many ways. In one scenario, those who need legal services will increasingly turn to the internet and will seek fast, expert, inexpensive legal advice from "electronic lawyers," which could potentially decimate traditional legal practice (Wall and Johnstone 1997). Perhaps the most fundamental question about the future of the legal profession is this: Will lawyers continue to be aligned principally with the forces of power and privilege, or will they become associated increasingly with challenges to inequality and injustice?

Key Terms and Concepts

ambulance chasers
American Bar Association
barrister
case method of legal education
cause lawyering
commercial/entrepreneurial style of lawyering
contingency fees
courtroom workgroup
disbarment
electronic lawyers
exculpatory evidence
glass ceiling
Juris Prudentes
lawyer-client confidentiality principle
overlawyering
power of attorney
pro bono
rainmakers
Socratic method
solicitor
traditional style of lawyering

Discussion Questions

1. Should pro bono work be required of all lawyers, whether they are in a firm or solo practitioners? What effect might such work have on society if all lawyers did even a small amount?

2. Discuss the dangers involved when corporate lawyers attempt to protect the interests of their corporate clients. How do they lose sight of what it means to be a *lawyer* when they settle cases confidentially that the public should know about?

3. Will it ever be possible for women to break through the "glass ceiling"? Why are people apprehensive about hiring a woman lawyer? What can women contribute to the legal world that men cannot? Do you think women tend to adapt to the "macho" culture, or transform it?

4. How important is it to have "professional responsibility" courses in law school? Are they effective? Do you agree with the decision made by the New York state bar association in the Garrow case that his lawyer, Frank Armani, was acting in the best interest of his client?

5. Will it ever be realistic to have a world of "electronic lawyers"? How do you see the legal profession in the twenty-first century? What is it that motivates most lawyers who practice law today? Will this change?

Chapter Eight

Legal Institutions and Processes: An Overview

Over the course of time, human beings have developed legal institutions to formally administer the law. A legal institution is a system with a patterned set of procedures and practices addressing matters of law. As societies become increasingly complex, different types of legal institutions evolve to address specific types of disputes or particular classes of people. This chapter identifies some key elements of major systems of justice within our society, with special emphasis on their social dimensions. The review that follows is a highly selective discussion, and only passing reference is made to some of the countless specific features of these systems. Its aim is to provide some sense of the basic nature of these coexisting systems of justice and some of the principal issues confronting them. The chapter looks at the following legal systems: criminal justice; juvenile justice; civil justice; regulatory justice; military justice; and informal justice. Each of the different systems of justice claims to address a particular class of offenses or disputes effectively and fairly.

Law and the Criminal Justice System

The branch of law and justice most visible to the general public is that pertaining to crime. The criminal justice system is widely featured in the media, even though many aspects of its operation are represented in a distorted manner (Bailey and Hale 1998; Jarvis and Joseph 1998). The decisions made by the criminal justice system are especially dramatic, sometimes literally involving questions of life and death.

In the recent era, many Americans have been frustrated and disappointed with the perceived failure of the criminal justice system to respond effectively to the crime problem (Jacob 1996, 30). At the same time, some Americans—typically holding liberal or progressive ideas—have been concerned with ensuring that full-fledged due process is accorded all those accused of law-breaking. A basic tension exists, then, between crime control as the primary objective of the criminal justice system and respect for due process as the primary obligation of the criminal justice system (Packer 1968). In addition, some tension exists between other objectives of the criminal justice system, including avenging wrong-doing and reaffirming society's basic moral commitments; being fair and imposing just desserts on lawbreakers; not doing more harm than good by intervening in the lives of minor offenders; rehabilitating criminals and restoring them to society as constructive citizens; and fostering reconciliation between offenders and victims. There are many active controversies in criminal justice, including the broad issue of whether the criminal justice system should emphasize aggressive policing and punishment or employ preventive and reconciliative strategies, which are more effective and more just (Fuller 1998; Eskridge 1996).

The origins of a criminal justice system go far back in history, to a time when a certain class of harmful acts came to be defined as violations of the king's peace, and the state began to process such offenses on behalf of the king (Gatrell et al. 1980). Over time, a system evolved with an enforcement component (policing), an adjudicatory component (the courts), and a correctional component (e.g., prisons), with the prosecutorial office sometimes regarded as a fourth branch of criminal justice (Friedman 1993). One of the distinctive features of the American criminal justice "system" is its fragmented character and absence of centralized control, which means it is not a coordinated, integrated system (Jacob 1996, 33). Criminal justice agencies and courts may be federal, state, or local; in a parallel vein, criminal law is formulated by Congress, state legislatures, and (regarding offenses) local councils. Accordingly, policy, practices, and political pressures vary considerably across all these lines.

Defining Crime

The basic elements of a legal conception of crime include the commission of a forbidden act (or, in certain circumstances, the failure to act) within a particular jurisdiction and criminal intent (evil intent, criminal purpose, or knowledge of the wrongfulness of the conduct).

Crimes vary greatly in terms of their seriousness and identifiable consequences. The most basic distinction has been between felonies and misdemeanors (although treason—aiding and abetting the enemy—and offenses—minor forms of law-breaking such as jay-walking—are also separate categories). Felonies are serious crimes, punishable by up to life in prison, or in some cases by death; conviction of a felony may entail loss of certain basic rights as a citizen. Misdemeanors are less serious offenses, typically punishable by a fine or no more than a year in jail; conviction of a misdemeanor does not result in a loss of citizenship rights.

The Police

For many people the police are "the law." The police are regarded as standing between a society based upon law and order and a society based upon crime and chaos. The police themselves, confronting the difficult if not impossible challenge of effectively controlling crime, often define their own mission in moral terms, as a battle of good versus evil (Herbert 1996). Conversely, a long tradition of suspicion of or outright hostility toward the police is also part of the American experience: on the frontier; in the early ethnic neighborhoods of new immigrants settled in big cities; among racial minorities generally; and among radicals and dissidents. Some see the police as agents of the people, primarily serving the needs of the community; others say that the police emerged in complex, modern societies as instruments of social control, created by and acting principally on behalf of the dominant classes (Robinson and Scaglion 1987). A number of different conceptions of the proper primary role of the police can be identified (Wilson 1968). The media generally have emphasized the crime fighter role, with the police aggressively pursuing major offenders. A second role conception is law enforcer, with police enforcing all laws—not just those pertaining to major crimes—in an even-handed manner. A third role model is watchman, with the police basically maintaining a presence in the community in the interest of preserving order and deterring crime. Finally, a fourth conception stresses the notion of the police as providers of social services. Of course in real life the police tend to play a mixture of roles, but the perceived primacy of one or the other of these role conceptions varies, with individual police officers themselves holding different views.

Discretionary Decision Making

The police have considerable discretion, or choice, in their job-related decision making (Smith and Visher 1981; Riksheim and Chermak 1993). Many factors—situational, attitudinal, and administrative (relating to department policy and structure)—affect their decision making. Research suggests that situational factors are especially influential in the arrest decision but that administrative factors are determinate for other kinds of decisions (Worden 1989). The police often use their discretion in positive ways, to enforce law more efficiently (disregarding minor, inconsequential violations of the law) and to mitigate the effects of harsh or unreasonable laws (by refusing to enforce them). The police in many cases provide useful services to citizens beyond what is required of them by their formal duties.

The worst abuses of police discretionary decision making might be summarized this way: bribery; bigotry; and brutality. First, throughout their history the police have too often been bribed (or corrupted), especially in relation to victimless crime laws (e.g., gambling; prostitution; drugs) (Kleinig 1996). This persistent corruption seems to reflect unusual opportunities for police to generate bribes; the existence of ineffective or unpopular laws; and the discrepancy between the police officer's considerable situational power and his or her income. Second, throughout their history many police officers have been bigoted and have enforced the law in a biased manner. In the American experience, there is a long (and ugly) history of predominantly white police officers treating black people differently (e.g., arresting them more readily) from white people. Among other consequences, such bigotry has promoted distrust of the police and has sometimes precipitated major race riots. Third, throughout their history the police have too often engaged in brutality (or the excessive use of force, beyond what was called for in the situation). Persons suspected of crimes have been beaten, sometimes as a means of extracting confessions from them. Police brutality, especially in conjunction with bigotry, has also contributed to hostility toward the police. Various types of reforms, guidelines, and internal or external investigations have attempted to address these extreme forms of abuse of police discretion.

Trends

The modern police force was established in the early part of the nineteenth century, but through much of that century and into the twentieth, police were often poorly educated, amoral, and unprofessional in their conduct (Walker 1980). Throughout the twentieth century a recurrent theme has been the need for more professional policing, and the push in this direction escalated following the release in 1967 of an influential Presidential Commission report calling for more educated police. A greater emphasis on higher education for the police followed, along with more sophisticated means of screening out those unsuited for policing. The police during the 1960s also had to learn to live with the constraints imposed upon them by a series of decisions by the U.S. Supreme Court under Chief Justice Warren; the most famous and controversial of these was the Miranda decision (1966), requiring the police to warn those accused of crimes of their rights. In a June 2000 decision (7–2), the U.S. Supreme Court reaffirmed the Miranda rule as an established aspect of American national culture (Greenhouse 2000d).

In still another basic shift, beginning in the early 1970s, minorities and women were actively recruited for policing. The expanded representation of minorities and women on police forces has enhanced the confidence of minorities and women in the police, since both groups have in the past experienced abuses or mistreatment at the hands of white male police officers. Although minority and female police officers have continued to experience some forms of discrimination and disadvantages in terms of promotions, they clearly enhance the effectiveness of the police in many aspects of policing. The evidence suggests that women perform very successfully as police officers, and on some criteria they outperform male officers (Senna and Siegel 1999, 220). Altogether, policing has experienced some significant changes.

In the recent era some special emphasis has been placed on community policing (Greene and Mastrofski 1988). The concept of community policing does not have a single meaning but generally refers to a deemphasis on legalistic policing and arrest and more emphasis on building rapport with community members, crime prevention, and victim assistance, with greater deference to the will of the community itself (Mastrofski, Worden, and Snipes 1995). Community-oriented policing certainly represents a significant shift in the philosophy of policing, although it remains to be seen whether it becomes the dominant model for police departments in the twenty-first century. Some commentators say that the movement to community policing was driven by the need of the police to enhance their legitimacy, or the need to increase community support of the police (Crank 1994). However, community policing calls for new controls on police discretion, in the view of other commentators (Livingston 1997). Because community police tend to have fewer constraints imposed on them, some commentators expressed concern that these police would make more decisions reflecting personal predilections and racial biases rather than basing decisions on legalistic grounds. Research has not generally lent support to those concerns, although community-oriented police apparently are less likely to make arrests.

Some emerging trends in policing have been identified (Bayley and Shearing 1996). First, a dramatic expansion of private policing has occurred, to the point where private police now outnumber public police in the United States and many other countries; also, there are more civilian support personnel for policing. Second, in addition to the wider adoption of community policing (as discussed above), the police have attempted to develop more efficient strategies for traditional crime-fighting and order-maintenance functions. Third, police have been subjected to more oversight and supervision from various government and civilian entities, which many police officers resent. The basic challenge faced by policing in the future is to respond effectively to the public's ongoing fear of crime without at the same time compromising human rights or intensifying the existing inequalities between the circumstances of the rich and the poor.

The Courts

The adjudicatory branch of government, or the courts, is the symbolic centerpiece of the American system of justice. The courts in the criminal justice system are formally organized to operate adversarially, with a "contest" between the prosecution and the defense, but in fact the vast majority of cases are disposed of (in most large jurisdictions) with some form of negotiation, or plea bargaining (Maynard 1984; Rosett and Cressey 1976). The image of a full-scale criminal trial is deeply embedded in Americans' collective consciousness because such trials—both real and dramatized—are featured in the media. But relative to the number of criminal cases where a trial could occur, only a small percentage (10 percent, in most jurisdictions) actually go to trial (Jacob 1996, 42).

The prosecutor and the defense attorney are typically portrayed as adversaries, but as some commentators point out, they are typically part of a "courtroom workgroup," more often committed to the smooth, efficient functioning of the court than to the public or the defendant (Neubauer 1999; Eisenstein, Flemming, and Nardulli 1999). In the lower courts, in particular, a form of "rough justice" is said to prevail, with mainly poor defendants hustled through the system with little real concern for their due process rights (Robertson 1974). The metaphor of the assembly line, then, has been applied to the operation of the courts. At every stage, the poor and minorities are at a disadvantage. As one classic example, middle class and wealthy people accused of crimes—even serious crimes—rarely sit in jail awaiting trial for any significant period of time. Rather, they are able to get out on bail, even if the bail amount is high. Historically, however, accused individuals who are poor have often been unable to make even modest bail and have sat in jail for many months awaiting disposition of their case or trial.

Many defendants who do go to trial opt for a bench trial before a judge, at least partly on the premise that they will face harsher consequences if convicted in a jury trial. This choice is always a gamble, as some research suggests that juries are more likely to acquit than are judges. Jury trials are not an option in most countries. Although Americans regard trial by jury as essential

Box 8.1

Jury Nullification

Juries sometimes vote their conscience (especially in political cases), even when that judgment is at odds with the evidence and the law; such "jury nullification" is celebrated by some, and criticized by others (Barkan 1983). Jury nullification has specifically been defended as a crucial instrument in protecting basic liberties (Lehman 1997); it has been criticized as the wrong answer to biases in the criminal justice system (Estrich 1998). Paul Butler (1995) has made a provocative argument in favor of black jurors exercising jury nullification powers to counter the demonstrable bias against black Americans built into the existing criminal justice system. For example, black jurors could refuse to vote for conviction in crack cocaine cases involving black defendants, on the grounds that the crime is victimless and a disproportionately high percentage of black defendants (relative to whites in parallel cases) are imprisoned on such charges. If the likely harm from conviction outweighs any likely harm from acquittal, the jury should acquit despite highly incriminating evidence.

to a true democracy, and it is guaranteed by the Bill of Rights, trial by jury has also been criticized as unnecessary, wasteful, and incompetent. Some critics have remarked that juries are not even typically composed of peers of the defendant (see Box 8.1).

A substantial body of sociolegal research has explored many aspects of the jury as an institution, including the dynamics of its decision making (Hastie 1993; King 1996). Many factors—including attributes of both defendants and jurors themselves—have been found to bias jury decisions.

Sentencing

If either a judge or jury find a defendant guilty, a sentence must be imposed, typically by the judge. Here, too, a substantial body of sociolegal research has investigated the bases for this important decision (Mears 1998; Tonry 1996; von Hirsch and Ashworth 1992). Judges in the past had considerable discretion in sentencing, and, as one consequence, there were significant disparities in sentences given offenders with similar records and attributes. Since the late 1970s the federal system and many state systems have adopted sentencing guidelines as one controversial constraint on judicial discretion (Alschuler 1991; Uelmen 1992). Sentencing guidelines use a number of criteria, such as the seriousness of the offense itself, mitigating circumstances (e.g., not using a weapon), the degree of injury, and the past record of the offender to specify a presumptive sentence for a particular offender. If judges choose to impose a sentence that departs from the guidelines, they are required to provide some written justification for doing so.

The introduction of sentencing guidelines in the United States has led to longer average prison sentences and has contributed to prison overcrowding (Tonry and Hatlestad 1997). The sentences prescribed by the U.S. Sentencing Commission do seem to correspond with those favored by the general public (Rossi and Berk 1997). Sentencing guidelines have been criticized on many grounds, including the claim that they create new sentencing disparities and interfere with the judge's application of common sense to cases (Stith and Cabranes 1998). Criminologists have criticized the harsh sentences of the recent guidelines era as out of proportion to the harm of the criminal conduct they address (McCoy 1997). Also, many judges have been critical of sentencing guidelines, on the argument that the best justice results if judges are entrusted with considerable leeway in imposing the most appropriate sentence in the case before them.

Those who have been convicted of crimes in the American system have the option of appealing the decision to a higher court; if they are able to raise a significant constitutional issue, the case may be appealed right up to the United States Supreme Court. Most appeals are based on an alleged violation of procedural due process rights. Although criminal conviction appeals have increased in the recent era and impose a considerable burden on appellate courts, they rarely result in calls for outright reversal of a conviction or a call for a retrial. Criminal case appellants who are able to secure the services of topflight attorneys willing to invest a significant amount of time in their cases are more likely to be successful on appeal.

Victims' Rights

In the earliest systems of justice, the victim of a crime was often at the center of the legal proceedings (Umbreit 1994). In the Western system of criminal justice, however, the victim, over time, came to be pushed aside, with no real voice in the proceedings, and was called only as a witness to be questioned on certain particulars of the crime. Since the early 1970s, victims' rights advocacy groups have had some success in promoting legislation that extends to victims more rights (for example, to provide a victim's impact statement) and greater sensitivity (for example, prohibiting defense attorneys in rape cases from questioning the victim of a rape on her past sexual history). Although support for crime victims might seem uncontroversial, some critics claim that these new rights end up seriously compromising the rights of those accused of crimes. For example, well-educated, articulate victims may be especially successful in persuading jurors to focus on emotional dimensions of their cases, and this can work against the interests of inarticulate, unsympathetic defendants being tried on circumstantial evidence.

The Correctional System

The correctional system is the final basic component of the criminal justice system. Although prisons are the most conspicuous feature of the correctional system, a substantial majority of those declared guilty of criminal charges are not sent to prison but are fined, put on probation (under court supervision), or briefly jailed. Those sent to prison are disproportionately from disadvantaged classes and, in the United States, are disproportionately black (McCoy 1997). The prison system has long been criticized as harming rather than rehabilitating most incarcerated offenders; nevertheless, in the recent era the prison population grew exponentially, in response to both increasing public and political demands to get tough with criminals and the requirements of the sentencing guidelines.

Conclusion

In a democratic society with a high crime rate, the criminal justice system inevitably confronts many challenges. The appropriate and inappropriate use of discretion at all stages of the criminal justice system is one major issue (Walker 1993). Ongoing evidence of various forms of racial and ethnic bias in the operation of this system is especially disturbing (Sampson and Lauritsen 1997). Social science theory and research can and should play an important role in shaping anticrime policies (Friedman and Fisher 1997). In the twenty-first century this system is sure to face ongoing pressures to improve its effectiveness and efficiency without becoming intrusive in the lives of ordinary citizens and without compromising basic rights of these citizens.

Law and the Juvenile Justice System

The juvenile justice system, by specific design, tends to receive substantially less attention than the criminal justice system. Juvenile proceedings are supposed to take place behind closed doors, and the names of juveniles accused of crimes are not supposed to appear in the news media, in order to protect young offenders from the stigma of being labeled a criminal. Nevertheless, juvenile justice itself has been an important societal preoccupation, and the juvenile justice system has been a target for criticism on various grounds.

Juveniles pose various challenges for a system of law. Traditionally, children were especially vulnerable before the law. On the one hand, they had no standing as plaintiffs in civil proceedings. Fathers, in particular, had almost unlimited control over other family members, including their children, whose legal status combined elements of noncitizen, slave, pet, and property. In the Massachusetts Bay Colony (in the mid-seventeenth century) a father could have a "stubborn or rebellious son" of at least sixteen years of age brought before a magistrate to be put to death (Beales 1985). Although this is certainly an extreme example, it shows how extraordinary was parental control over their children's lives. Until the recent era the law extended little protection to children abused by their parents, and children have not generally had rights regarding the basic conditions of their lives. On the other hand, juveniles who committed violations of the law, if they were past the age of infancy (in the common law tradition, age seven), were not formally defined as different from adult offenders. Children could be burned alive, drowned, or hanged, although it was not the norm to subject them to such harsh sanctions. Nevertheless, as late as the early part of the nineteenth century, there are cases on record of children as young as eight or nine being hung for petty crimes.

Children's Character

Philosophical views of children have varied over the ages. One historian says that prior to the fifteenth century, children were seen principally as miniature adults (Aries 1962). Another historian, however, says that among Puritans, children and youths were clearly differentiated from adults (Beales 1985). In some eras and societies, children have been regarded as inherently sinful, in need of vigilance and stern discipline from the earliest ages. In others, they have been seen as innocents in need of protection from the corrupting influences of the world.

When children come to the attention of the law, it has not always been obvious how they should be classified. Some children are clearly victims of neglect and abuse and need the protection of the law. Other children (especially those well into their teens) are clearly predators from whom society requires protection by law. Still other children (so-called status offenders) are viewed as engaged in behavior signaling that the law must take steps to protect them from themselves (e.g., running away from home; truancy; sexual promiscuity). In any number of cases, however, it is far from clear which of these categories is most appropriate for a particular child. Accordingly, considerable overlap may exist between the categories of neglected child, juvenile delinquent, and status offender.

Even when a child has clearly committed an offense that, if committed by an adult, would be regarded as a serious crime, the complicated metaphysical question of responsibility arises. That is, at what age does a child become truly capable of understanding the consequences of her or his actions to the point that the child should be held responsible for committing actions in violation of the law? Such questions continue to be debated vigorously. Different states have adopted different ages for protecting juveniles from adult sanctions or processing them as adults. In a case where two high school buddies committed a heinous crime (e.g., the rape and murder of two young girls), one has faced life imprisonment and the other incarceration for no more than a few years, with release by age 21, because one was just over and the other just under the cut-off age for juvenile disposition. No easy solution to the ultimate arbitrariness of these kinds of distinctions exists.

Establishment of Juvenile Courts

Through the course of the nineteenth century various social reform movements (notably, the Child-Saving Movement) called for recognizing that children were different from adults and so required different protections and procedures (Ryerson 1978). Although some initiatives for separate hearings and separate reformatories were adopted by the mid-nineteenth century, it was only in 1899 that a truly autonomous juvenile court was established in Chicago, Illinois. In the first quarter of the twentieth century, virtually all other American states established juvenile courts and a separate juvenile justice system. The official rationale of the reformers who promoted a separate juvenile justice system was that children were fundamentally different from adults, and it was in their interest as well as that of society to help them—through close supervision and rehabilitative programs—rather than to make punishment the priority. Although some scholars largely accept this standard account and view the establishment of the juvenile court as a "child-saving" progressive reform, others have argued that it was actually motivated by growing fear of hordes of immigrant children flooding into American cities and the desire to exercise greater control over them (as well as other problem children) (Platt 1977). In still another interpretation the juvenile court was established principally as a formalization of the general trend toward greater discretionary control over children (Sutton 1985). In all likelihood, then, some mixture of motives and objectives was involved.

The official rationale for establishing the juvenile justice system was that those below a certain age were either victims themselves (of circumstances) or insufficiently mature to be held responsible for their actions and that accordingly the juvenile court should take steps toward ensuring their rehabilitation and eventual return to society as constructive citizens. In line with this philosophy of the court acting in place of parents and for the best interest of the child, the juvenile justice system afforded juveniles brought before it few if any due process rights. Although the relative informality of the juvenile court proceedings may have benefitted some of the juveniles brought before the court, it also resulted in other juveniles being remanded to juvenile correctional facilities on the basis of slender or nonexistent evidence. Furthermore, despite the claim that juvenile correctional facilities were supposed to rehabilitate juvenile offenders, these facilities typically had many punitive and stigmatizing attributes, and were likely to be experienced as punishment by the juvenile inmates.

Extension of Due Process Rights

During the Warren Court era of the 1960s, a series of U.S. Supreme Court decisions extended more formal rights to juveniles brought before the juvenile courts: *Kent v. U.S.* (1966) prohibited these courts from making procedurally arbitrary decisions; the landmark *In Re Gault* (1967) established that juveniles were entitled to certain basic due process rights, such as notification of charges, protection against self-incrimination, the right to confront witnesses, and the right to have a written transcript of the proceedings; in a third case, *In Re Winship* (1970), the Court ruled that the standard of beyond a reasonable doubt must be applied in cases where a juvenile faces incarceration in a locked facility.

Although broader due process rights have been extended to juveniles accused of violating the law, it does not follow that these rights are uniformly implemented in practice, and the overall operation of the juvenile courts continues to be considerably more informal than that of the adult criminal courts. Much evidence of bias in the operation of juvenile justice can certainly be identified. A far higher percentage of male juveniles than females have always gotten in trouble with the law, but historically female juveniles were more likely than males to be processed by the juvenile justice system for sex-related behavior. In one view, then, the juvenile justice system has been a manifestation of male dominance and has been used against female juveniles to reinforce traditional role expectations for females (Alder 1984; Chesney-Lind 1978; Shelden 1998). Lower-class, inner-city youths, especially blacks and other minorities, have also been disproportionately brought into the juvenile justice system; the misdeeds of middle-class, suburban, white youths have traditionally been more likely to be overlooked or disposed of with informal discretion (Chambliss 1973b; Sampson and Laub 1993). It appears, then, that juvenile justice processing has been applied most vigorously to those segments of the juvenile population viewed as most threatening to the influential white middle class. It may be, however, that lower-class single-parent mothers may be more likely than middle-class parents to turn to the juvenile courts when they find themselves unable to control their children.

Cycles of Harshness and Lenience

The juvenile justice system continues to endure conflicting demands: to protect and nurture wayward (and abused) children; to grant juveniles, as young citizens, due process rights; to protect society from harmful predators; and so on. The juvenile justice system appears to have undergone alternating cycles emphasizing either harshness or lenience (Bernard 1992). In the punitive cycle (associated with a more conservative political environment), the general public has become fearful over youth crime, especially when it takes the form of extreme violence, and calls for tough measures to incapacitate and punish juvenile offenders. Protection from juvenile predators is the priority here. In the lenience cycle (associated with a more liberal political environment), the general public has become disenchanted with punitive measures (which are viewed as largely ineffective) and disturbed by revelations of severe abuse of juveniles in correctional facilities. The long-term needs of juveniles themselves—and, by extension, society—is the priority here. Both the perceived ineffectiveness and the harmfulness of subjecting juveniles to juvenile justice system processing calls for "radical nonintervention," which means that many minor forms of juvenile deviance and misbehavior are tolerated, and justice system processing is reserved for serious juvenile predators (Schur 1973). In the final era of the twentieth century the punitive cycle was dominant (Birch 1997; Geraghty and Drizin 1997; Small 1997). The juvenile court was described as a second-class criminal court that disproportionately imposed tough sanctions on minority youths (Feld 1999). These developments can be attributed to both the more conservative political environment of this period and the public perception (fostered by the media) of an increase in especially gruesome and violent crimes by juveniles (see Box 8.2).

A century after the establishment of the first juvenile court in Chicago, controversy over the future of the juvenile justice system was vigorous (Ainsworth 1991; O'Connor and Treat 1996). Those involved with juvenile justice were divided not only on the question of how far juveniles should be held morally and criminally responsible for their offenses, but also on whether the juvenile courts should be abolished because they were both ineffective and unfair or should be retained because they were more responsive to the special circumstances of children (Geraghty and Drizin 1997, 5). The twentieth century witnessed the establishment of a full-fledged juvenile justice system, but the twenty-first century has to contend with the troubled and somewhat unsatisfactory legacy of this history.

Law and the Civil Justice System

On the whole, less public and political attention has focused on the civil justice system than on the criminal justice system, although in the recent era

Box 8.2

Juvenile Waivers

In the late 1970s many states began to adopt procedures to facilitate the processing and punishing of serious juvenile offenders as adults. These waivers (or transfers) of juvenile cases to adult criminal courts reflect the action of state legislative bodies, responding to public pressure (Feiler and Sheley 1999). According to polls, the American public overwhelmingly (90 percent) supports such waivers for violent juvenile offenders, with at least two-thirds supporting waivers for juveniles who commit property and drug-related offenses (Wu 2000). Unsurprisingly, such support declines in the case of younger juvenile offenders; disturbingly, it increases if the juvenile is African American (Feiler and Sheley 1999).

Proponents of juvenile waivers to criminal court argue that they are a necessary measure against tough, dangerous juvenile offenders; they contribute to the deterrence of juvenile offenses; and they reflect the public will. Critics contend that waivers are ineffective and inappropriate; are applied inconsistently and in a discriminatory manner; and in the long term damage and make more threatening juveniles who will eventually be released into society (O'Connor and Treat 1996). The increasing reliance upon and support for waivers of juveniles to adult criminal courts is a major challenge to the original rationale for the establishment of a separate juvenile justice system.

the civil justice system has begun to attract more attention than in the past (Galanter et al. 1994). Major criminal trials are a staple of the media, and some—for example, the O. J. Simpson trial for murder—become a national obsession. Of course, there are at least some civil trials as well that generate considerable public interest and media attention: for example, when the President is sued for sexual harassment; when a superstar is caught up in an ugly divorce case; when a Fortune 500 corporation is ordered to pay hundreds of millions of dollars in fines and to pay for damages, and so on. The civil justice system has impact on the lives of large numbers of ordinary people, sometimes in profound ways.

The civil justice system is arguably the oldest of the different justice systems, since the earliest courts in ancient times were organized to provide remedies to those who could establish that they had been harmed by some other party. From this early time a primary objective for the civil justice system has been for the state to provide an orderly (nonviolent) mechanism for the resolution of interpersonal disputes. Increasingly in the modern era, disputes between individuals and organizations, or between different organizations, are involved. The civil law is concerned with private, not public, wrongs, and disputes between private parties (although the government is sometimes a party in these suits). Some civil justice issues—such as tort law reform and the challenge to no-fault divorce—have an increasingly public profile. In one definition, "Any court proceeding in which the objective is not the infliction by the state of punishment for unlawful acts is termed a civil proceeding"(Mayers 1973, 12).

The range of possible harms and disputes, then, is exceptionally broad. Of course, the vast majority of disputes—between husbands and wives, landlords and tenants, consumers and retailers, and so on—are resolved without resorting to law. Disputes are social constructs, not "things." They may be transformed into civil lawsuits by evolving through several stages: first, the recognition that a particular experience has been injurious (naming); second, attributing the injury to another (blaming); and third, asking for a remedy (claiming) (Felstiner, Abel, and Sarat 1989). Even when people do turn to the law, some form of settlement as opposed to a court trial is the norm. These settlements—for example, in the case of divorce—may occur in "the shadow of the law" (Mnookin and Kornhauser 1979). This notion means that the formal law greatly influences how people define their troubles and formulate their claims. Whether such an influence exists has been disputed (Jacob 1992).

Is There a Litigation Explosion?

The claim that Americans have for some time been too inclined to sue each other and that we have been experiencing a "litigation explosion" was recounted earlier in this text. It is difficult to reliably measure litigation across time and place, however, so this claim has been challenged (Friedman 1996b; Jacob 1996, 49). If the likelihood of formal litigation increases when people have proportionally more dealings with others with whom they are not on intimate terms, then we should expect more civil lawsuits in America as such patterns of contact increase; on the other hand, if formal litigation is viewed as economically inefficient by businesses, then we should expect less litigation in a highly developed capitalist society. Although civil filings in the United States increased at a rate several times the rate of increase in the population in the recent era, most of these cases involve petty disputes (often in small claims courts), domestic matters (mainly uncontested divorces), and estate matters (also typically uncontested) (Friedman 1996b, 56). Of some 20 million civil cases filed in a given year, then, only a very small proportion involve major litigation on substantial matters.

There has been an increase in certain types of civil litigation (e.g., rights-related; product liability; medical malpractice) as well as in the number of class action suits and multimillion dollar civil judgments. And some evidence suggests that civil litigation filings increase in the face of tort law reform, as prospective plaintiffs fear the new laws will limit their options (Marvell 1994). But the inclination to sue is also linked with such factors as class membership. Neither the very rich nor the very poor are likely to settle their disputes by turning to law; the upper middle class, however, has both the resources and the peer support to encourage a higher level of litigation (Silberman 1985). Obviously, the more serious a dispute is, the more likely it will lead to litigation. Also, if a lawyer is contacted, litigation is more likely (see Box 8.3).

Civil litigation in the contemporary era is more likely than in the past to involve class action suits, where large numbers of plaintiffs (e.g., consumers injured by a particular product; workers jeopardized by dangerous working conditions) join together in a lawsuit (Priest 1997). Corporations are the most common targets of these class action suits, and altogether some of the most significant and highest-stake civil litigation involves corporations.

Box 8.3

Some Major Types of Civil Law

The term *tort* is used for a private injury caused by one party to another (in the form of injury either to a person or to property). In classical legal terms, a tort involves a breach of duty (broadly defined) by one party toward another, with some form of injury resulting. A tort may be intentional—for example, in a case of defamation of character—although no violation of the criminal code is involved. A large percentage of tort actions, however, arise out of unintentional actions (or failures to act), such as negligence. Automobile accidents, for example, typically involve negligence, and are the most common basis for litigation in the United States (Jacob 1996, 59). If an injury of some kind is claimed, it must be shown that an act (or inaction) on the part of the party being sued is the proximate (direct and necessary) cause of the injury. Issues of contributory negligence on the part of the injured party may arise. In some cases the doctrine of *strict liability* is in effect. This means that the party being sued may be held liable if harm can be shown, even in the absence of any deliberate action on the part of this party. For example, this standard is applied if a consumer suffers some identifiable harm after using a defective product.

In addition to torts, the civil justice system covers a vast range of disputes arising out of all manner of business and personal dealings. Contracts are a central element of a complex, modern society, especially where many of one's dealings are with relative strangers. A contract has been defined, quite concisely, as "an enforceable promise about what is owed to and by people who have entered into some sort of exchange relationship with one another"(McIntyre 1994, 13). Many issues arise in connection with claims that the terms of a contract have not been properly fulfilled; the contract was signed in ignorance, or under some form of duress; or the contract is fraudulent or unconscionable on some grounds.

Another class of civil cases concerns issues pertaining to property. Property in complex, modern societies takes many forms, from real property (such as land) to intellectual property, such as a patent, copyrighted creative work, or trademark. In an immensely influential law review article in 1964 Charles Reich, then a professor at Yale Law School, identified new forms of government-created property—including welfare benefits; government employment; occupational licenses; franchises; government contracts, subsidies, and services—that in turn have become a basis of civil litigation (Minda 1995). Civil suits can arise over conflicting claims of possession of property or unauthorized use of someone's property. Cases contesting the validity of wills and trusts would also fit into this category.

Family law, of course, encompasses matters pertaining to separation, annulment, and divorce, as well as to custody issues. This may be the single most emotionally vulnerable realm of civil litigation, and one requiring arbitrators and judges to make painfully difficult decisions (Maccoby and Mnookin 1992).

Beyond these basic categories of civil litigation, one finds an almost endless range of other matters, including cases involving every imaginable form of commercial transaction and business arrangement, labor and management cases (including such matters as working conditions and job loss), and cases alleging violation of civil rights or other rights.

Judgments of Damages

The single most common remedy sought in a civil proceeding is monetary damages. Strictly speaking, a judicial finding of a monetary judgment is a declaration of the right of the winning party to such payment, although if it is not made voluntarily, a sheriff might seize and sell property belonging to the losing party to satisfy the judgment. These monetary damages are divided between compensation for direct losses and punitive damages for the wrong done to the plaintiff. As a rule, it is easier to establish a figure for compensatory damage (e.g., through hospital bills; lost wages) than an appropriate dollar figure for punitive damages. In the recent era, in particular, figures in the millions—occasionally, even in the billions—are sometimes awarded in civil cases. Civil litigation directed at major tobacco companies in the final years of the twentieth century was one high-profile instance of multibillion dollar judgments. Such outcomes are especially likely to be reported in the media, of course, but they are rare. Even in these cases, an appeals court often reduces, sometimes drastically, the size of the original award. The monetary damages in typical cases is several thousand dollars, not several million dollars (Jacob 1996, 49).

Many civil suits seek some form of remedy other than monetary damages: a divorce or custody of children; a job restored or an unfairly denied promotion granted; a contract enforced or voided. In some cases, plaintiffs seek an *injunction*, or an order that the other party either perform some act or cease engaging in some activity. An injunction is generally regarded as more extreme than the awarding of monetary damages, and it is not often granted by the courts.

Civil Court Proceedings

Just as is the case with the criminal justice system, civil cases may be pursued in state courts or federal court. Although the vast majority of civil lawsuits are heard in state courts, some increase in federal cases has occurred. A very small class of cases—for example, disputes on water rights between two states—might go directly to the United States Supreme Court. Most federal cases are heard in lower federal courts (district courts). Cases involving a federally granted right—for example, the right to be free of discrimination—as well as maritime cases arising at sea are civil matters heard in federal court. Cases involving citizens (or, increasingly, corporations) in different states (diversity cases) where an excess of $10,000 in monetary damages is sought may also be taken to federal courts. The balance of civil disputes are directed to a state court; minor matters are assigned to informal small claims courts, and those involving major issues and substantial financial claims are assigned to the formal civil court.

Although claimants in small claims courts make their own case without the assistance of a lawyer, formal civil court proceedings are difficult, if not impossible, for lay people to navigate. While major corporations and businesses have in-house counsel or pay major law firms retainers and large hourly fees to represent them, small businesses and ordinary citizens must typically pay their own lawyers. For some kinds of cases (e.g., divorce) a fixed fee rather than an hourly fee may be involved. Poor people who cannot afford such fees must turn to some form of legal aid, but such aid is not always readily available. The contingency fee system—where the attorney receives a percentage of the monetary damages recovered, if any, but nothing if the case is lost—has been justified as a means of enabling ordinary citizens to sue for harm incurred without having to pay legal fees they cannot afford, especially if the case is unsuccessful. On the other hand, the contingency fee system has also been criticized for encouraging greedy plaintiffs and lawyers to go after defendants with "deep pockets."

Specific procedures in the civil court systems of the various states vary somewhat, although the most basic elements are fairly uniform. Many civil complaints are filed without any serious expectation of taking the case to trial but rather as a tactic for securing a favorable judgment or settlement (Jacob 1996, 56). In fact, the vast majority of civil cases are resolved by a default judgment (i.e., a judgment on behalf of the plaintiff when the defendant fails to respond) or a negotiated settlement. If cases do go to trial, they may be heard by a judge or a jury. The use of juries in civil cases is rare outside of the United States and is also controversial on some grounds; some say that lay juries are not competent to understand issues in complex civil cases and are too prone to manipulation by lawyers playing on their sympathy. Juries are far more likely to be used in personal injury cases than in cases involving sophisticated business dealings.

The civil justice system differs from the criminal justice system in that it does not have large enforcement and vast correctional components. The civil justice system is mainly concentrated in the court. But the civil justice system is not wholly without enforcement and correctional dimensions. Sheriffs, for example, are empowered to make seizures of property to satisfy claims. Some civil cases—for example, failure to make child support payments—may result in jail time. (Figure 8.1 summarizes the way cases move through the civil, criminal, and juvenile justice systems.)

Millions of Americans in any given year will find themselves parties to a civil proceeding, from divorce to a major tort claim against a corporation. In the contemporary era major corporations and prestigious professionals such as doctors have sometimes bitterly complained that they are victims of a civil litigation system that is out of control. On balance, however, the evidence strongly suggests that the poor and powerless are more likely to be at a disadvantage through inadequate or nonexistent representation and through judgments against them that they can ill afford.

Law and the Administrative/ Regulatory Justice System

Administrative law and the regulatory system of justice is generally far less visible than either the criminal justice system or the civil justice system. Yet throughout much of the twentieth century, and especially in the final decades of the century, administrative law and regulatory justice became increasingly important and pervasive (Schwartz 1996). In one sense of the term administrative justice is nothing new, since administrative and judicial

Figure 8.1 How Cases Move Through the Criminal Justice System, the Juvenile Justice System, and the Civil Justice System*

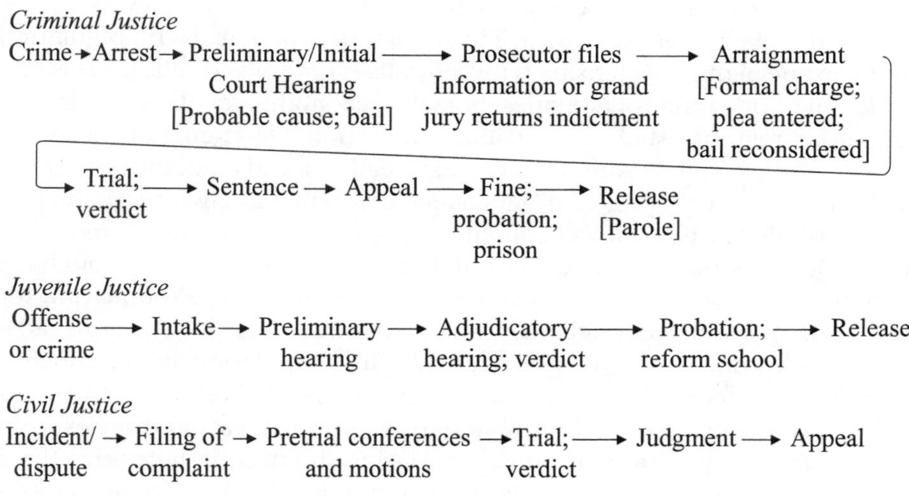

*Cases may be dropped, diverted, or settled at any stage of the process. Accordingly, the charts here provide only a rough approximation of the basic stages through which a case might move.

functions were often combined in an earlier time (for example, governors in the American colonies also served as judges) (Mayers 1973, 74). Here, the term administrative law refers to the body of law that both creates and governs administrative and regulatory agencies. The term administrative or regulatory justice refers to the various boards, commissions, and agencies that enforce rules and hold administrative hearings on, or adjudicate, cases in their particular jurisdiction. Regulatory law/justice specifically refers to the rules made and enforced by the regulatory agencies, although the terms administrative and regulatory law are sometimes used interchangeably (Carter 1983, 38). Examples of administrative agencies hearing cases could include the Immigration Service deportation hearings, a Workman's Compensation Board hearing relating to an on-the-job injury and disability payments, Equal Employment Opportunity Commission (EEOC) hearings on a claim of job discrimination, and National Labor Relations Board hearings on union complaints against management. Although any of these matters can be appealed to a court in the formal civil justice system, the vast majority of such matters are resolved on the administrative level; many factors (including costs) discourage appeals to the courts. Within administrative agencies, those who perform judicial functions ideally are not also involved in administrative functions—to avoid conflicts of interest—but in many state agencies such functions are not really separated (Mayers 1973, 71). One important form of administrative justice is carried out on both the federal and state level by various regulatory agencies, and such regulatory justice will be the focus of this section.

Economic Regulation Versus Social Regulation

Some form of marketplace regulation was characteristic of even ancient civilizations. Throughout the feudal period in Europe the market was heavily regulated on behalf of the Crown. The American experience with regulation has been one of ongoing tension between calls for more and calls for less regulation of a wide range of activities. So-called economic regulation (addressing market relations such as securities transactions) has generally been less resisted by the business community than so-called social regulation (addressing harmful consequences of productive activity such as environmental pollution). While most businesses benefit from the market stability promoted by economic regulation, social regulation tends to cut into profits. Although the Commerce clause of the American Constitution provided a foundation for regulation, the nineteenth century was dominated by a "laissez faire" economic philosophy and involved relatively little regulation in the modern sense. The first federal regulatory agency, the Interstate Commerce Commission (ICC), was created in 1887 by Congress to protect various parties from unfair rates and practices of railroads. During the twentieth century there were three major waves of regulatory activity: the Progressive era (1900–1914), when such acts as the Pure Food and Drug Act (1906) were passed, addressing unsafe production practices; the New Deal era (1930s), when agencies such as the Securities and Exchange Commission (SEC) were created, addressing unscrupulous market activities; and the Great Society era (late 1960s to early 1970s), when various agencies were created, such as the Environmental Protection Agency (EPA) and the Occupational Safety and Health Administration (OSHA), to address a range of unsafe business practices. Some other significant regulatory agencies, in addition to those named, include the Food and Drug Administration (FDA), the Federal Trade Commission (FTC), the Federal Aviation Agency (FAA), the Federal Communications Commission (FCC), and the Consumer Product Safety Commission.

The regulatory agencies are somewhat unusual entities within the American system of government because they have legislative, executive (enforcement), and judicial functions.

Legislative Functions

First, the regulatory agencies have been authorized by Congress to create specific rules within their area of responsibility (for example, the Environmental Protection Agency produces rules pertaining to environmental practices, and the Occupational Safety and Health Administration produces rules pertaining to workplace conditions). This authorization might seem to be in violation of a Constitutional prohibition against Congress delegating lawmaking powers to any other entity. But the Supreme Court has held that the rule making of regulatory agencies is essentially filling in details of laws, not lawmaking itself. As a practical matter, Congress (and state legislative bodies) cannot produce the countless specific standards and rules in the many different areas of activity overseen by the various regulatory agencies. Congress (or the state legislature) officially has oversight powers over this regulatory agency rule making, but it typically defers to the agencies' expertise.

Enforcement Functions

The regulatory agencies are empowered to enforce the rules they have created, but they are still bound by constitutional standards in this process. Regulatory enforcement styles vary greatly, and an ongoing debate divides those who favor agencies emphasizing compliance and those who favor agencies stressing deterrence, or the choice between persuasion and punishment (Braithwaite, Walker, and Grabosky 1987; Frank and Lombness 1988; Gunningham 1987; Kagan 1989). Both practical considerations (i.e., the vast number of businesses to be regulated, and the huge resources of at least some of these businesses) as well as political philosophy (e.g., progressive or conservative) influence choices that regulators make in this respect. Regulatory enforcement differs from conventional policing enforcement because it relies heavily on self-policing by those within its jurisdication. When violations of regulatory rules are brought to the attention of regulatory agencies, the notifications can come from many sources, including consumer complaints, government investigations, congressional committee investigations, business competitors, the media, and employees (Clinard and Yeager 1980, 81–83). Although regulatory agencies may actively initiate investigations, such investigation involves a complex, costly commitment, so more often than not an agency investigation is a reaction to complaints from others.

Judicial Functions

When it is determined that further action or hearings are appropriate, regulatory agencies can act informally in many circumstances, without observing due process guidelines (Friedrichs 1996). If the investigation uncovers a serious violation of criminal law, the regulatory agency can refer the matter to the Department of Justice for possible criminal prosecution. Regulatory agencies often prefer not to do this, for a variety of reasons (e.g., it is a concession of their failure to prevent such wrongdoing; they lose control of the case; it may be counterproductive in terms of long-term relations with the industry being regulated). More often, the regulatory agency holds its own hearings on violations. A fairly large body of law, codified by the Adminstrative Procedure Act (APA) in 1946, governs formal agency proceedings (Moore, Magaldi, and Gray 1987, 120). Agency hearings most typically take the form of quasi-criminal proceedings but are less formal than regular court hearings and trials (Metzger et al. 1986, 36). Such hearings are presided over by an administrative judge or hearing examiner, who is independent of agency personnel. Defendants can have attorneys, but they are not entitled to a jury trial. Administrative judges and hearing examiners are empowered to impose various orders or sanctions on defendants, including cease-and-desist orders (equivalent to injuctions); special orders (e.g., directives intended to correct past conduct or to call for product recalls); consent orders (negotiations regarding certain actions); summary orders (e.g., prevention of the sale of food); and license suspension or revocation (Clinard and Yeager 1980, 94; Frank and Lombness 1988). Also, they can impose fines.

Regulatory agency cases may be referred for criminal action or may lead to civil suits. Appeals from hearing decisions must first go through an internal agency appeal process and only then are eligible for appellate court review, although appellate courts have typically been reluctant to overturn agency decisions (Metzger et al. 1986, 37). When agency decisions are overturned, the basis for such reversals is likely to be a determination that the decision was fundamentally arbitrary, capricious, or discriminatory; was not based on substantial evidence; violated applicable constitutional safeguards; or exceeded the statutory authority of the agency.

Focus of Controversy

As suggested earlier, the administrative justice of regulatory agencies has been a focus of ongoing controversy. Many business interests and political conservatives have regarded the regulatory agencies as inefficient, ineffective governmental bureaucracies that interfere—with unfortunate economic consequences—in the operation of the free market. Regulators themselves are viewed as unelected, faceless bureaucrats rendering incompetent decisions. These interests favor abolishing most of the regulatory agencies or, at a minimum, stripping them of the means to interfere with and penalize businesses. The other side of the controversy comes from citizen/consumer/worker activists and political progressives, who are more likely to express concern over "agency capture," which here means that agencies are too much influenced by or even dominated by the industries they are supposed to regulate (in part, because the regulators often come out of those industries and expect to return to them). These interests typically favor adopting policies strengthening the autonomy or independence of regulatory agencies and arming them with powerful means to oversee (and if necessary punish) the various industries. This debate over regulatory agencies, and administrative justice generally, is sure to continue.

Law and the Military Justice System

The military has traditionally had laws of its own and has administered its own justice system, going back at least to the time of the ancient Romans (Bishop 1974, 3). During warfare, and occasionally as a consequence of an especially sensational case, military justice comes to the attention of the larger public. For the most part, however, military justice receives little public attention and interest (Bishop 1974; Keveles 1984, 284). Throughout history, the military has been the dominant political force in at least some countries, and has sometimes imposed its own autocratic and harsh form of justice on a whole society. Also, *military governments* have sometimes been imposed on defeated enemies by the victorious side, as was the case after World War II when a temporary government headed by American General Douglas MacArthur was imposed upon the defeated Japan.

Americans, however, have been traditionally leery of direct military involvement in affairs of state (as have citizens of other democratic nations), and for the most part some lines of separation between military and civil government affairs have been maintained. High-level military commanders have often been influential in state affairs, however, and some prominent generals (from Washington to Eisenhower) have become presidents (see Box 8.4).

Box 8.4

Martial Law

Constitutional, statutory, and executive provisions and powers allow for the declaration of *martial law* in a national emergency. Full martial law is most likely to be declared in a time of war or rebellion, or in the face of a serious threat of external invasion or internal insurrection. If full martial law is in effect, military commanders are granted broad powers to control governmental operations and to seize and detain (without trial) any parties deemed threatening to the state. Full martial law has been invoked infrequently in American history (for example, during the War of 1812, during the Civil War, and in Hawaii following the attack on Pearl Harbor) (Myren 1988, 54). Sometimes the President or one of the state governors calls out the national guard or the state militia to impose partial martial law in a temporary emergency situation (for example, following a natural disaster or in response to rioting and potentially violent protest demonstrations). In these cases the military supplements, but does not replace or supercede, the civilian system of justice. While such use of martial law is generally supported by most of the civilian population, it can also inspire controversy. In 1971, for example, the National Guard was called in at Kent State University (Ohio) in response to an antiwar demonstration, and several students were shot and killed by guardsmen (Davies 1973). This led to a firestorm of protest and demonstrations across the country.

Military justice typically refers to the ongoing administration of justice by military commanders, to those under their command. This system of justice has its roots in the Articles of War implemented by the Continental Congress in 1775, as well as in the Constitution, executive orders, and statutes. The Uniform Code of Military Justice, which has been revised periodically over the years, spells out the specific provisions of the relevant law. Although the civilian justice system has traditionally avoided interfering with military justice, the decisions of military courts are subject to review by federal courts, and in 1950 a Court of Military Appeals, made up of civilian appointees, was established to provide some oversight on decisions made within a purely military environment.

Military justice has jurisdiction over all those who are serving in one of the branches of the military, whether as draftees, enlisted members, or commissioned officers; it also has some jurisdiction over civilians serving with or accompanying military forces, and may be used in cases involving foreign spys. The principal rationale for military justice is to maintain the order and discipline necessary for the successful fulfillment of the military's mission. Obviously any form of aid to the enemy is regarded as an especially serious offense, but fundamental violations of military discipline are also treated seriously. The improper treatment of enemy captives or disposition of captured property, as well as misconduct as a prisoner of war, are also significant violations within the context of war.

Existing military law has been criticized as imposing a strong obligation of obedience to the commands of superior officers; this obligation can obviously conflict with principles proscribing blatantly illegal conduct. Mark Osiel (1999) calls for a transformation of military law that would stress tactical imagination, self-discipline, and loyalty to immediate comrades rather than blind obedience to superior orders.

Since the United States is not at war most of the time, military justice cases principally address violations of military discipline. Although some such violations are specifically spelled out—for example, failure to obey an order—a court martial is also possible for "conduct unbecoming an officer and a gentleman" (or gentlewoman), which is sufficiently vague to allow for fairly broad application (Myren 1988, 96). In the 1990s, in a series of episodes thoroughly embarrassing to the military, various officers (including several of high rank) were tried before military tribunals on sexual harassment charges. These charges reflected both a growing societal attention to sexual harassment and the increasingly coeducational character of the military forces. In some cases the criminal act of rape was charged; the military justice system also has the option of trying those under its jurisdiction for such criminal charges. Of course the most serious criminal charges, such as homicide, may be referred to the civilian justice system.

The military tribunals that hear court-martial cases are composed of superior officers, who are not typically the peers of those being tried (Mayers 1973, 82). Since these officers are chosen by the commanding officer within the particular jurisdiction, it is a legitimate concern that they may be controlled by this superior and may be more concerned with fulfilling military objectives than with doing justice. An unresolved question, then, is whether the somewhat authoritarian character of much military justice can be comfortably reconciled with expectations of full respect for individual rights and due process.

Informal Justice: Alternative Dispute Resolution and Mediation

Law and the formal systems of justice inspire much frustration, huge economic costs, and endless conflict. The formal system of justice is experienced by many as intimidating or inaccessible. It is widely believed, with some justification, that the powerful and privileged tend to have the advantage in this system of justice. In a now classic article entitled "Why the Haves Come Out Ahead: Speculations on the Limits of Legal Change," Marc Galanter (1974) argued that financially and organizationally stronger parties tend to prevail in litigation over weaker parties, especially to the extent that they are "repeat players" in the court system. Subsequent research has generally confirmed this thesis (e.g., Kritzer and Silbey 1999; Wheeler et al. 1987).

Of course, it has always been true, and continues to be true, that countless disputes between different parties are resolved informally, without turning to law. Even when cases or disputes do go before the formal system of law, they are most likely to be resolved informally. The great majority of criminal cases are settled by plea bargaining; the vast majority of civil cases are settled by negotiation (Emmelman 1996). As a general proposition, the more complex and developed a society is, the more it will rely on formal law and legal institutions to resolve disputes. Preliterate and less developed societies are more likely to resolve disputes informally.

American Tradition

Within the American tradition a commitment to informal justice on the part of some has always been a factor. As was noted elsewhere, the earliest American settlers were often hostile toward lawyers and formal legal institutions, especially if they had suffered from persecution in the Old World. Among the Puritans and the Quakers, for example, a strong bias in favor of informal justice prevailed. On the Western frontier, disputes were often settled outside the boundaries of formal law, and small Western ranchers in the modern era continue to seek justice outside the formal law in many cases (Ellickson 1991). As Jerold Auerbach (1983) recounts, not only these early communities but many later American communities as well—including utopian nineteenth-century communities (e.g., Oneida and the Mormon settlements); ethnic immigrant communities (e.g., Scandinavian and Chinese immigrants); and workforce/commercial communities (e.g., the labor movement and chambers of commerce)—rejected formal litigation and sought to resolve disputes by informal means. Over time, according to Auerbach, alternatives to formal law came to be manipulated by the state as a means of limiting the rights of the disadvantaged. Whether informal justice resulted in less authoritarian, fairer, and generally superior justice for the parties involved is a matter of interpretation and debate (Abel 1981, 1982; Fitzpatrick 1992b; Pavlich 1996; Sebba 1996). Religious and other community leaders who oversee these informal procedures obviously may administer capricious, biased, and even cruel outcomes; in the ideal circumstance, of course, they resolve disputes fairly, harmoniously, and efficiently.

The contemporary call for greater reliance upon informal justice—or alternative dispute resolution (ADR)—can be interpreted in different ways (Cimini 1997; Edwards 1986). On the one hand, alternative dispute resolution, typically some form of mediation, can be endorsed as a more humane, open, equitable, conciliatory, understandable, and efficient means of settling cases. The parties avoid the alienating, power-influenced, class-biased, conflict-oriented, argot-ridden, and often costly and time-consuming dimensions of the formal legal system. On the other hand, alternative dispute resolution, and informal justice generally, has been criticized on the grounds that it leads to a more arbitrary form of justice, governed more by biases than by due process; that it saves the state money at the expense of other parties; that it creates a lower tier of justice to resolve disputes of the underprivileged; that it puts the powerless at an even greater disadvantage than they face in the formal system of justice; and that it expands the scope of the state's involvement in people's lives (Abel 1981, 1982; Fiss 1984; Henry 1985). In this view, informal justice distracts people from the fundamental problems in society and transforms their troubles into interpersonal disputes. Accordingly, informal justice in a capitalist system may simply serve to mask inherent inequalities and help preserve the system rather than making it more equitable and fair.

Popular Justice

The term *informal justice* is sometimes used interchangeably with, or as parallel to, popular justice, vigilante justice, community justice, neighborhood justice, and private justice. These related terms, however, tend to have distinctive connotations. *Popular justice* is most closely associated with the form of justice administered within post-revolutionary societies, such as Russia, China, and Cuba after their communist revolutions. The essence of such justice is that it rejects the formal system of law and courts (viewed as instruments of capitalist class interests) and replaces it with popular tribunals made up of political leaders and representatives of the people, and these tribunals apply the principles of revolutionary doctrine and future objectives to dispose of cases. Although in the early stages of post-revolutionary societies, popular justice has often been embraced enthusiastically and has substantial participation and interest from ordinary citizens, the trend has been toward gradual reintroduction of increasingly formal systems of law. Although such popular justice may have advanced some revolutionary objectives and in at least some individual cases resulted in correcting past injustices, much injustice also clearly resulted. Arbitrary, and sometimes cruel, judgments were imposed on many people not protected by due process, and whole lives, families, and communities were effectively destroyed.

The term popular justice is not unique to communist societies, however, and in the American context, it has been applied to justice influenced or determined by popular (public) opinion which is sometimes at odds with the formal rule of law (Walker 1980). In the more extreme cases such popular justice has taken the form of *vigilante justice* (or mob justice) and lynch law. In the frontier West and in the traditional South, for example, a very rough form of vigilante or mob justice was sometimes administered, with vulnerable parties (e.g., black people in the South) subjected to flogging, expulsion, or lynching on the mere rumor or suspicion of some wrongdoing, without any attention to due process (Brown 1979). Vigilante justice was justified by frontier communities as necessary to maintain a civilized way of life in the absense of formal legal institutions, and among traditional Southerners as necessary to preserve their way of life in the face of interference by outside forces.

Community Justice

Community justice is a somewhat more neutral term for the administration of justice by a particular community, although the membership of a "community" is not always obvious (Bazemore 1997). Such justice is administered by lay people who are members of a community in some sense of the term (e.g., live in a common area; belong to a professional association; are part of a university) (Henry 1981, 186–188). The related term *neighborhood justice* refers to justice administered at neighborhood justice centers established in many American communities in the 1970s with federal funding. Trained mediators, who may or may not be lawyers, attempt to resolve disputes between parties who may have been referred to the center by the formal court, and have agreed to such a resolution of their case. The several hundred such centers tend to serve large metropolitan areas, however, and so do not typically involve neighbors—in the conventional sense of the term—administering justice for each other. Accordingly, they have been criticized as another means of expanding state control (Hofrichter 1987). Ideal objectives of these courts, such as lower costs and more informal, efficient resolution of cases, have not always been met (Tomasic and Feeley 1982). And the closely related term *private justice* refers to the resolution of disputes from within a private institution, typically a business (Henry 1981). Again, all these terms may be used interchangeably (see Box 8.5).

Although community justice institutions are supposed to implement the values of a particular community in a democratic fashion, the makeup of the community tribunal is not necessarily the outcome of democratic means of selection. Community courts typically have procedural guidelines but also have considerable discretion in how they interpret and carry out the guidelines. Professional associations, as noted elsewhere, have proceedings to discipline their members and in extreme cases to strip them of their license to practice. Such disciplinary bodies often have been viewed as more concerned with protecting the image and financial well-being of the profession than with administering justice to individuals and protecting the general public. Internal disciplinary hearings held by colleges are also examples of such community, or private, justice. For example, a coed who has been raped by a date may choose to take the matter to a college disciplinary tribunal rather than reporting it to the police, so she can avoid the stress of publicity and criminal justice proceedings. In some cases, however, the complainant may feel that the college is more concerned with protecting its reputation and avoiding publicity than with taking appropriate action against the accused; the accused may feel he has been subjected to accusations and stigmatization on the basis of a false case that could not hold up in a court of law.

A system of justice is not necessarily either formal or informal. Rather, a continuum between the highly formal and the thoroughly informal may be

Box 8.5

Private Justice and the World of Business

In a sociolegal classic, Stewart Macaulay (1963) demonstrated that businessmen found it more conducive to ongoing business relations to avoid formal, legalistic contracts in their dealings whenever possible. And private justice is often preferred by businesses when an employee has been caught stealing from the company, for a variety of reasons. It minimizes the chances of embarrassing publicity, saves time and money, contributes to more harmonious relations with employees generally, and increases the employer's control over employees.

If private justice can be potentially beneficial for both employer and employee (who avoids formal processing by the criminal justice system), it can also be administered abusively, especially if the employer is victim, prosecutor, judge, and jury (Henry 1981, 185). Due process and privacy rights of employees may be disregarded, and employees may suffer severe sanctions—including the loss of a job—on the basis of minimal evidence. Of course, employees who feel they have been unjustly treated by these procedures may turn to the civil courts and sue, although this choice involves substantial costs and risks.

said to exist (Norrie 1996). Formal law and informal law are often interdependent (Harrington 1985; Henry 1983). Civil courts sometimes require that parties attempt to resolve differences first through mediation (Clarke and Gordon 1997). The juvenile justice courts, as discussed above, have been a classic example of a system of justice combining informal and formal elements. Although the informalism of the juvenile courts traditionally has been justified as in the best interest of juveniles appearing before the court, recently, more formalism has been reintroduced to protect the rights of these juveniles.

Small Claims Court

Small claims courts are an example of a legal institution with both formal and informal dimensions (Conley and O'Barr 1990; Vidmar 1984). On the one hand, a judge presides over small claims court cases and imposes a decision on the parties involved. On the other hand, the proceedings are far more informal than those in conventional court hearings. Each party states her or his own case, and the judge directs questions to each of the parties. Cases that might go into small claims courts include disputes between neighbors (for example, regarding boundaries or nuisances); personal loans; shoddy goods; inadequately performed services; landlord/tenant matters (e.g., on securities); minor accidents involving cars; dog bites, or pet-related damages; and the like. Millions of Americans have been exposed to small claims court proceedings through TV shows such as "The People's Court," although research suggests that small claims court litigants often come to the court with unrealistic expectations of what the court will do for them and are then disappointed (O'Barr and Conley 1988).

Although ideally the small claims court allows ordinary individuals seeking nominal damages to obtain justice without incurring the formidable expenses involved in hiring a lawyer and suing in a formal civil court proceeding, in fact a disproportionate percentage of those who initiate small claims court proceedings are businesspeople trying to collect debts or landlords trying to collect rents, often from poor people (Conley and O'Barr 1990). When small claims court cases are mediated, some evidence indicates that minority females do less well than others (LaFree and Rack 1996).

Mediation and Arbitration

Any discussion of informal justice must also distinguish between some crucial terms. The term *adjudication* is most commonly applied to a formal system for resolving disputes, presided over by a judge, and accordingly is not typically associated with informal justice. *Arbitration* also involves a judge or third party imposing a resolution on a dispute, but typically it is more informal than adjudication. A key feature of arbitration is that the two parties to a dispute have mutually agreed to subject themselves to it. Binding arbitration means that the parties have agreed to abide by the ruling of the arbitrator. Labor/management disputes, for example, are not infrequently resolved by bringing in an arbitrator who resolves the dispute. *Mediation* gets to the essence of informal justice. A mediator is called in to attempt to clarify issues for the parties to a dispute, and possibly to suggest some forms of resolution. But the mediator is a facilitator only and does not impose a solution (Bush and Folger 1994).

Mediation has been increasingly used, for example, in domestic violence, divorce, and custody cases. Indeed, in many states couples seeking divorce are first required to subject themselves to mediation. Most reasonable people would agree that, other things being equal, it is preferable to have mediation rather than a judge-imposed solution in a case where a father and mother of minor children are disputing the custody of the children as a consequence of their divorce. Surely it would be better if the parents could be helped in working out a mutually acceptable custody arrangement between themselves rather than to battle out the custody issues in court, with the children sometimes called upon to testify against one or the other of their parents. In domestic violence cases, however, at least some feminists have raised the question of whether it is really fair and humane to subject the abused spouse (typically the wife) to an attempt to "mediate" over issues arising from the abuse, or whether mediation in these cases principally serves to allow a violent and abusive spouse (typically the husband) to avoid criminal prosecution (Bryan 1992). When parties to mediation have a long-standing relationship, they generally must choose between abandoning the relationship, negotiating a compromised and provisional settlement of their differences, and achieving a reconciliation oriented toward the restoration of their original relationship.

The call for informal justice has been based on both idealistic and practical grounds. Idealistically, informal justice has been justified as a fairer, more humane, and more democratic means of achieving justice, a repudiation of the bureaucratized, debasing, and inequitable formal legal system. In practical terms, informal justice has been promoted as a means of avoiding the costs and delays associated with the formal legal system. No sweeping generalizations about informal justice are likely to be accurate. One can find many circumstances where those involved fervently believe that it has produced a better and more just outcome, and many other circumstances where gross injustices have resulted. Informal justice must be evaluated cautiously, with attention to the specific form and context.

Conclusion

People have developed a range of institutions and procedures to address the many different kinds of harm that people do to one another and the disputes in which they engage. (Table 8.1 presents a brief comparison of the justice system discussion here.) Although many disputes are settled between people on their own, in a complex society various kinds of formal institutions and procedures have to be developed to attend to disputes that cannot (or should not) be so resolved. The formal procedures of these institutions are generally invoked in a small minority of cases; most are resolved by some form of informal procedure. But in view of the frustrations and costs associated with the formal procedures of justice, there are frequent calls for alternative dispute resolution, ideally as independent of the formal systems of justice as possible. All too often alternative dispute resolution has been coopted by the legal establishment. Formal and informal procedures for dispute resolution (and the disposition of cases involving harmful conduct) will always coexist. One of the questions for the future is whether the momentum promoting informal justice procedures will continue to grow; another is whether costly, frustrating, and inequitable aspects of the formal justice systems can be more successfully addressed and reformed.

Table 8.1 A Comparison of Justice Systems*

Justice System	*Objective/Focus*	*Basic Procedure*	*Adjudicator*	*Standard of Proof*
Criminal Justice	Controlling, preventing, and punishing crime	Adversarial trial; plea negotiation	Judge; jury	Beyond a reasonable doubt
Juvenile Justice	Controlling and rehabilitating juvenile offenders	More inquisitorial and informal	Judge; probation officer	Beyond a reasonable doubt; often discretionary
Civil Justice	Resolving disputes formally	Adversarial; negotiated	Judge; jury	Clear and convincing evidence; preponderance of evidence
Administrative Justice	Regulating important or dangerous activities	Administrative hearing	Admin. judge; hearing officer	Substantial evidence; often discretionary
Military Justice	Maintain order and discipline within military	Military court; hearing	Military tribunal; unit commander	From equivalent to criminal justice to discretionary
Informal Justice	Alternative to formal justice system for dispute resolution	Informal hearing	Arbitrator; mediator; community	Merits of case; mutual consent; often discretionary

*The different justice systems may use different procedures and standards, depending on the nature of the case being addressed; accordingly, this table should only be taken as an approximation of some key differences between them.

Key Terms and Concepts

adjudication
administrative law
agency capture
alternative dispute resolution
arbitration
community justice
community policing
felony
injunction
lenience cycle
mediation
military governments
misdemeanor
neighborhood justice
popular justice
private justice
punitive cycle
rough justice
status offenders
tort
vigilante justice

Discussion Questions

1. Discuss the concept of discretion in the criminal justice system, especially pertaining to police officers and judges. How much discretion should these professions be awarded? When offered too much, do you think police officers have a tendency to abuse it? Can judges impose more fair sentences on criminals if they can use their discretion, as opposed to relying on sentencing guidelines?
2. Should a juvenile who commits a serious crime, such as premeditated murder, still be treated as a juvenile and be subjected to the separate juvenile justice system? Explain.
3. Is the American civil litigation system really "out of control"? How does the system seem to be taken advantage of at times?
4. Discuss the positive and negative aspects of the administrative justice system. How can the power that these agencies have to function legislatively, executively, and judicially be both beneficial and possibly result in negative consequences?
5. What benefits does alternative dispute resolution bring to the American justice system? Should ADR be relied upon more often than it is? How could it possibly help such a highly litigious society?

Chapter Nine

Legal Culture and Legal Behavior

Law in our lives does not exist in a vacuum. Rather, people have varying degrees of knowledge about the law, they form attitudes toward law and legal institutions, and patterns of behavior in relation to law develop (Friedman 1975, 193). The term "legal culture" has been adopted to describe public knowledge and attitudes toward law, although patterns of behavior are typically not included as a part of legal culture (Ewick and Silbey 1992; Friedman and Scheiber 1996). In a recent formulation, Lawrence Friedman (1997, 34), the leading proponent of the concept, has written that legal culture "refers to ideas, values, expectations and attitudes towards law and legal institutions, which some public or some part of the public holds." People's ideas about law, in turn, are assumed to influence their behavior.

Legal Culture

Legal culture refers both to the ideas of elites and other special interests within society and to ideas held by "ordinary people," or the general public. Legal culture is significant because it has an impact on the legal system; changes in cultural attitudes can lead to changes in law. It is also true that changes in law can influence cultural attitudes. For example, the American movement toward desegregation reflected the discomfort of growing numbers of Americans with a segregated society, and this attitude influenced lawmakers. At the same time, the legal rulings and legal reforms—e.g., *Brown v. Board of Education* (1954) and the Civil Rights Act (1964)—also made legal discrimination less culturally acceptable over time. Furthermore, as Friedman (1997, 34) observes, changes in the social environment generate new demands on the legal system: "Somebody invents the motor car and later we see modifications in tort law, and a massive pile of new regulations: on drivers' licences, rules of the road, drunk driving, air bags, and so on."

Figure 9.1 American Legal Culture in Relation to Some Other Legal Cultures

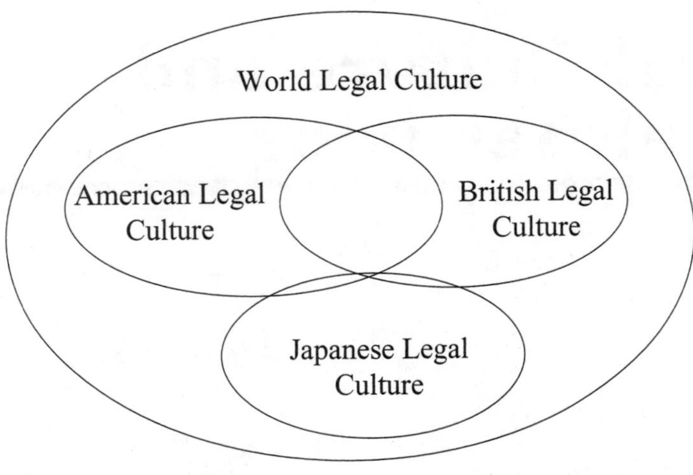

American legal culture differs in varying degrees from the legal cultures of other countries; for example, it differs somewhat from the legal culture of England and still more so from that of Japan. A study of American and Japanese responses to corporate lawbreaking found that Americans were more likely to favor punishments imposed on individual corporate executives, while Japanese respondents tended to focus more on extracting apologies from these corporate offenders (Sanders, Hamilton, and Yuasa 1998). These different responses reflect different cultural values in the United States and Japan. However, we may also be witnessing the emergence of a world legal culture (Friedman and Scheiber 1996, 6) (see Figure 9.1).

American Legal Culture

What are the elements of American legal culture? Certainly, Americans have been greatly interested in law and legal issues relative to other cultures, despite the fact that they hold contradictory attitudes toward law. Americans tend to venerate the rule of law and at the same time are often hostile to lawyers, burdensome legal proceedings, and state interventions in private lives. Some commentators claim that Americans are obsessed with legal rights and entitlements, and other commentators describe Americans as "law avoiders"(Engel and Munger 1996). Of course, in such a large country it is not surprising to find evidence of contradictory tendencies.

David Engel and Frank Munger (1996) have suggested that even though Americans talk easily about legal rights and entitlements, it does not necessarily mean that they will follow through by initiating legal action. Specifically, in their study of disabled individuals, they found that these Americans are often conflicted in their own minds about asserting legal rights extended to them by the Americans With Disabilities Act. Nevertheless, even if they do not choose to formally pursue these rights, they are influenced by the knowledge that they have such legal rights.

Despite the qualifications stated above, it is common to attribute litigiousness—or a willingness, even eagerness, to sue—to American legal culture. Does American culture really stress such conflict, or does it stress harmony? In a study of residents of a New York City suburb, M. P. Baumgartner (1988) found that people go to considerable lengths to resolve grievances without confrontation and without resorting to formal legal action. According to Baumgartner (1988, 127), "Moral minimalism dominates the suburbs. On a day-by-day basis, life is filled with efforts to deny, minimize, contain, and avoid conflict." Whether such moral minimalism signifies strong or weak social control within a particular community is a matter of some dispute (Schneider 1990). However, the findings of Baumgartner's study do challenge an image of Americans as relentlessly litigious. It is indisputable that there is a great deal of litigation in American society—proportionately far more than in many other developed nations. The sources of this "adversarial legalism" include, on the one hand, the nature of the political system, and on the other hand, the self-interested promotion of litigation by the large core of American lawyers (Kagan 1996).

The claim that Americans (1) have become more litigious than in the past; (2) are more litigious than people in other countries; and (3) are clearly in the midst of a "litigation explosion" has been challenged (Friedman 1996b). As suggested earlier in this text, litigation is not so easily—or obviously—defined. If litigation is thought of as active, contested lawsuits, some types of lawsuits are more common today and others are less common.

If Americans are not necessarily more likely to sue today than in the past, they are more likely to expect the law to address injustice and loss. Lawrence M. Friedman (1985, 5) identifies a demand for what he calls "total justice" or "a general expectation of recompense for injuries and loss" as an important emerging dimension of American legal culture. This expectation leads to demands for new legal rules or to the use of informal dispute resolution, and only sometimes to formal litigation.

In the final decades of the twentieth century, relatively strong support for a "get tough on crime" approach also emerged as an attribute of American legal culture (Scheingold 1997). In one interpretation, a move toward favoring harsher criminal sentencing reflected a reaction against more liberal social policies in other areas (Gaubatz 1995). Public support for harsh penalties is often based upon perceptions that have been influenced by the media but are based upon mistaken and distorted information about the reality of crime (Roberts and Stalans 1997). Whether a significant decline in the conventional crime rate would lead to changes in public attitudes toward punishing crime remains to be seen.

A basic tension exists, then, between American frustration with costly, inefficient lawsuits and American commitment to individual and social justice, and between a demand for both due process and respect for privacy and for efficient, tough crime control. Friedman (1990) has also argued that Americans have come to live in a "republic of choice," or a cultural environment in which they at least believe that they have many rights and many different choices. Modern technology and the increasing expectation of change have contributed to this situation.

Friedman's interpretation has been criticized on a number of grounds, including its overly optimistic assessment of American legal culture, its relative neglect of power, conflict, and inequality, and its overly generalized character (e.g., Herzog 1992). In response, Friedman (1992) argues that it is valid and necessary to formulate broad generalizations, even when one can find many exceptions to these generalizations, and that beliefs within a legal culture are not always consistent with objective evidence of actual conditions. He has conceded that he likes many of the achievements of American legal culture, including a spread of due process, the welfare state, laws against discrimination, no-fault divorce laws, and the expansion of liability (for harms they cause) for corporations and professionals (Friedman 1985, 151; 1992, 165). Of course, American legal culture can also be accused of complicity in the ongoing oppression of or discrimination against disadvantaged groups, social inequality, the tolerance of various forms of violence, and so on. Law, supported by cultural values, is an instrument that can both legitimate existing inequalities and provide means of resisting and challenging domination (Lazarus-Black and Hirsch 1994). Legal culture incorporates some contradictory tendencies, then.

American Legal Subcultures

Throughout its history, America has become increasingly multicultural, with a large influx of immigrants from all parts of the world. Although American law in principle is supposed to protect minorities, much evidence suggests that the law has been biased toward promoting the cultural values of the dominant (i.e., white Anglo-Saxon Protestant) group and promoting the assimilation of minorities into the American cultural mainstream (Norgren and Nanda 1996). According to Friedman (1984, 28), the idea of a single standard for all has, in recent decades, been in decline in American legal culture. What he calls "plural equality" refers to the acceptance of different standards or languages for different groups. For example, in a Wisconsin case, the U.S. Supreme Court upheld the right of the Amish to keep their children out of high school. Hispanic Americans, or Latinos, constitute an increasing percentage of the American population. For many Latinos Spanish is their primary, or exclusive, language, and this fact has sometimes led to legal conflicts in a society where English is the dominant language (Norgren and Nanda 1996). The "English only" norm has been challenged as discriminatory.

It is clear that not only individual Americans, but subcultures and different socioeconomic classes within American society have different attitudes toward law and legal institutions, ranging from uncritical support for them to a dedication to destroy them. Middle-class suburban Americans, for example, are regarded as highly supportive of law; improvident anarchists and survivalists have been antagonistic toward important dimensions of the legal system. The Mormons in America early in their history found themselves at odds with American law. For example, their practice of polygamy led to legal persecution by the American national government (Norgren and Nanda 1996). Most Mormons abandoned polygamy and adapted to the demands of the national legal norms, however, and became conservative supporters of the formal legal order.

The experience of African Americans with American law has been more complex. Slavery and its aftermath was discussed in Chapter 6. With good reason, inner-city African Americans have been less trusting of law and legal institutions than middle-class suburban white Americans. This issue is explored more fully later in this chapter.

Legal cultural values can also vary locally; that is, somewhat different norms, attitudes, and practices relating to law may prevail in different local communities (Kritzer and Zemans 1993). Accordingly, in some communities legal cases are more likely to be filed and formally addressed than in other communities (see Box 9.1).

Internal Legal Culture

The aspects of legal culture discussed so far pertain to the *lay legal culture* of the general public. In addition to the legal culture of the general public, there is also an *internal legal culture* (Friedman 1975, 223–224). This term refers to the values and attitudes of those within the legal profession toward law and the legal system. While considerable overlap exists between the internal legal culture and the popular, or lay, legal culture, differences can also be identified. For example, on the whole, the internal legal culture is more committed to the adversarial ethic—which calls upon criminal defense lawyers to make the best possible case, within the rules, for the client, regardless of how heinous the crime the client may have committed—than is the general public, which often cannot comprehend how lawyers can defend "those people." Those within the legal profession tend to be more oriented toward formal, logical legal reasoning than is the general public, which may be more oriented toward the human or emotional dimensions of cases.

Those within the legal profession are well positioned to translate their attitudes and values into social policy, especially if they are overrepresented among lawmakers, as they typically are. Roger Cotterrell (1997), in his critique of the concept of legal culture, makes a case for "legal ideology" instead, with this term specifically referring to the ideas about law coming from the state and from within the profession, whose power to impose these ideas on the general public is accordingly highlighted. Perhaps it is best to think of legal culture as having various different dimensions, with the legal ideology of the dominant group especially influential on (but not wholly determining) the law-related beliefs of the general public.

Finally, in a world moving toward "globalization," is American legal culture becoming more influential in the world at large? Yves Dezalay and Bryant Garth (1996) have argued that as international trade involving China has increased exponentially and as American-based multinationals are key players in this process, the role of Western formal law has become ever more dominant, and lawyers assume an increasingly central role in business conduct. In contrast, Richard Appelbaum (1998) argues that the Eastern preference for informal, extra-legal forms of business will successfully resist the Western, or American, influence. Appelbaum believes that "guanxi"—the traditional Chinese reliance upon gift-giving and bestowing of favors as a basis for business dealings—will continue to play a central role in the Eastern world and will not be displaced by formal legal practices. Guanxi was not successfully repressed by the communist regime and is evident in the new Asian economies.

Box 9.1

The Legal Culture of American Communities

In the recent era several anthropologists and sociologists have explored the legal culture of ordinary Americans living in particular communities. In a study of several small New England county courts Barbara Yngvesson (1993) found much concern with having rights vindicated by the law, as well as a certain measure of resistance to authority. People in these communities often bring complaints to the courts when they believe they have been abused or exploited by another person with whom they have some type of relationship; the court clerks must in many cases explain to these people that their complaint does not meet the appropriate legal criteria. Women, in particular, turn to the court in the hope that it will use its power to discipline a male partner who is abusing them. Sometimes the court clerk will offer some informal advice or will attempt to mediate the dispute involved.

In a study of legal consciousness in two small New England towns, Sally Engle Merry (1990) found that the townspeople turned to courts only reluctantly, when all else had failed in resolving some dispute or situation where they needed help. The plaintiffs who go to court do not think of their problems in terms of specific legal doctrines or rules but more in terms of basic rights involving their parental authority, their property, or some other matter of personal concern. Those who go to court as plaintiffs are disproportionately white, middle-aged, homeowners, and women of average means, with one or two years of college education. For Merry, the turn to courts does not reflect the collapse of community so much as it reflects American cultural values of individualism and egalitarianism, as well as policies adopted by the state in the recent era that encourage or at least facilitate initiating legal actions. People go to court to reaffirm their privacy rights as well as other rights. When poor people turn to the courts to pursue entitlements (e.g., disability payments), they are empowered in one sense, but, paradoxically, in another sense they increase their dependence on the state. Altogether, Merry regards the turn to courts as a form of searching for a new community and moral authority that will uphold and affirm such American cultural values as autonomy, self-reliance, and tolerance.

In a study conducted in a middle Atlantic state, Patricia Ewick and Susan Silbey (1998) found that their respondents did not spend much time thinking about law, but when they did, they experienced it in quite different ways:

1. An objective, disinterested realm.
2. A game, or terrain for tactical encounters.
3. A product of power.

Here, too, people tended to turn to the law only reluctantly, resolving disputes informally whenever they could. When people did turn to law it was typically when the alternatives didn't seem to work, and to assert values, rights, or some conception of justice. People were often frustrated by the law's inability to take their special, personal circumstances into account and to address their troubles effectively. Law, then, was not experienced as a uniformly positive force in people's lives, or one always deserving of deference and respect.

Law, Community, and Identity

The preceding discussion has suggested that the concept of legal culture is very broad. In a complex, heterogeneous society such as the United States, then, one can expect to find numerous coexisting (and sometimes overlapping) subcultures of attitudes and values pertaining to law. Much about these legal subcultures remains to be learned. But some studies have been made of the attitudes toward and understandings of law within particular communities.

The notion of community is central to the social existence of human beings. Almost all of us, unless we are hermits or living in very isolating circumstances, belong to one or more communities. Most of us find it necessary to orient ourselves toward the laws, rules, or norms of these several different communities to which we belong. This circumstance was described as one of legal pluralism. Obviously, then, people may experience conflicting demands—for example, from their religious community and from the political community of which they are a part. Also, communities can provide a means of resisting or confronting law, and sometimes communities actively organize to resist or challenge law.

The idea of community is often associated with a past when people are seen as having lived in close, caring communities; much concern in the present is expressed over the dissolution of such communities (Greenhouse 1988). Of course, communities in the past often imposed severe limitations on the freedom (and privacy) of their members; persecuted community members who deviated in any measurable way from community norms; and deliberately excluded from community membership those who were seen as different. Communities have specifically been in conflict with, and have engaged in the persecution of, other communities. Communities as a whole, then, have a mixed history of positive and negative contributions to the human experience.

In the present era, there has been a celebration of certain forms of community ties, and claims have been put forth on behalf of communities (for example, of minority group members, the disabled, or gay people). The term "identity politics" is sometimes used to describe the highlighting of ties to communities, especially communities that have historically been the targets of discrimination or persecution (Minow 1997). Cultural pluralism and an era of identity politics pose complex questions for law (Sarat and Kearns 1999). The paradox and challenge here is to determine when community membership should matter and when it should be irrelevant. On the one hand, the U.S. Supreme Court has prohibited the use of challenges in jury selection to specifically exclude members of a particular community from serving on the jury; on the other hand, the U.S. Census Bureau has attempted to classify and identify people by group (community) memberships, in part to provide data for addressing problems of discrimination.

Certainly, the identity of many people is an important function of their primary community memberships, and obviously people derive many benefits from belonging to communities. A basic question remains on how and when law should foster community, and when it should interfere with community (Mertz 1994a, 981). Historically, law has been organized mainly in terms of individuals as legal entities. When individuals invoke the law, such action has often separated them from the community and sometimes put them into conflict with the community. In the more recent era, the law has

Box 9.2

Community Values and the Case of Pornography

In certain kinds of cases, the law makes assumptions or claims about communities, and such assumptions or claims may or may not be correct. For example, one criterion for identifying pornographic material prohibited by law is that the material is "offensive to community standards" (Linz et al. 1995). This standard raises a number of problems. First, and obviously, much pornographic material is broadly—even nationally—distributed, but different communities across the nation are unlikely to embrace a single standard for what they find offensive. Within cities of any size, one can surely find smaller communities with quite different standards for what is offensive. Also in pornography cases the application of "community standards" has often relied upon inferences and intuitions as opposed to scientifically valid surveys of community standards, if only for practical reasons. Ironically, a study by Linz et al. (1995) found that sexually explicit material not generally offensive to a particular community was subjected to vigorous prosecution in the name of the law, while violent materials clearly offensive to the same community were not subject to legal prosecution. Accordingly, important discrepancies between the legal code and community standards for sex and violence can be established. When the law claims to be acting on behalf of the community—in the case of pornography, as well as in other situations—it does not necessarily follow that its actions are truly in accord with the values and preferences of the community. Inevitably, then, at least some part of the community is likely to be deeply offended by the law and may actively protest against it.

more often allowed—for example, in class action lawsuits—for whole communities to take legal action collectively. But the law remains principally focused on individuals.

Although the importance of individual rights has been stressed in American legal history, there is also a long history of recognizing the needs of communities. One significant claim in the present political environment holds that too much emphasis has been placed on individual rights at the expense of community needs (Elshtain 1995; Glendon 1991). Communitarians, who emphasize the necessity of recognizing and dealing with community rights and needs, call for achieving a better balance between individual rights and the needs of the community (Etzioni 1996b). To some critics it is far from obvious who makes up a community: A social group? A neighborhood? A town? A category of people (e.g., members of a particular racial or ethnic group)? A leading proponent of communitarianism, Amitai Etzioni (1996b), says a community is "a group of people who share affective bonds and a culture." Of course, such a definition does not fully solve the problem of identifying communities. Critics of communitarianism also hold that it is based on a false nostalgia for an imagined past of strong, supportive communities; represents a reactionary backlash against the success of formerly oppressed groups (e.g., women; racial minorities) in winning rights; and can easily lead to compromising or abandoning important civil rights and liberties (Newman and De Zoysa 1997; Walker 1998). Such concerns clearly have merit, but the broad endeavor of searching for an optimal balance between rights of individuals and perceived needs of communities is likely to continue in some form.

Law as Product: The Making of Laws

There are records of lawmaking from some of the earliest human societies that left a written record, and the inclination to make new laws has been an enduring feature of human history. Why do laws get made? This basic question has elicited different answers from different sources. The most conventional answer in elementary American civics lessons has been that law reflects the will of the people, implemented by their elected representatives. This notion can be regarded as a somewhat extreme example of a consensus, or functionalist, perspective on lawmaking. On the other end of the spectrum, radical (or leftist) adherents of conflict theory see the rich and powerful (elites) controlling and manipulating the lawmaking process for their own benefit and self-interest. Another view (pluralist), standing somewhere between these two extremes, sees lawmaking as a process involving competing interest groups who mobilize forces, with varying degrees of success, to pressure lawmakers to adopt laws they favor. In an attempt to find an alternative to the radical elitist and the pluralist perspective on lawmaking, William Chambliss (Chambliss and Zatz 1993) has advanced a dialectical theory of lawmaking, which says laws are adopted to resolve various contradictions, conflicts, and dilemmas confronting society in a particular historical context.

Public Demand and Moral Entrepreneurs

Altogether, legislative lawmaking reflects a complex mixture of interests and pressures, with a different mixture of factors involved in the introduction of particular laws (Mayhew 1986). In a study of the introduction of the Illinois Seat Belt law, for example, Maguire, Hinderliter and Faulkner (1990) found that moral entrepreneurs (auto safety activists) and special interests (the auto industry) were most responsible for how the law developed; the law was not a response to general public demand and objective facts. The "general public," although hardly a unified entity, may share some broad values or may sometimes be aroused about a particular concern, creating pressure for legislative action. Laws proscribing homicide obviously reflect a broad consensus that the willful taking of another person's life is intolerable in a civilized society. Recent laws enacted in response to general public demand include the Three-Strikes-and-You're-Out law (requiring mandatory life in prison following conviction for a third felony) and Megan's law (requiring community notification if a released sex offender is living in its midst). Both were adopted largely in response to especially heinous abductions, rapes, and murders of two young girls in highly publicized cases (Shichor and Sechrest 1997).

Moral entrepreneurs take it upon themselves to crusade actively for new laws. The Temperance Movement early in the twentieth century crusaded on behalf of the adoption of the Volstead Act, prohibiting the sale and distribution of liquor; Mothers Against Drunk Driving (MADD) mobilized to campaign for tougher penalties for those convicted on DUI (Driving Under the Influence) charges.

Lobbies

Those who lobby for new laws, modifications in existing laws, or the repeal of existing laws are not necessarily motivated by moralistic or public interest concerns. By the end of the twentieth century, interest groups were playing an increasingly important role in the lawmaking process in the United States (Koshner 1998). Much effective lobbying is carried out on behalf of various business or professional interests who are motivated primarily by self-interest or to protect the economic well-being of their constituency (Abramson 1998). Lobbying by a wide range of private interest groups increased exponentially in the recent era. Since no single private interest groups can stay at the heart of, or dominate, the lawmaking process, one influential study claimed that a hollow core is at the center of this process (Heinz et al. 1993). These lobbying interests may be more successful in blocking unwanted legislation than in initiating new legislation. Powerful economic interests often have considerable advantages in the legislative and administrative arena because politicians depend on their financial support for campaign expenses. In addition, various government agencies or entities may actively lobby on behalf of laws either because their expertise has led them to realize a need for the laws or because their own agency or operation can benefit with a bigger budget and increases in personnel (Luchansky and Gerber 1993). Legislative lawmakers themselves may take the initiative in proposing new laws, either on the basis of a perceived political advantage to themselves or perhaps because, as dedicated public servants, they perceive a need for the new law. Figure 9.2 outlines the stages in the making of statutory law.

Judges and the Executive Branch

Judges at least those in common law countries also make law. Specifically, the opinions of appellate court justices take the form of law; when the U.S. Supreme Court declares legalized segregation to be unconstitutional or requires that those accused of crimes be informed of their rights, it is making law. In the United States the justices of the United States Supreme Court, and other federal judges, are appointed for life, which is supposed to free them from the influence of political pressures or the public passions of the moment. However, their ideological commitments and past record of decisions are important factors in justices or judges being appointed in the first place. More often than not, judges remain reasonably faithful to these earlier commitments, and make rulings of law consistent with these commitments.

Where judges are elected and face re-election, it stands to reason that they may be influenced in their rulings by political considerations. Judge-made law is supposed to be based upon principled legal reasoning, although, as was noted earlier, there are basic disagreements over such matters as whether judges should largely defer to the intentions of legislators (and, on

Figure 9.2 The Making of Statutory Law

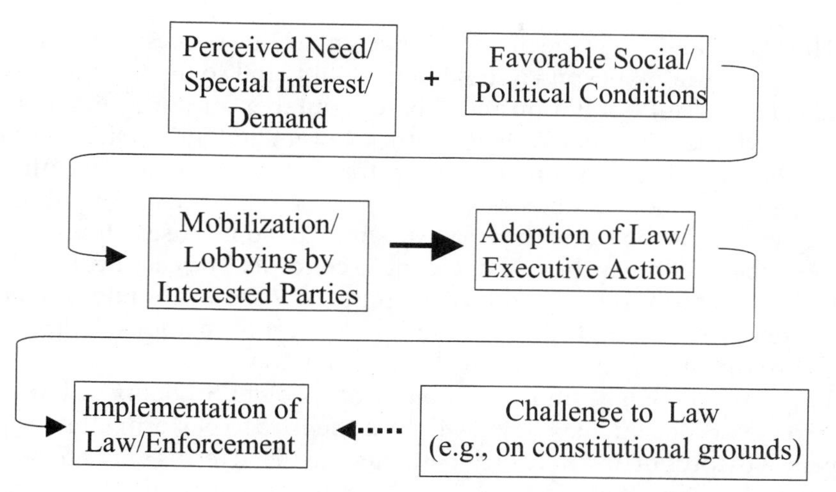

constitutional law, the Founding Fathers) or should take the law in new directions consistent with a perception of society's present needs.

Law in a real sense is also made by those in the executive branch of the government and by those in the administrative agencies. The executive branch often provides much of the expertise and initial drafting of laws adopted by legislative bodies and then uses its discretion in determining how (if at all) legislative law is enforced. Administrative or regulatory agencies (as discussed in Chapter 8) are empowered to adopt, enforce, and administer a broad range of administrative laws. Prosecutors become "crime creators" (i.e., create new categories of crime) through their discretionary power to interpret the law; for example, by extending the statutory prohibition against delivering drugs to a minor to a circumstance where pregnant women were using drugs, prosecutors effectively created the law of prenatal drug use (Maschke 1995). In general, prosecutors tend to be especially political in orientation and may be somewhat biased in their lawmaking function toward making law consistent with the perceived public will. Of course, other factors, including the prosecutor's own beliefs and convictions, will influence prosecutorial lawmaking.

Law as Communication

Much of law is inevitably expressed in words, and language is central to legal proceedings (Tiersma 1999). As O'Barr and Conley (1998, 129) put it

> language is the essential mechanism through which the power of law is realized, exercised, reproduced, and occasionally challenged and subverted. Most of the time, law is talk; the talk between disputants; the talk between

> lawyers and clients; the courtroom talk among lawyers, parties, judges, and witnesses; the legal talk that gets reduced to writing as statutes and judicial opinions. . . .

The words and language of law—for example, due process, equal protection, criminal intent, beyond a reasonable doubt, and so forth—may be subjected to endless interpretation and debate about their meaning, expressed in still more words (Levi and Walker 1990). Lawyers and judges must learn to choose their words in legal proceedings with great care, and ideally with technical precision, since the choice of one word over another can have immense consequences. At the same time, lawyers may in some cases choose words that will obscure things they do not want to concede. The case against President Clinton featured almost comical disputes over the legally relevant meaning of various terms and words, from "is" to "sexual relations." Altogether, words are the principal tools of the legal profession.

Law has a language and terminology of its own. Students of law must learn to master the language of law itself if they are to perform effectively as lawyers. A disproportionately high percentage of legal terms are Latin words. Lawyers are sometimes accused of invoking unfamiliar legal jargon to score technical points in a case rather than to communicate something clearly. Judges are sometimes accused of using language in their opinions that is ambiguous, subject to different interpretations. The language of ordinary litigants and witnesses is often at odds with the technical legal language lawyers and judges may insist upon, and these litigants are frustrated when their attempts to tell their stories in their own terms are interrupted by judges and lawyers insisting that they limit themselves to "legally relevant" answers (Conley and O'Barr 1990) (see Box 9.3).

Box 9.3

Forensic Linguistics

Roger Shuy (1993, 1998) is a linguist who has testified as an expert witness, or has been a consultant, in a large number of legal cases, as a result of a chance encounter with an attorney on an airplane in 1979. Linguists are trained to analyze and interpret the complex structure and patterns of verbal communications between human beings. Tape recordings of conversations or other forms of verbal communication are sometimes key pieces of evidence in legal cases. Accordingly, a linguist may analyze "speech acts" involving "offering, agreeing, threatening, admitting, lying, promising, and requesting"(Shuy 1993, xix). Has someone clearly solicited or agreed to accept a bribe, or not? Has someone attempted to extort money from another person or threatened that individual, or not? Has someone really conspired to commit murder or simply listened while another party spoke of committing murder? Has a suspect in a criminal case truly confessed, or not?

It is not the task of the linguist to determine guilt or innocence, but the linguist can analyze the use of language and can offer an expert opinion on whether particular verbal acts and exchanges support what is being alleged. A linguist can offer some basic principles for conducting effective and fair-minded interrogations and evaluating the use of deceptive language. A linguist can offer some guidelines for determining whether a confession is valid.

Language and Ideology

Judges today are sometimes monitored by advocacy groups and can get themselves into trouble by expressing "politically incorrect" or fundamentally insensitive sentiments and viewpoints. For example, some judges have been severely criticized and when they appeared to disparage the experiences of rape victims (Soothill, Walby, and Bagguley 1990). Lawyers have been accused of manipulating language as a means of tricking or confusing hostile witnesses. Victims of such crimes as rape may be led by a shrewd defense lawyer into using, or agreeing to the use of, terminology that reframes the rape in terms of a consensual encounter. The language of predominantly male judges and police when they speak to women making complaints in domestic dispute cases has all too often suggested a gender-based bias. The language of some law, then, is said to be biased and to covertly express a male outlook and male interests (O'Barr and Conley 1998, 3, 60–77; Beaman-Hall 1996). Andrew Taslitz (1999, 9) argues that men are taught to view language as a tool, or weapon, to achieve particular goals, while women learn to view language as a means of strengthening relationships and mediating disputes. The law, Taslitz suggests, promotes the invocation of patriarchal stories adopting a male-centered point of view, and the law is directly complicit in the silencing of women. He believes that legal procedures should be changed to prohibit the exploitation of race- and gender-based stereotypes in court proceedings; to restrict or eliminate male biases; and to promote forms of reasoning consistent with the experiences and outlook of women. The voices of women are too often silenced by the language and method of law.

The language of law, intertwined with ideology, played a key role in both the United States and South Africa in reinterpreting the history of indigenous peoples, stripping them of rights, and relegating them to "reservations" and "homelands" (Mertz 1988). The language of law, then, has been yet another device used to maintain or extend power.

Semiotics

Semiotics is the study of signs, or "linguistic codes." Dragan Milovanovic (1994, 144–145) has applied a critical semiotic perspective to law and the legal process as a means of exposing the uses of language and various signs by some powerful interests, at a cost to others with less power. His perspective includes the following assumptions:

Language is value laden, not neutral.

Language structures thought.

A political economy leads some forms of "discourse," or understandings of the world and ways of communicating, to be dominant over others.

Politicians, judges, psychiatrists, and the like are in a position to impose their form of discourse on others—citizens, defendants, patients—with less power.

Lawyers are manipulators of the dominant form of discourse or language.

Open and fair communication is possible only in a society where structural forms of inequality and exploitation have been eliminated.

Although virtually any form of legal communication has been interpreted in terms of signs, signs in the conventional sense play an important role in law. The term "official graffiti" has been applied to countless signs—such as the familiar "Stop" sign and "No Smoking" sign—that convey prohibitions, warnings, instructions, and the like (Hermer and Hunt 1996). In one interpretation such signs, which are differentiated from conventional graffiti by being legitimated by the state, reflect an overload of law in our environment, and become an efficient means of announcing rules and extending control over people's lives.

The Media

Law is communicated. When legislative bodies adopt new laws and judges issue new opinions, these new laws and opinions have to be communicated to the larger public. For the most part, this communication takes place through the media, which are quite selective about what they communicate. Accordingly, public knowledge of new law and legal rulings is incomplete and is biased in favor of the newsworthy. Law and news have actually been compared with each other (Ericson 1996). Both are oriented toward an event, which is dramatized, and toward individualizing problems; both are based in an institutional setting, claim to follow rules stressing objectivity and fairness, and dramatize what they produce. Overall, the news may have somewhat less credibility and legitimacy because of the large size of its audience and the immediacy of its communications. But the news plays an important role in shaping the way people make sense of the social order and of the law itself (Ericson, Baranek, and Chan 1991; Ericson 1996). The media's coverage of a trial may play an important role in determining its historical significance (Chiasson 1997). The news communicates much about law and legal institutions.

Television, in particular, has played a central role in shaping the way people think about legal issues in America, including such issues as abortion, euthanasia, homelessness, sexual abuse, divorce, and parental responsibility (Jarvis and Joseph 1998). Televised trials today expose a broad segment of the general public to the realities of legal proceedings, although the cases featured tend to be atypical; also, the public may actually be exposed to evidence not presented to the jury, which leads to different conclusions on the part of the public (Giles and Snyder 1999; Goldfarb 1998).

People also learn about law from other sources: observations and instructions from family and peers; the school curriculum; lessons in church; books; and direct experiences. Both the messages about law and the specific content of what one learns about law from these different sources may be contradictory and not easily reconciled, which contributes to some of the confusion about law.

Box 9.4

Law Stories

Lawyers have always used stories to inspire sympathy for their clients, by portraying them as heroes or victims in narratives highlighting emotional and empathetic dimensions of their experience. But law stories today may also focus on the experiences of lawyers themselves, of those who find themselves in a circumstance giving rise to legal action, and those who have been through the legal process. A collection of stories about law entitled *Outside the Law: Narratives on Justice* presents accounts of high-profile cases such as the O. J. Simpson case and the Susan Smith case (a young mother who drowned her two sons). It also reproduces first-person accounts from the father and the brother of a convicted murderer, who share their experience of his case. Another contributor constructs a fictional story to capture the character of justice in the workplace. Another writer provides an autobiographical tale of fleeing the Dominican Republic, where the dictator General Trujillo was the law. Another writer, a gay activist, contributes an essay on the troubled circumstances of gay people in America in relation to law. A juror explores her experiences in the jury room. A lawyer remembers his days trying voter discrimination cases in the South during the civil rights era. And a writer provides an account of a case of two young boys (ages ten and eleven) who were living in the projects in Chicago and who were sent to prison for dropping a five-year-old to his death out of a fourteenth-story window (Shreve and Shreve 1997).

Legal Narratives

In the recent era, a growing number of students of law have developed an interest in law as story, or narrative. One theme, explored earlier, looks at literature as a source of stories that often have much to teach about the nature of law. Another viewpoint focuses on law itself and legal cases, as stories that have to be understood in narrative terms. In trials, for example, the lawyers involved typically tell stories, with the objective of persuading the jury (or judge) to accept their story as the more persuasive one in the case. Ethnographic research has established, however, that laypeople who appear in court—as plaintiffs, defendants, or witnesses—tend to tell stories in a somewhat different form than do legal professionals (Conley and O'Barr 1990). Laypeople tell stories that include much legally irrelevant detail but seem to the person telling the story appropriate for understanding the sequence of events involved and how they provide an account of blameworthiness, or its absence. Stories, then, are central to the legal process, although stories in law take many different forms (see Box 9.4).

Legal Socialization

Newborn infants know nothing about law. The infant is an anarchist by default: that is, the infant is utterly indifferent to rules and order and simply does what he or she can to satisfy needs and curiosity (howling in the middle of the night for food or pushing a plate off the highchair tray). But over time, if human beings are to become social beings, they must be socialized to conform to the rules and expectations of society, and to acquire the values and attitudes of their primary group. Legal socialization eventually becomes a part of this process. It has been defined as "the process through which members of a society acquire its legal values, such as fairness, equality, and justice, and its norms of rule-governed behavior"(Cohn and White 1997, 152).

Legal socialization typically follows more urgent stages of socialization (such as toilet training, eating with a fork and spoon, learning to speak, and asking for something instead of taking it). As Judith Torney (1977, 134) has observed, "The socialization of children into the legal system includes diverse objectives: children must come to recognize laws, perceive their functions, accurately view their sources, develop appropriate attitudes toward those who enforce them, and guide their own behavior to conform to morality and legality." How, then, are people socialized about law? In part, we are taught specific lessons about the content and purpose of law, in school and at home; in part, we acquire understandings about and attitudes toward law through our exposure to law-related stories and accounts on television, in films, and in the print media; and in part we are socialized about law through our direct experiences as litigants, as victims, as defendants, or as jurors (see Table 9.1).

Table 9.1 Agents of Legal Socialization

General	*Specific*	*Specialized*
Family/Peers/ Professionals	Personal encounters/ experiences w/law	Internship/Apprenticeship in law-related occupation
School/Church	Courses addressing law; books addressing law	Law school; grad study in law-related areas; Police Academy
Media	TV shows; films; songs about law	Documentaries about law

In its earliest stages, the legal socialization of young children can hardly be separated from their instruction in matters of morality. According to the Swiss psychologist Jean Piaget (1932) and the American psychologist Lawrence Kohlberg (1969), in the earliest stages of life children are "premoral": that is, what feels good is good and what feels bad is bad. Children typically move on to the next stage of moral socialization—the conventional stage—where goodness is equated with what is approved of by peers and by other important figures in a child's life. A minority of children eventually move on to a principled stage of moral reasoning, where the morality of a particular action or circumstance is evaluated in terms of its relation to a coherent set of defensible moral principles.

The cognitive developmental model can be constrasted with other models for learning about or becoming oriented toward morality and law: in the accumulation model, children are simply the passive recipients of law-related information passed on by their parents and other sources within their environment; in the identification model, the child imitates the adults in her or his environment; in the role transfer model, the child takes on the role of a subordinate and generalizes from the role in the home to that in the political system (Torney 1977). And on another dimension, the psychologist Carol Gilligan (1982) has claimed that female children tend to engage in a form of moral reasonng that differs from that of male children, upon whom the classic sudies of moral reasoning are based. Whichever of these models, or combinations of models, is correct, an understanding of and images of law are acquired in the course of the socialization process.

At the very end of the twentieth century, American children, including quite young children, were inevitably exposed to representations of law and justice in the case of O. J. Simpson, the former football star accused of murdering his ex-wife and her visitor, and in the series of cases (culminating in the impeachment trial) directed at President Clinton. The television coverage and general discussion of these cases was so pervasive that few children (certainly of school age) could have avoided it. The possible long-term effects of this exposure on children's views of and attitudes toward law and legal institutions remain to be discovered.

Legal Behavior: Compliance and Discretion

Why do people obey, or disobey, the law, and should people always obey the law? This question was answered in part in the preceding section: they obey the law because they have learned to do so (or disobey because they have failed to learn to do so). Furthermore, they have learned and internalized values that persuade them that they should obey the law. Philosophers through the ages have grappled with the question of whether it is natural for human beings to conform or natural for them to behave in an antisocial way, and they have come up with different answers to this question. Philosophers have also contended with the question of whether human beings have the capacity to make freely willed, voluntary choices of how to behave or whether human behavior is simply determined by various forces acting upon individuals. Such questions remain, and there are competing conceptions of human nature and human will, as well as the position that no fundamental human nature exists. Is law the natural expression of the human tendency to conform and cooperate, or is law an alien set of restrictions imposed by the powerful on the weak? Such questions, alluded to earlier, arise here as well. However one answers the question of human nature and the nature of law, no serious observer would deny that human beings learn about law and acquire specific attitudes and values pertaining to law in the course of becoming socialized and educated.

Conformity

For the most part, we human beings become habituated to behaving in ways that conform with the law. In many respects conformity is the line of least resistance, or the easiest and most natural thing to do. Of course, another aspect of the legal socialization process is the acquisition of values and beliefs that are in conformity with the demands of the law. In addition to *internalization*(of values promoting conformity with law), people may also be

Box 9.5

Everybody Breaks the Law Some of the Time

Most of us like to think of ourselves as law-abiding, but most of us also violate certain laws. Among the more common violations of law, one could include parking illegally; speeding; failing to recycle; evading taxes; lying to customs agents; gambling illegally; smoking where prohibited; copying software illegally; and stealing TV signals (Adler and Lambert 1993). Such violations occur because people regard the laws involved as trivial, unnecessary, unfair, or unreasonable. Sometimes people violate laws simply because they can get away with it, and sometimes because they enjoy a small thrill by defying authority. Running red lights is certainly common; a psychologist in New York City observed one in four cars running a red light (Freedman 1975). When the Mayor of New York City called for a crackdown on jaywalking—an exceptionally common offense—many of those receiving summonses expressed disgust (Rohde 1998). If a society enforces too many laws that people are inclined to disregard, it may encourage a lack of respect for law.

influenced by *identification*, or a social bond with those who create and enforce the law. And the term *compliance* is applied to circumstances where people obey law or orders because they hope for reward or fear punishment (Kelman and Hamilton 1989). The concept of "legal behavior" can also be introduced here. Legal behavior has been defined as "any piece of voluntary conduct, influenced in any way by a norm, rule, decision, [or] order. . . ." (Friedman 1977, 115) (see Box 9.5).

In real life, then, a complex mixture of factors may influence people's behavior in relation to law. The law's basic appeal is *normative*, trying to persuade people to comply with law because they have a moral obligation to do so and because the values promoted by the law are consistent with their own. The law here also has an educational purpose: that is, it attempts to teach people the difference between right and wrong. Another strategy adopted by the law is *utilitarian*, or practical. For example, if you follow certain procedures, you will be granted a license to practice some professional calling, for which practice you may be well paid. Ultimately, however, law relies upon *coercion*; force, or the threat of force. Those who fail to comply with law face the prospect of a fine or prison or, in the extreme case, the death penalty.

Tom Tyler (1990), a psychologist, has produced a book entitled *Why People Obey the Law*. Tyler basically finds that normative (or moral) as opposed to instrumental (or practical) considerations are central to obedience of law. In particular, people are found to obey a law if it emanates from a source they regard as legitimate (legitimacy of law is discussed in the following section). More specifically, when people view the legal order as using fair procedures, they tend to view it as legitimate. In addition, people's personal morality—and the desire most people have to view themselves as moral beings—plays a central role in obedience to law, more so than fear of the consequences of being caught breaking laws. Although such findings may be helpful in understanding why middle class white women are less likely to engage in conventional forms of lawbreaking than lower class minority males, they are less helpful in understanding much white-collar crime. Nor does this approach to understanding why people obey law probe the question of how the legitimation of law is generated and promoted in the first place.

Tom Tyler and Kenneth Rasinski (1991) contend that people are more likely to comply with decisions of a court if they believe that the court has arrived at the ruling in a procedurally fair manner. Another scholar points out, however, that the court is able to elicit acceptance of its rulings, especially among opinion leaders, on account of its traditional prestige and institutional legitimacy, not because of the fairness of its procedures (Gibson 1989, 1991). Or compliance may simply reflect a rational calculation that it makes sense to comply, especially if one wants to avoid punishment (Gibson 1989, 492–493). A more narrowly focused study found that when the police acted in a procedurally fair manner in the course of making an arrest in domestic violence cases, repeat incidents of domestic violence were less likely to occur (Paternoster et al. 1997). Although the findings of studies of this type should be interpreted with some caution, they do strongly suggest a significant influence on the part of normative evaluations of law and legal proceedings.

Obeying Evil Orders

A related question arises: Why do people obey orders they should *not* obey, when the orders are intrinsically evil or immoral? In a famous social psychology experiment, Stanley Milgram (1974) set up a situation where subjects were instructed by the experimenter to administer an electrical shock to people (actually, the experimenter's stooges) who appeared to be failing in the performance of an assigned task. Most of the subjects obeyed the experimenter's instruction to administer shocks. This finding was interpreted to mean that most people would perform harmful (or evil) acts if the order to do so came from a legitimate authority figure. Although aspects of this experiment have been controversial, it remains immensely influential in the study of obedience to evil orders (Blass 2000).

H. C. Kelman and V. L. Hamilton (1989), in *Crimes of Obedience*, are among those who have addressed this question. The participation of a large number of Germans (and other nationals) in the Nazi Holocaust of World War II; the slaughter of several hundred Vietnamese villagers by Lt. William Calley and his troops during the Vietnam War; and the Watergate break-in (and cover-up) during the Nixon administration are three familiar examples of such crimes of obedience. Of course, there is no single answer to the question of why people obey evil orders, and many of the different forms of explanation for legal behavior outlined above come into play. Specific factors involved in crimes of obedience may range from personality to culture. Overall, however, those who engage in crimes of obedience tend to be people who feel obliged to obey orders, even if it requires them to suspend their own moral views. At least some of those who engage in such crimes—in all the cases referred to above—went beyond specific orders and undertook illegal or evil activities that seemed to them to advance the objectives of the organization. As to attributions of responsibility for such crimes of obedience, a survey found that Americans tend to be divided between those who blame the superiors who gave the orders and those who blame the people who obeyed the orders.

Deterrence

The coercive response of the law has several purposes: to avenge wrongdoing and to make a strong moral statement that certain behavior is wholly unacceptable in a civilized society; to incapacitate those who represent a danger to other members of society; and to deter. The concept of deterrence is important in criminal law (Paternoster 1987). The law basically attempts to deter on two different levels: general and specific. On the one hand, it hopes to deter members of the general public from breaking laws by making an example of lawbreakers who are caught, processed by the criminal justice system, and appropriately punished. On the other hand, it also hopes to deter the specific offender who is being punished from repeating the offense, or any criminal offense. Deterrence differs from incapacitation in that it addresses the psychological level whereas incapacitation addresses the physical aspect of misbehavior. Obviously, deterrence fails in a fairly high percentage of cases, as people continue to break laws despite being aware of the possibility of being subjected to penal sanctions, and lawbreakers who have been punished get out and commit new offenses in a significant percentage of cases.

The effectiveness of deterrence is linked with the particular character of the lawbreaking. In this sense so-called expressive crimes crimes committed for emotional reasons or in the heat of passion should be less affected by the threat of punitive sanctions than instrumental crimes, which are planned and carried out for gain (Chambliss 1967). But, again, many factors can enter into choices to comply with or ignore law, so there are many exceptions to any such proposition.

The effectiveness of deterrence has been linked principally with the certainty, severity, uniformity, and celerity of punishment. Perhaps the principal reason behind the laws frequent failure to deter behavior is the broad absence of certainty that any particular act of lawbreaking will result in identification, apprehension, and the imposition of some form of punishment. Indeed, for many offenses, the odds heavily favor the lawbreaker. Severity is less important, but if the punishment is excessively mild, the lawbreaking behavior is unlikely to be deterred. Uniformity refers to the notion that like offenders are accorded like sentences; with the adoption of the U.S. Sentencing Guidelines, greater uniformity has been achieved, although the deterrent value of this uniformity is still somewhat unclear. If one offender is sharing a cell with another offender, and the two offenders have generally identical records and have committed the same types of crime but are doing sentences that vary greatly in length, uniformity is obviously absent. In these circumstances the convicted person with the harsher sentence is likely to see the legal system as being as arbitrary as a lottery and to deeply resent that sentence.

Finally, celerity refers to the speed with which the punishment is imposed. Punishment or its threat is likely to be more effective as a deterrent the sooner after the lawbreaking episode it is applied. In our system of law, those accused of crimes are accorded due process; as a consequence, the punishment is often applied only long after the event, which by that time may seem like ancient history to the offender. In sum, then, a number of factors, or combinations of factors, influence the effectiveness of deterrence. Even if deterrence often fails, it is an overstatement to suggest that law can have no deterrent effect. After all, if no threat of punishment existed for tax evasion, much evidence suggests that fudging on taxes would be even more extensive than it is today.

Legitimation of the Legal System

If people do not believe in some fundamental way that they are obliged to comply with law—that the legal system and the legal authorities are deserving of compliance—then law as an instrument of social control is bound to fail. The idea of the legitimation of a legal system captures some of the principal concerns of this chapter. Every legal culture explicitly or implicitly adopts a view of what makes a legal system valid and deserving of support and obedience.

The German sociologist Max Weber ([1954] 1967, 1964, 1978) made some fundamental contributions to the concept of legitimacy. His use of the term in various places included notions of belief, claim, justification, promise, and self-justification. For present purposes, legitimacy is broadly construed in Weberian terms as that which is justified ("right") and demanding of support ("binding"). Compliance with a legal system as such should not be confused with legitimation; some degree of legitimation is required for the very emergence of, or continued endurance of, the legal system. Legitimation of a system implies, at a minimum, acceptance but need not necessarily mean absolute commitment. In contemporary society, legal-rational grounds for legitimation have achieved increasing significance, whereas in the past traditional authority and charismatic appeal were relatively more important bases for legitimation.

The concept of legitimation has been criticized. Alan Hyde (1983) has argued that the concept cannot be adequately operationalized (that is, put into a measurable form) and cannot be easily disentangled from other motives for obedience to law. Hyde asserts that habituation and rational, calculated self-interest explain obedience to law. While conceding some of the problems with the concept of legitimation, the author of this text (Friedrichs 1986b) has argued in response that the concept of legitimation is worth retaining with reference to the capacity of human beings to make autonomous moral assessments of the legal order (whether or not such assessments coincide with self-interest). More broadly, legitimacy may describe both a state of affairs and a process, and is generally considered to be at least a desirable and at most a necessary element of a stable and effective political (or legal) order (Friedrichs 1979). Ultimately, legitimacy involves explicit or implicit justifications for the authority of an order on the one hand, and the development of a sense of obligation on the part of subjects of that order, on the other.

When a significant percentage of the population no longer regards the legal system as legitimate, or worthy of their respect and obedience, then there is a legitimacy crisis (Friedrichs 1980). Such a crisis should not be confused with the related crisis in confidence, when a sizable proportion of the population experiences diminishing faith in the system's leadership, although the two types of crises may well affect each other (see Box 9.6).

Box 9.6

African Americans and Legitimation of the American Legal Order

It is well known that African Americans are disproportionately processed by the criminal justice system and make up a vastly disproportionate part of the American prison population. There is the staggering statistic that by the mid-1990s one out of three young black men, at any given point in time, was involved with the criminal justice system. (If these trends continue, by 2010 the majority of black men between 18 and 40 would be in prison) (Elikann 1996). Various explanations have been offered for this disparity (Wilbanks and Mann 1996). Some commentators have claimed that it principally reflects the higher levels of involvement in lawbreaking by young black men. Others have viewed it as a function of the similarly disproportionate representation of African Americans among the disadvantaged. A third form of explanation has viewed these outcomes as a consequence of racism and discriminatory decision making by predominantly white criminal justice personnel.

Although no one explanation may fully explain the disproportionate representation of black Americans in prison, a long and enduring history of discriminatory treatment surely plays a significant role. A response to this history is the relative absence of legitimacy of the legal system for many African Americans. Slavery, after all, was constructed and supported by this legal order, as was the systematic segregation of and discrimination against African Americans (especially in the South) in the century following the Civil War. African Americans have a historical legacy of a legal system, then, that did not extend basic rights to them, did not protect the rights they enjoyed, and was directly complicit in a denial of rights.

Despite *Brown v. Board of Education* (1954), the Civil Rights Act of 1964, affirmative action laws of the more recent era, and other such legal efforts to correct or make amends for past injustices, many African Americans have continued to experience various types of disadvantages. In the 1960s, and sporadically since then, a series of explosive riots occurred in African-American inner-city neighborhoods, clearly an expression of anger about enduring forms of racism and discrimination (especially on the part of the police) and frustration with the gap between the promise of equality and the reality of so many disadvantaged African-American lives. On some level, however, African-American patterns of lawbreaking can surely be linked with reservations about or the direct repudiation of the legitimation of the American legal system and of the corresponding obligation to comply with law (Davis 1974). This repudiation was most starkly articulated by black militants such as the Black Panthers in the late 1960s and early 1970s but seems to be broadly diffused, even when it is not specifically expressed.

The introduction of a "black rage" defense for criminal conduct also reflects the position that the experience of racial oppression generates an understandable sense of rage that may manifest itself in illegal behavior that can be linked with the idea of delegitimation of the legal order (Harris 1997). Two high-profile cases in the 1990s highlighted the distrust by African Americans of a white-dominated justice system: the beating of Rodney King by white police officers and the officers' subsequent acquittal in their first trial (with major protests and rioting in black neighborhoods in Los Angeles); and the not-guilty verdict by a predominantly African-American jury in the O. J. Simpson trial, a verdict based partly on evidence of racism by white police officer Mark Furhman, a key investigator of the crime (Gibbs 1996). A 1995 Gallup Poll found dramatic differences between ☞

☞ white Americans and African Americans on confidence in law enforcement (Johnson 1997, 12). Some 63 percent of whites expressed great confidence, as opposed to only 26 percent of African Americans. Only 8 percent of white Americans expressed little or no confidence, while more than a third—35 percent—of African Americans expressed this view. In a Canadian study of responses to a widely reported interracial homicide, it was found that well-educated African Americans who had had recent contact with the police were especially likely to perceive injustice in the response of the criminal justice system to this incident. In an American public poll undertaken in 1999, almost half the respondents (not simply African Americans) viewed the legal system as unfair to the poor and to minorities (Greenhouse 1999a). Perhaps only if the residual effects of the dismal history of white oppression of and exploitation of African Americans is resolved can we expect to witness a broader legitimation of the American legal order in the African-American community.

Legitimating Law: The Case of South Africa

The case of law and South Africa is discussed here because it illustrates in an especially striking way some of the themes pertaining to legal culture and legal behavior, and specifically the legitimation of law. The case of South Africa is a fascinating one for students of the sociolegal and comparative legal systems on more general terms. First, South Africa's official legal system cannot be easily classified in one of the principal families of law. Second, through much of its history over the past several hundred years, law was clearly one major means used by whites to dominate and oppress blacks. Third, South Africa represents a striking case of legal pluralism, insofar as a number of different systems of popular justice long coexisted with the official legal system. And fourth, South Africa's recent transformation into a democracy raises various important questions about the role of law in this process and about the appropriate legal response to the injustices of the past.

The democratization of South Africa in the early 1990s is surely one of the more dramatic occurrences of the recent era. More specifically, a country that had denied the great majority of its inhabitants (black South Africans) a vote held a democratic election in 1994, and Nelson Mandela became the first black South African president of the nation. It is all the more remarkable that only several years earlier, on February 11, 1990, Mandela had been released from prison after serving twenty-seven years of a life sentence on a treason charge.

Obviously the earliest form of law in the South African region was the tribal law of the indigenous peoples of South Africa. When Europeans, primarily Dutch, settled in South Africa from the seventeenth century on, they imposed a form of civil law. The British began settling in South Africa in the nineteenth century, and their political dominance for a time, following the Boer War early in the twentieth century, led to the increasing introduction of common law elements into the legal system, with trials basically modeled on the British pattern (Milton 1987, 36). From the beginning of the twentieth century, a series of laws were adopted that stripped black South Africans of rights to land ownership in most of South Africa and relocated most blacks to segregated areas, ultimately designated as "homelands"; the process of denying American Indians their dominance over the land and relocating them to reservations had parallels with the South African situation, although in South Africa blacks always far outnumbered whites (Mertz 1988).

When the Afrikaner Nationalist Party came to power in 1948, some of the British influences in the legal system diminished; for example, the jury system was abolished in the 1950s. The Afrikaners who dominated this party are whites descended from the early Dutch settlers. James Gibson and Amanda Gouws (1997, 173) observe that, "to a degree uncharacteristic of dictatorial regimes, South Africa relied heavily on law as an instrument of political repression during the dark days of apartheid." Largely through the institutions of law, then, the Nationalist Party created the notorious "apartheid" system, which imposed multiple forms of segregation, discrimination, and control on the black majority of the population (Davis 1986; Steytler, 1987). More specifically, apartheid included denial of South African citizenship and the vote to blacks; establishment of governmental control of land and of freedom of movement, especially with "pass laws" and "influx control"; segregation of facilities; and repression of dissent.

The white South African government, identifying with developed Western nations, claimed that it was in accord with "the rule of law," although its constitutional system and various legislative enactments and "extralegal" actions (e.g., death squads assassinating anti-apartheid activists) largely seemed to negate the claim (Foster, Sandler, and Davis 1987; Thompson 1986). The official system of law, claiming to adhere to the principles of legal positivism, was also used as a means of maintaining control over black South Africans; no bill of rights was in existence. Some seventeen million blacks, from the beginning of the twentieth century on, were believed to have been arrested and prosecuted under influx control and pass laws (Steytler 1987, 70). Blacks who ended up in one of the official courts typically found themselves in a thoroughly alien environment, facing a white judge, speaking a language they did not understand, and applying rules unfamiliar to them (Dlamini 1988).

Although in the final period of the apartheid regime many forms of "petty" apartheid were eliminated, a variety of measures, culminating with a "state of emergency" declaration in 1985, broadly extended the state's powers of social control (Milton 1987). Large numbers of blacks were shot down in protests, detained, tortured, and killed while in custody (Webster 1987). The principal thrust of the system of law surely seemed to many to be the maintenance of white power and privilege.

As noted earlier, however, a vast system of informal law, operating on various different levels, was also part of the black experience in South Africa (McCall 1995; Nina 1993; Pavlich 1992). These alternative systems of justice have been variously labeled popular justice, community justice, and private justice. A study of justice in a large black township, for example, found that it was "administered" by gangs; cultural movements; ad hoc neighborhood vigilante groups; community councils; and "Makgotla," which are unofficial people's courts operating under tribal authority, administering indigenous native law (Hund and Kotu-Rammopo 1983). If certain conduct (especially anti-state activity) defined as criminal by the official code of law was not so regarded by black South Africans, at least some conduct considered criminal (mundane street crime) in the townships was of no concern to the official legal system (Hund 1988). The white South African government, however, viewed emerging forms of popular justice (such as vigilante courts) as increasingly threatening toward the end of its regime, and tried to outlaw them (Nina 1993).

The great majority of black township residents turned to one of the informal mechanisms of social control with their grievances and accusations rather than to the formal system of justice established by whites, although at least a minority continued to rely upon the formal courts (McCall 1995). Mediation, rather than a judge-imposed ruling, was featured in the popular, or private, system of justice (Nina 1993). The popular justice of the Makgotla focuses more on issues of character than on the facts or the rules emphasized by the official system. However, such popular justice at least sometimes degenerates into a form of mob rule or vigilante justice. The "necklace"—placing a burning tire around the head of an accused person, leading to an especially tortured death—was the most notorious manifestation of this form of justice (Scheper-Hughes 1995). Furthermore, these courts typically reflected the patriarchal (or sexist) biases of the culture (Pavlich 1992). Such factors, as well as the fact that they all too often were both politically divisive and ineffective in addressing larger political issues, led to some deterioration of support for popular justice courts among black South Africans.

Although law was heavily implicated in the establishment and maintenance of apartheid, it also became a weapon—both as a sword and as a shield—in the struggle against apartheid, in part because there were few other weapons readily available and in part because elements of a historical commitment to "the rule of law" prevented its use solely and exclusively as an instrument for the protection of white political purposes (Abel 1995b). Those who challenged the apartheid system on some issue certainly lost many cases in the courts, but they also won some cases. The government's professed allegiance to the rule of law and its claim that the courts operated fairly was an important basis for its further claim to be legitimate and deserving of compliance (Davis 1986; Ellmann 1995; Gibson and Gouws 1997). Commitment to the rule of law at the end of the white regime could also be seen as a reflection of white concern about their own vulnerability in a post-apartheid society where no strong commitment to the rule of law had been established (Haysom and Kahanovitz 1987, 198). On the other hand, during the final period of white rule, it was said that black South Africans accorded government laws less legitimacy than virtually any other governed group, and large majorities expressed negative attitudes toward law and legal institutions (Human Sciences Research Council 1985; McCall 1995, 64–65; Steytler 1987, 68).

Although black South Africans certainly experienced many negative aspects of law during the apartheid era, various polls conducted during the more recent post-apartheid era suggested that they held more favorable views of the legal system than one would expect (Ellmann 1995; Gibson and Gouws 1997). According to a poll conducted in 1996, well after democratization, black South Africans were generally distrustful of all social institutions (except Nelson Mandela, the first black South African president), but the legal system came off less poorly than many other social institutions (Gibson and Gouws 1997). If at least some black South Africans had developed some confidence in the legal system (but not the police), it may be attributed to the fact that many other institutions of white South Africa were experienced as even less trustworthy and fair. Perhaps unsurprisingly, although white South Africans remained strongly committed to the rule of law following democratization, their trust in the legal system declined significantly (Gibson and Gouws 1997). Black South Africans, on the other hand, are far less committed to the rule of law, and are more concerned with substantive justice than with procedural formality.

Ultimately, white minority dominance of South Africa could not be sustained because such a system was too widely regarded as not legitimate or not deserving of respect and compliance. As one commentator observed near the end of the apartheid regime, "Perhaps more than any other state and social order, South Africa stands illegitimate and repressive before its own people" (Greenberg 1987, 1). Traditionally, the white minority in South Africa relied heavily upon Western racism intermixed with special elements of Afrikaner culture (including the theological rationales emanating from the Dutch Reformed Church) to promote its legitimacy claims. The pervasive level of control over the media and other sources of information was also a central element in promoting legitimating claims. In the final years of rule the white government attempted to maintain legitimacy and power by a mixture of reforms (e.g., eliminating petty forms of apartheid) and coercion (e.g., the Emergency Act, giving the police broad powers). Ultimately, a recognition developed in the last white government, under F. W. De Klerk, that democratization (with protections built in for the white minority) was the only viable means of resolving the ongoing legitimacy crisis.

In the years leading up to and those following the transition to democracy, South Africa was plagued with increasing crime and much violence in the black townships, with anxiety over this wave of crime overtaking earlier concerns about political violence (Hutton 1997). The township violence was widely, and understandably, condemned as "senseless" in light of the fall of the apartheid regime; an anthropologist responded by asking: "Did 'senseless violence' imply that the police were 'sensible' in their attacks and raids on Black townships? Was 'senseless violence' a racist code for irrational Black violence, as opposed to rational, sensible white violence?" (Scheper-Hughes 1995, 147). Despite the high level of concern about crime and violence, the policies of the criminal justice system—at odds with trends in many Western nations, including those of the United States—became more liberal. The death penalty (commonly imposed in apartheid South Africa) was abolished; magistrates received training in race and gender sensitivity; rehabilitation was stressed in sentencing, on the premise that many offenders were victims of apartheid (Hutton 1997). Whether such practices would endure in the long run, especially if rates of crime and violence continued to increase, was an open question.

In view of the historical role of law in the repression of black South Africans, it would have been understandable if the new government, elected following democratization with African National Congress leader Nelson Mandela as President, moved to abolish existing legal institutions. Mandela himself had been tried and convicted of treason and had been sentenced to life in prison (and served some 27 years in harsh conditions) by this legal system. Although a new constitution was adopted and reforms were instituted, much of the existing legal system was retained. Mandela's commitment to the rule of law was not necessarily embraced by all his associates, who for many years had operated outside the tradition of formal law. Retention of the legal system reflected the government's concern with potential chaos as a result of a wholesale abandonment of law and legal institutions; a need to retain a good measure of confidence from both South African whites and outside investors in the economy; and perhaps some respect on the part of Mandela and others for what had finally been accomplished through legal means.

The new government faced a large and sensitive challenge: What should it do about the many crimes, injustices, and human rights abuses perpetrated by or on behalf of the apartheid regime, as well as the opposition forces? More specifically, could it reconcile the potentially conflicting objectives of exposing the truth about past atrocities and penalizing the offenders (Berat and Shain 1995, 166)? In other words, was it only by offering amnesty to past offenders that one could hope to obtain true accounts of past crimes? If the government were to satisfy the understandable desire of past victims of these crimes (and their survivors) for avenging the wrongdoing, it could jeopardize support for the newly established democratic institutions (especially among anxious white South Africans). In one of its first acts, the new democratic government established a remarkable Truth and Reconciliation Commission, empowered to grant amnesty to those who confessed truthfully about past political crimes. Needless to say, the work of this Commission was controversial, with demands for justice sometimes conflicting with the pursuit of truth.

For South Africa, moving into the twenty-first century, the challenges would remain formidable. Would the post-Mandela presidents be able to maintain a level of support comparable to that enjoyed by this historically unique figure? Could the commitment to the rule of law be maintained while addressing past injustices and present inequalities? Would the black South African majority support and regard as legitimate a government unable to promote broader economic equality any time soon?

Conclusion

Law intersects with culture at many points, and legal behavior has many different dimensions. The notion of community (and identity) is one key feature of the broader terrain of legal culture. The fact that law has a language and law is communicated must also be understood as a critical aspect of legal culture. The process of lawmaking reflects some aspects of the legal culture but must also be seen in relation to specific institutional processes. And legal behavior cannot be separated from a consideration of legitimation as it relates to law. The case of South Africa illustrates some of the themes of the chapter and, as a fascinating case in its own right, can be linked with many issues explored in other chapters.

Key Terms and Concepts

accumulation model
apartheid
celerity
certainty
coercion
compliance
crime creators
deterrence
identification
identification model
identity politics
internal legal culture
internalization
legal culture
legal ideology
legal socialization
Makgotla
normative
official graffiti
republic of choice
role transfer model
severity
total justice
uniformity
utilitarian

Discussion Questions

1. With issues such as whether sexual and violent materials are offensive, who should ultimately decide? Does it make sense to let the law decide such an issue for the community? Could any problems arise if each community made its own laws based upon its values?
2. In what situations does the general public usually voice the greatest concern for new laws, or for changes to be made to existing ones? Do most laws seem to be a reflection of elitist control over the powerless, or are they more of a general consensus of the population? Explain.
3. Discuss the power behind the language of the law. How do legal professionals have an advantage over laypeople, especially in the courtroom?
4. Discuss the process of legal socialization. Through what means, and when, are most people oriented toward the law? Explain how the news or media play a part in how we learn about the law. Why do you think *most* people who obey the law do so? Do moral reasons tend to play more of a role than rational reasons?
5. Compare the role of legitimation in the case of African Americans and the law to the case of South Africans and the law. Are there any similarities to the cases?

Chapter Ten

Law in Flux: Law and Social Change

We want law to reflect basic values, to be a source of stability, to withstand the shifting winds of fashion and passions of the moment. At the same time, we want law to evolve with transformations in social attitudes and societal needs, to be flexible in new circumstances, to lead society in the direction of emerging goals and aspirations. Is law best thought of as responding to changes in the larger society or as an active instrument of those changes? Where is law heading as we move through the twenty-first century, and what will it look like in the future? Of course, law is endlessly complex and multifaceted. Some aspects of law do endure with little if any real change over centuries; other parts of law undergo dramatic changes, sometimes within a relatively short space of time. Law is clearly both an object of social change and an instrument of social change. Some dimensions of law will change little, if at all, as we move through the twenty-first century, whereas other dimensions of law will change dramatically.

What is social change? Many of the changes in society are superficial, cosmetic, and insubstantial. Styles, fashions, and fads come and go. Yet, certain forms of social change are fundamental, structural, and consequential. Revolutions and major reforms can bring into being far-reaching and enduring changes. One of the ways in which the modern world is said to be different from the ancient and traditional world is that people have come to expect (and often insist upon) change in many aspects of their existence.

Many members of modern society welcome change, but others are resistant to at least some forms of change. Tensions and conflicts inevitably arise between those who are promoting social change (e.g., feminists) and those who are opposing it (e.g., traditionalists). Thus, law is used by some to promote social change that they want to see come into being; law is bitterly attacked by others for promoting social change they find distressing. Law is viewed by some as an instrument that should be used to lead the way in improving social conditions; law is viewed by others as an entity that should maintain the traditional values of society in defiance of passions of the moment. Some changes originate from without the legal system, others from within it (Friedman 1975, 270). Change may affect only the legal system itself, or it may have an impact within the larger society. Legal change, then, occurs on many different levels and takes many different forms.

Legal change may take a liberal, or progressive, direction, but it may also take a conservative, or reactionary, direction. In the liberal view, law should be reformed to promote more equality, broader opportunities, more protective rights, and so on. For conservatives, law should only be changed when it expands personal freedom, supports free enterprise, and reinforces traditional values. Conservatives typically view liberal legal initiatives as restricting individual rights, interfering with a capitalist economy, and reinforcing dependency or tolerating predatory crime. Liberals typically view conservative legal initiatives as protecting socially destructive rights (such as gun ownership), making the rich richer and the poor poorer, rendering those accused of crimes vulnerable to unjustly imposed punishment by the state, and depriving citizens of important privacy rights (e.g., the right to have an abortion). Legal change is a function of power, and all too often the powerful and privileged have used their influence on law to protect or extend their own interests. The historical path of legal change in America has been complex and contradictory. Americans have experienced cycles during which many progressive initiatives have been advanced, and other cycles during which reactionary measures have been dominant.

Should law be used as an instrument of social change and as a means of promoting good behavior? Those at the ideological extremes—anarchists and reactionaries—generally oppose such use of law. Radical anarchists regard legal reform within the existing system as an illusion. Law in its very form favors the advantaged, and the social system itself has to be radically transformed. As Peter Kropotkin ([1927] 1966, 295), a leading theorist of anarchism, puts it: "No more laws! No more judges! Liberty, equality, and practical human sympathy are the only effectual barriers we can oppose to the antisocial instincts of certain among us." He has defined anarchism as "a principle or theory of life and conduct under which society is conceived without government—harmony in such a society being obtained, not by submission to law, or by obedience to any authority, but by free agreements . . ." (Kropotkin [1910] 1971, xi). On the other hand, the reactionary Nicholas Murray Butler (1923), a president of Columbia University, spoke out early in the twentieth century against the Fifteenth Amendment to the Constitution (extending the universal franchise) and the Eighteenth Amendment (prohibiting trade in liquor) as doing more harm than good and contributing to the general lawlessness in the country.

Law is both an object of social change and an instrument of social change, a dependent variable and an independent variable (E. Levine 1990). These two dimensions of law and social change are intimately interrelated, and cannot be easily separated. That is, when social conditions change, laws over time are likely to reflect such changes, but at the same time those welcoming social change or having some vested interest in it will often actively campaign for legal reforms that could speed up the pace of the desired social change. If, on the one hand, the civil rights laws of the 1960s reflected changing attitudes within society, they were also intended to promote racial integration and the demise of racial prejudice. If welfare law reforms of the 1990s reflected changing social attitudes about poverty and dependency, the reforms were also implemented with the claim that they could help bring

Box 10.1

Founding Fathers of Law and Society on Legal Reform

The pioneering students of law and society were intensely interested in the question of law and social change. Their views were discussed in earlier chapters, on jurisprudence and on the sociology of law. But some of their key ideas can be briefly reviewed here. For Sir Henry Maine ([1861] 1970), the primary law-related transformation over time can be found in a shift in law from the centrality of status (related to group membership) to contract (related to voluntary individual agreements). While it seems indisputable that contracts have become more important in a complex, modern society, it is worth noting that in the recent era, status (e.g., gender; race; disability) has also been important in a growing body of law. For Karl Marx (Cain and Hunt 1979), law evolved into its modern form in conjunction with the rise of capitalism; the transformation of society to communism should lead to the obliteration of law. As we know, the attempt to eliminate law in post-revolutionary societies had largely devastating consequences and could not be sustained in the long run. For Herbert Spencer (1898), it was a mistake to use law as a means of assisting the disadvantaged because this interfered with the laws of nature and the principle of survival of the fittest. Although Spencer's advice was largely disregarded in the twentieth century, conservatives have continued to embrace and promote this position (with recent welfare law reforms at least partially reflecting this). For Emile Durkheim ([1893] 1984), the principal change over time was from a system of law with repressive (or punitive) legal sanctions to one with restitutive (or compensatory) sanctions. This claim has been challenged, since much law in the modern world seems to be oriented toward controlling and exploiting people. For Max Weber ([1954] 1967), law in contemporary bureaucratic, capitalist society takes on an increasingly rational orientation, with an emphasis on objectivity, predictability, and instrumentality. The rationalization of the law is far from complete, however, and many irrational elements still survive.

about desirable changes in the behavior and attitudes of welfare recipients. Accordingly, any separation of law as object of social change and law as instrument of social change, for purposes of discussion, is inevitably somewhat arbitrary (see Box 10.1).

Law and social change has been an ongoing preoccupation of contemporary students of law and society. For some, especially those with a positivistic or functionalist orientation, social scientists should dispassionately formulate law-like propositions about law and social change that can be subjected to empirical testing. These themes were discussed in Chapter 5 but can be briefly reviewed here. Donald Black (1976) has formulated a series of propositions about the relation between law and certain social variables, with the idea that these propositions can be tested. For example, Black predicts that law varies inversely with other forms of social control. This proposition inevitably suggests that as other forms of social control decline, more law will have to be introduced in response. Richard Lempert and Joseph Sanders (1986) attempt to demonstrate how social science research can enable us to understand law and social change. For example, such research provides some evidence of the impact of legal reforms (e.g., the Civil Rights Act of 1964) on the enduring problem of racial inequality. Although these sociologists are committed to a scientific approach to understanding law and social change, they also express the faith that this approach can provide a foundation for promoting greater justice within society.

At the same time, some students of law and society have rejected the social science approach to understanding law and social change in favor of critique and interpretation. Richard Quinney's (1974) *Critique of Legal Order* seeks to expose some of the many ways in which contemporary American law is exploitative and oppressive, calling for a basic societal transformation to overcome these conditions. Richard Delgado and Jean Stefanic (1994), in *Failed Revolutions: Social Reform and the Limits of Legal Imagination*, suggest that only a fundamental transformation in consciousness, not legal reform by itself, is likely to produce long-term change in a progressive direction. Boaventura de Sousa Santos' (1995) *Toward a New Common Sense: Law, Science and Politics in the Paradigmatic Transition* seeks to expose the collapse of modernity and the emergence of a postmodern world, with a call for moving law in a whole new, emancipatory direction in the future. These students of law and society call for their readers' active engagement in the process of legal and societal transformation.

Law As an Object of Social Change

Law changes over time. Law as an institution tends to become increasingly formal and complex as a society evolves and expands. Many factors contribute to the changes in law. First, the increasing size of the population alone tends to impose some pressures for change. The kind of law needed to govern a teeming city with millions of people is bound to be different from the kind of "law" called for in the case of a small, nomadic tribe. As a general rule, as people shift from small rural communities to urban centers, there is a need for new forms and types of law to respond to the special conditions of city life. Over time, for example, you need laws to allow people to live together in close proximity without constant conflicts, and you need legal institutions that can process large numbers of defendants and litigants at the same time. In a parallel vein, with the emergence of a modern capitalist system, and of increasing numbers of large, complex organizations (such as industrial corporations), law must change to adapt to the realities of these new conditions. Over time, a vast complex of laws has developed in the realm of contracts, for example, since they are one key feature of this type of economy; a similar growth and expansion has occurred in the realm of corporate law, or the conditions governing corporations.

The introduction of ever more complex forms of technology inevitably produces a need for new laws. As one obvious example, the introduction of the automobile ultimately led to many new traffic laws. In the more recent era, the introduction of computers, and the very rapid spread of the Internet, has generated a demand for laws to respond to the whole new set of conditions created. The increasing capacity of sophisticated medical technology to keep people "alive" indefinitely is another example of an area where technology generates a need for new laws (for example, on the proper role of physicians in allowing, or even facilitating, death).

Table 10.1 Factors Contributing to Legal Reform

Factors Contributing to Legal Reform
Growth of society (e.g., population growth)
New economic system (e.g., capitalism)
New technology (e.g., computers)
New social conditions (e.g., urbanism)
Moral entrepreneurs (e.g., Mothers Against Drunk Driving)
Special interest groups (e.g., corporate lobbyists)
Public interest considerations (e.g., communicated by idealistic legislators)

Law changes, too, because groups of people perceive a discrepancy between what their values or their sense of rights calls for and what the existing law permits or tolerates. Prohibition, early in the twentieth century, with its ban on the sale and distribution of liquor, came into being largely because supporters of the Temperance Movement campaigned for it over a long period of time. In the more recent era, Mothers Against Drunk Driving (MADD) has mobilized, with some success, for tougher laws against drunk drivers. Of course, the fact that some particular interest group in society mobilizes to bring new laws into existence or to repeal existing laws does not mean that such efforts are uniformly successful. The Pro-Life Movement in America, for example, has not been able to bring about the outlawing of abortion, despite relentless campaigning on the issue over a period of decades.

Law changes for many reasons, only some of which have been suggested here. (Table 10.1 lists a number of factors contributing to legal reform.) Law changes because new sets of conditions may make such change necessary simply as a practical matter. For example, although the occasional dispute in a simple society can be handled by community leaders on an ad hoc basis, the processing of thousands of cases in a large contemporary urban justice system requires some form of a legal bureaucratic organization. Law changes because it is in the interest of parties who are in a position to determine or influence the nature of law to promote certain changes. The corporate business community, for example, has promoted changes in product liability law to minimize their exposure to consumer lawsuits. Somewhat idealistically, we like to believe that law changes because some people in a position to implement change (for example, legislators or appellate court justices) arrive at the conclusion that the best interests of society as a whole are served by a change in law, the legal process, or legal institutions. But much evidence can be marshalled to demonstrate that politics, power, and special interests have played a larger role in bringing about legal change than have principled and altruistic objectives (see Box 10.2).

Efforts to reform law typically encounter many forms of resistance. Steven Vago (1994, 244–250) has efficiently identified many of these sources of resistance. They include social, economic, cultural, and psychological factors. In social terms, the upper class tends to resist legal reform that might compromise its advantages, and there are always specific parties who have a vested interest in maintaining the status quo (Handler 1978). If enough is at stake in a proposed legal reform, parties whose vested interests are threatened are likely to form an organized opposition to the proposed legal reform.

Box 10.2

Social Science Research and Legal Change

Does social science research promote legal change? At various points in this text such an impact has been suggested. In the wake of research on the unreliability of eyewitness testimony, for example, various jurisdictions have made some changes in the law, to allow psychologists to testify on this unreliability or to modify instructions for juries (Tanford 1991). Rule-making commissions have apparently been more receptive to making changes in response to social science findings than have courts; in some cases, courts have even changed law in a direction at odds with social science research (Tanford 1991). Social science research, then, can be an agent of legal change, although not uniformly and not in a single direction.

The opposition to legal reform may be based on ideology, morality, or religious belief, as well as on economic or practical interests, or possibly some combination of both types of factors. The National Rifle Association (NRA), as one example, has had a long history of successfully organizing opposition to proposed gun control laws, although in the recent era it has been somewhat less successful in this regard; the NRA campaign against gun control reflects a combination of vested interests (of gun manufacturers and dealers) and ideology (the belief that citizens are constitutionally entitled to possess firearms without restrictions).

The source of resistance to legal reform may be specifically economic. This economic interest may reflect a desire to protect economic advantage, or a perceived lack of economic resources necessary to finance the reform. Corporations and businesses have long opposed legal reforms of all kinds that are perceived to cut into profit margins; such reforms include the imposition of new taxes and the setting of new liability, safety, or antipollution standards. Since wealthy corporations and business associations typically have large economic resources available to them, for advertising campaigns or the like, these efforts have often been successful. Citizen and taxpayer advocacy groups have opposed legal reforms that are viewed as too costly, such as the extension of comprehensive, universal healthcare coverage.

Cultural resistance to legal reform reflects concern with perceived threats to traditional customs and values. Indigenous peoples in colonial societies, for example, have often resisted legal reforms imposed upon them by colonial governments when these reforms were at odds with their traditional way of life. When members of a particular group subscribe to the ethnocentric view that their way of life is superior to that of other people, they are likely to resist legal change that is viewed as influenced by external cultural values. Plain superstition may also play a role in resistance to legal change.

Finally, one can identify some psychological sources of resistance to legal reform. People are likely to resist legal reforms that are at odds with their personality, moral orientation, personal perceptions, or ingrained patterns of behavior. If someone has been accustomed to driving without a seatbelt for many years and does not regard such driving as especially risky, that individual may well oppose a law requiring people to wear a seatbelt. Of course, an individual is not typically able to do much to stop a new law from being passed—unless the individual happens to occupy a crucial position within the political system—but individuals often express their unhappiness with new laws simply by refusing to comply with them.

Law As an Instrument of Social Change

Does law also change the social and human world, or does it simply reflect changes in this world? New laws and legal reform efforts are uniformly introduced or initiated with the professed aim of improving society in some way and promoting better human behavior. It is widely believed that major U.S. Supreme Court decisions, and major new legislative reforms, lead to social change. The Warren Court of the 1950s and 1960s made many landmark decisions regarded as inspiring significant social and political reforms (Horwitz 1998). Although most scholarly attention has focused on the U.S. Supreme Court as a source of social change, the lower federal courts and the state courts can also play a key role in these changes (Schultz 1998).

Michael W. McCann (1994) argues that litigation and court decisions made a significant difference in addressing pay equity issues. Women (and minorities) through much of the twentieth century were systematically paid less than white males for the same job. In the final decades of the century, these inequities began to be challenged in litigation at least partially inspired by the Feminist Movement. In the landmark decision *County of Washington, Oregon, v. Gunther* (1981), the U.S. Supreme Court supported claims of female prison guards for pay equity with male guards. Although subsequent court decisions in pay equity cases often interpreted claims in such cases somewhat narrowly, McCann claims that on balance the litigation and court actions did make a measurable difference in bringing about much broader pay equity for females and minorities. Even when the courts did not rule favorably on behalf of pay equity litigants, the legal activity itself proved useful in achieving pay equity objectives. It was not just prison guards, but prisoners themselves, who were affected by court rulings (Feeley and Rubin 1998). Until the mid-1960s the courts largely adopted a hands-off policy toward prison conditions, but subsequently they made a series of rulings requiring changes in prison conditions and an extension of rights of prisoners.

On the other hand, Gerald N. Rosenberg (1991) concludes that the courts have little significant influence on social change. He reaches this controversial conclusion about two of the most famous U.S. Supreme Court decisions—the *Brown v. Board of Education* (1954) decision on segregation and the *Roe v. Wade* (1973) decision on abortion—as well as about less famous decisions. These decisions are seen as largely reflecting change in society during the period in question; changes following the handing down of the decisions, then, reflect these other social forces. Since such change often occurs only years after the opinion is handed down, intervening social forces must be at work. Certainly, the hopes of legal reform activists have often been dashed, or severely compromised, in the years following a victory in the courts. Despite the obliteration of legal segregation and discrimination following the *Brown* decision, by some measures *de facto* segregation (following white flight and other factors) actually increased in subsequent decades, and racial division as well as racism was not eliminated, and was sometimes intensified.

What are the conditions under which law is most likely to promote social change? William Evan (1965), writing from a functionalist perspective, contends the law is most likely to promote social change when it emanates from an authoritative source; it has an acceptable rationale; practical models for compliance have been identified; changes in patterns of enforcement are instituted over a reasonably brief period of time; enforcement agents are committed to change; positive as well as negative sanctions are used; and enforcement of the new law is reasonable. The emphasis in the conflict or critical perspective on the impact of legal change is very different, however (Chambliss 1973a; Kairys 1998). It says that, to the extent that those in power have direct (or indirect) control over resources, they are in a position to impose their will on the powerless. If members of society adapt to legal reforms imposed on them by those in power, it is largely a matter of being coerced or manipulated into making such adaptations. The imposition of law is unlikely to be total, however, and various forms of resistance can arise to the extent that legal changes are experienced as inequitable or exploitative in some way.

A conflict approach can be applied to understanding how law itself changes. In a dialectical perspective on lawmaking, advanced by William Chambliss (e.g., Chambliss and Zatz 1993), the introduction of new laws is viewed as a process directed toward the resolution of various contradictions, conflicts, and dilemmas confronting society in a particular historical context. For example, the introduction of laws regulating the meat packing industry in the early twentieth century and the more recent antipollution laws can be explained in terms of a resolution of conflicts between a public increasingly angry about unhealthy meat (or dangerous forms of pollution) and the short-term economic interests of meatpacking corporations (or corporate polluters); the new laws helped resolve conflicts by reassuring the public, on the one hand, while protecting long-term economic interests of major corporations, on the other.

Legal Reforms and Their Impact

Specific legal reforms are best understood both in terms of circumstances producing them and their impact on social conditions or patterns of behavior. Some legal reform movements come into being because a class of people (or advocates on their behalf) challenge their disadvantaged status. More law has been introduced and passed on behalf of the powerful and privileged, however. Does law succeed in diminishing inequality, or does it merely create the appearance of doing so? In the paragraphs that follow, a number of areas of law that addressed issues of inequality—especially economic inequality—are reviewed.

Labor Law

Throughout most of history employers have had a tremendous advantage over employees, and this advantage was largely supported by law. In the early part of the nineteenth century, most working people did not even have a right to vote; attempts at that time to form labor unions were treated by the courts as a form of criminal conspiracy and as an illegal attempt to interfere with free trade (Turkel 1996, 155). Although an 1841 case in Massachusetts established a precedent for the legal establishment of labor unions, the American courts (including the U.S. Supreme Court) were more often than not hostile toward labor interests throughout the nineteenth century and into the early part of the twentieth century. In an 1895 decision, *In Re Debs*, the U.S. Supreme Court upheld a contempt citation against an important labor leader involved in a strike against the Pullman Railroad Car Company, and this decision reflected an enduring lack of support for a broad-based unionism (Papke 1999). The courts further ruled that the Sherman Antitrust Act was applicable to labor unions and that legislative bodies (including Congress) had limited authority to pass laws governing employer/employee relations.

Beginning in the latter part of the nineteenth century, labor/management conflict produced considerable disorder and sometimes erupted into violence. Following World War I, and especially as a consequence of the onset of the Great Depression in the 1930s, the U.S. Supreme Court (e.g., in *American Foundries v. Tri-City Council*, 1921) and the U.S. Congress (e.g., with the Norris-LaGuardia Act of 1932) made decisions or laws more favorable to labor, extending to workers the right to organize and to strike without outside interference. A landmark law, the National Labor Relations Act (Wagner Act), was adopted in 1935, but its real meaning has been interpreted in conflicting ways. In the conventional interpretation, this act, by establishing a National Labor Relations Board and requiring management to engage in collective bargaining with unionized workers on all issues pertaining to the wages and conditions of work, effectively put workers (collectively) on an equal footing with management. In a dissenting interpretation, however, the Wagner Act was really intended to defeat union radicalism, and through a series of appellate court opinions has been interpreted in a manner that continues to give management the upper hand in most disputes (Klare 1978). In a backlash against the growing power of labor unions in the mid-twentieth century, the Labor Management Relations Act (Taft-Hartley Act) of 1948 declared certain union activities as unfair labor practices. Although legal reforms between the end of the nineteenth century and the end of the twentieth century indisputably led to the improvement of some of the circumstances of employees, the notion that management and labor settle disputes as equals can certainly be challenged. Furthermore, changes in the American economy during the final decades of the twentieth century led to a decline in the proportion of American workers represented by unions, with a proportional decline in union power.

Welfare Law

Throughout most of history, the poor and the disabled either have been ignored by the law or have been persecuted in the name of the law (Trattner

1999). Traditionally, poverty was regarded as a natural condition, and the poor were left to their own devices and private charity. The transient poor and the homeless poor, if they had no family to take them in, were often expelled from the community, sent to workhouses, put into stocks for public shaming, or thrown into debtors' prison. All of these practices within the English tradition, except debtors' prison, were widely adopted by the American colonies (Hall 1989, 28–30; Katz 1986). The policy of extending some form of financial aid to dependent people evolved gradually throughout the nineteenth century. In the United States, pensions made available to Civil War veterans provided one model for government welfare, although this form of relief turned out to be costly and often corrupt (Skocpol 1992). Workmen's compensation for disabilities arising out of work was quite broadly supported. Over time, with the support of women's associations, government welfare was extended by law to a broader class of dependent people, especially women and children. In the 1930s, during the Depression, the Social Security system was introduced, and during the 1960s Medicaid and Medicare were implemented. These forms of welfare were clearly effective in reducing the poverty rate among the elderly. Although the Warren Court of the 1960s extended some constitutional protections to the poor, it never identified welfare benefits as a constitutional right (Bussiere 1997).

Welfare as such came to be identified through much of the twentieth century with the extension of economic benefits to the dependent poor, especially single women and their children (Aid to Families With Dependent Children, or AFDC) (Teles 1996). Politically, it has always been more difficult to secure broad support for benefit programs for "targeted" populations (e.g., the poor) than for broad classes of people. Accordingly, there has been some debate over whether the poor are best helped by programs specifically focusing on their needs or by being incorporated into programs benefiting the middle class as well (Greenstein 1991; Skocpol 1992). Scholars have different interpretations of what welfare means for the poor and why welfare expanded through much of the twentieth century. Is welfare a form of charity, a practical inducement, or a right and, accordingly, a new form of property? To conservatives, bloated welfare programs represent a misguided, and counterproductive, liberal philosophy and do more harm than good. To moderates and liberals, welfare programs are an expression of compassion and a contemporary form of civic obligation; ideally, they enable individuals and families to rise out of poverty. In a well-known progressive or radical interpretation, welfare is a device used by those in power to control the poor, and welfare is extended more broadly in times of unrest to quell an uprising, while it is reduced (or withdrawn) in more stable times (Piven and Cloward 1971).

In 1964, in the face of considerable social unrest, President Johnson signed into law the "War on Poverty" called for by President Kennedy. But this war became somewhat neglected over time, in part because of the enormous distraction of another war, that in Vietnam. In the view of some, the principal beneficiaries of this war on poverty were government bureaucrats on different levels for whom it provided employment. Nevertheless, evidence has been marshalled to support the claim that the war on poverty programs of the Johnson administration did have some impact in reducing poverty (Jencks 1992). The long-term benefits of welfare in generally reducing poverty are far less clear.

Through much of its history, the contemporary American welfare system was attacked from many different vantage points—as counterproductive and riddled with corruption and, conversely, as administered in a mean and demeaning way (Zasloff 1998). There have been many myths about the attributes of those receiving welfare. For example, welfare was alleged to include a significant proportion of able-bodied but lazy men, women with many children, and people living well on their welfare income. Welfare was specifically blamed for promoting a dramatic increase in the breakup of families, the growing number of single mothers, and a rise in the rate of illegitimate births, although contrary evidence strongly suggested that these developments occurred independently of expanding welfare benefits and were linked more closely with shifting cultural values (Jencks 1992; Stoesz 1997). In the late 1960s and early 1970s, a welfare rights movement succeeded in winning a series of court cases recognizing legal entitlements and due process for welfare applicants; the dramatic expansion of the welfare rolls, at least in some places (for example, in New York City), was one consequence of this movement. But by the end of the twentieth century, the conservative viewpoint, with its central claim that the welfare system fosters a debilitating form of dependency and is wasteful and ineffective on many levels, came to prevail. In August 1996, President Clinton signed into law the Personal Responsibility and Work Opportunity Act (PRWOA), ending the traditional system of welfare entitlements. In addition to imposing time limits and other restrictions on receipt of welfare, this law called for most welfare recipients to be integrated into the workforce. Various states and cities implemented parallel welfare reform policies of their own.

While a majority of Americans apparently believed that legal reforms to welfare law had all too often done more harm than good and had certainly not reduced poverty in any significant way, many Americans were also uncomfortable with dumping large numbers of people into a situation where they would be desperately strapped for basic economic resources (and could be pressed into committing crimes to provide for themselves and their families) (Edelman 1997, 53). Various welfare-to-work programs in the past have failed because they were based upon the false premise that the principal problem with the poor is that they lack a commitment to work; an alternative interpretation suggests that welfare dependency is much more a function of the deterioration of the low-wage labor market in many poor neighborhoods (Handler and Hasenfeld 1997). With the beginning of a new century, it was still far from clear what the real impact of legal reform of welfare would be over time, or whether the problem of poverty had to be addressed in other ways.

Civil Rights Law

No legal reform movement in America in the twentieth century had a higher social profile or was more fully documented than the civil rights movement. Although the origins of the civil rights movement can be traced far back, the major stages of the movement took place between the mid-1950s and the mid-1960s. The civil rights movement launched a basic challenge to legally sanctioned discrimination against African-American citizens, with segregated schools as the single most visible symbol of this segregation. The

Box 10.3

Hate Crimes

The concept of hate crime or bias crime was introduced in about 1980, as one more response to a long and ugly history of racism and intolerance. Hate or bias crime laws imposed stronger punishments on offenders who committed crimes motivated by hate or bias. Frederick Lawrence (1999) argues in favor of these laws. He contends that crimes motivated by bias or hate injure the immediate victim, the target community, and society at large in ways exceeding the injury of parallel crimes not motivated by hate. Such crimes merit greater punishment because they represent an attack on racial harmony and equality, two of the highest values of Americans' society. Lawrence argues that hate crime laws do not necessarily conflict with Americans' commitment to free speech, since we can clearly distinguish between bias crime, a form of behavior, and racist speech, a form of expression.

James B. Jacobs and Kimberly Potter (1998) argue against the idea of a special category of hate crime or bias crime. They contend that (1) key terms in such laws, such as "prejudice," are ambiguous (2) harsher punishments for minorities, who disproportionately commit interracial crimes, are the likely practical consequence of such laws (3) existing law already has provisions for providing harsher punishment for more harmful crimes and (4) the hate crime laws were adopted in response to an alleged but actually nonexistent new epidemic of hate crime.

celebrated *Brown v. Board of Education* (1954) decision, declaring official segregation unconstitutional, is typically credited with having played a significant role in bringing about an end to such segregation, despite substantial resistance from Southern courts (Sanders 1995). The adoption of a strategy of nonviolent protest, primarily under the inspirational leadership of the Reverend Martin Luther King Jr. was a noteworthy attribute of the civil rights movement. This movement (with the help of television news broadcasts) drew the attention of the country to the Southern resistance to implementing *Brown v. Board of Education* and to the many demeaning and unjust dimensions of segregation. Accordingly, it contributed to a transformation of the political environment and passage of the Civil Rights Act of 1964 and the Voting Rights Act of 1965. The Supreme Court decision in *Swann v. Charlotte-Mecklenburg Board of Education* (1971) authorized the controversial practice of busing children as a means of achieving integration. Although these laws were successful in sweeping away legal (or formal) discrimination and in promoting integration at least in certain circumstances, they have been far less successful in legislating racism and its consequences out of existence (see Box 10.3).

Women's Rights and the Equal Rights Amendment

Throughout most of history, women have not enjoyed the same rights as men. Under traditional law, and in the English common law, women were treated as subordinate to or virtually the property of fathers or husbands (Dusky 1996). In general, women in the American colonies were somewhat better off under law than those in England—perhaps because there were fewer women and accordingly women were valued more—but they were still at a substantial disadvantage. Married women could not own property, sue, or enter into a contract independently of their husbands. They also could not vote. For all but the most serious crimes, women were regarded as acting on behalf of, or under the influence of, their husbands (Bartlett 1991). Although some women challenged the inferior legal status of women, little changed until the present era. From the early nineteenth century on, it is true, some rights of property ownership were granted to women as well as more equal standing in legal proceedings, but it is likely that such reforms served the interests of the larger society and of men who wanted to shield assets from creditors, not the interests of women.

The suffragist movement of the nineteenth century emerged, in part, out of the experience of women with the abolitionist movement (Dubois 1998; Dusky 1996, 258). Again, the ultimate success of this movement early in the twentieth century in obtaining the vote for women has been viewed more as a reflection of the desire of white middle-class males to retain political clout in the face of the growing hordes of European immigrants than as a full-fledged recognition of the inherent political rights of women.

Only with the emergence of the contemporary feminist movement (primarily from the early 1970s on) has there been a more fundamental extension of equal legal rights to women. Just as the suffragist movement emerged in part out of the abolitionist movement, the contemporary feminist movement was influenced by the involvement of women in the civil rights movement and the success of that movement in challenging unjust laws. Most states revised their laws to remove blatant forms of gender bias, and the United States Supreme Court, in a series of decisions, struck down formal biases against women in the operation of the justice system and in both criminal and civil law proceedings.

Throughout the 1970s, into the early 1980s, feminists campaigned for the adoption of an Equal Rights Amendment (ERA) to the U.S. Constitution, which would have prohibited as unconstitutional any form of discrimination against individuals for reasons of gender. This effort failed, however, in 1982. Various reasons have been given for failure of the ERA to pass (Hoff-Wilson 1986; Mansbridge 1986). Not only many men but a large number of women as well opposed the ERA, on various grounds. Some argued that it was simply not necessary because state laws already prohibited significant forms of discrimination. Some feared that it would deprive women of certain privileges (from alimony to exclusion from the draft). Some stated an ideological objection to treating men and women alike. For at least some, the principal significance of the ERA was symbolic: it would assert, once and for all, that women were not subordinate to men and were entitled to the same rights as men. Whether an Equal Rights Amendment, if ratified, would have had a measurable positive impact on the lives of women is open to dispute.

Despite the removal of many specific forms of gender bias from law, the legal status of women by the end of the twentieth century was declared "still unequal," with many forms of discrimination still in effect (Dusky 1996; Landrine and Klonoff 1997). As long as significant economic and social differences divide the sexes, treating men and women alike under law will not produce true equality (Barker, Kirk, and Sah 1998). Traditional sexist attitudes have proved more enduring than formal laws. Many unresolved issues remain, regarding pregnancy discrimination, custody, post-divorce property settlement, unequal compensation and promotion policies, comparable worth, taxation (especially as applied to benefits), and the overall treatment of physically and sexually abused women.

Equal Opportunity and Affirmative Action

Although America historically has been celebrated as the "land of opportunity," it has hardly been a land of *equal* opportunity. In response to the Civil Rights Movement and the Feminist Movement, laws have been introduced to provide more equal opportunity for those belonging to categories or groups that have been victims of discrimination (e.g., minorities and women). Affirmative action has been an especially controversial legal response to the historical reality of unequal opportunity (Mosley and Capaldi 1996). Ideally, it is intended to correct for some of the consequences of past discrimination and to produce much-needed diversity in influential occupations. The term affirmative action has been applied to programs calling for aggressive recruitment of and extension of special programs to minorities and underrepresented groups as well as for specific quotas for such groups; the latter form of affirmative action has been far more controversial than the recruitment and special program form (Hall 1989, 330).

For groups victimized by discrimination, for example, African Americans and women, the original objective was to challenge laws and associated norms that specifically supported discrimination. Prior to 1964, activist members of these groups and their leaders were campaigning for race- and gender-blind policies. In the late 1960s and early 1970s, however, with most of the formal barriers gone, concern shifted to addressing the dramatic underrepresentation of people of color and women in elite educational institutions, prestigious professions, and business management. One scholar believes that the urban race riots of the late 1960s prompted government and business leaders to adopt policies that might promote higher levels of hiring of African Americans, with the hope that this would reduce the level of anger and bitterness expressed by these riots (Skrentny 1996). The Republican Nixon administration perceived a political benefit in supporting race-based affirmative action, since it would help pit two strong Democrat constituencies—union members and blacks—against each other. Once the affirmative action programs were in place, various managers and bureaucrats charged with hiring more people of color found it to be in their interest to implement affirmative action programs.

The U.S. Supreme Court, beginning with the Bakke decision in 1978, handed down a series of decisions upholding some kinds of affirmative action programs (those involving preferences, for example) while striking down others (those involving rigid quotas, for example) (Hall 1989, 331). In the latter half of the 1990s, affirmative action programs, which had come to include women along with more traditional disadvantaged groups, were the target of a significant backlash (Chavez 1998). In California, for example, voters supported an initiative to eliminate policies specifically assigning preference by race or gender; a significant decline in successful state university applications by traditional minorities was one consequence of this new law. Some constituencies increasingly attacked affirmative action as a form of reverse discrimination, as promoting interracial resentment and conflict, as no longer justifiable (especially in the case of women), and as stigmatizing and counterproductive (by putting people in positions for which they were not qualified, and in which they would fail). In particular, some challenged policies that might favor affluent women and people of color over economically disadvantaged others, including white males (Kahlenberg 1996).

Former presidents of two elite universities, Princeton and Harvard, produced a study late in this period documenting the success of affirmative action in bringing African Americans into leading educational institutions and in contributing to their representation in influential and prestigious occupations (Bowen and Bok 1998). Some evidence suggested that for affirmative action programs to be successful, both the diversity and the integration rationales had to be combined (Jacobs 1998). But in a new century that would witness a great proportional growth in the size of the nonwhite population and a growing proportion of women in most fields, the long-term fate of affirmative action law remained unsettled. It seemed likely, however, that affirmative action laws would be increasingly phased out.

Domestic Violence and Child Abuse

Another series of legal reforms has been inspired by the desire to protect vulnerable victims of directly harmful behavior who are regarded as not having been adequately protected by traditional law. Women (and children) have been victims of male violence through the ages, especially in the form of domestic violence (including child abuse) and rape. Historically, a patriarchal, male-dominated system of law largely refrained from intervening in cases of domestic violence and did not treat rape with the seriousness that it would have had if the victims had been men, not women. In the nineteenth century the North Carolina court of appeals could still uphold, for a period of time, the right of husbands to physically chastise their wives, and even when the courts abandoned this position, they reaffirmed their reluctance to intervene in matters of "family government." The contemporary Feminist Movement, from the early 1970s on, played an important role in highlighting the many dimensions of violence toward women and in promoting changes in societal attitudes toward such violence and changes in law and the justice system response to such violence.

In the case of domestic violence, the evidence holds that women are far more likely than men to be seriously injured (or killed) by their spouses (or partners). Some 1,500 women in the United States are killed annually in domestic violence situations, and it has been estimated that close to two million are physically assaulted annually (Dusky 1996, 356; Tjaden and Thoennes 1998). Traditionally, local police have been reluctant to make arrests when responding to domestic violence situations. This reluctance has been rationalized, at least in part, by the claim that an arrest would make a bad situation even worse. Pioneering research undertaken in the 1980s indicated that less violence rather than more followed arrest, although one of the researchers involved cautioned about adopting policy based on this work (Sherman 1992). On the basis of such research, however, as well as in response to feminist demands for greater accountability in domestic violence cases, at least some states adopted mandatory arrest policies; only a small percentage of the arrested offenders are actually prosecuted and convicted, however (Martin 1994). Linda Mills (1999) finds that physically abused women are best off not when the state undertakes mandatory intervention but when these women become willing partners with the state in the investigation and prosecution of their abusers.

Legal "orders of protection," or restraining orders, are granted more commonly today to individuals who live separately from a physically abusive partner. Women are more likely than men to seek such orders and tend to believe that such orders reflect support from and protection by the legal system (Ptacek 1999). Nevertheless, periodic reports of women (and children) who are killed by an estranged husband (or partner), despite having an order of protection, show that such orders can hardly guarantee safety.

The Violence Against Women Act was adopted in 1994, to extend increasing protection to women and children in abusive circumstances. It provided funding for shelters for battered women, a national hotline for victims, training on domestic violence for law enforcement officers, and support for state initiatives against domestic violence. It also facilitated bringing civil suits against abusers, especially in the absence of criminal prosecution. This expanded federal involvement with domestic violence is inevitably controversial. In May 2000, the U.S. Supreme Court invalidated the provision of the Violence Against Women Act that allowed victims of gender-based violence to sue their attackers in federal court (Greenhouse 2000c). The narrow majority (5–4) rejected the claim that this provision was constitutionally valid as a form of regulating interstate commerce or to ensure Fourteenth Amendment equal protection.

The provision of shelters for abused women, as well as other services and forms of support, has benefited many victims, but no such initiatives can guarantee safety from enraged, violent men. Furthermore, over time, some states began to retreat from viewing battered women as victims of male domination in need of protection; instead, they took a "family conflict" view calling for therapeutic intervention for the whole family (Dixon 1995, 361). The single most famous twentieth century case of domestic violence was probably that of former professional football star O. J. Simpson, who was tried for the murder of his estranged wife Nicole (and her visitor, Ron Goldman). Although Simpson was acquitted by a controversial jury verdict, evidence emerged in the trial (and a subsequent, civil proceeding against him) that he had committed earlier acts of domestic abuse against his wife and had been treated with excessive lenience by law enforcement officers.

The "Battered Women Syndrome" is another controversial outcome of the changing legal environment in response to domestic violence (Downs 1996; Maguigan 1998). A relatively small number of women have offered as a defense for killing a husband (or male partner) that they had been victims of a pattern of violent conduct over a significant period of time and that they had no realistic option to protect themselves (and their children) other than to kill their abuser. This defense, when offered, has not been uniformly successful, but at a minimum it has inspired more attention to the desperate circumstances in which some women find themselves. A movement to gain clemency for battered women convicted of killing their male partners gained some momentum in the final years of the twentieth century (Gagne 1998). The battered woman's defense itself is not formally recognized by law, incidentally; rather, "Battered Women Syndrome" refers to the introduction of expert testimony in certain criminal and civil proceedings (Maguigan 1998). Historically, the law has made it difficult for women to claim self-defense when they kill male partners; in part, this reflects a male-influenced interpretation of threat and reasonable behavior in response to threat (Gillespie 1989; Dixon 1995).

The physical and sexual abuse of children received rather limited attention from the legal system until the recent era (from the late 1960s on) (Pfohl 1977). The corporal punishment of children was generally regarded as a parental prerogative, and even obligation, and only in the most extreme cases would the state intervene when children were abused or neglected. In the contemporary era legal obligations were imposed upon third parties (such as doctors and teachers) to report cases of abused children that came to their attention, and state agencies assumed greater responsibility in removing abused children from their homes (Ashford 1994). Social agencies and the courts have remained somewhat reluctant to take a child away from a natural parent permanently, however; consequently, one periodically reads about tragic cases of an abused child known to child services agencies beaten to death by a parent, or a child returned by the court to an abusive parent and then killed. Many cases of severe child abuse never do come to the attention of the courts, and altogether the law has failed to protect many children from severe abuse.

Rape Law

Rape, too, has been subject to significant legal reform in the recent era. According to Susan Brownmiller's (1975) classic *Against Our Will*, the rape of a married woman in an earlier time was treated as adultery, and of an unmarried woman as a property crime against her father (since her bridal price declined in value). Indeed, the resolution of a rape case involving an unmarried woman sometimes took the form of marrying her off to the rapist. Furthermore, rape in a male-dominated society was openly accepted in some situations, such as war, where the women of the losing side were raped. Unfortunately, these practices are not extinct in the contemporary era. The courts in the Anglo-American tradition did not treat rape with the seriousness it might have been accorded if the victims had been men. The British justice Lord Hale declared that rape was the easiest charge to make and the hardest to prove. Corroboration (in the form of witness testimony or physical evidence) was required to obtain convictions in a rape case, which was not true for other types of physical assault. A larger culture that often blamed rape victims for their experience, as well as a justice system culture that treated their claims with skepticism or exposed them to demeaning forms of cross-examination, discouraged many victims from reporting the crime in the first place. Unsurprisingly, the rate of convictions in rape cases, or in the small percentage that resulted in arrest and trial, was typically low.

In the 1970s the feminist movement began mobilizing to change the perception of rape and the legal response to it. First, an ongoing enterprise involving such activities as "Take Back the Night" promoted attention to the devastating impact of rape on victims and its threat to women generally. Then feminists lobbied successfully for various reforms of existing rape laws. These reforms included (1) redefining rape to emphasize its violent nature; (2) removing the corroboration requirement; (3) adding a "rape shield" provision ordinarily prohibiting the introduction of evidence (or cross-examination) about the victim's past sexual conduct; (4) protecting children from sexual exploitation (while diminishing legal attention to consensual teenage sex); and (5) increasing the certainty of appropriate penalties (Berger, Searles, and Neuman 1988; Horney and Spohn 1991). Furthermore, laws in many states prohibiting the prosecution of husbands for raping their wives were eliminated (Gross 1991). Significant changes were introduced as well in the justice system handling of rape cases. For example, specially trained female officers were more likely to interview rape victims. Outside the formal justice system, various support services such as "rape crisis centers" were introduced.

It was the hope of those who promoted rape reform that reforms in the legal system's response to rape would transform public perceptions of rape, would diminish the trauma for victims in pursuing rape cases, and ideally would deter rape itself (Estrich 1987; Berger, Neuman, and Searles 1994). Scholarly studies of the impact of rape law reform, however, have found that entrenched attitudes and practices within the justice system tend to limit the practical effect of the reforms (Marsh, Geist, and Caplan 1982; Horney and Spohn 1991; Berger, Neuman, and Searles 1994). For the most part, then, the rape law reforms had somewhat limited effects on arrest policies and justice system processing of rape cases; such reform seems to have had limited impact on the rape rate or the conviction rate in rape cases, and it did not necessarily persuade a higher percentage of women to report rape cases to the authorities. To the extent that patterns of rape and victim reporting changed, other factors in the larger social environment are probably responsible. However, at a minimum, the rape law reforms have made an important symbolic statement about the seriousness of rape as a crime against women, and these reforms have somewhat reduced the trauma for many rape victims of pursuing their cases through the justice system (see Box 10.4).

Homosexuality and the Rights of Gay People

Societal attitudes toward homosexuality have varied considerably across history and across different cultures (Eskridge 1999; Richards 1999). In American culture solicitation for and engaging in homosexual relations was criminalized. Homosexuals through most of American history stayed "in the closet," not only to avoid the profound social stigma typically imposed on homosexuals but also because the law afforded them no protection if they were discriminated against, fired from a job, or denied a lease, for example. The emergence of a highly visible gay activist movement in the final decades of the twentieth century was one of the more remarkable social developments of this period (Adam 1987; Altman 1982). Gay activists (and sympathizers) were able to achieve many changes in laws pertaining to homosexuals, especially enacting laws to protect them against discrimination on the basis of sexual preference (Rayside 1998). At the same time, these efforts encountered considerable resistance, and many initiatives on behalf of gay rights were defeated. By century's end, approximately half the American states had decriminalized consensual sexual relations between homosexuals, and half

Box 10.4

Sexual Harassment and the Law

While sexual harassment (overwhelmingly of women, by men) has been an age-old problem, only in the recent era (beginning about 1975), largely as a consequence of the efforts of committed feminists, did the law address it (Belknap and Erez 1997). What had been a private trouble became a public issue as the boundaries between private and public eroded (Roth 1999). Although sexual harassment remains a common occurrence, it rarely leads to a legal response. Many complex and contentious issues continue to be debated in relation to sexual harassment, including these: How is it best defined? Should it be permissible to explore a plaintiff's sexual history? What about same-sex harassment? How can proscriptions on a hostile work environment be reconciled with free speech rights (Stein 1999)? Sexual harassment has been a problem in various work settings, including the military. High-profile cases in the recent era involved a prominent senator, Robert Packwood; a prospective U.S. Supreme Court Justice (Clarence Thomas, subsequently confirmed); and a President, Bill Clinton (LeMoncheck and Hajdin 1997). Despite the success of some sexual harassment lawsuits, some commentators suggest that there is still a wide schism between the law and women's experience of sexual harassment (Belknap and Erez 1997; Schulhofer 1998). This was likely to remain a contentious area of law for some time to come in the twenty-first century.

In *Davis v. Monroe County Board of Education* (1999), a divided (5–4) U.S. Supreme Court found against a school board in a district where school authorities had failed to respond to repeated complaints on behalf of a fifth-grade female student who was sexually harassed by a fellow student. Although dissenters on the Court expressed concern that a precedent would be established involving the Court in the inevitable squabbles of immature children, the majority asserted that the extreme circumstances in the case before them warranted a decision on behalf of the plaintiff.

Student-on-student sexual harassment has been a common occurrence on college campuses, but many colleges and universities have chosen to avoid responding in a substantial way (Williams 1999). Colleges have historically done little to protect students from sexual harassment (Franke 1998). In the wake of the *Davis* decision, colleges need to ensure that they have an effective sexual harassment policy in place; they need to investigate complaints of harassment; and they need to successfully resolve cases where sexual harassment is found to have occurred.

had not. In an important U.S. Supreme Court decision, *Bowers v. Hardwick* (1986), the Court upheld the right of states to criminalize such behavior if they so chose. However, even where such laws remained on the books, they were highly unlikely to be enforced. Past practices of vice squad officers actively seeking to make arrests for homosexual solicitation had been largely if not wholly abandoned, in the face of court rulings declaring such police actions a form of impermissible entrapment.

The overall reform of laws pertaining to homosexuals reflected, and possibly influenced, a general increase of societal tolerance of gays. In a 1996 case, *Romer v. Evans*, the U.S. Supreme Court ruled for the first time that some laws discriminating against homosexuals were in violation of the equal protection clause of the Fourteenth Amendment (Keen and Goldberg 1998). But such tolerance was hardly uniform, with fundamentalist religious groups especially likely to denounce homosexuality. From the 1980s on, an increase of "gay bashing" was reported, possibly both as a form of backlash against gay rights and a function of identifying gays with the AIDS plague. Overall, the general public was highly resistant to extending rights to marriage or adoption to gay couples, and legislators largely concurred. The state of Vermont, in 2000, adopted a law recognizing civil unions between members of the same sex, but it remained to be seen whether this would pave the way for a general legal recognition of same-sex marriages. An initiative by President Clinton, shortly after he first came to office, to abolish formal discrimination against gays in the military precipitated a firestorm of controversy, and a more modest reform ("Don't ask, don't tell") was ultimately adopted (Rayside 1998). At the outset of the new century, it was difficult to say whether the significant progress made by gays toward achieving protection and some recognition of rights would continue to move forward until no formal legal differention between people on the basis of sexual preference existed, or whether the existing legal reforms represented the basic limits of what a predominantly heterosexual population would tolerate.

Victimless Crimes

Still another set of legal reforms has focused on so-called victimless crimes. The concept of victimless crime has been applied to activities that are by definition consensual and nonpredatory (Schur 1965; Meier and Geis 1997). Among the activities included in this category are consensual homosexual activity and a range of other consensual sexual activities, from fornication to adultery. Others are public drunkenness, illicit drugs, prostitution, pornography, and gambling. Responding to such activities has historically absorbed a significant percentage of the resources of criminal justice systems. The characterization of crimes as "victimless" has been challenged, however, with the claim that society as a whole, certain neighborhoods in particular, and many innocent parties (e.g., loved ones) suffer significant consequences from the existence of such "victimless" crimes as alcohol abuse, illicit drug use, gambling, pornography, and prostitution. Laws proscribing such activities have been promoted on grounds of protecting people from themselves, as well as protecting in some sense the other entities or parties just identified. Even if the activities listed are not in themselves predatory, most of them are regarded as linked with predatory crime and certainly with organized crime activity. In varying degrees, these activities are in violation of religious values or proscriptions, and many people believe that societal tolerance of such activities fosters the erosion of the social and moral order.

Throughout much of the twentieth century, victimless crime laws were at the heart of vigorous controversy, and this has also been a dynamic area of law in the sense of much change in one direction or the other. Opponents of laws against victimless crime claim that they infringe on individual liberty and privacy rights; they make lawbreakers out of large numbers of conventional members of society; they stigmatize such conventional members of society and sometimes push them into further deviance or criminality; they promote disrespect for law and the criminal justice system (and consequently

Box 10.5

Changing the Legal Drinking Age

While overall levels of alcohol consumption began to decline in the 1970s, the extent of alcohol consumption among young people and such phenomena as high rates of binge drinking on college campuses were a source of serious concern (Wechsler 1996). At what age should young people be allowed to drink legally? State laws on the legal age for drinking, typically ranging from 18 to 21, have been inconsistent through much of the century (Mooney and Gramling 1993). For example, in New York the age was 18; in the neighboring state of Connecticut it was 21. Large numbers of young people driving across the state line from Connecticut to drink in New York resulted in many fatal crashes. A nationwide minimum drinking age of 21 was adopted in the 1980s, in response to growing public concern with teenage drunken drivers.

Michael and Margaret Smith (1999) call for lowering the drinking age to 18. They argue that the existing policy has obviously failed, as is evident from violations of the law on campuses all across the country and from reported increases in binge drinking. The existing policy, they claim, may enhance the attractiveness of alcohol to young people as "forbidden fruit." This policy is inconsistent with other legal policies on age (for example, the voting age and the age for military service). It has soured relations between students and the police, resulted in police records for otherwise promising students, has discouraged faculty (who are concerned about becoming complicit in illegal activity) from socializing with students, and has led to less public, more dangerous student partying.

diminish cooperation); they deflect attention from underlying causes of deviant behavior; they impose an enormous burden on the criminal justice system and on taxpayers; the laws themselves, rather than the activities, promote predatory crime (e.g., when a drug addict commits a mugging to obtain money to pay the exorbitant price of illegal substances); the laws themselves, rather than the activities, provide opportunities for organized crime to exploit; they negate a large source of tax revenue; and they simply don't work.

Alcohol

The celebrated attempt early in the twentieth century to legally abolish alcohol from American life, Prohibition, was discussed earlier (Pegram 1998). It is often cited as the classic case to illustrate the proposition that one cannot legislate morality, since millions of Americans flagrantly violated the proscriptions on liquor during Prohibition; it was repealed in 1933. In one sense, the failure of law to sweep alcohol off the face of American life has been very costly, as alcoholism is highly correlated with a wide range of crimes, auto accidents (and accidents of all kinds), domestic violence, family discord, suicide, unemployment, and the like (Goode 1997, 175–198). On the other hand, the majority of American adults cherish the right to drink alcohol in moderation and believe that neither they nor others suffer any significant negative consequences. A "new temperance movement" emerged in the more recent era (from the 1970s on), with the objective of limiting access to alcohol and attempting to persuade especially vulnerable parties (e.g., pregnant women) not to drink (Gusfield 1996). The success of this movement has been somewhat limited (see Box 10.5).

The reform of law in response to alcohol use that has directly harmful consequences, such as drunk driving, also moved in the direction of a tougher response, with harsher sanctions. Such reforms importantly reflected lobbying efforts by MADD (Mothers Against Drunk Driving), an organization founded by a woman whose young daughter was killed by a drunken driver. Although the call for tougher penalties against drunk drivers was certainly understandable in terms of the human devastation caused by them, those who have studied the problem are not wholly in agreement about the most effective strategies for deterring drunken drivers (Jacobs 1989; Ross 1992a).

On public drunkenness and alcohol consumption more generally, there is ongoing social and cultural ambivalence and contradictions. The majority of American adults enjoy social drinking on some level and expect to have the right to engage in such drinking. Americans as a whole are also concerned about the harmful consequences of drinking to excess. Drinking problems continue to be characterized by some as a consequence of poor character and moral irresponsiblity, and by many others as a symptom of a sickness (alcoholism). It seems that the problems associated with alcohol consumption would have to be addressed principally as cultural and medical problems and that the legal response would have to play a more limited role.

Illicit Drugs

During the first half of the twentieth century a series of laws were passed with the objective of criminalizing the sale and distribution of a range of drugs, such as heroin and marijuana. Some earlier efforts at prohibition or control of narcotics seemed to have been inspired by racism and fear of corrupt foreign influences, such as Chinese opium dens (Meier and Geis 1997, 87–88). The Harrison Tax Act (1914) established a basic framework for the illegal status of heroin and other so-called hard drugs. Although growing concern about narcotics addiction played some role, such legislation was not based upon scientific evidence of the harmfulness of using narcotics. The Marijuana Tax Act (1937) provided a basis for declaring the sale, distribution, and possession of marijuana illegal in every state in the union (Musto 1973). Historically, marijuana had been quite easily available and little controlled in many parts of the country. In the 1930s, however, the Depression gave rise to considerable social unrest; by some accounts, the land-holding classes out West were concerned about their poorly paid laborers getting high on readily available marijuana and making trouble. Also, the newly revived liquor industry, following repeal of Prohibition, was anxious about competition from marijuana. It is worth noting that in the 1920s marijuana was legal in many places, and alcohol was not; a decade or so later, the situation was reversed. An ambitious commissioner of the Federal Bureau of Narcotics, Harry Anslinger, testified before Congress that marijuana was a dangerous substance and had to be controlled; he claimed that it caused some users to go berserk and commit violent acts. Various forces, then, were involved in promoting laws criminalizing marijuana, but serious scientific or medical research into the actual effects of marijuana use was not a factor. Indeed, when commissions of scientists and physicians were eventually called upon to provide some guidance on this question, they did not, for the most part, claim that hard evidence showed any significant harmful effect.

Through most of the twentieth century, certain drugs (such as heroin, cocaine, and marijuana) were treated as illegal substances, and people dealing in or acquiring these drugs faced harsh penal sanctions. Millions have been arrested and hundreds of thousands have gone to prison or jail. The existence of these laws has obviously not deterred large numbers of people from involvement with these drugs. As is well known, a great upsurge of usage generally occurred in the latter part of the 1960s and the early 1970s. Various reasons have been given for the dramatic increase in illicit drug usage, but the very fact of illegal status may well have played a role in promoting drug use as a specific act of defiance toward the established order and its leadership. On the one hand, an aggressively fought "war on drugs," especially from the 1980s on, led to a huge volume of arrests and long prison sentences for drug offenders. On the other hand, groups and individuals reflecting a broad range of ideological commitments have called for abolishing or at least reforming the existing drug laws (*National Review* 1996; Goode 1998; Miller 1991).

Despite some relatively minor changes—such as decriminalizing possession of small amounts of marijuana in some jurisdictions and permitting a few people to legally obtain marijuana for medical reasons—the basic criminal laws pertaining to drugs have changed little, or have been made harsher (DiChiari and Galliher 1994). The government's emphasis on a criminal justice system response to drugs, as opposed to an approach placing much more emphasis on education and treatment programs, has been widely criticized. In at least one interpretation, the war on drugs has provided politicians with a symbolic opportunity to blame America's problems on a "dangerous class" disproportionately made up of young urban blacks and new immigrants, who are especially vulnerable to criminal justice processing (Gordon 1994). The War on Drugs is politically successful, we are told, because it sustains racial antagonism, plays into the media's need for theater, and serves the purposes of religiously oriented, conservative coalition politics (Baggins 1998).

A number of prominent scholars and social commentators have called for some form of legalization of drugs, on the premise that the costs of the war on drugs have far outweighed any identifiable benefits, but a serious movement toward legalization seems politically untenable in the foreseeable future (Ryan 1998). Even though the existing drug laws have obviously failed to deter millions of Americans from at least experimenting with one or more illicit drugs, the critics of legalization argue that drug use and addiction would become even more of a problem in the absence of legal controls. A truly effective reform of drug laws in a direction that would win broad public support remains a formidable challenge.

Pornography

Although pornography is not so easily defined, it is most commonly associated with the explicit representation of sexual activity or sex organs in a manner intended to stimulate sexual lust. Sexually explicit representations of human beings have existed since time immemorial, but the widespread proliferation of pornography is largely a modern phenomenon (Kendrick 1987).

In the American experience, there has been a long history of attempts to ban or suppress pornography by law. These efforts have come up against challenges based on the claim that they violate First Amendment guarantees of freedom of speech and press. In one classic case in 1933, Federal Judge John M. Woolsey ruled that James Joyce's *Ulysses* (considered by some the greatest literary creation of the twentieth century) could not be legally banned, despite the sexually provocative character of Molly Bloom's famous soliloquy (deGrazia 1992, 29–30). Previously, it had been illegal to bring this book into the United States, on the claim that it was pornographic.

Over a period of several decades, the United States Supreme Court attempted to articulate a legal test for discriminating between valid free speech or literature and pornography subject to legal restrictions (Lindgren 1993). These tests included concepts such as "without redeeming social value" and "offensive to community standards," but no such tests could resolve conclusively the challenge of discriminating between pornography and some form of protected free expression. Justice Potter Stewart famously observed, with regard to pornography, "I know it when I see it." From the late 1960s on, pornography became a major growth industry in America; by the 1990s it was an $8 billion industry, as measured by estimated spending on hard-core videos, peep shows, live sex acts, adult cable programming, sexual devices, computer porn, and sex magazines (Schlosser 1997, 44). Although many restrictive laws existed, they were often not enforced or were readily evaded.

Traditional and conservative forces had a long history of calling for the suppression of pornography, and from the 1970s on an influential faction of the feminist movement joined this call. Law professor Catherine MacKinnon and writer Andrea Dworkin were leading figures in this feminist attack on pornography, and they drafted legislation outlawing pornography on the grounds that it was inherently harmful to women, demeaning them and promoting rape and other forms of abuse toward them (Childress 1991). Although laws along these lines were adopted in Indianapolis and Minneapolis, these laws were later overturned on constitutional grounds. Feminists themselves were somewhat divided on this issue, with opponents of the anti-pornography efforts arguing that censorship precedents from the outlawing of pornography could ultimately be used to suppress other unpopular forms of free expression, including feminist writings; that the characterization of women as victims of pornography was disempowering and denied to women their freedom of choice; and that other issues were of far more pressing concern to most women (Lacombe 1994). The claims of traditionalists and anti-pornography feminists—that exposure to pornography promotes violent abuse of women and other harmful social consequences—has not generally been supported by the empirical research. Rather, social science research suggests that exposure to representations of violence (whether or not in the form of pornography) is harmful, but exposure to sexually explicit material per se is not harmful (Childress 1991).

At least on one point, a high level of consensus is achieved: pornography directed at children or using children in any way cannot be legally tolerated. At the end of the twentieth century the growing traffic in pornography (including kiddie porn) in the largely unregulated realm of cyberspace was generating some concern (Wallace and Mangan 1996). By any measure the boundaries of sexually explicit forms of expression that would be legally tolerated had expanded considerably by the end of the twentieth century, but the appropriate role of law in the regulation or suppression of pornography continued to be a contested matter.

Gambling

The American history of gambling is filled with contradictory legal policies (Skolnick 1978; W. Thompson 1994). Moral entrepreneurs were for a long time successful in having most forms of gambling outlawed in most parts of the United States (Nevada was a glaring exception). Of course, violation of antigambling laws was especially pervasive, and in many American neighborhoods bookmaking and numbers games were large-scale enterprises. In the last several decades of the twentieth century, however, one state after another not only legalized certain forms of gambling—especially off-track betting and lotteries—but actively promoted gambling that was run by and ideally benefited state programs (for example, programs for education or for the elderly). The movement toward legalization was partly driven by recognition of the futility of many existing antigambling laws but also by the irresistible temptation to raise state revenue without imposing or raising taxes directly (typically unpopular with voters). The primary movers behind legalized gambling, then, were gaming industry interests and political officials or legislators seeking profits or a relatively painless source of state revenue, not citizens (Goodman 1996).

By the latter part of the 1990s Americans were spending some $400 billion a year on legalized gambling, and this gambling was producing some $40 billion in revenue. But it was far from clear that legalized gambling enhanced the overall economy of states that adopted and aggressively promoted it (Goodman 1996). Furthermore, legalized gambling incurred many costs, ranging from deflecting discretionary income from other legitimate businesses (such as restaurants and theaters); promoting crime and criminal justice system expenditures; and producing personal tragedies for addictive gamblers, their families, and those with whom they had personal and business relationships.

Legalized gambling has been characterized as a "regressive tax," in the sense that those with modest or low incomes contribute disproportionately to this revenue. Gambling entrepreneurs who seek licensing for casino operations typically encounter a certain amount of resistance. Many citizens continue to regard gambling as inherently immoral, as addictive and personally destructive to some individuals, and as corrupting or damaging to neighborhoods, governments, and society generally. Although the momentum in the final decades of the twentieth century was toward broader legalization of gambling, much ambivalence or active opposition to this trend survives.

Conclusion

It should be evident from this review of legal reform that law is indeed both a dependent and an independent variable. Citizens, organizations, and government functionaries have conflicting agendas about legal reform (see Table 10.2). Law both reflects changing social conditions and plays a role in transforming social conditions. Law is attacked for not playing a more dynamic role in promoting social change on some of these issues, and also attacked for doing more social harm than good in relation to these issues. The calls for more (or tougher) law versus less (or milder) law on victimless crime issues is especially intense and divisive. The laws on victimless crime inevitably engage people's most fundamental beliefs about morality and human nature. It seems likely that victimless crime law in the twenty-first century will continue to be contested terrain and subject to significant change and reform.

Table 10.2 Conflicting Agendas in Relation to Legal Reform

More formal law	vs.	Less formal law
More regulation	vs.	Less regulation
Crime control	vs.	Due process
Expanded individual rights	vs.	Greater community responsibility

Basic Trends in Law and Social Change in America

American law and the American legal system undergo constant change, but it is difficult to make broad generalizations about the nature of such change because for almost every trend, one can find a countertrend. It is indisputable that over time Americans have become reliant upon more law—or at least more secular, formal law—as an inevitable response to the increasing size, heterogeneity, and complexity of American society. A countertrend of turning to alternative forms of dispute resolution has, however, also been a characteristic of the recent era in American law, in part as a response to the frustrations and costs associated with reliance upon formal law. Two basic questions arise about this countertrend: Just how far can it go in an increasingly large, complex, and heterogeneous society? And to what extent does the turn to informal law in some form really represent a fundamental break with formal law, as opposed to a means to extend the scope and discretion involved in law?

Historically, the formal legal system has all too often worked to the advantage of the powerful and the privileged. A movement toward greater reliance on informal law, then, could in at least some circumstances be helpful to powerless and poorer people; in many other circumstances, however, it could provide broader opportunities to take advantage of them.

Regulatory Law

American law and the American legal system have experienced a general move toward more regulation of commercial and professional activities, with the formation of various regulatory agencies (such as the Interstate Commerce Commission, or ICC; the Securities and Exchange Commission, or SEC; and the Environmental Protection Agency, or EPA). The growth of regulatory law also reflects the recognition, in an increasingly large and complex society of mutually interdependent people, that one cannot allow entrepreneurs and organizations the freedom to do whatever they wish. Here, too, there is a significant countertrend: regulatory law and agencies have been persistently attacked as a counterproductive, inefficient, and unnecessary force in a free market economy. Accordingly, Americans tend to experience cycles of regulation and deregulation, with higher levels of regulatory law generally correlated with good business cycles, and declines with poor economic conditions. When he first ran for president in 1980, Ronald Reagan attempted to implement at least some cuts in regulatory agencies or regulatory law. The tension between more regulation and less regulation is likely to persist in a society that both demands clean air and does not want to pay higher prices or taxes.

Due Process

Due process rights have been generally expanded in American law; some say that the expansion is a function of a more inclusive and more confident society. The Warren Court of the 1960s handed down a series of decisions significantly expanding the due process rights of defendants in criminal cases; the *Gideon v. Wainwright* (1963) decision, ensuring indigents of legal representation, and the *Miranda v. Arizona* decision (1966), requiring that warnings on rights be given to those being accused of crimes, are among the most famous of these. This trend has sought to make amends for the inequities and injustices typically encountered by criminal defendants through most of history. When people perceive that crime is rising, however, a countertrend emerges, calling for the curtailment of rights of those accused of crimes (and even more so of those convicted of having committed crimes). Over the long term, alternating cycles of crime control and due process have occurred, although the crime control cycle has seemed to be entrenched in the more recent era. On the one hand, the U.S. Supreme Court in various cases has tended to narrow the scope of the due process rulings, without specifically overruling them. On the other hand, the U.S. Congress and various state legislative bodies have passed numerous "tough on crime" laws, such as the Three-Strikes-and-You're-Out law (mandating life in prison following conviction in a third felony case) and Megan's law (calling for community notification when a convicted sex offender is released from prison). This tension between realizing crime control and due process objectives is sure to endure as well.

Entitlements and Rights

The general movement toward an expansion of individual rights and group entitlements is also a significant trend within American law. Again, this trend could be interpreted as belated acknowledgment within American law of the many disadvantages experienced by individuals (and groups) such as women, African Americans, gay people, the disabled, the elderly, and so forth. But here, too, there is a countertrend in calls for more responsibility toward the welfare of the community itself and the imposition of a higher degree of personal responsibility on individuals, including those coming from substantially disadvantaged homes. The welfare reform movement could be viewed, at least in part, as a demand for greater individual accountability and diminished individual entitlement. The backlash against affirmative action, at the end of the twentieth century, is a symptom of the countertrend on behalf of individual rights and against group-based entitlements. The search for an optimal balance between individual rights and responsibility, group entitlements, and the needs of the larger community or society was also sure to continue in the twenty-first century.

Technology

Throughout the twentieth century, the law had to contend with new forms of technology that required new laws. In the early part of the century, the automobile and the telephone generated new law; at the end of the century, cyberspace and biogenetic engineering were generating the need for new law (Gold 1996; Susskind 1996). Whether the law should facilitate the use of new forms of technology or should impose constraints on it, was an enduring source of controversy (see Box 10.6).

Law in the Twenty-First Century

The idea of a society without law has been the dream of various social philosophers, with Karl Marx probably the most famous of these. In a utopian society, there would be no need for law because human beings would live together in a state of perpetual harmony and in a spirit of cooperation and sharing. In a certain sense, preliterate human societies and, in the context of modern societies, some families and small communities (such as communes) live without law, unless one stretches the meaning of the term law so broadly that it encompasses any and all norms governing human conduct. Earlier in this book, however, some space was devoted to the disastrous consequences in a recent era for example, in Russia and in China of efforts to establish large-scale societies without law. If the hope for a society without laws has not become entirely extinct (there are, after all, still anarchists in our midst), it has few believers.

Most serious thinkers would concede that law in some form is an absolutely necessary and wholly unavoidable feature of any complex modern society. And many commentators celebrate the general expansion of law during the twentieth century as one of the great achievements of the century. On the other hand, even among the many who concede the inevitability and accomplishments of law, some insist that there is altogether too much law, that the excessive growth of law has to be combated vigorously, and that we can and should find ways to reduce the scope of law s presence in our lives and to rid legal institutions of cumbersome forms of red tape, confusion, and delay. Some argue that we presently have laws that we do not need or that do more harm than good (for example, laws prohibting the distribution and use of marijuana and other illicit drugs). Others believe that we are presently lacking some laws we need to prevent egregious harm to other beings (for example, laws prohibiting abortion). If history provides any lesson, we can expect battles over such issues to continue. On another front, it seems likely that vigorous debate will continue for some time on whether we have too much regu-

Box 10.6

Law and the Internet

The term *Internet* refers to linked, federally subsidized computer networks, all running on the same protocols. Between 1990 and the year 2000, Internet users increased from approximately 1.3 million to over 200 million (Sunstein 2000, 38). This increase is certainly astonishing, although it is likely that for some time to come, the Internet will continue to compete with television, books, magazines, and the like, as sources of information and entertainment (Sunstein 2000, 42). The Internet only became commercial in the 1990s; at the beginning of the twenty-first century, its commercial uses were expanding at lightning speed.

The Internet has important implications for the future of privacy, free speech, and the circulation of ideas and information. Commentators today are somewhat divided on whether the Internet is likely to extend or diminish individual freedom and control (Sunstein 2000). Andrew Shapiro (1999) believes that the Internet makes it more difficult for dictatorial leaders to achieve the kind of control over political dissent that Hitler and Stalin accomplished, since it provides a means for dissidents to communicate with the outside world and convey information not easily blocked by the government. Of course, states may continue to crack down on offensive aspects of Internet transmissions: for example, political dissidence in China; sexual exploitation of minors in the United States.

The Internet also has the potential to greatly expand public access to legal decision making—for example, of regulatory agencies—and to allow public participation in the legal decision-making processes (Johnson 1998). At present, Internet access is still quite unevenly distributed in society, and it has the potential for intensifying inequalities. Harvard law professor Lawrence Lessig (1999b) argues that the Internet will increasingly become a means through which software programs will achieve pervasive control over our lives. Lessig's choice of the term "code" for his book deliberately calls attention to parallel objectives of both legal codes and software codes to dictate how we live. Of course, software is different from law in important ways, including the absence of a punitive mechanism. In cyberspace, however, code is alleged to achieve the control of law. When people go on-line, they are sacrificing freedom and privacy, and sophisticated software can track much about them through their on-line transactions. Although many commentators suggest that the Internet is making information of all kinds much more easily available, Lessig suggests that password-driven software has the potential to bill those who access this information, and eventually all forms of accessing information and knowledge on the Internet will become costly. At present, the Internet seems to have expanded the capacity of people to infringe on copyrighted material; for example, the music industry is threatened when people download music from the Internet rather than purchasing CDs.

Altogether, the Internet will have important impacts on many dimensions of law, just as early technologies did (Katsh 1995). Legal education itself is likely to be available increasingly through the Internet, possibly threatening traditional law schools. Richard Susskind (1996) suggests that the nature of legal practice will be transformed, and lawyers will increasingly become "legal information engineers."

Some specific legal issues arising as a consequence of the new information technology include governance of the Internet; technology and surveillance; data protection; supervision of users; computer fraud and hacking; the nature of software monopoly (Microsoft case); and remedies for internet libel (Lloyd 1997; Harmon 1998). For some of these issues, traditional legal theories and principles are applicable; for other issues, this is not the case.

latory law or too little in such areas as environmental protection, worker safety, and consumer product liability.

The ultimate crisis for a legal system comes when a significant proportion of its constituency lose fundamental faith in it and no longer believe they have an obligation to comply. The collapse of the Soviet Union in the final years of the twentieth century was one famous case attesting to the potential for a legitimacy crisis in a large-scale society to contribute to the transformation of that society and its legal system. The transformation of South Africa, early in the last decade of the century, from an undemocratic system wholly dominated by a white minority to an electoral democracy was also importantly linked to a legitimacy crisis. In the twenty-first century, if there are increasing expectations of the legal system that the system cannot effectively address, that could contribute to a loss of belief in, and support for, the system.

Lawrence Friedman (1985) has written of the increasing expectation through the twentieth century that the legal system will provide a just resolution to every wrong and denial of a right. If such a trend continues into the twenty-first century, disenchantment with and disappointment with the legal system is likely to increase. If the view that the law systematically favors some segments of society over others expands, this could also contribute to the emergence of a legitimacy crisis. Although the perceived legitimation of the political (and economic) system is not necessarily synonymous with the perceived legitimation of the legal system, they are closely related. Accordingly, the fate of law is in important ways tied to the fate of the larger political economy; however, law and the legal system might continue to enjoy support even when the political system loses it if law is viewed as autonomous (or independent) and a critically important instrument for addressing the limitations or injustices of the political economy.

Science

Early in the twentieth century the German sociologist Max Weber advanced the thesis that rationalization was becoming increasingly critical to the operation of the legal system. That is, law was becoming increasingly oriented toward rational, logical procedures and moving away from a focus on divine right and superstition. Not everyone is convinced that all our problems have rational solutions, and Paul Campos (1998, viii) refers to our "irrational worship of rationality."

In the twentieth century, indisputably, reliance upon science (and scientific evidence) has become more important generally within law. One projection for the future of law in the twenty-first century envisions a continued and growing emphasis upon science and a scientific approach. Some say that the courts in the last part of the twentieth century, for example, increasingly administered a form of "technocratic justice," moving away from traditional legal values and practices. Technocratic justice, in this context, refers to reliance upon scientific and technical knowledge and the realization of practical objectives as the basis for legal decision making (Heydebrand 1979, 33; Stryker 1989, 342). It is not evident, however, that legal institutions rely increasingly upon technocratic (scientific/technical) expertise in a uniform way, and in at least some instances such reliance has apparently been reduced (Stryker 1989).

Tensions and conflicts over the proper place, and scope, of science in the legal process are likely to continue.

In general, however, scientific evidence has been introduced into legal cases more often than in the past, despite the fact that law and science are rooted in different cultural systems and have somewhat different approaches to establishing "truth" (Goldberg 1994; Jasanoff 1995; Reece 1998). In the twentieth century, science sometimes clashed with religious values within a legal setting. Early in the century the famous Scopes trial—featuring a confrontation between evolutionary theory and religion—highlighted this clash. Although the religious perspective was at least formally triumphant in that particular trial, which took place in the Bible Belt, science generally became an increasingly dominant force within law during the course of the century. Since different forms of expertise and criteria for truth claims can be found within science, the handling of scientific evidence and testimony within the legal system is often complicated or troublesome.

For most of the twentieth century the Frye Test dominated judicial thinking about the admissibility of scientific evidence. In this test, the criteria for accepting expert opinion into evidence depended upon whether it had gained general acceptance in its particular field (or among the expert's peers). In a 1993 case, *Daubert v. Merrill Dow Pharmaceuticals, Inc.*, the U.S. Supreme Court rejected sole reliance upon peer review and instead called upon courts to assess the validity of scientific testimony or evidence on the basis of (1) whether the reasoning or methodology underlying the testimony or evidence is scientifically valid, and (2) whether that reasoning or methodology can be properly applied to the facts in the case.

Many legal proceedings rely heavily upon the testimony of expert witnesses, especially those with scientific credentials. The validity of relying upon such scientific expertise has been challenged. For example, Margaret Hagen (1997) claims that psychiatrists and psychologists testifying in legal cases have often grotesquely subverted the search for justice. They have put themselves forth as experts when their opinions have no solid scientific basis. Hagen invokes various "horror stories" of psychiatrists or psychologists testifying about repressed memory and past lives in support of dubious claims about alleged criminal behavior, and offering many different grounds for excusing people from criminal responsibility. Others believe, however, that properly credentialed experts can provide judges and jurors with immense assistance in resolving questions on such issues as insanity, competence, and custody.

Lie detector (or polygraph) tests have been used in the American legal system as one means of discriminating between truth and untruth in both criminal and civil law cases. David Lykken (1998) asserts that no scientifically acceptable estimate of the accuracy of lie detector tests exists. George Dery (1999) argues that polygraph evidence has been estimated to be up to 90 percent reliable, and in any case is more reliable than many forms of evidence (for example, psychiatric testimony; fingerprint evidence; eyewitness testimony; and handwriting identification) that have been found admissible in American courts of law. Since 1988, it has been illegal for most private sector employers to require that employees take a lie detector test. In about half the American states, lie detector evidence can be introduced under some circumstances, and Federal courts have historically considered such evidence on a case-by-case basis.

The increasing introduction of DNA evidence beginning late in the twentieth century is one significant example of growing reliance upon scientific evidence. By the year 2000, some sixty men had been released from American prisons because DNA evidence established that they had been wrongly convicted of the crimes for which they were sent to prison (Boyer 2000). Of course, DNA evidence was also used to establish guilt in many cases, including cases that had been unsolved for years. In the celebrated O. J. Simpson case, DNA evidence was introduced by the prosecution in its attempt to establish the guilt of the accused, but this evidence was successfully challenged by defense lawyers attacking the way the evidence was collected, handled, and stored. Although DNA evidence can still be contested, then, it is likely to play an increasingly important role in criminal cases.

In a world of complex (and sometimes disturbing) new scientific developments—for example, in the realms of nuclear fission and fusion; human genetics; and artificial intelligence—it was inevitable that scientific expertise would be needed to contend with the legal (and moral) issues arising out of these developments (Goldberg 1994). Although it seems likely that scientific innovations and breakthroughs will become incorporated into the operation of the system of law, two basic questions arise: Just how far will the scientific approach to justice go, and is scientific justice superior to traditional human justice? On the first point, will there eventually be a point where sophisticated computers discriminate between true and false testimony and render verdicts? Even if such a movement toward a scientific justice is possible, is it desirable? Or will it produce a wholly dehumanized form of justice? The nature of scientific criteria for truth and legal criteria for truth may be fundamentally incompatible (Jasanoff 1995). Certainly, scientific evidence is often misunderstood or distorted in court proceedings to achieve some legal end.

Alternative visions of the future have been put forward. Boaventura de Sousa Santos (1995) views science, scientific rationality, and the scientific method itself as in the throes of a severe crisis. More generally, he believes that the paradigm of modernity has exhausted itself and can no longer provide people with an appropriate framework for making sense of their world or for creating a viable future. The divide between the modern, developed states and underdeveloped states is one critical dimension of the global environment. Santos draws attention to the fundamental hypocrisy of the United States (and some other Western nations) in promoting standards of human rights for other countries while refusing to be held accountable to such standards. Accordingly, a new politics of rights is called for. Santos provides a basis for a radical challenge to the conventional, mainstream, Eurocentric traditions of thinking about law and society.

Globalization

Globalization has been one of the dominant themes of the recent era (Teubner 1997), and there are many reasons to believe that pressures for globalization will intensify. Globalization is sometimes regarded as a force promoting the spread of Western standards of living to other parts of the world; alternatively, some warn that globalization can contribute to greater concentrations of power and a greater divide between the rich and the poor (Silbey 1997). It is far from clear that the Western legal model—as opposed to

Box 10.7

Law, Human Rights, and the International Criminal Court

In 1948 the Universal Declaration of Human Rights was produced, under the sponsorship of the United Nations. This document articulates the basic rights that all humans are entitled to and that all states should strive to protect (Evans 1998). Unfortunately, the second half of the twentieth century witnessed pervasive violations of human rights in countries all over the world. The broader implementation of human rights will surely be one of the major challenges of the twenty-first century (Symonides 1998; Lauren 1998; Dunne and Wheeler 1999). Many commentators believe that any broad international implementation of human rights will require fostering democracy and tolerance and more effectively addressing economic development, poverty, education, genocide, terrorism, and refugee problems. Globalization has both positive and negative effects on the promotion of human rights, as it may adversely affect indigenous peoples while broadening the opportunities for women.

A permanent International Criminal Court (ICC) was established in 1998, through adoption of a treaty by the international community (Duffy 1999). This court was to address alleged war crimes, genocidal crimes, and crimes against humanity. The United States was one of the few countries to vote in opposition to establishing the court, on the rationale that it feared politically motivated prosecutions would be directed against Americans serving in various parts of the world. It remains to be seen how effective this court will be in addressing the challenges of state crimes.

an Eastern, or Chinese, legal model—will prevail as the world becomes globalized (Appelbaum 1998). In the realm of law, it seems safely predictable that international law and transnational law will assume increasing importance in the years ahead. On the other hand, globalization confronts a countertrend of revived ethnic nationalism and localism. Some aspects of law, then, will reflect a shift to the global and the transnational; other aspects of law will reflect intensified local and ethnic concerns. These tensions and conflicts are sure to be an important story in the twenty-first century.

The Future of Law

The perpetual gaps between the haves and the have-nots on all levels (i.e., between countries; between social groups; between individuals) will likely endure as one of the major challenges for law in the twenty-first century. By at least some measures, the gaps actually widened toward the end of the twentieth century. This piece of data provides some support for Marx's celebrated prediction that, under capitalism, the rich would get richer and the poor would get poorer; of course, Marx was wrong about many things. To the extent that law is viewed as complicit in maintaining or perpetuating social inequalty, it will be the target of ongoing hostility and challenge from the disadvantaged and their allies. Conversely, law may continue to be viewed as a potentially powerful instrument for promoting greater social equality and the fairer distribution of scarce resources (see Box 10.7).

On the future of law, then, the only thing one can assert with some degree of confidence is that law will change, in ways large and small, as we move through the twenty-first century. It is far from clear, however, exactly what form the changes will take. By understanding as fully as possible the character and nature of law in our lives, we should be better prepared to understand the legal changes we are sure to encounter and, ideally, to contribute to these changes in a constructive way.

Key Terms and Concepts

Battered Women Syndrome
Equal Rights Amendment (ERA)
Frye Test
globalization
Harrison Tax Act (1914)
Labor Management Relations Act (Taft-Hartley Act)
legitimacy crisis
Marijuana Tax Act (1937)
National Labor Relations Act (Wagner Act)
Personal Responsibility and Work Opportunity Act
technocratic justice

Discussion Questions

1. Explain how law is both an independent and a dependent variable in relation to social change. Review the conditions under which law is most likely to promote social change, as well as the sources of resistance to legal reform. Which views do you tend to agree with the most? Why?

2. What message did President Clinton send to America when he signed the Personal Responsibility and Work Opportunity Act (PRWOA) in 1996? How would such an action substantiate the claim cited on numerous occasions throughout the text that laws and the legal system make the rich richer and the poor poorer?

3. Why does it seem that domestic violence and rape, two of the most violent acts known to exist (usually against women), are among the hardest for our legal system to control? Would the laws be any different, or the reforms of greater significance, if *men* were the primary targets of violence?

4. Why don't laws seem to deter drug users? Would legalization of at least marijuana be a step in the right direction in our "war on drugs"? Would an emphasis on education and treatment programs, instead of an emphasis on a criminal justice system response, make more of a difference?

5. Does the administration of "technocratic justice" have the potential to create a more "exact" system of legal decision making? What are the pros and cons of the movement toward more reliance upon science within our system?

Appendix A

Case Briefing: A Rudimentary Skill in Legal Analysis

Even students new to the study of law can acquire a basic practical understanding of legal analysis (and reasoning) in the form of case briefing. In reading appellate court opinions, what should one look for? Here, in outline form, are some of the elements of case briefing.

I. Preliminary Questions:

A. Type of case: Is it a criminal case or a civil case? In American case opinions a case entitled "*U.S. v.* . . ." or "*Commonwealth of PA. v.* . . ." indicates a criminal case, prosecuted in the state's name, while a case entitled "*Smith v. Jones,*" involving private parties, indicates a civil proceeding (the "*v.,*" of course, stands for "versus"). But as the state may be a party to a civil proceeding, the appearance of the state in the case title does not guarantee that the case is a criminal proceeding. Ultimately, of course, the answer to this question must be found in the nature of the case (i.e., is it about burglary or divorce?).

B. Parties to the Case: Who is being charged, by whom, or who is suing who else? Who is the defendant, and who is the prosecutor—or plaintiff?

C. Court Hearing Case: Which court has produced the opinion? One should be able to determine the answer to this—e.g., is it the United States Supreme Court or the Supreme Court of some state?—from the captioning of the case.

D. Time/Place: When did the case occur, and where? Importantly, on this point, one should not confuse the year given in the captioning of the case with the year when the incident giving rise to the case occurred. The first-mentioned year refers to the year when the appellate court opinion was handed down. In many cases the appellate court opinion is handed down a few years after the original incident in the case. The date of the original incident should be found in the Court's summary of the facts of the case.

E. Where can the opinion be found? If one finds the following: *State v. Tages*, Court of Appeals of Arizona (1969) 10 Ariz. App. 127, 457 P.2d 289—this indicates that the opinion can be found in two different "reporters" of cases; the number preceding the abbreviated reporter title is the volume, the number following it is the first page of the published opinion (if a second page number is given, it is calling attention to a part of the opinion that is being discussed). Both sources are provided mainly because some law libraries—or lawyers—may subscribe to only one of these reporters.

F. How did the case get to the present court? The published opinion will not typically provide an answer to this question, but one should understand the difference between cases that reach state supreme courts on the basis of a mandatory right of appeal and cases that reach the U. S. Supreme Court on a Writ of Certiorari, which means that the Court has exercised its discretion (on the basis of the votes of at least four justices) to have the case sent up and to hear it.

II. Basic Facts in Case: At or near the outset of the appellate court opinion, one should find a summary of the principal facts in the case. Of course, it is the trial court and its jury (or, if it is a bench trial, the judge) that determines the facts in a legal case. Appellate courts generally accept the trial court's findings on the facts, although the appellate court may determine that some legal error occurred in the process of arriving at the facts or attempting to apply law to them. However, in any given case an almost endless string of facts could be produced. The student of law must learn to discriminate between facts that are deemed legally relevant and those that are legally irrelevant. In a case involving a contractual dispute the defendant's height may well be legally irrelevant; on the other hand, in a criminal case involving an eyewitness description or forensic evidence indicating a perpetrator of a certain size, the defendant's height may be highly relevant.

III. Legal Provisions: What rules of law are cited in the opinion as applicable to the case? For example, a particular statutory law on homicide, or on grounds for divorce, might be cited. In addition, are any Constitutional provisions cited? For example, in a case involving Search and Seizure, the Fourth Amendment of the Constitution arises and is going to be cited.

IV. Issue: If a case is appealed to a higher court, it cannot be appealed solely on the basis that the appellant was unhappy with the decision in the case. The court of appeals must be presented with one or more issues upon which the case is appealed. A *substantive* issue pertains to the law invoked in the case in the first place, and claims that it was misapplied. For example, someone convicted of selling pornographic books may claim that the statute criminalizing pornography does not apply to the books in question, which are claimed to be a legitimate form of artistic expression. In a case of this nature a Constitutional issue may also be invoked, on the claim that the prosecution and conviction violated a First Amendment right to free speech. A *procedural* issue, on the other hand, addresses alleged error in the justice system procedure. For example, someone convicted of a crime may claim that he was not given the Miranda warning (on the right to remain silent) at the point of arrest; or that the incriminating evidence was improperly seized; or that the judge allowed inadmissible testimony to be given at the trial; or that the jury was improperly charged. A specific appeal may raise both substantive and procedural issues—more than one in each case—in the hope that on at least one of these issues the court of appeals will agree with the appellant and reverse the judgment.

V. Decisions (Holding): Judges (unlike some professors) cannot equivocate; at the end of the trial they must make a decision (or administer the jury's decision) and declare who has won and who has lost. The holding in the case should be clearly stated at the end of the opinion. The holding in the case, however, may only represent a partial victory for one side: for example, a defendant in a criminal case may be found guilty of one charge but not another; a plaintiff in a civil case may be granted only part of what the original lawsuit demanded.

VI. Reasoning: In the American legal system the court of appeals is generally expected to provide reasons for its holding. A court of appeals may refuse to consider an appeal without providing a reason for doing so. In important and novel cases, however, the court of appeals is likely to provide some chain of reasoning for its decision, or holding. One or more legal principles may be enunciated as well, as keys to the holding. And in the American common law tradition one or more precedents (or earlier, similar cases) may be cited in support of the holding in the present case. (The important issues surrounding the citation of precedents, and the principle of stare decisis, are discussed in Chapter 2.) In addition to precedents, other sources may be cited in support of a holding. In the past, in particular, it was not uncommon to cite traditional authority (e.g., the Bible; a prominent legal sage, such as Coke); in the modern era appellate court judges have been more likely to cite the findings of empirical research.

VII. Separate Opinions: A court of appeals always issues an opinion on behalf of the court (based on the vote of the majority of the justices on the court), but appellate court justices may also opt to deliver separate opinions of their own. In a *concurring* opinion the justice agrees with the holding of the court but has adopted a different line of reasoning or may want to express reservations on some implications of the holding. In a *dissenting* opinion the justice disagrees with the holding and expresses reasons for this disagreement. Although only the court's opinion has any binding legal force, both concurring and dissenting justices take the trouble to formulate their opinions at least in part because they hope their line of reasoning will be adopted in future cases on the issue at hand.

VIII. Policy Analysis/Sociohistorical Analysis: In the context of a law and society focus one wants to go beyond the internal legal elements of an appellate court opinion. Although one will not necessarily—or even probably—find the answers to questions posed by the analysis in the opinion, ideally one finds ways to answer them. First, what is the sociohistorical context of the case? For example, if one looks at opinions in nineteenth-century cases involving divorce or the abuse of wives, one can only clearly understand them if one knows something about norms and values pertaining to marital relations and rights in that time (and place). Second, what are the extralegal influences on the opinion? In other words, what considerations other than strictly legal considerations contributed to the reasoning and holding of the court? Again, one may not be able to identify these factors, but hypothetically they might include: political or religious beliefs of the justice; bigotry, racism, and sexism; personality factors or personal connections to parties to the case; and so on. Third, what is the historical significance of the case? At least some cases have an immense impact on subsequent historical developments. For example, the *Dred Scott* (1857) decision of the U. S. Supreme Court, upholding the notion of slaves as property, was one of the precipitants of the Civil War. Fourth, what are the policy implications of the case? For example, the *Miranda* (1966) decision requiring the provision of a warning to remain silent to people being arrested changed police policy. Finally, what does a normative evaluation of the case produce? In other words, do you think the court's ruling was good or bad, ethically and morally justifiable, or not? Of course on this level personal, subjective evaluation enters. For example, Americans are sharply divided on whether the *Roe v. Wade* (1973) decision, striking down laws prohibiting abortion, was a good or bad decision.

IX. Legal terminology: Law has a language, or a long list of terms, that are invoked in legal opinions. Students of law must learn this language. In the American legal system Latin terms in particular are quite common. *Mens rea*—the thing in the mind, or criminal intent—and *bona fide*—in good faith—are just two of the more familiar of these terms.

Appendix B

Law in Our Lives: Films

Countless films and documentaries have been produced that feature lawyers or legal proceedings, or address legal issues. The listing below is quite selective. For example, it does not include documentaries on purely technical legal matters (e.g., "How to Commence a Civil Litigation," "Power Cross-Examination," "Practical Evidence" and "Client Interviewing"). Law and the legal profession have been exceptionally popular topics for feature films, so the listing here too is quite selective, weighted toward more recent films. Cinemania (a Microsoft CD-ROM software product) can be used to search for feature films with law-related themes. First Search is especially useful in searching for documentary films on law-related themes. This listing was compiled with some assistance from Karen Heckman of the University of Scranton Media Research Center, and Sarah Buckley.

Principal distributors of documentaries listed here are:

- Insight Media, 2162 Broadway, New York, NY 10024-6620; Tel: (212) 721-6316; Fax: (212) 799-5309; www.insight.media.com
- Films for the Humanities & Sciences (FHS), PO Box 2053, Princeton, NJ 08543-2053; Tel: (800) 257-5126; Fax: (609) 275-3767; http://www.films.com

Chapter 1: Introduction

Documentaries:

—*For the People* [Impact of the Constitution in Three Cases]
60 min., BQK4914 [FHS]

—*Contemporary Life v. the Constitution*
60 min., BQK4915 [FHS]

—*The Bill of Rights: A Living Document*
30 min., BQK8097 [FHS]

—*Fourteen Days in May: The Capital Punishment Debate*
88 min., BQK7431 [FHS]

—*The Right to Kill*
58 min., 1989 [American Portrait Films]

—*Michigan v. Kevorkian: The Trial of Dr. Death*
50 min., 1994, #3S370 [Insight]

—*Pleading Insane*
50 min., 1994, #3S385 [Insight]

—*In the Shadow of Watergate: Campaign Finance* Reform
26 min., #CGJ8832 [Insight]

Chapter 2: Law: Its Meaning and Logic

Documentaries:

—*Overview of the Legal System*
28 min., 1988, #GR34 [Insight]

—*Law and the Legal System*
29 min., 1989 [RMI Media Productions]

—*Our Legal System*
1993, #GR518 [Insight]

—*The U.S. Constitution: Origins in Classical Greece*
14 min., 1989 [American Hellenic Alliance]

—*The Judicial Branch of Government*
1996, #GR456 [Insight]

—*Interpreting the Law: The Role of the Supreme Court*
60 min., 1989, #3S103 [Insight]

—*Strictly Speaking* [On Original Intent]
60 min., BQK4912 [FHS]

—*Mr. Justice Douglas*
52 min., 1972 [Carousel Films]

—*Justice Harry A. Blackmun, Man in the Middle*
60 min., BQK4907 [FHS]

—*Mr. Justice Brennan*
60 min., BQKa4909 [FHS]

—*Justice Sandra Day O'Connor*
60 min., BQK4913 [FHS]

—*Justice Lewis F. Powell*
60 min., BQK4916 [FHS]

Chapter 3: Law, Justice, and the Moral Order

Documentaries:

— *God and the Constitution*
60 min., BQK4911 [FHS]

— *Legislating Morality: There Oughta Be a Law!*

28 min., BQK6387 [FHS]

— *Sex for Sale: Should Prostitution Be Legal?*
15 min., BQK7634 [FHS]

Chapter 4: Jurisprudence and the Study of Law

Documentaries:

—*Natural Law: What It Is & Why We Need It*
1997 [International Catholic Univ.]

—*Ronald Dworkin: The Meaning of the Constitution*
60 min., BQK4910 [FHS]

—*Blind Justice: Women and the Law*
30 min., BQK1608 [FHS]

Chapter 5: The Law and Society Movement

Chapter 6: Comparative and Historical Perspectives on Law and Society

Documentaries:

—*The Criminal Justice System: U.S. vs. England*
48 min., 1995, #GR523 [Insight]

—*China's Legal System*
30 min., 1991, #3S194 [Insight]

—*Incident at Oglala*
90 min., 1992 [Live Home Video]

—*The Road to Brown*
58 min., 1990 [California Newsreel]

—*Brown v. Board of Education*
Mac/Windows CD-ROM, 1996, #3S297 [Insight]

—*The Nuremberg War Crimes Trial*
60 min., 1996, #GR532 [Insight]

Chapter 7: The Legal Profession

Feature Films:

The Accused (1988)
Anatomy of a Murder (1958)
The Big Easy (1987)
Cape Fear (1961) (1991)
A Civil Action (1998)
Class Action (1991)
The Client (1994)
Defenseless (1990)
Erin Brockovich (2000)

Fair Game (1995)
A Few Good Men (1991)
The Firm (1993)
Guilty As Sin (1993)
Inherit the Wind (1960)
Jagged Edge (1985)
Judicial Consent (1994)
Judgment at Nuremberg (1961)
And Justice for All (1979)
To Kill a Mockingbird (1962)
Legal Eagles (1986)
Love Crimes (1991)
Music Box (1989)
My Cousin Vinny (1990)
Other People's Money (1991)
The Pelican Brief (1993)
Philadelphia (1993)
Physical Evidence (1988)
Primal Fear (1996)
Reversal of Fortune (1990)
Suspect (1987)
The Verdict (1982)
Witness for the Prosecution (1957)
Young Mr. Lincoln (1939)

Documentaries:

—*Alan Dershowitz: A Portrait in the First Person*
24 min., BQK5220 [FHS]
—*Attorneys for the Unpopular*
28 min., BQK5402 [FHS]
—*The Defenders*
50 min., 1996, #3S341 [Insight]
—*Justice Is a Constant Struggle*
28 min., 1987 [Univ. of Calif. Media]
—*Lawyers on Trial*
29 min., BQK6385 [FHS]
—*The Good That Lawyers Do*
56 min., 1999 [Washington Univ. School of Law]
—*Conflicts of Interest and Other Ethical Issues for Attorneys*
64 min., 1992 [Bar Association of San Francisco]

Chapter 8: Legal Institutions and Processes: An Overview

Documentaries:

—*Understanding the Criminal Justice System*
3 volumes, 20 min. each, 1996, #3S299 [Insight]

—*In the Eyes of the Law*
25 min., 1995, #GR500 [Insight]

—*The Rodney King Case: What the Jury Saw in* California v. Powell
120 min., 1992, #3544 [Insight]

—*And Justice for All?*
60 min., BQK5033 [FHS]

—*Plea Bargains: Dealing for Justice*
26 min., BQK4593 [FHS]

—*Crime and Punishment in America*
120 min., 1997 [PBS Home Video]

—*Civil Law: Understanding Your Rights, Remedies, and Obligations*
45 min., 1983, #3S20 [Insight]

—*Anatomy of a Libel Trial: Carol Burnett v. National Enquirer*
24 min., 1983, #32289 [Insight]

—*Understanding the Juvenile Justice System*
3 volumes, 20 min. each, 1996, #GRS19 [Insight]

—*Family Mediation: We Can Work It Out*
29 min., #CGJ8904 [Insight]

—*Restorative Justice: For Victims, Communities and Offenders*
25 min. [U. of Minn.]

—*Restorative Justice: Victim Empowerment Through Mediation and Dialogue*
20 min. [U. of Minn.]

Chapter 9: Legal Culture and Legal Behaviors

Documentaries:

—*The Rule of Law*
52 min., 1989, #GR22 [Insight]

—*The Trial of Socrates*
29 min., 1971, #GR33 [Insight]

—*Democracy in a Different Voice: Lani Guinier*
54 min., 1995, #GR508 [Insight]

—*The American Civil Liberties Union: A History*
57 min., BQK7613 [FHS]

—*The Executive Branch of Government*
30 min., BQK8093 [FHS]

—*The Judicial Branch of Government*
35 min., BQK8277 [FHS]

—*Lawmakers, Lawmaking, and the Law*
60 min, BQK6185-87 [FHS]

—*How a Bill Becomes a Law*
30 min., BQK8094 [FHS]

Chapter 10: Law in Flux: Law and Social Change

Documentaries:

—*We, the People: The Growth of the Constitution*
13 min., 1992 [New Dimension Media]

—*Gender Justice: Women's Rights Are Human Rights*
41 min., 1996 [Unitarian Universalist]

—*Sexual Harassment: Crossing the Line*
30 min., BQK8032 [FHS]

—*All in a Day's Work* [Sexual Harassment]
25 min., 1993 [Institute for Labor]

—*Affirmative Action: The History of an Idea*
56 min., BQK6552 [FHS]

—*Legitimating Morality: Affirmative Action and the Burden of History*
29 min., #CGJ6388 [Insight]

—*Hate on Trial: Challenging the First Amendment*
3 Parts: 49, 70, 23 min., CGJ6853 [Insight]

—*DNA: A Question of Reliability*
48 min., 1995, #GR496 [Insight]

—*Technology and Legal Issues: Ownership and Copyright on the Web*
60 min., 1997, #3S381 [Insight]

—*The Constitution in Cyberspace Law*
68 min., 1996 [Sweet Pea Productions]

—*Cyberspace: Freedom or Regulation?*
29 min., BQK6392 [FHS]

Appendix C

Law in Our Lives on the Internet

The Internet is expanding and evolving daily, and has become a vast storehouse of information and communication. The listing below is provisional and highly selective. It includes a number of Web sites and net-related resources that are deemed especially relevant to the focus of this book. Since Web sites often have links with other, related sites, this listing merely provides certain points of departure for searches for information pertaining to law in our lives. In light of the exceptionally dynamic character of the net, no claim is made here that all the sites listed are still being maintained as you read this note. This listing was compiled with assistance from Kara Kosiorowski, Ann Marie Lutz, and Martyna Sleszynska. The following book provided basic information: James Evans, *Law on the Net* (Berkeley, CA: Nolo Press, 1996) (updated on a CD-ROM version). Some additional books or sources that should prove helpful to those making law-related searches on the net include:

Biehl, Kathy. 2000. *The Lawyer's Guide to Internet Legal Research.* Lanham, MD: Scarecrow Press.

Halvorson, R. R., and Reva Basch. 2000. *Law of the Super Searchers: The Online Secrets of Top Legal Researchers.* Medford, NJ: Cyberage Books.

Long, Judy A. 2000. *Legal Research Using the Internet.* Albany, NY: West Legal Studies.

Web Sites of Selected Law-Related Organizations

— American Bar Association
  http://www.abanet.org

— American Civil Liberties Union
  http://www.aclu.org

— Academy of Criminal Justice Sciences
  http://www.acjs.org

— American Judicature Society
  http://www.ajs.org

— American Society of Criminology
http://www.asc41.com
— Association of Trial Lawyers
http://www.atlanet.org
— Bureau of Justice Statistics
http://www.ojp.usdoj.bjs
— Center on Crime, Communities, and Culture
http://www.soros.org/crime/pfdv
— Community Court Forum
http://www.communitycourts.org
— Community Policing Information
http://www.communitypolicing.org.index.html
— Death Penalty Information Center
http://www.essential.org/dpic/
— Federal Judicial Center
http://www.fjc.gov
— Government Agency Links
http://www.fjc.gov/govlinks.html
— Graduate School Information
http://www.clas.ufl.edu/CLAS/american-universities.html
— Handgun Control, Inc.
http://www.handguncontrol.org
— International Perspectives on Justice
http://pap01.adt.jjay.cuny.edu
— Justice Information Center
http://www.ncjrs.org
— Juvenile Justice Clearinghouse
http://ncjrs.org/ojjhome.htm
— Law School Information
http://www.jmls.edu/law/schools/us
— Law and Society Association
http://www.lawandsociety.org
— Lindesmith Center Library (Drug Issues)
http://www.lindesmith.org
— Mothers Against Drunk Driving (MADD)
http://www.madd.org
— National Association of Criminal Defense Lawyers
http://www.criminaljustice.org
— National Center for State Courts
http://www.ncsc.dni.us

—National Clearinghouse for Alcohol and Drug Information
http://www.health.org
—National Consortium on Violence Research
http://www.heinz.cmu.edu/ncovr
—National District Attorneys Association
http://www.ndaa-apri.org
—National Drugs and Crime Clearinghouse
http://www.ncjrs.org
—National Institute of Justice (NIJ)
http://www.ojp.usdoj.gov/ni
—National Rifle Association
http://www.nra.org/
—National Victim Center (NVC)
http://www.nvc.org
—Prison Reform Information
http://caq.com/prison.html
—Southern Poverty Law Center
http://www.splcenter.org
—U.S. Dept. of Justice
http://www.usdoj.gov
—U.S. Federal Courts
http://www.uscourts.gov
—U.S. Supreme Court
http://www.law.cornell.edu/supct/

General Information on Law and Law-Related Topics

—The 'Lectric Law Library
http://www.inter-law.com
—Nolo Press: Self-Help Law and Access to Law
http://www.nolopress.com
—Quicklaw American Internet Law Library
htp://www.currentlegal.com/lawlibrary/
—Yahoo Law
http://www.yahoo.com/government/law/

Legislative Activity and Appellate Court Opinions

—U.S. Congress
http://thomas.loc.gov/
—U.S. Supreme Court
http:/www.law.cornell.edu.supct/supct.table.html

Listservers and Newsgroups

Numerous listservers address law-related issues. These lists include Abortion and Reproductive Rights; Americans With Disabilities Act; Animal Rights Alert; Child Abuse; Civil Rights Law; Criminal Justice; Dispute Resolution; Environmental Law; Family Law; Feminism and the Law; Free Speech Law; Future Law; History of Law; International Law; Juvenile Justice; Law Schools; Legal Ethics; Miscarriages of Justice; Gaylaw; National Organization for the Reform of Marijuana Laws; Poverty Law; Violence; Youth Rights.

Especially relevant listservers include:

— Law and Society: Discussion about law and society issues

To subscribe by e-mail: listserv@polecat.law.indiana.edu

Subject: ANYTHING

Message: subscribe Law And our name

— Legal Studies: Discussion about law-related teaching at the undergraduate level

To subscribe by e-mail: listserv@listserv.law.cornell.edu

Subject: ANYTHING

Message: subscribe LegalStudies our name

— Law and Politics Book Reviews: Reviews of books on law and politics, broadly defined

To Subscribe by e-mail: listser@listserver.acns.nwu.edu

Subject: anything

Message: subscribe LPBR-L our name

— New Law Books: Information on newly published legal texts

To subscribe by e-mail: listserve@lawlib.wuacc.edu

Subject: ANYTHING

Message: subscribe newlawbooks-| our name

— Psychology and Law: Discussion of issues involving the interaction of psychology and law

To subscribe by e-mail: listserv@utepvm.ep.utexas.edu

Subject: ANYTHING

Message: PsyLaw L our name

Numerous newsgroups also address legal issues, including many of the same listed above for listservers. Newsgroups include Alt.Censorship, Misc.Legal, and Talk.Abortion.

For a guide to some of the other listservers listed above and additional newsgroups, and how to subscribe to or access them, see: James Evans, *Law on the Net* (Berkeley: Nolo Press, 1996; 1997).

Web Sites on Some Selected Law and Society Issues

Annotated Guide to Some Broadly Focused Web Sites:

— Law and Justice

http://www.ilj.org

- This Web site provides information about an Institute for Law and Justice.

— Law and Morality

http://www.unquietmind.com/mislaid_v.html

- This Web site provides a brief view of how law interacts with moral views. It also has a table of contents that can link you to other web sites on aggression, crime, social injustice, and related topics.

— Law and Religion

http://www.law.edu.religion.html

- This Web site provides a discussion of the relationship between law and religion. It also provides descriptions of college courses on this topic, and other related information.

— Legal Ethics

http://www.nobc.org

http://www.condor.depaul.edu:80/ethics/ethb20.html

- Both of these sites provide basic information about legal ethics issues, and links to related sites.

— Poverty, Politics, and Jurisprudence

http://www.cato.org/pubs/pas/pa049es.html

- This Web site provides information about the activities of the Legal Services Corporation, and offers links to Web sites related to poverty, politics, and law.

— Social Injustice

http://www.bfsr.org.sj.html

- This Web site provides a list of organizations concerned with social justice issues (e.g., the American Civil Liberties Union; the Children's Defense Fund).

— Sociolegal Studies

http://www.osu.edu/units/law/socio.htm

- This Web site provides some information about a Center for Sociolegal Studies.

Web sites on Legal Issues:

— Biotech Law

http://biotechlaw.arinet.com

— The Copyright Web site

http://www.benedict.com/

— Cyberlaw

http://www.portal.com/~cyberlaw/cylw_home.html

— Deathnet [Right to Die]

http://www.islandnet.com/~deathnet/

— Divorce Home Page
  http://www.primenet.com/~dean/
— Firearms
  http://www.portal.com/~chan/firearms.faq.htm/
— Peacenet
  http://www.igc.apc.org/peacenet/
— Sexual Harassment
  http://www.vix.com/pub/men/harass/harass.html
— Women's Rights and Resources
  http://sunsite.unc.edu/cheryb/women/wresources.html

References

Abel, Richard L. 1981. "Conservative Conflict and the Reproduction of Capitalism: The Role of Informal Justice." *International Journal of the Sociology of Law* 9: 245–267.

———. 1982. *The Politics of Informal Justice*. New York: Academic Press.

———. 1986. "Lawyers." Pp. 369–444, in Leon Lipson and Stanton Wheeler, eds. *Law and the Social Sciences*. New York: Russell Sage Foundation.

———. 1988. "United States: The Contradictions of Professionalism." Pp. 186–243, in Richard L. Abel and Philip S. C. Lewis, eds. *Lawyers in Society*. Berkeley, CA: University of California Press.

———. 1989. *American Lawyers*. New York: Oxford University Press.

———. 1995a. *The Law & Society Reader.* New York: New York University Press.

———. 1995b. *Politics by Other Means: Law in the Struggle Against Apartheid, 1980–1994*. New York: Routledge.

Abel, Richard L., and Philip S. C. Lewis. 1995. *Lawyers in Society: An Overview.* Berkeley, CA: University of California Press.

Abel, Richard L. and Philip S.C. Lewis, eds. 1988, 1989. *Lawyers in Society,* Vols. I–III. Berkeley, CA: University of California PRess.

Abraham, Henry J. 1973. *The Judiciary: The Supreme Court in the Governmental Process*. 3rd ed. Boston: Allyn & Bacon.

Abrams, Floyd. 1985. "Why We Should Change the Libel Law." *The New York Times Magazine* (September 29): 34, 87, 90, 92–93.

Abrams, Kathryn. 1991. "Hearing the Call of Stories." *California Law Review* 79: 971–1054.

Abramson, Jill. 1988. "For Women Lawyers, an Uphill Struggle." *The New York Times Magazine* (March 6): 36–37; 73–75.

———. 1998. "The Business of Persuasion Thrives in Nation's Capital." *The New York Times* (September 29): A1.

Adam, Barry D. 1987. *The Rise of a Gay and Lesbian Movement*. Boston: Twayne Publishers.

Adler, Mortimer J., and Charles Van Doren. 1977. *Great Treasury of Western Thought*. New York: R. R. Bowker.

Adler, Stephen J., and Wade Lambert. 1993. "Just About Everyone Violates Some Laws, Even Model Citizens." *Wall Street Journal* (March 17): 1.

Aichele, Gary J. 1990. *Legal Realism and Twentieth Century Jurisprudence*. New York: Garland.

Ainsworth, Janet E. 1991. "Re-Imagining Childhood and Reconstructing the Legal Order: The Case for Abolishing the Juvenile Courts." *North Carolina Law Review* 69: 1083–1133.

Alder, Christine. 1984. "Gender Bias in Juvenile Diversion." *Crime & Delinquency* 30: 400–414.

Alderman, Ellen, and Caroline Kennedy. 1995. *The Right to Privacy*. New York: Alfred Knopf.

Alibrandt, Tom, and Frank H. Armani. 1991. *Privileged Information*. New York: HarperCollins.

Allegretti, Joseph G. 1996. *The Lawyer's Calling: Christian Faith and Legal Practice*. New York: Paulist Press.

Allen, Mike. 1999. "Beyond the Bar Exam." *The New York Times* (July 11): 4/3.

Alper, Benedict S., and Lawrence T. Nichols. 1981. *Beyond the Courtroom: Programs in Community Justice and Conflict Resolution*. Lexington, MA: Lexington Books.

Alpert, Geoffrey, ed. 1980. *Legal Rights of Prisoners*. Beverly Hills, CA: Sage.

Alschuler, Albert W. 1991. "The Failure of Sentencing Guidelines: Plea for Less Aggregation." *University of Chicago Review* 58: 901–952.

Altman, Andrew. 1990. *Critical Legal Studies: A Liberal Critique*. Princeton, NJ: Princeton University Press.

Altman, Dennis. 1982. *The Homosexualization of America, the Americanization of the Homosexual*. New York: St. Martin's Press.

Andrews, Lori B. 1999. *The Clone Age: Adventures in the New World of Reproductive Technology*. New York: Henry Holt.

Anleu, Sharyn L. Roach. 1992. "Critiquing the Law: Themes and Dilemmas in Anglo-American Feminist Legal Theory." *Journal of Law and Society* 19: 423–440.

Appelbaum, Richard P. 1998. "The Future of Law in a Global Economy." *Social & Legal Studies* 7: 172–192.

Applebome, Peter. 1995. "The Pariah as Cheat: Bombing Case Rekindles Debate Among Lawyers." *The New York Times* (April 28): A28.

Aquinas, Thomas. [1266–1272] 1993. *The Treatise on Law* (R. J. Henleu, ed.). Notre Dame, IN: University of Notre Dame Press.

Aries, Phillipe. 1962. *Centuries of Childhood*. New York: Vintage.

Armstrong, Troy L., Michael H. Guilfoyle, and Ada Pecos Melton. 1996. "Traditional Approaches to Tribal Justice: History and Current Practice." Pp. 46–53, in Marianne A. Nielsen and Robert Silverman, eds. *Native Americans, Crime, and Justice*. Boulder, CO: Westview Press.

Arnold, Bruce L., and Fiona M. Kay. 1995. "Social Capital, Violations of Trust and the Vulnerability of Isolates: The Social Organization of Law Practice and Professional Self-Regulation." *International Journal of the Sociology of Law* 23: 321–346.

Ashford, Jose B. 1994. "Child Maltreatment Interventions: Developments in Law, Prevention, and Treatment." *Criminal Justice Review* 19: 271–285.

Auerbach, Jerold. 1976. *Unequal Justice: Lawyers and Social Change in Modern America*. London: Oxford University Press.

———. 1983. *Justice Without Law? Resolving Disputes Without Lawyers*. New York: Oxford University Press.

Austin, John. [1832] 1954. *The Province of Jurisprudence Determined*. (H. L. A. Hart, ed.). London: Weidenfeld & Nicolson.

Bach, Amy. 1995. "Nolo Contendere." *New York* (December 11): 49–55.

Bachman, Walt. 1995. *Law v. Life: What Lawyers Are Afraid to Say About the Legal Profession*. Rhinebeck, NY: Four Directions Press.

Baer, Judith A. 1999. *Our Lives Before the Law: Constructing a Feminist Jurisprudence*. Princeton, NJ: Princeton University Press.

Bailey, Frankie Y., and Donna C. Hale. 1998. *Popular Culture, Crime, and Justice*. Belmont, CA: West/Wadsworth.

Baird, Robert M., and Stuart E. Rosenbaum, eds. 1997. *Same-Sex Marriage: The Moral and Legal Debate*. Amherst, NY: Prometheus Books.

Baggins, David. 1998. *Drug Hate and the Corruption of American Justice*. Westport, CT: Greenwood Publishing.

Bandes, Susan. 1999. *The Passions of Law*. New York: New York University Press.

Barkan, Steven E. 1983. "Jury Nullification in Political Trials." *Social Problems* 31: 28–44.

Barker, Christine R., Elizabeth A. Kirk, and Monica Sah, eds. 1998. *Gender Perceptions and the Law*. Brookfield, VT: Ashgate Publishing Co.

Barreto, Humberto, Thomas A. Husted, and Ann D. Witte. 1984. "The New Law and Economics: Present and Future." *ABF Research Journal* 1984: 253–266.

Barthel, Joan. 1977. *A Death in Canaan*. New York: Dell.

Bartlett, Katharine T. 1991. *Gender and Law: Theory, Doctrine, Commentary*. New York: New York University Press.

Baumgartner, M. P. 1988. *The Moral Order of a Suburb*. New York: Oxford University Press.

Baumgartner, M. P., ed. 1999. *The Social Organization of Law*. 2nd ed. San Diego, CA: Academic Press.

Bayley, David H., and Clifford D. Shearing. 1996. "The Future of Policing." *Law & Society Review* 30: 585–606.

Bazemore, Gordon. 1997. "The Community in Community Justice: Issues, Themes, and Questions for the New Neighborhood Sanctioning Models." *The Justice System Journal* 19: 193–228.

Beales, Ross W. 1985. "In Search of the Historical Child: Miniature Adulthood and Youth in Colonial New England." Pp. 7–26, in N. Ray Hiner and Joseph M. Hawes, eds. *Growing Up in America: Children in Historical Perspective*. Urbana, IL: University of Illinois Press.

Beaman-Hall, Lori. 1996. "Legal Ethnography: Exploring the Gendered Nature of Legal Method." *Critical Criminology* 7: 53–74.

Beccaria, C. [1764] 1988. *On Crimes and Punishments*. New York: MacMillan.

Becker, Howard S. 1963. *Outsiders*. New York: The Free Press.

Beckett, Katherine. 1997. *Making Crime Pay: Law and Order in Contemporary American Politics*. New York: Oxford University Press.

Bedau, Hugo Adam. 1998. *The Death Penalty in America: Current Controversies*. New York: Oxford University Press.

Beirne, Piers, and Alan Hunt. 1988. "Law and the Constitution of Soviet Society: The Case of Comrade Lenin." *Law & Society Review* 22: 575–614.

Beirne, Piers, and Richard Quinney, eds. 1982. *Marxism and Law*. New York: John Wiley & Sons.

Beirne, Piers, and Robert Sharlet. 1980. *Pashukanis: Selected Writings on Marxism and Law*. London: Academic Press.

Belknap, Joanne, and Edna Erez. 1997. "Redefining Sexual Harassment: Confronting Sexism in the 21st Century." *The Justice Professional* 10: 143–159.

Bell, Derrick A., Jr. 1980. *Race, Racism, and American Law*. 2nd ed. Boston: Little Brown.

———. 1987. *And We Are Not Saved: The Elusive Quest for Racial Justice*. New York: Basic Books.

———. 1992. *Faces at the Bottom of the Well*. New York: Basic Books.

Bender, Leslie. 1990. "Feminist (Re)torts: Thoughts on the Liability Crisis, Mass Torts, Power, and Responsibility." *Duke Law Journal* (September): 848–912.

Bentham, Jeremy. [1776] 1960. *A Fragment on Government*. (W. Harrison, ed.). Oxford, UK: Basil Blackwell.

———. [1789] 1970. *An Introduction to the Principles of Morals and Legislation*. (J. H. Burns and H. L. A. Hart, eds.). London: Athlone Press.

Ben-Yehuda, Nachman. 1997. "Political Assassination Events as a Cross-Cultural Form of Alternative Justice." *International Journal of Comparative Sociology* 38: 25–47.

Berat, Lynn, and Yossi Shain. 1995. "Retribution or Truth-Telling in South Africa? Legacies of the Transitional Phase." *Law & Social Inquiry* 20: 163–189.

Berger, Curtis J., and Vivian Berger. 1999. "Academic Discipline: A Guide to Fair Process for University Students." *Columbia Law Review* 99: 289–355.

Berger, Ronald J., W. Lawrence Neuman, and Patricia Searles. 1994. "The Impact of Rape Law Reform: An Aggregate Analysis of Police Reports and Arrests." *Criminal Justice Review* 19: 1–22.

Berger, Ronald J., Patricia Searles, and W. Lawrence Neuman. 1988. "The Dimensions of Rape Reform Legislation." *Law & Society Review* 22: 329–357.

Berlin, Ira. 1998. *Many Thousands Gone: The First Two Centuries of Slavery in North America*. Cambridge, MA: The Belknap Press.

Berman, Harold J. 1963. *Justice in the U.S.S.R.: An Interpretation of Soviet Law*. New York: Vintage.

———. 1966. *Soviet Criminal Law and Procedure: The RSFSR Codes*. Cambridge, MA: Harvard University Press.

———. 1974. *The Interaction of Law and Religion*. Nashville, TN: Abingdon Press.

———. 1983. *Law and Revolution: The Formation of the Western Legal Tradition*. Cambridge, MA: Harvard University Press.

———. 1993. *Faith and Order: The Reconciliation of Law and Religion*. Atlanta: Scholars Press.

Berman, Jesse. 1969. "The Cuban Popular Tribunals." *Columbia Law Review* 69: 1317–1354.

Bernard, Thomas J. 1983. *The Consensus-Conflict Debate*. New York: Columbia University Press.

———. 1992. *The Cycle of Juvenile Justice*. New York: Oxford University Press.

Bernstein, Anita. 1996. "A Feminist Revisit to the First-Year Curriculum." *Journal of Legal Education* 46: 217–232.

Bernstein, Emily M. 1996. "Law School Women Question the Teaching." *The New York Times* (June 5): B10.

Bernstein, Nina. 1996. "With Colleges Holding Court, Discretion Vies With Fairness." *The New York Times* (May 5): A1.

Berrigan, Daniel. 1970. *The Trial of the Catonsville Nine*. Boston: Beacon Press.

Besharov, Douglas J., ed. 1990. *Legal Services for the Poor: Time for Reform*. Washington, DC: The AEI Press.

Bierbrauer, Gunter. 1994. "Toward an Understanding of Legal Culture: Variation in Individualism and Collectivism Between Kurds, Lebanese, and Germans." *Law & Society Review* 28: 243–264.

Binion, Gayle. 1997. "On Politics, Constitutional Interpretations, and Abortion Rights Jurisprudence." *Law & Society Review* 31: 845–870.

Birch, Sharon. 1997. *Determinate Sentencing: Examining the Growing Use of the Tougher Juvenile Incarceration Penalty*. Austin: Texas Criminal Justice Policy Council.

Bishop, Joseph, Jr. 1974. *Justice Under Fire: A Study of Military Law*. New York: Charterhouse.

Bix, Brian. 1996. "Natural Law Theory." Pp. 223–240, in Dennis Patterson, ed. *A Companion to Philosophy of Law and Legal Theory*. Cambridge, MA: Blackwell Publishers.

Black, Amy E., and Stanley Rothman. 1998. "Shall We Kill All the Lawyers First? Insider and Outsider Views of the Legal Profession." *Harvard Journal of Law and Public Policy* 21: 835–860.

Black, Donald. 1976. *The Behavior of Law*. New York: Academic Press.

———. 1983. "Crime as Social Control." *American Sociological Review* 48: 34–45.

———. 1989. *Sociological Justice*. New York: Oxford University Press.

———. 1993. *The Social Structure of Right and Wrong*. San Diego, CA: Academic Press.

———. 1995. "The Epistemology of Pure Sociology." *Law and Social Inquiry* 20: 829–870.

Black, Jonathan, ed. 1971. *Radical Lawyers*. New York: Avon.

Blackstone, William. [1765–1769] 1979. *Commentaries on the Laws of England*. Chicago: University of Chicago Press.

Blasius, Mark. 1994. *Gay and Lesbian Politics: Sexuality and the Emergence of a New Ethic*. Philadelphia: Temple University Press.

Blass, Thomas, ed. 2000. *Obedience to Authority: Current Perspectives on the Milgram Paradigm*. Mahwah, NJ: Lawrence Erlbaum Associates.

Blee, Kathleen M. 1999. "The Perils of Privilege." *Law & Social Inquiry* 24: 993–998.

Blum, John Morton. 1991. *Years of Discord: American Politics and Society, 1961–1974*. New York: W. W. Norton.

Blumberg, Abraham. 1967. "The Practice of Law as a Confidence Game: Organizational Cooptation of a Profession." *Law & Society Review* 1: 15–39.

Bodenheimer, Edgar. 1974. *Jurisprudence: The Philosophy and Method of Law*. Rev. ed. Cambridge, MA: Harvard University Press.

Bogoch, Bryna. 1997. "Gendered Lawyering: Difference and Dominance in Lawyer–Client Interaction." *Law & Society Review* 31: 677–712.

Bohannon, Paul. 1967a. "The Differing Realms of Law." Pp. 45–58, in Paul Bohannon, ed. *Law and Warfare*. Garden City, NY: The Natural History Press.

Bohannon, Paul, ed. 1967b. *Law and Warfare*. Garden City, NY: The Natural History Press.

Bok, Derek. 1983. "A Flawed System of Law Practice and Training." *Journal of Legal Education* 33: 570–585.

Bonsignore, John, Ethan Katsh, Peter d'Errico, Ronald M. Pipkin, Stephen Arons, and Janet Rifkin, eds. 1998. *Before the Law*. 6th ed. Boston: Houghton Mifflin Co.

Bordewich, Fergus M. 1996. "Revolution in Indian Country." *American Heritage* (July/August): 34–46.

Bork, Robert. 1990. *The Tempting of America*. New York: The Free Press.

Bowen, William G., and Derek Bok. 1998. *The Shape of the River: Long-Term Consequences of Considering Race in College and University Admissions*. Princeton, NJ: Princeton University Press.

Boyer, Peter. 2000. "DNA on Trial." *The New Yorker* (January 17): 42–53.

Braithwaite, John, J. Walker, and Peter Grabosky. 1987. "An Enforcement Taxonomy of Regulatory Agencies." *Law and Policy* 9: 315–343.

Branch, Taylor. 1988. *Parting the Waters: America in the King Years, 1954–1963*. New York: Simon & Schuster.

———. 1998. *Pillar of Fire: America in the King Years, 1963–1968*. New York: Simon & Schuster.

Brint, Michael, and William Weaver, eds. 1991. *Pragmatism in Law and Society*. Boulder, CO: Westview Press.

Bronner, Ethan. 1999. "In a Revolution of Rules, Campuses Go Full Circle." *The New York Times* (March 3): A1.

Brooke, James. 1996. "Lawsuit Tests Lethal Power of Words." *The New York Times* (February 14): A12.

Brooks, Peter, and Paul Gewirtz. 1996. *Law's Stories: Narrative and Rhetoric in the Law*. New Haven, CT: Yale University Press.

Brown, Dee. 1971. *Bury My Heart at Wounded Knee*. New York: Holt, Rinehart & Winston.

Brown, Esther L. 1938. *Lawyers and the Promotion of Justice*. New York: Russell Sage Foundation.

Brown, Richard M. 1979. "Historical Patterns of American Violence." Pp. 19–48, in H. D. Graham and Ted Robert Gurr, eds. *Violence in America*. Beverly Hills, CA: Sage.

Brownmiller, Susan. 1975. *Against Our Will: Men, Women, and Rape*. New York: Simon & Schuster.

Brownsword, Roger, W. R. Cornish, and Margaret Llewelyn. 1998. "Human Genetics and the Law: Regulating a Revolution." *The Modern Law Review* 61: 593–597.

Bryan, Penelope E. 1992. "Killing Us Softly: Divorce Mediation and the Politics of Power." *Buffalo Law Review* 40: 441–523.

Buchanan, Allen E. 1982. *Marx and Justice: The Radical Critique of Liberalism*. Totowa, NJ: Rowman & Littlefield.

Burman, Sandra B., and Barbara E. Harrell-Bond, eds. 1979. *The Imposition of Law*. New York: Academic Press.

Burrage, Michael. 1988. "Revolution and the Collective Action of French, American, and English Legal Professionals." *Law & Social Inquiry* 13: 225–277.

Burton, Steven J. 1985. *An Introduction to Law and Legal Reasoning*. Boston, MA: Little, Brown & Co.

Bush, Robert A., and Joseph P. Folger. 1994. *The Promise of Mediation: Responding to Conflict Through Empowerment and Recognition*. San Francisco, CA: Jossey-Bass.

Bussiere, Elizabeth. 1997. *(Dis)Entitling the Poor: The Warren Court, Welfare Rights, and the American Political Tradition*. University Park: Penn State University Press.

Butler, Nicholas Murray. 1923. "Law and Lawlessness." Pp. 158–175, in Laurence Veysey, ed. 1970. *Law and Resistance: American Attitudes Toward Authority*. New York: Harper & Row.

Butler, Paul. 1995. "Racially Based Jury Nullification: Black Power in the Original Justice System." *The Yale Law Journal* 105: 677–726.

Caenegem, R. C. van. 1988. *The Birth of the English Common Law*. 2nd ed. Cambridge, UK: Cambridge University Press.

———. 1992. *An Historical Introduction to Private Law*. Cambridge, UK: Cambridge University Press.

Cahn, Edmund. 1949. *The Sense of Injustice*. Bloomington, IN: Indiana University Press.

Cain, Maureen, and Christine Harrington. 1994. *Lawyers in a Postmodern World: Translation and Transgression*. Buckingham, UK: Open University Press.

Cain, Maureen, and Alan Hunt, eds. 1979. *Marx and Engels on Law*. London: Academic Press.

Calabresi, Guido. 1970. *The Cost of Accidents*. New Haven, CT: Yale University Press.

Calabresi, Guido, and Phillip Bobbitt. 1978. *Tragic Choices*. New York: W. W. Norton & Co.

Campos, Paul F. 1998. *Jurismania: The Madness of American Law*. New York: Oxford University Press.

Cantor, Robert. 1973. "New Laws for a New Society." *Cuba Resource Center Newsletter* 3: 3–9, 12–20.

Caplow, Stacy. 1999. "Still in the Dark: Disappointing Images of Women Lawyers in the Movies." *Women's Rights Law Reporter* 20: 55–71.

Caputo, Philip. 1977. *A Rumor of War*. New York: Henry Holt & Co.

Carlin, Jerome E. 1962. *Lawyers on Their Own: A Study of Individual Practitioners in Chicago*. New Brunswick, NJ: Rutgers University Press.

———. 1994. *Lawyers on Their Own: The Solo Practitioner in an Urban Setting*. San Francisco, CA: Austin & Winfield Publishers.

Carlson, Rhonda. 1997. *Introduction to Paralegalism*. Chicago: Irwin.

Carrington, Paul. 1984. "Of Law and the River." *Journal of Legal Education* 34: 222–238.

Carter, Lief H. 1983. *Administrative Law and Politics: Cases and Comments*. Boston: Little Brown.

———. 1998. *Reason in Law*. 5th ed. New York: Longman.

Carter, Stephen. 1993. *The Culture of Disbelief: How American Law and Politics Trivialize Religious Devotion*. New York: Basic.

———. 1998. *The Dissent of the Governed: A Meditation on Law, Religion, and Loyalty*. Cambridge, MA: Harvard University Press.

Carty, Anthony, ed. 1990. *Post-modern Law*. Edinburgh, UK: Edinburgh University Press.

Chamallas, Martha. 1999. *Introduction to Feminist Legal Thought*. New York: Aspen Law & Business.

Chambliss, William J. 1967. "Types of Deviance and the Effectiveness of Legal Sanctions." *Wisconsin Law Review* (Summer): 703–714.

———. 1973a. *Sociological Readings in the Conflict Perspective*. Reading, MA: Addison-Wesley Publishing.

———. 1973b. "The Saints and the Roughnecks." *Society* 11: 24–31.

Chambliss, William J., and Robert Seidman. 1982. *Law, Order, and Power.* 2nd ed. Reading, MA: Addison-Wesley Publishing Co.

Chambliss, William J., and Marjorie Zatz. 1993. *Making Law: The State, the Law, and Structural Contradictions*. Bloomington, IN: Indiana University Press.

Chase, Anthony. 1997. *Law and History: The Evolution of the American Legal System*. New York: New Press.

Chavez, Lydia. 1998. *The Color Blind: The Battle to End Affirmative Action*. Berkeley, CA: University of California Press.

Chemerinsky, Erwin. 1985. "Pedagogy Without Purpose: An Essay on Professional Responsibility Courses and Casebooks." *ABF Research Journal* 189–199.

Chesney-Lind, Meda. 1978. "Judicial Paternalism and the Female Status Offender: Training Women to Know Their Place." Pp. 376–391, in Barry Krisberg and James Austin, eds. *The Children of Ishmael*. Palo Alto, CA: Mayfield Publishing Co.

Chi, Bonnie, and Emile Chi. 1979. "Crime and Punishment in China." *The New York Times Magazine* (October 7): 48–70.

Chiasson, Lloyd, Jr., ed. 1997. *The Press on Trial: Crimes and Trials as Media Events*. Westport, CT: Greenwood.

Childress, Steven Alan. 1991. "Reel Rape Speech: Violent Pornography and the Politics of Harm." *Law & Society Review* 25: 177–214.

Cimini, Joseph F. 1997. "Alternative Dispute Resolution in the Criminal Justice Process." *The Justice Professional* 10: 105–125.

Clarke, Stevens H., and Elizabeth Ellen Gordon. 1997. "Public Sponsorship of Private Settling: Court-Ordered Civil Case Mediation." *The Justice System Journal* 19: 311–339.

Clinard, Marshall B., and Peter C. Yeager. 1980. *Corporate Crime*. New York: Free Press.

Clinton, Robert L. 1997. *God and Man in the Law: The Foundations of Anglo-American Constitutionalism*. Lawrence, KS: University Press of Kansas.

Cloud, John. 1997. "Ivy League Gomorrah?" *Time* (September 22): 70.

———. 1999. "Law on Bended Knee." *Time* (September 13): 32–33.

Coase, Ronald. 1960. "The Problem of Social Cost." *Journal of Law and Economics* 3: 1–44.

Coblentz, Stanton A. 1970. *The Militant Dissenters*. New York: A. S. Barnes.

Cochran, Robert F., Jr. 1997. "Christian Perspectives on Law and Legal Scholarship."*Journal of Legal Education* 47: 1–18.

Cohen, Adam. 1999. "Meet the Mediator." *Time* (December 13): 72.

Cohen, Esther. 1986. "Law, Folklore and Animal Lore." *Past and Present* 110: 6–37.

Cohen, Felix. 1935. "Transcendental Nonsense and the Functional Approach." *Columbia Law Review* 35: 809–849.

Cohen, Marshall, ed. 1984. *Ronald Dworkin and Contemporary Jurisprudence*. Totowa, NJ: Rowman & Allenheld.

Cohen, Roger. 2000. "A European Identity: Nation-State Losing Ground." *The New York Times* (January 14): A3.

Cohen, Ronald L. 1986. *Justice: Views From the Social Sciences*. New York: Plenum.

Cohn, Ellen S., and Susan O. White. 1990. *Legal Socialization: A Study of Norms and Rules*. New York: Springer-Verlag.

———. 1997. "Legal Socialization Effects on Democratization." *International Social Science Journal* 152: 151–172.

Coleman, Jules L., and Brian Leiter. 1996. "Legal Positivism." Pp. 241–260, in Dennis Patterson, ed. *A Companion to Philosophy of Law and Legal Theory*. Cambridge, MA: Blackwell Publishers.

Collett, Teresa Stanton. 1999. "Authentic Pluralism: The Case for Including Religiously Affiliated Schools in Publicly-Funded Voucher Systems." *Focus on Law Studies* (Fall): 4, 6.

Collier, Jane F. 1994. "Intertwined Histories: Islamic Law and Western Imperialism." *Law & Society Review* 28: 395–408.

Comaroff, John. 1991. "Re-Marx on Repression and the Rule of Law." *Law & Social Inquiry* 15: 671–678.

Conley, John, and William M. O'Barr. 1990. *Rules Versus Relationships: The Ethnography of Legal Discourse*. Chicago: University of Chicago Press.

———. 1998. *Just Words: Law, Language, and Power.* Chicago: University of Chicago Press.

Connery, Donald S. 1977. *Guilty Until Proven Innocent*. New York: G. P. Putnam's Sons.

Conot, Robert. 1983. *Justice at Nuremberg*. New York: Harper & Row.

Constable, Marianne. 1994. *The Law of the Other: The Mixed Jury and Changing Conceptions of Citizenship, Law, and Knowledge*. Chicago: University of Chicago Press.

Conte, Alba. 1990. *Sexual Harassment in the Workplace: Law and Practice*. New York: Wiley Law Publications.

Cook, Kimberly J. 1998. *Divided Passions: Public Opinion on Abortion and the Death Penalty.* Boston: Northeastern University Press.

Cooter, R., and T. Ulen. 1987. *Law and Economics*. Glenview, IL: Scott, Foresman.

Cotterrell, Roger. 1986. *The Sociology of Law: An Introduction*. London: Butterworths.

———. 1989. *The Politics of Jurisprudence: A Critical Introduction to Legal Philosophy*. Philadelphia: University of Pennsylvania Press.

———. 1991. "The Durkheimian Tradition in the Sociology of Law." *Law & Society Review* 25: 923–945.

———. 1997. "The Concept of Legal Culture." Pp. 13–32, in David Nelken, ed. *Comparing Legal Cultures*. Aldershot, UK: Dartmouth.

———. 1998. "Why Must Legal Ideas Be Interpreted Sociologically?" *Journal of Law and Society* 25: 171–192.

Cotton, Samuel L. 1998. *Silent Terror: A Journey Into Contemporary African Slavery.* New York: Harlem River Press.

Cover, Robert M. 1983. "The Supreme Court 1982 Term—Foreword: *Nomos* and Narrative." *Harvard Law Review* 97: 4–68.

———. 1986. "Violence and the Word." *Yale Law Review* 95: 1601–1629.

Cox, Archibald. 1978. *The Role of the Supreme Court in American Government*. London: Oxford University Press.

Cramton, Roger. 1978. "The Ordinary Religion of the Law School Classroom." *Journal of Legal Education* 34: 155–167.

Crank, John P. 1994. "Watchman and Community: Myth and Institutionalization in Policing." *Law & Society Review* 28: 325–351.

Crenshaw, Kimberle. 1989. "Demarginalizing the Intersection of Race and Sex: A Black Feminist Critique of Antidiscrimination Doctrine, Feminist

Theory and Antiracist Doctrine." *University of Chicago Legal Forum* 189: 139–142.

Crocker, David A. 1998. "Transitional Justice and International Civil Society: Toward a Normative Framework." *Constellations* 5: 492–517.

Crosette, Barbara. 1999. "Testing the Limits of Tolerance as Cultures Mix." *The New York Times* (March 6): B9.

Current Biography. 1993. "Richard Posner." Pp. 471–474, in J. Graham, ed. *Current Biography*. New York: H. W. Wilson.

———. 1994. "Catharine MacKinnon." Pp. 364–367, in J. Graham, ed. *Current Biography*. New York: H. W. Wilson.

Custer, Lawrence B. 1986. "Ordeal by Touch." *American Heritage* (April/May): 93–97.

Dalton, Harlon L., Scott Burris, and the New York AIDS Law Project. 1987. *AIDS and the Law: A Guide for the Public*. New Haven, CT: Yale University Press.

D'Amato, Anthony. 1984. *Jurisprudence: A Descriptive and Normative Analysis of Law*. Boston: Martinus Nijhoff.

———. 1987. *International Law: Process and Prospect*. Dobbs Ferry, NY: Transactional Publishers.

Daniels, Cynthia R. 1993. *At Women's Expense: State Power and the Politics of Fetal Rights*. Cambridge, MA: Harvard University Press.

Davies, Peter. 1973. *The Truth About Kent State*. New York: Farrar Straus Giroux.

Davis, D. M. 1986. "Political Trials and Civil Liberties in South Africa." *Natal University Law and Society Review* 1: 87–98.

Davis, F. James. 1962. "Law as a Type of Social Control." Pp. 39–61, in F. James Davis, Henry H. Foster, Jr., C. Ray Jeffery, and E. Eugene Davis. *Society and the Law: New Meanings for an Old Profession*. New York: Free Press.

Davis, John. 1974. "Justification for No Obligation: Views of Black Males Toward Crime and the Criminal Law." *Issues in Criminology* 9: 69–87.

Deakin, Simon. 1996. "Law and Economics." Pp. 106–134, in Philip A. Thomas, ed. *Legal Frontiers*. Aldershot, UK: Dartmouth Publishing Co.

Dear, John. 1997. *Apostle of Peace: Essays in Honor of Daniel Berrigan*. Maryknoll, NY: Orbis Books.

deGrazia, Edward. 1992. *Girls Lean Back Everywhere: The Law of Obscenity and the Assault on Genius*. New York: Random House.

Delgado, Richard. 1989. "Storytelling for Oppositionists and Others: A Plea for Narrative." *Michigan Law Review* 87: 2411–2441.

Delgado, Richard, ed. 1995. *Critical Race Theory: The Cutting Edge*. Philadelphia: Temple University Press.

Delgado, Richard, and Jean Stefanic. 1994. *Failed Revolutions: Social Reform and the Limits of Legal Imagination*. Boulder, CO: Westview Press.

DePalma, Anthony. 1992. "Court Grants Boy Wish to Select His Parents." *The New York Times* (September 26): A1.

———. 1997. "Murderer's Sex Tapes Put Canadian Lawyer at Risk." *The New York Times* (February 24): A4.

d'Errico, Peter. 1975. "The Law Is Terror Put Into Words." *Learning and the Law*. Chicago: American Bar Association.

Dershowitz, Alan M. 1994. *The Abuse Excuse*. Boston: Little Brown & Co.

Dery, George M., III. 1999. "Mouse Hunting With an Elephant Gun: The Supreme Court's Overkill in Upholding a Categorical Rejection to Polygraph Evidence in *United States v. Scheffer." American Journal of Criminal Law* 26: 227–256.

Dezalay, Yves, and Bryant Garth. 1996. *Dealing in Virtue: International Commercial Arbitration and the Construction of a Transnational Legal Order.* Chicago: University of Chicago Press.

Diamond, Stanley. 1973. "The Rule of Law Versus the Order of Custom." Pp. 318–343, in Donald Black and Maureen Mileski, eds. *The Social Organization of Law.* New York: Seminar Press.

DiChiari, Albert, and John F. Galliher. 1994. "Dissonance and Contradictions in the Origins of Marijuana Decriminalization." *Law & Society Review* 28: 41–77.

Dickstein, Morris, ed. 1999. *The Revival of Pragmatism: New Essays on Social Thought, Law, and Culture.* Durham, NC: Duke University Press.

DiFonzo, J. Herbie. 1997. *Beneath the Fault Line: The Popular and Legal Culture of Divorce in Twentieth Century America.* Charlottesville: University Press of Virginia.

Dixon, Jo. 1995. "The Nexus of Sex, Spousal Violence, and the State." *Law & Society Review* 29: 359–376.

Dixon, Jo, and Carroll Seron. 1995. "Stratification in the Legal Profession: Sex, Sector, and Salary." *Law & Society Review* 29: 381–412.

Dlamini, C. R. M. 1988. "The Influence of Race on the Administration of Justice." *South African Journal of Human Rights* 4: 37–54.

Dolgin, Janet L. 1997. *Defining the Family: Law, Technology and Reproduction in an Uneasy Age.* New York: New York University Press.

Donohue, John J. 1988. "Law and Economics: The Road Not Taken." *Law & Society Review* 22: 903–929.

Douglas, William O. 1974. *Go East, Young Man: The Early Years.* New York: Random House.

———. 1980. *The Court Years: 1939–1975.* New York: Random House.

Douzinas, Costas, Ronnie Warrington, and Shaun McVeigh. 1991. *Postmodern Jurisprudence.* London, UK: Routledge.

Downie, Leonard, Jr. 1971. *Justice Denied: The Case for Reform of the Courts.* Baltimore: Penguin.

Downs, Donald Alexander. 1996. *More Than Victims: Battered Women, the Syndrome Society, and the Law.* Chicago: University of Chicago Press.

Drachman, Virginia G. 1998. *Sisters in Law: Women Lawyers in Modern American History.* Cambridge, MA: Harvard University Press.

Dubnoff, Caren. 1999. "The Inclusion of Religious Schools in Public Voucher Systems Is Unconstitutional." *Focus on Law Studies* (Fall): 5, 6.

Dubois, Ellen Carol. 1998. *Women's Suffrage and Women's Rights.* New York: New York University Press.

Duffy, Helen. 1999. "Toward Eradicating Impunity: The Establishment of an International Criminal Court." *Social Justice* 26: 115–124.

Dugger, Celia W. 1996. "Tug of Taboos: African Genital Rite vs. U.S. Law." *The New York Times* (December 28): A1.

Dunne, Timothy, and Nicholas J. Wheeler, eds. 1999. *Human Rights in Global Politics.* New York: Cambridge University Press.

Durkheim, Emile. [1893] 1984. *The Division of Labor in Society.* New York: The Free Press.

———. [1897] 1951. *Suicide*. New York: Free Press.

Dusky, Lorraine. 1996. *Still Unequal: The Shameful Truth About Women and Justice in America*. New York: Crown Publishers, Inc.

Duxbury, Neil. 1995. *Patterns of American Jurisprudence*. Oxford: Oxford University Press.

Dworkin, Gerald, R. G. Frey, and Sissela Bok. 1998. *Euthanasia and Physician-Assisted Suicide*. Cambridge, UK: Cambridge University Press.

Dworkin, Ronald. 1977. *Taking Rights Seriously*. Cambridge, MA: Harvard University Press.

———. 1985. *A Matter of Principle*. Cambridge, MA: Harvard University Press.

———. 1986. *Law's Empire*. Cambridge, MA: Harvard University Press.

———. 1993. *Life's Dominion*. New York: Alfred A. Knopf.

———. 1996. *Freedom's Law*. Cambridge, MA: Harvard University Press.

Edelman, Peter. 1997. "The Worst Thing Bill Clinton Has Done." *The Atlantic Monthly* (March): 43–58.

Edwards, Harry T. 1986. "Alternative Dispute Resolution: Panacea or Anathema?" *Harvard Law Review* 99: 668–684.

Egan, Timothy. 1998a. "New Prosperity Brings New Conflict in Indian Country." *The New York Times* (March 8): A1.

———. 1998b. "Backlash Growing as Indians Make a Stand for Sovereignty." *The New York Times* (March 9): A1.

Ehrlich, Eugen. [1913] 1936. *Fundamental Principles of the Sociology of Law*. New York: Russel & Russel.

———. 1922. "The Sociology of Law." *Harvard Law Review* 36: 130–145.

Ehrlich, J. W. 1959. *Ehrlich's Blackstone*. New York: Capricorn.

Eisen, A. 1978. "The Meanings and Confusions of Weberian Rationality." *British Journal of Sociology* 29: 57–69.

Eisenstein, James, Roy B. Flemming, and Peter F. Nardulli. 1999. *The Contours of Justice: Communities and Their Courts*. Lanham, MD: University Press of America.

Elikann, Peter T. 1996. *The Tough-on-Crime Myth*. New York: Plenum Press.

Elkins, James R. 1979. "The Paradox of a Life in Law." *University of Pittsburgh Law Review* 40: 129–168.

———. 1985a. "On the Emergence of Narrative Jurisprudence: The Humanistic Perspective Finds a New Path." *Legal Studies Forum* 9: 123–156.

———. 1985b. "Ethics: Professionalism, Craft, and Failure." *Kentucky Law Journal* 73: 937–965.

———. 1985c. "The Pedagogy of Ethics." *The Journal of the Legal Profession* 10: 37–83.

Elkins, James, ed. 1990. "Pedagogy of Narrative: A Symposium." *Journal of Legal Education* 40: 1–250.

Ellickson, Robert C. 1991. *Order Without Law: How Neighbors Settle Disputes*. Cambridge, MA: Harvard University Press.

Elliott, Dorinda. 1996. "A Land Without Lawyers: But Not Enough Law." *Newsweek* (April 1): 50.

Ellis, Kate, Nan D. Hunter, Beth Jaker, Barbara O'Dair, and Abby Tallmer, eds. 1986. *Caught Looking: Feminism, Pornography, and Censorship*. New York: The Real Comet Press.

Ellmann, Stephen. 1995. "Law and Legitimacy in South Africa." *Law & Social Inquiry* 20: 407–479.

Elshtain, Jean Bethke. 1995. *Democracies on Trial*. New York: Basic.

Ely, John Hart. 1990. "The American War in Indochina, Part I: The (Troubled) Constitutionality of the War They Told Us About." *Stanford Law Review* 42: 877–926.

Emmelman, Debra S. 1996. "Trial by Plea Bargain: Case Settlement as a Product of Recursive Decision-Making." *Law & Society Review* 30: 335–360.

Engel, David M., and Frank W. Munger. 1996. "Rights, Remembrance, and the Reconciliation of Difference." *Law & Society Review* 30: 7–53.

Epstein, Cynthia. 1993. *Women in Law*. 2nd ed. Urbana, IL: University of Illinois Press.

Epstein, Lee, and Joseph F. Kobylka. 1992. *The Supreme Court and Legal Change: Abortion and the Death Penalty.* Chapel Hill, NC: University of North Carolina Press.

Erickson, Nancy S., and Nadine Taub. 1990. "Final Report: Sex Bias in the Teaching of Criminal Law." *Rutgers Law Review* 42: 312–608.

Ericson, Richard V. 1996. "Why Law Is Like News." Pp. 195–230, in David Nelken, ed. *Law as Communication*. Aldershot, UK: Dartmouth.

Ericson, Richard V., Patricia M. Baranek, and Janet B. L. Chan. 1991. *Representing Order, Crime, Law, and Justice in the News Media*. Toronto: University of Toronto Press.

Erikson, Kai T. 1966. *Wayward Puritans: A Study in the Sociology of Deviance.* New York: John Wiley & Sons.

Erlanger, Howard S., Mia Cahill, Charles R. Epp, and Kathleen M. Haines. 1996. "Law Student Idealism and Job Choice: Some New Data on an Old Question." *Law & Society Review* 30: 851–864.

Erlanger, Steven. 1992. "Two Novelties in Russian Courts: Defense Lawyers and Jury Trials." *The New York Times* (May 1): A1, A8.

Eskridge, Chris W. 1996. *Criminal Justice: Concepts and Issues.* Los Angeles, CA: Roxbury Publishing Co.

Eskridge, William N., Jr. 1994. *Dynamic Statutory Interpretation*. Cambridge, MA: Harvard University Press.

———. 1999. *Gaylaw: Challenging the Apartheid of the Closet.* Cambridge, MA: Harvard University Press.

Estrich, Susan. 1986. "Rape." *The Yale Law Journal* 95: 1087–1184.

———. 1987. *Real Rape*. Cambridge, MA: Harvard University Press.

———. 1998. *Getting Away With Murder: How Politics Is Destroying the Criminal Justice System*. Cambridge, MA: Harvard University Press.

Etzioni, Amitai. 1968. *The Active Society.* New York: The Free Press.

———. 1996a. "The Responsive Community: A Communitarian Perspective." *American Sociological Review* 61: 1–11.

———. 1996b. "The Attack on Community: The Grooved Debate." *Society* 32: 12–17.

Evan, William M. 1965. "Law as an Instrument of Social Change." Pp. 285–293, in Alvin W. Gouldner and S. M. Miller, eds. *Applied Sociology: Opportunities and Problems*. New York: The Free Press.

———. 1980. *The Sociology of Law: A Social–Structural Perspective*. New York: The Free Press.

———. 1990. *Social Structure and Law: Theoretical and Empirical Perspectives*. Newbury Park, CA: Sage.

Evans, Tony, ed. 1998. *Human Rights Fifty Years Ago: A Reappraisal*. Manchester, UK: Manchester University Press.

Ewick, Patricia, Robert A. Kagan, and Austin Sarat, eds. 1999. *Social Science, Social Policy, and the Law*. New York: Russell Sage Foundation.

Ewick, Patricia, and Susan S. Silbey. 1992. "Conformity, Contestation, and Resistance: An Account of Legal Consciousness." *New England Law Review* 3: 731–749.

———. 1995. "Subversive Stories and Hegemonic Tales: Toward a Sociology of Narrative." *Law & Society Review* 29: 197–226.

———. 1998. *The Common Place of Law: Stories From Everyday Life*. Chicago: University of Chicago Press.

Ewing, Sally. 1987. "Formal Justice and the Spirit of Capitalism: Max Weber's Sociology of Law." *Law & Society Review* 21: 487–512.

Faigman, David L., David H. Kaye, Michael J. Saks, and Joseph Sanders. 1997. *Modern Scientific Evidence: The Law and Science of Expert Testimony*. Volumes I & II. St. Paul, MN: West.

Falk, Richard A. 1971. "The Question of War Crimes: A Statement of Perspective." Pp. 3–10, in Richard A. Falk, Gabriel Kolko, and Robert Jay Lifton, eds. *Crimes of War*. New York: Vintage Books.

Falk, Richard A., Gabriel Kolko, and Robert J. Lifton, eds. 1971. *Crimes of War*. New York: Vintage Books.

Fanon, Frantz. 1968. *The Wretched of the Earth*. New York: Grove Press.

Farber, Daniel A., and Suzanna Sherry. 1997. *Beyond All Reason: The Radical Assault on Truth in American Law*. New York: Oxford University Press.

Fay, E. Stewart. 1937. *Hanged by a Comma*. London: Lovat Dickson.

Feeley, Malcolm M., and Edward L. Rubin. 1998. *Judicial Policy Making and the Modern State: How the Courts Reformed America's Prisons*. New York: Cambridge University Press.

Feibleman, James. 1985. *Justice, Law and Culture*. Boston: Martinus Nijhoff.

Feiler, Stephen M., and Joseph F. Sheley. 1999. "Legal and Racial Elements of Public Willingness to Transfer Juvenile Offenders to Adult Court." *Journal of Criminal Justice* 27: 55–64.

Feinberg, Joel, and Hyman Gross. 1977. *Justice: Selected Readings*. Princeton, NJ: Princeton University Press.

Feld, Barry C. 1999. *Bad Kids: Race and the Transformation of the Juvenile Court*. New York: Oxford University Press.

Felstiner, William. 1998. "Justice, Power, and Lawyers." Pp. 55–79, in Bryant G. Garth and Austin Sarat, eds. *Justice and Power in Sociolegal Studies*. Chicago: Northwestern University Press.

Felstiner, William, Richard L. Abel, and Austin Sarat. 1989. "The Emergence and Transformation of Disputes: Naming, Blaming, and Claiming." Pp. 468–470, in J. Bonsignore et al., *Before the Law*. 4th ed. Dallas: Houghton Mifflin.

Felstiner, William, and Austin Sarat. 1995. *Divorce Lawyers and Their Clients: Power and Meaning in the Legal Process*. New York: Oxford University Press.

Ferguson, Robert A. 1984. *Law and Letters in American Culture*. Cambridge, MA: Harvard University Press.

Fields, Charles B., and Richter H. Moore Jr. 1996. *Comparative Criminal Justice*. Prospect Heights, IL: Waveland Press.

Finder, Alan. 1999. "Drive Drunk, Lose the Car? Law Principle Faces a Test." *The New York Times* (February 24): B1.

Findlay, Mark. 1989. "Show Trials in China: After Tiananmen Square." *Journal of Law and Society* 16: 352–359.

Finnis, John. 1980. *Natural Law and Natural Rights*. Oxford, UK: Clarendon Press.

Fish, Stanley. 1997. "Mission Impossible: Settling the Just Bounds Between Church and State."*Columbia Law Review* 97: 2255–2333.

Fiske, Edward. 1983. "President of Harvard Brands Legal System Costly and Complex." *The New York Times* (April 22): A1.

Fiss, Owen. 1984. "Against Settlement." *Yale Law Review* 93: 1073–1090.

———. 1986. "The Death of Law?" *Cornell Law Review* 72: 1–16.

Fitzpatrick, Peter. 1992a. *The Mythology of Modern Law*. New York: Routledge.

———. 1992b. "The Impossibility of Popular Justice." *Social & Legal Studies* 1: 199–215.

Flaherty, Julie. 1999. "14-Hour Days? Some Lawyers Say No." *The New York Times* (October 6): G1.

Fleming, John. 1967. *An Introduction to the Law of Torts*. Oxford: Clarendon Press.

Fleming, Macklin. 1997. *Lawyers, Money, and Success: The Consequences of Dollar Obsession*. Westport, CT: Greenwood Publishing Group.

Fletcher, George P. 1996. *Basic Concepts of Legal Thought*. New York: Oxford University Press.

Flood, John. 1985. *The Legal Profession in the United States*. 3rd ed. Chicago: American Bar Foundation.

———. 1991. "Doing Business: The Management of Uncertainty in Lawyers' Work." *Law & Society Review* 25: 41–71.

———. 1994. "Shark Tanks, Sweatshops, and the Lawyer as Hero? Fact as Fiction." *Journal of Law and Society* 21: 396–405.

Fluehr-Lobban, Carolyn. 1987. "Islamization of Law in the Sudan." *Legal Studies Forum* 11: 189–204.

Footlick, Jerrold. 1977. "Too Much Law?" *Newsweek* (January 10): 42–47.

———. 1978. "Lawyers on Trial." *Newsweek* (December 11): 98–100.

Foster, D. H., D. Sandler, and D. M. Davis. 1987. "Detention, Torture and the Criminal Justice Process in South Africa." *International Journal of the Sociology of Law* 15: 105–120.

Foster, Kenneth R., and Peter W. Huber. 1997. *Judging Science: Scientific Knowledge and the Federal Courts*. Cambridge, MA: MIT Press.

Foucault, Michel. 1977. *Discipline and Punish: The Birth of the Prison*. New York: Vintage Books.

Frank, Jerome. 1930. *Law and the Modern Mind*. Garden City, NY: Anchor.

———. 1949. *Courts on Trial*. Princeton, NJ: Princeton University Press.

Frank, Nancy, and Michael Lombness. 1988. *Controlling Corporate Illegality*. Cincinnati, OH: Anderson.

Franke, Ann H. 1998. "The Message From the Supreme Court: Clarify Sexual-Harassment Policies." *Chronicle of Higher Education* (July 17): B6–7.

Frankford, David M. 1995. "Social Structure of Right and Wrong: Normativity Without Agents." *Law and Social Inquiry* 20: 787–828.

Freedman, Jonathan. 1975. "Running the Red." *New York* (November 17): 117–119.

Freeland, Richard. 1997. "Islamic Law: An Introduction." *New Law Journal* (June 13): 893–896.

Freeman, Michael. 1996. *Children's Rights: A Comparative Perspective*. Aldershot, UK: Dartmouth.

French, Howard W. 1999. "Japan's Troubling Trend: Rising Teenage Crime." *The New York Times* (October 12): A6.

Freund, Paul A. 1961. *The Supreme Court of the United States*. Cleveland, OH: World Publishing.

Fried, Joseph P. 1999. "Gun Marketing Is Issue in Trial Against Makers." *The New York Times* (January 6): A1.

———. 2000. "Paralegals: Occupation Is New Top in Growth." *The New York Times* (March 12): 46.

Friedman, Lawrence M. [1973] 1986. *A History of American Law*. New York: Simon and Schuster.

———. 1975. *The Legal System*. New York: Russell Sage.

———. 1977. *Law and Society: An Introduction*. Englewood Cliffs, NJ: Prentice Hall.

———. 1984. "Two Faces of Law." *Wisconsin Law Review* 1984: 13–34.

———. 1985. *Total Justice*. New York: Russell Sage Foundation.

———. 1986. "The Law and Society Movement." *Stanford Law Review* 38: 763–780.

———. 1990. *The Republic of Choice: Law, Authority, and Culture*. Cambridge, MA: Harvard University Press.

———. 1992. "I Hear a Cacophony: Herzog and *The Republic of Choice*." *Law & Social Inquiry* 17: 159–166.

———. 1993. *Crime and Punishment in American History*. New York: Basic.

———. 1996a. "Borders: On the Emerging Sociology of Transnational Law." *Stanford Journal of International Law* 32: 65–90.

———. 1996b. "Are We a Litigious People?" Pp. 53–78, in L. M. Friedman and H. N. Scheiber, eds. *Legal Culture and the Legal Profession*. Boulder, CO: Westview Press.

———. 1997. "The Concept of Legal Culture: A Reply." Pp. 33–40, in David Nelken, ed. *Comparing Legal Cultures*. Aldershot, UK: Dartmouth.

———. 1998a. *American Law: An Introduction*. 2nd ed. New York: W. W. Norton & Co.

———. 1998b. "Law Reviews and Legal Scholarship: Some Comments." *Denver University Law Review* 75: 661–668.

Friedman, Lawrence M., and George Fisher, eds. 1997. *The Crime Conundrum: Essays on Criminal Justice*. Boulder, CO: Westview Press.

Friedman, Lawrence M., and Stewart Macaulay. 1969. *Law and the Behavioral Sciences*. Indianapolis, IN: Bobbs-Merrill.

Friedman, Lawrence M., and Harry Scheiber. 1996. *Legal Culture and the Legal Profession*. Boulder, CO: Westview Press.

Friedmann, W. 1972. *Law in a Changing Society*. 2nd ed. New York: Columbia University Press.

Friedrich, Carl J. 1963. *The Philosophy of Law in Historical Perspective*. 2nd ed. Chicago: University of Chicago Press.

Friedrichs, David O. 1979. "The Law and the Legitimacy Crisis: A Critical Issue for Criminal Justice." Pp. 290–311, in R. G. Iacovetta and Dae H. Chang, eds. *Critical Issues in Criminal Justice*. Durham, NC: Carolina Academic Press.

———. 1980. "The Legitimacy Crisis in the United States: A Conceptual Analysis." *Social Problems* 27: 540–555.

———. 1981. "The Problem of Reconciling Divergent Perspectives on Urban Crime: Personal Experience, Social Ideology, and Scholarly Research." *Qualitative Sociology* 4: 217–228.

———. 1986a. "Critical Legal Studies and the Critique of Criminal Justice." *Criminal Justice Review* 11: 15–22.

———. 1986b. "The Concept of Legitimation and the Legal Order: A Response to Hyde's Critique." *Justice Quarterly* 3: 33–50.

———. 1990a. "Narrative Jurisprudence and Other Heresies: Legal Education at the Margin." *Journal of Legal Education* 40: 3–18.

———. 1990b. "Law in South Africa and the Legitimacy Crisis." *International Journal of Comparative and Applied Criminal Justice* 14: 189–199.

———. 1996. *Trusted Criminals: White Collar Crime in Contemporary Society*. Belmont, CA: ITP/Wadsworth Publishing Co.

Friend, Tad. 1995. "The Untouchables." *The New York Times Magazine* (October 16): 27; 101.

Fuller, John R. 1998. *Criminal Justice: A Peacemaking Perspective*. Boston: Allyn & Bacon.

Fuller, Lon L. 1940. *The Law in Quest of Itself*. Boston: Beacon Press.

———. 1967. *Legal Fictions*. Stanford, CA: Stanford University Press.

———. 1968. *Anatomy of the Law*. New York: New American Library.

———. 1969. *The Morality of Law*. New Haven: Yale University Press.

———. 1981. *The Principles of Social Order*. Durham, NC: Duke University Press.

Gagne, Patricia. 1998. *Battered Women's Justice: The Movement for Clemency and the Politics of Self-Defense*. New York: Twayne Publishers.

Galanter, Marc. 1974. "Why the Haves Come Out Ahead: Speculations on the Limits of Legal Change." *Law & Society Review* 9: 95–160.

———. 1985. "The Legal Malaise; or, Justice Observed." *Law & Society Review* 19: 537–556.

Galanter, Marc, Bryant Garth, Deborah Hensler, and Frances Kahn Zemans. 1994. "How to Improve Civil Justice Policy." *Judicature* 77: 185; 229–230.

Galanter, Marc, and Thomas M. Palay. 1991. *Tournament of Lawyers: The Transformation of the Big Law Firms*. Chicago: University of Chicago Press.

Garth, Bryant, and Austin Sarat, eds. 1998a. *Justice and Power in Sociolegal Studies*. Chicago: Northwestern University Press.

———. 1998b. *How Does Law Matter?* Chicago: Northwestern University Press.

Garth, Bryant, and Joyce Sterling. 1998. "From Legal Realism to Law & Society: Reshaping Law for the Last Stages of the Social Activist Stage." *Law & Society Review* 32: 409–472.

Gatrell, V., B. Lenham, and G. Parker. 1980. *Crime and the Law: The Social History of Crime in Western Europe Since 1500*. London: Europa.

Gaubatz, Kathlyn Taylor. 1995. *Crime in the Public Mind*. Ann Arbor: University of Michigan Press.

Gaylin, Willard. 1974. *Partial Justice: A Study of Bias in Sentencing*. New York: Vintage.

Gaylord, Mark S., and Paul Levine. 1997. "The Criminalization of Official Profiteering: Law-Making in the People's Republic of China." *International Journal of the Sociology of Law* 25: 117–134.

Geis, Gilbert. 1964. "Sociology and Sociological Jurisprudence: Admixtures of Lore and Law." *Kentucky Law Journal* 52: 267–293.

George, Robert P. 1996. *The Autonomy of Law: Essays on Legal Positivism*. Oxford: Clarendon Press.

———. 1999. *In Defense of Natural Law*. New York: Oxford University Press.

Geraghty, Thomas F., and Steven A. Drizin, eds. 1997. "Symposium on the Future of the Juvenile Court." *Journal of Criminal Law & Criminology* 88: 1–241.

Gessner, Volkmar, and John M. Thomas. 1988. "Sociolegal Research and Policy Studies: A Review of the Issues." *Law & Policy* 10: 85–95.

Gibbs, Jack P. 1989. *Control: Sociology's Central Notion*. Champaign, IL: University of Illinois Press.

Gibbs, Jewelle Taylor. 1996. *Race and Justice: Rodney King and O. J. Simpson in a House Divided*. San Francisco: Jossey-Bass.

Gibson, James L. 1989. "Understandings of Justice: Institutional Legitimacy, Procedural Justice, and Political Tolerance." *Law & Society Review* 25: 469–496.

———. 1991. "Institutional Legitimacy, Procedural Justice, and Compliance with Supreme Court Decisions: A Question of Causality." *Law & Society Review* 25: 631–635.

Gibson, James L., and Gregory A. Caldeira. 1996. "The Legal Culture of Europe." *Law & Society Review* 30: 55–85.

Gibson, James L., and Amanda Gouws. 1997. "Support for the Rule of Law in the Emerging South African Democracy." *International Social Science Journal* 152: 173–193.

Giles, Robert, and Robert W. Snyder, eds. 1999. *Governing the Courts: Free Press, Fair Trials, and Journalistic Performance*. New Brunswick, NJ: Transaction Publishers.

Gillespie, Cynthia K. 1989. *Justifiable Homicide: Battered Women, Self-Defense, and the Law*. Columbus, OH: Ohio State University Press.

Gilligan, Carol. 1982. *In a Different Voice*. Cambridge, MA: Harvard University Press.

Gilmore, Grant. 1977. *The Ages of American Law*. New Haven: Yale University Press.

Gitlin, Todd. 1987. *The Sixties: Years of Hope, Days of Rage*. New York: Bantam.

Glaberson, William. 1998a. "A Law School Where Jesus Is the Ultimate Case Study." *The New York Times* (November 25): A1.

———. 1998b. "In a Judicial 'What If,' Indians Revisit a Case." *The New York Times* (October 26): A12.

Gleick, James. 2000. "Patently Absurd." *The New York Times* (March 12): 44–49.

Glendon, Mary Ann. 1991. *Rights Talk: The Impoverishment of Political Discourse*. New York: Free Press.

———. 1994. *A Nation Under Lawyers: How the Crisis in the Legal Profession is Transforming American Society*. New York: Farrar, Straus and Giroux.

Godwin, Mike. 1998. *Cyber Rights: Defending Free Speech in the Digital Age*. New York: Random House.

Gold, E. Richard. 1996. *Body Parts: Property Rights and the Ownership of Human Biological Materials*. Washington, DC: Georgetown University Press.

Goldberg, Carey. 1998. "Vermont Court Takes Up Gay Marriage." *The New York Times* (November 19): A20.

———. 1999. "Redefining a Marriage Made New in Vermont." *The New York Times* (December 12): 4/3.

Goldberg, Stephanie. 1992. "The Law, a New Theory Holds, Has a White Voice." *The New York Times* (July 17): A23.

Goldberg, Steven. 1994. *Culture Clash: Law and Science in America*. New York: New York University Press.

Goldberg-Ambrose, Carole. 1994. "Of Native Americans and Tribal Members: The Impact of Law on Indian Group Life." *Law & Society Review* 28: 1123–1143.

Goldfarb, Ronald. 1998. *TV or Not TV: Television, Justice, and the Courts*. New York: New York University Press.

Golding, Martin P., ed. 1966. *The Nature of Law: Readings in Legal Philosophy*. New York: Random House.

———. 1975. *Philosophy of Law*. Englewood Cliffs, NJ: Prentice Hall.

———. 1986. "Jurisprudence and Legal Philosophy in Twentieth Century America: Major Trends and Developments." *Journal of Legal Education* 36: 441–480.

Goldman, Sheldon, and Thomas P. Jahnige. 1971. *The Federal Courts as a Political System*. New York: Harper & Row.

Goldstein, L. 1992. *Feminist Jurisprudence: The Difference Debate*. Lanham, MD: Rowman & Littlefield.

Goldstein, Robert J. 1996. *Burning the Flag: The Great 1989–1990 American Flag Desecration*. Kent, OH: Kent State University Press.

Goode, Erich. 1997. *Deviant Behavior.* 5th ed. Upper Saddle River, NJ: Prentice Hall.

———. 1998. "Strange Bedfellows: Ideology, Politics, and Drug Legalization." *Society* (May/June): 17–27.

Goodman, Robert. 1996. *The Luck Business: The Devastating Consequences and Broken Promises of America's Gambling Explosion*. New York: The Free Press.

Gordon, Diane. 1994. *The Return of the Dangerous Classes: Drug Prohibition and Policy Politics*. New York: W. W. Norton.

Gordon, Robert. 1985. "Letter." *Journal of Legal Education* 35: 1–9, 13–16.

Gose, Ben. 1996. "Brown University's Handling of Date-Rape Case Leaves Many Questioning Campus Policies." *The Chronicle of Higher Education* (October 11): A53–A54.

———. 1998. "Some Colleges Extend Their Codes of Conduct to Off-Campus Behavior." *The Chronicle of Higher Education* (October 8): A51–A52.

Gottfredson, Michael, and Michael Hindelang. 1979. "A Study of *The Behavior of Law*." *American Sociological Review* 44: 3–18.

Gouldner, Alvin W. 1966. *Enter Plato*. Part II. New York: Harper Torchbooks.

Grace, Clive, and Philip Wilkinson. 1978. *Sociological Inquiry and Legal Phenomena*. New York: St. Martin's Press.

Graglia, Lino A. 1976. *Disaster by Decree: The Supreme Court Decisions on Race and the Schools*. Ithaca, NY: Cornell University Press.

Graham, Fred P. 1970. *The Due Process Revolution: The Warren Court's Impact on Criminal Law*. New York: Hayden Book Co.

Graham, Hugh David, and Ted Robert Gurr. 1969. *Violence in America: Historical and Comparative Perspectives*. New York: New American Library.

Granfield, Robert. 1992. *Making Elite Lawyers: Visions of Law at Harvard and Beyond*. New York: Routledge, Chapman and Hall.

Green, Mark J. 1978. *The Other Government: The Unseen Power of Washington Lawyers*. Rev. ed. New York: W. W. Norton & Co.

Greenberg, David F. 1983. "Donald Black's Sociology of Law: A Critique." *Law & Society Review* 17: 337–368.

Greenberg, Martin S., and R. Barry Ruback. 1982. *Social Psychology of the Criminal Justice System*. Monterey, CA: Brooks/Cole.

Greenberg, S. 1987. *Legitimating the Illegitimate*. Berkeley, CA: University of California Press.

Greene, Jack R., and Stephen D. Mastrofski, eds. 1988. *Community Policing: Rhetoric or Reality*. New York: Praeger.

Greene, Kathanne W. 1989. *Affirmative Action and Principles of Justice*. New York: Greenwood Press.

Greenfield, Steve, and Guy Osborn. 1995. "Where Cultures Collide: The Characterization of Law and Lawyers in Film." *International Journal of the Sociology of Law* 23: 107–130.

Greenhouse, Carol J. 1988. "Courting Difference: Issues of Interpretation and Comparison in the Study of Legal Ideologies." *Law & Society Review* 22: 687–707.

Greenhouse, Linda. 1999a. "47% in Poll View Legal System as Unfair to Poor and Minorities." *The New York Times* (February 24): A12.

———. 1999b. "States Are Given New Legal Shield by Supreme Court." *The New York Times* (June 24): A1.

———. 1999c. "Cases Give Court Chances to Define Church and State." *The New York Times* (September 19): A1.

———. 2000a. "Supreme Court Shields States From Lawsuits on Age Bias." *The New York Times* (January 12): A1.

———. 2000b. "Weighing Restrictions on Legal Aid for Poor." *The New York Times* (April 4): A20.

———. 2000c. "Women Lose Right to Sue Attackers in Federal Court." *The New York Times* (May 16): A1.

———. 2000d. "Justices Reaffirm Miranda Rule, 7–2; A Part of Culture." *The New York Times* (June 27): A1.

Greenstein, Robert. 1991. "Relieving Poverty: An Alternative View." *The Brookings Review* (Summer): 34–35.

Grey, Thomas C. 1983. "Langdell's Orthodoxy." *University of Pittsburgh Law Review* 45: 1–53.

———. 1996. "Modern American Legal Thought." *The Yale Law Journal* 106: 493–517.

Griffiths, John. 1986. "What Is Legal Pluralism?" *Journal of Legal Pluralism* 24: 1–55.

Grilliot, Harold J. 1979. *Introduction to Law and the Legal System*. 2nd ed. Boston: Houghton Mifflin.

Gross, Edward. 1998. "Lawyers and Their Discontents." *Society* (November/December): 26–31.

Gross, Hyman. 1979. *A Theory of Criminal Justice*. New York: Oxford University Press.

Gross, Jane. 1993. "A Killer in Law School: Admirable or Abominable?" *The New York Times* (September 13): A14.

Gross, Joseph J. 1991. "Marital Rape—A Crime? A Comparative Law Study of the Laws of the United States and the State of Israel." *International Journal of Comparative and Applied Criminal Justice* 15: 207–216.

Guest, Stephen. 1997. *Ronald Dworkin*. 2nd ed. Edinburgh, UK: Edinburgh University Press.

Guinier, Lani, Michelle Fine, and Jane Balin. 1997. *Becoming Gentlemen: Women, Law School, and Institutional Change*. Boston, MA: Beacon Press.

Gunningham, Neal. 1987. "Negotiated Non-Compliance: A Case Study of Regulatory Failure." *Law & Policy* 9: 69–93.

Gusfield, Joseph R. 1963. *Symbolic Crusade: Status Politics and the American Temperance Movement*. Urbana, IL: University of Illinois Press.

———. 1996. *Contested Meanings: The Construction of Alcohol Problems*. Madison: University of Wisconsin Press.

Haar, Charles M. 1965. *The Golden Age of American Law*. New York: George Braziller.

Habermas, Jurgen. 1970. *Legitimation Crisis*. Boston: Beacon Press.

———. 1996. *Between Facts and Norms: Contributions to a Discourse Theory of Law and Democracy*. Cambridge, MA: The MIT Press.

Hagan, J., M. Huxter, and P. Parker. 1988. "Class Structure and Legal Practice: Inequality and Mobility Among Toronto Lawyers." *Law & Society Review* 22: 9–56.

Hagan, John, and Fiona Kay. 1995. *Gender in Practice: A Study of Lawyers' Lives*. New York: Oxford University Press.

Hagen, Margaret A. 1997. *Whores of the Court: The Fraud of Psychiatric Testimony and the Rape of American Justice*. New York: Reganbooks.

Hajjar, Lisa. 1997. "Cause Lawyering in Transnational Perspective: National Conflict and Human Rights in Israel/Palestine." *Law & Society Review* 31: 473–504.

Hall, Kermit L. 1989. *The Magic Mirror: Law in American History*. New York: Oxford University Press.

Halliday, Terence, and Lucien Karpik, eds. 1997. *Lawyers and the Rise of Western Political Liberalism: Legal Professions and the Constitution of Modern Politics*. Oxford, UK: Oxford University Press.

Hamilton, V. Lee, and Joseph Sanders. 1992. *Everyday Justice: Responsibility and the Individual in Japan and the United States*. New Haven, CT: Yale University Press.

Handler, Joel F. 1978. *Social Movements and the Legal System: A Theory of Law Reform and Social Change*. New York: Academic Press.

———. 1990. *Law and the Search for Community*. Philadelphia: University of Pennsylvania Press.

———. 1992. "Postmodernism, Protest, and the New Social Movements." *Law & Society Review* 26: 697–732.

Handler, Joel, and Yeheskel Hasenfeld. 1997. *We the Poor People: Work, Poverty, and Welfare*. New Haven, CT: Yale University Press.

Harding, Alan. 1973. *A Social History of English Law*. Gloucester, MA: Peter Smith.

Harmon, Amy. 1998. "The Law Where There Is No Land." *The New York Times* (March 16): D1.

Harnett, Bertram. 1984. *Law, Lawyers, and Laymen: Making Sense of the American Legal System*. San Diego, CA: Harcourt Brace Jovanovich.

Harnsberger, Richard S. 1997. "Reflections About Law Reviews and American Legal Scholarship." *Nebraska Law Review* 76: 681–707.

Harr, Jonathan. 1995. *A Civil Action*. New York: Vintage.

Harrington, Christine. 1985. *Shadow Justice: The Ideology and Institutionalization of Alternatives to Courts*. Westport, CT: Greenwood Press.

Harrington, Michael. 1973. *Socialism*. New York: Bantam.

Harris, Paul. 1997. *Black Rage Confronts the Law*. New York: New York University Press.

Harris, Whitney R. [1954] 1995. *Tyranny on Trial: The Evidence at Nuremberg*. New York: Barnes & Noble Books.

Hart, H. L. A. 1961. *The Concept of Law*. Oxford: Clarendon Press.

———. 1963. *Law, Liberty, and Morality*. New York: Vintage.

Hart, Henry, and Albert Sacks. 1958. *The Legal Process: Basic Problems in the Making and Application of Law*. Cambridge, MA: Harvard University Press.

Hasnas, John. 1995. "The Myth of the Rule of Law." *Wisconsin Law Review* (1995): 199–234.

Hastie, Reid, ed. 1993. *Inside the Juror*. New York: Cambridge University Press.

Haward, L. R. C. 1981. *Forensic Psychology*. North Pomfret, VT: Batsford.

Haysom, N., and S. Kahanovitz. 1987. "Courts and the State Emergency." Pp. 187–198, in G. Moss and I. Obery, eds. *South Africa Review 4*. Johannesburg, RSA: Ravan Press.

Hazard, John N. 1990. "Where Are the Peril Points?" *Law and Social Inquiry* 15: 521–534.

Heald, Paul J., ed. 1998. *Literature and Legal Problem Solving: Law and Literature as Ethical Discourse*. Durham, NC: Carolina Academic Press.

Heilbrun, Carolyn, and Judith Resnik. 1999. "Covergences: Law, Literature, and Feminism." *The Yale Law Journal* 99: 1913–1956.

Heinz, John P., and Edward O. Laumann. 1982. *Chicago Lawyers: The Social Structure of the Bar*. New York: Russell Sage.

———. 1997. "The Constituencies of Elite Urban Lawyers." *Law & Society Review* 31: 441–472.

Heinz, John P., Edward O. Laumann, Robert L. Nelson, and Ethan Michelson. 1998. "The Changing Character of Lawyers' Work: Chicago in 1975 and 1995." *Law & Society Review* 32: 751–775.

Heinz, John P., Edward O. Laumann, Robert L. Nelson, and Robert H. Salisbury. 1993. *The Hollow Core: Private Interests in National Policy Making*. Cambridge, MA: Harvard University Press.

Heller, Agnes. 1987. *Beyond Justice*. Cambridge, MA: Basil Blackwell.

Heller, Scott. 1987. "Research on Coerced Behavior Leads Berkeley Sociologist to Key Role as Expert Witness in Controversial Lawsuit." *Chronicle of Higher Education* (April 8): 13–14.

Helmholz, R. H., Charles M. Gray, John H. Langbein, Eben Moglen, Henry E. Smith, and Albert W. Alschuler. 1997. *The Privilege Against Self-Incrimination: Its Origin and Development*. Chicago: University of Chicago Press.

Henriques, Diana B. 1999. "S.E.C. Is Making Lawyers Walk in Client's Shoes." *The New York Times* (June 1): C1.

Henry, Stuart. 1981. "Decentralized Justice: Private v. Democratic Informality." Pp. 179–191, in S. Henry, ed. *Informal Institutions: Alternative Networks in the Corporate State*. New York: St. Martin's Press.

———. 1983. *Private Justice: Towards Integrated Theorizing in the Sociology of Law*. Boston: Routledge & Kegan Paul.

———. 1985. "Community Justice, Capitalist Society, and Human Agency: The Dialectics of Collective Law in the Cooperative." *Law & Society Review* 19: 303–327.

Herbert, Steve. 1996. "Morality in Law Enforcement: Chasing 'Bad Guys' with the Los Angeles Police Department." *Law & Society Review* 30: 799–818.

Herman, Shael. 1993. *The Louisiana Civil Code: A European Legacy for the United States*. New Orleans, LA: Louisiana Bar Foundation.

Hermer, Joe, and Alan Hunt. 1996. "Official Graffiti of the Everyday." *Law & Society Review* 30: 455–480.

Herzog, Don. 1992. "I Hear a Rhapsody: A Reading of *The Republic of Choice*." *Law & Social Inquiry* 17: 147–158.

Heumann, Milton. 1978. *Plea Bargaining: The Experiences of Prosecutors, Judges, and Defense Attorneys*. Chicago: University of Chicago Press.

Heydebrand, Wolf. 1979. "The Technocratic Administration of Justice." Pp. 29–64, in Steven Spitzer, ed. *Research in Law and Society* 2. Greenwich, CT: JAI Press.

Heydebrand, Wolf, and Carroll Seron. 1981. "The Double Bind of the Capitalist Judicial System." *International Journal of the Sociology of Law* 9: 407–437.

———. 1991. *Rationalizing Justice: The Political Economy of Federal District Courts*. Albany: State University of New York Press.

Higginbotham, Leon, Jr. 1978. *In the Matter of Color: Race and the American Legal Process: The Colonial Period*. New York: Oxford University Press.

———. 1996. *Shades of Freedom: Racial Politics and Presumptions of the American Legal Process*. New York: Oxford University Press.

Higgins, Michael. 1998. "Taking the Best Shot." *ABA Journal* 84:79–81.

Hilton, N. Zoe. 1993. *Legal Responses to Wife Assault*. Newbury Park, CA: Sage.

Hipkin, Brian. 1980. "State, Law, and Politics in China." Pp. 201–220, in Susan S. Silbey, ed. *Research in Law and Sociology*. Volume III. Greenwich, CT: JAI Press, Inc.

Hirsch, Susan F. 1998. *Pronouncing and Persevering: Gender and the Discourses of Disputing in an African Islamic Court*. Chicago: University of Chicago Press.

Hirst, Paul Q. 1986. *Law, Socialism and Democracy*. London: Allen & Unwin.

Hirst, Paul Q., and Phil Jones. 1987. "The Critical Resources of Established Jurisprudence." *Journal of Law and Society* 14: 21–32.

Hobbes, Thomas. [1651] 1958. *Leviathan*. Indianapolis, IN: Bobbs-Merrill.

Hoebel, E. Adamson. [1954] 1967. *The Law of Primitive Man*. Cambridge, MA: Harvard University Press.

———. 1960. *The Cheyennes*. New York: Holt, Rinehart and Winston.

Hoff-Wilson, Joan. 1986. *Rights of Passage: The Past and Future of the ERA*. Bloomington: Indiana University Press.

Hofrichter, Richard. 1987. *Neighborhood Justice in Capitalist Society: An Expansion of the Informal State*. New York: Greenwood Press.

Holmes, Oliver Wendell, Jr. 1881. *The Common Law*. Boston: Little, Brown and Co.

———. 1897. "The Path of the Law." *Harvard Law Review* 10: 457–478.

Honeyball, Simon, and James Walter. 1998. *Integrity, Community, and Interpretation: A Critical Analysis of Ronald Dworkin's Theory of Law*. Brookfield, VT: Ashgate Publishing Co.

Horney, Julie, and Cassia Spohn. 1991. "Rape Law Reform and Instrumental Change in Six Urban Jurisdictions." *Law & Society Review* 25: 117–153.

Horwitz, Morton J. 1977. *The Transformation of American Law, 1780–1860*. Cambridge, MA: Harvard University Press.

———. 1998. *The Warren Court and the Pursuit of Justice*. New York: Hill & Wang.

Horwitz, Paul. 1997. "Scientology in Court: A Comparative Analysis and Some Thoughts on Selected Issues in Law and Religion." *DePaul Law Review* 47: 85–152.

Howard, Michael, George J. Andreopoulos, and Mark R. Shulman. 1994. *The Laws of War: Constraints on Warfare in the Western World*. New Haven: Yale University Press.

Howard, Philip K. 1994. *The Death of Common Sense: How Law Is Suffocating America*. New York: Warner Books.

Huber, Peter. 1993. *Galileo's Revenge: Junk Science in the Courtroom*. New York: Basic Books.

Human Sciences Research Council. 1985. *The South African Society*. Pretoria, RSA: Human Sciences Research Council.

Hund, John. 1988. "Formal Justice and Township Justice." Pp. 203–216, in J. Hund, ed. *Law and Justice in South Africa*. Johannesburg, RSA: Centre for Intergroup Studies.

Hund, John, and M. Kotu-Rammopo. 1983. "Justice in a South African Township: The Sociology of Makgotla." *Comparative and International Law Journal of South Africa* 16: 179–208.

Hunt, Alan. 1990. "The Big Fear: Law Confronts Postmodernism." *McGill Law Journal* 35: 507–540.

———. 1993. *Explorations in Law and Society: Toward a Constitutive Theory of Law*. New York: Routledge.

Hurst, James Willard. 1950. *The Growth of American Law*. Boston: Little, Brown & Co.

Hutchinson, Allan C., ed. 1989. *Critical Legal Studies*. Totowa, NJ: Rowman & Littlefield.

Hutchinson, Allan C., and P. Monahan, eds. 1987. *The Rule of Law: Ideal or Ideology*. Toronto: Carswell.

Hutton, Neil. 1997. "Sentencing in the New South Africa: The Prospects for Reform." *International Journal of the Sociology of Law* 25: 315–335.

Hyde, Alan. 1983. "The Concept of Legitimation in the Sociology of Law." *Wisconsin Law Review* 1983: 370–426.

Hyman, Dick. 1977. *It's Against the Law*. Pleasantville, NY: Reader's Digest.

Institute for Civil Justice. 1997. *Annual Report: 1996–1997*. Santa Monica, CA: Rand.

Inverarity, James M. 1992. "Sociology of Law." Pp. 2026–2029, in E. F. Borgatta and Maria Borgatta, eds. *Encyclopedia of Sociology*. New York: MacMillan Publishing Co.

Inverarity, James M., Pat Lauderdale, and Barry C. Feld. 1983. *Law and Society: Sociological Perspectives on Criminal Law*. Boston: Little Brown.

Irons, Peter. 1981. "The Relegalization of Cuba." *ALSA Forum* 5: 20–36.

Israel, Jerold H., Yale Kamisar, and Wayne R. LaFave. 1993. *Criminal Procedure and the Constitution*. St. Paul, MN: West Publishing Co.

Jackson, Emily. 1992. "Catharine MacKinnon and Feminist Jurisprudence: A Critical Appraisal." *Journal of Law and Society* 19: 195–213.

Jackson, Robert H. 1955. *The Supreme Court in the American System of Government*. New York: Harper.

Jacob, Herbert. 1978. *Justice in America: Courts, Lawyers, and the Judicial Process*. 3rd ed. Boston: Little Brown.

———. 1992. "The Elusive Shadow of Law." *Law & Society Review* 26: 565–590.

———. 1995. *Law and Politics in the United States*. Reading, MA: Addison-Wesley.

———. 1996. "Courts and Politics in the United States." Pp. 16–80, in H. Jacob, E. Blankenburg, H. M. Kritzer, D. M. Provine, and J. Sanders. *Courts, Law, and Politics in Comparative Perspective*. New Haven, CT: Yale University Press.

Jacob, Herbert, Erhard Blankenburg, Herbert M. Kritzer, Doris Marie Provine, and Joseph Sanders. 1995. *Courts, Law and Politics in Comparative Perspective*. New Haven, CT: Yale University Press.

Jacobs, James B. 1989. *Drunk Driving: An American Dilemma*. Chicago: University of Chicago Press.

Jacobs, James B., and Kimberly Potter. 1998. *Hate Crimes: Criminal Law and Identity Politics*. New York: Oxford University Press.

Jacobs, Lesley A. 1998. "Integration, Diversity, and Affirmative Action." *Law & Society Review* 32: 725–746.

Jacoby, Susan. 1983. *Wild Justice: The Evolution of Revenge*. New York: Harper & Row.

Jaffa, Harry V. 1994. *Original Intent and the Framers of the Constitution*. Washington, DC: Regnery Gateway.

Jamieson, Dale. 1991. "The Poverty of Postmodernist Theory." *The University of Colorado Law Review* 62: 577–595.

Jarvis, Robert M., and Paul R. Joseph. 1998. *Prime Time Law: Fictional Television as Legal Narrative*. Durham, NC: Carolina Academic Press.

Jasanoff, Sheila. 1995. *Science at the Bar: Law, Science, and Technology*. Cambridge, MA: Harvard University Press.

Jefferson, Thomas. [1781] 1998. *Notes on the State of Virginia*. New York: Viking Penguin.

Jeffery, C. Ray. 1962. "The Legal Profession." Pp. 313–356, in F. James Davis, Henry H. Foster Jr., C. Ray Jeffery, and E. Eugene Davis. *Society and the Law: New Meanings for an Old Profession*. New York: Free Press.

Jencks, Christopher. 1992. *Rethinking Social Policy: Race, Poverty and the Underclass*. Cambridge, MA: Harvard University Press.

Jenkins, Iredell. 1980. *Social Order and the Limits of Law: A Theoretical Essay*. Princeton, NJ: Princeton University Press.

Jenkins, Pamela J., and Steve Kroll-Smith. 1996. *Witnessing for Sociology: Sociologists in Court*. Westport, CT: Praeger.

Ji, Wei-Dong. 1989. "The Sociology of Law in China: Overview and Trends." *Law & Society Review* 23: 903–914.

Johnson, Harry M., ed. 1978. *Social System and Legal Process*. San Francisco: Jossey-Bass Publishers.

Johnson, Jean. 1997. "Americans' Views on Crime and Law Enforcement." *NIJ Journal* (September): 9–14.

Johnson, Stephen M. 1998. "The Internet Changes Everything: Revolutionizing Public Participation and Access to Government Information Through the Internet." *Administrative Law Review* 50: 277–337.

Jones, Howard. 1987. *Mutiny on the Amistad: The Saga of a Slave Revolt and Its Impact on American Abolition, Law, and Diplomacy*. New York: Oxford University Press.

Josephy, Alvin M., Jr. 1971. *Red Power: The American Indians' Fight for Freedom*. New York: McGraw Hill.

Kagan, Robert A. 1989. "Understanding Regulatory Enforcement." *Law & Policy* 11: 89–119.

———. 1995. "What Socio-Legal Scholars Should Do When There Is Too Much Law to Study." *Journal of Law and Society* 22: 140–148.

———. 1996. "American Lawyers, Legal Cultures, and Adversarial Legalism." Pp. 53–78, in Lawrence M. Friedman and Harry N. Scheiber, eds. *Legal Culture and the Legal Profession*. Boulder, CO: Westview Press.

Kahlenberg, Richard D. 1992. *Broken Contract: A Memoir of Harvard Law School*. Boston: Faber & Faber.

———. 1996. *The Remedy: Class, Race, and Affirmative Action*. New York: Basic Books.

Kahn, Paul W. 1997. *The Reign of Law: Marbury v. Madison and the Construction of America*. New Haven, CT: Yale University Press.

Kairys, David. 1998. *The Politics of Law: A Progressive Critique*. New York: Basic.

Kalman, Laura. 1986. *Legal Realism at Yale: 1927–1960*. Chapel Hill, NC: University of North Carolina Press.

Kalven, Harry. 1988. *A Worthy Tradition: Freedom of Speech in America*. New York: Harper & Row.

Kalven, Harry, and Hans Zeisel. 1966. *The American Jury*. Boston: Little, Brown & Co.

Kant, Immanuel. [1785] 1998. *Groundwork of the Metaphysics of Morals*. (Translated and edited by Mary Gregor). Cambridge, UK: Cambridge University Press.

———. [1788] 1998. *Critique of Practical Reason*. Milwaukee, WI: Marquette University Press.

Kapardis, Andreas. 1997. *Psychology and Law: A Critical Introduction*. New York: Cambridge University Press.

Kappeler, Victor E., Mark Blumberg, and Gary W. Potter. 1996. *The Mythology of Crime and Criminal Justice*. 2nd ed. Prospect Heights, IL: Waveland Press.

Karlen, Delmar. 1967. *Anglo-American Criminal Justice*. New York: Oxford University Press.

Katsh, M. Ethan. 1995. *Law in a Digital World*. New York: Oxford University Press.

———. 1998. *Taking Sides: Clashing Views on Controversial Legal Issues*. Guilford, CT: Dushkin.

Katz, Jack. 1982. *Poor People's Lawyers in Transition*. New Brunswick, NJ: Rutgers University Press.

Katz, Leo. 1987. *Bad Acts and Guilty Minds: Conundrums of the Criminal Law*. Chicago: The University of Chicago Press.

Katz, Michael B. 1986. *In the Shadow of the Poorhouse: A Social History of Welfare in America*. New York: Basic Books.

Kauzlarich, David, and Ronald C. Kramer. 1998. *Crimes of the American Nuclear State: At Home and Abroad*. Boston: Northeastern University Press.

Kay, Fiona. 1997. "Flight From Law: A Competing Risks Model of Departures From Law Firms." *Law & Society Review* 31: 301–335.

Kay, Fiona, and John Hagan. 1998. "Raising the Bar: The Gender Stratification of Law-Firm Capital." *American Sociological Review* 63: 728–743.

Keen, Lisa, and Suzanne B. Goldberg. 1998. *Strangers to the Land: Gay People on Trial*. Ann Arbor: The University of Michigan Press.

Kellogg, Frederick R. 1986. "Law, Morals and Justice Holmes." *Judicature* 69: 214–217.

Kelly, J. M. 1992. *A Short History of Western Legal Theory*. Oxford, UK: Clarendon Press.

Kelly, Michael J. 1994. *Lives of Lawyers: Journeys in the Organizations of Practice*. Ann Arbor: University of Michigan Press.

Kelman, Herbert, and V. Lee Hamilton. 1989. *Crimes of Obedience: Toward a Social Psychology of Authority and Responsibility*. New Haven, CT: Yale University Press.

Kelman, Mark. 1987. *A Guide to Critical Legal Studies*. Cambridge, UK: Harvard University Press.

Kelsen, Hans. [1934] 1967. *Pure Theory of Law*. Berkeley: University of California Press.

———. 1955. *The Communist Theory of Law*. London: Stevens & Sons.

Kempers, Margot. 1989. "There's Losing and Winning: Ironies of the Maine Indian Land Claim." *Legal Studies Forum* 13: 267–300.

Kendrick, Walter. 1987. *The Secret Museum: Pornography in Modern Culture*. New York: Viking.

Kennedy, Duncan. 1983. *Legal Education and the Reproduction of Hierarchy: A Polemic Against the System*. Cambridge, MA: Afar.

———. 1997. *A Critique of Adjudication (fin de siecle)*. Cambridge, MA: Harvard University Press.

Kennedy, Paul, and George J. Andreopoulos. 1994. "The Laws of War: Some Concluding Reflections." Pp. 214–225, in Michael Howard, George J. Andreopoulos, and Mark R. Shulman, eds. *The Laws of War*. New Haven, CT: Yale University Press.

Kennedy, Randall. 1997. *Race, Crime and Law*. New York: Pantheon.

Kephart, William M., and William W. Zellner. 1991. *Extraordinary Groups*. 4th ed. New York: St. Martin's Press.

Kerruish, Valerie. 1988. "Coherence, Integrity, and Equality in *Law's Empire:* A Dialectical Review of Ronald Dworkin." *International Journal of the Sociology of Law* 16: 51–73.

———. 1991. *Jurisprudence as Ideology*. London: Routledge.

Kessler, Mark. 1987. *Legal Services for the Poor: A Comparative and Contemporary Analysis of Interorganizational Politics*. New York: Greenwood Press.

———. 1990. "Legal Mobilization for Social Reform: Power and the Politics of Agenda Setting." *Law & Society Review* 24: 121–143.

Keveles, Gary. 1984. "Individual Rights Under Military Justice: Past, Present, and Future." *ALSA Forum* 8: 284–315.

Kidder, Robert L. 1983. *Connecting Law and Society*. Englewood Cliffs, NJ: Prentice Hall.

Kidder, Robert L., and John A. Hostetler. 1990. "Managing Ideologies: Harmony as Ideology in Amish and Japanese Societies." *Law & Society Review* 24: 893–922.

Kilborn, Peter T. 1995. "Hard Times for Legal Aid, and Getting Harder." *The New York Times* (October 7): 6.

King, Martin Luther, Jr. 1963. *Letter From Birmingham City Jail*. Philadelphia: American Friends Service Committee.

King, Michael. 1993. "The Truth About Autopoieses." *Journal of Law and Society* 20: 218–236.

King, Nancy J., ed. 1996. "Jury Research and Reform." *Judicature* 79: 214–289.

Kitch, Edmund. 1986. "Law and the Economic Order." Pp. 109–150, in Leon Lipson and Stanton Wheeler, eds. *Law and the Social Sciences*. New York: Russell Sage Foundation.

Klafter, Craig Evan. 1993. *Reason Over Precedents: Origins of American Legal Thought*. Westport, CT: Greenwood Press.

Klare, Karl. 1978. "Judicial Deradicalization of the Wagner Act and the Origins of Modern Legal Consciousness, 1937–1941." Pp. 138–168, in Piers Beirne and Richard Quinney, eds. *Marxism and Law*. New York: John Wiley.

Kleinig, John. 1996. *The Ethics of Policing*. Cambridge, UK: Cambridge University Press.

Klinck, Dennis R. 1992. *The Word of the Law*. Ottawa, ON: Carleton University Press.

Kluger, Richard. 1975. *Simple Justice: The History of Brown v. Board of Education and Black America's Struggle for Equality*. New York: Alfred A. Knopf.

Kohan, John. 1992. "The Party on Trial." *Time* (July 20): 66–67.

Kohlberg, Lawrence. 1969. "The Cognitive-Developmental Approach to Socialization." Pp. 347–480, in David Goslin, ed. *Handbook of Socialization Theory and Research*. Chicago: Rand McNally.

———. 1981. *The Philosophy of Moral Development: Moral Stages and the Idea of Justice*. Volume I. San Francisco: Harper & Row.

Koshner, Andrew Jay. 1998. *Solving the Puzzle of Interest Group Litigation*. Westport, CT: Greenwood Press.

Kramnick, Isaac, and Lawrence Moore. 1996. *The Godless Constitution: The Case Against Religious Correctness*. New York: W. W. Norton & Co.

Kress, Ken. 1987. "The Interpretive Turn." *Ethics* 97: 834–860.

Kritz, Neil J., ed. 1995. *Transitional Justice: How Emerging Democracies Reckon With Former Regimes*. Washington, DC: United States Institute of Peace Press.

Kritzer, Herbert M. 1999. *Lawyers and Nonlawyers at Work*. Ann Arbor: University of Michigan Press.

Kritzer, Herbert M., and Susan S. Silbey. 1999. "Special Symposium Issue: Do the Haves Still Come Out Ahead? Twenty-Five Years Later." *Law & Society Review* 33: 803–1123.

Kritzer, Herbert M., and Frances Kahn Zemans. 1993. "Local Legal Culture and the Control of Litigation."*Law & Society Review* 27: 535–557.

Kronman, Anthony. 1993. *The Lost Lawyer: Failing Ideals of the Legal Profession*. Cambridge, MA: The Belknap Press of Harvard University Press.

Kropotkin, Peter. [1910] 1971. "Anarchism." Quoted in Marshall Shatz, ed. *The Essential Works of Anarchism*. New York: Bantam.

———. [1927] 1966. "Law, the Supporter of Crime." Pp. 289–295, in Leonard I. Krimerman and Lewis Perry, eds. *Patterns of Anarchy*. New York: Anchor.

Kunen, James Simon. 1983. *"How Can You Defend Those People?"* New York: Random House.

Kusha, Hamid R. 1998. "Revisiting the Islamic Shariah Law in Deterring Criminality: Is There a Lesson for Western Criminology?" *Crime and Justice International* 14: 9–10, 24–26.

Kyle, Ken, and Pat Lauderdale. 2000. "The Rule of Law or Unruly Law? Reflections on the Study of Political Trials." *Humanity and Society* 24: 52–73.

Lacombe, Dany. 1994. *Blue Politics: Pornography and the Law in the Age of Feminism*. Toronto: University of Toronto Press.

Ladany, Laszlo. 1992. *Law and Legality in China*. Honolulu: University of Honolulu Press.

LaFree, Gary, and Christine Rack. 1996. "The Effects of Participants' Ethnicity and Gender on Monetary Outcomes in Mediated and Adjudicated Civil Cases." *Law & Society Review* 30: 767–797.

Landon, Donald D. 1990. *Country Lawyers: The Impact of Context on Professional Practice*. New York: Praeger.

Landrine, Hope, and Elizabeth A. Klonoff. 1997. *Discrimination Against Women: Prevalence, Consequences, Remedies*. Beverly Hills, CA: Sage.

Langdell, Christopher Columbus. 1871. *Selection of Cases on the Law of Contracts*. Boston: Little, Brown & Co.

Langum, David J. 1999. *William M. Kunstler: The Most Hated Lawyer in America*. New York: New York University Press.

LaPiana, William P. 1995. "Honor Langdell!" *Law & Social Inquiry* 20: 761–764.

Lauderdale, Pat. 1997. "Indigenous North American Jurisprudence." *International Journal of Comparative Sociology* 38: 131–148.

Lauren, Paul Gordon. 1998. *The Evolution of International Human Rights: Visions Seen*. Philadelphia: University of Pennsylvania Press.

Lawrence, Charles R. 1998. "Race and Affirmative Action: A Critical Race Perspective." Pp. 312–327, in David Kairys, ed. *The Politics of Law: A Progressive Critique*. 3rd ed. New York: Basic Books.

Lawrence, Frederick M. 1999. *Punishing Hate: Bias Crime Under American Law*. Cambridge, MA: Harvard University Press.

Lazarus-Black, Mindie, and Susan F. Hirsch. 1994. *Contested States: Law, Hegemony and Resistance*. New York: Routledge.

Lefcourt, Robert, ed. 1971. *Law Against the People*. New York: Vintage.

Lehman, Godfrey D. 1997. *We the Jury: The Impact of Jurors on Our Basic Freedoms*. Amherst, NY: Prometheus Books.

LeMoncheck, Linda, and Mane Hajdin. 1997. *Sexual Harassment: A Debate*. Lanham, MD: Rowman & Littlefield.

Lempert, Richard, and Joseph Sanders. 1986. *An Invitation to Law and Social Science: Desert, Disputes, and Distribution*. New York: Longman.

Leng, Shao-chuan. 1977. "The Role of Law in the People's Republic of China as Reflecting Mao Tse-Tung's Influence." *Journal of Criminal Law & Criminology* 68: 356–373.

Leo, John. 1983. "A New Furor Over Pedophilia." *Time* (January 17): 47.

Leo, Richard A. 1996. "Miranda's Revenge: Police Interrogation as a Confidence Game." *Law & Society Review* 30: 259–288.

Leo, Richard A., and George C. Thomas III, eds. 1998. *The Miranda Debate: Law, Justice, and Policing*. Boston: Northeastern University Press.

Lerner, Melvin J. 1975. "The Justice Motive in Social Behavior: Introduction." *The Journal of Social Issues* 31: 1–20.

Lerner, M. J., and S. C. Lerner. 1981. *The Justice Motive in Social Behavior.* New York: Plenum Publishing Co.

Lessan, Gloria, and Joseph F. Sheley. 1992. "Does Law Behave? A Macrolevel Test of Black's Propositions on Change in Law." *Social Forces* 70: 655–678.

Lessig, Lawrence. 1999a. "The Law of the Horse: What Cyberlaw Might Teach." *Harvard Law Review* 113: 501–549.

———. 1999b. *Code—and Other Laws of Cyberspace*. New York: Basic Books.

Levi, Edward H. 1949. *An Introduction to Legal Reasoning*. Chicago: The University of Chicago Press.

Levi, Judith N., and Anne G. Walker, eds. 1990. *Language in the Judicial Process*. London: Plenum Press.

Levin, Harvey. 1985. *The People's Court*. New York: Quill.

Levine, Evyatar. 1990. *Legal Justice and Social Change: A Philosophy of Law.* Jerusalem: Rubin Mass Ltd.

Levine, Felice J. 1990. "Goose Bumps and 'The Search for Signs of Intelligent Life' in Sociolegal Studies: After Twenty-Five Years." *Law & Society Review* 24: 7–33.

Levine, Martin L. 1988. *Age Discrimination and the Mandatory Retirement Controversy*. Baltimore: Johns Hopkins University Press.

Levine, Murray. 1999. "The Legal Culture Must Assimilate the Scientific Culture, and Vice Versa?" *Law & Policy* 21: 71–89.

Levit, Nancy. 1998. *The Gender Line: Men, Women, and the Law*. New York: New York University Press.

Levy, Leonard. 1993. *Blasphemy: Verbal Offense Against the Sacred from Moses to Salman Rushdie*. New York: Alfred Knopf.

Lewin, Tamar. 1988. "Feminist Scholars Spurring a Rethinking of Law." *The New York Times* (September 30): B9.

———. 1989. "Women Say They Face Obstacles as Lawyers." *The New York Times* (December 4): A21.

Lewis, Neil. 1997. "For Black Scholars Wedded to Prism of Race, New and Separate Goals." *The New York Times* (May 5): B9.

———. 1998. "Switching Sides on Free Speech." *The New York Times* (April 25): E1.

Lewis, Orlando. 1967. *The Development of American Prisons and Prison Customs, 1776–1845*. Montclair, NJ: Patterson Smith.

Lewis, Paul. 2000. "The Artist's Friend Turned Enemy: A Backlash Against the Copyright." *The New York Times* (January 8): B9.

Lieberman, Jethro. 1978. *Crisis at the Bar: Lawyers' Unethical Ethics and What to Do About It*. New York: W. W. Norton.

———. 1981. *The Litigious Society*. New York: Basic.

Lind, E. Allan, and Tom R. Tyler. 1988. *The Social Psychology of Procedural Justice*. New York: Plenum.

Lindgren, James. 1993. "Defining Pornography." *University of Pennsylvania Law Review* 141: 1153–1276.

Linowitz, Sol. 1994. *The Betrayed Profession: Lawyering at the End of the Twentieth Century*. New York: Charles Scribner's Sons.

Linz, Daniel, Edward Donnerstein, Bradley J. Shafer, Kenneth C. Land, Patricia L. McCall, and Arthur C. Graesser. 1995. "Discrepancies Between the Legal Code and Community Standards for Sex and Violence: An Empirical Challenge to Traditional Assumptions in Obscenity Laws." *Law & Society Review* 29: 127–168.

Lipson, Leon, and Stanton Wheeler, eds. 1986. *Law and the Social Sciences*. New York: Russell Sage Foundation.

Litowitz, Douglas E. 1997. *Postmodern Philosophy and Law*. Lawrence: University Press of Kansas.

Littleton, Christine A. 1987. "In Search of a Feminist Jurisprudence."*Harvard Women's Law Journal* 10: 1–7.

Lively, Kit. 1997. "Campus Drug Arrests Increased 18 Per Cent in 1995; Reports of Other Crimes Fell." *The Chronicle of Higher Education* (March 21): A44–A45.

Livingston, Debra. 1997. "Police Discretion and the Quality of Life in Public Places: Courts, Communities, and the New Policing." *Columbia Law Review* 97: 551–672.

Llewellyn, Karl. [1930] 1951. *The Bramble Bush*. Dobbs Ferry, NY: Oceana Publications.

———. 1962. *Jurisprudence: Realism in Theory and Practice*. Chicago: University of Chicago Press.

Llewellyn, Karl N., and E. Adamson Hoebel. 1941. *The Cheyenne Way: Conflict and Case Law in Primitive Jurisprudence*. Norman: University of Oklahoma Press.

Lloyd, Dennis. 1970. *The Idea of Law*. Baltimore: Penguin.

Lloyd, Ian J. 1997. *Information Technology Law*. London: Butterworths.

Lloyd-Bostock, Sally. 1988. *Law in Practice—Applications of Psychology in Legal Decision-Making and Legal Skills*. London: Routledge.

———. 1996. "Law and Psychology: Their Theoretical and Working Relationship." Pp. 265–296, in Philip A. Thomas, ed. *Legal Frontiers*. Aldershot, UK: Dartmouth Publishing Co.

Locke, John. [1689] 1988. *Two Treatises on Government*. P. Laslett, ed. New York: Cambridge University Press.

———. [1690] 1965. *Treatise on Civil Government*. New York: Irvington Publishing Co.

Loewith, Karl. 1960. *Max Weber and Karl Marx*. London: George Allen & Unwin.

Lohr, Steve. 1982. "Tokyo Air Crash: Why Japanese Do Not Sue." *The New York Times* (March 10): A1.

Lony, Robert E. 1990. *Censorship*. New York: H. W. Wilson.

Lopez, Ian F. Haney. 1996. *White by Law: The Legal Construction of Race*. New York: New York University Press.

Lotito, M. J., M. J. Soltis, and R. Pimentel. 1992. *The Americans With Disabilities Act*. Northridge, CA: M. H. Wright and Associates.

Luban, David. 1988. *Lawyers and Justice: An Ethical Study*. Princeton, NJ: Princeton University Press.

———. 1994. *Legal Modernism*. Ann Arbor: The University of Michigan Press.

Luchansky, Bill, and J. Gerber. 1993. "Constructing State Autonomy: The Federal Trade Commission and the Celler-Kefauver Act." *Sociological Perspectives* 36: 217–240.

Lukes, Steven, and Andrew Scull, eds. 1983. *Durkheim and the Law.* Oxford, UK: Martin Robertson.

Lykken, David T. 1998. *A Tremor in the Blood: Uses and Abuses of the Lie Detector.* New York: Plenum Trade.

Lyons, William. 1999. *The Politics of Community Policing*. Ann Arbor: University of Michigan Press.

Ma, Yue. 1995. "Crime in China: Characteristics, Causes, and Control Strategies." *International Journal of Comparative and Applied Criminal Justice* 19: 247–256.

Macaulay, Stewart. 1963. "Non-Contractual Relations in Business: A Preliminary Study." *American Sociological Review* 28: 55–66.

———. 1986. "Private Government." Pp. 445–518, in Leon Lipson and Stanton Wheeler, eds. *Law and the Social Sciences*. Beverly Hills, CA: Sage.

———. 1987. "Images of Law in Everyday Life: The Lessons of School, Entertainment, and Spectator Sports." *Law & Society Review* 21: 185–218.

Macaulay, Stewart, Lawrence M. Friedman, and John Stookey, eds. 1995. *Law and Society: Readings on the Social Study of Law.* New York: W. W. Norton & Co.

Maccoby, Eleanor E., and Robert Mnookin. 1992. *Dividing the Child: Social and Legal Dilemmas of Custody*. Cambridge, MA: Harvard University Press.

MacCormick, Neil. 1996. "Law and Philosophy: The Rediscovery of Practical Reason." Pp. 41–65, in Philip A. Thomas, ed. *Legal Frontiers*. Aldershot, UK: Dartmouth Publishing Co.

Machan, Tibor R. 1995. "Posner's Rortyite (Pragmatic) Jurisprudence." *The American Journal of Jurisprudence* 40: 361–375.

Machiavelli, Niccolo. [1513] 1976. *The Prince*. Paramus, NJ: Prentice Hall.

MacKinnon, Catharine A. 1979. *The Sexual Harassment of Working Women*. New Haven, CT: Yale University Press.

———. 1987. *Feminism Unmodified: Discourses on Life and Law.* Cambridge, MA: Harvard University Press.

———. 1989. *Toward a Feminist Theory of the State*. Cambridge, MA: Harvard University Press.

———. 1993. *Only Words.* Cambridge, MA: Harvard University Press.

Maguigan, Holly. 1998. "It's Time to Move Beyond the Battered Woman Syndrome." *Criminal Justice Ethics* (Winter/Spring): 50–57.

Maguire, Brendan, Rebecca Hinderliter, and William Faulkner. 1990. "The Illinois Seat Belt Law: A Sociology of Law Analysis." *Humanity & Society* 14: 395–418.

Maine, Henry. [1861] 1970. *Ancient Law.* Glouster, MA: Peter Smith.

Maire, Jonathan Edward. 1995. "The Possibility of a Christian Jurisprudence." *The American Journal of Jurisprudence* 40: 101–156.

Malinowski, Bronislaw. 1926. *Crime and Custom in Savage Society.* London: Routledge & Kegan Paul.

Malloy, Robin Paul, and Christopher K. Braun, eds. 1995. *Law and Economics: New and Critical Perspectives*. New York: Peter Lang.

Mangan, Katherine S. 2000. "Ave Maria: A Seriously Catholic Law School." *The Chronicle of Higher Education* (February 18): A18–29.

Mangan, Mary. 1998. "Making Future Lawyers Squirm: Law Schools Focus on Ethical Dilemmas." *The Chronicle of Higher Education* (March 20): A12–13.

Mann, Coramae Richey. 1993. *Unequal Justice: A Question of Color.* Bloomington: Indiana University Press.

Manning, Bayless. 1977. "Hyperlexis: Our National Disease." *Northwestern University Law Review* 71: 767–782.

Mansbridge, Jane J. 1986. *Why We Lost the ERA*. Chicago: University of Chicago Press.

Marcuse, Herbert. 1966. "Ethics and Revolution." Pp. 133–148, in Richard T. DeGeorge, ed. *Ethics and Society*. Garden City, NY: Doubleday & Co.

Margolick, David. 1983. "The Trouble With American Law School." *The New York Times Magazine* (May 22): 20–38.

———. 1984. "Burger Says Lawyers Make Legal Help Too Costly."*The New York Times* (February 13): A13.

———. 1990. "Ignorance of L. A. Law Is No Excuse for Lawyers." *The New York Times* (May 6): 27.

———. 1991. "Sizing Up the Talk of Natural Law: Many Ideologies Discover a Precept." *The New York Times* (September 12): A22.

———. 1993a. "Horror's Stigma Still Clings to a Disbarred Lawyer." *The New York Times* (May 15): 21.

———. 1993b. "Still Radical After All These Years." *The New York Times* (July 6): B1; B2.

Marks, Paula Mitchell. 1998. *In a Barren Land: American Indian Dispossession and Survival*. New York: William Morrow & Co.

Marsh, Jeanne, Alison Geist, and Nathan Caplan. 1982. *Rape and the Limits of Law Reform*. Boston: Auburn House.

Marshall, James. 1966. *Law and Psychology in Conflict*. Garden City, NY: Doubleday.

———. 1968. *Intention: In Law and Society*. USA: Minerva.

Martin, Douglas. 1988. "The Rise and Fall of the Class-Action Lawsuit." *The New York Times* (January 8): B7.

Martin, Margaret. 1994. "Mandatory Arrest for Domestic Violence: The Courts' Response." *Criminal Justice Review* 19: 212–227.

Marvell, Thomas B. 1994. "Tort Caseload Trends and the Impact of Tort Reforms." *The Justice System Journal* 17: 193–204.

Marx, Karl. [1867] 1962. *Capital*. F. Engels, ed. Moscow: Foreign Language Publishing House.

Maschke, Karen J. 1995. "Prosecutors as Crime Creators: The Case of Prenatal Drug Use." *Criminal Justice Review* 20: 21–33.

Masters, Roger D. 1990. "Law, Biology, and the Sense of Injustice: An Inquiry." *Gruyter Institute for Law and Behavioral Research* 3: 1; 4–6.

Mastrofski, Stephen D., Robert F. Worden, and Jeffrey B. Snipes. 1995. "Law Enforcement in a Time of Community Policing." *Criminology* 33: 539–563.

Matsuda, Mari J., Charles P. Lawrence III, Richard Delgado, and Kimberle Williams Crenshaw. 1993. *Words That Wound: Critical Race Theory, Assaultive Speech, and the First Amendment*. Boulder, CO: Westview Press.

Matthews, Anne. 1993. "The Campus Crime Wave." *The New York Times Magazine* (March 7): 38, 42, 47.

Mayers, Lewis. 1973. *The Machinery of Justice*. Totowa, NJ: Littlefield, Adams & Co.

Mayes, G. Randolph. 1989. "The Internal Aspect of Law: Rethinking Hart's Contribution to Legal Positivism." *Social Theory and Practice* 15: 231–255.

Mayhew, David R. 1986. "Legislation." Pp. 259–286, in Leon Lipson and Stanton Wheeler, eds. *Law and the Social Sciences*. New York: Russell Sage.

Maynard, Douglas W. 1984. *Inside Plea Bargaining*. New York: Plenum Press.

McAdams, A. James, ed. 1997. *Transitional Justice and the Rule of Law in New Democracies*. Notre Dame, IN: University of Notre Dame Press.

McCaffery, Edward J. 1997. "Ronald Dworkin, Inside-Out." *California Law Review* 85: 1043–1086.

McCall, George J. 1995. "Use of Law in a South African Black Township." *International Journal of the Sociology of Law* 23: 59–78.

McCann, Michael W. 1994. *Rights at Work: Pay Equity Reform and the Politics of Legal Mobilization*. Chicago: University of Chicago Press.

McCoy, Candace. 1997. "Sentencing (and) the Underclass." *Law & Society Review* 31: 589–612.

McGlynn, Clare, ed. 1998. *Legal Feminisms: Theory and Practice*. Brookfield, VT: Ashgate Publishing Co.

McIntyre, Lisa J. 1987. *The Public Defender: The Practice of Law in the Shadows of Repute*. Chicago: University of Chicago Press.

———. 1994. *Law in the Sociological Enterprise: A Reconstruction*. Boulder, CO: Westview Press.

McKay, Robert. 1985. "What Law Schools Can and Should Do (and Sometimes Do)." *New York Law School Law Review* 30: 491–516.

McLaughlin, Robert H. 1999. "From the Field to the Courthouse: Should Social Science Research Be Privileged?" *Law & Social Inquiry* 24: 927–966.

McNamara, M. Francis. 1960. *Ragbag of Legal Quotations*. Albany, NY: Matthew Bender Co.

———. 1967. *2000 Famous Legal Quotations*. Rochester, NY: Aqueduct Books.

McNamara, Robert. 1995. *In Retrospect: The Tragedy and Lessons of Vietnam*. New York: Times Books.

McWhirter, Darien, and Jon Bible. 1992. *Privacy as a Constitutional Right*. New York: Quorum Books.

Mears, Daniel F. 1998. "The Sociology of Sentencing: Reconceptualizing Decision-Making Processes and Outcomes." *Law & Society Review* 32: 667–724.

Medema, Steven G., ed. 1998. *Coasean Economics: Law and Economics and the New Institutional Economics*. Norwell, MA: Kluwer Academic Publishers.

Meier, Barry, and Jill Abramson. 1998. "Tobacco War's New Front: Lawyers Fight for Big Fees." *The New York Times* (June 9): A1.

Meier, Barry, and Richard A. Oppel Jr. 1999. "State's Big Suits Against Industry Bring Battle on Contingency Fees." *The New York Times* (October 15): A1.

Meier, Robert F., and Gilbert Geis. 1997. *Victimless Crime? Prostitution, Drugs, Homosexuality, Abortion*. Los Angeles: Roxbury.

Meinhold, Stephen S., and Charles D. Hadley. 1995. "Lawyers as Political Party Activists." *Social Science Quarterly* 76: 364–380.

Mello, Michael. 1996. "The Centrality of Professional Ethics to the (Smart) Practice of Criminal Law, and the Confessions of a Professional Responsibility Professor." *Criminal Law Bulletin* 32: 168–171.

Mendels, Pamela. 1999. "Decision Is Expected Today on Anti-Pornography Law." *The New York Times* (February 1): C4.

Menkel-Meadow, Carrie. 1985. "Portia in a Different Voice: Speculations on the Women's Lawyering Process." *Berkeley Women's Law Journal* 1: 39–55.

Mensch, Elizabeth. 1998. "The History of Mainstream Legal Thought." Pp. 23–53, in David Kairys, ed. *The Politics of Law: A Progressive Critique*. 3rd ed. New York: Basic Books.

Mercuro, N., and S. G. Medema. 1997. *Economics and the Law: From Posner to Post-Modernism*. Princeton, NJ: Princeton University Press.

Merry, Sally Engle. 1988. "Legal Pluralism." *Law & Society Review* 22: 869–901.

———. 1990. *Getting Justice and Getting Even: Legal Consciousness Among Working-Class Americans*. Chicago: University of Chicago Press.

Merryman, John Henry. 1969. *The Civil Law Tradition*. Stanford, CA: Stanford University Press.

Mertz, Elizabeth. 1988. "The Uses of History: Language, Ideology, and Law in the United States and South Africa." *Law & Society Review* 22: 661–685.

———. 1994a. "Legal Loci and Places in the Heart: Community and Identity in Sociolegal Studies." *Law & Society Review* 28: 971–992.

———. 1994b. "A New Social Constructionism for Sociolegal Studies." *Law & Society Review* 28: 1243–1265.

Metzger, M. B., J. P. Mallor, T. B. Barnes, and M. J. Phillips. 1986. *Business Law and the Regulatory Environment: Concepts and Cases*. 6th ed. Homewood, IL: Irwin.

Metzloff, Thomas B., and David B. Wilkins, eds. 1995. "Teaching Legal Ethics." *Law and Contemporary Problems* 58: 1–370.

Michalowski, Raymond J. 1995. "Between Citizens and the Socialist State: The Negotiation of Legal Practice in Socialist Cuba." *Law & Society Review* 29: 65–101.

Michalowski, Raymond J., and Ronald C. Kramer. 1987. "The Space Between the Laws: The Problem of Corporate Crime in a Transnational Context." *Social Problems* 34: 34–53.

Milgram, Stanley. 1974. *Obedience to Authority: An Experimental View*. New York: Harper & Row.

Mill, John Stuart. [1859] 1963. "On Liberty." Pp. 127–242, in *The Six Great Humanistic Essays of John Stuart Mill*. New York: Washington Square Press.

Miller, Richard. 1991. *The Case for Legalizing Drugs*. New York: Praeger.

Mills, C. Wright. 1959. *The Power Elite*. New York: Oxford University Press.

Mills, James. 1971. *On the Edge*. New York: Doubleday.

Mills, Linda G. 1999. "Killing Her Softly: Intimate Abuse and the Violence of State Intervention." *Harvard Law Review* 113: 551–613.

Milovanovic, Dragan. 1981. "The Commodity-Exchange Theory of Law: In Search of a Perspective." *Social Justice* (Winter): 41–49.

———. 1994. *A Primer in the Sociology of Law*. 2nd ed. New York: Harrow & Heston.

Milton, J. R. L. 1987. "Criminal Law in South Africa, 1976–1986." Pp. 34–54, in T. W. Bennett et al. *Alta Juridica*. Cape Town, RSA: Juta & Co.

Minda, Gary. 1995. *Postmodern Legal Movements: Law and Jurisprudence at Century's End*. New York: New York University Press.

Minow, Martha. 1990. *Making All the Difference*. Ithaca, NY: Cornell University Press.

———. 1997. *Not Only for Myself: Identity, Politics, and Law*. New York: The New Press.

———. 1998. *Between Vengeance and Forgiveness: Facing History After Genocide and Mass Violence*. Boston: Beacon Press.

Mitchell, Basil. 1970. *Law, Morality, and Religion in a Secular Society*. London: Oxford University Press.

Miyazawa, Setsuo. 1987. "Taking Kawashima Seriously: A Review of Japanese Research on Japanese Legal Consciousness and Disputing Behavior." *Law & Society Review* 21: 219–241.

Mnookin, Robert H., and Lewis Kornhauser. 1979. "Bargaining in the Shadow of Law." *Yale Law Journal* 88: 750–797.

Monahan, John, and Laurens Walker. 1994. *Social Science in Law: Cases and Materials*. Westbury, NY: The Foundation Press.

Montesquieu, Baron Charles de. [1748] 1886. *The Spirit of Laws*. Cincinnati, OH: Robert Clarke & Co.

Mooney, Christopher F. 1990. *Boundaries Dimly Perceived: Law, Religion, Education and the Common Good*. Notre Dame, IN: University of Notre Dame Press.

Mooney, Linda A., and Robert Gramling. 1993. "The Differential Effects of the Minimum Drinking Age Law." *Sociological Inquiry* 63: 330–338.

Moore, G. A., A. M. Magaldi, and J. A. Gray. 1987. *The Legal Environment of Business: A Contextual Approach*. Cincinnati, OH: Southwestern Publishing.

Moore, Richter H., Jr. 1996. "Islamic Legal Systems: Traditional (Saudi Arabia), Contemporary (Bahrain), and Evolving (Pakistan)." Pp. 390–410, in Charles B. Fields and Richter H. Moore Jr. *Comparative Criminal Justice: Traditional and Nontraditional Systems of Law and Social Control*. Prospect Heights, IL: Waveland Press.

Moore, Sally Falk. 1986. "Legal Systems of the World: An Introductory Guide to Classifications, Typological Interpretations, and Bibliographical Resources." Pp. 11–62, in Leon Lipson and Stanton Wheeler, eds. *Law and the Social Sciences*. New York: Russell Sage Foundation.

Morawetz, Thomas. 1980. *The Philosophy of Law: An Introduction*. New York: MacMillan.

Morris, Thomas D. 1996. *Southern Slavery and the Law, 1619–1860*. Chapel Hill, NC: University of North Carolina Press.

Morrison, Wayne. 1997. *Jurisprudence: From the Greeks to Post-Modernism*. London: Cavendish.

Morse, Stephen. 1985. "Excusing the Crazy: The Insanity Defense Reconsidered." *Southern California Law Review* 58: 777–838.

Mosley, Albert G., and Nicholas Capaldi. 1996. *Affirmative Action: Social Justice or Unfair Preference?* Lanham, MD: Rowman & Littlefield.

Moss, Debra Cassens. 1988. "Would This Happen to a Man?" *ABA Journal* (June 1): 50–55.

Mueller, Ingo. 1991. *Hitler's Justice: The Courts of the Third Reich*. Cambridge, MA: Harvard University Press.

Munger, Frank. 1998. "Mapping Law and Society." Pp. 21–80, in A. Sarat et al., eds. *Crossing Boundaries: Traditions and Transformations in Law and Society Research*. Chicago: Northwestern University Press.

Murphy, Jeffrie G., and Jules L. Coleman. 1990. *Philosophy of Law: An Introduction to Jurisprudence*. Boulder, CO: Westview Press.

Murphy, W. T. 1997. *The Oldest Social Science? Configurations of Law and Modernity*. Oxford, UK: Clarendon Press.

Musto, David F. 1973. *The American Disease: Origins of Narcotic Control*. New Haven, CT: Yale University Press.

Myren, Richard A. 1988. *Law and Justice: An Introduction*. Pacific Grove, CA: Brooks/Cole.

Nader, Laura. 1997. *Law in Culture and Society*. Berkeley: University of California Press.

Nader, Laura, and Harry F. Todd Jr., eds. 1978. *The Disputing Process: Law in Ten Societies*. New York: Columbia University Press.

Nader, Ralph, and Wesley J. Smith. 1996. *No Contest: Corporate Lawyers and the Perversion of Justice in America*. New York: Random House.

Nagel, Stuart S. 1969. *The Legal Process From a Behavioral Perspective*. Homewood, IL: The Dorsey Press.

Napier-Andrews, Nigel. 1976. *This Is the Law?* Garden City, NY: Doubleday.

National Review. 1996. "The War on Drugs Is Lost." *National Review* (February 12): 34–48.

Nelken, David, ed. 1997. *Comparing Legal Cultures*. Brookfield, VT: Dartmouth Publishing.

Nelken, David. 1998. "Blinding Insights? The Limits of a Reflexive Sociology of Law." *Journal of Law and Society* 25: 407–426.

Nelkin, Dorothy, and Lori Andrews. 1999. "Whose Genes Are They, Anyway?" *Chronicle of Higher Education* (May 21): B6.

Nelson, Robert. 1988. *Partners With Power: The Social Transformation of the Large Law Firm*. Berkeley: University of California Press.

Nelson, Robert, and John P. Heinz. 1988. "Lawyers and the Structure of Influence in Washington." *Law and Society Review* 22: 237–300.

Neubauer, David W. 1999. *America's Courts and the Criminal Justice System*. 6th ed. Belmont, CA: Wadsworth.

Newman, Graeme. 1976. *Comparative Deviance*. New York: Elsevier Scientific Publishing Co.

Newman, Otto, and Richard De Zoysa. 1997. "Communitarianism: The New Panacea?" *Sociological Perspectives* 40: 623–638.

Nielsen, Marianne O. 1996. "Contextualization for Native American Crime and Criminal Justice Involvement." Pp. 10–19, in M. O. Nielsen and R. A. Silverman, eds. *Native Americans, Crime, and Justice*. Boulder, CO: Westview Press.

Nina, Daniel. 1993. "Community Justice in a Volatile South Africa: Containing Community Conflict, Clermont, Natal." *Social Justice* 20 (3–4): 129–142.

Nonet, Philippe, and Philip Selznick. 1978. *Law and Society in Transition*. New York: Harper Colophon.

Noonan, John T. Jr. [1976] 1994. "Virginia Liberators." Pp. 524–529, in John Bonsignore et al., eds. *Before the Law*. 5th ed. Boston: Houghton Mifflin.

———. 1976. *Persons and Masks of the Law*. New York: Farrar, Straus & Giroux.

Noreau, Pierre, and Andre-Jean Arnaud. 1998. "The Sociology of Law in France: Trends and Paradigms." *Journal of Law and Society* 25: 257–283.

Norgren, Jill, and Serena Nanda. 1996. *American Cultural Pluralism and Law*. 2nd ed. Westport, CT: Praeger.

Norrie, Alan. 1996. "From Law to Popular Justice: Beyond Antinominalism." *Social & Legal Studies* 5: 383–404.

Nozick, Robert. 1974. *Amnesty, State and Utopia*. New York: Basic Books.

Nunn, Kenneth B. 1997. "Law as a Eurocentric Enterprise." *Law and Inequality* 15: 323–373.

O'Barr, William M., and John M. Conley. 1988. "Law Expectations of the Civil Justice System." *Law & Society Review* 22: 137–161.

———. 1998. *Just Words: Law, Language, and Power*. Chicago: University of Chicago Press.

O'Connor, Jennifer M., and Lucinda K. Treat. 1996. "Getting Smart About Getting Tough: Juvenile Justice and the Possibility of Progressive Reform." *American Criminal Law Review* 33: 1299–1344.

O'Connor, John J., Cardinal. 1984. "Human Lives, Human Rights." *The New York Times* (October 16): B2.

O'Connor, Karen. 1996. *No Neutral Ground? Abortion Politics in an Age of Absolutes*. Boulder, CO: Westview Press.

O'Hagan, Timothy C. 1984. *The End of Law?* Oxford: Blackwell.

Oliverio, Annamarie. 1997. "The State of Injustice: The Politics of Terrorism and the Production of Order." *International Journal of Comparative Sociology* 38: 48–63.

Olsen, Frances E. 1995. *Feminist Legal Theory*. Volumes I and II. New York: Washington Square Press.

Olson, Marvin E., ed. 1970. *Power in Societies*. New York: The MacMillan Co.

Olson, Walter. 1997. *The Excuse Factory*. New York: The Free Press.

Osiel, Mark J. 1999. *Obeying Orders: Atrocity, Military Discipline & the Law of War*. New Brunswick, NJ: Transaction Publishers.

Packer, Herbert. 1968. *The Limits of the Criminal Sanction*. Palo Alto, CA: Stanford University Press.

Papke, David Ray, ed. 1987. *Framing the Criminal: Crime, Cultural Work and the Loss of Critical Perspective, 1830–1900*. Hamden, CT: Archon Books.

———. 1991. *Narrative and the Legal Discourse*. Liverpool, UK: Deborah Charles Publishers.

———. 1995. "Prime-Time Lawyers." IU–Indianapolis Alumni Magazine (Spring): 2–8.

———. 1998. *Heretics in the Temple: Americans Who Reject the Nation's Legal Faith*. New York: New York University Press.

———. 1999. *The Pullman Case: The Clash of Labor and Capital in Industrial America*. Lawrence: Kansas University Press.

Parsa, T. Z. 1999. "The Drudge Report." *New York* (June 21): 24–31.

Parsons, Ronald A. 1998. "That Which Governs: An Essay on the Nature of Law and Its Relation to Justice." *South Dakota Law Review* 43: 172–187.

Paternoster, Raymond. 1987. "The Deterrent Effect of the Perceived Certainty and Severity of Punishment: A Review of the Evidence." *Justice Quarterly* 4: 173–217.

Paternoster, Raymond, Robert Brame, Ronet Bachman, and Lawrence W. Sherman. 1997. "Do Fair Procedures Matter? The Effects of Procedural Justice on Spouse Assault." *Law & Society Review* 31: 163–204.

Patterson, Dennis.1992."Postmodernism/Feminism/Law." *Cornell Law Review* 77: 254–317.

———. 1996a. *Law and Truth*. New York: Oxford University Press.

Patterson, Dennis, ed. 1996b. *A Companion to Philosophy of Law and Legal Theory*. Cambridge, MA: Blackwell.

Pavlak, Thomas J. 1981. "Political Science." Pp. 89–136, in Gordon E. Misner, ed. *Criminal Justice Studies: Their Transdisciplinary Nature*. St. Louis, MO: The C. V. Mosby Co.

Pavlich, George. 1992. "People's Courts, Postmodern Difference, and Socialist Justice in South Africa." *Social Justice* 19: 29–45.

———. 1996. *Justice Fragmented: Mediating Community Disputes Under Postmodern Conditions*. London: Routledge.

Pegram, Thomas R. 1998. *Battling Demon Rum: The Struggle for a Dry America, 1800–1933*. Chicago: Ivan R. Dee.

Pence, Gregory E. 1998. *Who's Afraid of Human Cloning?* Lanham, MD: Rowman and Littlefield.

Pepinsky, Harold E., and Paul Jesilow. 1984. *Myths That Cause Crime*. Cabin John, MD: Seven Locks Press.

Perez-Pena, Richard. 1999. "Lawyers Abandon Legislatures for Greener Pastures." *The New York Times* (February 21): Sect. 4, 3.

Petersen, Melody. 1998. "The Short End of Long Hours." *The New York Times* (July 18): D1.

Pfohl, Stephen. 1977. "The 'Discovery' of Child Abuse." *Social Problems* 24: 310–323.

Pfuhl, Erdwin, Jr., and David L. Altheide. 1987. "TV Mediation of Disputes and Injustices." *Justice Quarterly* 4: 99–116.

Piaget, Jean. 1932. *The Moral Judgment of the Child*. New York: Keegan Paul Trench, Trubner.

Pierce, Jennifer L. 1995. *Gender Trials: Emotional Lives in Contemporary Law Firms*. Berkeley: University of California Press.

Pipes, Daniel. 1990. *The Rushdie Affair.* New York: Carol Publishing Co.

Piven, Francis Fox, and Richard Cloward. 1971. *Regulating the Poor.* New York: Vintage.

Platt, Anthony. 1977. *The Child Savers: The Invention of Delinquency*. 2nd ed. Chicago: University of Chicago Press.

Podgorecki, Adam. 1974. *Law and Society*. London: Routledge and Kegan Paul.

Podgorecki, Adam, and Christopher J. Whelan, eds. 1981. *Sociological Approaches to Law*. London: Croom Helm.

Polinsky, A. M. 1989. *An Introduction to Law and Economics*. Boston, MA: Little Brown.

Pommersheim, Frank. 1995. "Tribal Courts: Providers of Justice and Protectors of Sovereignty." *Judicature* 79: 110–112.

Posner, Richard A. 1986. "Law and Literature: A Relation Reargued." *Virginia Law Review* 72: 1351–1392.

———. 1987. "What Am I? A Potted Plant?" *The New Republic* (September 28): 23–25.

———. 1988. *Law and Literature: A Misunderstood Relation*. Cambridge, MA: Harvard University Press.

———. 1990. *The Problems of Jurisprudence*. Cambridge, MA: Harvard University Press.

———. 1992. *Sex and Reason*. Cambridge, MA: Harvard University Press.

———. 1995a. *Overcoming Law*. Cambridge, MA: Harvard University Press.

———. 1995b. *Aging and Old Age*. Chicago: University of Chicago Press.

———. 1998. *The Economic Analysis of Law*. 4th ed. Boston, MA: Little Brown.

———. 1999a. *The Problematics of Moral and Legal Theory*. Cambridge, MA: Harvard University Press.

———. 1999b. *An Affair of State: The Investigation, Impeachment, and Trial of President Clinton*. Cambridge, MA: Harvard University Press.

Post, G. Gordon. 1963. *An Introduction to the Law*. Englewood Cliffs, NJ: Prentice Hall.

Pound, Roscoe. 1907. "The Need of a Sociological Jurisprudence." *The Green Bag* 19: 607–615.

———. 1908. "Mechanical Jurisprudence." *Columbia Law Review* 8: 605–623.

———. 1910. "Law in Books and Law in Action." *American Law Review* 44: 12–36.

———. 1942. *Social Control Through Law*. New Haven, CT: Yale University Press.

———. 1943. "A Survey of Social Interests." *Harvard Law Review* 57: 1–39.

———. 1945. "A Survey of Public Interests." *Harvard Law Review* 58: 909–929.

Powers, David S. 1992. "On Judicial Review in Islamic Law." *Law & Society Review* 26: 315–341.

Prest, Wilfrid R. 1986. *The Rise of the Barristers: A Social History of the English Bar, 1590–1640*. Oxford, UK: Clarendon Press.

Priest, George L. 1997. "Procedural Versus Substantive Controls of Mass Tort Class Actions." *Journal of Legal Studies* 26: 521–573.

Provine, Doris Marie. 1996. "Courts in the Political Process in France." Pp. 177–248, in H. Jacob, E. Blankenburg, H. M. Kritzer, D. M. Provine, and J. Sanders, eds. *Courts, Law, and Politics in Comparative Perspective*. New Haven: Yale University Press.

———. 1999. "Revolutionizing Rights: Epp's Comparative Perspective." *Law and Social Inquiry* 24: 1125–1140.

Ptacek, James. 1999. *Battered Women in the Courtroom: The Power of Judicial Response*. Boston: Northeastern University Press.

Quinney, Richard. 1974. *Critique of Legal Order*. Boston: Little Brown.

———. 1991. "The Way to Peace: On Crime, Suffering and Service." Pp. 3–13, in H. E. Pepinsky and R. Quinney, eds. *Criminology as Peacemaking*. Bloomington: Indiana University Press.

Rabin, R. L., and S. D. Sugarman, eds. 1993. *Smoking Policy: Law, Politics and Culture*. New York: Oxford University Press.

Radcliffe-Brown, A. 1922. *The Andaman Islanders*. Cambridge, UK: The University Press.

Rae, Scott. 1994. *The Ethics of Commercial Motherhood: Brave New Families*. Westport, CT: Praeger.

Raphael, D. D. 1980. *Justice and Liberty*. Athlone Press.

Rawls, John. 1971. *A Theory of Justice*. Cambridge, MA: Harvard University Press.

Ray, Laura Krugman. 1999. "Autobiography and Opinion: The Romantic Jurisprudence of Justice William O. Douglas." *University of Pittsburgh Law Review* 60: 707–744.

Rayside, David. 1998. *On the Fringe: Gays and Lesbians in Politics*. Ithaca, NY: Cornell University Press.

Raz, Joseph. 1979. *The Authority of Law: Essays on Law and Morality*. Oxford: Clarendon Press.

Re, Edward D. 1994. "The Causes of Popular Dissatisfaction With the Legal Profession." *St. John's Law Review* 68: 85–136.

Reasons, Charles, Bonnie Bray, and Duncan Chappell. 1989. "Ideology, Ethics and the Business of Law: Varying Perceptions of the Ethics of the Legal Profession." *Legal Studies Forum* 13: 171–188.

Redfield, Robert. 1967. "Primitive Law." Pp. 3–24, in Paul Bohannon, ed. *Law and Warfare: Studies in the Anthropology of Conflict*. Garden City, NY: The Natural History Press.

Reece, Helen, ed. 1998. *Law and Science: Current Legal Issues, 1998*. Volume I. New York: Oxford University Press.

Reich, Charles. 1964. "The New Property." *Yale Law Journal* 73: 733–787.

Reichel, Philip A. 1999. *Comparative Criminal Justice Systems: A Topical Approach*. 2nd ed. Upper Saddle River, NJ: Prentice Hall.

Reiman, Jeffrey. 1990. *Justice and Modern Moral Philosophy*. New Haven, CT: Yale University Press.

Reisman, W. Michael. 1996. "Myres S. McDougal: Architect of a Jurisprudence for a Free Society." *Mississippi Law Journal* 66: 15–26.

———. 1999. *Law in Brief Encounters*. New Haven, CT: Yale University Press.

Rembar, Charles. 1980. *The Law of the Land: The Evolution of Our Legal System*. New York: Simon & Schuster.

Renner, Karl. [1904] 1949. *The Institutions of Private Law and Their Functions*. (O. Kahn-Freund, ed.) London: Routledge and Kegan Paul.

Rhodes, Susan L. 1992. "Prison Reform and Prison Life: Four Books on the Process of Court-Ordered Change." *Law & Society Review* 26: 189–218.

Richards, David A. S. 1999. *Identity and the Case for Gay Rights*. Chicago: University of Chicago Press.

Richardson, Lynda. 1998. "Wave of Laws Aimed at People With H.I.V." *The New York Times* (September 25): A1.

Riksheim, Eric, and Steven Chermak. 1993. "Causes of Police Behavior Revisited." *Journal of Criminal Justice* 21: 353–382.

Robel, Lauren. 1989. "Pornography and Existing Law." Pp. 178–197, in Susan Gubar and Joan Hoff, eds. *For Adult Users Only*. Bloomington: Indiana University Press.

Roberts, Julian V., and Loretta J. Stalans. 1997. *Public Opinion, Crime, and Criminal Justice*. Boulder, CO: Westview Press.

Robertson, John A. 1974. *Rough Justice: Perspectives on Lower Criminal Courts*. Boston: Little, Brown.

Robinson, Cyril D., and Richard Scaglion. 1987. "The Origin and Evolution of the Police Function in Society: Notes Toward a Theory." *Law & Society Review* 21: 109–153.

Robinson, Daniel N. 1980. *Psychology and Law: Can Justice Survive the Social Sciences?* New York: Oxford.

Robinson, Paul A., and John M. Darley. 1995. *Justice, Liability, and Blame: Community Views and the Criminal Law*. Boulder, CO: Westview Press.

Robson, Ruthann. 1998. *Sappho Goes to Law School: Fragments in Lesbian Legal Theory*. New York: Columbia University Press.

Rodes, Robert F., Jr. 1976. *The Legal Enterprise*. Port Washington, NY: Kennikat Press.

Rohde, David. 1998. "Officer Apprehends a Perpetrator. The Charge Is Jaywalking." *The New York Times* (February 14): B1.

———. 1999. "Critical Shortage of Lawyers for Poor Seen." *The New York Times* (December 12): B3.

Rojek, Dean C. 1985. "The Criminal Process in the People's Republic of China." *Justice Quarterly* 2: 117–125.

Rokumoto, Kahel. 1988. "The Present State of Japanese Practicing Attorneys: On the Way to Full Professionalization. " Pp. 160–199, in Richard L. Abel and Philip S. C. Lewis, eds. *Lawyers in Society: The Civil World*. Volume II. Berkeley: University of California Press.

———. 1994. *Sociological Theories of Law*. New York: New York University Press.

Roleff, Tamara L. 1996. *The Legal System: Opposing Viewpoints*. San Diego, CA: Greenhaven Press.

Rosen, Lawrence. 1989. *The Anthropology of Justice: Law as Culture in Islamic Society*. Cambridge, UK: Cambridge University Press.

———. 1992. "Law and Indigenous Peoples." *Law and Social Inquiry* 17: 363–371.

Rosen, Paul L. 1972. *The Supreme Court and Social Science*. Urbana: University of Illinois Press.

Rosenau, Pauline Marie. 1992. *Post-Modernism and the Social Sciences: Insights, Inroads, and Intrusions*. Princeton, NJ: Princeton University Press.

Rosenberg, Gerald N. 1991. *The Hollow Hope: Can Courts Bring About Social Change?* Chicago: University of Chicago Press.

Rosenfeld, Michel, and Andrew Arato. 1998. *Habermas on Law and Democracy*. Berkeley: University of California Press.

Rosenthal, Elisabeth. 1998. "A Day in Court, and Justice, Sometimes, for the Chinese." *The New York Times* (April 27): A1.

———. 2000. "In China's Legal Evolution, the Lawyers Are Handcuffed." *The New York Times* (January 6): A1.

Rosett, Arthur, and Donald R. Cressey. 1976. *Justice by Consent: Plea Bargains in the American Courthouse*. Philadelphia: J. B. Lippincott Company.

Ross, H. Laurence. 1992a. *Confronting Drunk Driving: Social Policy for Saving Lives*. New Haven, CT: Yale University Press.

———. 1992b. "The Law and Drunk Driving." *Law & Society Review* 26: 219–230.

Ross, H. Laurence, and Robert B. Voas. 1989. *The New Philadelphia Story: The Effects of Severe Penalties for Drunk Driving*. Washington, DC: AAA Foundation for Traffic Safety.

Rossi, Peter H., and Richard A. Berk. 1997. *Just Punishments: Federal Guidelines and Public Views Compared*. New York: De Gruyter.

Roth, Andrew, and Jonathan Roth. 1989. *Devil's Advocates: The Unnatural History of Lawyers*. Berkeley, CA: Nolo Press.

Roth, Louise Marie. 1999. "The Right to Privacy Is Political: Power, the Boundary Between Public and Private, and Sexual Harassment." *Law & Social Inquiry* 24: 45–71.

Rousseau, Jean-Jacques. [1762] 1978. *On the Social Contract*. New York: St. Martin's Press.

Rubin, Leslie G. 1997. *Justice v. Law in Greek Political Thought*. Lanham, MD: Rowman & Littlefield Publishers.

Russell, Katharine K. 1998. *The Color of Crime: Racial Hoaxes, White Fear, Black Protectionism, Police Harassment, and Other Macroaggressions*. New York: New York University Press.

Ryan, Kevin F. 1998. "Clinging to Failure: The Rise and Continued Life of U.S. Drug Policy." *Law & Society Review* 32: 221–242.

Ryerson, Ellen. 1978. *The Best-Laid Plans: America's Juvenile Court Experiment*. New York: Hill and Wang.

Sack, Peter, and Jonathan Aleck, eds. 1992. *Law and Anthropology*. New York: New York University Press.

Sadurski, Wojciech. 1984. "Social Justice and Legal Justice." *Law and Philosophy* 3: 329–354.

Sales, Bruce D., and Saleem Shah. 1996. *Mental Health and Law*. Durham, NC: Carolina Academic Press.

Salter, Michael. 1997. "Habermas's New Contribution to Legal Scholarship." *Journal of Law and Society* 24: 285–305.

Samaha, Joel. 1974. *Law and Order in Historical Perspective*. New York: Academic Press.

Sampson, Robert J., and John Laub. 1993. "Structural Variations in Juvenile Court Processing: Inequality, the Underclass, and Social Control." *Law & Society Review* 27: 285–311.

Sampson, Robert J., and Janet L. Lauritsen. 1997. "Racial and Ethnic Disparities in Crime and Criminal Justice in the United States." Pp. 311–374, in M. Tonry, ed. *Crime and Justice: A Review of the Research*. Volume 21. Chicago: University of Chicago Press.

Sanders, Francine. 1995. "*Brown v. Board of Education:* An Empirical Examination of Its Effects on Federal District Courts." *Law & Society Review* 29: 731–755.

Sanders, Joseph. 1996. "Courts and Law in Japan." Pp. 315–388, in H. Jacob, E. Blankenburg, N. M. Kritzer, D. M. Provine, and J. Sanders. *Courts, Law, and Politics in Comparative Perspective*. New Haven, CT: Yale University Press.

Sanders, Joseph, and V. Lee Hamilton. 1992. *Everyday Justice: Responsibility for the Individual in Japan and the United States*. New Haven, CT: Yale University Press.

Sanders, Joseph, V. Lee Hamilton, and Toshiyuki Yuasa. 1998. "The Institutionalization of Sanctions for Wrongdoing Inside Organizations: Public Judgments in Japan, Russia, and the United States." *Law & Society Review* 32: 871–930.

Santos, Boaventura de Sousa. 1995. *Toward a New Common Sense: Law, Science and Politics in the Paradigmatic Transition*. London: Routledge.

Sarat, Austin. 1998. "President's Column: Every Good Discipline Deserves a Canon, or How Can We Fight If We Aren't Armed?" *Law & Society Newsletter,* November, p. 2.

Sarat, Austin, Marianne Constable, David Engel, Valerie Hans, and Susan Lawrence, eds. 1998a. *Everyday Practices and Trouble Cases*. Chicago: Northwestern University Press.

——. 1998b. *Crossing Boundaries: Traditions and Transformations in Law and Society Research*. Chicago: Northwestern University Press.

Sarat, Austin, and William F. Felstiner. 1995. *Divorce Lawyers and Their Clients: Power and Meaning in the Legal Process*. New York: Oxford University Press.

Sarat, Austin, and Thomas R. Kearns, eds. 1993. *The Fate of Law*. Ann Arbor: University of Michigan Press.

——. 1995. *Law in Everyday Life*. Ann Arbor: University of Michigan Press.

——. 1997. *Legal Rights: Historical and Philosophical Perspectives*. Ann Arbor: University of Michigan Press.

——. 1999. *Cultural Pluralism, Identity Politics, and the Law*. Ann Arbor: University of Michigan Press.

Sarat, Austin, and Stuart Scheingold, eds. 1998. *Cause Lawyering*. New York: Oxford.

Sarat, Austin, and Susan S. Silbey. 1988. "The Pull of the Policy Audience." *Law & Policy* 10: 97–168.

Sartre, Jean-Paul. 1968. "Preface" to Frantz Fanon, *The Wretched of the Earth*. New York: Grove Press.

Saunders, David. 1997. *Anti-Lawyers: Religion and the Critics of Law and State*. New York: Routledge.

Savigny, Friedrich Karl von. [1831] 1986. *On the Vocation of Our Age for Legislation and Jurisprudence*. Birmingham, AL: Legal Classics Library.

Sayer, John William. 1997. *Ghost Dancing the Law: The Wounded Knee Trials*. Cambridge, MA: Harvard University Press.

Schauer, Frederick, and Virginia J. Wise. 1997. "Legal Positivism as Legal Information." *Cornell Law Review* 82: 1080–1100.

Schechter, R. E. 1990. "A Retrospective on the Reagan FTC: Musings on the Role of an Administrative Agency." *Administrative Law Review* (Fall): 489–517.

Scheck, Barry, Peter Neufeld, and Jim Dwyer. 2000. *Actual Innocence*. New York: Doubleday & Co.

Scheingold, Stuart A. 1997. *Politics, Crime Control and Culture*. Brookfield, VT: Ashgate.

Scheper-Hughes, Nancy. 1995. "Who's the Killer? Popular Justice and Human Rights in a South African Squatter Camp." *Social Justice* 22: 143–164.

Scheppele, Kim Lane. 1994. "Legal Theory and Social Theory." Pp. 383–406, in John Hagan and Karen S. Cook, eds. *Annual Review of Sociology*. Volume 20. Palo Alto, CA: Annual Reviews.

Scheuerman, William E. 1999. "Kenneth Starr's Rule of Law—and Ours." *Constellations* 6: 137–141.

Schlag, Pierre. 1987. "The Brilliant, the Curious, and the Wrong." *Stanford Law Review* 39: 917–927.

———. 1999. *The Enchantment of Reason*. Durham, NC: Duke University Press.

Schlegel, John Henry. 1984. "Notes Toward an Intimate, Opinionated, and Affectionate History of the Conference on Critical Legal Studies." *Stanford Law Review* 36: 391–412.

———. 1995a. *American Legal Realism and Empirical Social Science*. Chapel Hill: University of North Carolina Press.

———. 1995b. "Damn! Langdell!" *Law and Social Inquiry* 20: 765–770.

Schlosser, Eric. 1997. "The Business of Pornography." *U.S. News & World Report* (February 10): 43–52.

Schnayerson, Robert. 1986. *The Illustrated History of the Supreme Court of the United States*. New York: Harry Abrams.

Schneider, Carl E. 1990. "Social Structure and Social Control: On *The Moral Order of a Suburb*." *Law & Society Review* 24: 875–886.

Schneyer, Ted. 1991. "Professional Discipline for Law Firms?" *Cornell Law Review* 77: 1–46.

Schulhofer, Stephen J. 1998. *Unwanted Sex: The Culture of Intimidation and the Failure of Law*. Cambridge, MA: Harvard University Press.

Schultz, David A., ed. 1998. *Leveraging the Law: Using the Courts to Achieve Social Change*. New York: Peter Lang.

Schur, Edwin M. 1965. *Crimes Without Victims*. Englewood Cliffs, NJ: Prentice Hall.

———. 1968. *Law and Society: A Sociological View*. New York: Random House.

———. 1973. *Radical Non-Intervention: Rethinking the Delinquency Problem*. Englewood Cliffs, NJ: Prentice Hall.

Schwartz, Bernard. 1974. *The Law in America*. New York: American Heritage Books.

———. 1996. "Administrative Law." Pp. 130–150, in Alan B. Morrison, ed. *Fundamentals of American Law*. New York: Oxford University Press.

———. 1997. *The Book of Legal Lists*. New York: Oxford University Press.

Schwartz, Richard D. 1978. "Moral Order and Sociology of Law: Trends, Problems and Prospects." Pp. 577–601, in R. Turner, J. Coleman, and R. C. Fox, eds. *Annual Review of Sociology*. Volume 4. Palo Alto, CA: Annual Reviews.

Schwarz, Philip J. 1988. *Twice Condemned: Slaves and the Criminal Laws of Virginia, 1705–1865*. Baton Rouge: Louisiana University Press.

Sebba, Leslie, ed. 1996. *Social Control and Justice: Inside or Outside the Law?* Jerusalem: The Magnes Press.

Sebok, Anthony J. 1997. "*The Path of the Law* 100 Years Later: Holmes's Influence on Modern Jurisprudence." *Brooklyn Law Review* 63: 1–5.

———. 1998. *Legal Positivism in American Jurisprudence*. New York: Cambridge University Press.

Segal, Bernard. 1983. "American Bar Association." *The Guide to American Law*. St. Paul, MN: West.

Selznick, Philip. 1992. *The Moral Commonwealth: Social Theory and the Promise of Community*. Berkeley: University of California Press.

Senna, Joseph J., and Larry J. Siegel. 1999. *Introduction to Criminal Justice*. 9th ed. Belmont, CA: West/Wadsworth.

Seron, Carroll. 1993. "New Strategies for Getting Clients: Urban and Suburban Lawyers' Views." *Law & Society Review* 27: 399–418.

———. 1996. *The Business of Practicing Law: The Work Lives of Solo and Small Firm Lawyers*. Philadelphia: Temple University Press.

Shaffer, Thomas L., and Robert S. Redmount. 1977. *Lawyers, Law Students and People*. Colorado Springs, CO: Sheppard's.

Shamir, Ronen. 1995. *Managing Legal Uncertainty: Elite Lawyers in the New Deal*. Durham, NC: Duke University Press.

Shapiro, Andrew. 1999. *The Control Revolution*. Cambridge, MA: Perseus.

Shapiro, Fred R. 1993. *The Oxford Dictionary of American Legal Quotations*. New York: Oxford University Press.

Shapiro, Fred R., and Jane Garry, eds. 1998. *An Oxford Anthology of Legal Stories*. New York: Oxford University Press.

Sharlet, Robert, and Piers Beirne. 1984. "In Search of Vyshinsky: The Paradox of Law and Terror." *International Journal of the Sociology of Law* 12: 153–177.

Shea, Christopher. 1997. "Natural Law Theory Is at the Crux of a Nasty Intellectual Debate." *The Chronicle of Higher Education* (February 7): A14–15.

Shelden, Randall G. 1998. "Gender Bias in the Juvenile Justice System." *Juvenile and Family Court Journal* (Winter): 11–25.

Sheleff, Leon S. 1997. *Social Cohesion and Legal Coercion: A Critique of Weber, Durkheim, and Marx*. Atlanta, GA: Rodopi.

Sherman, Lawrence W. 1992. *Policing Domestic Violence: Experiments and Dilemmas*. New York: Free Press.

Shichor, David, and John W. Heeren. 1989. "Social Control in Socialist Societies: An Analysis of Five Major Characteristics." *Legal Studies Forum* 13: 215–238.

Shichor, David, and D. K. Sechrest, eds. 1997. *Three Strikes and You're Out*. Thousand Oaks, CA: Sage.

Shiell, Timothy C. 1993. *Legal Philosophy: Selected Readings*. Fort Worth, TX: Harcourt Brace.

———. 1998. *Campus Hate Speech on Trial*. Lawrence: University Press of Kansas.

Shklar, Judith N. [1964] 1986. *Legalism: Law, Morals, and Political Trials*. Cambridge, MA: Harvard University Press.

———. 1990. *The Faces of Injustice*. New Haven, CT: Yale University Press.

Shook, Michael D., and Jeffrey D. Meyer. 1995. *Legal Briefs*. New York: MacMillan.

Shrager, David S., and Elizabeth Frost. 1986. *The Quotable Lawyer*. New York: Facts on File.

Schreve, Susan Richards, and Porter Shreve, eds. 1997. *Outside the Law: Narratives on Justice*. Boston: Beacon.

Shuy, Roger W. 1993. *Language Crimes: The Use and Abuse of Language Evidence in the Courtroom*. Oxford, UK: Blackwell.

———. 1998. *The Language of Confession, Interrogation, and Deception*. Thousand Oaks, CA: Sage.

Sierra, Maria Teresa. 1995. "Indian Rights and Customary Law in Mexico: A Study of the Navahos in the Sierra de Puebla." *Law & Society Review* 29: 227–254.

Silberman, Laurence H. 1998. "Will Lawyering Strangle Democratic Capitalism? A Retrospective." *Harvard Journal of Law & Public Policy* 21: 607–621.

Silberman, Matthew. 1985. *The Civil Justice Process: A Sequential Model of the Mobilization of Law*. Orlando, FL: Academic Press.

Silbey, Susan S. 1997. "Let Them Eat Cake: Globalization, Postmodern Colonialism, and the Possibilities of Justice." *Law & Society Review* 31: 207–235.

Silbey, Susan S., and Austin Sarat. 1987. "Critical Traditions in Law and Society Research." *Law & Society Review* 21: 165–174.

Simon, David. 1999. *Elite Deviance*. 6th ed. Boston: Allyn & Bacon.

Simon, James F. 1980. *Independent Journey: The Life of William O. Douglas*. New York: Harper & Row.

Simon, Rita James. 1968. *The Sociology of Law: Interdisciplinary Readings*. San Francisco: Chandler.

Simon, Rita James, and James P. Lynch. 1989. "The Sociology of Law: Where We Have Been and Where We Might Be Going." *Law & Society Review* 23: 825–847.

Simon, William H. 1998. "The Kaye Scholer Affair: The Lawyer's Duty of Candor and the Bar's Temptations of Evasion and Apology." *Law & Social Inquiry* 23: 243–296.

Simpson, A. W. B. 1984. *Cannibalism and the Common Law: The Story of the Tragic Last Voyage of the Mignonette*. Chicago: University of Chicago Press.

———. 1988. *Invitation to Law*. Oxford: Blackwell.

Singer, Joseph William. 1984. "The Player and the Cards: Nihilism and Legal Theory." *Yale Law Review* 94: 1–70.

Singer, Simon. 1996. *Recriminalizing Delinquency: Violent Juvenile Crime and Juvenile Justice Reform*. Cambridge, UK: Cambridge University Press.

Skedsvold, Paula R., and Tammy L. Mann. 1996. "The Affirmative Action Debate: What's Fair in Policy and Programs?" *Journal of Social Issues* 52: 1–160.

Skocpol, Theda. 1992. *Protecting Soldiers and Mothers: The Political Origins of Social Policy in the United States*. Cambridge, MA: Harvard University Press.

Skolnick, Jerome H. 1965. "The Sociology of Law in America: Overview and Trends." *Law and Society* (Summer): 4–38.

———. 1966. *Justice Without Trial*. New York: Wiley.

———. 1978. *House of Cards: Legalization and Control of Casino Gambling*. Boston: Little Brown.

Skrentny, John David. 1996. *The Ironies of Affirmative Action: Politics, Culture, and Justice in America*. Chicago: University of Chicago Press.

Small, Mark, ed. 1997. "Juvenile Justice." *Behavioral Sciences & the Law* 15: 119–213.

Smart, Carol. 1989. *Feminism and the Power of Law*. New York: Routledge.

Smigel, Erwin. 1969. *The Wall Street Lawyer*. Bloomington: Indiana University Press.

Smith, Christopher. 1993. *Courts, Politics, and the Judicial Process*. Chicago: Nelson-Hall.

Smith, Douglas A., and Christy A. Visher. 1981. "Street-level Justice: Situational Determinants of Police Arrest Decisions." *Social Problems* 29: 167–177.

Smith, K. W., and K. A. Kinsey. 1987. "Understanding Taxpayers' Behavior: A Conceptual Framework With Implications for Research." *Law & Society Review* 21: 639–663.

Smith, Michael Clay, and Margaret D. Smith. 1999. "Treat Students as Adults: Set the Drinking Age at 18, Not 21." *The Chronicle of Higher Education* (March 12): B8.

Smith, Patricia, ed. 1993. *Feminist Jurisprudence*. New York: Oxford University Press.

Smith, Steven D. 1997. "Natural Law and Contemporary Moral Thought: A Guide From the Perplexed." *The American Journal of Jurisprudence* 42: 299–330.

Snyder, Francis. 1996. "Law and Anthropology." Pp. 135–179, in Philip A. Thomas, ed. *Legal Frontiers*. Aldershot, UK: Dartmouth.

Soifer, Avram. 1988. "Beyond Mirrors: Lawrence Friedman's Moving Pictures." *Law & Society Review* 22: 995–1016.

———. 1992. "Reflections on the 40th Anniversary of Hurst's *Growth of American Law*." *Law and Social Inquiry* 17: 167–179.

Solinger, Rickie, ed. 1998. *Abortion Wars: A Half Century of Struggle, 1950–2000*. Berkeley: University of California Press.

Solzhenitsyn, Aleksandr I. (1976) *The Gulag Archipelago: 1918–1956*. (Volumes V–VII). New York: Harper & Row.

Soothill, Keith, Sylvia Walby, and Paul Bagguley. 1990. "Judges, the Media, and Rape." *Journal of Law and Society* 17: 211–233.

Spaeth, Harold J., and Jeffrey A Segal. 1999. *Majority Rule or Minority Will: Adherence to Precedent on the U.S. Supreme Court*. New York: Cambridge University Press.

Spangler, Eve. 1986. *Lawyers for Hire*. New Haven, CT: Yale University Press.

Spencer, Herbert. 1898. *The Principles of Sociology*. Volume II. New York: D. Appleton & Co.

Spitzer, Steven. 1975. "Punishment and Social Organization: A Study of Durkheim's Theory of Penal Evolution." *Law & Society Review* 9: 613–635.

Spohn, Cassia, and Julie Horney. 1991. "The Law's the Law, but Fair Is Fair: Rape Shield Laws and Officials' Assessments of Sexual History Evidence." *Criminology* 29: 137–161.

Stanely, Alessandra. 1992. "Selling Voters on Bush, Nemesis of Lawyers." *The New York Times* (August 31): A1.

Stein, Laura W. 1999. *Sexual Harassment in America: A Documentary History*. Westport, CT: Greenwood Press.

Steinhoff, Patricia G. 1993. "Pursuing the Japanese Police." *Law & Society Review* 27: 827–850.

Stevens, Robert B. 1983. *Law School: Legal Education in America From the 1850s to the 1980s*. Chapel Hill: University of North Carolina Press.

Steytler, Nico C. 1987. "Criminal Justice and the Apartheid State." Pp. 68–84, in A. J. Rycroft, L. S. Boule, M. K. Robertson, and F. R. Stiller, eds. *Race and the Law in South Africa*. Cape Town, RSA: Juta & Co.

Stick, John. 1986. "Can Nihilism Be Pragmatic?" *Harvard Law Review* 100: 332–401.

Stith, Kate, and Jose A. Cabranes. 1998. *Fear of Judging: Sentencing Guidelines in the Federal Courts*. Chicago: University of Chicago Press.

Stoesz, David. 1997. "Welfare Behaviorism." *Society* (April/May): 68–77.

Stover, Robert V. 1989. *Making It and Breaking It: The Fate of Public Interest Commitment During Law School*. (H. Erlanger, ed.). Urbana: University of Illinois Press.

Strick, Ann. 1978. *Injustice for All*. New York: Penguin.

Stryker, Robin. 1989. "Limits on Technocratization of the Law: The Elimination of the National Labor Relations Board's Division of Economic Research." *American Sociological Review* 54: 341–358.

Subin, Harry I. 1987. "The Criminal Lawyer's Different Mission: Reflections on the Right to Present a False Case." *Georgetown Journal of Legal Ethics* 1: 125–136.

Sugarman, David, ed. 1981. *Legality, Ideology and the State*. London: Academic Press.

Summers, Robert S. 1972. *Law: Its Nature, Functions, and Limits*. 2nd ed. Englewood Cliffs, NJ: Prentice-Hall.

———. 1997. "How Law Is Formal and Why It Matters." *Cornell Law Review* 82: 1165–1229.

Sumner, William Graham. [1906] 1960. *Folkways*. New York: Mentor.

Sunstein, Cass R. 1996. *Legal Reasoning and Political Conflict*. New York: Oxford University Press.

———. 1999. *One Case at a Time: Judicial Minimalism on the Supreme Court*. Cambridge, MA: Harvard University Press.

———. 2000. "Code Comfort." *The New Republic* (January 10): 37–43.

Susskind, Richard. 1996. *The Future of Law: Facing the Challenge of Information Technology*. Oxford, UK: Clarendon Press.

Sussman, Erika. 1998. "Contending With Culture: An Analysis of the Female Genital Mutilation Act of 1996." *Cornell International Law Journal* 31: 194–270.

Sutherland, Arthur E. 1967. *The Law at Harvard*. Cambridge, MA: Harvard University Press.

Sutton, John P. 1985. "The Juvenile Court and Social Welfare: Dynamics of Progressive Reform." *Law & Society Review* 19: 107–145.

Symonides, Janusz, ed. 1998. *Human Rights: New Dimensions and Challenges*. Brookfield, VT: Ashgate Publishing Co.

Tamanaha, Brian Z. 1993. "The Folly of the 'Social Scientific' Concept of Legal Pluralism." *Journal of Law & Society* 20: 192–217.

———. 1997. *Realistic Social-Legal Theory: Pragmatism and a Social Theory of Law*. New York: Oxford University Press.

Tanford, J. Alexander. 1991. "Law Reform by Courts, Legislators, and Commissions Following Empirical Research on Jury Instructions." *Law & Society Review* 25: 155–175.

Tannenbaum, Frank. 1946. *Slave and Citizen*. New York: Alfred A. Knopf.

Tanner, Harold. 1995. "Policing, Punishment, and the Individual: Criminal Justice in China." *Law and Social Inquiry* 20: 277–303.

Tarpley, Joan R. 1997. "Bad Witches: A Cut on the Clitoris With the Instruments of Institutional Power and Politics." *West Virginia Law Review* 100: 297–352.

Taslitz, Andrew E. 1999. *Rape and the Culture of the Courtroom*. New York: New York University Press.

Tay, Alice Erh-Soon. 1990. "Communist Visions, Communist Realities, and the Role of Law." *Journal of Law & Society* 17: 155–169.

Taylor, E. L. Hedbden. 1969. *The Christian Philosophy of Law, Politics and the State*. Nutley, NJ: The Craig Press.

Taylor, Ian. 1999. "Criminology Post-Maastricht." *Crime, Law, & Social Change* 30: 333–346.

Taylor, Stuart, Jr. 1983. "Ethics and the Law: A Case History." *The New York Times* (January 9): 31–33, 46–49.

———. 1988. "Court, 8–0, Refuses to Curb Criticism of Public Figures." *The New York Times* (February 25): A1.

Taylor, Telford. 1970. *Nuremberg and Vietnam: An American Tragedy*. New York: Bantam.

Teles, Steven M. 1996. *Whose Welfare? AFDC and Elite Politics*. Lawrence: University of Kansas Press.

Terrill, Richard J. 1992. *World Criminal Justice Systems: A Survey*. 2nd ed. Cincinnati, OH: Anderson Publishing Co.

Terry, Don. 1998. "Mother Rages Against Indifference." *The New York Times* (August 24): A10.

Teubner, Gunther, ed. 1997. *Global Law Without a State*. Aldershot, UK: Dartmouth.

Tewksbury, William J. 1967. "The Ordeal as a Vehicle for Divine Intervention in Medieval Europe." Pp. 267–270, in Paul Bohannon, ed. *Law and Warfare*. New York: The Natural History Press.

Thomas, Philip A., ed. 1996. *Legal Frontiers*. Aldershot, UK: Dartmouth.

———. 1997. *Socio-Legal Studies*. Aldershot, UK: Dartmouth.

Thompson, E. P. 1978. *Whigs and Hunters: The Origin of the Black Act*. London: Penguin.

Thompson, H. 1986. "The Role of the Rule of Law in the Liberal State." *Natal University Law and Society Review* 1: 126–137.

Thompson, William N. 1994. *Legalized Gambling*. Santa Barbara, CA: ABC-Clio.

Thornton, Margaret. 1996. *Dissonance and Distrust: Women in the Legal Profession*. Melbourne, Australia: Oxford University Press.

Tiersma, Peter M. 1999. *Legal Language*. Chicago: University of Chicago Press.

Tigar, Michael E., and Madeleine R. Levy. 1977. *Law and the Rise of Capitalism*. New York: Monthly Review Press.

Timasheff, N. S. [1939] 1974. *An Introduction to the Sociology of Law*. Westport, CT: Greenwood Press.

Time. 1978. "TV Wins a Crucial Case." *Time* (August 21): 85.

Tjaden, Patricia, and Nancy Thoennes. 1998. "Stalking in America: Findings from the National Violence Against Women Survey." *NIJ CDL Research in Brief* (April): 1–19.

Tocqueville, Alexis de. [1835–1840] 1945. *Democracy in America*. Volumes I & II. P. Bradley, ed. New York: Alfred A. Knopf.

Tomasic, Roman. 1985. *The Sociology of Law*. London: Sage.

Tomasic, Roman, and Malcolm Feeley, eds. 1982. *Neighborhood Justice*. New York: Longman.

Tonry, Michael. 1996. *Sentencing Matters*. New York: Oxford University Press.

Tonry, Michael, and Kathleen Hatlestad, eds. 1997. *Sentencing Reform in Overcrowded Times: A Comparative Perspective*. New York: Oxford University Press.

Toobin, Jeffrey. 1998. "The Trouble With Sex." *The New Yorker* (February 18): 48–55.

Torney, Judith. 1977. "Socialization and Attitudes Toward the Legal System." Pp. 134–144, in June Louin Tapp and Felice J. Levine, eds. *Law, Justice, and the Individual in Society: Psychological and Legal Issues*. New York: Holt, Rinehart & Winston.

Touster, Saul. 1993. "Holmes' Common Law: A Centennial View." *The American Scholar* (Autumn, 1982): 521–531.

Trattner, Walter I. 1999. *From Poor Law to Welfare State*. New York: Free Press.

Tremper, Charles Robert. 1987. "Sanguinity and Disillusionment Where Law Meets Social Science." *Law and Human Behavior* 11: 267–276.

Trevino, A. Javier. 1996. *The Sociology of Law: Classical and Contemporary Perspectives*. New York: St. Martin's.

Trubek, David M. 1986. "Max Weber's Tragic Modernism and the Study of Law in Society." *Law & Society Review* 20: 573–598.

Tsosie, Rebecca. 1997. "American Indians and the Politics of Recognition: Soifer on Law, Pluralism, and Group Identity." *Law and Social Inquiry* 22: 359–388.

Turk, Austin T. 1969. *Criminality and Legal Order*. Chicago: Rand McNally Co.

Turkel, Gerald. 1990. "Michel Foucault: Law, Power, and Knowledge." *Journal of Law & Society* 17: 170–192.

———. 1996. *Law and Society: Critical Approaches*. Boston: Allyn & Bacon.

Turner, Stephen, and Regis A. Factor. 1994. *Max Weber: The Lawyer as Social Thinker*. London: Routledge.

Turow, Scott. 1977. *One L*. New York: G. P. Putnam's Sons.

———. 1997. "The High Court's 20-Year-Old Mistake." *The New York Times* (October 12): Op-Ed Page.

Tushnet, Mark. 1977. "Perspectives on the Development of American Law: A Critical Review of Friedman's *A History of American Law*." *Wisconsin Law Review* 1977: 81–109.

———. 1991. "Critical Legal Studies: A Political History." *The Yale Law Journal* 100: 1315–1544.

———. 1998. "Is Judicial Review Good for the Left?" *Dissent* (Winter): 65–70.

Tyler, Patrick E. 1999. "Tobacco-Busting Lawyers on Near Gold-Dusted Trails." *The New York Times* (March 10): A1.

Tyler, Tom R. 1990. *Why People Obey the Law*. New Haven, CT: Yale University Press.

———. 1998. "Justice and Power in Civil Dispute Processing." Pp. 309–346, in Bryant Garth and Austin Sarat, eds. *Justice and Power in Sociolegal Studies*. Chicago, IL: Northwestern University Press.

Tyler, Tom R., Robert J. Boeckmann, Heather J. Smith, and Yuen J. Huo. 1997. *Social Justice in a Diverse Society*. Boulder, CO: Westview Press.

Tyler, Tom R., and Kenneth Rasinski. 1991. "Procedural Justice, Institutional Legitimacy, and the Acceptance of Unpopular U.S. Supreme Court Decisions: A Reply to Gibson." *Law & Society Review* 25: 621–635.

Uelmen, Gerald F. 1992. "Federal Sentencing Guidelines: A Cure Worse than the Disease." *American Criminal Law Review* 29: 899–905.

Ulmer, Jeffery, and John H. Kramer. 1996. "Court Communities Under Sentencing Guidelines: Dilemmas for Formal Rationality and Sentencing Disparity." *Criminology* 34: 383–407.

Umbreit, Mark S. 1994. *Victim Meets Offender: The Impact of Restorative Justice and Mediation*. Monsey, NY: Criminal Justice Press.

Underwood, Barbara D. 1981. "Against Dichotomy." *The Yale Law Journal* 90: 1004–1007.

Upham, Frank K. 1987. *Law and Social Change in Postwar Japan*. Cambridge, MA: Harvard University Press.

Uviller, H. Richard. 1999. *The Tilted Playing Field: Is Criminal Justice Unfair?* New Haven, CT: Yale University Press.

Vago, Steven. 1994. *Law & Society*. 4th ed. Englewood Cliffs, NJ: Prentice Hall.

Vagts, Detlev. 1996. "The International Legal Profession: A Need for More Governance?" *The American Journal of International Law* 90: 250–261.

Valencia-Weber, Gloria. 1994. "American Indian Law and History: Instructional Mirrors." *Journal of Legal Education* 44: 251–266.

Vandevelde, Kenneth J. 1996. *Thinking Like a Lawyer: An Introduction to Legal Reasoning*. Boulder, CO: Westview Press.

Van Hoy, Jerry. 1997a. *Franchise Legal Firms and the Transformation of Personal Legal Services*. Westport, CT: Quorum Books.

——. 1997b. "The Practice Dynamics of Solo and Small Firm Lawyers." *Law & Society Review* 31: 377–387.

Vidmar, Neil. 1984. "The Small Claims Court: A Reconceptualization of Disputes and an Empirical Investigation." *Law & Society Review* 18: 515–550.

Vincent, Andrew. 1996. "Law and Politics." Pp. 106–134, in Philip A. Thomas, ed. *Legal Frontiers*. Aldershot, UK: Dartmouth Publishing Co.

Von Benda-Beckmann, Keebet. 1989. "Comment on Simon and Lynch." *Law & Society Review* 23: 849–856.

Von Glahn, Gerhard. 1992. *Law Among Nations: An Introduction to Public International Law*. 6th ed. New York: MacMillan.

Von Hirsch, Andrew, and Andrew Ashworth, eds. 1992. *Principled Sentencing*. Boston: Northeastern University Press.

Voss, Frederick. 1989. *Portraits of American Law*. Washington, DC: National Portrait Gallery.

Wagatsuma, Hiroshi, and Arthur Rosett. 1986. "The Implications of Apology: Law and Culture in Japan and the United States." *Law & Society Review* 20: 461–507.

Walker, Samuel. 1980. *Popular Justice: A History of American Criminal Justice*. New York: Oxford University Press.

———. 1990. *In Defense of American Liberties: A History of the ACLU*. New York: Oxford University Press.

———. 1993. *Taming the System: The Control of Discretion in Criminal Justice, 1950–1990*. New York: Oxford.

———. 1998. *The Rights Revolution: Rights and Community in Modern America*. New York: Oxford University Press.

Wall, David S., and Johnstone, Jennifer. 1997. "The Industrialization of Legal Practice and the Rise of the New Electronic Lawyer: The Impact of Technology on Legal Practice in the U.K." *International Journal of the Sociology of Law* 25: 95–116.

Wallace, Harvey, and Cliff Roberson. 1996. *Principles of Criminal Law*. White Plains, NY: Longman.

Wallace, Jonathan, and Mark Mangan. 1996. *Sex, Laws, and Cyberspace*. Indianapolis, IN: IOG Books Worldwide.

Ward, Richard. 1997a. "Public Security in Modern China." *Crime & Justice International* (April): 5–8.

———. 1997b. "China's Police: New Laws and Duties." *Crime & Justice International* (May): 12–17.

Watson, Alan. 1995. *The Spirit of Roman Law*. Athens: The University of Georgia Press.

Weber, Max. 1949. *The Methodology of the Social Sciences*. New York: The Free Press.

———. [1954] 1967. *On Law in Economy and Society.* (Max Rheinstein, ed.) New York: Simon & Schuster.

———. 1964. *The Theory of Social and Economic Organization.* (A. M. Henderson and T. L. Parsons, transl.) New York: Free Press.

———. 1978. *Economy and Society.* Volumes I & II. (Guenther Roth and Claus Wittich, eds.) Berkeley: University of California Press.

Webster, D. 1987. "Repression and the State of Emergency." Pp. 141–172, in G. Moss and J. Obery, eds. *South Africa Review 4.* Johannesburg, RSA: Ravan Press.

Wechsler, Henry. 1996. "Alcohol and the American College Campus." *Change* (July/August): 20–25, 60.

Weinberg, Lee S., and Judith W. Weinberg. 1980. *Law and Society: An Interdisciplinary Introduction.* Lanham, MD: University Press of America.

Weinreb, Lloyd L. 1977. *Denial of Justice: Criminal Process in the United States.* New York: The Free Press.

———. 1987. *Law and Justice.* Cambridge, MA: Harvard University Press.

Weisberg, Richard H. 1984. *The Failure of the Word.* New Haven, CT: Yale University Press.

———. 1992. *Poethics and Other Strategies of Law and Literature.* New York: Columbia University Press.

Wellman, Carl. 1995. *Real Rights.* New York: Oxford University Press.

West, Robin. 1985. "Authority, Autonomy, and Choice: The Rule of Consent in the Moral and Political Visions of Franz Kafka and Richard Posner." *Harvard Law Review* 99: 384–428.

———. 1988. "Jurisprudence and Gender." *University of Chicago Law Review* 55: 1–72.

———. 1997. *Caring for Justice.* New York: New York University Press.

West, Thomas G. 1998. *Vindicating the Founders: Race, Sex, Class, and Justice in the Origins of America.* Lanham, MD: Rowman & Littlefield.

Westermann, Ted D., and James W. Burfeind. 1991. *Crime and Justice in Two Societies: Japan and the United States.* Pacific Grove, CA: Brooks/Cole Publishing Co.

Westermarck, E. A. 1906. *The Origin and Development of Moral Ideas.* New York: MacMillan.

Weyler, Rex. 1992. *Blood of the Land: The Government and Corporate War Against First Nations.* Philadelphia: New Society Publishers.

Wheeler, Stanton, Bliss Cartwright, Robert A. Kagan, and Lawrence M. Friedman. 1987. "Do the Haves Come Out Ahead? Winning and Losing in State Supreme Courts, 1870–1970." *Law & Society Review* 21: 403–445.

White, G. Edward. 1972. "From Sociological Jurisprudence to Realism: Jurisprudence and Social Change in Early Twentieth Century America." *Virginia Law Review* 58: 999–1028.

———. 1976. *The American Judicial Tradition.* New York: Oxford University Press.

———. 1988. "The Anti-Judge: William O. Douglas and the Ambiguities of Individuality." *Virginia Law Review* 74: 17–86.

White, James Boyd. [1973] 1985. *The Legal Imagination.* Abridged ed. Chicago: University of Chicago Press.

———. 1984. *When Words Lose Their Meaning: Constitutions and Reconstitutions of Language, Character, and Community.* Chicago: University of Chicago Press.

Wiehl, Lis. 1989. "Louisiana Begins to Slip Its Ties to France." *The New York Times* (October 13): B5.

Wilbanks, William, and Coramae Richey Mann. 1996. "Racism in the Criminal Justice System: Two Sides of a Controversy." Pp. 54–64, in Chris W. Eskridge, ed. *Criminal Justice: Concepts and Issues*. 2nd ed. Los Angeles: Roxbury.

Williams, Patricia J. 1991. *The Alchemy of Race and Rights*. Cambridge, MA: Harvard University Press.

Williams, Robert A., Jr. 1990. *The American Indian in Western Legal Thought: The Discourses of Conquest*. New York: Oxford University Press.

Williams, Verna L. 1999. "A New Harassment Ruling: Implications for Colleges." *The Chronicle of Higher Education* (June 14): A56.

Wilson, James Q. 1968. *Varieties of Police Behavior.* Cambridge, MA: Harvard University Press.

———. 1997. *Moral Judgment: Does the Abuse Excuse Threaten Our Legal System?* New York: Basic Books.

Winkler, Karen S. 1988. "Controversial Judge and Legal Theorist Jumps Into the Debate on Law and Literature." *The Chronicle of Higher Education* 35: 5–6.

Wise, Steven M. 1999. *Rattling the Cage: Toward Legal Rights for Animals*. Cambridge, MA: Perseus Books.

Wishman, Seymour. 1981. *Confessions of a Criminal Lawyer.* New York: Times Books.

Witte, John, Jr. 1996. "Law, Religion, and Human Rights." *Columbia Human Rights Law Review* 28: 1–31.

Wolfson, Mark. 1995. "The Legislative Impact of Social Movement Organizations: The Anti-Drunken-Driving Movement and the 21-Year-Old Drinking Age." *Social Science Quarterly* 76: 311–327.

Wolfson, Nicholas. 1997. *Hate Speech, Sex Speech, Free Speech*. Westport, CT: Praeger.

Wood, Arthur Lewis. 1967. *Criminal Lawyer.* New Haven, CT: College and University Press.

Woodward, C. Vann. 1957. *The Strange Career of Jim Crow.* New York: Oxford University Press.

Worden, Robert E. 1989. "Situational and Attitudinal Explanations of Police Behavior: A Theoretical Appraisal and Empirical Assessment." *Law & Society Review* 23: 667–711.

Wortley, Scot, John Hagan, and Ross MacMillan. 1997. "Just Des(s)erts: The Racial Polarization of Perceptions of Criminal Justice." *Law & Society Review* 31: 637–676.

Wrightsman, Lawrence S. 1991. *Psychology and the Legal System*. 2nd ed. Pacific Grove, CA: Brooks/Cole.

Wrong, Dennis H. 1995. "Conscience and Culture." *Dissent* (Winter): 127–130.

Wu, Bohsiu. 2000. "Determinants of Public Opinion Toward Juvenile Waiver Decisions." *Juvenile and Family Court Journal* 51: 9–20.

Wueste, Daniel E. 1986. "Fuller's Processual Philosophy of Law." *Cornell Law Review* 71: 1205–1230.

Wunder, John R., ed. 1996. *Recent Legal Issues for American Indians, 1968 to the Present*. New York: Garland.

Xu, Xinyi. 1995. "The Impact of Western Forms of Social Control on China: A Preliminary Evaluation." *Crime, Law and Social Change* 23: 67–87.

Yang, Kun. 1989. "Law and Society Studies in Korea: Beyond the Hahm Thesis." *Law & Society Review* 23: 893–901.

Yarnold, Barbara M. 1992. *Politics and the Courts: Toward a General Theory of Public Law*. New York: Praeger.

Yisheng, Dai. 1997. "Haves vs. Have Nots: One of the Factors Causing Crime in China." *Crime & Justice International* (February): 23–25.

Yngvesson, Barbara. 1993. *Virtuous Citizens, Disruptive Subjects: Order and Complaint in a New England Court*. New York: Routledge.

Zane, John M. 1927. *The Story of Law*. Garden City, NY: Garden City Publishing.

Zasloff, Jonathan. 1998. "Children, Families, and Bureaucrats: A Prehistory of Welfare Reform." *Journal of Law and Politics* 14: 225–317.

Zatz, Marjorie S. 1994. *Producing Legality: Law and Socialism in Cuba*. New York: Routledge.

Zellner, William W. 1995. *Counter Cultures: A Sociological Analysis*. New York: St. Martin's Press.

Zimmerman, Richard. 1998. "Law Reviews: A Foray Through a Strange World." *Emory Law Review* 47: 660–695.

Zorn, Jean G. 1990. "Lawyers, Anthropologists, and the Study of Law: Encounters in the New Guinea Highlands." *Law and Social Inquiry* 15: 271–304.

Subject Index

Explanatory Note: The fullest definition of certain key terms indexed on more than one page are indicated by boldface type. Most proper names, whether of subjects or authors of works cited, can be found in the Name Index, but a few proper names, of individuals discussed in boxes, are listed here as well.

A

B

C

F

G

H

I

M

T

U

V

W

X, Y

Z

Name Index

C

D

E

F

G

H

I

J

K

L

M

N

O

P

Q

R

S

T

ULYSSES S. GRANT

General and President

Ulysses S. Grant:

ILLUSTRATED BY WILLIAM MOYERS

General and President

JOSEPH OLGIN

HOUGHTON MIFFLIN COMPANY · BOSTON

NEW YORK · ATLANTA · GENEVA, ILL. · DALLAS · PALO ALTO

Contents

Library of Congress Catalog Card No. 67–10460

CHAPTER 1

Horses! Horses! Horses!

Horses! Horses! Horses! How little Ulysses loved his four-legged friends! There were always teams of horses waiting patiently in the yard outside his father's tannery.

Jesse Grant, Ulysses' father, had built a new business in the village of Georgetown, Ohio. Georgetown was twenty-five miles east of Point Pleasant, where Ulysses had been born almost four years ago on April 27, 1822. Mr. Grant had also built a fine two-story brick house near the tannery.

Ulysses had grown into a fine, husky boy. He had no fear at all of the workhorses that filled the yard. He loved to walk down the path, holding their reins and looking up into their faces. He was a rather silent boy, taking completely after his mother, Hannah Simpson Grant.

"Hannah, look!" Mrs. Hamner, a neighbor of the Grants, called one day. "Ulysses is playing under the horses' legs. They'll crush him to death!"

Mrs. Grant only smiled. "Horses seem to understand Ulysses," she said quietly.

Just then Ulysses began to swing happily on a horse's tail.

Mrs. Hamner shouted in alarm, "Please, Hannah, take the child away from that animal! If it kicks back with that ironshod hoof . . ."

"Calm yourself," Mrs. Grant said. "The Good Lord watches over my son. He'll be safe."

On Ulysses' fourth birthday, Mr. Grant hitched up his best horse to the buggy. "In honor of Ulysses' birthday," he said, "we will drive to Point Pleasant for a picnic. I want to show Ulysses the place where he was born."

It was a lovely day. Here and there men were cutting down trees to clear their land. The sound of axes and the smell of burning brush filled the air.

"Look, Hannah," Mr. Grant said. "New people are flooding into Ohio. You know what that means — new homes, new demands for leather, shoes, harnesses. My tannery will help fill these needs." Mrs. Grant smiled at her eager husband.

Ulysses looked with great interest at the modest one-family wooden house in which he had been born. It stood on the banks of the beautiful Ohio River.

"I know what you're thinking, son," Mr. Grant said. "Our new house is so much nicer than this one."

Ulysses shrugged his shoulders. "We have more horses at our new house," he said.

Suddenly Mr. Grant laughed. "Hannah,

do you remember the hard time we had choosing Ulysses' name? Everyone in the family wanted a different one."

Ulysses had heard the story many times of how his name had finally been picked from names written on slips of paper placed in Grandpa Simpson's hat. "I'm glad you picked *Ulysses,*" he said. "I like my name."

"But *Hiram* was the first name drawn," Mrs. Grant told him. "Ulysses is really your middle name."

"No one ever calls him Hiram, and no one ever will," Mr. Grant said. "It just doesn't seem to fit him."

The Grants had a lovely picnic on the banks of the Ohio. Ulysses watched the busy river traffic flowing up and down the river. The white steamers pressing against the sunlit current made a pretty sight.

Mr. Grant pointed across the broad Ohio to Maysville, Kentucky, and said, "Someday we must visit your Uncle Peter. I used to work in his tannery before I went into business for myself. He is a very rich man."

"Does he have many horses?" Ulysses asked.

The two grown-ups laughed, and the family started back to Georgetown.

A few days later Mr. Grant announced a great event. "Today we'll go to see the circus that's in town. We'll have a fine time. Ulysses will love seeing the wild animals."

The Grants dressed in their Sunday best and drove down to the Square. Circus music blared. Barkers' voices shouted the wonders to be seen in the big tent. Mrs. Grant went inside to meet Mrs. Hamner and several other women from the church she attended. Mr. Grant walked around the circus grounds, holding his young son by the hand. He was so proud of Ulysses that he boasted about him to anyone who would listen.

"My son has no fear of anything," he bragged. "What other boy his age would dare to play right under a horse's legs and swing on his tail?"

A young man standing nearby heard Mr. Grant's remarks. "I'll bet he'd cry if I fired

this gun near him," he said, moving up closer.

"Nonsense," Mr. Grant said. "I know my son. Here, give me that gun." He carefully held the rifle with the barrel pointing upward so no one could get hurt. He placed Ulysses' finger around the trigger. Then he pressed it down slowly with his own finger. Boom! The gun exploded with an ear-shattering crash. Several people winced and closed their eyes. A young lady clapped her hands over her ears and gave a cry of alarm.

But Ulysses hardly moved. He remained completely calm. Not so his father. "There, didn't I tell you the boy was brave?" he bragged.

The youth who owned the gun had to admit that Mr. Grant was right. "That son of yours has nerves of iron — better nerves than I have, and I'll be voting in the next election."

Mr. Grant then took Ulysses to see the wild animals. The boy stared at the lions and the tigers. Somehow he didn't seem as interested in them as his father had thought he would be.

"Horses, let's go see the horses!" said Ulysses.

Mr. Grant laughed and took him into the main tent, where they joined Mrs. Grant in the stands. The ringmaster, dressed in a black outfit with a high silk hat, was snapping his long whip at a little black pony that was prancing around the ring.

"Who wants to ride the pony?" the ringmaster called out.

Ulysses, who was usually very quiet, cried out, "Let *me* ride the pony! Let *me!*"

"Oh, no," Mrs. Grant said, "he's too frisky, Ulysses."

"Yes, yes, let me, let me," Ulysses begged.

"All right," Mr. Grant said. "You may ride the pony around the ring, but I'll hold you."

Ulysses was overjoyed as his father put him on the pony's back. "Gee-up," he yelled, laughing and jumping up and down with joy.

"I never saw Ulysses so happy," Mr. Grant said later as they drove home. "That boy surely loves horses."

Mrs. Grant looked down at her son. "Yes, and horses seem to love Ulysses, too."

CHAPTER 2

Schoolboy Adventures

In the fall Ulysses' father entered him in the village school. It was not a free school. Mr. Grant paid a dollar and fifty cents for a thirteen-week term. Other boys' fathers gave corn, wheat, flax, or tobacco in exchange for their sons' schooling. The teacher was old Mr. Barney. He taught reading, writing, arithmetic, and little else. All the pupils were in one room, from little Ulysses to big, brawny axemen. The number of whippings Mr. Barney gave astonished Ulysses. Dust blew from the boys' jackets all day, and broken switches flew about the room.

Ulysses behaved very well. Although he wasn't the smartest boy in the school, he was good at arithmetic, never failed any of his subjects, and was promoted each term. By the time he was ten, he had a reputation of being bashful, quiet, but very determined.

One day his friends Jimmy Sanderson and Johnny Marshall and his cousin Dan Ammen decided to have a little fun with Ulysses.

"Let's see if we can get his new top away from him," Dan whispered when Mr. White, their strict new teacher, left the room. The three boys set upon Ulysses, who fought back strongly. They managed to wrestle him to the floor, but they couldn't get at the top.

Ulysses kicked wildly about, laughing and shouting, "You might as well stop trying! You can't make me give it up!"

Just then Mr. White came back into the room. The other boys had heard him coming. Quickly they ran back to their seats. Ulysses was caught flat on the floor, still shouting and kicking. A silence fell over the room as Mr. White seized Ulysses by one ear.

"Who else was mixed up in this disgraceful affair?" he roared at him.

Ulysses grew pale, but he wouldn't tell who the boys were.

"Perhaps a taste of the switch will loosen your tongue," said Mr. White.

Ulysses took the switching manfully, still refusing to tell on his friends.

After school Ulysses and Dan went for a horseback ride to a nearby fishing stream. On the way Ulysses decided to be a little more daring than usual. He stood up on the horse's back and rode, balancing himself with the long reins.

"Dan!" he shouted. "This is fun! Why don't you try it?"

"Not me," Dan said. "I can't ride well enough to risk my neck doing that."

When they arrived at the stream, they stared in surprise. It had rained the night before. The brook was now racing wildly and overflowing its banks.

"We'd better not fish here today," Dan said. "It looks dangerous."

Ulysses laughed. "After facing Mr. White today, nothing scares me," he said.

He noticed a log jutting out into the stream. "I'm going to crawl out there," he said. "Fishing is best over rushing water."

"Don't," Dan warned. "If you fall in, you'll be sorry."

But Ulysses, fishing rod in hand, was already crawling out onto the log. The rushing water under him made him dizzy. For a moment he wanted to crawl back, but he shook his head and began to inch forward again. Suddenly the log shifted and began to roll. Ulysses held on hard, but it was no use. He was thrown head first into the water and swept along like a piece of driftwood.

"Help! Help!" Dan screamed. But there was no one around to help the boys.

Ulysses was powerless against the force of the stream. He knew he had to save himself quickly or he'd be badly cut on the sharp rocks.

"The bend!" he shouted. "The willow tree!"

Dan saw what Ulysses meant. He ran at top speed to the bend in the stream. A huge willow tree spread its branches across the stream at this point. Praying hard that he would be in time, Dan crawled out on the lowest branch and hooked his legs firmly around it. Just then Ulysses came hurtling by. Dan reached down and caught hold of Ulysses' shirt. If the shirt ripped, Ulysses was lost. But the shirt held, and Ulysses reached up, grasped the branch, and managed to pull himself from the water. The branch creaked under the weight of the two boys. Slowly, ever so slowly, Ulysses and Dan crept along it until they reached the bank. There they collapsed, exhausted.

"What a day this has been," Ulysses sighed. "I'd better go home and stay in bed. This isn't my lucky day."

But that night, when Jimmy and Dan reminded him that there was a carnival in town, Ulysses was ready for further adventure.

By now Ulysses was considered one of the

best riders in Georgetown. Many farmers brought him their wild colts to tame. At the carnival Ulysses watched carefully when the ringmaster offered five dollars to anyone who could ride a trick colt. Young men and boys, one after another, tried. All were quickly knocked off by the colt's bucking and wheeling. Ulysses suspected the colt's back had been greased. Still, he suddenly got up and said to his friends, "I think I know how to handle this colt."

"Don't try it," Jimmy whispered. "You'll make a fool of yourself."

Ulysses shook his head. "I must try it," he said quietly.

The crowd grew tense as Ulysses entered the ring and jumped up on the colt's back. The colt began to buck and twist wildly. When it reared up on its hind legs, Ulysses dug his heels into its flanks. When it put its head down and kicked with its hind legs, he threw his arms around its neck and ground in his bare toes behind its shoulder blades. The crowd began to cheer.

Ulysses gritted his teeth and held on. The ringmaster was angry. He hadn't expected that he would have to pay anyone the five dollars he had offered. He decided to try a trick to unseat the boy. Suddenly he tossed a monkey onto Ulysses' shoulder. The frightened monkey pulled his hair and scratched his neck. But Ulysses only set his jaw and held on. By now he was sorry he had taken on the task, but he wouldn't give up. Around and around the ring he whirled.

"Had enough, boy?" the ringmaster shouted.

Ulysses stubbornly shook his head. It was plain to see that he would never have enough. Unwillingly, the ringmaster announced that Ulysses had won.

A great cheer went up as Ulysses took the five-dollar prize. He was breathing hard, his body was sore and bruised, but he hadn't quit. He dragged himself back to the stands to watch the rest of the performance.

Ulysses soon found that he wasn't through with being the center of attention. Next, a turbaned gentleman appeared in the ring. As the ringmaster blindfolded him, he announced that Professor Ben Ali from India could tell a person's future from the bumps on the person's head. Several people came forward and one at a time sat in the chair in front of Ben Ali. The professor passed his fingers over each one's head and told what his future would be. Finally the ringmaster beckoned to Ulysses. This time Ulysses was bashful, but his friends pushed him to his feet. He felt silly as the professor's long fingers played over his skull.

Then Professor Ben Ali astounded everyone by announcing, "Ladies and gentlemen, this boy has a most unusual head. This boy will be a great man. I predict that one day he will be the President of these United States of America!"

Ulysses fled from the chair, embarrassed. The professor had made a fool of him. He, Ulysses, great? President? It could never happen.

But Mr. Grant, proud of his son, wasn't so modest. When Ulysses arrived home and told him about Professor Ben Ali's prediction, Mr. Grant said, "President? Why, of course. My son could easily be President someday."

CHAPTER 3

Traveling Far and Wide

The moment Ulysses feared came when he was twelve years old. His father wanted him to work in the tannery and learn the trade. Ulysses said he would rather become a teamster and bring wood from the nearby forest.

Mr. Grant laughed. "You're too young, son. You couldn't load the heavy wood onto the wagon."

"The men cutting the trees could load it for me. The men at the tannery could unload it back here."

Mr. Grant shook his head. "It's out of the question. You're not tall enough even to harness the horses yourself, although I must admit you can ride better than most grown-ups. However, we'll talk about it tonight."

Ulysses ran to the barn. He grabbed a heavy leather harness and dragged it over to the manger. He climbed up on the manger and struggled until he had put the harness over Blackie, one of the horses that had not yet been trained. He overturned a basket, stood on it, and threw the collar over the horse's head. Then he hitched Blackie to a wagon. For an hour he patiently taught the horse to respond to the rein. Then he set out for the woods.

"I'll show Father I'm big enough to be a teamster," he said to himself. He cut brush and loaded it all through the hot day. He made trip after trip from the woods to the tannery yard. That evening he showed his father the huge pile of brush. In spite of himself Mr. Grant had to chuckle.

"I guess you can be a teamster, all right," he said. "Son, you have the most stubborn determination I ever saw."

From that time on, Ulysses was a wagon driver for his father. Of course, he was too small to load and unload the heavy logs, but he could handle the team better than any man.

When his father opened up a livery business, Ulysses also began to drive people to nearby villages. Mr. Grant gave him a letter which stated that Ulysses had his father's permission to drive a carriage and that he wasn't a runaway from home. Ulysses soon began to drive to more distant places such as Cincinnati. Once he drove across the whole state to Toledo. He loved to drive through the wild countryside — through forests, over rivers, and over distant hills. When by mistake he sometimes passed a place he was looking for, he never liked to turn back along the same road. Instead he would go on until he found another route that would take him back to where he wanted to go. Often he would strike out cross-country to find new ways back to Georgetown.

"Aren't you afraid to let such a young boy

ride so far?" a neighbor asked Mrs. Grant.

"No, he can take care of himself. My boy will manage," Mrs. Grant said proudly.

And manage he did. Ulysses always kept calm in the face of danger.

One day he was driving some young ladies to Ripley. It had been raining hard and the White River was at high flood. Nevertheless, Ulysses drove the horses in at the ford and began the crossing. Soon the water was over

the wheels. The girls began to fear for their lives.

"Turn back, Ulysses," they shrieked, "or we'll all be drowned!"

"Don't shout," Ulysses said. "You'll scare the horses. I'll get you across safely." Sure of himself, Ulysses calmly urged the horses through the rushing water to the safety of the opposite shore.

Mr. Grant now took on a new job. He contracted to build the new county jail in Georgetown Square. This meant hiring men to haul the huge logs from the woods to Georgetown.

"I'll do the hauling," Ulysses said. "Just buy me Dave. He's that powerful, big horse that Mr. Devore owns."

"This job is much too heavy for you," Mr. Grant said.

"Get me Dave and I'll do it," Ulysses insisted.

Mr. Grant bought the horse. Ulysses hitched Dave and another horse to the heavy wagon.

Mr. Grant had hired a man to go along with Ulysses. "When the boy gets tired, I want you to handle the team," Mr. Grant told him.

After a week, the man quit. "That boy never gets tired, or if he does, he won't admit it," he said. "He understands the team and manages it better than I do."

One day Ulysses came home with the usual load of heavy logs. "I won't go back tomorrow," he said. "The men weren't cutting any more logs today. These were left over from yesterday."

Mr. Grant was astonished. "How did you get the logs loaded if no one was there to help you?"

"Oh, Dave and I loaded," Ulysses explained. "I took a chain and hitched it to the ends of the logs. Dave dragged them onto a tree that was half felled and lying at a slant. I backed up the wagon to the tree and then Dave pulled the logs off onto the wagon. There was hardly anything to it, Father."

Mr. Grant's chest swelled with pride. "I

don't know anyone else who would have thought of that," he said. "Ulysses, you have a good head for figuring out problems."

"Ulysses did something like that when he was only six," Mrs. Grant broke in. "He was bringing home a sack of meal on horseback and he fell asleep. The first thing he knew, he and the sack tumbled to the ground."

"I had almost forgotten about that," Ulysses said, laughing. "But it was nothing at all to roll the sack up a sloping tree trunk and slide it off onto the horse's back."

"I don't know," Mr. Grant said. "Maybe Professor Ben Ali will turn out to be right yet!"

However, one day Ulysses made a deal that Mr. Grant wasn't proud of. A farmer named Ralston owned a horse that Ulysses wanted. Ralston was asking twenty-five dollars for it.

"The horse is not worth twenty-five dollars," Mr. Grant said. "Offer Mr. Ralston twenty dollars first, then raise your offer to twenty-two if he wants more. Pay him the full price only if you can't get the horse for less."

Ulysses was too straightforward in his deal. "Mr. Ralston," he said, "my father said to offer you twenty dollars for the horse, to raise the offer to twenty-two if you wouldn't take twenty, and to give you twenty-five if you wouldn't take less. What do you want for the horse?"

"Twenty-five dollars, I reckon," said the farmer.

The whole town laughed when it heard the story.

Ulysses traveled far and wide over the countryside, delivering goods and passengers. He once drove as far as Louisville, Kentucky, to deliver a team. When he was ready to travel back home on the river steamer, the captain refused to let him come aboard.

"Sorry," the captain said. "I've been in trouble before for allowing runaway boys on my boat."

"But I'm not a runaway!" Ulysses protested. "I work for my father in his livery

business in Georgetown, Ohio. I just drove a team of horses to Louisville for him."

"You *must* be a runaway," the captain repeated. "No one would trust a youngster like you to deliver a team to a place over a hundred miles from home."

Ulysses then showed him the letter of permission from his father. The steamboat skipper slapped Ulysses on the back. "Come aboard as my guest," he said. "If you can do a man's work at your age, you'll travel free of charge on your homeward trip."

Not all of Ulysses' trips went so smoothly. Once he had to drive a Mr. Payne of Georgetown to Flat Rock, Kentucky, and back — a round trip of over a hundred and forty miles. On the return trip Ulysses saw a colt that he liked. He traded one of his horses for it, hitched the colt to his team, and set out again. Trouble started right away. The colt was not used to a harness and was easily excited. When it caught sight of a dog in the road, it began to kick wildly. Before he knew what was happening, Ulysses had a runaway team on his hands.

"Whoa! Whoa there!" Ulysses shouted. The horses only ran faster. Ulysses pulled up on the reins with all his might and managed to stop the team at the edge of a ravine. A foot more and the carriage would have tumbled into it.

"I've had enough!" Mr. Payne shouted. Pale and trembling, he jumped from the carriage. "I won't ride any farther with that wild animal. I'll wait for another wagon to take me into Maysville."

Ulysses begged Mr. Payne to get back into the carriage. He had never failed to deliver a passenger safely before. "I'll tame the colt," Ulysses promised. But Mr. Payne hopped aboard the next wagon that passed.

"I'll fix you, Mr. Colt," Ulysses said. He whipped out a big handkerchief and blindfolded the colt. "Now you won't be able to see anything to frighten you."

Ulysses made the trip to Maysville safely. There he exchanged the excitable colt for another horse. The next day he convinced Mr. Payne that he should rejoin him for the trip home. They arrived in Georgetown without further trouble. Ulysses had kept clear his record of never failing in a mission.

CHAPTER 4

The Skating Contest

In the winter of 1836, when Ulysses was fourteen years old, his father sent him to Maysville, Kentucky, to a private school run by two gentlemen named Mr. Richardson and Mr. Rand. "You have learned everything you can from our Georgetown school," Mr. Grant said. "I want you to have the best education I can afford."

"But Father," Ulysses protested, "I hate to leave all my friends. I won't know anyone in Maysville."

"You won't be lonely," his father assured

him. "You can live with my brother Peter's widow while attending the academy."

Ulysses arrived at the new school determined to make new friends. He found that he liked most of the pupils, and soon Ted Brewster and Richard Wadsworth, another boy from Ohio, became his close friends. But Jeff Bradley, a tall Kentucky boy, seemed to delight in making fun of him.

"You're quite small for a fourteen-year-old," Jeff said to Ulysses one day. "You look more like ten."

Ulysses' cheeks flamed. He was sensitive about his short stature. He swallowed hard, but he couldn't think of anything to say.

The main sport of the boys during the cold winter months was skating on the nearby river. One Saturday morning as Ulysses and his friends were putting on their skates, Ted said, "We're going to have our annual ice-skating contest next Saturday. Why don't you enter, Ulysses? You're the best skater from Ohio. Maybe you could beat the Kentucky champion."

Ulysses shook his head. "I could never beat Jeff Bradley. His family is so wealthy that he took private skating lessons from an expert."

"Just the same," Richard said, "I'm sure you could beat Jeff."

Jeff came up just in time to hear the last remark. "Huh," he snorted. "I could beat Ulysses on one foot. Look at his old rusty skates. Mine are imported from Europe. See this razor-sharp edge."

This time Ulysses had an answer ready. "I've heard it's the person *on* the skates that wins races," he said quietly.

Jeff drew his lips tightly together. "In that case," he said, "perhaps you would like to bet some small sum — let's say a hundred dollars — that you can beat me."

Ulysses swallowed hard. A hundred dollars! At no time had Ulysses had even a tenth of that amount. "Why trifle with that petty sum?" he asked. "I'll beat you for nothing."

Several boys laughed. Jeff's face turned a

bright red. "Don't forget to be here for the race," he warned, "or I'll come and get you."

"I'll be here," Ulysses answered.

All that week he trained faithfully.

"Make the race a long one," Ted advised Ulysses. "Jeff is faster than you, but you have more endurance."

"And more courage, too," Richard added. "I've never seen you give up on anything once you've started."

Ulysses' blue eyes blazed. "Jeff will know he's in a race," he promised.

On Saturday the entire school came out to see the contest. The boys broke up into two camps — the group from Kentucky all rooting for Jeff, and the Ohio boys all championing Ulysses. Old Professor Richardson was there to act as referee. He brought both boys to the starting line.

"How far will you race?" he asked.

Jeff pointed to an old stump about two hundred yards away. "Up to the stump and back — if Ulysses doesn't quit before that."

Ulysses took a deep breath. "Across the

river and back," he said, "unless, of course, Jeff is too weak to skate that far."

"Enough of this nonsense," Professor Richardson said. "It is not good sportsmanship. Jeff, are you willing to race across the river and back? It's over a mile."

Jeff couldn't refuse now. "All right," he said quickly.

"Ready, boys?" Professor Richardson asked, raising his pistol.

Bang! The race was on.

Ulysses set out as fast as he could, but Jeff sprang forward as though shot from a cannon. His friends yelled, "You're 'way ahead of him, Jeff! He hasn't a chance!"

Ulysses' heart sank as Jeff gained a big lead. Why had he let his friends talk him into this race? He had been a good skater in Georgetown. But did he have a chance against a skater who had taken private lessons? His rusty skates were no match for the best steel in Europe. Well, he *would* have a chance if he didn't give up. He bent his body against the cold wind and skated steadily on.

Jeff reached the other side of the river about two hundred yards in the lead. Returning, he swept past Ulysses, who was still struggling to finish the first lap. Jeff shouted something to him, but Ulysses didn't bother to answer. He was saving his breath for the battle ahead.

Now Ulysses touched the other side and started back. He felt stronger now. He had found his second wind. Although he was still

far behind, he noticed that Jeff's smooth glide was becoming choppy. "He's tiring," Ulysses thought. "Now is my chance to cut down his lead." Slowly but surely he began to overtake him. Halfway back he had cut Jeff's lead to less than fifty yards. He heard wild yells from the shore.

"Come on, Jeff!"

"Come on, Ulysses!"

Ulysses' short legs began to churn faster.

With a quarter of the way left to go, he was only ten yards behind. His breath began to come hard. A tight band of iron seemed to bind his chest. His mouth was so dry he could hardly swallow.

"I've got to catch him! I've just got to!" he told himself.

With a hundred yards left to go, he drew even with Jeff. Never had he been so tired. Each skate seemed to weigh a hundred pounds. He gulped in huge mouthfuls of air. Jeff made a final desperate spurt and forged a little ahead of Ulysses. Ulysses hurled himself forward with his last bit of energy. A string along the finish line flashed up at him. He flung himself at it and felt it snap across his chest. Then he fell forward.

Professor Richardson's strong arms caught him. "Easy, lad. Easy does it," he said. "Breathe in as much air as you can. No, no, you can't lie down. You must keep moving."

Gradually Ulysses' head began to clear. He'd won! He'd won! He couldn't quite believe it. The pain in his chest was gone.

The heavy feeling was beginning to leave his legs. He stumbled over to congratulate Jeff.

Jeff looked at him with a new respect in his eyes. "I didn't think you could do it, Grant," he said. "But I guess I was beaten by a better man."

"Not better," Ulysses said modestly, "just luckier."

CHAPTER 5

West Point

After a year at the Richardson and Rand School, Ulysses' father entered him in the Presbyterian Academy at Ripley, Ohio.

One day Mr. Grant spoke seriously to Ulysses about his future. "You're getting older, son," he said. "You're sixteen now. Why not work in the tannery after school and learn the trade? Someday it will be yours."

"I'll work at the tannery if you want me to, Father, but I don't like that type of work. There's one thing I'm sure of — I won't work one day at it after I'm of age."

"What do you want to be?" Mr. Grant asked.

Ulysses' eyes sparkled. "A river trader, Father. I want to work on the steamboats."

Mr. Grant shook his head. "It's a wild,

hard life. I want no boy of mine to work on the riverboats."

Soon afterwards Ulysses' father received a letter from a congressman of the Grants' Ohio district. Mr. Grant opened it with trembling fingers.

"Ulysses, I've been able to get you an appointment to the Military Academy at West Point, New York! You will train to be an officer in the United States Army."

"But I won't go," Ulysses protested.

"I think you will," Mr. Grant said.

"I thought so too, if *he* did," Ulysses later told his friend Jimmy Sanderson sadly.

Now he would have to leave Georgetown and the people he loved, to live far away in the East among strangers. Maybe his father would change his mind. But he didn't.

Ulysses and Jimmy tacked the initials *H.U.G.*, for *Hiram Ulysses Grant,* on Ulysses' trunk.

"I don't like the way that looks," Ulysses said. "They'll call me Hug!" They removed the tacks and made a new pattern — *U.H.G.*

As Ulysses prepared to leave, he thought about a boy he knew who had failed to pass his examinations at West Point. The boy's angry father had felt the family had been disgraced. Would that happen to him too? He couldn't bear the thought of failure. He would pass all right. Then he would resign from the Army. He didn't want to be a soldier. A farmer, a riverboat trader, perhaps — a soldier, never!

On May 15, 1839, at the age of seventeen, Ulysses left for West Point. He looked forward with great interest to seeing the two largest cities on the American continent — New York and Philadelphia. On the other hand, he almost hoped he would meet with a slight accident so he wouldn't have to go to West Point. But nothing unusual happened to him on the trip, except that he rode on railroad trains for the first time in his life. He was very much impressed with Philadelphia and New York, which he explored for several days before heading unwillingly for West Point.

The Military Academy was situated on the bluffs high above the Hudson River. Ulysses left the river steamer and walked slowly to the admissions office. He signed the register *Ulysses Hiram Grant.*

The officer in charge looked at the signature and said, "We are expecting no one by that name. We have a Ulysses *Simpson* Grant, of Ohio, appointed here."

Ulysses tried to explain that *Simpson* was his mother's maiden name, but not his middle name. The officer would not listen. "The only changes recognized by the United States Army have to be made by the War Department," he said stiffly.

Thereafter Ulysses signed his name as *U. S. Grant.*

A list of the new cadets was posted on the wall. When a group of upperclassmen passed by and noticed the name *U. S. Grant,* they laughed.

"United States Grant — that's quite a name!" said one of them.

"No, let's call him Uncle Sam Grant,"

said a cadet by the name of William T. Sherman.

Ulysses was to know Sherman much better at another time and another place.

Life soon became hard for the new cadets. The upperclassmen barked orders at them all day long.

"Stand up straight, you object!"

"Salute! Stomach in! Shoulders back!"

"Sit down! Keep quiet!"

There were drums beating most of the time — drums to announce it was time to get up — time to eat — time to drill. Drums, drums, drums!

On July first, Ulysses passed his entrance examination easily. Now he was measured for a uniform — sheep-gray coat, military cap, and white pants. "I didn't want to come here," he said to himself. "But now that I'm here, I'll stay."

One day the great General Winfield Scott visited West Point. The cadets stood at attention as the General reviewed them. Ulysses stared at "Old Fuss and Feathers" in

his handsome uniform decorated with medals and shining brass and braid.

"I'd hate to be a big general," he thought, "and have to dress like that every day. I don't think I'd ever be comfortable."

"Stand up straight, you beast!" an upperclassman hissed. Ulysses was jolted back to the present.

He liked his roommate, Rufe Ingals. The two spent many happy hours in the little room under the eaves on the fourth floor of the north barracks. Ulysses loved to look out

at the broad Hudson River flowing majestically far below the window. He was lonesome for his home and friends back in Georgetown, but he no longer dreamed of becoming a riverboat trader.

In January he passed his final examination. He was a real West Pointer now. His trial period was over.

As always, Ulysses was good in mathematics, but French was hard for him. He stood twenty-seventh in his class of sixty. He received his share of poor marks. He was amazed to hear that a Robert E. Lee of Virginia had graduated from West Point ten years earlier without getting even one red mark.

"No one will ever equal *that* record," Ulysses said to his friend George Deshon.

"*We* certainly won't, if we get caught having our chicken roast tonight," George answered.

That night while the boys were roasting their chicken in the fireplace in George's room, a knock on the door brought them both to their feet. Ulysses quickly covered the chicken with ashes.

The Officer of the Day entered. Ulysses and George stood stiffly at attention with their backs to the fireplace and their hearts hammering. Would the officer notice the chicken? If he did, they would be severely punished or maybe even expelled. Slowly the officer's eyes swept the room. Ulysses mopped his forehead as the officer left.

"Good thing I covered the bird with ashes," said Ulysses.

"Yes," said George. "But that fellow must have had a cold or he would have smelled it." The chicken, ashes and all, tasted delicious. Soon there was nothing left of it but a few scattered bones.

Ulysses may not have been a perfect student, but he was the most daring horseman at West Point. One day he heard that the riding master intended to have a big horse called York put to death. York was so wild no one could manage him.

"Let me try," Ulysses begged the riding

master. To everyone's surprise Ulysses tamed the animal. After that he saved many other unmanageable horses from a like fate.

At the end of two years Ulysses left for home on a ten-week leave. His family had moved to Bethel, Ohio, where his father now had a large wholesale tannery. Mr. Grant was pleased with his son's record at West Point. Ulysses stood twenty-fourth in his class now. He looked fine in his military uniform. As usual, Mrs. Grant didn't talk much. "Ulysses, you stand much straighter," was all she said.

"Yes, Mother, that's the first thing they taught me to do," Ulysses told her.

Ulysses discussed his future with his father. "I've changed my mind about becoming a riverboat trader. When I graduate, I'll try to get an appointment to the Academy as a mathematics teacher. After I serve four years at that post, I'll resign from the Army and teach mathematics at some college."

"That sounds like a good plan, son," said Mr. Grant.

Ulysses returned to West Point and soon was busy with his studies again.

One day in mathematics class one of his friends pushed a small alarm clock into Ulysses' hands at the very moment the instructor said, "Cadet Grant to the blackboard!"

Ulysses hurriedly stuffed the clock inside his shirt, went to the front of the room, and began to explain the problem on the board. A clanging sound suddenly filled the room.

"Close the door so we won't hear that noise!" the instructor ordered. *Ring, ring, ring,* the disturbing sound continued.

Ulysses well knew what had happened. His friend had played a prank on him. He had set the alarm on the clock.

Ring, ring, ring. The instructor looked around the room, trying to discover where the sound was coming from. Ulysses kept right on talking and explaining the problem on the board. *Ring, ring, ring.* Finally Ulysses outtalked the alarm clock.

The class had a hearty laugh after the period was over. But Ulysses said he hoped he would never hear another alarm clock for at least ten years.

The years passed swiftly, and Ulysses was now a senior. His roommate for his final year was Fred Dent of Missouri. Ulysses and Fred once had a violent argument and stripped for a fight, but before any blows were struck, they both began to laugh and the fight was forgotten.

Finally the week of graduation exercises arrived. One afternoon was devoted to an exhibition of horsemanship. The riding arena was filled to capacity. The superintendent of the Academy was there, along with many generals, congressmen, and other distinguished guests.

One by one, the cadets put their horses through their paces. Then Sergeant Herschberger, the riding master, called out, "Cadet Grant!"

Ulysses, mounted on big, powerful York, rode to the end of the arena. Sergeant Herschberger raised the jumping bar to a height of five feet, six and a half inches.

"If Cadet Grant makes this jump, it will be a new West Point record," he announced.

Ulysses patted York's head. He thought of the many horses he had tamed back in Georgetown. He thought of the time he had ridden the wild colt with a monkey clinging to his shoulder. He took a deep breath. "We can do it, old fellow," he whispered into York's ear.

A tense silence fell over the arena as the big horse started forward at a full gallop. As they approached the bar, Ulysses felt York gather himself for the terrific leap.

"Over, boy!" Ulysses shouted as York leaped upward and outward toward the bar.

Ulysses and York appeared welded together as they cleared the height. A tremendous roar of applause rang through the arena.

"Well done," Sergeant Herschberger said to Ulysses later. It was the highest form of praise the gruff sergeant ever gave. Ulysses knew the riding master was well pleased. "That record will stand for twenty-five years at least," the sergeant added. And he was right.

At graduation Ulysses stood twenty-first in the group of thirty-nine cadets who had finished the four years. He learned he would have to serve in the Army for a while before he could apply for a position as a mathematics teacher at the Academy. He was appointed a second lieutenant in the Fourth Infantry Regiment, stationed at Jefferson Barracks, near St. Louis, Missouri.

Ulysses looked back as he left West Point. "I'll be back here soon as a mathematics teacher," he promised himself. But he was wrong. There was another far different assignment in store for him.

CHAPTER 6

Rumors of War

The prospect of war with Mexico interfered with Ulysses' ambition to become a college professor.

The Mexican territory of Texas, which was largely settled by Americans from the South, had revolted against Mexico. In 1836, after a hard fight, Texas had won its independence.

As a Mexican territory, the southern border of Texas had been the Nueces River. Now Texas claimed the Rio Grande, much farther south, as its boundary, and the United States supported this claim. Texas had voted to become part of the United States, but the matter had not yet been settled because many Northerners did not want another slave state in the Union. In addition to Texas, the United States hoped finally to gain California and the vast New Mexico territory, which also belonged to Mexico.

Ulysses considered the proposed war against Mexico unjust. He and many other people thought that it was unfair for a big country to go to war with a small one in order to get some of its territory. However, he was a soldier of the United States Army, and he would do his duty if his country called.

During his stay at Jefferson Barracks in Missouri, Ulysses had visited his classmate friend Fred Dent. The Dent family lived in a beautiful mansion called White Haven about five miles west of the regiment's headquarters. There Ulysses had met Fred's sister Julia, and before long they had become good friends. Ulysses thoroughly enjoyed these visits.

In May, 1844, there were rumors that Ulysses' regiment would be moved soon. He received a twenty-day leave to visit his family. While Ulysses was home, one of his friends wrote him that the Fourth Infantry had been ordered to Fort Jessup, Louisiana.

Ulysses hurried back to Jefferson Barracks and obtained from his commanding officer a few days extra leave. Then he mounted his favorite horse and set out for White Haven. He was dressed in his best uniform and had taken extra care with his shaving and with combing his hair. Ulysses had something very important to say to Julia Dent.

When he reached Gravois Creek, which lay between Jefferson Barracks and White Haven, he brought his horse up short. The creek was usually a quiet stream. Now, due to recent heavy rain, it was an angry torrent. What should he do? Perhaps a few miles downstream he could find a shallow ford. But he was in too much of a hurry to see Julia. He plunged his horse straight into the swirling water.

"Easy there, old fellow," he spoke to the frightened animal, tightening the reins. "Just keep your head above water and keep swimming. We'll make it." They finally did, but

Ulysses was wet to the skin. His newly pressed uniform was limp and soggy. His smart military cap had been washed away. His hair, that he had combed so carefully, was a sight. Still, he rode on quickly and soon reached White Haven. He went directly to Fred's room.

"What happened to you?" Fred asked in surprise.

"Too long a story," Ulysses snapped. "Lend me one of your suits. I'm soaked through."

When Fred saw Ulysses in the borrowed clothes, he couldn't help laughing.

"My suit's much too big for you, Ulysses."

"It does make me look like a scarecrow," Ulysses admitted, "but I can't help it. Where's Julia?"

"She's in the garden," Fred said with a twinkle in his eye. "Don't be offended if she thinks you're dressed for a masquerade party."

Ulysses hurried to the garden. Julia, surprised and happy, ran to meet him. She didn't

seem to notice his rather strange appearance.

"Ulysses!" she cried. "I'm so glad you're back. I missed you."

"And — and I missed you too, Julia," Ulysses stammered, suddenly finding it hard to breathe. All the fine words he had prepared for this occasion suddenly left his mind. "Julia — would you — could you —" Somehow he couldn't finish.

"Of course, silly," Julia answered.

Ulysses felt ten feet tall. "All right, that settles it," he said. "We're engaged. We'll be married as soon as possible." Little did he know that they would have to wait four years before they could be married.

In Louisiana, Ulysses' regiment began to prepare for war. The climate at Camp Salubrity, as the men called it, was wonderful. Ulysses' health improved greatly in the fresh, cool air. The cough he had been troubled with while he was at West Point disappeared. He gained weight and looked every inch the rugged soldier.

The regiment was next transferred to New

Orleans. There the training became more vigorous. In September, 1845, the regiment was ordered to Corpus Christi, in the part of Texas still claimed by Mexico. War was surely coming.

CHAPTER 7

Wild Horses, Wolves, and Outlaws

The army in Texas was under the command of General Zachary Taylor, "Old Rough and Ready." Lieutenant Grant liked him. He noticed General Taylor had little use for pomp and finery. He rarely wore his fancy uniforms and decorations. "He's all soldier," Grant thought. "When war comes, we'll be in good hands."

The army needed many horses for transportation. Grant was interested in the methods used to get them. Huge bands of wild horses roamed the plains of Texas. They were descended from the horses which had been brought over from Spain by Cortez. They were big, handsome animals with bushy tails and manes. The Mexican cowhands who worked in Texas were experienced at catching them with lassos. As war had not been officially declared, the army hired the Mexicans to capture the wild horses. They would rope the horses around their necks and drag them into a huge corral. There they would brand them with the Army brand. Then the hard work of breaking them into pulling the wagons would begin. Just when a five-horse team seemed ready, the horses would suddenly balk or run off wildly. The process would begin all over again, and again, and again. Finally, after much sweat and strain, the army had enough horses to pull its supplies and ammunition.

One day Lieutenant Grant was given a special assignment. He and Lieutenants Benjamin and Auger were to accompany the army paymaster to San Antonio and Austin

with money for the troops stationed there.

"This is a wild, unsettled country," the commander warned. "It's full of hostile Indians and outlaws. If you fall into their hands, don't expect to come out alive. They never take prisoners."

Grant checked his side arms. "We'll have to be on the lookout every second."

"I'm taking my rifle along," Benjamin said. "I hear there are packs of wolves roaming the countryside."

"I'll take mine, too," Auger echoed. "Wolves, Indians, outlaws — we ought to have a relaxing time!"

They set out through the prairie grass, which grew as high as a man mounted on a horse. There were no trails.

"Let's follow the San Antonio River wherever possible," Grant suggested. "There might be some settlements on the river." But mile after mile went by without a single sign of human beings. Suddenly Grant pulled up his horse. "There are some houses over there," he said, pointing.

But when the men arrived, they found no people in the little huts.

"Where could they be?" Ulysses wondered.

"There's some smoke coming out of an underground cave," Benjamin shouted.

They investigated and found a few settlers hiding in the cave. "We're not safe in our houses," one of them said. "The Indians would kill us all."

"I wouldn't want to live like that," Ulysses remarked as they journeyed on. "Living in a damp cave, ugh! I need fresh air and sunshine."

They delivered the payroll to the San Antonio and Austin troops without further incident. The paymaster stayed behind and the three young officers started back. They slept out for several nights on the prairie. Finally they sighted a large village. They took out their map. After one glance at it Benjamin said, "No use going there. That's the village of Goliad."

"Why not?" asked Auger.

"Because Santa Anna, the Mexican general, massacred all the people living there. It happened in 1836 when Texas was fighting for its independence. Santa Anna wiped out the Alamo the same year."

The Alamo was an abandoned Spanish mission in San Antonio. It had sometimes been used as a fort by the Texans. There a small band of Texans led by William Barret Travis and James Bowie, and including the famous scout Davy Crockett, had fought an army of over five thousand Mexicans. The Americans were killed to the last man. Sam Houston later avenged the brave defenders of the Alamo. He defeated Santa Anna's army at the Battle of San Jacinto, and Texas won its independence.

Grant and his men decided to take a look at Goliad, and there they received a pleasant surprise. A man whom they knew from New Orleans had come to settle there.

"The American Army will be here soon," he said. "That will be enough protection for me and my family. Stay with us tonight, gentlemen."

"I think I'll *have* to stay," Lieutenant Auger moaned. He had suddenly broken out in a severe sweat. "I'm afraid I have the fever."

"You'll be better in the morning," Grant said. "After a good night's rest you'll be fine."

But in the morning Auger was worse. "Go on ahead, boys," he said. "Another military party should be along in a few days. I'll go back with it."

"No," Grant said. "We'll wait another day or two. Then if you're not better, we'll have to leave. We can't afford to be absent without permission, even if we can explain."

The next day Auger was still too sick to travel.

"I'll tell you what," Benjamin said to Grant. "While we're detained here, let's go hunting down by the creek. There's plenty of wild game in that wooded area."

Grant didn't care to go hunting, but when Benjamin added that their sick friend needed some fresh, nourishing meat, he agreed to go.

As they moved through the tall prairie

grass, they scared up a herd of deer and antelope. The animals bounded off in great leaps. Benjamin didn't even have time to raise his gun to his shoulder.

"I'd rather catch a few wild turkeys," he muttered as they stationed themselves at the creek. "Sh, I think I hear a flock of them."

Suddenly the air was full of wild turkeys. Benjamin shot several of them, but Grant only raised his rifle.

"Shoot!" Benjamin urged him. "You can't miss at this range."

Grant dropped his gun. "I can't," he said. "It doesn't seem sporting."

Benjamin laughed. "Lucky we don't have to depend on you for food, or we'd all starve."

"I don't like useless killing," Grant said. "We have enough food now. Why kill more of those harmless birds?"

After waiting in Goliad several more days, Grant and Benjamin had to leave.

"We'll get back just in time to avoid being absent without permission," Grant said. They made Auger as comfortable as possible and rode off into the wilderness.

Grant became worried as they rode mile after mile through the tall prairie grass. "Our view is limited by this high growth," he said. "An enemy could shoot us without our even seeing him." Before Benjamin could answer, the silence was broken by the howling of a wolf. Grant's horse reared up on its hind legs in fear.

"That wolf was close by!" said Grant.

Suddenly there was another howl from the opposite direction. Grant drew his gun. "We've got to be careful," he said. "These wolves often travel in packs. I've heard that hungry wolf packs have devoured entire parties of horses and men."

Benjamin didn't seem afraid as the howling continued. "Did you have many wolves in Ohio?" he asked.

Grant shook his head. "They were all cleared out by the settlers before I was born."

"I'm used to them," Benjamin said. "Back in Indiana where I come from, the country is still infested with wolves."

The savage baying continued. Grant secretly hoped Benjamin would suggest turning back. After all, they were only two against what seemed to be at least a hundred wolves. It was wiser to be absent without leave than be devoured. But Benjamin rode on as though he were on parade. At last he noticed Grant's uneasiness and reined up his horse.

"How many wolves do you think there are in that pack, Grant?"

Grant supposed there were a hundred, judging by the horrible howling, but he didn't want to let his friend know he was alarmed.

"Oh, about twenty," he said casually.

Benjamin spurred up his horse. "We'll soon see," he said. "They should be up ahead of us in that clearing."

To Grant's surprise, they found that only two wolves had been making all the racket. Both ran off as soon as they saw the men. Grant thought a moment and then said slowly, "This will teach me a lesson I'll never forget — there are always more of the enemy before they are counted."

As they rode on, Grant's spirits rose. Someday, he knew, this wilderness would be settled. Texas had been admitted into the Union on December 29, 1845. It would become a great American state.

They sighted thousands of wild horses during this part of the trip.

"They're as numerous as the buffaloes used to be on the great plains of the Midwest," Benjamin said.

Grant nodded. "Yes, and I'm afraid they'll suffer the same fate as the buffaloes, once greedy men come in here and kill them off."

After riding for several days and sleeping out on the open prairie at night, they reached Corpus Christi.

In March, General Taylor gave orders for his army to march southward to the Rio Grande. Grant began to feel excited as the troops neared Mexico. Just north of the Rio Grande the army halted at a small stream lined with trees. Suddenly the horse Grant was riding, which had recently been captured from a wild herd, reared up on its hind legs and gave a loud whinny.

"Control your animal," Grant's captain warned. "The enemy may be lying in ambush on the other side."

Grant patted his horse's neck to calm him down. As he did so, confidence surged through him. "Once we get across," he said, "we'll have clear sailing until we reach the Rio Grande."

"It sounds fairly simple the way you put it, Lieutenant Grant," the captain snapped, "but may I remind you we're not over this river yet!"

Suddenly the blare of bugles filled the air. The sounds seemed to be coming from many different places in the woods on the opposite shore.

"There must be at least ten thousand troops over there!" Grant gasped. "We have less than two thousand. We haven't a —"

Lieutenant Benjamin didn't give Grant a chance to finish. "Remember the wolves," he said.

Grant had to grin. He did remember: there are always more of the enemy before they are counted.

Benjamin was right, for in spite of the bugle blasts, no troops appeared. The army crossed the stream without firing a shot, forged ahead, and soon reached the Rio Grande. There General Taylor ordered the army to halt and build a fort.

The Mexicans sent a message ordering the Americans to leave, reminding them that the boundary between Texas and Mexico was not the Rio Grande but the Nueces River much farther north. The Americans refused to go.

The Mexicans crossed the Rio Grande and attacked a small American scouting party, killing or wounding sixteen men. General Taylor ordered his army to pursue the Mexicans. The war had begun.

CHAPTER 8

The Mexican War

Young Lieutenant Grant fought the first battle of his life on May 8, 1846, at Palo Alto, Texas. He wondered how he would act under fire. When the moment came, he was so busy fighting he didn't have time to think. The tall grass in which the action was fought soon caught fire from the burning shells. A cloud of heavy smoke arose. Under cover of the billowing, choking fumes, Grant's regiment got behind the enemy's forces on their left flank. The surprised Mexicans were forced to retreat and change their line of battle.

The next day a fierce action was fought at Resaca de la Palma. There Grant saw how his general, "Old Rough and Ready" Zachary Taylor, behaved under fire. The action was hottest at the point where the General sat mounted on his horse. Taylor's officers begged him to retreat.

"No," grunted the old, gruff leader. "Let us ride forward a little. Then the cannon balls will fall behind us."

Grant was filled with admiration at the coolness shown by the General. "I wonder if someday I might be half as good a leader of men," he thought.

Soon Grant was appointed assistant quartermaster of the regiment. His duty was to see that his section of the army had food and clothes. Grant was disappointed with this assignment because he wanted to fight. However, in his new post he learned many valuable lessons in how to keep an army supplied during a campaign. They were to serve him in good stead many years later in a far more important war.

On May 13, the United States officially declared war on Mexico. General Taylor ordered his troops across the Rio Grande and in September marched against the city of Monterrey. As a quartermaster, Grant did not have to fight. However, he believed that in war the post of danger is the post of duty. He mounted his horse, rode to the front, and took part in the thickest part of the action. He was saddened when two of his comrades from West Point were killed.

When the American forces had nearly reached the center of the city, Grant's detachment found itself cut off and without ammunition.

"We'll be lost if we don't get some ammunition," the Colonel said. "Who will volunteer to take a message to headquarters?"

"I'll volunteer," Grant piped up. He leaped onto his horse and raced past the enemy lines in Comanche Indian style — his body shielded from the Mexicans by his horse. He clung to the side of the animal, one foot over the saddle and both hands clutching

the horse's mane. The enemy directed a rain of fire at him. He prayed that the horse would not be hit. By some miracle neither Grant nor his horse was even grazed by a bullet, and soon they were safely through to headquarters. The commanding General was amazed.

"Where did you learn to ride like that, Lieutenant?" he asked.

"It's too long a story," Grant gasped. "May we have ammunition sent immediately?"

The ammunition was soon on its way to the surrounded men. Before long the Mexicans surrendered Monterrey.

Although the Americans seemed to be winning the war, the Mexicans kept right on fighting. It became clear that the Americans would have to take Mexico City to end the war. President Polk decided that General Winfield Scott, Commander in Chief of the United States Army, should be given the assignment of capturing the Mexican capital.

In March, 1847, Grant's regiment was ordered to join General Scott's troops, which had landed near Veracruz. While General

Taylor's army fought off the Mexicans sent to attack Scott's forces, General Scott advanced toward Mexico City.

Grant fought bravely in the battles that brought General Scott's army nearer and nearer the capital.

At the battle of Molino del Rey, on September 8, 1847, Grant helped capture an old stone powder mill crowded with Mexicans. He had left his supply wagons to fight when he saw a friend shot through the shoulder. As he rushed into the mill waving his gun, he stumbled over a fallen American soldier. To his horror he saw that it was Fred Dent, his future brother-in-law. He breathed a sigh of relief as he found Fred was still alive and only wounded in the thigh.

Suddenly he heard a shout: "Look out, Grant!" Grant jumped to his feet and turned to face two Mexican soldiers who were aiming their guns at him. He protected Fred with his body as two American soldiers fired from behind him and shot the Mexicans.

For his gallantry at Molino del Rey, Grant

was promoted to the rank of first lieutenant.

On September 13, the Americans captured the hilltop fortress of Chapultepec and then began the final march on Mexico City, now only three miles away. At one point on the road the American advance was held up by Mexicans hidden behind a strong barrier. A headlong charge would have taken the lives of many men. Grant took a half dozen men, circled behind the enemy, and opened fire. The disorganized Mexicans retreated, and the way was open for the Americans to advance to the gates of the city.

There the Mexicans were entrenched behind a strong barricade and could not be dislodged. Cannonballs bounced harmlessly off the heavy wet logs. Grant noticed a church near the gate.

"If we could get a cannon up to that belfry," Grant said, "we could fire into the Mexicans behind the gate."

"Impossible," said the Colonel. "Look at those deep, wide ditches between us and the church. How would you get a heavy gun over those ditches, much less up into a belfry?"

"We'll take the gun apart," Grant said.

Grant and several volunteers dismantled the gun and reached the church without being seen by the enemy. They carried the weapon piece by piece up into the belfry and put it together again. They aimed it at the soldiers guarding the gate less than a thousand feet away. The surprised Mexicans did not know where the cannonballs were coming from.

Grant's division commander sent for Grant during the action. "Good work, Lieutenant," he said. "Get another gun up there, and we'll get in easily." Grant knew there was no more room in the little belfry for another gun, but he did not contradict his superior. Instead, he went back and directed the fire down at the enemy with greater accuracy. The Mexicans soon fled, and the army charged into Mexico City.

After a bitter struggle the battle was won, and the war was over. Mexico surrendered. The Rio Grande was established as the southern and western border of Texas. Mexico also surrendered the territories of New Mexico and California. The United States was now a great power which stretched from the Atlantic to the Pacific.

CHAPTER 9

Climbing the Volcano

The peace treaty was signed in Mexico in February, 1848. However, it would take time for it to reach Washington. There it would have to be approved by the President and then ratified by the Senate. Lieutenant Grant and the rest of the American soldiers settled down for the long wait. Now that the exciting action of the war was over, time hung heavily on their hands.

One spring morning Lieutenant Z. B. Towers, one of Grant's friends, came running into Grant's quarters.

"We've got it!" he shouted, waving a paper.

"Got what, Z. B.?" Grant asked.

"We've got permission to climb the highest volcano on the American continent, Popocatepetl! Want to come?"

"Try and stop me!" Grant exclaimed. "I'm for anything that will get us away from here for awhile."

"All right, get your horse and meet us at the supply depot in an hour."

Grant joined the other officers who were going on the expedition. Most of them were close friends. The party was made up of Lieutenants Towers, Anderson, and Stone, Captain Porter, and a few others Grant did not know. They rode through the countryside to the little village of Ozumba, near the base of the volcano. Grant looked up in awe at the towering peak of the mountain which was the crater of Popocatepetl.

"Think we can make it?" Z. B. asked.

"With no trouble at all," Grant answered — but he had his doubts.

They hired two guides and two pack animals for the climb. Grant as usual made friends with the animals.

"Good boy, Pedro," he whispered as he held out a lump of sugar to one of the donkeys.

"No wonder animals like you," Z. B. said. "You bribe them with sugar and carrots."

"I feel sorry for this little fellow," said Grant. "Those sacks of barley he's carrying on each side are bigger than he is."

"Let us save our breath for the climb," Santos, the head guide, broke in. "It is a very hard task we are facing. Our first stop is the shepherd's hut called Vacqueria. We will reach it by nightfall."

The party began the slow climb. The path was narrow and winding. In some places it was only a few feet wide. On one side rocky walls rose almost straight up. On the other side the land fell steeply away. Grant held his breath as he looked down after they had climbed a half mile. Hundreds of feet below was a racing mountain torrent. He patted his horse's mane. "Be careful, boy," he warned. "I'd hate to slip off this ledge. My life depends on your steady hoofs."

The party continued to climb slowly. The weather, which had been beautiful and clear, became cloudy. A cold wind sprang up.

"This is bad," Santos declared. "If we

should run into a storm now . . ." He shook his head at the thought.

Suddenly there was a howl from the rear. Grant turned and stared in horror as little Pedro lost his footing and tumbled off the ledge. The donkey rolled over and over down the mountainside and finally landed with a splash in the river below.

Grant felt sad, but there was nothing he could do. "Awful," he said. "We'll never see poor little Pedro again. He must have been torn to pieces by that fall."

The party continued upward, all except Juan, Pedro's master. "I am too sad to go

on," he said. "I loved that Pedro like a son. I shall go back and look for his body."

A few hours later the tired party reached Vacqueria.

"Not much of a shelter," Grant remarked. "The roof is gone on one side, and the other side is full of holes."

"I guess no one has lived in it for a long time," Z. B. said.

"You are right," Santos replied. "The old shepherd died many years ago. All the cattle he took care of are now wild. They roam the mountainside, and no one can catch them."

The men started a fire and settled down to eat their supper. Grant was silent.

"I can't stop thinking about poor Pedro," he said at last.

"Well anyway, Grant, he didn't suffer," Captain Porter comforted him. "The fall must have broken his neck instantly."

"Listen!" said Santos suddenly. "I hear someone shouting on the path below."

The men turned and looked down. They could hardly believe what they saw. There, trotting up the path, led by his master, was little Pedro.

"The barley bags!" Juan called. "They broke his fall and saved his life!"

Grant patted Pedro's neck and dug deep into his pockets for sugar cubes. "Here, Pedro," he said, "If anyone deserves a reward, you do."

The men lay down to sleep in the one-room hut.

"Get a good rest, everyone," Captain Porter said. "We'll need all our strength tomorrow. From here on, we have to go on foot."

No one slept a wink that night. A wind sprang up, and it began to rain. Grant and his friends were soaked to the skin. They would have had as much protection if there had been no roof at all. The wind rose to a gale. The freezing rain slanted in. It began to hail.

"What luck!" Grant said. "It'll be a miracle if we don't catch pneumonia."

"This rain is bad enough, but it could be

worse," Z. B. said. "What if it were snowing?"

"That's what's worrying me," Anderson muttered. "I hope it's not snowing higher up on the slope. It's cold enough to snow."

The next morning at dawn a freezing rain was still falling. The men left their horses in Juan's care and started out on foot. The wind was so strong it took their breath away.

"We won't let a little hurricane stop us," Grant gasped.

As they climbed higher, the weather grew even worse. Soon they ran into a blinding snowstorm, and drifts began to pile up across the trail.

"We must turn back," Santos warned.

"He's right," Anderson said. "The footing is much too slippery. If one of us falls over the side, he won't be as lucky as Pedro."

"Unless he lands on his thick head!" Z. B. shot back. "What ever made us leave our nice warm base?"

"We'd better go back to Vacqueria and try again after the storm," Captain Porter decided.

"I'd rather fall off the mountain than spend another night in that uncomfortable place!" Grant protested.

As the men slipped and slid down the trail, there was a sudden lull in the storm. The sun came out and reflected blindingly from the snow. However, when they finally reached the shepherd's hut, the storm struck again. It grew very dark, and the howling wind rose to a scream.

Quickly they mounted their horses and rode down the winding path back to the village of Ozumba. There they bedded down for some rest.

In the middle of the night Grant heard someone moan. He sat up and tried to open his eyes. The pain in them was agonizing. He soon found that all the others were suffering from the same eye trouble. What had caused it Grant didn't know. Whether it was the piercing wind or the blinding snow didn't seem to matter. All he knew was that the pain in his eyes was almost unbearable.

For the next three days the party remained at Ozumba. Little by little, the men recovered enough so they could bear to keep their eyes open in the bright light of day. Then they moved on about six miles to the village of Amecameca. There they were treated by the local doctor. Fortunately, no one's eyes had been seriously hurt.

They stayed in the village until everyone's eyes were free of pain. The sun shone brightly, and the men could see the summit of the volcano beckoning to them again. Lieutenant Anderson and Captain Porter decided to go back and try again to get to the top of the volcano. Grant wanted to go too, but Captain Porter would not allow it. "Your eyes still bother you at times. You might risk blindness if you went with us," he reminded Grant.

Grant finally agreed to go instead with the rest of the men to visit the great caves of Mexico, ninety miles away. When they got back to Mexico City, they found that on their second try Anderson and Porter had reached the top of the volcano with little trouble.

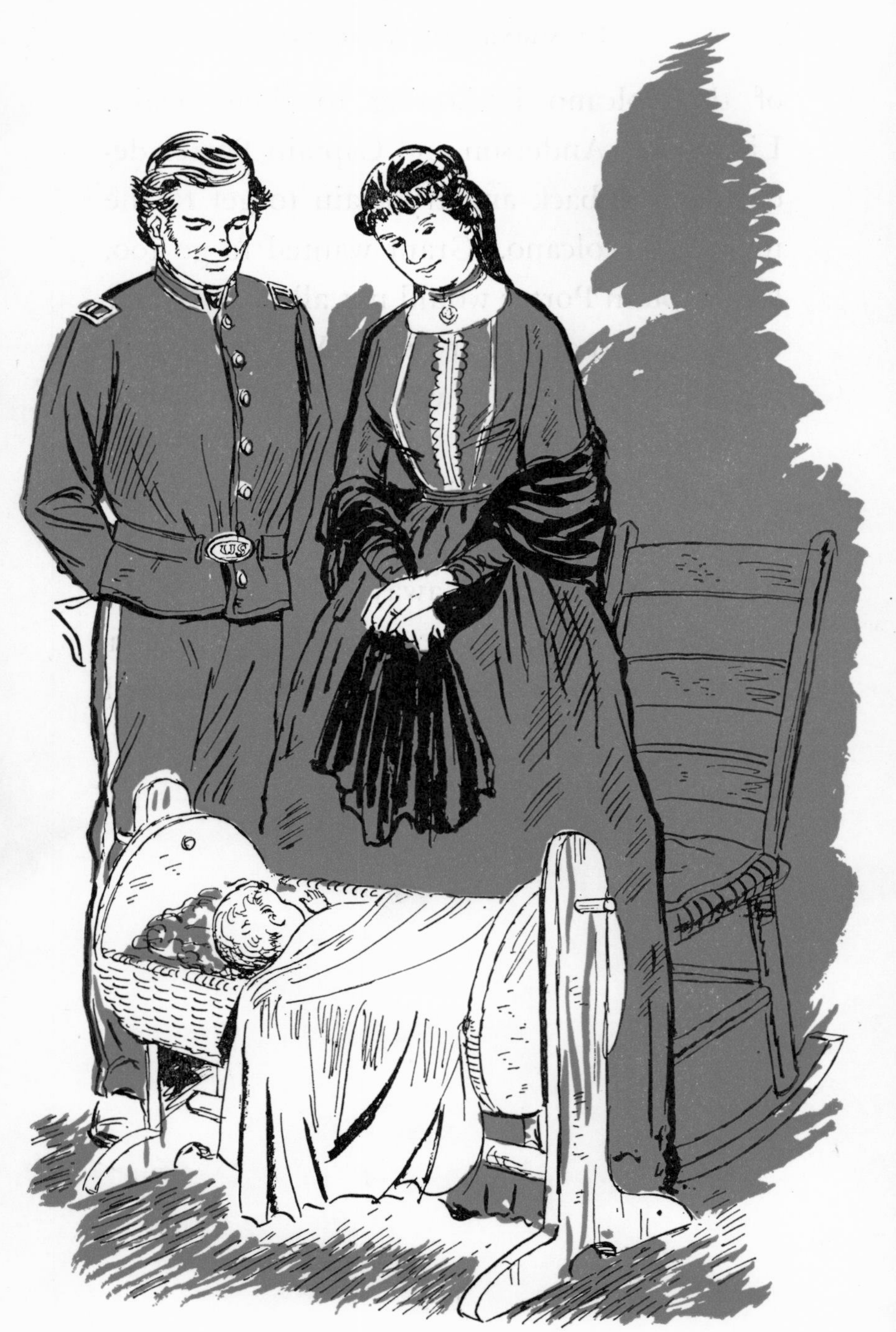

CHAPTER 10

Grant Resigns from the Army

Grant waited impatiently for the orders that would let him go back to St. Louis to keep a promise he had made. Finally the orders for his leave came through. Lieutenant Grant hurried back to St. Louis to marry Julia Dent.

Ulysses and Julia enjoyed several years of happy life together while he was stationed at Army camps in the East. Their first child, a son, was born, and the Grants named him Frederick Dent.

In the spring of 1852, Grant received bad news. The War Department was sending

Grant's regiment, the Fourth Infantry, to Fort Vancouver on the Pacific Coast. Grant knew that the California gold rush had made the cost of living very high in the West. He was not sure his Army pay was large enough to support his family there. Julia and little Fred would have to be left behind.

"Don't worry, Julia," he said. "I'll go into some business ventures to make some extra money. Before you know it, I'll be able to send for you."

"I know you'll try, Ulysses," Julia said.

Grant, who was again to be the regimental quartermaster, left New York with the Fourth Infantry on the first leg of the voyage. The seven hundred men who made up the regiment crowded onto the tiny steamer which was to take them to the Isthmus of Panama. The trip was uncomfortable but uneventful, and they soon reached the Atlantic side of the Isthmus. There Grant met with a bad setback. The contractor who was supposed to provide the mules, dugouts, and canoes to transport the troops across the Isthmus was nowhere to be found. Grant rolled up his sleeves and got to work.

"As quartermaster, I'm responsible for getting our men and equipment across the Isthmus, and I'm going to do it," he promised himself.

He scared up as much emergency transportation as he could, and the regiment started across the steamy, tropical jungle. It was slow going all the way. To make matters worse, many of the men caught cholera, and some died.

Once on the Pacific Coast, he had hospital tents erected for the sick men. Then his real work began. He made arrangements to bury the dead. He rented a steamer and put on board all the soldiers who had escaped the cholera.

"We'll wait here," he said, "until our sick men recover their health."

It was over six weeks before the regiment could sail. Grant looked back at the Isthmus from the ship's bow and thought, "I hope I never see this place again."

The regiment arrived at Vancouver Barracks in September. Grant found that prices were even higher than he had expected. His Army pay was certainly too small to support his family there. A second son, Ulysses junior, had been born soon after he had left for the Pacific Coast.

"Why, my pay as a lieutenant wouldn't even hire a cook," he said. "A man could get twice as much working as a civilian. Well, wishing won't bring my family out here. I'll have to get busy on making that extra money." All that winter he planned, and by planting time he was ready. In partnership with several other officers, he rented some choice land along the Columbia River. He bought horses, farm implements, and seed.

"Gentlemen," he said, "now you will see the advantage of being brought up in a small Ohio town. I have the biggest green thumb in the Army!"

Young Lieutenant Johnson gloated. "With food prices so high, the potatoes we plant will yield a small fortune," he said.

They plowed the land, planted the seeds, and prayed. It seemed that their prayers were answered. The sun shone warm and bright. Just enough rain fell. Their crop was going to be a huge success. Grant seemed to be walking on air as he looked at the fields.

"Only a few weeks now and we can start digging potatoes," he thought. "What a wonderful thing it will be to send for Julia and the children."

Then it started to rain.

"Nothing to worry about," Grant said cheerfully as the river began to rise. "Rain will only make our potatoes bigger."

The rain turned into a cloudburst. The Columbia River overran its banks and destroyed most of the precious crop.

"We're ruined," said Lieutenant Johnson.

"Not at all," Grant replied. "We can still save some of the crop. Half a crop is better than none."

But the potatoes that escaped the flood were never dug. Many other people on the Pacific Coast had also planted potatoes. The market was so glutted that the price of potatoes fell to almost nothing.

"It really won't pay to dig the rest of the crop," Grant said. "So — I guess the flood saved us a great deal of work."

The men were discouraged. "We're licked," they said.

"A little bad luck can't beat us, gentlemen," Grant replied. "I hear that ice is scarce in San Francisco. This winter we'll cut one hundred tons and send it there by steamer.

That ought to bring us a handsome profit."

Some of the men decided to quit, but a few joined Grant. As soon as the river was frozen, they set to work. With the help of hired men from nearby towns and with much back-breaking labor, they cut the ice and carted it on board a rented steamer.

But again the weather turned. The ship met storms and headwinds. By the time it docked at San Francisco, shiploads of ice from Alaska had already arrived. The market for ice was broken. Grant and his friends lost every cent of their investment.

Grant, however, had just begun to fight. Undaunted, he and Lieutenant Johnson bought a load of hogs and shipped them to San Francisco. There they ran into another falling market.

"Well," Grant said, trying not to show his disappointment, "at least we weren't wiped out on this venture. We only lost several hundred dollars. I'm sure our chickens will do better. They need fresh poultry in San Francisco."

No one else would join Grant this time, so he bought a load of chickens himself and shipped them by steamer. Bad news arrived a few weeks later. Due to some sickness, all the chickens had died during the voyage.

Grant was getting desperate. "Everything I touch can't fail," he said.

While he and several other officers were on leave in San Francisco, they hit upon a good idea. Hotel rooms were scarce.

"Let's go into the hotel business," Grant said. "We can hire an agent to run it for us."

"I'm willing to try one more time," Lieutenant Johnson said.

They found a nice rooming house, which they rented and turned into a hotel.

"This time we'll make money," Grant said. "I am so lonesome to see Julia and the children." But it was not to be. The agent they had hired to run the hotel turned out to be dishonest and ran away with the profits.

"I'm finished with all business ventures," Lieutenant Johnson said. "There seems to be a curse on us."

In 1853 Grant was promoted to captain, but the extra salary he made was not half enough to enable him to send for his family. To make matters worse, he was transferred to a lonely post at Humboldt Bay, California. There was no chance even to try to make extra money at that base.

Finally, overcome with homesickness and boredom, he resigned from the Army in the spring of 1854. He took a ship to New York and landed there without a penny in his pocket. He borrowed some money from a West Point friend to pay his hotel bill. He sent a wire to Ohio for funds, and his father sent him the money to get home. At last Grant was able to rejoin his family. He was a civilian for the first time since he had left for West Point as a boy of seventeen.

"Don't worry, Julia," he said to his wife. "Although we haven't any money, I'll find work to support our family. I'm strong and eager."

"I'm not worried," Julia said. "I have confidence in you, Ulysses."

CHAPTER 11

Hard Times

Grant's father-in-law came to the rescue of the Grant family. He gave his daughter sixty acres of land near St. Louis. When Ulysses drove out with Julia to see the land, he tried not to show his keen disappointment. A forest of trees and underbrush covered the sixty acres. However, he was determined to become a farmer.

"Well, with a couple of sharp axes and a little work, I'll hack a good farm out of this wilderness," he said.

Julia didn't answer, but Ulysses could tell that his wife would back him in anything he tried to do.

"I won't let her down," he promised himself. Bright and early the next day he set to work. For the next two years he toiled on the land. He cut down the trees and hauled wagonloads of timber to St. Louis. There he sold the wood to anyone who would buy it. When he ran into former Army friends, he couldn't help comparing their smart Army uniforms with his own ragged work clothes. He wore an old battered hat and his faded Army overcoat.

He never complained. "It's honest work," he said.

When he had enough land cleared, he squared logs and built a house. It was a proud day for Grant when Julia and the children moved in.

"The worst is over now!" he told them. "I have enough land cleared for the spring planting. I'll raise a bumper crop. Money will come rolling in. We'll be prosperous."

Grant watched over his crops like a mother tending her baby. The results were excellent. The spring and summer weather were fine for growing. But as Grant prepared to harvest his first crop, the business depression of 1857 hit the country. Farm prices dropped to almost nothing. The year's work was wasted.

"Well," said Grant, "we can't expect to prosper while the rest of our country is in trouble. We'll just have to take our hard knocks along with the rest."

The next season a cold snap hit the crop and ruined it. Grant tried to appear cheerful. "Our luck is bound to turn soon," he said.

Julia looked anxiously at her husband. "Ulysses, you're working too hard. You don't look well. I'm going to call the doctor."

Grant tried to protest, but Julia insisted, and soon the doctor arrived. "You must go to bed and rest, Mr. Grant," the doctor ordered. "You have a high fever."

"I'll be up and around in a few days," Grant promised. But he was confined to his bed for six months. Sadly, he made his decision. "A farmer who can't do hard work isn't much use on a farm," he said.

The Grants sold their farm and took a cottage in St. Louis as part payment. There Grant tried the real-estate business. He wasn't very good at it. Collecting rents and selling houses didn't even cover expenses. Grant tried unsuccessfully to get a job as a county engineer. One day Julia brought him more bad news. The man who had bought their farm couldn't make the payments, so there would be no more income from that source.

Grant squared his shoulders. No matter how bad things got, he was determined to keep trying. Finally he secured a job as a clerk in the St. Louis Customs House. The Grants were happy at last. Ulysses had a steady job. While it didn't pay much, money would be coming in regularly. After a few weeks a new customs collector was appointed. He fired the entire staff, including Ulysses.

Grant still refused to be discouraged. "I'll find something better," he said.

He walked the streets of St. Louis, looking for work. One day he met a former West Point acquaintance, William Tecumseh Sherman. To Grant's surprise, Sherman looked rather shabby.

"What happened, Bill?" Grant asked.

Sherman shrugged his shoulders. "I left the Army and took a banking position. As you see, I failed completely."

Grant sighed. "I haven't been a success either, since I left the Army. But cheer up, things are bound to get better."

Sherman shook his head. "One thing is sure, West Point training is useless in civilian life. It doesn't prepare you for anything but the Army."

Grant couldn't argue the point. The two

men parted, promising to keep in touch with each other.

In 1860 Grant finally reached a new low. He was thirty-eight years old. He had a wife and four children to support. A daughter, Nelly, and another son, Jesse, had been born after Grant resigned from the Army. He was in debt and unable to find work. Much against his will, he swallowed his pride and asked his father for a job. Mr. Grant placed him in his leather goods store in Galena, Illinois. The store was managed by Ulysses' two younger brothers.

"Those must have been terrible days for you, Ulysses," one of his brothers remarked.

"Not at all," said Grant. "They were happy days. I was doing the best I could to support my family. No man could do more than that."

When Julia's sister-in-law tried to console her, she said, "We will not always be in this condition. Ulysses is a very able man. My confidence in him has never wavered, not even once, and Ulysses knows that."

"I surely do, Julia," Grant said. "And that's why, even though I've had some hard times in my life, I know we'll come out of this one with colors flying. I never saw the moment when I wasn't sure I would come out ahead in the end."

Union gunboats on the Mississippi

CHAPTER 12

Unconditional Surrender

Grant's struggles made him think about the working man. He began to hate slavery. His wife's father owned many slaves, and he had given Grant a slave to help him in his farm work. But Grant knew deep down in his heart that slavery was wrong. In 1859, when he had had to give up his farm, he could have sold his slave for a thousand dollars.

"I need the money desperately," he had said. "But I will have papers drawn up to give this man his freedom. No man should be a slave to another."

Meanwhile, dark clouds of trouble had

rolled over the United States. Several bitter disputes had arisen between the states. Unless they were settled, they would surely lead to war. Many Southern states felt they could leave the Union any time they wanted to. They argued that they had joined the United States on their own, and they could leave if they were dissatisfied. The North and the South were divided over the question of whether to allow slavery in the new territories gained through the Mexican War and through other means. The South felt its economic way of life depended on slavery, and it wanted to have slavery extended throughout the new states and territories. The North wanted no slavery in the new states. Much violence and fighting had occurred over this issue.

Another cause of trouble was the Abolitionists. They were people who wanted all slavery abolished — everywhere in the country. John Brown, one of the leading Abolitionists, was hung for leading a bloody raid on the military arsenal in Harpers Ferry,

Virginia. He had hoped to secure weapons and lead the slaves to rise up and free themselves from their masters.

In 1851 Harriet Beecher Stowe had written a book called *Uncle Tom's Cabin.* Although the book was fiction, it inflamed the North by picturing the cruelty of slaveowners to helpless slaves.

When Abraham Lincoln was elected President in 1860, the South became alarmed. Lincoln was a firm believer that the Union must be preserved. He said that a house divided against itself cannot stand, and that the Government could not permanently endure half slave and half free.

A month after Lincoln's election, on December 20, 1860, South Carolina seceded from the Union. Before Lincoln was inaugurated on March 4, 1861, Mississippi, Florida, Alabama, Georgia, Louisiana, and Texas had joined South Carolina. Virginia, Arkansas, North Carolina, and Tennessee seceded later the same year. The states that had withdrawn from the Union called their organization the

Confederate States of America. They named Jefferson Davis as their President and made Richmond, Virginia, their capital.

In April, President Lincoln sent a naval expedition with supplies to Fort Sumter, a federal fort at the harbor of Charleston, South Carolina. Before the expedition arrived, Confederate troops shelled the fort and forced its surrender. The terrible war had begun.

Grant offered his services to the Union, hoping to be reappointed to the regular Army. His request was put in an old file and somehow overlooked. He was disappointed when he didn't receive a prompt reply from the War Department. Even though he had no commission, as a service to his country he trained a volunteer company in Galena. After many hard weeks of drilling, the group went off to join an Illinois regiment. Grant trained another group of volunteers — still no news from Washington. He refused to be discouraged.

"My chance will come one day," he said. And it did.

Frederick, Grant's eldest son, came running to him, waving a telegram. "Father!" he shouted. "A message from the War Department for you! What does it say?"

With trembling fingers Grant opened the telegram. He quickly read it, then handed it to his son. Frederick took one look and began to jump up and down. "You've been appointed a colonel!" he shouted. "Colonel Grant, yippee!"

Grant took the news calmly. He knew the regiment to which he was being assigned — The Twenty-first Illinois. The men were wild, raw troops who had run their previous colonel out of camp.

"Do you think you can handle them?" Julia asked anxiously.

Grant smiled. "Never was a wild colt I couldn't handle, so these boys should not be too difficult."

He arrived at camp in his old clothes, for he didn't have the money to buy a new uniform. He had a red bandanna handkerchief tied around his waist instead of a sash. He

had thrust an old, borrowed cavalry sabre through it.

The wild young soldiers laughed when they saw their new commanding officer. One of them began to show off. He got behind Grant and began sparring at his back. Another recruit gave the show-off a hard push. He lost his balance, stumbled, and hit Grant behind the shoulders. Grant whirled around. The look in his steady blue eyes caused an instant hush to fall over the group.

"Men, go to your quarters," the new colonel said simply. And the men went.

There was something about their new leader that won the soldiers' respect. Grant trained the men hard, but he was just and fair. Soon he wrote to Julia in New Jersey, where the family had gone to stay for the duration of the war: "I have been lucky enough to be appointed a brigadier general, but I still can't afford to buy a new uniform."

General Grant was assigned to the Western army. Its aim was to gain control of the Mississippi down to the Gulf of Mexico. If this could be done, the Confederacy would be split in two, and the end of the war would be hastened.

General Grant set up his headquarters at Cairo, Illinois. He had the good fortune to work with Commander Foote of the Navy, who had several gunboats on the Mississippi River near Cairo.

"Our first task," Grant told Foote, "is to clear the Confederate forces from the Cumberland and Tennessee Rivers."

In January, 1862, they mounted an attack on Fort Henry on the Tennessee River. Commander Foote's gunboats shelled it from the river. Grant's army moved toward it over land. It was raining hard, and the mud was a foot deep. Grant pushed his men stubbornly on. When they arrived at the fort, he found that the Confederates had abandoned it and retired to Fort Donelson. The weather turned colder, and freezing rain and sleet made the roads almost impassable. The men wanted to rest, but Grant would not allow it. "On to Fort Donelson," he ordered. "Remember, the Southerners are less used to cold weather than we are."

Grant then met with Commander Foote on his gunboat.

"This is their strongest position yet," Foote said. "They have twenty thousand men. They are well equipped and have plenty of food and ammunition. They'll be hard to beat."

"We'll beat them," Grant said. "We'll move against them at once."

"But it's snowing," the commander protested. "Your men won't be able to get through."

"We'll get through," Grant said. "You just shell them from the river."

Grant made good his promise. The weather was freezing, but he ordered his men to throw away their blankets and overcoats. "We won't need them," he said. "We'll use the Confederates' own equipment, if we move fast enough."

The men suffered terribly. Grant gave orders that no fires were to be built, for the

Southerners would see them. "We must surprise the enemy," he said. "They won't be expecting anyone to march over land in weather like this."

Then came bad news from Commander Foote. The guns of Fort Donelson had found the range of the commander's gunboats. Several of the warships had been damaged, and Foote himself had been wounded. Grant rushed to visit his ally.

Foote was lying in the ship's hospital, discouraged. "Call off the attack, General," he said. "Our gunboats can't help you this time."

"Never!" said Grant.

When Grant arrived back on shore, he found everything in confusion. The Confederates had ripped through his lines. His men had panicked and were running for their lives. Grant leaped into their midst, waving his sword. "Hold fast, boys!" he shouted. "They're not attacking. They're trying to escape. Drive them back to the fort!"

Grant's men were inspired by the spirit of

their leader. They stopped their retreat and, charging headlong at the enemy, forced the Confederates back into Fort Donelson.

A message arrived from General Buckner, the commander of the Southern forces, asking for terms of surrender. Grant replied in a manner which captured the imagination of the whole nation: "No terms except an unconditional and immediate surrender can be accepted."

General Buckner, who had served with Grant in Mexico, knew that Grant meant what he said. The North had won its first great victory.

The country was electrified. Grant's new nickname, "Unconditional Surrender" Grant, was on everyone's lips. Back in Washington, President Lincoln smiled. "Never heard much about him before," he said, "but I have a feeling we'll hear plenty more of him before this conflict is ended." He then promoted Grant to the post of major general.

CHAPTER 13

Victory in the West

In the spring of 1862, Grant defeated the Confederates at the Battle of Shiloh. The first day of fighting was disastrous for the Union forces. The Confederates drove them back, smashed their lines, and took over their camp. During the heat of the action Grant appeared calm and unconcerned. His men couldn't help being inspired by the courage of their leader. But in spite of his outward appearance, Grant was busy thinking of how to turn defeat into victory. He still was confident that his men could whip the enemy.

The next morning Grant ordered an attack. He rode up and down the lines, urging his troops on. The men cheered at the sight of their quiet leader and renewed the battle. The Confederates were surprised while they were celebrating their supposed victory in the Union camp. They had to give up the ground they had won the day before and soon were retreating in panic. Grant had won another important battle for the North.

But Union losses at Shiloh had been heavy. In spite of his victory, Grant had made some enemies. Several congressmen complained to Lincoln about him, urging that he be replaced. Lincoln refused, saying, "I can't spare this man — he fights!"

Knowing that the President was behind him made Grant even more confident. After several minor victories he took on his biggest job so far — the capture of the city of Vicksburg. This action would clear the last Confederate stronghold from the Mississippi River.

General Pemberton was the Confederate

commander at Vicksburg. Knowing the importance of this city, Robert E. Lee, the South's commander in chief, took no chances. He sent another powerful army under General Joseph E. Johnson, one of the South's best and bravest generals, to help Pemberton. Grant had to act quickly. If the two Southern armies were united, they could overpower his forces.

He first attacked Pemberton's army. In two hard battles he defeated it and chased it back to Vicksburg. Then he turned on the advancing troops of General Johnson. He beat them in three desperate battles and sent them fleeing back away from Vicksburg. In twenty days and in five different battles, Grant had beaten two strong armies.

The defenders of Vicksburg fought bravely. Grant's troops surrounded the city and cut off all supplies. Then, after weakening the garrison by starvation, Grant attacked again. This time, after a terrible struggle, Vicksburg surrendered.

On the day before, July 3, 1863, the North

had won the Battle of Gettysburg in Pennsylvania. For the first time the North began to see hope of victory. The Union would be saved.

General Grant rested his tired troops. He thanked his main assistants, General McPherson and his old friend General William T. Sherman. "We are welding a winning team, men," he said. "The Mississippi is now clear to the Gulf of Mexico. Our next task is to open a path for our army division trapped in Chattanooga, Tennessee. If we can beat the Southern armies in that section, the stretch of country between the Mississippi and the Allegheny Mountains will be clear."

While the troops were resting, Grant received a letter of thanks from President Lincoln. Congress also sent him a note of thanks, as well as the legislatures of many states. All their praise had little effect on the quiet commander. He had never been a man of many words, and words did not impress him.

Grant was busy making his plans to help the Northern army surrounded in Chattanooga, Tennessee, by strong Confederate forces. The Northern army was under the command of General Rosecrans. Grant replaced him with General George H. Thomas. He sent Thomas a message, urging him to hold Chattanooga at all costs. General Thomas, one of the bravest of the Union generals, assured Grant he would hold Chattanooga "till we starve." But the Union situation was desperate. The Confederates held positions on nearby Lookout Mountain and Missionary Ridge, from which they commanded the supply routes into the city. They planned to starve Thomas and his men into surrender. Grant found that he could supply Thomas by one isolated mountain road. He sent men and supplies up the narrow, winding path. The soldiers called it the "cracker line," but it supplied the starving Northern soldiers with food.

Then Grant's men hit the Confederates surrounding Chattanooga. Grant sent troops swarming up the side of Lookout Mountain, forcing back the enemy in a fierce battle

US
US
US
US

fought above the clouds. Then he ordered an assault on Missionary Ridge, in which his men swept everything before them. The Southerners were soon scattered in retreat.

President Lincoln and the country were now convinced that the simple, modest Ulysses S. Grant was the North's greatest soldier. On President Lincoln's personal recommendation, Grant was made commander in chief of all the Northern armies. He was ordered to Washington to receive his new commission.

Grant hurried East to meet Abraham Lincoln. He knew his hardest work was still ahead of him. He would have to fight the great General Robert E. Lee, who for three years had defeated all four generals the army of the Potomac had sent against the army of Virginia. He had seen General Lee fight in the Mexican War. Lee would be the toughest foe he would ever meet.

CHAPTER 14

Grant Against Lee

General Grant took his eldest son, Frederick, with him to Washington. When they arrived at the White House, they found a lively party going on. At first, Grant was too bashful to enter.

"Frederick," he said, "I can't go in there among those grand ladies and gentlemen. I'd rather face a regiment of soldiers."

Frederick laughed. "Father, to me, you're a greater man than all those gentlemen put together. Besides, you have no choice. President Lincoln is waiting for you."

Grant took a deep breath and entered the East Room. Abraham Lincoln came toward him. He clasped Grant's hand.

"Welcome, General," he said. "I've never had the pleasure of meeting the man to whom the whole country is indebted."

Grant blushed. President Lincoln saw that he was ill at ease. After presenting Grant's commission to him, he took him to his private office. "This is better, Mr. President," Grant sighed. "I feel more at ease."

He told Lincoln his plans for winning the war. "We have worked too much apart up to the present. We've been a balky team — no two pulling together. I intend to make the army of the Potomac a smooth-working organization, all for one and one for all."

Lincoln smiled. "Tell me more, General."

"I plan to hurl myself at Lee, to keep smashing armies at him, to give him no rest, no chance to reinforce his men. I plan to take *no backward step*."

The President was deeply impressed. "With such a plan, General, and with such a man to run it, I know our country is in safe hands. I will sleep better tonight."

In May, 1864, Grant's army started forward. It was never to stop until General Robert E. Lee was defeated.

General Meade was the commanding general of the army of the Potomac, but Grant, the commander in chief of all the armies, made the army of the Potomac his headquarters. He ate and slept with the men and shared their dangers.

"Give the enemy no rest," he ordered his generals. His voice was often heard above the roar of battle. His commands thrilled his men. "Strike the enemy hard, and keep striking him. The war must be ended. We must end it now. Make our opponents defend themselves. We must not defend ourselves from the enemy."

After a terrible battle at Spotsylvania, Virginia, Grant wrote: "I propose to fight it out on this line if it takes all summer."

Thirteen months after President Lincoln appointed Grant commander in chief, the end came. General Sherman had marched his army through Georgia to the sea. General Thomas, at Nashville, Tennessee, had held back the Western armies of the Confederacy and kept them from reinforcing General Lee. General Sheridan's cavalry had cut behind Lee's beaten army, preventing its retreat. Finally, General Lee agreed to surrender.

On April 9, 1865, Lee met Grant in a little farmhouse at Appomattox, Virginia, and surrendered himself and his entire army. Grant, dressed in a simple soldier's blouse, without a sword, shook hands with his great opponent. Lee was dressed in a splendid uniform. He carried his sword and wore all his decorations. Grant's only marks of rank were his shoulder straps bearing the insignia of a general.

Grant offered the Southerners the most generous terms. He even allowed the cavalry men to keep their horses. "They'll need them for the spring plowing," he said.

Each officer was to give his word that he would not take up arms again against the United States. The company and regimental commanders were to sign a like promise for the men of their command.

Grant then sent a telegram to Secretary of War Stanton: "General Lee surrendered the Army of Northern Virginia this afternoon on terms proposed by myself."

After the surrender, the Union soldiers wanted to fire cannons in salute to Grant. He stopped them, saying, "It will hurt the feelings of our gallant foes, who have become our countrymen again."

The war was finally over, but terrible events still lay ahead. President Lincoln invited General Grant and his wife to attend the theater with him on the evening of April 14. Grant declined the invitation respectfully. He explained that he and his wife had made plans to visit their children in New Jersey. That night, as President Lincoln watched the performance, he was assassinated by a half-crazed actor, John Wilkes Booth. It was rumored that the conspirators had planned to kill General Grant also. The country was plunged into sadness.

In spite of the tragedy, life had to go on. Andrew Johnson, the Vice-President, became

President. In Washington, Grant reviewed the Army as it marched for the last time. The great parade continued for two days. Then the Army was disbanded, and the men went home.

Due to the great services of Ulysses S. Grant and many other brave men, the Union was forever secure.

CHAPTER 15

President of the United States

After the war Ulysses S. Grant became a national hero. But all the honors that were heaped upon him did not change him from the simple, modest man he had always been. He remained generous to the defeated Southerners. Some congressmen wanted to have a huge painting of Lee's surrender placed in the White House. Grant objected: "I can never consent to having any picture placed in the capital to commemorate a victory in which our own countrymen were the losers."

He kept his word to General Lee that the Confederate leaders were not to be punished.

That promise wasn't easy to keep. After Abraham Lincoln was killed, many people in the North had cried for revenge: "We must hang Lee and all the Southern leaders. That will teach the South a lesson and avenge the murder of our President."

But Grant could not be moved from his terms of surrender. "General Lee and the other leaders are gentlemen," he said. "They are not to be held responsible for the actions of a few maniacs. I gave Lee my word, and I intend to keep it. Besides, Abraham Lincoln would not want us to shed blood to avenge him. Do you not remember his words, 'With malice toward none, with charity for all'? No, gentlemen, no Southerner will be harmed as long as he keeps his word not to take up arms against the United States again."

Grant did not like President Johnson. He disagreed with the way he handled the reconstruction of the South. However, when Johnson appointed him Secretary of War, he agreed to serve on a temporary basis.

When President Johnson's term ran out, Grant was the Republican party's choice for President. Again, Grant did his duty when called upon.

"If the people elect me, I must serve," he said.

Grant did no campaigning. He did not make a single speech or a single promise in order to get votes, yet he won the election easily. On March 4, 1869, he was inaugurated President of the United States. All the great men of the country were there — judges, senators, generals. But to the new President, the members of his own family were the most important people present. He remembered that only eight years ago he had walked the streets of St. Louis, penniless and friendless. Even then his family had had faith in him. He had justified that faith. His daughter, Nell, stood by his side as he gave his inaugural address. She seemed to be the proudest youngster in the whole country as she gazed at her father.

Grant's inaugural speech was short and to

the point. He promised to serve the nation as loyally as he had served it in the past.

When Grant became President, many congressmen wanted his rank of General in Chief kept in waiting for him. "We will not fill this position," they said. "We created it for you alone. We will hold it for you until you have finished your term as President."

Grant refused the honor. "I cannot consent to such an arrangement. I couldn't sleep at night if I felt I was depriving General Sherman of a promotion which he has earned as fairly as I have earned mine." He insisted that Sherman should succeed him, and he did.

Grant set to work at once to change Washington from a mudhole into a great city. He called in architects and builders from all parts of the world. Soon the capital of the United States became a city Americans could boast about. Washington could now compare in beauty, if not in size, with London, Paris, Berlin, and the other great capitals of the world.

Many angry people had been saying Great Britain should be made to pay for the damage done to Northern shipping during the Civil War. England had given shelter to Confederate warships that had sunk many Northern ships and almost ruined United States commerce. Many of these raiders had been built and outfitted in British ports. "If England does not pay, we should go to war and force her to," the warlike politicians said.

"No," President Grant answered them. "I shall never fire another shot in anger. I have had too much of war. I want peace — but peace with honor for all people." He tried a new plan. He suggested arbitration instead of war. Great Britain agreed, and a court was set up at Geneva, Switzerland. The United States, Great Britain, Italy, Switzerland, and Brazil sent representatives. After the facts were heard, the court decided that the United States was right and that Great Britain should pay fifteen million dollars for the damage she had done to the United States. Great Britain paid, and the rest of the world looked on in wonder. Perhaps the quiet man from Ohio had found a new way to settle troubles between nations.

One of the important changes that Grant made during his administration had to do with the way Indian affairs were handled. Many of the Indian agents were selfish men who lined their own pockets with money instead of helping the Indians. Sometimes they sold whiskey to the Indians and then robbed them.

Grant pointed out that the Quakers had lived in peace with the Indians in the early settlement of Pennsylvania, while their neighbors in other settlements were always at war with the Indians. The Quakers were known to be against all violence and war and were noted for their honesty and fair dealings. Grant therefore appointed Quakers as Indian agents. During Grant's term as President there were far fewer Indian outbreaks.

In June, 1872, Grant was again nominated for President and again elected. During his second term of office his administration was charged with corruption. Grant, who was honest and fair himself, was heartbroken. He trusted all people and believed they were as honest as he was. Sometimes he had made mistakes by putting his trust in the wrong men. Many of the officials he had trusted had turned out to be dishonest. Grant was quick to act. "Let no guilty man escape," he said. "Men who use their high offices to line their own pockets should be punished."

At the end of his second term as President, Grant was ready to bow out of public life. He refused to allow an attempt to nominate him for a third term. "Choose someone else," he said. "Let me be a plain citizen of my country."

The United States ship Indiana, *Europe-bound in 1887, carrying the Grants*

CHAPTER 16

Around the World

For sixteen years Grant had been busy day and night in the service of his country. Now he decided to rest. He and his wife set sail for a vacation abroad. They took their son Jesse with them. The Grants especially wanted to see their daughter, Nellie, who had married an Englishman.

Grant longed for a quiet life, but it was not to be. Everywhere, people wanted to welcome him. In England he was invited to Windsor Castle by the Queen. When he traveled to the continent of Europe, he visited the President of France and also the Emperor of Germany.

While in Austria he was shown the famous

ruins of an old Roman camp near the city of Salzburg. The people of this area had a strange custom. In honor of a visiting celebrity, they would open up an old grave of a Roman soldier dead for over two thousand years. Grant did not like this custom. He was not impressed by the ancient ashes. "I am a practical man," he said. "I prefer to see a living dog to a dead lion."

However, he looked over the ruins of the Roman military camp very carefully. "The Romans were great soldiers," he said. "But these ruins show the futility of war. The Romans fought and died for a cause they believed in. These ancient ruins show that nothing permanent is really accomplished by bloodshed. It seems we haven't learned much by past mistakes. Even to this day, the path of glory leads but to the grave."

In Switzerland he visited the city of Geneva. At a luncheon in his honor he said, "I have never been more happy than to visit the city where the United States' claims against Great Britain were settled without bloodshed. I hope the principle of nations settling differences around the peace table will be resorted to by all other countries. This could be the means of continuing peace to all mankind."

From Switzerland the Grants crossed into northern Italy by way of the Simplon Pass. This road had been built over a mountain ten thousand feet high by the great French military genius, Napoleon.

"This road will be a monument to Napoleon's engineering skill long after his military deeds are forgotten," Grant said to his wife.

Mrs. Grant shuddered as they passed over an alarmingly high bridge. "I can't bear to look down," she said. "If this bridge should break, we'd fall into a hole over a mile deep."

Grant laughed. "No fear of that," he said. "Napoleon did his work well. This bridge had to be strong enough to support an army with all its heavy equipment. I think it will hold the weight of our carriage very well."

Mrs. Grant was still worried as she gazed at

the jagged snow-covered mountain peaks towering over them. "I've heard there are many dangerous avalanches in this area. What if a snowslide starts?"

Grant held her hand tightly. "Napoleon thought of that, too. There are twenty houses of refuge built into the solid cliff walls, where we could find shelter from an avalanche."

When they reached the top of the pass, they stopped and looked down through a gorge at the town they had started from, twenty

miles away. The great height at which they were standing made even Grant tremble a little.

"This reminds me of our attempt to climb Popocatepetl," he said. "I doubt if my little donkey, Pedro, could have survived a fall from here, even if he had ten barley bags to protect him."

Grant pictured in his mind how hard it must have been to move an army over the pass and marveled again at Napoleon's imagination and genius. "I'm glad I never had

to face him in battle," he thought. "Fighting Robert E. Lee was bad enough."

In Italy the Grants visited the ruins of Pompeii. This city had been destroyed and buried by a great eruption of the volcano Vesuvius in A.D. 79. The volcano was still active, and fire and lava belched from its crater day and night. In Grant's honor the authorities dug up one of the buried houses. "From now on it will be called the Grant House," they said.

Grant searched through the house with great interest. Everything in it was just as it had been on the terrible day when the sea of ashes and cinders from Vesuvius had buried it. He found a few trinkets and a loaf of bread wrapped in a cloth. "This bread must be rather stale," he said, smiling. "I'm getting hungry, so let's get back to where *I* can excavate a real beefsteak!"

In Egypt, Grant was presented with a high-spirited Arabian horse. As he mounted it, the horse began to rear and buck. One of the handlers was afraid Grant would be thrown.

"Don't worry," said Grant. "If I can mount a horse, I can ride him."

Though Grant was now getting rather tired of traveling, he still could not rest. Other rulers insisted that he visit their countries. In St. Petersburg the Russians welcomed him with open arms and invited the Grants to a grand party.

Grant enjoyed talking with people of all classes, but he liked most of all to talk to people of the working class. When he returned to England, the workers gave him a wonderful welcome. "I know what it means to toil and sweat over a day's work," Grant told them. "I have been a laboring man all my life."

The Grants now wanted to come home, but the President of the United States, Rutherford B. Hayes, asked the General to continue his trip to the Far East as an ambassador of goodwill. Grant apologized to his wife. "I know I am in retirement," he said, "but the President still wants me to serve the country."

"Then of course you must do so," Mrs. Grant answered.

Grant continued his travels in a trip around the world. He visited India, Siam, China, and Japan. Always he studied the people. He was more impressed by people than by all the great natural wonders of the world.

A United States warship took him to Nagasaki, where he visited the Emperor of Japan. This was the first time in history that an emperor of Japan had talked to a foreigner. Grant took advantage of this chance to try to make peace between Japan and China. Due to Grant's efforts, war between the two countries was set aside in favor of the peace table.

There was a great reception for the Grants when they finally crossed the Pacific and landed at San Francisco.

"I enjoyed all the countries of the world," Grant said. "But now I am in the best land of all — my home, the U. S. A. I will never leave it again."

CHAPTER 17

The Hardest Fight of All

In 1880 the Republican convention again tried to nominate Grant for a third term as President. On the first ballot he received more votes than any other candidate. His friends began to hope. However, the plan did not succeed. There was too much feeling against a third term for any President.

Now came the saddest part of Grant's life. He invested all his money in a Wall Street brokerage firm, along with one of his sons and several other partners. But one of his trusted partners had been dishonest. He had invested in worthless stocks and bonds, and the brokerage business failed. Many people, including Grant, lost all their money. On the day before the business failed, the dishonest partner had told Grant that if he could raise one hundred and fifty thousand dollars, the business could be saved. Grant borrowed the money from William K. Vanderbilt, one of the richest men in the country. When that money was lost too, Grant told his wife, "We must pay him back by all means." Mrs. Grant agreed.

Grant sold his house and all his personal property. He paid Mr. Vanderbilt every cent he owed him. Grant was now wiped out to the last penny, but he felt better. "I care more for my reputation," he said, "than for all the money and material wealth in the world."

Misfortune soon followed upon misfortune. Grant developed cancer of the throat. Knowing he was dying, he decided to write his memoirs to make some money for his family. He started to write his book in New

York City, but he became so ill and weak he was taken to a cottage at Mount McGregor, in the Adirondack Mountains. The doctors thought that the clear mountain air would prolong his life. On the trip up to Mount McGregor, the train passed West Point. Grant stared across the river at the place where he had spent four years as a

youth. He turned around and looked until he could no longer see the buildings.

"I have many memories of my early life back there," he said to his son. "Some of the friends I made there have already crossed to the other side of life's river. They will be waiting to greet me when I cross over soon."

Grant seemed to rally for a while in the cool, clear air of Mount McGregor. Soon he became very weak again. However, whenever he could, he visited a little white tent on the front lawn. It was occupied by a former Union soldier, who still wore his faded blue uniform. He had been employed to keep strangers from annoying the sick man while he was working on his book.

Messages of sympathy came to Grant from every state and from foreign countries as well. One of the most cheering was from a Democratic convention held in Vicksburg, Mississippi. The convention had passed a resolution of sympathy for Grant's illness and a hope for his recovery. Grant was pleased. "Even my former enemies are pulling for

me," he said. "It shows that the scars of war are healing."

Little by little, Grant became much weaker, but he grimly kept on writing. He fought so hard that one of his doctors said, "General Grant never knew defeat, and it begins to look as if neither death nor doctors will defeat him."

Another event cheered Grant up. An old man traveled all the way from Illinois, on foot. He was tired and weather-beaten. His clothes and shoes were in tatters. He prayed outside Grant's house all night and then left. He refused to give his name but said, "Grant took care of me many times when I fought under him in the past. I want to pray for him now."

Grant's condition grew much worse as he fought the greatest battle of his life. His wife urged him to stop work on his book. "The writing is weakening you too much," she said. But Grant, once started, would not turn back on the road. Though he was in great pain, he stuck to his task.

Mark Twain, the great American writer and humorist, was to publish the memoirs. "Ulysses will never finish the book," he told Mrs. Grant. "It is impossible for a man so weak and exhausted to continue writing."

"My Ulysses will finish any task he starts," Mrs. Grant told him proudly.

One day, with barely enough strength to hold the pen, Grant finished his memoirs. Four days later, on July 23, 1885, he died. He had completed his last task. His family received five hundred thousand dollars for the book, and they would be comfortable.

Grant was buried in Riverside Park, New York City, on a rise overlooking the Hudson River. His magnificent tomb is now visited by many thousands of people each year.

Ulysses S. Grant typifies the best in American life. From a poor, humble schoolboy he rose to be President of the United States. His life has inspired many other American boys who, though born in humble circumstances, rose to the top by following Grant's code—determination, self-sacrifice, and above all, hard work!

Author's Note

Ulysses S. Grant was a great military genius. He tried many innovations and proved them successful under combat conditions. However, his greatest quality was his stubborn habit of never admitting or accepting defeat. Many times, in his private as well as his military life, he faced hardships and disasters that would have caused a lesser man to give up. Grant never! As soon as he was able, he would be back fighting until he achieved victory. Whether it was a struggle to support his family, or a life and death battle, Grant could be counted on to grit his teeth and endure until the objective was won.

History has produced many leaders who could achieve their goals when good fortune and the odds were in their favor. Grant was one of the select few who had a greater quality. He would persevere and win when all odds were against him. Once he set his mind on a course of action, nothing could deter nor stop him until he received an unconditional surrender from his opponent.

Although all the facts in my biography of Grant are true, I often had to imagine what the conversations were. For instance, when Grant and his companions climbed the volcano, there is no record of what they actually said. The same holds true of Grant's childhood and earlier Army life. However, in his later life as head of the Army and as President, we have a good record of his words that are now famous.

In the times that lie ahead, our country would do well to produce another man with the qualities of Ulysses S. Grant!

JOSEPH OLGIN

Pronunciation Key

Alamo (al′ uh mo)
Amecameca (uh may′ kuh may′ kuh)
Appomattox (ap′ oh mat′ uks)
Cairo (kair′ oh)
Chapultepec (chah pool′ tay pek′)
Chattanooga (chat′ uh noo′ guh)
Corpus Christi (kawr′ pus krihs′ tee)
Goliad (go′ lee add′)
Molino del Rey (mo leen′ oh del ray′)
Monterrey (mon′ tuh ray′)
Nagasaki (nah′ guh sah′ kee)
Nueces (noo ay′ sehs)
Palo Alto (pal′ oh al′ toh)
Pompeii (pom pay′)
Popocatepetl (poh′ poh kuh tay′ pet'l)
Resaca de la Palma (reh sah′ kah day lah pahl′ mah)
Rio Grande (ree′ oh grand′)
San Jacinto (san juh sin′ toh)
Shiloh (shy′ loh)
Veracruz (vair′ uh krooz′)

ABCDEFGHIJ—R—73210/69876

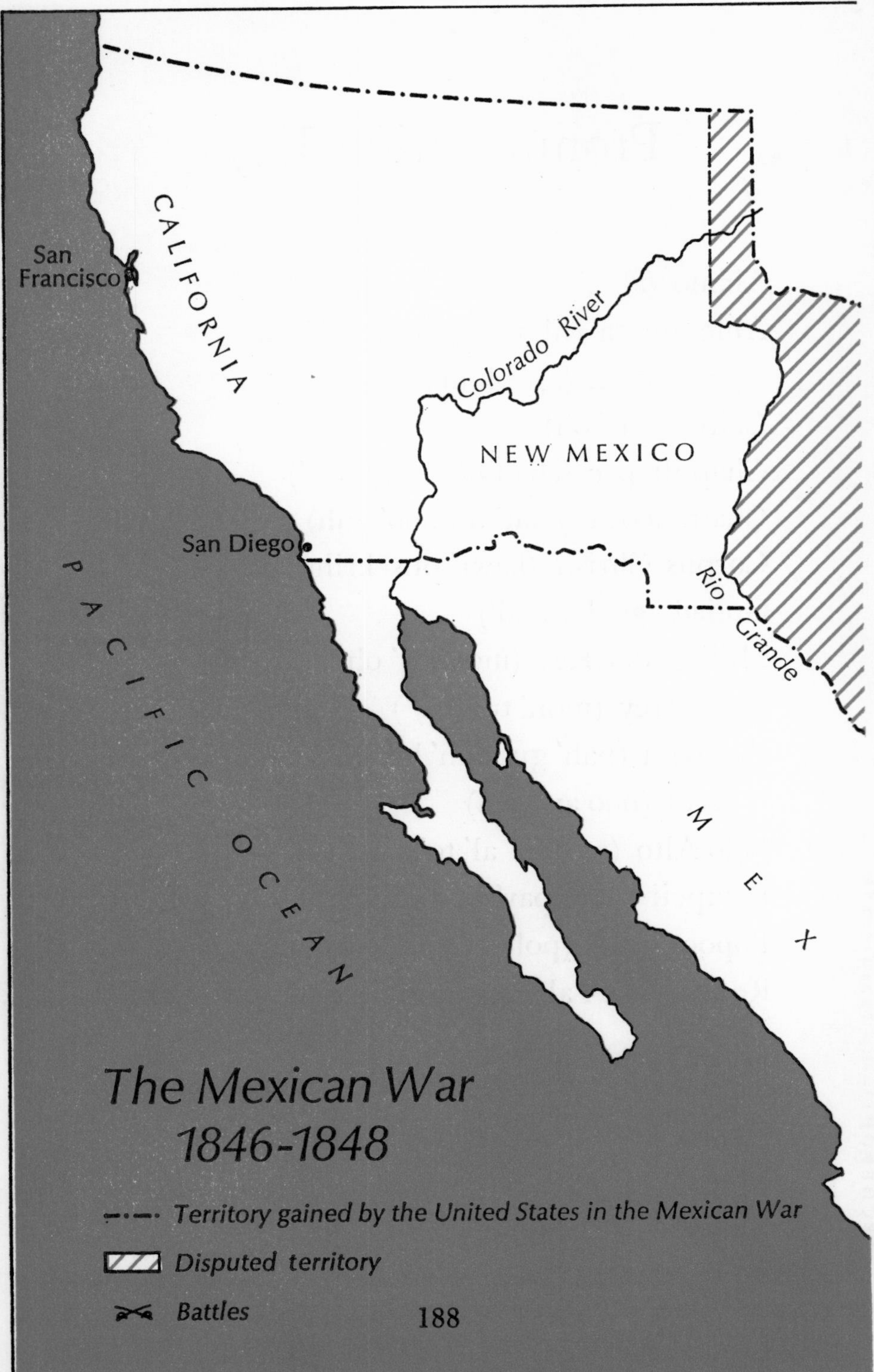
CALIFORNIA
San Francisco
Colorado River
NEW MEXICO
San Diego
Rio Grande
PACIFIC OCEAN
MEX
The Mexican War
1846-1848
Territory gained by the United States in the Mexican War
Disputed territory
Battles

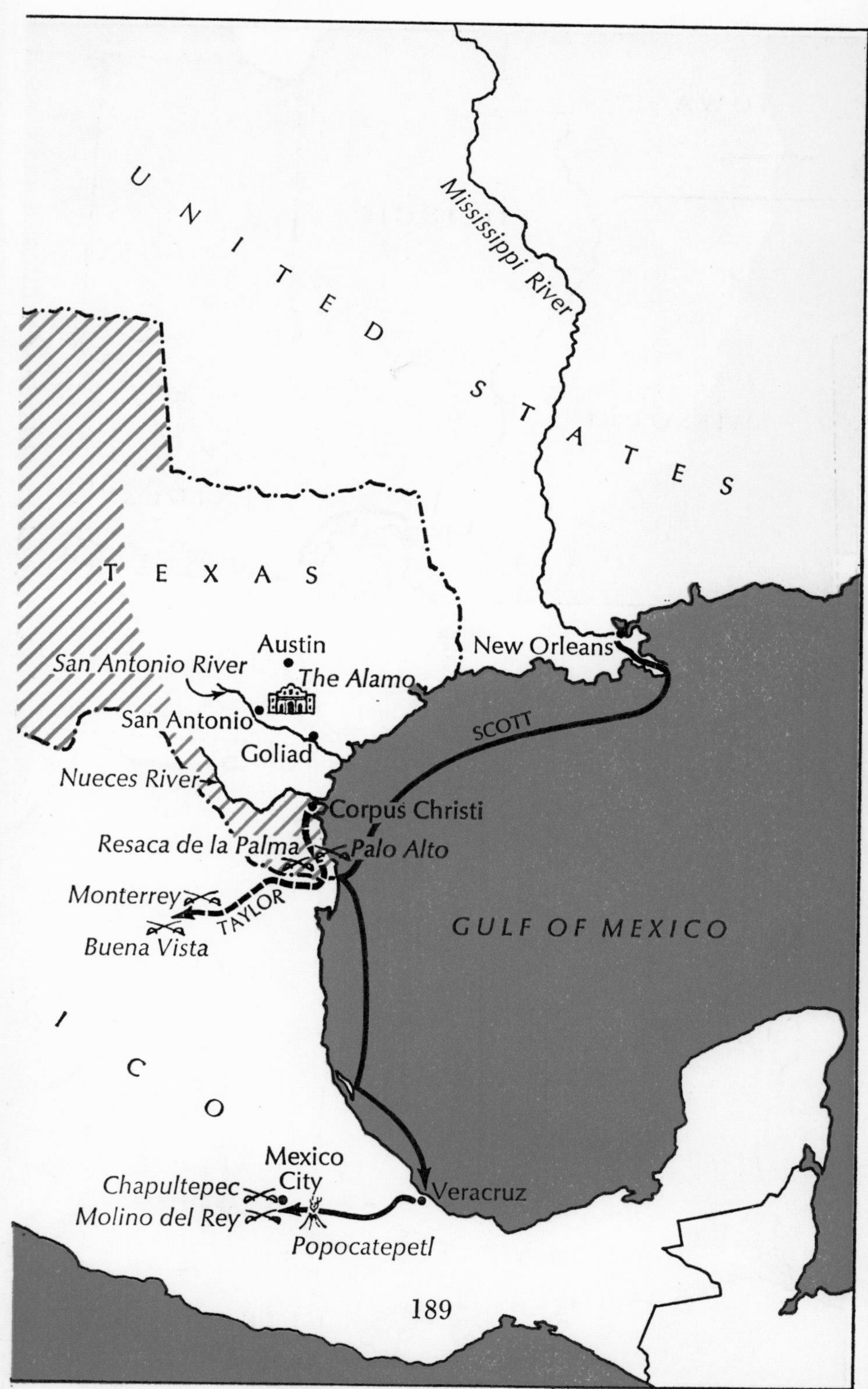
UNITED STATES
Mississippi River
TEXAS
Austin
San Antonio River
The Alamo
San Antonio
Goliad
New Orleans
SCOTT
Nueces River
Corpus Christi
Resaca de la Palma
Palo Alto
Monterrey
TAYLOR
Buena Vista
GULF OF MEXICO
ICO
Mexico City
Chapultepec
Molino del Rey
Veracruz
Popocatepetl

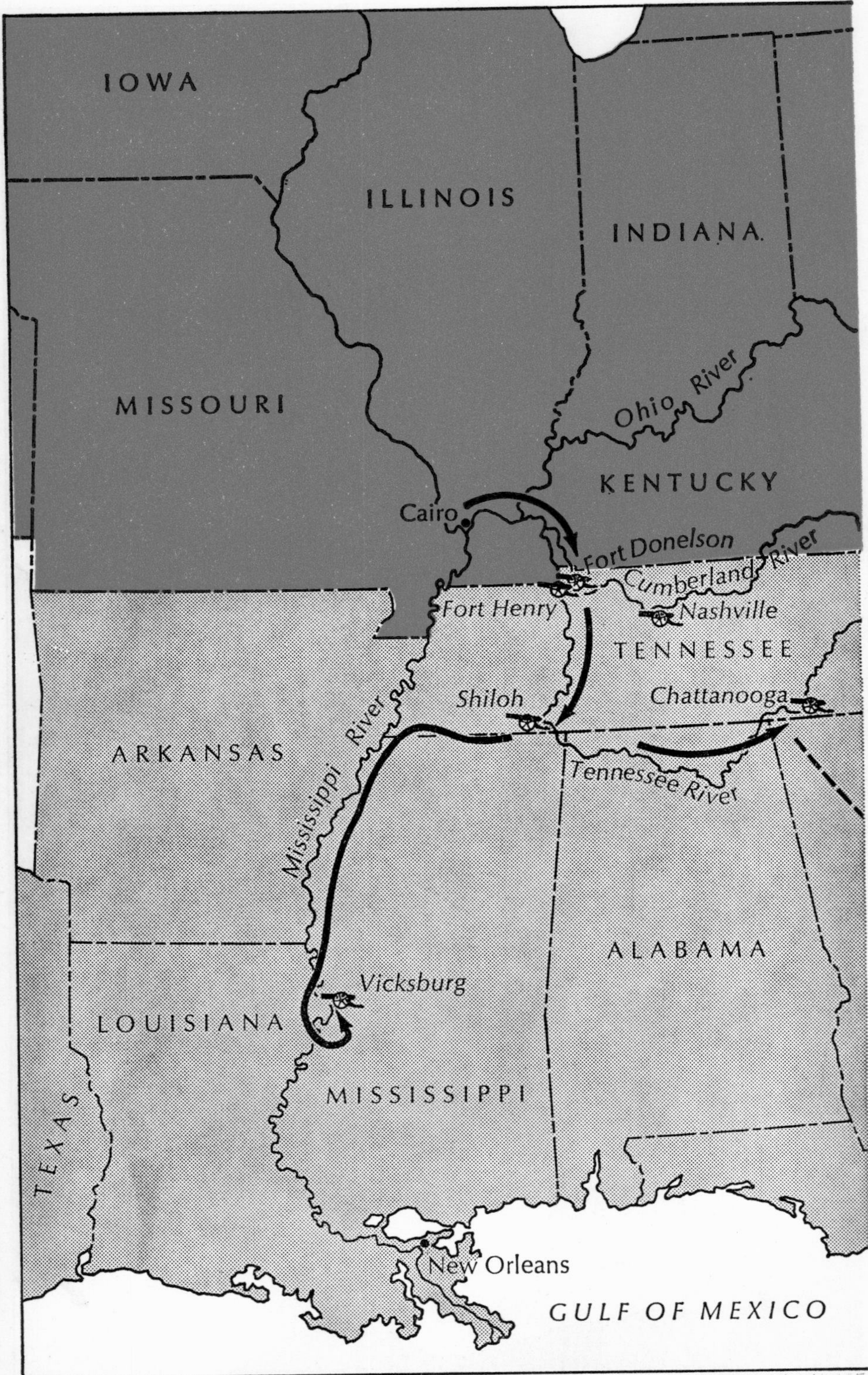
IOWA
ILLINOIS
INDIANA
MISSOURI
Ohio River
KENTUCKY
Cairo
Fort Donelson
Cumberland River
Fort Henry
Nashville
TENNESSEE
Shiloh
Chattanooga
ARKANSAS
Mississippi River
Tennessee River
ALABAMA
Vicksburg
LOUISIANA
MISSISSIPPI
TEXAS
New Orleans
GULF OF MEXICO

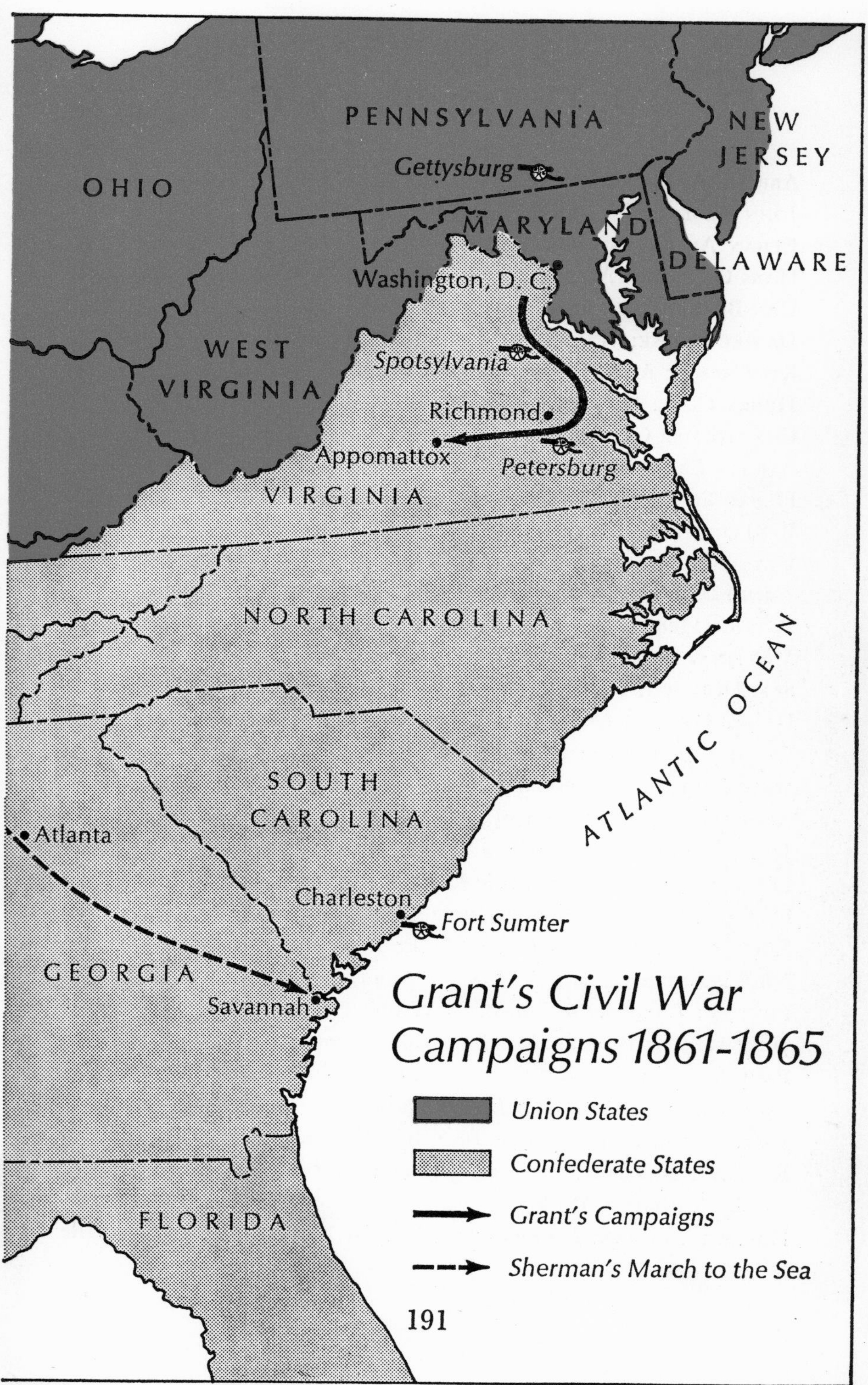
PENNSYLVANIA
NEW JERSEY
OHIO
Gettysburg
MARYLAND
DELAWARE
Washington, D. C.
WEST VIRGINIA
Spotsylvania
Richmond
Appomattox
Petersburg
VIRGINIA
NORTH CAROLINA
ATLANTIC OCEAN
SOUTH CAROLINA
Atlanta
Charleston
Fort Sumter
GEORGIA
Savannah
FLORIDA
Grant's Civil War Campaigns 1861-1865
Union States
Confederate States
Grant's Campaigns
Sherman's March to the Sea

PIPER BOOKS

ABIGAIL ADAMS: *The President's Lady,* by Regina Z. Kelly
JOHN ALDEN: *Steadfast Pilgrim,* by Cecile Pepin Edwards
ETHAN ALLEN: *Green Mountain Hero,* by Sheldon N. Ripley
HANS CHRISTIAN ANDERSEN: *Fairy Tale Author,* by Shannon Garst
DAN BEARD: *Boy Scout Pioneer,* by Jerry Seibert
DANIEL BOONE: *Wilderness Trailblazer,* by Miriam E. Mason
KIT CARSON: *Mountain Scout,* by Donald E. Worcester
HENRY CLAY: *Statesman and Patriot,* by Regina Z. Kelly
CHRISTOPHER COLUMBUS: *Sailor and Dreamer,* by Bernadine Bailey
AMELIA EARHART: *First Lady of the Air,* by Jerry Seibert
HENRY FORD: *Maker of the Model T,* by Miriam Gilbert
BENJAMIN FRANKLIN: *First Great American,* by John Tottle
ULYSSES S. GRANT: *General and President,* by Joseph Olgin
JOHN HANCOCK: *Friend of Freedom,* by Jeannette C. Nolan
PATRICK HENRY: *Voice of Liberty,* by William Percival Jones
MATTHEW HENSON: *Arctic Hero,* by Sheldon N. Ripley
SAM HOUSTON: *Friend of the Indians,* by Joseph Olgin
HENRY HUDSON: *Explorer of the North,* by Dorothea J. Snow
THOMAS JEFFERSON: *Champion of the People,* by Joseph Olgin
JOHN PAUL JONES: *Soldier of the Sea,* by Donald E. Worcester
ABRAHAM LINCOLN: *Man of Courage,* by Bernadine Bailey
JAMES MADISON: *Statesman and President,* by Regina Z. Kelly
FERDINAND MAGELLAN: *Noble Captain,* by Katharine Wilkie
HORACE MANN: *Sower of Learning,* by Cecile Pepin Edwards
KING PHILIP: *Loyal Indian,* by Cecile Pepin Edwards
JUAN PONCE DE LEON: *First in the Land,* by Bernadine Bailey
PONTIAC: *Lion in the Forest,* by Wilma Pitchford Hays
JOHN WESLEY POWELL: *Canyon's Conqueror,* by Marian T. Place
PAUL REVERE: *Colonial Craftsman,* by Regina Z. Kelly
SACAJAWEA: *Guide to Lewis and Clark,* by Jerry Seibert
JOHN SMITH: *Man of Adventure,* by Miriam E. Mason
ROBERT LOUIS STEVENSON: *Storyteller and Adventurer,* by Katharine Wilkie
HARRIET TUBMAN: *Flame of Freedom,* by Frances T. Humphreville